INTERNATIONAL
ENVIRONMENTAL
LAW

INTERNATIONAL ENVIRONMENTAL LAW

TEXT, CASES AND MATERIALS

MALGOSIA FITZMAURICE

Chair of Public International Law, Queen Mary University of London, UK

MEAGAN S. WONG

Lecturer, School of Law, University of Essex, UK

JOSEPH CRAMPIN

*Lecturer, University of Glasgow and
Associate Lecturer, University College London, UK*

Cheltenham, UK • Northampton, MA, USA

Cover illustration: Childhood. Pasture Day.
1979 (Bērnība. Ganu diena.1979) by Leonīds
Āriņš (1907–1991) reproduced with permission
by Monika Bērzs-Bērziņa and Tukums Museum
(inventory designation: TMNM 29054 Mgl 464),
photographer Valdis Jansons.

Published by
Edward Elgar Publishing Limited
The Lypiatts
15 Lansdown Road
Cheltenham
Glos GL50 2JA
UK

Edward Elgar Publishing, Inc.
William Pratt House
9 Dewey Court
Northampton
Massachusetts 01060
USA

A catalogue record for this book
is available from the British Library

Library of Congress Control Number:
2020952082

Printed on elemental chlorine free (ECF)
recycled paper containing 30% Post-Consumer Waste

ISBN 978 1 78536 780 9 (cased)
ISBN 978 1 78536 781 6 (eBook)
ISBN 978 1 78536 791 5 (paperback)

Printed and bound in the USA

CONTENTS

PART IV   ENVIRONMENTAL LAW AND INTERNATIONAL LAW

PREFACE

There has developed, over the second half of the 20th century, a vast and complex body of legal rules and principles of international law dedicated to addressing environmental concerns. Environmental challenges are not, by their nature, restricted to national jurisdiction and so require international cooperation to understand and resolve. In some cases, these challenges are among the most pressing and important problems facing the world. To name just a few: marine pollution, rapid loss in biodiversity and climate change.

The aim of this book is to provide a comprehensive source to a broad range of legal instruments and case law relevant to, *inter alia*, the protection and regulation of the environment. By introducing and highlighting the most important instruments and cases of environmental law, it seeks to provide students, policy-makers, government advisors, non-legal experts, scientists and civil society, with a broad understanding of the existing legal framework and soft-law instruments and selected case law that is accessible and easy to use.

Each chapter of the book sets out the various treaties, soft-law instruments and case law on the topic. Excerpts of important provisions of relevant instruments or passages from cases are provided. These excerpts are, however, highly selective. Due to the wealth of material, and often lengthy and highly technical nature of many legal provisions, it is not possible to reproduce treaties in their entirety. While passages are selected to bring out the most salient points, this is not meant to, nor could it, replace the need to examine the primary materials in their entirety. Each chapter also provides a bibliography that is not intended to be comprehensive but focuses on a selection of important and recent scholarship.

The selection of material, while comprehensive, is not exhaustive. International environmental law is a dynamic and evolving field, and this precludes any such ambition. The selection, and overall focus of the book, identifies the most important structural features of the field, since these are both unlikely to change in the near future and provide the structure for understanding the dynamics behind and context within which new developments occur. Areas of development that are currently the subject of negotiation, or otherwise works in progress, are only lightly touched upon, and it is not the aim of this book to predict or speculate on their final outcome. Similarly, as a book concerned with the international regulation of the environment, it does not reproduce regulation at the national or EU level.

The book is a collaborative effort of the authors. Initial drafts of Chapters 2, 4, 5, 6, 7, 8, 9, 10 and 17 were by Malgosia Fitzmaurice, Chapters 11, 12, 13, 14, 18, 19 and 21 were by Meagan Wong, and Chapters 15, 16 and 20 were by Joseph Crampin. The authors wish to thank Dr Niccolò Lanzoni for his invaluable input in the chapter on the management of hazardous waste and the permanent sovereignty over natural resources, respectively.

ACKNOWLEDGEMENTS

The authors would like to acknowledge and thank for their endorsements from Judge María Teresa Infante Caffi, International Tribunal for the Law of the Sea and University of Chile, Chile; Dr Nilüfer Oral, Senior Fellow, NUS Centre for International Law and Member, International Law Commission; Professor Philippe Sands QC, University College London, UK; and Professor Sean D. Murphy, Manatt/Ahn Professor of International Law, George Washington University, USA and Member, International Law Commission.

TABLE OF CASES

TABLE OF LEGISLATION

1
Introduction

1.1 HISTORY OF INTERNATIONAL ENVIRONMENTAL LAW

International environmental law has undergone major development since the start of the 20th century.[1] States in the late 19th and early 20th century entered into agreements to regulate questions of conservation of natural resources or for the management of transboundary issues affecting rivers and lakes, but these covered discrete issues on an ad hoc basis. The principal change has been the development of a distinct field of law, bounded by its own principles and institutions, dedicated to the protection of the environment. Together with the development of a regime of environmental law has been a large expansion in treaties and other forms of international regulation at the global, regional and bilateral levels addressing an increasing range of environmental concerns.

1.1.1 Early Development

Early examples of regulation of the environment under international law concerned the conservation and use of migratory species. The use of bilateral treaties to manage the exploitation and right to regulate the exploitation of fisheries is longstanding.[2] Specific concerns over overfishing developed in the second half of the 19th century, several treaties concluded to ensuring the better regulation and management of fisheries.[3] This period saw a shift in emphasis in international conventions, away from an earlier model in which agreements were concerned with the grant of rights to foreign nationals to exploit fisheries and to delimit the extent of the territorial state's power to regulate the overexploitation of its fisheries[4] and towards agreements designed to harmonise regulations for both nationals and foreign fishermen to protect against overexploitation. An early example of this is the 1867 Convention Between France and

---

[1]   See P Sands and J Peel, *Principles of International Environmental Law* (4th edn, CUP 2018) Chapter 2.

[2]   Examples dating from as early as the 14th century can be found: see AP Daggett, 'The Regulation of Maritime Fisheries by Treaty' (1934) 28 AJIL 693.

[3]   North Sea Fisheries (Overfishing Convention) 1882.

[4]   *North Atlantic Fisheries Arbitration (Great Britain, USA)* (1910) XI RIAA 167.

Great Britain Relative to Fisheries, which sought to protect the overexploitation of oysters by prohibiting fishing except within certain periods.[5]

Protection of marine mammals by international treaty also began in this period, in the case of fur-seals by a treaty of 1911.[6] After the First World War, the conservation and management of whales became a matter of serious concern, and two treaties were concluded in 1931 and 1937 under the auspices of the League of Nations to regulate whaling. These sought, rather unsuccessfully, to restrict the number of whales that could be caught and introduced prohibitions on the killing of certain species of whales and calves. Despite their limitations, these conventions provided the foundations of the subsequent 1946 International Convention for the Regulation of Whaling.[7]

The protection of birds[8] can be traced to the 1902 Convention to Protect Birds Useful to Agriculture. This prohibited the killing of certain species of birds deemed useful to agriculture, such as insectivores, as well as prohibiting the destruction of their nests or eggs. More general treaties protecting wildlife were concluded in European colonies in Africa[9]and in the Americas.[10]

During this early period, significant arbitral awards contributed to the development of the field. The first of these is the *Pacific Fur Seal Arbitration (United States of America v. Great Britain)*, which addressed the question of whether the USA had the sovereign right to exercise jurisdiction over fur-seals outside its territorial waters, among other reasons, in order to protect them from overexploitation. The claim was based on the protection of a living resource as an economic asset, rather than for conservation *per se*. The tribunal rejected the claim, but, on the request of the parties, proposed regulations which they could adopt concurrently in order to protect the fur-seal population in the region, which included prohibitions on the killing of seals in certain areas or at certain periods of the year.

The most significant decision of the early environmental law decisions was the decision of the tribunal in the *Trail Smelter Arbitration (United States v. Canada)*. The case concerned transboundary air pollution caused by sulphur fumes emitted by a smelter in Canada resulting in damage in the United States. The decision is primarily known for its articulation of the principle under international law that no state may use its territory in a manner that causes harm to other states (*sic utere iure tuo ut alterum non laedas*). This principle of no transboundary harm has been significant in the development of the 'no harm' and 'prevention principles',[11] which lie at the foundations of much of modern environmental law.

---

[5]   See also 1885 Regulation of Salmon Fishery in the Rhine River Basin; 1923 Pacific Halibut Convention.

[6]   North Pacific Fur Seal Convention (Washington, 7 July 1911).

[7]   161 UNTS 72. See further Chapter 11.

[8]   1902 Convention to Protect Birds Useful to Agriculture (Paris, 19 March 1902). See Chapter 12.

[9]   1900 Convention Destinée à Assurer la Conservation des Diverses Espèces Animales Vivant à l'Etat Sauvage en Afrique qui sont Utiles à l'Homme ou Inoffensive (London, 19 May 1900); 1933 Convention on the Preservation of Fauna and Flora in their Natural State 172 LNTS 242.

[10]   1940 Convention on Nature Protection and Wildlife Preservation in the Western Hemisphere 161 UNTS 193.

[11]   See Chapter 4.

The establishment of the United Nations in 1945 provided institutional support for the protection of the environment. The Food and Agriculture Organization (FAO), a specialised agency of the UN, has among its purposes the 'the conservation of natural resources and the adoption of improved methods of agricultural production'.[12] Another specialised agency, the United Nations Education, Scientific and Cultural Organization (UNESCO), played an instrumental role in the foundation of the International Union for Conservation of Nature and Natural Resources (IUCN), which has contributed to the development of the law on the international protection of wildlife. Another UN specialised agency, the International Maritime Organization (IMO), has also proved highly influential in matters affecting the protection of the marine environment,[13] including overseeing the conclusion of treaties to combat oil pollution, creating regimes for liability for oil pollution, and the creation of an oil compensation fund.[14] In addition, the Economic and Social Council (ECOSOC) created the UN Conference on the Conservation and Utilization of Resources (UNCCUR), which, although unremarkable in itself, represents the first of many UN conferences addressing environmental issues. The UN General Assembly was also seised of environmental matters in this period, notably in matters concerning sovereignty over natural resources.[15]

1.1.2   From Stockholm to Rio

Following developments in the UN, in 1968 the UN General Assembly passed a resolution on Problems of the Human Environment, convening the United Nations Conference on the Human Environment (Stockholm Conference). The conference was held in 1972, attended by 114 states and various intergovernmental organisations and non-governmental actors, and it is 'generally seen as the foundational moment of modern environmental law'.[16] The result of the Conference was the adoption of a resolution on institutional and financial matters, the 'Declaration on the Human Environment' (Stockholm Declaration) and 'Action Plan for the Human Environment'. Following a recommendation (no 4) in the 'Action Plan', the UN General Assembly shortly thereafter established the UN Environment Programme (UNEP), which has acted as a catalyst for the subsequent development of international environmental norms. The Stockholm Declaration was the most famous and important outcome of the Conference. It articulates 26 principles that have provided guidance to the development of environmental law as a unified field of legal activity, and which have, in certain cases, become customary international law.

The Stockholm Conference also provided impetus to the already accelerating process of concluding environmental conventions. In the period shortly after Stockholm, several major environmental treaties were adopted, including the 1972 London Convention, the International

---

[12]   FAO Constitution, art 2(c).

[13]   See Chapter 10.

[14]   See Chapter 17.

[15]   See Chapter 3.

[16]   P-M Dupuy and J Viñuales, *International Environmental Law* (2nd edn, CUP 2018) 9.

Convention on Prohibition of Pollution from Ships 1973 and its 1978 Protocol (MARPOL),[17] and 1973 Convention on International Trade in Endangered Species of Wild Fauna and Flora (CITES).[18] The UNEP also established the Regional Seas Programme, under which many regional treaties on environmental matters affecting regional seas have been concluded.[19] Included among numerous other developments post-Stockholm are the 1978 UNEP 'Draft Principles of Conduct in the Field of the Environment', the 1981 Montevideo Programme, and the 1982 World Charter for Nature. In 1983, the World Commission on Environment and Development was established by the UN General Assembly. The Commission, led by Gro Harlem Brundtland, published its report in 1987. The Brundtland Report gave prominence to several key concepts in environmental law, including sustainable development and intergenerational equity, and was an important precursor to the 1992 UN Conference on Environment and Development (UNCED) held at Rio in 1992.

A different development of environmental law in the late 1970s and 1980s involved its expansion into the regulation by treaty of atmospheric harm.[20] In 1979, the Convention on Long-Range Transboundary Air Pollution (LRTAP) was concluded under the auspices of the UN Economic Commission for Europe. The LRTAP sought to protect states from harmful air pollution, particularly of substances responsible for causing acid rain. The LRTAP was followed in 1985 by the Vienna Convention on the Protection of the Ozone Layer and its 1987 Montreal Protocol. These treaties were notable not only for their effective expansion of the environmental regime to address new challenges, but also for their use of new and innovative techniques, including the use of economic tools, financial and technical cooperation, and specific targets for emissions reduction. The 1987 Montreal Protocol, widely regarded as a great success in environmental regulation, has become a model for other areas of environmental law, including air pollution, climate change,[21] and non-compliance procedures.[22] Other notable developments in this period include the strengthening of environmental impact assessment as a precautionary measure, reflected in the 1987 UNEP Goals and Principles of Environmental Impact Assessment and 1991 Espoo Convention on Environmental Impact Assessment in a Transboundary Context.[23]

Of the post-Stockholm developments affecting the protection of the environment, the most significant is the 1982 UN Convention on the Law of the Sea (UNCLOS). Intended as a Constitution for the Oceans, UNCLOS provides the foundations for the international norms on all matters on the protection of the environment in connection with the oceans. These include protection of the marine environment *per se*, from various forms of pollution,[24]

---

[17]   See Chapter 10.

[18]   See Chapter 12.

[19]   See Chapter 10.

[20]   See Chapter 15.

[21]   See Chapter 16.

[22]   See Chapter 18.

[23]   See Chapter 9.

[24]   See Chapter 10.

protection of fisheries and marine mammals,[25] specific provisions reinforcing international norms on responsibility and liability,[26] a system of compulsory inter-state dispute settlement,[27] and the constitution of the International Seabed Authority to regulate activities on the seabed.

1.1.3   Towards the Present: Rio and its Aftermath

Following the Brundtland Report, in 1989 the UN General Assembly convened a new Conference on Environment and Development (UNCED). The Conference was held at Rio in 1992. The outcome of the UNCED was the adoption of three non-binding instruments and the conclusion of two international conventions. The non-binding instruments were the Declaration on Environment and Development (Rio Declaration), a Non-Legally Binding Authoritative Statement of Principles for a Global Consensus on the Management, Conservation and Sustainable Development of All Types of Forest (UNCED Forest Principles), and Agenda 21. The two treaties were the Convention on Biological Diversity (CBD)[28] (adopted in 2000) and the UN Framework Convention on Climate Change (UNFCCC) (adopted in 1992).[29] In addition, Rio precipitated the conclusion of several treaties and protocols designed to replace or update older environmental regimes established in the 1960s and 1970s.

The Rio Declaration comprises 27 principles and, together with Agenda 21, formed a new model, in line with the Brundtland Report, integrating environmental and development issues. The Rio Declaration reaffirmed principles concluded at Stockholm, notably Principle 2 of the Rio Declaration reflects Principle 21 of the Stockholm Declaration, which balanced the sovereign right to exploit natural resources with the duty to ensure that activities within their jurisdiction do not damage the environment of other states or of areas beyond national jurisdiction. The Rio Declaration also recognises several new or emerging principles of great importance to international environmental law. These include: intergenerational equity (Principle 3), sustainable development (Principle 4),[30] 'common but differentiated responsibilities' (Principle 7), public participation and access to environmental information (Principle 10),[31] the precautionary approach (Principle 15),[32] polluter-pays principle (Principle 16),[33] environmental impact assessment (Principle 17),[34] and the special protection of the

---

[25]   Both under UNCLOS and, in respect of fisheries, notably also the 1995 Agreement on Straddling Fish Stocks, which implements the 1982 United Nations Agreement for the Implementation of the Provisions of the United Nations Convention on the Law of the Sea: see Chapter 11.

[26]   See Chapter 17.

[27]   See Chapter 19.

[28]   See Chapter 12.

[29]   See Chapter 16.

[30]   See Chapter 2.

[31]   See Chapter 9.

[32]   See Chapter 5.

[33]   See Chapter 7.

[34]   See Chapter 9.

environment in armed conflict (Principle 24).[35] Principle 1 of the Rio Declaration is notable for stopping short of endorsing a specific human right to a healthy environment, but it has proved an important catalyst for the integration of the environment into matters concerning human rights.[36]

In 1998, the idea of public participation was enshrined in the Aarhus Convention, concluded under the UNECE, giving effect to Principle 10. This represents an important shift in the recognition of a procedural right to a healthy environment and is part of a broader, post-Rio trend, involving the greater participation of non-state actors in international environmental law.

The most significant regime to emerge from Rio has been that governing climate change. Notwithstanding the serious challenges in creating adequate legal regimes to address the issue, the UNFCCC remains the foundation of the international climate change regime. It was supplemented in 1997 by the Kyoto Protocol, which had operative force between 2008 and 2012, and reflected the model of the ozone layer regime that the participants at Rio consciously adopted. The current legal approach to climate change is found in the 2015 Paris Agreement and represents a significant departure from the approach taken under Kyoto, rejecting harder regulation at the international level in favour of softer norms with greater discretion in their implementation at the national level.

The period post-Rio has also seen significant advances in the codification of the law of international watercourses, including the conclusion of the International Law Commission's (ILC) examination of the subject, which resulted in the 1997 Convention on the Law of Non-navigational uses of international watercourses.[37] The ILC has included within its work a number of other environmental law matters. This has resulted in the 2001 Draft Articles on the Prevention of Transboundary Harm from Hazardous Activities,[38] and the 2006 Draft principles on the allocation of loss in the case of transboundary harm arising out of hazardous activities.[39] On its current agenda are the protection of the environment in armed conflicts, protection of the atmosphere, and sea-level rise.

On the anniversaries of Rio in 2002 and 2012, the UN has held summits marking the event. The 2002 Johannesburg World Summit on Development reaffirmed in the Declaration on Sustainable Development the commitment to sustainable development. In 2012, Rio+20 sought to discuss new matters, including the development of a 'green economy', but did not produce any clear commitments from states in order to achieve this end. Following Rio+20, the UN General Assembly adopted 17 Sustainable Development Goals together with targets for meeting them, as part of a new plan called *Transforming Our World: The 2030 Agenda for Sustainable Development*. According to Sands and Peel, the 'SDGs indicate the extent to which – in the more than two decades since UNCED – international environmental law

---

[35] See Chapter 21.

[36] See Chapter 8.

[37] See Chapter 13.

[38] See Chapter 4.

[39] See Chapter 17.

has evolved and become more widely integrated with the development agenda as a whole'. Three other developments since Rio are worth noting. The first is the increase in international litigation before the ICJ, under UNCLOS, and in inter-state arbitration that raises environmental law issues. Notable decisions before the ICJ raising environmental matters include: the Legality of the Threat or Use of Nuclear Weapons,[40] *Gabčíkovo-Nagymaros Project (Hungary v. Slovakia)*,[41] *Pulp Mills on the River Uruguay (Argentina v. Uruguay)*,[42] *Whaling in the Antarctic (Australia v. Japan: New Zealand intervening)*[43] and *Certain Activities Carried Out by Nicaragua in the Border Area (Costa Rica v. Nicaragua)* and *Construction of a Road in Costa Rica along the San Juan River (Nicaragua v. Costa Rica)*.[44]

The second is the advancement of the process of integrating international environmental law with international economic law, in particular international trade law.[45] The overlap between trade law and environmental law is not new, and goes back to the 1948 General Agreement on Tariffs and Trade, but, post-Rio, the interrelationship between the two regimes has arisen, increasingly, in international trade dispute settlement fora at the WTO.

The third is the integration with international human rights law.[46] This arises both in the context of the development of a 'right to a healthy environment' and the integration of environmental issues affecting the enjoyment of other human rights. Human rights litigation, moreover, provides a new and increasingly popular avenue in which individuals can directly influence the development of environmental law at the international law, and secure the enforcement of environmental standards.

New directions in the protection of the environment continue to emerge. Some of these follow from the dynamic nature of environmental treaties. For example, the Conference of the Parties under the UNFCCC meets annually to make progress in tackling climate change. The 26th such meeting, CoP26, has continued to make strides in this regard.

A nascent, but potentially very significant, new development is the articulation of an international crime of 'ecocide' in June 2021. It is the work of independent legal experts, a fact which reflects the broader practical role that civil society plays in the creation of international environmental law. The crime is proposed as an amendment to the Rome Statute of the International Criminal Court, and it seeks to create criminal liability for 'unlawful or wanton acts committed with knowledge that there is a substantial likelihood of severe and either widespread or long-term damage to the environment being caused by those acts'.[47] If it obtains suf-

---

[40]   Legality of the Threat or Use of Nuclear Weapons, Advisory Opinion, ICJ Reports 226 (1996).

[41]   *Gabcikovo-Nagymaros Project (Hungary v. Slovakia)*, ICJ Reports 7 (1997).

[42]   *Pulp Mills on the River Uruguay (Argentina v. Uruguay)*, ICJ Reports 14 (2010).

[43]   *Whaling in the Antarctic (Australia v. Japan: New Zealand intervening)*, Judgment, ICJ Reports 226 (2014)

[44]   *Certain Activities Carried Out by Nicaragua in the Border Area (Costa Rica v. Nicaragua)* and *Construction of a Road in Costa Rica along the San Juan River (Nicaragua v. Costa Rica)*, ICJ Reports 665 (2015).

[45]   See Chapter 20.

[46]   See Chapter 8.

[47]   'Independent Expert Panel for the Legal Definition of Ecocide: Commentary and Core Text' (Stop Ecocide Foundation, June 2021) https://www.stopecocide.earth/legal-definition accessed 6 November 2021.

ficient support from states, it could open new avenues for environmental protection, beyond the areas covered in this book.

1.2   SOURCES OF INTERNATIONAL ENVIRONMENTAL LAW

As a branch of international law, the sources of international environmental law are first to be found in the sources of public international law. The list of sources enumerated in Article 38(1) of the ICJ Statute contain the generally recognised sources of international law, and provide as follows:

1. The Court, whose function is to decide in accordance with international law such disputes as are submitted to it, shall apply:
   a. international conventions, whether general or particular, establishing rules expressly recognized by the contesting states;
   b. international custom, as evidence of a general practice accepted as law;
   c. the general principles of law recognized by civilized nations;
   d. subject to the provisions of Article 59, judicial decisions and the teachings of the most highly qualified publicists of the various nations, as subsidiary means for the determination of rules of law.

Of these sources, the first three are formal sources of law, while the decisions of courts and highly qualified publicists are only 'subsidiary means for the determination of rules of law'. Two uncertainties surround the list of sources: first, there is uncertainty about the particular sources contained in Article 38, notably the identification of rules of custom and general principles of law; and, second, there is a difficult issue of whether the list is exhaustive, or whether there are other sources of international law beyond those recognised in the statute.

Treaties (referred to in Article 38 as 'international conventions') are the main source of specific rights and obligations in international law, and this is particularly true of international environmental law. The law governing treaties is set out in the Vienna Convention on the Law of Treaties 1969 (VCLT),[48] and the vast majority of its rules are accepted as reflecting customary international law.[49] The principal norm governing treaties is *pacta sunt servanda*, defined in Article 26, VCLT, as: 'Every treaty in force is binding upon the parties to it and must be performed in good faith.' Specific rules govern the capacity of states and authority of state agents to conclude treaties (arts 6, 7, 8), the process of concluding a treaty by which a state consents to be bound (arts 9–17), and when a treaty enters into force (art 24). The VCLT rules on the process of treaty-making provide default rules, but allow for a great deal of flexibility for parties to make their own arrangements. In practice most treaties, and in particular most

---

[48]   1155 UNTS 331.

[49]   *Legal Consequences for States of the Continued Presence of South Africa in Namibia (South West Africa) notwithstanding Security Council Resolution 276 (1970)*, ICJ Reports 16; 47 (1971).

treaties arising from a formal process of negotiation and conclusion (which is characteristic of environmental treaties), contain their own operative clauses, usually at the end of a treaty, that contain special rules governing such questions for the particular treaty. The VCLT contains rules governing certain general issues of performance, such as questions over conflicts between the treaty and internal law, non-retroactivity of treaty and effects on third states (arts 27–41). The VCLT also contains special rules on the validity of treaties (arts 48–53), grounds for termination or withdrawal (arts 54–64) and process and effects of invalidity, termination and withdrawal (arts 65–72).

The law of treaties governs all treaties of whatever type and under whatever name. A treaty is defined in art 2 as: 'an international agreement concluded between States in written form and governed by international law, whether embodied in a single instrument or in two or more related instruments and whatever its particular designation.' A treaty may be titled 'convention', 'act', 'declaration', 'protocol', or by any other name, but are all subject to the same rules. As a matter of conventional practice, however, different names carry particular designations as to the nature of the instrument, although the terms are not always used in a stable way. For example, 'convention' is typically used for treaties concluded following conferences convened by an international organisation, and 'protocol' is used for a supplementary agreement that implements or amends an earlier treaty of which it may form an integral part. These designations, however, are not determinative. A distinction is also often made between 'law-making' treaties (*traités loi*) and 'contractual' treaties (*traités contrat*). The former denote treaties, usually concluded between or open to adherence by a large number of parties, that lay down general rules governing the relations between the parties. Contractual treaties, on the other hand, contain specific obligations, owed between the parties, of a synallagmatic character. Many environmental treaties are of the former kind, establishing general legal regimes to address particular environmental problems. As a matter of international law, the distinction between the two types of treaty does not carry specific legal consequences in itself, although the different types of norms typically contained within such treaties may have different consequences.

Customary international law encompasses norms of international law derived from patterns of state behaviour. It is understood to have two elements, restated recently by the ILC: 'To determine the existence and content of a rule of customary international law, it is necessary to ascertain whether there is a general practice that is accepted as law (opinio juris).'[50] The ILC has also clarified the approach to the assessment of evidence for the existence of a customary rule:[51]

1. In assessing evidence for the purpose of ascertaining whether there is a general practice and whether that practice is accepted as law (opinio juris), regard must be had to the

---

[50] ILC Draft Conclusions on identification of customary international law, with commentaries (2018) Ybk ILC, vol. II, Conclusion 2.

[51] Ibid., Conclusion 3.

overall context, the nature of the rule and the particular circumstances in which the evidence in question is to be found.

2. Each of the two constituent elements is to be separately ascertained. This requires an assessment of evidence for each element.

State practice may take the form of 'diplomatic acts and correspondence; conduct in connection with resolutions adopted by an international organization or at an intergovernmental conference; conduct in connection with treaties; executive conduct, including operational conduct "on the ground"; legislative and administrative acts; and decisions of national courts'.[52] To amount to a custom, the practice must be widespread and general.[53]

The development and practice of international environmental law has not been driven, for the most part, by customary international law. Custom, nonetheless, is an important source of environmental norms, since it is the main source of obligations under international law that are universal in scope. Unlike a treaty, which only binds the parties to it, rules of custom bind all states. The only exception to this is the case of the 'persistent objector', namely the rule that a state which persistently objects to a customary rule both prior to its formation and after its crystallisation is not bound by the customary rule.[54] The persistent objector rule is, however, of potentially limited application in the environmental context, given that such norms may be *erga omnes* due to their communitarian character.[55] Although treaties rather than custom are the main source of environmental obligations, certain significant rules of international environmental law are understood to be customary law, including the no harm rule, principle of prevention and duty to make an environmental impact assessment. Another significant aspect of custom is that it provides the default set of rules on the international responsibility of states to make reparation for internationally wrongful acts.

The third source of international law are general principles of law. According to the ILC in its ongoing work on the topic, the requirement for a general principle to exist is that 'it must be recognised by the community'. There is a degree of uncertainty as to what counts as a 'general principle'. There is a broad understanding that general principles of law were included to enable the International Court of Justice to draw upon general principles found in national

---

[52]   Ibid., Conclusion 6(2).

[53]   Ibid., Conclusion 8.

[54]   *Anglo-Norwegian Fisheries*, ICJ Reports 116, 131 (1951).

[55]   'Seabed Advisory Opinion', Responsibilities and Obligations of States Sponsoring Persons and Entities with Respect to Activities in the Area, Advisory Opinion, Case No. 17, ITLOS Reports 10 (Seabed Dispute Chamber) (1 February 2011), para. 180.

legal systems in order to fill gaps in international law. This understanding of general principles has recently been endorsed by the ILC, which adopted the proposition:[56]

> To determine the existence and content of a general principle of law derived from national legal systems, it is necessary to ascertain:
> (a) the existence of a principle common to the various legal systems of the world; and
> (b) its transposition to the international legal system.

The existence of a second kind of category, namely general principles of international law, is more unclear. These principles are, in the words of the Special Rapporteur, 'principles which find their origin exclusively within the international legal system'.[57] There is, however, disagreement over what distinguishes these 'general principles of international law' from principles of customary law, and thus whether they constitute a truly separate category or ought to be subject to different standards for their identification from customary norms. The category has yet to be endorsed by the ILC. According to the Special Rapporteur, there are three ways principles of international law might arise: (1) they may arise from widespread recognition in treaties (for instance in their Preambles) or other international instruments such as General Assembly Resolutions;[58] (2) they may be principles which underlie general rules of customary or conventional law;[59] or (3) they may be 'inherent in the basic features and fundamental requirements of the international legal system'.[60] Although this category is still in need of further clarification by the ILC, it is notable that many 'principles' of environmental law sit more easily in this second category of general principle than in the first.

Recourse to principles has been important in the development of international environmental law. The principle of good faith[61] pervades numerous aspects of environmental procedural norms, including obligations to cooperate, consult and notify neighbouring states as part of the norms on preventing or taking precautionary measures to prevent environmental harm.[62] The 'no harm' principle itself is founded upon the general principle of *sic utere tuo ut alien non laedas* (a state is not allowed to use, or permit the use of, its territory to cause harm to the territory (or interests) of another state),[63] and is connected with the broader category of abuse of rights. Several of the principles elaborated in the Stockholm and Rio Declarations fall within

---

[56]   ILC, 'General Principles of Law: Text and titles of draft conclusions 1, 2 and 4 provisionally adopted by the Drafting Committee' (28 July 2021) A/CN.4/L.955, Draft Conclusion 4.

[57]   ILC Special Rapporteur Vázquez-Bermúdez, 'Second report on general principles of law' (9 April 2021) A/CN.4/741, para. 114.

[58]   Ibid., para. 122.

[59]   Ibid., para. 138.

[60]   Ibid., para. 146.

[61]   See Bin Cheng, *General Principles of Law as Applied by International Courts and Tribunals* (1953, reprint, CUP 2006); Robert Kolb, *Good Faith in International Law* (Hart 2017).

[62]   See chs 4, 5, 9.

[63]   J Brunée, '*Sic utere tuo ut alien non laedas*' MPEIL.

this category, including, for example, the polluter-pays principle.[64] Good faith and *sic utere tuo* are principles established within international law more generally, while other principles are unique to environmental law.

The legal effects of principles in environmental law are difficult to state with certainty. As noted by the Tribunal in *Iron Rhine*, there is 'considerable debate' as to what the legal effects of environmental law principles are.[65] They may be reflected in a customary rule or rules, and therefore constitute a rule of decision in particular cases. Alternatively, the principle may not yet be sufficiently precise to provide a basis for deciding cases in a particular way. Environmental principles may nevertheless provide coherence to the interpretation of environmental norms contained in treaties or customary law. They also provide a frame of reference for the coherent development of international environmental law.[66]

Customary rules and general principles of law may be reflected in rules or principles found in treaties. A treaty may reflect a rule of customary international law if it codified an existing customary rule, its conclusion led to the crystallisation of a rule of custom that was still developing at the time of the treaty's conclusion, or has given rise to a general practice accepted as law.[67] The attitudes of the parties to the treaty and practice and acceptance of non-parties determine whether a given treaty rule is also a rule of custom.

Custom and general principles are also related to the legal effects of resolutions or other acts of international organisations. Unless the acts of an international organisation are the result of a specific power to make binding decisions,[68] their acts and resolutions are not legally binding. Nor does the recognition of a principle of international law, in itself, create a rule of customary international law. Such recognition may nonetheless provide evidence of *opinio juris* for a customary rule.[69] A customary rule may be inferred from a series of resolutions which show 'the gradual evolution of the *opinio juris* required for the establishment of a new rule'.[70] It may also materially contribute to the development of custom by providing impetus to the creation of a general practice.[71]

---

[64]   ILC Special Rapporteur 'Second Report' (n 57) para. 135.

[65]   *Award in the Arbitration regarding the Iron Rhine ('Ijzeren Rijn') Railway between the Kingdom of Belgium and the Kingdom of the Netherlands (Belgium vs. the Netherlands)*, XXVII RIAA 35–125 (24 May 2005), para. 58.

[66]   MM Mbengue and B McGarry, 'General Principles of International Environmental Law in the Case Law of International Courts and Tribunals' in M Andenas, M Fitzmaurice, A Tanzi, and J Wouters (eds), *General Principles and the Coherence of International Law* (Brill 2019).

[67]   ILC Draft Conclusions on custom (n 51), Conclusion 11(1).

[68]   E.g. the UN Security Council under its Chapter VII powers.

[69]   ILC Draft Conclusions on custom (n 51), Conclusion 10(2).

[70]   Legality of the Threat or Use of Nuclear Weapons, Advisory Opinion, ICJ Reports 226 (1996), para. 70. For an example of this, see *Legal Consequences of the Separation of the Chagos Archipelago from Mauritius in 1965*, Advisory Proceedings, ICJ Reports 95 (2019).

[71]   Ibid., Conclusion 12(2).

The distinction between legally binding and non-legally binding instruments is closely related to the difference between 'hard' and 'soft' law.[72] The key to the distinction is that 'soft' law is not binding, and 'hard law' is. Often, the descriptors 'hard' and 'soft' are attached to the form of particular instruments: a treaty is hard law, and a General Assembly Resolution is soft law. On this classification, many significant instruments of international law, such as the Stockholm or Rio Declarations are soft law. A non-binding, soft law instrument may, as observed above, be a catalyst for, or the material source of, a rule of customary international law, and thus although the instrument is soft, it may contain binding norms. Another view of soft law is that it refers to the characteristics of the content of the norm rather than the form of the instrument in which it is contained. A norm which is clear and definite, imposing clear obligations with consequences if breached is hard, while vague and indeterminate provisions are soft. This applies to norms, even if contained in a hard instrument, notably a treaty. It is also possible to distinguish between hard and soft principles. While the interchangeable terminology is unhelpful, the composite descriptions of norms as binding/non-binding and hard/soft instruments/norms is an attempt to capture nuances that can be overlooked in the traditional categorisation of sources, namely that various kinds of norms exist in international law, possessing diverse legal effects, and this divergence exists across different kinds of instruments.[73]

Last, the decisions of international courts and tribunals have a significant influence on the development of international law, even if they are not strictly a 'source of law' within the meaning of Article 38(1). International decisions are only 'binding' on the parties to the decision,[74] and their denomination as 'subsidiary' reflects the fact that international law does not have a strict doctrine of *stare decisis*. However, they are 'regarded as evidence of the law',[75] and the process of applying techniques of legal reasoning to determine the scope and content of principles and rules is significant for the crystallisation of norms of international law. For example, the decision of the arbitral tribunal in *Trail Smelter* had a significant influence on the development of the 'no harm' principle, and several decisions of various international courts and tribunals have clarified and developed areas of international environmental law.

1.3 OUTLINE OF THE BOOK

This book aims to provide a comprehensive introductory resource to a broad range of legal instruments and case law relevant to the protection and regulation of the environment. It is divided into four parts:

Part I examines the main principles of international environmental law. Chapter 2 addresses 'Sustainable Development'. Chapter 3 covers 'Permanent Sovereignty Over Natural Resources'.

---

[72] See discussion in A Boyle, 'Soft Law in International Law-Making' in M Evans, *International Law* (5th edn, OUP 2018).

[73] Baxter 'International Law in her Infinite Variety' (1980) 29 ICLQ 549.

[74] Article 59, ICJ Statute.

[75] J Crawford, *Brownlie's Principles of Public International Law* (8th edn, OUP 2012) 37.

Chapter 4 examines the 'no harm' principle and its broader manifestation in the principle of prevention. Chapter 5 addresses the nature and role of the precautionary principle. Chapter 6 examines the polluter-pays principle. Chapter 7 covers the concept of intergenerational equity. Chapter 8 addresses the issue of the existence of substantive interactions between environmental law and human rights norms, including the right to a healthy environment. Chapter 9 covers the manifestation of these principles in the requirement to conduct environmental impact assessments, and rights of public participation in environmental decision-making.

Part II examines the main areas of substantive environmental regulation: the protection of the marine environment (Chapter 10); conservation of marine living resources (Chapter 11); biodiversity (Chapter 12); international watercourses (Chapter 13); the management of hazardous waste (Chapter 14); atmospheric protection (Chapter 15); and climate change (Chapter 16).

Part III covers the implementation of environmental law: responsibility and liability (Chapter 17); non-compliance procedures (Chapter 18); and dispute settlement (Chapter 19).

Part IV addresses relations between environmental law and other areas of international law, in particular: trade and the environment (Chapter 20); and the environment and armed conflict (Chapter 21).

The chapters are organised as follows. Every chapter provides an introduction to the topic and to the most important documents. Extracts from documents are divided by their material source into the following categories: 'legally binding instruments', 'non-legally binding instruments' and 'case law'. In chapters where there are fewer documents overall, the chapters are divided by category of instrument only. In larger chapters which encompass subjects that contain important and distinct sub-topics, the chapter is divided first by sub-topic and the documents from each category of material are then provided. For example, the chapter on the atmospheric protection is sub-divided into 'air pollution' and 'ozone protection'. Extracts are ordered chronologically according to the date of the legal instrument or judicial decision, in order that readers may see the pattern of development.

Each chapter contains a list of further reading. It is recommended, in addition to the works listed in the chapters, for the reader to consult for each and every topic the following textbooks: A Boyle and C Redgwell (eds), *Birnie, Boyle and Redgwell's International Law and the Environment* (4th edn, Oxford University Press 2021); Pierre-Marie Dupuy and Jorge E Viñuales (eds), *International Environmental Law* (2nd edn, Cambridge University Press 2018); Philippe Sands and Jacqueline Peel (eds), *Principles of International Environmental Law* (4th edn, Cambridge University Press 2018); Lavanya Rajamani and Jacqueline Peel (eds), *The Oxford Handbook of International Environmental Law* (2nd edn, Oxford University Press 2021); Malgosia Fitzmaurice, Panos Merkouris and Marcel Brus (eds), *Edward Elgar Handbook on International Environmental Law* (2nd edn, Edward Elgar 2021).

PART I
GENERAL PRINCIPLES AND APPROACHES

2
Sustainable development

2.1   INTRODUCTION

Sustainable development (SD) is a core principle of international environmental law. However, notwithstanding numerous publications on this subject, the concept remains oblique and ill defined. The most well known and relied upon definition of this concept is one coined by Gro Harlem Brundtland, who was a chair of the United Nations World Commission on Environment and Development (WCED), which published in 1987 the report, *Our Common Future* (also known as the 'Brundtland Report').[1] The definition submitted by the Commission is as follows: 'development which meets the needs of current generations without compromising the ability of future generations to meet their own needs'. This definition is very catchy but does not really say what is the precise content of the concept of sustainable development, which is far more complex than indicated by this definition.

The fundamental formulation of this concept was included in the 1992 Rio Declaration on Environment and Development in Principle 4, the so-called principle of integration:

> In order to achieve sustainable development, environmental protection shall constitute an integral part of the development process and cannot be considered in isolation from it.[2]

The aim of Principle 4 was to secure environmental interests while taking developmental decisions within the national and international structures. However, the formulation in Principle 4 does not solve the problem of reconciliation of economic development and environmental protection per se.

In general, it is accepted that the concept of sustainable development is based on three pillars: environmental protection; economic development; and social concerns. This formulation was crystallised in 2002 during the Johannesburg Summit on Sustainable Development in two main documents adopted there: the Declaration on Sustainable Development[3] and

---

[1]   *Report of the World Commission on Environment and Development: 'Our Common Future'* (1987) http://www.un-documents.net/our-common-future.pdf.

[2]   Rio Declaration on Environment and Development (1992) A/CONF.156.26 (Vol. I) http://www.unep.org/documents.multilingual/default.asp?documentid=78&articleid=1163.

[3]   Johannesburg Declaration on Sustainable Development (2002) A/CONF.199/20 http://www.un-documents.net/jburgdec.htm.

the Plan of Implementation of the World Summit on Sustainable Development.[4] It is also found in the other milestones of the development of international environmental law, i.e. the Rio+20 'Future We Want' – and 'Transforming Our World: The 2030 Agenda for Sustainable Development'.[5]

The concept of SD was further defined by the International Law Association, which is a private body, in 'New Delhi Declaration on Principles of International Law Related to Sustainable Development'. There are several elements of the concept of SD: the 'need' to take into account the interests of present and future generations; the principle of sustainable use of natural resources; the duty to take into account the interests of other states while exploiting states' own resources; and the duty of states to incorporate into their developmental policies environmental considerations. Some of the components of the principle of SD are lacking a well-defined normative content (such as the principle of intergenerational equity). The most well-defined element is sustainable utilisation, which deals with such issues as closed and open seasons for taking natural living resources, the size of fishing gear, etc.

It may be said that the milestone events of the development of SD clearly indicate that the environment's role has become secondary to economic development. The main element of SD at present is the eradication of poverty, a main theme of the Johannesburg Summit, the Rio+20 and the 2013 Agenda for Sustainable Development.

The classical definition of the principle of common but differentiated responsibilities (CBDR) is contained in Principle 7 of the Rio Declaration:

> States shall cooperate in a spirit of global partnership to conserve, protect and restore the health and integrity of the Earth's ecosystem. In view of the different contributions to global environmental degradation, States have common but differentiated responsibilities. The developed countries acknowledge the responsibility that they bear in the international pursuit to sustainable development in view of the pressures their societies place on the global environment and of the technologies and financial resources they command.

This principle as formulated in the Rio Declaration is an expression of an equitable approach that embodies the principle of fairness in international environmental law. The formulation of this principle was a subject of grave disagreement during the Rio conference between developed and developing countries. Most industrialised countries adhered to the view that the principle of CBDR applied only in the context of global environmental issuers, whilst developing countries assumed responsibility within the context of the pressures their societies place on the global environment and of the technologies and financial resources they command. There are many different ways to implement the principle of CBDR in international instruments. Multilateral environmental agreements (MEAs) contain numerous provisions which are aimed at remedying inequities in the position between states. Some MEAs contain

---

[4]   Plan of Implementation of the World Summit on Sustainable Development (2002) http://www.un.org/esa/sustdev/documents/WSSD_POI_PD/English/WSSD_PlanImpl.pdf.

[5]   Transforming our world: the 2030 Agenda for Sustainable Development (2015) A/RES/70/1 http://www.un.org/ga/search/view_doc.asp?symbol=A/RES/70/1&Lang=E.

special funds to assist developing states, such as the 1987 Montreal Protocol on Substances that Deplete the Ozone Layer. The same Protocol as well as the climate regime are based on a different timetable for developed and developing countries to eradicate certain substances. The Johannesburg Summit Plan of Implementation referred to the principle of CBDR. At this forum this principle resulted in a rather robust debate between developed and developing countries. Outside treaty regimes, the legal content of this principle remains controversial.

In general, it may also be said that sustainable development has an unclear status in international law. It is still unclear whether it is a norm of customary international law (CIL); of general principle of law as formulated in Article 38 of the Statute of the International Court of Justice; or just a concept without much legal content. However, it is an incontrovertible conclusion that SD is the most important building block of international environmental law.

2.2   NON-BINDING INSTRUMENTS

The Johannesburg Declaration on Sustainable Development

From our origins to the future
1.   We, the representatives of the peoples of the world, assembled at the World Summit on Sustainable Development in Johannesburg, South Africa, from 2 to 4 September 2002, reaffirm our commitment to sustainable development.
2.   We commit ourselves to building a humane, equitable and caring global society, cognizant of the need for human dignity for all.
3.   At the beginning of this Summit, the children of the world spoke to us in a simple yet clear voice that the future belongs to them, and accordingly challenged all of us to ensure that through our actions they will inherit a world free of the indignity and indecency occasioned by poverty, environmental degradation and patterns of unsustainable development.
4.   As part of our response to these children, who represent our collective future, all of us, coming from every corner of the world, informed by different life experiences, are united and moved by a deeply felt sense that we urgently need to create a new and brighter world of hope.
5.   Accordingly, we assume a collective responsibility to advance and strengthen the interdependent and mutually reinforcing pillars of sustainable development — economic development, social development and environmental protection — at the local, national, regional and global levels.
6.   From this continent, the cradle of humanity, we declare, through the Plan of Implementation of the World Summit on Sustainable Development and the present Declaration, our responsibility to one another, to the greater community of life and to our children.

7.   Recognizing that humankind is at a crossroads, we have united in a common resolve to make a determined effort to respond positively to the need to produce a practical and visible plan to bring about poverty eradication and human development.

From Stockholm to Rio de Janeiro to Johannesburg

8.   Thirty years ago, in Stockholm, we agreed on the urgent need to respond to the problem of environmental deterioration. Ten years ago, at the United Nations Conference on Environment and Development, held in Rio de Janeiro, we agreed that the protection of the environment and social and economic development are fundamental to sustainable development, based on the Rio Principles. To achieve such development, we adopted the global programme entitled Agenda 21 and the Rio Declaration on Environment and Development, to which we reaffirm our commitment. The Rio Conference was a significant milestone that set a new agenda for sustainable development.

9.   Between Rio and Johannesburg, the world's nations have met in several major conferences under the auspices of the United Nations, including the International Conference on Financing for Development, as well as the Doha Ministerial Conference. These conferences defined for the world a comprehensive vision for the future of humanity.

10.   At the Johannesburg Summit, we have achieved much in bringing together a rich tapestry of peoples and views in a constructive search for a common path towards a world that respects and implements the vision of sustainable development. The Johannesburg Summit has also confirmed that significant progress has been made towards achieving a global consensus and partnership among all the people of our planet.

The challenges we face

11.   We recognize that poverty eradication, changing consumption and production patterns and protecting and managing the natural resource base for economic and social development are overarching objectives of and essential requirements for sustainable development.

12.   The deep fault line that divides human society between the rich and the poor and the ever-increasing gap between the developed and developing worlds pose a major threat to global prosperity, security and stability.

13.   The global environment continues to suffer. Loss of biodiversity continues, fish stocks continue to be depleted, desertification claims more and more fertile land, the adverse effects of climate change are already evident, natural disasters are more frequent and more devastating, and developing countries more vulnerable, and air, water and marine pollution continue to rob millions of a decent life.

14.   Globalization has added a new dimension to these challenges. The rapid integration of markets, mobility of capital and significant increases in investment flows around the world have opened new challenges and opportunities for the pursuit of sustainable development. But the benefits and costs of globalization are unevenly distributed, with developing countries facing special difficulties in meeting this challenge.

15.   We risk the entrenchment of these global disparities and unless we act in a manner that fundamentally changes their lives the poor of the world may lose confidence in their representatives and the democratic systems to which we remain committed, seeing their representatives as nothing more than sounding brass or tinkling cymbals.

Our commitment to sustainable development

16.   We are determined to ensure that our rich diversity, which is our collective strength, will be used for constructive partnership for change and for the achievement of the common goal of sustainable development.

17.   Recognizing the importance of building human solidarity, we urge the promotion of dialogue and cooperation among the world's civilizations and peoples, irrespective of race, disabilities, religion, language, culture or tradition.

18.   We welcome the focus of the Johannesburg Summit on the indivisibility of human dignity and are resolved, through decisions on targets, timetables and partnerships, to speedily increase access to such basic requirements as clean water, sanitation, adequate shelter, energy, health care, food security and the protection of biodiversity. At the same time, we will work together to help one another gain access to financial resources, benefit from the opening of markets, ensure capacity-building, use modern technology to bring about development and make sure that there is technology transfer, human resource development, education and training to banish underdevelopment forever.

19.   We reaffirm our pledge to place particular focus on, and give priority attention to, the fight against the worldwide conditions that pose severe threats to the sustainable development of our people, which include: chronic hunger; malnutrition; foreign occupation; armed conflict; illicit drug problems; organized crime; corruption; natural disasters; illicit arms trafficking; trafficking in persons; terrorism; intolerance and incitement to racial, ethnic, religious and other hatreds; xenophobia; and endemic, communicable and chronic diseases, in particular HIV/AIDS, malaria and tuberculosis.

20.   We are committed to ensuring that women's empowerment, emancipation and gender equality are integrated in all the activities encompassed within Agenda 21, the Millennium Development Goals and the Plan of Implementation of the Summit.

21.   We recognize the reality that global society has the means and is endowed with the resources to address the challenges of poverty eradication and sustainable development confronting all humanity. Together, we will take extra steps to ensure that these available resources are used to the benefit of humanity.

22.   In this regard, to contribute to the achievement of our development goals and targets, we urge developed countries that have not done so to make concrete efforts reach the internationally agreed levels of official development assistance.

23.   We welcome and support the emergence of stronger regional groupings and alliances, such as the New Partnership for Africa's Development, to promote regional cooperation, improved international cooperation and sustainable development.

24.   We shall continue to pay special attention to the developmental needs of small island developing States and the least developed countries.

25.   We reaffirm the vital role of the indigenous peoples in sustainable development.

26. We recognize that sustainable development requires a long-term perspective and broad-based participation in policy formulation, decision-making and implementation at all levels. As social partners, we will continue to work for stable partnerships with all major groups, respecting the independent, important roles of each of them.

27. We agree that in pursuit of its legitimate activities the private sector, including both large and small companies, has a duty to contribute to the evolution of equitable and sustainable communities and societies.

28. We also agree to provide assistance to increase income-generating employment opportunities, taking into account the Declaration on Fundamental Principles and Rights at Work of the International Labour Organization.

29. We agree that there is a need for private sector corporations to enforce corporate accountability, which should take place within a transparent and stable regulatory environment.

30. We undertake to strengthen and improve governance at all levels for the effective implementation of Agenda 21, the Millennium development goals and the Plan of Implementation of the Summit.

Multilateralism is the future

31. To achieve our goals of sustainable development, we need more effective, democratic and accountable international and multilateral institutions.

32. We reaffirm our commitment to the principles and purposes of the Charter of the United Nations and international law, as well as to the strengthening of multilateralism. We support the leadership role of the United Nations as the most universal and representative organization in the world, which is best placed to promote sustainable development.

33. We further commit ourselves to monitor progress at regular intervals towards the achievement of our sustainable development goals and objectives.

Making it happen!

34. We are in agreement that this must be an inclusive process, involving all the major groups and Governments that participated in the historic Johannesburg Summit.

35. We commit ourselves to act together, united by a common determination to save our planet, promote human development and achieve universal prosperity and peace.

36. We commit ourselves to the Plan of Implementation of the World Summit on Sustainable Development and to expediting the achievement of the time-bound, socio-economic and environmental targets contained therein.

37. From the African continent, the cradle of humankind, we solemnly pledge to the peoples of the world and the generations that will surely inherit this Earth that we are determined to ensure that our collective hope for sustainable development is realized.

Transforming Our World: The 2030 Agenda for Sustainable Development

… The 17 Sustainable Development Goals and 169 targets which we are announcing today demonstrate the scale and ambition of this new universal Agenda. They seek to build on the Millennium Development Goals and complete what these did not achieve. They seek to realize the human rights of all and to achieve gender equality and the empowerment of all women and girls. They are integrated and indivisible and balance the three dimensions of sustainable development: the economic, social and environmental.

The Goals and targets will stimulate action over the next fifteen years in areas of critical importance for humanity and the planet:

People
We are determined to end poverty and hunger, in all their forms and dimensions, and to ensure that all human beings can fulfil their potential in dignity and equality and in a healthy environment.

Planet
We are determined to protect the planet from degradation, including through sustainable consumption and production, sustainably managing its natural resources and taking urgent action on climate change, so that it can support the needs of the present and future generations.

Prosperity
We are determined to ensure that all human beings can enjoy prosperous and fulfilling lives and that economic, social and technological progress occurs in harmony with nature.

Peace
We are determined to foster peaceful, just and inclusive societies which are free from fear and violence. There can be no sustainable development without peace and no peace without sustainable development.

Partnership
We are determined to mobilize the means required to implement this Agenda through a revitalized Global Partnership for Sustainable Development, based on a spirit of strengthened global solidarity, focused in particular on the needs of the poorest and most vulnerable and with the participation of all countries, all stakeholders and all people.

The interlinkages and integrated nature of the Sustainable Development Goals are of crucial importance in ensuring that the purpose of the new Agenda is realized. If we realize our ambitions across the full extent of the Agenda, the lives of all will be profoundly improved and our world will be transformed for the better.

[…]

2.   On behalf of the peoples we serve, we have adopted a historic decision on a com-
       prehensive, far-reaching and people-centred set of universal and transformative
       Goals and targets. We commit ourselves to working tirelessly for the full imple-
       mentation of this Agenda by 2030. We recognize that eradicating poverty in all its
       forms and dimensions, including extreme poverty, is the greatest global challenge
       and an indispensable requirement for sustainable development. We are committed
       to achieving sustainable development in its three dimensions – economic, social
       and environmental – in a balanced and integrated manner. We will also build upon
       the achievements of the Millennium Development Goals and seek to address their
       unfinished business.

3.   We resolve, between now and 2030, to end poverty and hunger everywhere;
       to combat inequalities within and among countries; to build peaceful, just and
       inclusive societies; to protect human rights and promote gender equality and the
       empowerment of women and girls; and to ensure the lasting protection of the
       planet and its natural resources. We resolve also to create conditions for sustaina-
       ble, inclusive and sustained economic growth, shared prosperity and decent work
       for all, taking into account different levels of national development and capacities.

[…]

7.   In these Goals and targets, we are setting out a supremely ambitious and transfor-
       mational vision. We envisage a world free of poverty, hunger, disease and want,
       where all life can thrive. We envisage a world free of fear and violence. A world
       with universal literacy. A world with equitable and universal access to quality
       education at all levels, to health care and social protection, where physical, mental
       and social well-being are assured. A world where we reaffirm our commitments
       regarding the human right to safe drinking water and sanitation and where there
       is improved hygiene; and where food is sufficient, safe, affordable and nutritious.
       A world where human habitats are safe, resilient and sustainable and where there is
       universal access to affordable, reliable and sustainable energy.

8.   We envisage a world of universal respect for human rights and human dignity, the
       rule of law, justice, equality and non-discrimination; of respect for race, ethnicity
       and cultural diversity; and of equal opportunity permitting the full realization of
       human potential and contributing to shared prosperity. A world which invests in
       its children and in which every child grows up free from violence and exploitation.
       A world in which every woman and girl enjoys full gender equality and all legal,
       social and economic barriers to their empowerment have been removed. A just,
       equitable, tolerant, open and socially inclusive world in which the needs of the most
       vulnerable are met.

9.   We envisage a world in which every country enjoys sustained, inclusive and sus-
       tainable economic growth and decent work for all. A world in which consumption
       and production patterns and use of all natural resources – from air to land, from
       rivers, lakes and aquifers to oceans and seas – are sustainable. One in which democ-
       racy, good governance and the rule of law as well as an enabling environment at
       national and international levels, are essential for sustainable development, includ-
       ing sustained and inclusive economic growth, social development, environmental
       protection and the eradication of poverty and hunger. One in which development

and the application of technology are climate-sensitive, respect biodiversity and are resilient. One in which humanity lives in harmony with nature and in which wildlife and other living species are protected.

[…]

55.   The SDGs and targets are integrated and indivisible, global in nature and universally applicable, taking into account different national realities, capacities and levels of development and respecting national policies and priorities. Targets are defined as aspirational and global, with each government setting its own national targets guided by the global level of ambition but taking into account national circumstances. Each government will also decide how these aspirational and global targets should be incorporated in national planning processes, policies and strategies. It is important to recognize the link between sustainable development and other relevant ongoing processes in the economic, social and environmental fields.

[…]

Sustainable Development Goals
Goal 1. End poverty in all its forms everywhere
Goal 2. End hunger, achieve food security and improved nutrition and promote sustainable agriculture
Goal 3. Ensure healthy lives and promote well-being for all at all ages
Goal 4. Ensure inclusive and equitable quality education and promote lifelong learning opportunities for all
Goal 5. Achieve gender equality and empower all women and girls
Goal 6. Ensure availability and sustainable management of water and sanitation for all
Goal 7. Ensure access to affordable, reliable, sustainable and modern energy for all
Goal 8. Promote sustained, inclusive and sustainable economic growth, full and productive employment and decent work for all
Goal 9. Build resilient infrastructure, promote inclusive and sustainable industrialization and foster innovation
Goal 10. Reduce inequality within and among countries
Goal 11. Make cities and human settlements inclusive, safe, resilient and sustainable
Goal 12. Ensure sustainable consumption and production patterns
Goal 13. Take urgent action to combat climate change and its impacts*
Goal 14. Conserve and sustainably use the oceans, seas and marine resources for sustainable development
Goal 15. Protect, restore and promote sustainable use of terrestrial ecosystems, sustainably manage forests, combat desertification, and halt and reverse land degradation and halt biodiversity loss
Goal 16. Promote peaceful and inclusive societies for sustainable development, provide access to justice for all and build effective, accountable and inclusive institutions at all levels

Goal 17. Strengthen the means of implementation and revitalize the global partnership for sustainable development

* Acknowledging that the United Nations Framework Convention on Climate Change is the primary international, intergovernmental forum for negotiating the global response to climate change.

2.3   CASE LAW

CASE
ICJ, Gabčíkovo-Nagymaros Project (Hungary v. Slovakia), ICJ Reports 7 (1997)

140. It is clear that the Project's impact upon, and its implications for, the environment are of necessity a key issue. The numerous scientific reports which have been presented to the Court by the Parties – even if their conclusions are often contradictory – provide abundant evidence that this impact and these implications are considerable. In order to evaluate the environmental risks, current standards must be taken into consideration. This is not only allowed by the wording of Articles 15 and 19, but even prescribed, to the extent that these articles impose a continuing – and thus necessarily evolving – obligation on the parties to maintain the quality of the water of the Danube and to protect nature. The Court is mindful that, in the field of environmental protection, vigilance and prevention are required on account of the often irreversible character of damage to the environment and of the limitations inherent in the very mechanism of reparation of this type of damage. Throughout the ages, mankind has, for economic and other reasons, constantly interfered with nature. In the past, this was often done without consideration of the effects upon the environment. Owing to new scientific insights and to a growing awareness of the risks for mankind – for present and future generations – of pursuit of such interventions at an unconsidered and unabated pace, new norms and standards have been developed, set forth in a great number of instruments during the last two decades. Such new norms have to be taken into consideration, and such new standards given proper weight, not only when States contemplate new activities but also when continuing with activities begun in the past. This need to reconcile economic development with protection of the environment is aptly expressed in the concept of sustainable development. For the purposes of the present case, this means that the Parties together should look afresh at the effects on the environment of the operation of the Gabcikovo power plant. In particular they must find a satisfactory solution for the volume of water to be released into the old bed of the Danube and into the side-arms on both sides of the river.

CASE
RIAA, *Award in the Arbitration regarding the Iron Rhine ('Ijzeren Rijn') Railway between the Kingdom of Belgium and the Kingdom of the Netherlands (Belgium vs. the Netherlands)*, XXVII RIAA 35–125 (24 May 2005)

59. Since the Stockholm Conference on the Environment in 1972 there been a marked development of international law relating to the protection of the environment. Today, both international and EC law require the integration of appropriate environmental measures in the design and implementation of economic development activities. Principle 4 of the Rio Declaration on Environment and Development, adopted in 1992 (31 I.L.M. p. 874, at p. 877), which reflects this trend, provides that 'environmental protection shall constitute an integral part of the development process and cannot be considered in isolation from it'. Importantly, these emerging principles now integrate environmental protection into the development process. Environmental law and the law on development stand not as alternatives but as mutually reinforcing, integral concepts, which require that where development may cause significant harm to the environment there is a duty to prevent, or at least mitigate, such harm (...). This duty, in the opinion of the Tribunal, has now become a principle of general international law. This principle applies not only in autonomous activities but also in activities undertaken in implementation of specific treaties between the Parties. The Tribunal would recall the observation of the International Court of Justice in the *Gabčíkovo-Nagymaros* case that

> [t]his need to reconcile economic development with protection of the environment is aptly expressed in the concept of sustainable development(...) [And in that context the Court further clarified that] new norms have to be taken into consideration, and new standards given proper weight, not only when States contemplate new activities but also when continuing with activities begun in the past (Ibid.).

In the view of the Tribunal this dictum applies equally to the Iron Rhine railway.

QUESTIONS

1. Please reflect on and explain the role and usefulness of the concept of SD in relation to the protection of the environment.
2. Has the concept of SD achieved the balance between all three pillars: environmental protection; economic development; and social issues?
3. What, if any, is the normative content of the concept of SD?

FURTHER READING

BOOKS

A Boyle and D Freestone (eds), *International Law and Sustainable Development: Past Achievements and Future Challenges* (Oxford University Press 1999)

D French, *International Law and Policy of Sustainable Development* (Manchester University Press 2005)

D French and L Kotzé (eds), *Sustainable Development Goals: Law, Theory and Implementation* (Edward Elgar 2018)

C Voigt, *Sustainable Development as a Principle of International Law: Resolving Conflicts Between Climate Measures and WTO Law* (Brill/Nijhoff 2009)

CHAPTERS

V Barral, 'The Principle of Sustainable Development' in L Krämer and E Orlando (eds), *Principles of Environmental Law* (Edward Elgar 2018)

D Barstow Magraw and LD Hawke, 'Sustainable Development' in D Bodansky, J Brunnée and E Hey (eds), *The Oxford Handbook of International Environmental Law* (Oxford University Press 2008)

ARTICLES

V Barral, 'Sustainable Development in International Law: Nature and Operation of an Evolutive Legal Norm' (2012) 23 EJIL 377

RE Kim and K Bosselmann, 'Operationalizing Sustainable Development' (2015) 24 Rev Euro Comp & Int Env Law 194

P Sands, 'International Law in the Field of Sustainable Development' (1994) 64 BYBIL 303

N Schrijver, 'The Evolution of Sustainable Development in International Law' (2007) 329 RCADI 217

3
Permanent sovereignty over natural resources

3.1   INTRODUCTION

At the international level, the first mention to the right of free access to natural resources 'on equal terms' dates back to the years of the Second World War, when the Allies' war effort made evident the dependence of industrialised states on overseas raw materials.[1]

With the end of the conflict and the start of the decolonisation process, the right to the free use of natural resources would lie at the core of the opposition between the Western and the Soviet blocs. In fact, third world states, rich in natural resources, weaponised the right in question as an instrument of political and economic struggle. In the context of the Cold War, the clash shifted within the UN General Assembly, where the principle of permanent sovereignty over natural resources (PSNR) began to be shaped one UN Resolution at a time.[2]

In 1958, the UN General Assembly established the Commission on PSNR 'to conduct a full survey of this basic constituent of the right to self-determination'.[3] The work of the Commission led to the adoption of the Declaration on PSNR, which, listed under eight paragraphs, spells out the rights stemming from the principle at hand.[4] It is worth noting that the principle is framed here in a strictly political and economic dimension, as one of the cornerstones for the establishment of a 'new international economic order'.[5]

However, the versatility of the PSNR principle is immediately clear: between the second half of the 1960s and the first half of the 1970s, the latter was first elaborated as a corollary of the

---

[1]   The Atlantic Charter, Yearbook of the United Nations 1946–47 (New York, 1947), p. 2.

[2]   Starting from UN General Assembly Resolution on Integrated Economic Development and Commercial Agreements, A/RES/523(VI) (1952).

[3]   UN General Assembly Resolution on Recommendations Concerning International Respect for the Rights of Peoples and Nations to Self-determination, A/RES/1314(XIII) (1958), para. 1.

[4]   UN General Assembly Resolution on Permanent Sovereignty over Natural Resources, A/RES/1803(XVII) (1962).

[5]   In this vein, see UN General Assembly Resolution on Declaration on the Establishment of a New International Economic Order, A/RES/3201(1974) and UN General Assembly Resolution on Programme of Action on the Establishment of a New International Economic Order, A/RES/3202(1974).

principle of peoples' self-determination,[6] and then, as international environmental law took its first steps, as the source of a general obligation on the cooperative and responsible management of natural resources. It is no coincidence, therefore, that Principle 21 of the Declaration of Stockholm of 1972 places states' right to exploit their natural resources alongside with 'the responsibility to ensure that activities within their jurisdiction or control do not cause damage to the environment of other States or of areas beyond the limits of national jurisdiction'.[7] This 'environmental dimension' expands and deepens the 'duty-side' of the PSNR principle. As Prof. Schrijver puts it, 'the emphasis of the principle of sovereignty over natural resources gradually shifted from a primarily rights-based to a qualified concept encompassing duties as well as rights'.[8]

Under this bidimensional reinterpretation, that is, as a source of both rights and duties, the PSNR has since taken hold as a general principle of international environmental law. As such, in tandem with other and potentially encroaching concepts, such as 'sustainable development', 'sustainable use', 'maximum sustainable yield' and the like, it is recalled in a number of international legal instruments. Among the binding ones, the United Nations Convention on the Law of the Sea,[9] the Convention on Biological Diversity,[10] the Energy Charter Treaty,[11] and the Protocol Against the Illegal Exploitation of Natural Resources[12] stand out.

Despite the fact that, since the fall of the Berlin Wall, its political and economic dimension has progressively lost relevance, the PSNR principle is today recognised as customary in nature both by the international scholarship[13] and jurisprudence.[14] Its 'right side' has remained prevalent as an articulation of the principle of peoples' self-determination, especially in relation

---

[6]   See Article 1 of both the International Covenant on Civil and Political Rights, 999 UNTS 171 (1966) and the International Covenant on Economic, Social and Cultural Rights, 993 UNTS 3 (1966).

[7]   United Nations Conference on the Human Environment, Stockholm, 5–16 June 1972, Declaration of the United Nations Conference on the Human Environment.

[8]   Schrijver, Nico J., 'Natural Resources, Permanent Sovereignty over', in Rüdiger Wolfrum (ed.), *Max Planck Encyclopedia of Public International Law* (2008), para. 2.

[9]   Article 193 of the United Nations Convention on the Law of the Sea, 1833 UNTS 3 (1982).

[10]   Article 15 of the Convention on Biological Diversity, 1760 UNTS 79 (1992).

[11]   Article 18 of the Energy Charter Treaty, 2080 UNTS 95 (1994).

[12]   Protocol Against the Illegal Exploitation of Natural Resources (2006).

[13]   *Inter alia*, see Stephan Hobe, 'Evolution of the Principle on Permanent Sovereignty over Natural Resources', in Bungenberg, Marc and Hobe, Stephan (eds), *Permanent Sovereignty over Natural Resources* (Heidelberg, New York, Dordrecht, London: 2015), p. 11.

[14]   *Inter alia*, see *Armed Activities on the Territory of the Congo (Democratic Republic of the Congo v. Uganda)*, Judgment, ICJ Reports 168 (2005), para. 244.

to the Palestinian question[15] and the rights of indigenous people,[16] while its 'duty side' has developed as a source of states' responsibility of careful and forward-thinking managing of their natural resources.

It is believed that, far from being an outdated heritage of the Cold War era, the PSNR represents a principle of current importance, in particular in the light of the common challenges that environmental exploitation and resource scarcity pose before us.

3.2   LEGAL INSTRUMENTS

3.2.1   Legally Binding Instruments

3.2.1.1   International
1966 International Covenant on Civil and Political Rights, 999 UNTS 171; 1966 International Covenant on Economic, Social and Cultural Rights, 993 UNTS 3

Article 1
1.   All peoples have the right of self-determination. By virtue of that right they freely determine their political status and freely pursue their economic, social and cultural development.
2.   All peoples may, for their own ends, freely dispose of their natural wealth and resources without prejudice to any obligations arising out of international economic co-operation, based upon the principle of mutual benefit, and international law. In no case may a people be deprived of its own means of subsistence.
3.   The States Parties to the present Covenant, including those having responsibility for the administration of Non-Self-Governing and Trust Territories, shall promote the realization of the right of self-determination, and shall respect that right, in conformity with the provisions of the Charter of the United Nations.

1968 African Convention on the Conservation of Nature and Natural Resources, 1001 UNTS 3

Preamble
Re-affirming that States have, in accordance with the Charter of the United Nations and the principles of international law, a sovereign right to exploit their own resources pursuant to their environmental and developmental policies, and the responsibility to ensure that activities within their jurisdiction or control do not cause damage to the environment of other States or of areas beyond the limits of national jurisdiction.

---

[15]   See, for instance, UN General Assembly Resolution on Permanent Sovereignty of the Palestinian People in the Occupied Palestinian Territory, including East Jerusalem, and of the Arab Population in the occupied Syrian Golan over their Natural Resources, A/RES/52/207 (1997).

[16]   See, for instance, United Nations General Assembly Resolution on Declaration on the Rights of Indigenous Peoples, A/RES/61/295 (2007).

1978 Treaty for Amazonian Cooperation, 1202 UNTS 71

Preamble
Conscious that both socio-economic development as well as conservation of the environment are responsibilities inherent in the sovereignty of each State, and that cooperation among the Contracting Parties shall facilitate fulfillment of these responsibilities, by continuing and expanding the joint efforts being made for the ecological conservation of the Amazon region
  [...]

Article IV
The Contracting Parties declare that the exclusive use and utilization of natural resources within their respective territories is a right inherent in the sovereignty of each state and that the exercise of this right shall not be subject to any restrictions other than those arising from International Law.

1981 African Charter on Human and Peoples' Rights, 1520 UNTS 217

Article 21 (*Right to Free Disposal of Wealth and Natural Resources*)
1.   All peoples shall freely dispose of their wealth and natural resources. This right shall be exercised in the exclusive interest of the people. In no case shall a people be deprived of it
2.   In case of spoilation, the dispossessed people shall have the right to the lawful recovery of its property as well as to an adequate compensation.
3.   The free disposal of wealth and natural resources shall be exercised without prejudice to the obligation of promoting international economic cooperation based on mutual respect, equitable exchange and the principles of international law.
4.   State Parties to the present Charter shall individually and collectively exercise the right to free disposal of their wealth and natural resources with a view to strengthening African Unity and solidarity.
5.   State Parties to the present Charter shall undertake to eliminate all forms of foreign exploitation particularly that practised by international monopolies so as to enable their peoples to fully benefit from the advantages derived from their national resources.

1982 United Nations Convention on the Law of the Sea, 1833 UNTS 3

Article 193 (*Sovereign right of States to exploit their natural resources*)
States have the sovereign right to exploit their natural resources pursuant to their environmental policies and in accordance with their duty to protect and preserve the marine environment.

1992 Convention on Biological Diversity, 1760 UNTS 79

Article 15 (*Access to Genetic Resources*)
1.   Recognizing the sovereign rights of States over their natural resources, the authority to determine access to genetic resources rests with the national governments
      and is subject to national legislation.

1992 United Nations Framework Convention on Climate Change, 1771 UNTS 107

Preamble
Recalling also that States have, in accordance with the Charter of the United Nations
and the principles of international law, the sovereign right to exploit their own resources
pursuant to their own environmental and developmental policies, and the responsibility
to ensure that activities within their jurisdiction or control do not cause damage to the
environment of other States or of areas beyond the limits of national jurisdiction.

2006 Protocol Against the Illegal Exploitation of Natural Resources

Preamble
   We, Heads of State and of Government of the Member States of the International
Conference on the Great Lakes Region;
   [...]

Considering that permanent sovereignty over natural resources is an inalienable right of the
people, which must be exercised in the interest of their national development and of the
well-being of the population of the State concerned, without prejudice to the obligations
arising out of international economic cooperation, based upon the principle of mutual
interest and international law;
   Considering that the illegal exploitation of natural resources in the Great Lakes Region
is one of the factors causing or aggravating endemic conflicts and persistent insecurity
in the Region, and represents, at the same time, a major obstacle to the attainment of
the Millennium Development Goals; Deeply concerned about the negative impact of the
illegal exploitation of natural resources, which aggravates environmental degradation and
deprives States of the resources needed to fight poverty;
   [...]

Agree as follows:

Chapter I (*General Provisions*)

Article 1 (*Definitions*)
For the purposes of this Protocol, unless the context otherwise requires, the following
mean:
   [...]

"Permanent Sovereignty over Natural Resources": the permanent authority and competence exercised by a State over natural resources on its territory according to the principle of international law as enshrined in the UN General Assembly Resolution 1803 (XVII) of 1962;

Article 2 (*Objectives*)

The objectives of this Protocol are:

1. To promote and strengthen, in each Member State, the development of effective mechanisms to prevent, curb and eradicate the illegal exploitation of natural resources;
2. To intensify and revitalize cooperation among Member State with a view to achieving more efficient and sustainable measures against the illegal exploitation of natural resources;
3. To promote the harmonization by Member States of their national legislations, policies and procedures against the illegal exploitation of natural resources.

Article 3 (*Permanent Sovereignty over Natural Resources*)

1. Member States shall freely dispose of their natural resources. This right shall be exercised in the exclusive interest of the people. In no case, the populations shall a State be deprived of it.
2. In case of spoliation, the dispossessed Member State shall have the right to the lawful recovery of its property, as well as to adequate compensation.
3. The free disposal of wealth and natural resources shall be exercised without prejudice to the obligation of promoting international economic cooperation, based on mutual respect, equitable exchange and the principles of international law.
4. Member States shall develop and implement a participatory and transparent mechanism for the exploitation of natural resources, according to their respective economic and social systems.

Article 4 (*Infringement of the Right to Permanent Sovereignty of States over Natural Resources*)

The illegal exploitation of natural resources shall be considered as a violation of the right of Member States to permanent sovereignty over their natural resources, and contrary to the spirit and principles of the United Nations Charter, the Declaration on the Right to Development adopted by the United Nations General Assembly, the Constitutive Act of the African Union and the African Charter on Human and Peoples' Rights.

Table 3.1 Other notable treaties

1994	United Nations Convention to Combat Desertification in those Countries Experiencing Serious Drought and/or Desertification, Particularly in Africa, 1954 UNTS 3
1999	Protocol on Water and Health to the 1992 Convention on the Protection and Use of Transboundary Watercourses and International Lakes, 2331 UNTS 302
2001	Stockholm Convention on Persistent Organic Pollutants, 2256 UNTS 119

3.2.1.2   Non-binding instruments

UN General Assembly Resolution on Right to Exploit Freely Natural Wealth and Resources, A/RES/626(VII) (1952)

The General Assembly,

Bearing in mind the need for encouraging the under-developed countries in the proper use and exploitation of their natural wealth and resources,

Considering that the economic development of the under-developed countries is one of the fundamental requisites for the strengthening of universal peace,

Remembering that the right of peoples freely to use and exploit their natural wealth and resources is inherent in their sovereignty and is in accordance with the Purposes and Principles of the Charter of the United Nations,

1.   *Recommends* all Member States, in the exercise of their right freely to use and exploit their natural wealth and resources wherever deemed desirable by them for their own progress and economic development, to have due regard, consistently with their sovereignty, to the need for maintaining the flow of capital in conditions of security, mutual confidence and economic co-operation among nations;

2.   *Further recommends* all Member States to refrain from acts, direct or indirect, designed to impede the exercise of the sovereignty of any State over its natural resources.

UN General Assembly Resolution on Permanent Sovereignty over Natural Resources, A/RES/1803(XVII)(1962)

The General Assembly,
   [...]
Declares that:

1.   The right of peoples and nations to permanent sovereignty over their natural wealth and resources must be exercised in the interest of their national development and of the well-being of the people of the State concerned.

2.   The exploration, development and disposition of such resources, as well as the import of the foreign capital required for these purposes, should be in conformity with the rules and conditions which the peoples and nations freely consider to be necessary or desirable with regard to the authorization, restriction or prohibition of such activities.

3.   In cases where authorization is granted, the capital imported and the earnings on that capital shall be governed by the terms thereof, by the national legislation in force, and by international law. The profits derived must be shared in the proportions freely agreed upon, in each case, between the investors and the recipient State, due care being taken to ensure that there is no impairment, for any reason, of that State's sovereignty over its natural wealth and resources.

4.   Nationalization, expropriation or requisitioning shall be based on grounds or reasons of public utility, security or the national interest which are recognized as overriding purely individual or private interests, both domestic and foreign. In such cases the owner shall be paid appropriate compensation, in accordance with

the rules in force in the State taking such measures in the exercise of its sovereignty and in accordance with international law. In any case where the question of compensation gives rise to a controversy, the national jurisdiction of the State taking such measures shall be exhausted. However, upon agreement by sovereign States and other parties concerned, settlement of the dispute should be made through arbitration or international adjudication.

5. The free and beneficial exercise of the sovereignty of peoples and nations over their natural resources must be furthered by the mutual respect of States based on their sovereign equality.

6. International co-operation for the economic development of developing countries, whether in the form of public or private capital investments, exchange of goods and services, technical assistance, or exchange of scientific information, shall be such as to further their independent national development and shall be based upon respect for their sovereignty over their natural wealth and resources.

7. Violation of the rights of peoples and nations to sovereignty over their natural wealth and resources is contrary to the spirit and principles of the Charter of the United Nations and hinders the development of international co-operation and the maintenance of peace.

8. Foreign investment agreements freely entered into by or between sovereign States shall be observed in good faith; States and international organizations shall strictly and conscientiously respect the sovereignty of peoples and nations over their natural wealth and resources in accordance with the Charter and the principles set forth in the present resolution.

UN General Assembly Resolution on Permanent Sovereignty over Natural Resources, A/RES/3171(XXVIII) (1973)

The General Assembly,

Reiterating that the inalienable right of each State to the full exercise of national sovereignty over its natural resources has been repeatedly recognized by the international community in numerous resolutions of various organs of the United Nations,

Reiterating also that an intrinsic condition of the exercise of the sovereignty of every State is that it be exercised fully and effectively over all the natural resources of the State, whether found on land or in the sea,

Reaffirming the inviolable principle that every country has the right to adopt the economic and social system which it deems most favourable to its development,

Recalling its resolutions 1803 (XVII) of 14 December 1962, 2158 (XXI) of 25 November 1966, 2386 (XXIII) of 19 November 1968, 2625 (XXV) of 24 October 1970, 2692 (XXV) of 11 December 1970 and 3016 (XXVII) of 18 December 1972, and Security Council resolution 330 (1973) of 21 March 1973, which relate to permanent sovereignty over natural resources,

Recalling, in particular, the Declaration on Principles of International Law concerning Friendly Relations and Co-operation among States in accordance with the Charter of the United Nations, which proclaims that no State may use or encourage the use of economic, political or any other type of measures to coerce another State in order to obtain from it the subordination of the exercise of its sovereign rights and to secure from it advantages of any kind,

Considering that the full exercise by each State of sovereignty over its natural resources is an essential condition for achieving the objectives and targets of the Second United Nations Development Decade, and that this exercise requires that action by States aimed at achieving a better utilization and use of those resources must cover all stages, from exploration to marketing,

Taking note of section VII of the Economic Declaration adopted by the Fourth Conference of Heads of State or Government of Non-Aligned Countries, held at Algiers from 5 to 9 September 1973,

Taking note also of the report of the Secretary-General on permanent sovereignty over natural resources,

1. *Strongly reaffirms* the inalienable rights of States to permanent sovereignty over all their natural resources, on land within their international boundaries as well as those in the sea-bed and the subsoil thereof within their national jurisdiction and in the superjacent waters;

2. *Supports resolutely* the efforts of the developing countries and of the peoples of the territories under colonial and racial domination and foreign occupation in their struggle to regain effective control over their natural resources;

3. *Affirms* that the application of the principle of nationalization carried out by States, as an expression of their sovereignty in order to safeguard their natural resources, implies that each State is entitled to determine the amount of possible compensation and the mode of payment, and that any disputes which might arise should be settled in accordance with the national legislation of each. State carrying out such measures;

United Nations General Assembly Resolution on
Declaration on the Rights of Indigenous Peoples, A/RES/61/295 (2007)

Preamble

Convinced that control by indigenous peoples over developments affecting them and their lands, territories and resources will enable them to maintain and strengthen their institutions, cultures and traditions, and to promote their development in accordance with their aspirations and needs,

Article 26

1. Indigenous peoples have the right to the lands, territories and resources which they have traditionally owned, occupied or otherwise used or acquired.

2. Indigenous peoples have the right to own, use, develop and control the lands, territories and resources that they possess by reason of traditional ownership or other traditional occupation or use, as well as those which they have otherwise acquired.

3. States shall give legal recognition and protection to these lands, territories and resources. Such recognition shall be conducted with due respect to the customs, traditions and land tenure systems of the indigenous peoples concerned.

Article 27

States shall establish and implement, in conjunction with indigenous peoples concerned, a fair, independent, impartial, open and transparent process, giving due recognition to indigenous peoples' laws, traditions, customs and land tenure systems, to recognize and adjudicate the rights of indigenous peoples pertaining to their lands, territories and resources, including those which were traditionally owned or otherwise occupied or used. Indigenous peoples shall have the right to participate in this process.

Table 3.2 Other relevant UN General Assembly Resolutions

UN General Assembly Resolution on Integrated Economic Development and Commercial Agreements, A/RES/523(VI) (1952);
UN General Assembly Resolution on the Right of Peoples and Nations to Self-Determination, A/RES/637(VII) (1952);
UN General Assembly Resolution on the Right to Exploit Freely Natural Wealth and Resources, A/RES/1720(XVI) (1952);
UN General Assembly Resolution on Recommendations Concerning International Respect for the Rights of Peoples and Nations to Self-determination, A/RES/1314(XIII) (1958);
UN General Assembly Resolution on Declaration on the Granting of Independence to Colonial Countries and Peoples, A/RES/1514(XV) (1960);
UN General Assembly Resolution on Concerted Action for Economic Development of Economically Less Developed Countries, A/RES/1515(XV) (1960);
UN General Assembly Resolution on Permanent Sovereignty over Natural Resources, A/RES/1720(XVI) (1961);
UN General Assembly Resolution on Permanent Sovereignty over Natural Resources, A/RES/2158(XXI) (1966);
UN General Assembly Resolution on Permanent Sovereignty over Natural Resources, A/RES/2386(XXIII) (1969);
UN General Assembly Resolution on Declaration on Social Progress and Development, 2542 A/RES/(XXIV)(1969);
UN General Assembly Resolution on Declaration on Principles of International Law concerning Friendly Relations and Co-operation among States in accordance with the Charter of the United Nations, A/RES/2625(XXV) (1970);
UN General Assembly Resolution on International Development Strategy for the Second United Nations Development Decade, A/RES/2626(XXV) (1970);
UN General Assembly Resolution on Permanent Sovereignty over Natural Resources of Developing Countries and Expansion of Domestic Sources of Accumulation for Economic Development, A/RES/2692(XXV) (1970);
UN General Assembly Resolution on Development and Environment, A/RES/2849(XXVI) (1971);
United Nations Conference on the Human Environment, Stockholm, 5–16 June 1972, Declaration of the United Nations Conference on the Human Environment ('Stockholm Declaration');
UN General Assembly Resolution on Permanent Sovereignty over Natural Resources of Developing Countries, A/RES/3016(XXVII) (1972);
UN General Assembly Resolution on Preservation and Further Development of Cultural Values, A/RES/3148(XXVIII) (1973);

3.3   CASE LAW

ADVISORY OPINION
ICJ, Legal Consequences for States of the Continued Presence of South Africa in Namibia (South West Africa) notwithstanding Security Council Resolution 276, Advisory Opinion, ICJ Reports 16 (1971)

Furthermore, the subsequent development of international law in regard to non-self-governing territories, as enshrined in the Charter of the United Nations, made the principle of self-determination applicable to all [...] "territories whose peoples have not yet attained a full measure of self-government" (Art. 73). Thus it clearly embraced territories under a colonial régime. [...] A further important stage in this development was the Declaration on the Granting of Independence to Colonial Countries and Peoples (General Assembly resolution 1514 (XV) of 14 December 1960), which embraces all peoples and territories which "have not yet attained independence". [...] Today, only two out of fifteen, excluding Namibia, remain under United Nations tutelage. This is but a manifestation of the general development which has led to the birth of so many new States (para. 52).

[...] These developments leave little doubt that the ultimate objective of the sacred trust was the self-determination and independence of the peoples concerned. In this domain, as elsewhere, the *corpus iuris gentium* has been considerably enriched, and this the Court, if it is faithfully to discharge its functions, may not ignore (para. 53).

CASE
ICJ, *Fisheries Jurisdiction (United Kingdom v. Iceland)*, Merits, Judgment, ICJ Reports 3 (1974)

DISSENTING OPINION OF JUDGE PETRÉN, PP. 161–162

[A]ttention has been drawn to the recent resolutions of United Nations organs concerning permanent sovereignty over natural resources. In its resolution 3016 (XXVII) of 18 December 1972, the General Assembly reaffirmed the right of States to permanent sovereignty over all their natural resources, on land within their national boundaries as well as those found in the sea-bed and the subsoil thereof within their national jurisdiction and in the superjacent waters [...].

[...]

[T]he complexity of the circumstances in which resolution 3016 (XXVII) was adopted, the statements accompanying the vote and the well-known attitude of certain States regarding fishery zones do not justify the conclusion that the resolution was passed by a large majority of States with the intention of creating a new binding rule of law [...].

ADVISORY OPINION
ICJ, Western Sahara, Advisory Opinion, ICJ Reports 12 (1975)

The principle of self-determination as a right of peoples, and its application for the purpose of bringing all colonial situations to a speedy end, were enunciated in the Declaration on the Granting of Independence to Colonial Countries and Peoples, General Assembly resolution 1514 (XV). In this resolution the General Assembly proclaims "the necessity of bringing to a speedy and unconditional end colonialism in all its forms and manifestations". To this end the resolution provides *inter alia*:

2. All peoples have the right to self-determination; by virtue of that right they freely determine their political status and freely pursue their economic, social and cultural development (para. 55).

[...]

General Assembly resolution 2625 (XXV), "Declaration on Principles of International Law concerning Friendly Relations and Co-operation among States in accordance with the Charter of the United Nations" – to which reference was also made in the proceedings – mentions other possibilities besides independence, association or integration. But in doing so it reiterates the basic need to take account of the wishes of the people concerned:

"The establishment of a sovereign and independent State, the free association or integration with an independent State or the emergence into any other political status freely determined by a people constitute modes of implementing the right of self-determination by that people" (para. 58).

CASE
ILM, *Award on the Merits in Dispute between Texaco Overseas Petroleum Company/California Asiatic Oil Co. and the Government of the Libyan Arab Republic (Texaco v. Libya)*, 17 ILM 1 (1977)

[T]he absence of any binding force of the resolution of the General Assembly of the United Nations implies that such resolutions must be accepted by the members of the United Nations in order to be legally binding. In this respect, the Tribunal notes that [...] Resolution 1803 (XVII) of 14 December 1962 was supported by a majority of Member States representing all of the various groups [...] (para. 86);

On the basis of the circumstances of adoption mentioned above and by expressing an *opinio juris communis*, Resolution 1803(XVII) seems to this Tribunal to reflect the state of customary law existing in this field. Indeed, on the occasion of the vote on a resolution finding the existence of customary rule, the States concerned clearly express their views. The consensus by a majority of States belonging to the various representative groups indicates without the slightest doubt universal recognition of the rules therein incorporated [...] (para. 87);

[R]esolution 1803(XVII) appears to a large extent as the expression of a real general will [...] (para. 88).

[O]ne should note that the principle of good faith, which had already been mentioned in

Resolution 1803(XVII), has an important place even in Resolution 3281(XXIX) called "The Charter of Economic Rights and Duties of States". One should conclude that a sovereign State which nationalizes cannot disregard the commitments undertaken by the contracting State: to decide otherwise would in fact recognize that all contractual commitments undertaken by a State have been undertaken under a purely permissive condition on its part and are therefore lacing of any legal force and any binding effect (para. 91).

CASE
ILM, *Arbitral Tribunal: Award in Dispute between Libyan American Oil Company (Liamco) and the Government of the Libyan Arab Republic Relating to Petroleum Concessions*, 20 ILM 1 (1981), p. 78

It has been contended by the Libyan Government [...] that it rejects arbitration as contrary to the heart of its sovereignty. [...] More generally, Resolution No. 1803(XVII) of the United Nations General Assembly [...] while proclaiming the permanent sovereignty of peoples and nations over their natural resources, confirms the obligation of the State to respect arbitration agreements (Section I, paras 1 and 4).

CASE
ICCPR, *Human Rights Committee, Chief Bernard Ominayak and the Lubicon Lake Band v. Canada* (Communication No. 167/1984), CCPR/C/38/D/167/1984 (1990), para. 13.3

[T]he Committee reaffirm[s] that the Covenant recognizes and protects in most resolute terms a people's right of self-determination and its right to dispose of its natural resources, as an essential condition for the effective guarantee and observance of individual human rights and for the promotion and strengthening of those rights.

CASE
ICJ, *East Timor (Portugal v. Australia)*, Judgment, ICJ Reports 90 (1995)

29: In the Court's view, Portugal's assertion that the right of peoples to self-determination, as it evolved from the Charter and from United Nations practice, has an *erga omnes* character is irreproachable. The principle of self-determination of peoples has been recognized by the United Nations Charter and in the jurisprudence of the Court [...]; it is one of the essential principles of contemporary international law.

DISSENTING OPINION OF JUDGE WEERAMANTRY

I am also in agreement with the Court's observations in regard to the right to self-determination of the people of East Timor, their right to permanent sovereignty over their natural resources, and the *erga omnes* nature of these rights. The stress laid by the Court on self-determination as "one of the essential principles of contemporary international law"

(Judgment, para. 29) has my complete and unqualified support (p. 142).

[...]

Australia is party to a treaty which deals, *inter alia*, with resources acknowledgedly belonging to the East Timorese people, who are acknowledgedly a non-self-governing people. So long as they continue to be a non-self-governing people, those resources will continue to belong to them by incontrovertible principles of the law of nations. At such time as they achieve self-determination, they may deal with these resources in such manner as they freely choose. Until such time, the international legal system protects their rights for them, and must take serious note of any event by which their rights are disposed of, or otherwise dealt with, without their consent. Indeed, the deepest significance of the right of a non-self-governing people to permanent sovereignty over natural resources lies in the fact that the international community is under an obligation to protect these assets for them. [...] If East Timor is still a non-self-governing territory, every member of the community of nations, including Australia, is under a duty to recognize its right to self-determination and permanent sovereignty over its natural resources (pp. 153–154).

[...]

The central principle around which this case revolves is the principle of self-determination, and its ancillary, the principle of permanent sovereignty over natural resources (p. 193).

[...]

As the General Assembly has stressed, the right to permanent sovereignty over natural resources is "a basic constituent of the right to selfdetermination" (resolution 1803 (XVII) of 14 December 1962). So, also, in resolution 1515 (XV) of 15 December 1960, the General Assembly recommended that "the sovereign right of every State to dispose of its wealth and its natural resources should be respected". Sovereignty over their economic resources is, for any people, an important component of the totality of their sovereignty. For a fledgling nation, this is particularly so. This is the wisdom underlying the doctrine of permanent sovereignty over natural resources, and the wisdom which underlies the protection of this resource for a non-self-governing people until they achieve self-determination. [...] This right is described by the General Assembly, in its resolution on Permanent Sovereignty over Natural Resources, as "the inalienable right of all States freely to dispose of their natural wealth and resources in accordance with their national interests..." (General Assembly resolution 1803 (XVII)) [...] [S]elf-determination includes by very definition the right of permanent sovereignty over natural resources (pp. 197–199).

[...]

In the result I would reaffirm the importance of the right of the people of East Timor to self-determination and to permanent sovereignty over natural resources, and would stress that, in regard to rights so important to contemporary international law, the duty of respect for them extends beyond mere recognition, to a duty to abstain from any State action which is incompatible with those rights or which would impair or nullify them (p. 204).

[...]

The obligations to respect self-determination and the right to permanent sovereignty over natural resources are among th[o]se [of customary international law] and extend far further than mere compliance with specific rules or directions and the avoidance of prohibited conduct (p. 210).

[...]

[...] The right to permanent sovereignty over natural resources is a basic constituent of the right to self-determination[; t]he rights to self-determination and permanent sovereignty over natural resources are recognized as rights *erga omnes*, under well-established principles of international law [...] (p. 221).

DISSENTING OPINION OF JUDGE SKUBIESZEWSKI

The status of the Territory of East Timor as non-self-governing, and the right of the people of East Timor to self-determination, including its right to permanent sovereignty over wealth and natural resources, which are recognized by the United Nations, require observance by all Members of the United Nations (para. 58(2)).

[...]

The Court has not been asked to adjudicate or make a declaration on non-recognition in regard to the Indonesian control over East Timor. But let me restate the question: can the Court avoid this issue when it states certain principles? Non-recognition might protect or indeed does protect the rights to self-determination and to permanent sovereignty over natural resources. Any country has the corresponding duty to respect these rights and no act of recognition can release it from that duty (para. 131).

[...]

The non-self-governing status of the Territory of East Timor, and the right of the people of East Timor to self-determination, including its right to permanent sovereignty over natural wealth and resources, which are recognized by the United Nations, require observance by all Members of the United Nations (para. 167(2)).

CASE
ACHPR, *Social and Economic Rights Action Center and the Center for Economic and Social Rights v. Nigeria* (Communication No. 155/96) (May 27 2002), para. 56

The origin of this provision [Article 21 of the African Charter] may be traced to colonialism, during which the human and material resources of Africa were largely exploited for the benefit of outside powers, creating tragedy for Africans themselves, depriving them of their birthright and alienating them from the land. The aftermath of colonial exploitation has left Africa's precious resources and people still vulnerable to foreign misappropriation. The drafters of the Charter obviously wanted to remind African governments of the continent's painful legacy and restore co-operative economic development to its traditional place at the heart of African Society.

CASE

ICJ, *Armed Activities on the Territory of the Congo (Democratic Republic of the Congo v. Uganda)*, Judgment, ICJ Reports 168 (2005), para. 244

The Court recalls that the principle of permanent sovereignty over natural resources is expressed in General Assembly resolution 1803 (XVII) of 14 December 1962 and further elaborated in the Declaration on the Establishment of a New International Economic Order (General Assembly resolution 3201 (S.VI) of 1 May 1974) and the Charter of Economic Rights and Duties of States (General Assembly resolution 3281 (XXIX) of 12 December 1974). While recognizing the importance of this principle, which is a principle of customary international law [...]

DECLARATION OF JUDGE KOROMA, PARA. 11

Another issue that was pleaded before the Court relates to permanent sovereignty over natural resources. The Court's acknowledgment of the customary law character of General Assembly resolution 1803 (XVII) of 14 December 1962, on permanent sovereignty over natural resources, is not without significance, for [...] resolution 1803 (XVII), it should be recalled, confirmed the "right of peoples and nations to permanent sovereignty over their natural wealth and resources". It makes clear that such resources should be exploited "in the interest of ... the well-being of the people of the State concerned". These rights and interests remain in effect at all times, including during armed conflict and during occupation. The Security Council in resolution 1291 (2000) reaffirmed the sovereignty of the DRC over its natural resources, and noted with concern reports of the illegal exploitation of the country's assets and the potential consequences of these actions on the security conditions and continuation of hostilities. Accordingly, in my view, the exploitation of the natural resources of a State by the forces of occupation contravenes the principle of permanent sovereignty over natural resources, as well as the Hague Regulations of 1907 and the Fourth Geneva Convention of 1949.

DISSENTING OPINION OF JUDGE AD HOC KATEKA PARA. 56

The [permanent sovereignty over natural resources (PSNR)] concept is embodied in General Assembly resolution 1803 (XVII) of 1962. The PSNR was adopted in the era of decolonization and the assertion of the rights of newly independent States. It thus would be inappropriate to invoke this concept in a case involving two African countries. This remark is made without prejudice to the right of States to own and or dispose of their natural resources as they wish.

CASE
ICJ, *Pulp Mills on the River Uruguay (Argentina v. Uruguay)*, ICJ Reports 14 (2010)
Joint Dissenting Opinion of Judges Al-Khasawneh and Simma, para. 26

A final observation: in matters related to the use of shared natural resources and the possibility of transboundary harm, the most notable feature that one observes is the extreme elasticity and generality of the substantive principles involved. Permanent sovereignty over natural resources, equitable and rational utilization of these resources, the duty not to cause significant or appreciable harm, the principle of sustainable development, etc., all reflect this generality.

CASE
***African Commission on Human and Peoples' Rights v. Republic of Kenya*, (Application No. 006/2012) (2017)**

The Court notes, in general terms, that the Charter does not define the notion of "peoples". In this regard, the point has been made that the drafters of the Charter deliberately omitted to define the notion in order to permit a certain flexibility in the application and subsequent interpretation by future users of the legal instruments [...] (para. 196).

It is generally accepted that, in the context of the struggle against foreign domination in all its forms, the Charter primarily targets the peoples comprising the populations of the countries struggling to attain independence and national sovereignty (para. 197).

In the circumstances, the question is whether the notion "people" used by the Charter covers not only the population as the constituent elements of the State, but also the ethnic groups or communities identified as forming part of the said population within a constituted State. In other words, the question that arises is whether the enjoyment of the rights unquestionably recognised for the constituent peoples of the population of a given State can be extended to include sub-state ethnic groups and communities that are part of that population (para. 198).

In the view of the Court, the answer to this question is in the affirmative, provided such groups or communities do not call into question the sovereignty and territorial integrity of the State without the latter's consent. It would in fact be difficult to understand that the States which are the authors of the Charter intended, for example, to automatically recognise for the ethnic groups and communities that constitute their population, the right to self-determination and independence guaranteed under Article 20 (1) of the Charter, which in this case would amount to a veritable right to secession. On the other hand, nothing prevents other peoples' rights, such as the right to development (Article 22), the right to peace and security (Article 23) or the right to a healthy environment (Article 24) from being recognised, where necessary, specifically for the ethnic groups and communities that constitute the population of a State (para. 199).

In the instant case, one of the rights at issue is the right of peoples to freely dispose of their wealth and natural resources guaranteed under Article 21 of the Charter. In essence, as indicated above, the Applicant alleges that the Respondent violated the aforesaid right insofar as, following the expulsion of the Ogieks from the Mau Forest, they were deprived of their traditional food resources (para. 201). The Court recalls, in this regard, that it has already recognised for the Ogieks a number of rights to their ancestral land, namely, the right to use (*usus*) and the right to enjoy the produce of the land (*fructus*), which presuppose the right of access to and occupation of the land. In so far as those rights have been violated by the Respondent, the Court holds that the latter has also violated Article 21 of the Charter since the Ogieks have been deprived of the right to enjoy and freely dispose of the abundance of food produced by their ancestral lands (para. 200).

CASE
ESCR, *Inter-American Court of Human Rights, Case of the Kaliña and Lokono Peoples v. Suriname, Merits, Reparations and Costs*, Judgment (25 November 2015)

The Court recalls its case law in this regard in the sense that Article 21 of the American Convention protects the close relationship that the indigenous peoples have with their lands, as well as with the natural resources within those lands, and the incorporeal elements that are derived from them. [...] (para. 129).

The Court has considered that, owing to their very existence, the indigenous peoples have a right to live freely in their territories. In addition, the close relationship that the indigenous peoples have with the land should be recognized and understood as the essential basis of their culture, spiritual life, integrity and economic system (para. 130).

QUESTIONS

1. How many 'dimensions' of the PSNR principle can you enumerate? To which one does UN Resolution 1803(1962) refer?
2. Why is it said that the PSNR principle has both a 'right' and a 'duty' side? Which one is most relevant with respect to international environmental law?
3. Would you consider the PSNR principle still relevant today? Why?

FURTHER READING

BOOKS

M Bungenberg and S Hobe (eds), *Permanent Sovereignty over Natural Resources* (Heidelberg 2015)
NJ Schrijver, *Sovereignty over Natural Resources: Balancing Rights and Duties* (Cambridge University Press 2008)

CHAPTERS

SR Chowdhury, 'Permanent Sovereignty over Natural Resources' in K Hossain and SR Chowdhury (eds), *Permanent Sovereignty over Natural Resources in International Law: Principle and Practice* (St Martin's Press 1984)
NJ Schrijver, 'Global Resources Management and the Environment' in S Daws and TG Weiss (eds), *The Oxford Handbook of the United Nations* (2nd edn, Oxford University Press 2007)

NJ Schrijver, 'Natural Resources, Permanent Sovereignty over' in R Wolfrum (ed.), *Max Planck Encyclopedia of Public International Law* (2008)

ARTICLES

SK Banerjee, 'The Concept of Permanent Sovereignty Over Natural Resources: An Analysis' (1968) 8 Indian Journal of International Law 515

YT Chekera and VO Nmehielle, 'The International Law Principle of Permanent Sovereignty over Natural Resources as an Instrument for Development: The Case of Zimbabwean Diamonds' (2013) 6 African Journal of Legal Studies 69

L Cotula, 'Reconsidering Sovereignty, Ownership and Consent in Natural Resource Contracts: From Concepts to Practice' (2018) 9 European Yearbook of International Economic Law 143

E Duruigbo, 'Permanent Sovereignty over Natural Resources and People's Ownership of Natural Resources in International Law' (2006) 38 George Washington International Law Review 33

KN Gess, 'Permanent Sovereignty over Natural Resources: An Analytical Review of the United Nations Declaration and Its Genesis' (1964) 13 International and Comparative Law Quarterly 398

P Gümplová, 'Sovereignty over Natural Resources: A Normative Reinterpretation' (2020) 9 Global Constitutionalism 7

JN Hyde, 'Permanent Sovereignty Over Wealth and Resources' (1956) 50 American Journal of International Law 854

LA Miranda, 'The Role of International Law in Intrastate Natural Resource Allocation: Sovereignty, Human Rights, and Peoples-Based Development' (2012) 45 Vanderbilt Journal of Transnational Law 785

R Pereira, 'Permanent Sovereignty Over Natural Resources in the 21st Century: Natural Resource Governance and the Right to Self-Determination of Indigenous Peoples Under International Law' (2013) 14 Melbourne Journal of International Law 1

SM Schwebel, 'The Story of the UN's Declaration on Permanent Sovereignty over Natural Resources' (1963) 49 American Bar Association Journal 463

4
Prevention of transboundary harm

4.1   INTRODUCTION

The prevention of environmental harm is preferable to repairing damage after it has occurred.[1] This is because it is in the nature of environmental harm that restoration of the *status quo ante* is very costly and difficult, if not impossible. Environmental harm can be irreversible, and there are many instances of this, such as the extinction of species. International law, therefore, has developed a principle – the principle of prevention – that dictates that states should take steps to prevent environmental harm arising from their actions. The objective is to avoid harm, rather than remedy it. The principle of prevention is particularly closely associated with, and developed from, the 'no-harm' principle, requiring that a state not engage in or permit activities which cause transboundary harm, and it is possible to understand the former as encompassing the latter principle. The principle of prevention may also be closely connected with the idea of 'abuse of rights', in particular as the limit on the right of states to permanent sovereignty over their natural resources.[2] It also exists alongside, and overlaps with, the principle of precaution, and its relationship with the precautionary principle is complicated.[3]

The origins of the principle can be traced to the *Trail Smelter Arbitration*, in which an arbitral tribunal provided an articulation of a requirement on states to prevent the infliction of transboundary environmental harm on neighbouring states.[4] The principle of 'no harm' to neighbouring states has developed over the course of the 20th century from an idea grounded in 'good neighbourliness' into a general requirement of prevention of environmental harm, and it is now understood to have become the 'cornerstone of international environmental law'.[5] The first major step in this direction was made in Principle 21 of the Stockholm Declaration

[1]   Leslie-Anne Duvic-Paoli, *The Prevention Principle in International Environmental Law* (CUP 2018) Chapter 1.

[2]   Ibid., 16.

[3]   Ibid., 263ff.

[4]   *Trail Smelter Arbitration (United States v. Canada)*, 3 RIAA 1905 (1938 and 1941).

[5]   Duvic-Paoli (n 1) Chapter 2.

1972. This recognised, on the one hand, that states have sovereign rights to exploit their own natural resources, but that there are limits to that right in respect of environmental harm:[6]

> Principle 21.
> States have the sovereign right to exploit their own resources pursuant to their own environmental policies, and the responsibility to ensure that activities within their jurisdiction or control do not cause damage to the environment of other States or of areas beyond the limits of national jurisdiction.

It has since been enshrined in various international treaties (in particular those concerned with transboundary issues, such as watercourse treaties, but also in treaty provisions whose object is environmental harm of general concern to the international community, rather than harm limited to other states)[7] and received recognition in international declarations and other soft law instruments, as well as the jurisprudence of international tribunals.[8] As the principle has developed, it has come be understood that the obligation of prevention exists alongside other specific procedural obligations, notably environmental impact assessments.[9]

The prevention principle's most significant elaboration within a transboundary context has been by the International Law Commission in its 2001 Draft Articles on the Prevention of Transboundary Harm from Hazardous Activities. Moreover, its analysis of the obligation of prevention provides an important source of the content of the principle of prevention in general, and may be said to 'clarify the standards of care expected, but not made explicit, by Principle 21'.[10] Responsibility not to cause transboundary harm is focused on 'harm; not environmental interference (e.g. emissions into the atmosphere). Environmental interference may cause harm to the environment, persons and property'.[11] The ILC's threshold for harm is that it must be 'significant', and this reflects the position in modern international law. Any harm below this threshold will not result in a state's responsibility.[12]

The ILC Draft Articles provide for the realisation of the duty to prevent harm through several procedural obligations that reflect the obligation's content, as generally understood. As several cases have made clear, the procedural obligations of prevention are ones of due diligence. Confusion has arisen, however, over the connection between the procedural aspects of the prevention principle and the duty to prevent. The former are referred to as procedural

---

[6]　Declaration of the United Nations Conference on the Human Environment 1972 (16 June 1972) UN Doc A/CONF.48/14/Rev. 1, 3, reprinted in 11 ILM 1416 (1972).

[7]　See e.g. Chapter 10 (marine environment), Chapter 15 (atmospheric protection).

[8]　See Duvic-Paoli (n 1) Chapters 3–5.

[9]　On Environmental Impact Assessment, see Chapter 8.

[10]　L-A Duvic-Paoli, 'Principle of prevention' in L Krämer and E Orlando (eds), *Principles of Environmental Law* (EE 2018) 104.

[11]　R Lefeber, 'Responsibility not to cause transboundary environmental harm' in Krämer and E Orlando (n 10) 87.

[12]　See Chapter 17.

obligations as they 'contribute to operationalising the "substantive" obligation of prevention'.[13] However, such a differentiation has been challenged.[14] (Brunée 2016). Judgments of the court in the *Pulp Mills on the River Uruguay* case and the *Costa Rica v. Nicaragua* cases have led to lack of certainty 'whether violation of a "procedural" obligation necessary to discharge State from its due diligence obligation automatically leads to a breach of "substantive" obligation to prevent'.[15] In *Pulp Mills*, the court responded in the negative. Judges Al-Kasawneh and Simma in their Joint Dissenting Opinion have criticised the court for missing the opportunity to draw adequate conclusions regarding the link between procedural and substantive obligation.

A general difficulty arising in connection with the prevention principle is its relation with other environmental law principles. As noted above, the relationship with the precautionary principle is not altogether clear, but another area of confusion concerns its connection with cooperation. The ILC makes clear that cooperation is a central element for the operation of the prevention principle, and it has been said of the two that: 'If due diligence is the first rule of transboundary environmental risk management, cooperation is the second.'[16] However, as Craik explains: 'While distinct obligations, the duty to prevent harm and the duty to cooperate operate simultaneously. However, scant attention has been paid to how these duties relate to one another.'[17]

4.2 LEGAL INSTRUMENTS

4.2.1 Legally Binding Instruments

1985 Vienna Convention for the Protection of the Ozone Layer, 1513 UNTS 293

Article 2 General Obligations

1. The Parties shall take appropriate measures in accordance with the provision of this Convention and of those protocols in force to which they are a party to protect human health and the environment against adverse effects resulting or likely to result from human activities which modify or are likely to modify the ozone layer.

2. To this end the Parties shall, in accordance with the means at their disposal and their capabilities:

...

---

[13]   Duvic-Paoli (n 10) 168.

[14]   See Jutta Brunée, 'International Environmental Law and Community Interests: Procedural Aspects', in Eyal Benvenisti and Georg Nolte (eds), *Community Interests in International Law* (OUP 2018).

[15]   Duvic-Paoli (n 10) 168–69.

[16]   P Birnie, A Boyle and C Redgwell, *International Law and the Environment* (4th edn, OUP 2021) 200.

[17]   N Craik, 'The Duty to Cooperate in International Environmental Law: Constraining State Discretion through Due Respect' (2020) Yearbook of International Environmental Law.

(b)   Adopt appropriate legislative or administrative measures and co-operate in har-
        monising appropriate politics to control, limit, reduce, or prevent human activities
        under their jurisdiction or control should it be found that these activities have or
        are likely to have adverse effects resulting from modification or likely modification
        of the ozone layer;

1982 United Nations Convention on the Law of the Sea, 1833 UNTS 3

Article 207
Pollution from land-based sources
1.   States shall adopt laws and regulations to prevent, reduce and control pollution
        of the marine environment from land-based sources, including rivers, estuaries,
        pipelines and outfall structures, taking into account internationally agreed rules,
        standards and recommended practices and procedures.
2.   States shall take other measures as may be necessary to prevent, reduce and control
        such pollution.

1992 Convention on the Protection and Use of Transboundary Watercourses and International Lakes, 1936 UNTS 269

Article 2 General Provisions
1.   The Parties shall take all appropriate measures to prevent, control and reduce any
        transboundary impact.
2.   The Parties shall, in particular, take all appropriate measures:
        (a)   To prevent, control and reduce pollution of waters causing or likely to cause
                transboundary impact;
        (b)   To ensure that transboundary waters are used with the aim of ecologically
                sound and rational water management, conservation of water resources
                and environmental protection;
        (c)   To ensure that transboundary waters are used in a reasonable and equitable
                way, taking into account their transboundary character, in the case of activ-
                ities which cause or are likely to cause transboundary impact;
        (d)   To ensure conservation and, where necessary, restoration of ecosystems.

4.2.2   Non-Binding Instruments

'Charter of Economic Rights and Duties of States' UNGA Res 3281 (XXVII) (1974)

Article 30
All states have the responsibility to ensure that activities within their jurisdiction or control
do not cause damage to the environment of other states or of areas beyond the limits of
national jurisdiction.

UNEP Draft Principles of Conduct in the Field of the Environment for the Guidance of States in the Conservation and Harmonious Utilization of Natural Resources Shared by Two or More States 1978

Principle 3

1.   States have, in accordance with the Charter of the United Nations and the principles of international law, the sovereign right to exploit their own resources pursuant to their own environmental policies, and the responsibility to ensure that activities within their jurisdiction or control do not cause damage to the environment of other States or of areas beyond the limits of national jurisdiction.

Rio Declaration on Environment and Development 1992 (UN Conference on Environment and Development) (14 June 1992) UN Doc A/CONF.151/126/Rev.1 vol. I, 3

Principle 2

States have, in accordance with the Charter of the United Nations and the principles of international law, the sovereign right to exploit their own resources pursuant to their own environmental and developmental policies, and the responsibility to ensure that activities within their jurisdiction or control do not cause damage to the environment of other States or of areas beyond the limits of national jurisdiction.

Draft Articles on the Prevention of Transboundary Harm from Hazardous Activities, 12 December 2001, UNGA Res 56/82 UN Doc A/RES/56/82

Article 1. Scope

The present articles apply to activities not prohibited by international law which involve a risk of causing significant transboundary harm through their physical consequences.

Article 2. Use of terms

For the purposes of the present articles:

(a)   "Risk of causing significant transboundary harm" includes risks taking the form of a high probability of causing significant transboundary harm and a low probability of causing disastrous transboundary harm;

(b)   "Harm" means harm caused to persons, property or the environment;

(c)   "Transboundary harm" means harm caused in the territory of or in other places under the jurisdiction or control of a State other than the State of origin, whether or not the States concerned share a common border;

(d)   "State of origin" means the State in the territory or otherwise under the jurisdiction or control of which the activities referred to in article 1 are planned or are carried out;

(e)   "State likely to be affected" means the State or States in the territory of which there is the risk of significant transboundary harm or which have jurisdiction or control over any other place where there is such a risk;

(f)   "States concerned" means the State of origin and the State likely to be affected.

Article 3. Prevention

The State of origin shall take all appropriate measures to prevent significant transboundary harm or at any event to minimize the risk thereof.

Commentary

(3)   This article, together with article 4, provides the basic foundation for the articles on prevention. The articles set out the more specific obligations of States to prevent significant transboundary harm or at any event to minimize the risk thereof. The article thus emphasizes the primary duty of the State of origin to prevent significant transboundary harm; and only in case this is not fully possible it should exert its best efforts to minimize the risk thereof. The phrase "at any event" is intended to express priority in favour of the duty of prevention. The word "minimize" should be understood in this context as meaning to pursue the aim of reducing to the lowest point the possibility of harm.

[…]

(7)   The obligation of the State of origin to take preventive or minimization measures is one of due diligence. It is the conduct of the State of origin that will determine whether the State has complied with its obligation under the present articles. The duty of due diligence involved, however, is not intended to guarantee that significant harm be totally prevented, if it is not possible to do so. In that eventuality, the State of origin is required, as noted above, to exert its best possible efforts to minimize the risk. In this sense, it does not guarantee that the harm would not occur.

[…]

(10)   In the context of the present articles, due diligence is manifested in reasonable efforts by a State to inform itself of factual and legal components that relate foreseeably to a contemplated procedure and to take appropriate measures, in timely fashion, to address them. Thus, States are under an obligation to take unilateral measures to prevent significant transboundary harm or at any event to minimize the risk thereof arising out of activities within the scope of article 1. Such measures include, first, formulating policies designed to prevent significant transboundary harm or to minimize the risk thereof and, secondly, implementing those policies. Such policies are expressed in legislation and administrative regulations and implemented through various enforcement mechanisms.

(11)   The standard of due diligence against which the conduct of the State of origin should be examined is that which is generally considered to be appropriate and proportional to the degree of risk of transboundary harm in the particular instance. For example, activities which may be considered ultrahazardous require a much higher standard of care in designing policies and a much higher degree of vigour on the part of the State to enforce them. Issues such as the size of the operation; its location, special climate conditions, materials used in the activity, and whether the conclusions drawn from the application of these factors in a specific case are reasonable, are among the factors to be considered in determining the due diligence requirement in each instance. What would be considered a reasonable standard of

care or due diligence may change with time; what might be considered an appropriate and reasonable procedure, standard or rule at one point in time may not be considered as such at some point in the future. Hence, due diligence in ensuring safety requires a State to keep abreast of technological changes and scientific developments.

[...]

4.3 CASE LAW

CASE
RIAA, *Trail Smelter Arbitration (United States v. Canada)*, 3 RIAA 1905 (1938 and 1941)

p. 1965:
[...] under the principles of international law [...] no State has the right to use or permit the use of its territory in such a manner as to cause injury by fumes in or to the territory of another or the properties or persons therein, when the case is of serious consequence and the injury is established by clear and convincing evidence.

CASE
ICJ, *Corfu Channel (United Kingdom v. Albania)*, Merits, Judgment, ICJ Reports 22 (1949)

p. 22:
The obligations incumbent upon the Albanian authorities consisted in notifying, for the benefit of shipping in general, the existence of a minefield in Albanian territorial waters and in warning the approaching British warships of the imminent danger to which the minefield exposed them. Such obligations are based, not on the Hague Convention of 1907, No. VTII, which is applicable in time of war, but on certain general and well-recognized principles, namely: elementary considerations of humanity, even more exacting in peace than in war; the principle of the freedom of maritime communication; and every State's obligation not to allow knowingly its territory to be used for acts contrary to the rights of other States.

ADVISORY OPINION
ICJ, Legality of the Threat or Use of Nuclear Weapons, Advisory Opinion, ICJ Reports 226 (1996)

29. The Court recognizes that the environment is under daily threat and that the use of nuclear weapons could constitute a catastrophe for the environment. The Court also recognizes that the environment is not an abstraction but represents the living space, the quality of life and the very health of human beings, including generations unborn. The existence of the general obligation of States to ensure that activities

within their jurisdiction and control respect the environment of other States or of areas beyond national control is now part of the corpus of international law relating to the environment.

CASE
ICJ, *Gabčíkovo-Nagymaros Project (Hungary v. Slovakia)*, ICJ Reports 7 (1997)

53. The Court has no difficulty in acknowledging that the concerns expressed by Hungary for its natural environment in the region affected by the
Gabčíkovo-Nagymaros Project related to an "essential interest" of that State, within
the meaning given to that expression in Article 33 of the Draft of the International
Law Commission.

The Commission, in its Commentary, indicated that one should not, in that context, reduce an "essential interest" to a matter only of the "existence" of the State, and that the whole question was, ultimately, to be judged in the light of the particular case (see Yearbook of the International Law Commission, 1980, Vol. II, Part 2, p. 49, para. 32); at the same time, it included among the situations that could occasion a state of necessity, "a grave danger to ... the ecological preservation of al1 or some of [the] territory [of a State]" (ibid., p. 35, para. 3); and specified, with reference to State practice, that "It is primarily in the last two decades that safeguarding the ecological balance has come to be considered an 'essential interest' of al1 States" (ibid., p. 39, para. 14).

The Court recalls that it has recently had occasion to stress, in the following terms, the great significance that it attaches to respect for the environment, not only for States but also for the whole of mankind:

"the environment is not an abstraction but represents the living space, the
quality of life and the very health of human beings, including generations unborn. The existence of the general obligation of States to ensure that activities
within their jurisdiction and control respect the environment of other States or
of areas beyond national control is now part of the corpus of international law
relating to the environment" (Legality of the Threat or Use of Nuclear Weapons,
Advisory Opinion, ICJ Reports 1996, pp. 241–242, para. 29).

[...]

140. [...] The Court is mindful that, in the field of environmental protection, vigilance and
prevention are required on account of the often irreversible character of damage to
the environment and of the limitations inherent in the very mechanism of reparation
of this type of damage.

> ### CASE
> ITLOS, *MOX Plant (Ireland v. United Kingdom)*, Provisional Measures, Case No. 10, ITLOS Reports 95 (3 December 2001)

82. [...] the duty to cooperate is a fundamental principle in the prevention of pollution of the marine environment under Part XII of the Convention and general international law.

> ### CASE
> ITLOS, *Land Reclamation By Singapore in and Around the Straits of Johor (Malaysia v. Singapore)*, Provisional Measures, Case No. 12, ITLOS Reports 10 (8 October 2003)

1. Unanimously,

Malaysia and Singapore shall cooperate and shall, for this purpose, enter into consultations forthwith in order to:

(a) establish promptly a group of independent experts with the mandate

    (i) to conduct a study, on terms of reference to be agreed by Malaysia and Singapore, to determine, within a period not exceeding one year from the date of this Order, the effects of Singapore's land reclamation and to propose, as appropriate, measures to deal with any adverse effects of such land reclamation;

    (ii) to prepare, as soon as possible, an interim report on the subject of infilling works in Area D at Pulau Tekong;

(b) exchange, on a regular basis, information on, and assess risks or effects of, Singapore's land reclamation works;

(c) implement the commitments noted in this Order and avoid any action incompatible with their effective implementation, and, without prejudice to their positions on any issue before the Annex VII arbitral tribunal, consult with a view to reaching a prompt agreement on such temporary measures with respect to Area D at Pulau Tekong, including suspension or adjustment, as may be found necessary to ensure that the infilling operations pending completion of the study referred to in subparagraph (a) (i) with respect to that area do not prejudice Singapore's ability to implement the commitments referred to in paragraphs 85 to 87.

CASE
PCA, *Case Concerning the Auditing of Accounts Between the Kingdom of the Netherlands and the French Republic pursuant to the Additional Protocol of 25 September 1991 to the Convention on the Protection of the Rhine Against Pollution by Chlorides of 3 December 1976*, (Netherlands v. France), Award, PCA Case No. 2002–02 (12 March 2004) (*'Rhine Chlorides'*)

59. Since the Stockholm Conference on the Environment in 1972 there has been a marked development of international law relating to the protection of the environment. Today, both international and EC law require the integration of appropriate environmental measures in the design and implementation of economic development activities. Principle 4 of the Rio Declaration on Environment and Development, adopted in 1992 (31 I.L.M. p. 874, at p. 877), which reflects this trend, provides that "environmental protection shall constitute an integral part of the development process and cannot be considered in isolation from it." Importantly, these emerging principles now integrate environmental protection into the development process. Environmental law and the law on development stand not as alternatives but as mutually reinforcing, integral concepts, which require that where development may cause significant harm to the environment there is a duty to prevent, or at least mitigate, such harm (see paragraph 222). This duty, in the opinion of the Tribunal, has now become a principle of general international law. This principle applies not only in autonomous activities but also in activities undertaken in implementation of specific treaties between the Parties. The Tribunal would recall the observation of the International Court of Justice in the Gabčíkovo-Nagymaros case that "[t]his need to reconcile economic development with protection of the environment is aptly expressed in the concept of sustainable development" (Gabčíkovo-Nagymaros (Hungary/Slovakia), Judgment, ICJ Reports 1997, p. 7 at p. 78, para. 140). And in that context the Court further clarified that "new norms have to be taken into consideration, and ... new standards given proper weight, not only when States contemplate new activities but also when continuing with activities begun in the past" (ibid.). In the view of the Tribunal this dictum applies equally to the Iron Rhine railway.

[...]

222. The use of the Iron Rhine railway started some 120 years ago and it is now envisaged and requested by Belgium at a substantially increased and intensified level. Such new use is susceptible of having an adverse impact on the environment and causing harm to it. Today, in international environmental law, a growing emphasis is being put on the duty of prevention. Much of international environmental law has been formulated by reference to the impact that activities in one territory may have on the territory of another. The International Court of Justice expressed the view that "[t]he existence of the general obligation of States to ensure that activities within their jurisdiction and control respect the environment of other States or of areas beyond national control is now part of the corpus of international law relating to the

environment" (Legality of the Threat or Use of Nuclear Weapons, Advisory Opinion, ICJ Reports 1996 (I), p. 226 at pp. 241–242, para. 29).

223. Applying the principles of international environmental law, the Tribunal observes that it is faced, in the instant case, not with a situation of a transboundary effect of the economic activity in the territory of one state on the territory of another state, but with the effect of the exercise of a treaty-guaranteed right of one state in the territory of another state and a possible impact of such exercise on the territory of the latter state. The Tribunal is of the view that, by analogy, where a state exercises a right under international law within the territory of another state, considerations of environmental protection also apply. The exercise of Belgium's right of transit, as it has formulated its request, thus may well necessitate measures by the Netherlands to protect the environment to which Belgium will have to contribute as an integral element of its request. The reactivation of the Iron Rhine railway cannot be viewed in isolation from the environmental protection measures necessitated by the intended use of the railway line. These measures are to be fully integrated into the project and its costs.

CASE
ICJ, *Pulp Mills on the River Uruguay (Argentina v. Uruguay)*, ICJ Reports 14 (2010)

101. The Court points out that the principle of prevention, as a customary rule, has its origins in the due diligence that is required of a State in its territory. It is "every State's obligation not to allow knowingly its territory to be used for acts contrary to the rights of other States" (*Corfu Channel (United Kingdom v. Albania)*, Merits, Judgment, ICJ Reports 1949, p. 22). A State is thus obliged to use all the means at its disposal in order to avoid activities which take place in its territory, or in any area under its jurisdiction, causing significant damage to the environment of another State. This Court has established that this obligation "is now part of the corpus of international law relating to the environment" (Legality of the Threat or Use of Nuclear Weapons, Advisory Opinion, ICJ Reports 1996 (I), p. 242, para. 29).

102. In the view of the Court, the obligation to inform CARU allows for the initiation of co-operation between the Parties which is necessary in order to fulfil the obligation of prevention. This first procedural stage results in the 1975 Statute not being applied to activities which would appear to cause damage only to the State in whose territory they are carried out.

[...]

113. In the opinion of the Court, the obligation to notify is intended to create the conditions for successful co-operation between the parties, enabling them to assess the plan's impact on the river on the basis of the fullest possible information and, if necessary, to negotiate the adjustments needed to avoid the potential damage that it might cause.

[...]

119. The Court notes that the environmental impact assessments which are necessary to reach a decision on any plan that is liable to cause significant transboundary harm to another State must be notified by the party concerned to the other party, through CARU, pursuant to Article 7, second and third paragraphs, of the 1975 Statute. This notification is intended to enable the notified party to participate in the process of ensuring that the assessment is complete, so that it can then consider the plan and its effects with a full knowledge of the facts (Article 8 of the 1975 Statute).

120. The Court observes that this notification must take place before the State concerned decides on the environmental viability of the plan, taking due account of the environmental impact assessment submitted to it.

[...]

197. Thirdly, the obligation to "preserve the aquatic environment, and in particular to prevent pollution by prescribing appropriate rules and measures" is an obligation to act with due diligence in respect of all activities which take place under the jurisdiction and control of each party. It is an obligation which entails not only the adoption of appropriate rules and measures, but also a certain level of vigilance in their enforcement and the exercise of administrative control applicable to public and private operators, such as the monitoring of activities undertaken by such operators, to safeguard the rights of the other party. The responsibility of a party to the 1975 Statute would therefore be engaged if it was shown that it had failed to act diligently and thus take all appropriate measures to enforce its relevant regulations on a public or private operator under its jurisdiction. The obligation of due diligence under Article 41 (a) in the adoption and enforcement of appropriate rules and measures is further reinforced by the requirement that such rules and measures must be "in accordance with applicable international agreements" and "in keeping, where relevant, with the guidelines and recommendations of international technical bodies". This requirement has the advantage of ensuring that the rules and measures adopted by the parties both have to conform to applicable international agreements and to take account of internationally agreed technical standards.

[...]

204. It is the opinion of the Court that in order for the Parties properly to comply with their obligations under Article 41 (a) and (b) of the 1975 Statute, they must, for the purposes of protecting and preserving the aquatic environment with respect to activities which may be liable to cause transboundary harm, carry out an environmental impact assessment. As the Court has observed in the case concerning the Dispute Regarding Navigational and Related Rights,

> "there are situations in which the parties' intent upon conclusion of the treaty was, or may be presumed to have been, to give the terms used — or some

of them — a meaning or content capable of evolving, not one fixed once and for all, so as to make allowance for, among other things, developments in international law" (Dispute Regarding Navigational and Related Rights (*Costa Rica v. Nicaragua*), Judgment, ICJ Reports 2009, p. 242, para. 64).

In this sense, the obligation to protect and preserve, under Article 41 (a) of the Statute, has to be interpreted in accordance with a practice, which in recent years has gained so much acceptance among States that it may now be considered a requirement under general international law to undertake an environmental impact assessment where there is a risk that the proposed industrial activity may have a significant adverse impact in a transboundary context, in particular, on a shared resource. Moreover, due diligence, and the duty of vigilance and prevention which it implies, would not be considered to have been exercised, if a party planning works liable to affect the régime of the river or the quality of its waters did not undertake an environmental impact assessment on the potential effects of such works.

JOINT DISSENTING OPINION OF JUDGES AL-KHASAWNEH AND SIMMA

26. A final observation: in matters related to the use of shared natural resources and the possibility of transboundary harm, the most notable feature that one observes is the extreme elasticity and generality of the substantive principles involved. Permanent sovereignty over natural resources, equitable and rational utilization of these resources, the duty not to cause significant or appreciable harm, the principle of sustainable development, etc., all reflect this generality. The problem is further compounded by the fact that these principles are frequently, where there is a dispute, in a state of tension with each other. Clearly in such situations, respect for procedural obligations assumes considerable importance and comes to the forefront as being an essential indicator of whether, in a concrete case, substantive obligations were or were not breached. Thus, the conclusion whereby non-compliance with the pertinent procedural obligations has eventually had no effect on compliance with the substantive obligations is a proposition that cannot be easily accepted. For example, had there been compliance with the steps laid down in Articles 7 to 12 of the 1975 Statute, this could have led to the choice of a more suitable site for the pulp mills. Conversely, in the absence of such compliance, the situation that was obtained was obviously no different from a fait accompli.

27. The Court does recognize a functional link between procedural and substantive obligations laid down by the 1975 Statute (see Judgment, para. 79). However, the Court does not give full weight to this interdependence, neither when assessing whether a breach of Article 41 of the 1975 Statute has occurred nor in determining the appropriate remedies for the breach of Articles 7 to 12 thereof. According to the Court, as long as compliance with substantive obligations has been assured (or at least lack of it not proved), the breach of procedural obligations would not matter very much and hence a declaration to that effect constitutes appropriate satisfaction; this is not the proper way to pay due regard to the interrelation of procedure and substance.

ADVISORY OPINION
ITLOS, Responsibilities and Obligations of States Sponsoring Persons and Entities with Respect to Activities in the Area, Advisory Opinion, Case No. 17, ITLOS Reports 10 (Seabed Dispute Chamber) (1 February 2011)

131. Having established that under the Nodules Regulations and the Sulphides Regulations, both sponsoring States and the Authority are under an obligation to apply the precautionary approach in respect of activities in the Area, it is appropriate to point out that the precautionary approach is also an integral part of the general obligation of due diligence of sponsoring States, which is applicable even outside the scope of the Regulations. The due diligence obligation of the sponsoring States requires them to take all appropriate measures to prevent damage that might result from the activities of contractors that they sponsor. This obligation applies in situations where scientific evidence concerning the scope and potential negative impact of the activity in question is insufficient but where there are plausible indications of potential risks. A sponsoring State would not meet its obligation of due diligence if it disregarded those risks. Such disregard would amount to a failure to comply with the precautionary approach.

CASE
PCA, *Indus Waters Kishenanga Arbitration (Pakistan v. India)*, Partial Award, PCA Case No. 2011–01 (18 February 2013)

450. Applied to large-scale construction projects, the principle of sustainable development translates, as the International Court of Justice recently put it in Pulp Mills, into "a requirement under general international law to undertake an environmental impact assessment where there is a risk that the proposed industrial activity may have a significant adverse impact in a transboundary context, in particular, on a shared resource." The International Court of Justice affirmed that "due diligence, and the duty of vigilance and prevention which it implies, would not be considered to have been exercised, if a party planning works liable to affect the regime of the river or the quality of its waters did not undertake an environmental impact assessment on the potential effects of such works." Finally, the International Court of Justice emphasized that such duties of due diligence, vigilance and prevention continue "once operations have started and, where necessary, throughout the life of the project."

451. Similarly, this Court recalls the acknowledgement by the Tribunal in the Iron Rhine arbitration of the "principle of general international law" that States have "a duty to prevent, or at least mitigate" significant harm to the environment when pursuing large-scale construction activities. As the Iron Rhine Tribunal determined, this principle "applies not only in autonomous activities but also in activities undertaken in implementation of specific treaties," such as, it may be said, the present Treaty.

CASE
ICJ, *Certain Activities Carried Out by Nicaragua in the Border Area (Costa Rica v. Nicaragua)* **and** *Construction of a Road in Costa Rica along the San Juan River (Nicaragua v. Costa Rica)*, **ICJ Reports 665 (2015)**

104. As the Court has had occasion to emphasize in its Judgment in the case concerning Pulp Mills on the River Uruguay (*Argentina v. Uruguay*):

> "the principle of prevention, as a customary rule, has its origins in the due diligence that is required of a State in its territory. It is 'every State's obligation not to allow knowingly its territory to be used for acts contrary to the rights of other States' (Corfu Channel (*United Kingdom v. Albania*), Merits, Judgment, ICJ Reports 1949, p. 22). A State is thus obliged to use all the means at its disposal in order to avoid activities which take place in its territory, or in any area under its jurisdiction, causing significant damage to the environment of another State." (Judgment, ICJ Reports 2010 (I), pp. 55–56, para. 101.)

Furthermore, the Court concluded in that case that

> "it may now be considered a requirement under general international law to undertake an environmental impact assessment where there is a risk that the proposed industrial activity may have a significant adverse impact in a transboundary context, in particular, on a shared resource" (ibid., p. 83, para. 204).

Although the Court's statement in the Pulp Mills case refers to industrial activities, the underlying principle applies generally to proposed activities which may have a significant adverse impact in a transboundary context. Thus, to fulfil its obligation to exercise due diligence in preventing significant transboundary environmental harm, a State must, before embarking on an activity having the potential adversely to affect the environment of another State, ascertain if there is a risk of significant transboundary harm, which would trigger the requirement to carry out an environmental impact assessment.

Determination of the content of the environmental impact assessment should be made in light of the specific circumstances of each case. As the Court held in the Pulp Mills case:

> "it is for each State to determine in its domestic legislation or in the authorization process for the project, the specific content of the environmental impact assessment required in each case, having regard to the nature and magnitude of the proposed development and its likely adverse impact on the environment as well as to the need to exercise due diligence in conducting such an assessment" (ICJ Reports 2010 (I), p. 83, para. 205).

If the environmental impact assessment confirms that there is a risk of significant transboundary harm, the State planning to undertake the activity is required, in conformity with its due diligence obligation, to notify and consult in good faith with the potentially affected State, where that is necessary to determine the appropriate measures to prevent or mitigate that risk.

SEPARATE OPINION JUDGE DONOGHUE

21. First, the Judgment could be read to suggest that there is only one circumstance in which the State of origin must notify potentially affected States — when the State of origin's environmental impact assessment confirms that there is a risk of significant transboundary harm. A similar trigger for notification appears in Article 8 of the International Law Commission's 2001 Draft Articles on Prevention of Transboundary Harm from Hazardous Activities. However, due diligence may call for notification of a potentially affected State at a different stage in the process. For example, input from a potentially affected State may be necessary in order for the State of origin to make a reliable assessment of the risk of transboundary environmental harm. The Espoo Convention (Art. 3) calls for notification of a potentially affected State before the environmental impact assessment takes place, thereby allowing that State to participate in that assessment.

22. The facts in the *Nicaragua v. Costa Rica* case illustrate the importance of notification before the environmental impact assessment is complete. Only Nicaragua is in a position to take measurements or samples from the San Juan River, or to authorize such activities by Costa Rica. Consequently, it is difficult to see how Costa Rica could conduct a sufficient assessment of the impact on the river without seeking input from its neighbour.

ADVISORY OPINION
ITLOS, Request for an Advisory Opinion Submitted by the Sub-Regional Fisheries Commission (SRFC), Advisory Opinion, Case No. 21, ITLOS Reports 4 (2 April 2015)

138. While the nature of the laws, regulations and measures that are to be adopted by the flag State is left to be determined by each flag State in accordance with its legal system, the flag State nevertheless has the obligation to include in them enforcement mechanisms to monitor and secure compliance with these laws and regulations. Sanctions applicable to involvement in IUU fishing activities must be sufficient to deter violations and to deprive offenders of the benefits accruing from their IUU fishing activities.

[...]

216. The Tribunal notes in this regard that, while the SRFC Member States and other States Parties to the Convention have sovereign rights to explore, exploit, conserve and manage the living resources in their exclusive economic zones, in exercising their rights and performing their duties under the Convention in their respective exclusive economic zones, they must have due regard to the rights and duties of one another. This flows from articles 56, paragraph 2, and 58, paragraph 3, of the Convention and from the States Parties' obligation to protect and preserve the marine environment, a fundamental principle underlined in articles 192 and 193 of the

Convention and referred to in the fourth paragraph of its preamble. The Tribunal recalls in this connection that living resources and marine life are part of the marine environment and that, as the Tribunal stated in the *Southern Bluefin Tuna Cases*, "the conservation of the living resources of the sea is an element in the protection and preservation of the marine environment" (*Southern Bluefin Tuna (New Zealand v. Japan; Australia v. Japan), Provisional Measures, Order of 27 August 1999, ITLOS Reports 1999*, p. 280, at p. 295, para. 70).

CASE
PCA, *South China Sea Arbitration (Philippines v. China)*, Final Award, PCA Case No. 2013–19 (12 July 2016)

960. The Tribunal thus considers the harvesting of sea turtles, species threatened with extinction, to constitute a harm to the marine environment as such. The Tribunal further has no doubt that the harvesting of corals and giant clams from the waters surrounding Scarborough Shoal and features in the Spratly Islands, on the scale that appears in the record before it, has a harmful impact on the fragile marine environment. The Tribunal therefore considers that a failure to take measures to prevent these practices would constitute a breach of Articles 192 and 194(5) of the Convention, and turns now to consider China's responsibility for such breaches.

961. The vessels involved in the incidents described above were all Chinese flag vessels, under the jurisdiction and control of China. In the Tribunal's view, where a State is aware that vessels flying its flag are engaged in the harvest of species recognised internationally as being threatened with extinction or are inflicting significant damage on rare or fragile ecosystems or the habitat of depleted, threatened, or endangered species, its obligations under the Convention include a duty to adopt rules and measures to prevent such acts and to maintain a level of vigilance in enforcing those rules and measures.

...

974. In 2000, the People's Republic of China updated its Fisheries Law, Article 30 of which prohibits the "use of explosives, poisons, electricity and any other means in fishing that impairs the fishery resources."

...

1152. Adopting appropriate rules and measures is one component of the due diligence required by States under the Convention. States are also required to adopt a certain level of vigilance in the enforcement and control of the rules, but there is little in the record to suggest that China has failed to do so with respect to dynamite and cyanide fishing.

ADVISORY OPINION
IACtHR, The Environment and Human Rights (State obligations in relation to the environment in the context of the protection and guarantee of the rights to life and to personal integrity – interpretation and scope of Articles 4(1) and 5(1) of the American Convention on Human Rights), Advisory Opinion, OC-23/17 (15 November 2017), Series A No. 23

128. Under environmental law, the principle of prevention has meant that States have the "responsibility to ensure that activities within their jurisdiction or control do not cause damage to the environment of other States or of areas beyond the limits of national jurisdiction." This principle was explicitly established in the Stockholm and Rio Declarations on the environment and is linked to the international obligation to exercise due diligence so as not to cause or permit damage to other States (supra paras 95 to 103).

129. The principle of prevention of environmental damage forms part of international customary law. This protection encompasses not only the land, water and atmosphere, but also includes flora and fauna. Specifically, in relation to State obligations with regard to the sea, the United Nations Convention on the Law of the Sea establishes that "States have the obligation to protect and preserve the marine environment," and imposes a specific obligation "to prevent, reduce and control pollution of the marine environment." The Cartagena Convention that Colombia mentions in its request also establishes this obligation.

130. Bearing in mind that, frequently, it is not possible to restore the situation that existed before environmental damage occurred, prevention should be the main policy as regards environmental protection. The Court will now examine: (1) the sphere of application of the principle of prevention; (2) the type of damage that must be prevented; and (3) the measures States must take to comply with this obligation.

B.1.A SPHERE OF APPLICATION OF THE OBLIGATION OF PREVENTION

131. Under environmental law, the principle of prevention is applicable with regard to activities which take place in a State's territory, or in any area under its jurisdiction, that cause damage to the environment of another State, or in relation to damage that may occur in areas that are not part of the territory of any specific State, such as on the high seas.

[...]

B.1.B TYPE OF DAMAGE TO BE PREVENTED

134. The wording of the obligation of prevention established in the Stockholm and Rio Declarations does not describe the type of environmental damage that should be prevented. However, many treaties that include an obligation to prevent environmental damage do condition this obligation to a certain degree of severity of the harm that could be caused. Thus, for example, the Convention on the Law of the Non-Navigational Uses of International Watercourses, the Vienna Convention for Protection of the Ozone Layer, the United Nations Framework Convention on Climate Change, and the Protocol to the Antarctic Treaty on Environmental Protection establish the obligation to prevent significant damage. Similarly, the Convention on Biological Diversity indicates an obligation to prevent "significant adverse effects on biological diversity." In Europe, the Convention on Environmental Impact Assessment in a Transboundary Context establishes as a standard the prevention of "significant adverse transboundary environmental impact," and the Convention on the Protection and Use of Transboundary Watercourses and International Lakes establishes the obligation to prevent "any significant adverse effect."

135. The International Court of Justice has indicated that the obligation of prevention arises when there is risk of "significant damage." According to this Court, the significant nature of a risk may be determined based on the nature and size of the project and the context in which it is implemented.

136. Similarly, the International Law Commission's draft articles on prevention of transboundary harm from hazardous activities only refer to those activities that may involve significant transboundary harm. Thus, the ILC indicated that "the term 'significant' was not without ambiguity and a determination ha[d] to be made in each specific case. [...] It [should] be understood that 'significant' is something more than 'detectable' but need not be at the level of 'serious' or 'substantial.' The harm must lead to a real detrimental effect on matters such as, for example, human health, industry, property, environment or agriculture in other States. Such detrimental effects must be susceptible of being measured by factual and objective standards." In addition, the International Law Commission indicated that a State of origin is not responsible for preventing risks that are not foreseeable. However, it also noted that States have the continuing obligation to identify activities which involve significant risk.

137. Accordingly, there is consensus in international environmental provisions that the obligation of prevention requires that the harm or damage attain a certain level.

138. At the same time, in the context of human rights, the Inter-American Court has indicated that the American Convention cannot be interpreted in a way that prevents a State from issuing any type of concession for the exploration for natural resources or their extraction. In this regard, it has indicated that the acceptable level of impact, revealed by environmental impact assessments, that would allow a State to

grant a concession in indigenous territory may differ in each case, without it ever being permissible to negate the ability of members of indigenous and tribal peoples to ensure their own survival.

[...]

140. Based on the above, the Court concludes that States must take measures to prevent significant harm or damage to the environment, within or outside their territory. In the Court's opinion, any harm to the environment that may involve a violation of the rights to life and to personal integrity, in accordance with the meaning and scope of those rights as previously defined (supra paras 108 to 114) must be considered significant harm. The existence of significant harm in these terms is something that must be determined in each specific case, based on the particular circumstances.

QUESTIONS

1. Analyse the difference between the principle of prevention and precaution. Is it the same?
2. If there is a separate principle of precaution, do we need a principle of prevention?
3. What are the characteristic features of the principle of prevention?

FURTHER READING

BOOKS

P Birnie, A Boyle and C Redgwell, *International Law and the Environment* (4th edn, Oxford University Press 2021)

R Bratspies and R Miller, *Transboundary Harm in International Law: Lessons from the Trail Smelter Arbitration* (Cambridge University Press 2006)

N Craik, *The International Law of Environmental Impact Assessment* (Cambridge University Press 2008)

L-A Duvic-Paoli, *The Prevention Principle in International Environmental Law* (Cambridge University Press 2018)

X Hanquin, *Transboundary Damage in International Environmental Law* (Cambridge University Press 2003)

S Jayakumar and others (eds), *Transboundary Pollution: Evolving Issues of International Law and Policy* (Edward Elgar 2015)

A Nollkaemper, *The Legal Regime for Transboundary Pollution: Between Discretion and Constraint* (Martinus Nijhoff 1993)

N de Sadeleer, *Environmental Law Principles: From Political Slogans to Legal Rules* (2nd edn, Oxford University Press 2020)

E Scotford, *Environmental Principles and the Evolution of Environmental Law* (Hart 2017)

CHAPTERS

L-A Duvic-Paoli, 'Principle of Prevention' in L Krämer and E Orlando (eds), *Principles of Environmental Law* (Edward Elgar 2018)

D French, 'Trail Smelter' in C Miles and E Bjorge (eds), *Landmark Cases in International Law* (Hart 2017)

G Handl, 'Transboundary Impacts' in D Bodansky, J Brunnée and E Hey (eds), *The Oxford Handbook of International Environmental Law* (Oxford University Press 2008)

T Koivurova, 'Due Diligence' in *Max Planck Encyclopedia of Public International Law* (Oxford University Press 2007)

R Lefeber, 'Responsibility not to Cause Transboundary Environmental Harm' in L Krämer and E Orlando (eds), *Principles of Environmental Law* (Edward Elgar 2018)

ARTICLES

N Craik, 'The Duty to Cooperate in International Environmental Law: Constraining State Discretion through Due Respect' (2020) Yearbook of International Environmental Law

G Handl, 'Territorial Sovereignty and the Problem of Transnational Pollution' (1975) 69 AJIL 50

P Okowa, 'Procedural Obligations in International Environmental Law' (1996) 67 Br YB Int'l L 275

5
The precautionary principle

5.1   INTRODUCTION

The precautionary principle became central to international environmental law discourse in the 1980s, although it originated much earlier, in particular within the principle of 'Vorsorgeprinzip' applied in West Germany. Following increased recognition in international instruments, receiving its first mention in a treaty in the 1985 Vienna Convention on the Protection of the Ozone Layer, it was enshrined in Principle 15 of the 1992 Rio Declaration, which represents its classical formulation. Since then, it has been expressly recognised and invoked in numerous other international and regional instruments, and relied upon in submissions in international litigation.

As Meinhard Schröder observes, 'The precautionary principle is the idea that environmentally sensitive activities should be avoided and precautionary measures taken, even in situations where there is potential hazard but scientific uncertainty as to the impact of the environmentally sensitive activity.'[1] The nature of this principle is still debated, and it has been said that, 'Rather than ushering in an era of relatively certainty, with the provision of a new principle to help guide the international community through increasingly difficult international environmental problems, the complete opposite happened, and the exact status of the principle, or what it means is commonly held to be uncertain.'[2]

Part of the cause of the debates over the principle arises from its potentially far-reaching consequences for state action, and, consequently, the incursion upon freedom of action or incurrence of costs. Three uncertainties surrounding the principle are notable. First, there is uncertainty as to its legal status. Although it has been argued that the principle forms part of customary international law, this has tended not to find favour in the case law of international courts and tribunals. Another way of understanding the principle is to view it as an 'approach', but this leaves its legal effects vague.

Second, its content is disputed. It is possible to draw a broad distinction between 'weak' and 'strong' versions of the precautionary principle. Within the 'weak' version, the principle

---

[1]   M Schröder, 'Precautionary Approach/Principle' in *Max Planck Encyclopedia of Public International Law* (2014) para. 2.

[2]   Alexander Gillespie, 'The Precautionary Principle and the 21st Century: A Case Study of Noise Pollution in the Ocean', *The International Journal of Marine and Coastal Law* 22, 2007, 61.

operates as a justification or excuse for states adopting measures to protect the environment on a precautionary basis in situations of uncertainty, i.e. where lack of certainty would otherwise make a case of the need for the measures very difficult, and precludes reliance upon a lack of scientific knowledge as a justification, in itself, for *not* taking measures to prevent potentially serious, but uncertain, threats.[3] The 'strong' versions, on the other hand, elevate the principle to an obligation to anticipate and adopt early, proportionate, preventive measures in the face of such threats.[4] Another consequence of the 'strong' form of the precautionary principle may be to reverse the burden of proof, but this is disputed in the case law. Differences also exist between different formulations with regard to the degree of anticipation required, that is, to put it another way, whether (and if so how and where to draw) the threshold at which the precautionary principle is engaged.[5]

A third difficulty arises over how to understand the relation between the precautionary principle and other principles of environmental law, notably the principle of prevention. Duvic-Paoli notes that their relationship is 'perhaps the most difficult to articulate at present under international environmental law'.[6] Both are aimed at the same object, namely avoiding harm, and thus they may be seen as representing a single principle. However, they do not share the same normative status, which has resulted in a tendency in international law (unlike, e.g., EU law) to regard them as different principles.[7] Moreover, the precise logics of prevention and precaution differ: prevention pertains to risks that are assessable, precaution to risks that are unable to be assessed. Duvic-Paoli contends, however, that while the two principles may be distinguishable, they are linked on a continuum, both in light of their shared rationale and the 'fact that scientific knowledge does not rely on a strict certainty-uncertainty dichotomy'.[8] In practice, both principles often run together, including as part of a joint foundation for environmental impact assessment.

Despite these uncertainties, the precautionary principle is an important tool in protecting against environmental harm and constitutes one of the major frames through which environmental law must be understood. Moreover, its importance extends beyond environmental law since it provides a guide to risk management in situations of uncertainty in general, and thus can have an influence upon other areas of international law.

---

[3]   See e.g. the Rio Declaration.

[4]   See e.g. the 1991 Bamako Convention.

[5]   See discussion in P Sands and J Peel, *Principles of International Environmental Law* (4th edn, CUP 2018) 231–233.

[6]   L-A Duvic-Paoli, *The Prevention Principle in International Environmental Law* (CUP 2018) 263.

[7]   As recognised in the ILA Committee on Legal Principles Relating to Climate Change, 'Second Report', 75th Session 2012, at 28.

[8]   Duvic-Paoli (n 6) 273.

5.2   LEGAL INSTRUMENTS

5.2.1   Legally Binding Instruments

5.2.1.1   International
1985 Vienna Convention for the Protection of the Ozone Layer, 1513 UNTS 293

Preamble
Mindful also of the precautionary measures for the protection of the ozone layer which have already been taken at the national and international levels,
     Aware that measures to protect the ozone layer from modifications due to human activities require international co-operation and action, and should be based on relevant scientific and technical considerations,

1987 Montreal Protocol on Substances that Deplete the Ozone Layer, 1522 UNTS 3

Preamble
Conscious of the potential climatic effects of emissions of these substances,
     Aware that measures taken to protect the ozone layer from depletion should be based on relevant scientific knowledge, taking into account technical and economic considerations,
     Determined to protect the ozone layer by taking precautionary measures to control equitably total global emissions of substances that deplete it, with the ultimate objective of their elimination on the basis of developments in scientific knowledge, taking into account technical and economic considerations and bearing in mind the developmental needs of developing countries,

1992 Convention on Biological Diversity, 1760 UNTS 79

Preamble
[W]here there is a threat of significant reduction or loss of biological diversity, lack of full scientific certainty should not be used as a reason for postponing measures to avoid or minimize such a threat.

1992 UN Framework Convention on Climate Change, 1771 UNTS 107

Article 3.3
The Parties should take precautionary measures to anticipate, prevent or minimize the causes of climate change and mitigate its adverse effects. Where there are threats of serious or irreversible damage, lack of full scientific certainty should not be used as a reason for postponing such measures, taking into account that policies and measures to deal with climate change should be cost-effective so as to ensure global benefits at the lowest possible cost.

1995 Agreement on Straddling Fish Stocks, 2167 UNTS 88

Article 5 General Principles

In order to conserve and manage straddling fish stocks and highly migratory fish stocks, coastal States and States fishing on the high seas shall, in giving effect to their duty to cooperate in accordance with the Convention:

[...]

(c) $\quad$ apply the precautionary approach in accordance with article 6;

Article 6

Application of the precautionary approach

1. $\quad$ States shall apply the precautionary approach widely to conservation, management and exploitation of straddling fish stocks and highly migratory fish stocks in order to protect the living marine resources and preserve the marine environment.

2. $\quad$ States shall be more cautious when information is uncertain, unreliable or inadequate. The absence of adequate scientific information shall not be used as a reason for postponing or failing to take conservation and management measures.

3. $\quad$ In implementing the precautionary approach, States shall:

(a) $\quad$ improve decision-making for fishery resource conservation and management by obtaining and sharing the best scientific information available and implementing improved techniques for dealing with risk and uncertainty;

(b) $\quad$ apply the guidelines set out in Annex II and determine, on the basis of the best scientific information available, stock-specific reference points and the action to be taken if they are exceeded;

(c) $\quad$ take into account, *inter alia*, uncertainties relating to the size and productivity of the stocks, reference points, stock condition in relation to such reference points, levels and distribution of fishing mortality and the impact of fishing activities on non-target and associated or dependent species, as well as existing and predicted oceanic, environmental and socio-economic conditions; and

(d) $\quad$ develop data collection and research programmes to assess the impact of fishing on non-target and associated or dependent species and their environment, and adopt plans which are necessary to ensure the conservation of such species and to protect habitats of special concern.

4. $\quad$ States shall take measures to ensure that, when reference points are approached, they will not be exceeded. In the event that they are exceeded, States shall, without delay, take the action determined under paragraph 3 (b) to restore the stocks.

5. $\quad$ Where the status of target stocks or non-target or associated or dependent species is of concern, States shall subject such stocks and species to enhanced monitoring in order to review their status and the efficacy of conservation and management measures. They shall revise those measures regularly in the light of new information.

6. $\quad$ For new or exploratory fisheries, States shall adopt as soon as possible cautious conservation and management measures, including, *inter alia*, catch limits and effort limits. Such measures shall remain in force until there are sufficient data

to allow assessment of the impact of the fisheries on the long-term sustainability of the stocks, whereupon conservation and management measures based on that assessment shall be implemented. The latter measures shall, if appropriate, allow for the gradual development of the fisheries.

7.   If a natural phenomenon has a significant adverse impact on the status of strad-dling fish stocks or highly migratory fish stocks, States shall adopt conservation and management measures on an emergency basis to ensure that fishing activity does not exacerbate such adverse impact. States shall also adopt such measures on an emergency basis where fishing activity presents a serious threat to the sustainability of such stocks. Measures taken on an emergency basis shall be temporary and shall be based on the best scientific evidence available.

2000 Cartagena Protocol on Biosafety to the Convention on Biological Diversity, 2226 UNTS 208

Preamble

[...]

Reaffirming the precautionary approach contained in Principle 15 of the Rio Declaration on Environment and Development,

[...]

Article 1 Objective
In accordance with the precautionary approach contained in Principle 15 of the Rio Declaration on Environment and Development, the objective of this Protocol is to contribute to ensuring an adequate level of protection in the field of the safe transfer, handling and use of living modified organisms resulting from modern biotechnology that may have adverse effects on the conservation and sustainable use of biological diversity, taking also into account risks to human health, and specifically focusing on transboundary movements.

Table 5.1   Other international treaties

Stockholm Convention on Persistent Organic Pollutants, amended in 2009, entered into force on 17 May 2004, art. 1
London Protocol to the Convention on the Prevention of Marine Pollution from Dumping of Wastes and Other Matter (with its 2006 amendments), entered into force on 24 March 2006, preamble and art. 3.1
International Convention on Control of Harmful Anti-fouling Systems on Ships, entered into force on 17 September 2008
Agreement on the Application of Sanitary and Phytosanitary Measures, 15 April 1994, 1867 UNTS 493

5.2.1.2   Regional and bilateral

1991 Bamako Convention on the Ban of the Import into Africa and the Control of Transboundary Movement and Management of Hazardous Wastes Within Africa, 2101 UNTS 177

Article 4(3)

...

(f)   Each Party shall strive to adopt and implement the preventive, precautionary approach to pollution problems which entails, *inter alia*, preventing the release into the environment of substances which may cause harm to humans or the environment without waiting for scientific proof regarding such harm. The Parties shall cooperate with each other in taking the appropriate measures to implement the precautionary principle to pollution prevention through the application of clean production methods, rather than the pursuit of permissible emissions approach based on assimilative capacity assumption;

1992 Convention on the Protection and Use of Transboundary Watercourses and International Lakes, 1936 UNTS 269

Article 2

...

5.   In taking the measures referred to in paragraphs 1 and 2 of this article, the Parties shall be guided by the following principles:

   (a)   The precautionary principle, by virtue of which action to avoid the potential transboundary impact of the release of hazardous substances shall not be postponed on the ground that scientific research has not fully proved a causal link between those substances, on the one hand, and the potential transboundary impact, on the other hand;

Treaty on the Functioning of the European Union (Consolidated Version) OJ C 326/47

Article 191

2.   Union policy on the environment shall aim at a high level of protection taking into account the diversity of situations in the various regions of the Union. It shall be based on the precautionary principle and on the principles that preventive action should be taken, that environmental damage should as a priority be rectified at source and that the polluter should pay.

Table 5.2   Other regional treaties with precautionary principle

Convention for the Protection of the Marine Environment of the North-East Atlantic (22 September 1992, entered into force 25 March 1998) 2354 UNTS 67 (OSPAR Convention)
Convention on the Protection of the Marine Environment of the Baltic Sea Area 1992 (Helsinki Convention)
Framework Convention for the Protection of the Marine Environment of the Caspian Sea (Tehran Convention) (4 November 2003, entered into force 12 August 2006)
Convention on Co-Operation for the Protection and Sustainable Use of the River Danube (29 June 1994)
Convention on the Protection of the Rhine (entered into force 1 January 2003)
EU–Canada Comprehensive and Economic Trade Agreement (signed 30 October 2016, not yet in force but provisional application 21 September 2017) OJ L 11/23
1994 Oslo Protocol on Further Reduction of Sulphur Emissions (15 June 1994, entered into force 5 August 1998)
Regional Agreement on Access to Information, Public Participation and Justice in Environmental Matters in Latin America and the Caribbean (4 March 2018, entered into force 22 April 2021) ('Escazú Agreement')

5.2.2   Non-Binding Instruments

5.2.2.1   International

World Charter for Nature, UNGA Res 37/7 (28 October 1982)

11.   [...]

    (b)   Activities which are likely to pose a significant risk to nature shall be preceded by an exhaustive examination; their proponents shall demonstrate that their expected benefits outweigh potential damage to nature; and where potential adverse effects are not fully understood, the activity should not proceed.

1992 Rio Declaration on Environment and Development A/CONF.151/26 (vol. I)

Principle 15

In order to protect the environment, the precautionary approach shall be widely applied by States according to their capabilities. Where there are threats of serious or irreversible damage, lack of full scientific certainty shall not be used as a reason for postponing cost-effective measures to prevent environmental degradation.

Earth Charter 2000, para 6: Prevent harm as the best method of environmental protection and, when knowledge is limited, apply a precautionary approach.

a.   Take action to avoid the possibility of serious or irreversible environmental harm even when scientific knowledge is incomplete or inconclusive.

...

c.   Ensure that decision making addresses the cumulative, long-term, indirect, long distance, and global consequences of human activities.

Draft articles on Prevention of Transboundary Harm from Hazardous Activities, with commentaries (2001) Yearbook of the International Law Commission, 2001, vol. II, Part Two

Article 10. Factors involved in an equitable balance of interests
In order to achieve an equitable balance of interests as referred to in paragraph 2 of article 9, the States concerned shall take into account all relevant factors and circumstances, including:
[…]

(c)   the risk of significant harm to the environment and the availability of means of preventing such harm, or minimizing the risk thereof or restoring the environment;

Commentary
(5)   Subparagraph (c) compares, in the same fashion as subparagraph (a), the risk of significant harm to the environment and the availability of means of preventing such harm, or minimizing the risk thereof and the possibility of restoring the environment. It is necessary to emphasize the particular importance of protection of the environment. Principle 15 of the Rio Declaration is relevant to this subparagraph.

[…]

(7)   According to the Rio Declaration, the precautionary principle constitutes a very general rule of conduct of prudence. It implies the need for States to review their obligations of prevention in a continuous manner to keep abreast of the advances in scientific knowledge.

IUCN Guidelines for Applying the Precautionary Principle to Biodiversity Conservation and Natural Resource Management, As approved by the 67th meeting of the IUCN Council 14–16 May 2007

Introduction
[…] it must be borne in mind that the precautionary principle is generally only relevant where the following elements are present:

First, in situations where there is uncertainty. Where the threat is relatively certain (i.e. a causal link between an action and environmental damage can be established, the probability of occurrence can be calculated, and the damage insured against), measures may also need to be taken. However, these should be seen as preventive, not precautionary measures; and

Second, where there is a threat of environmental damage. Where there is no indication of a threat of environmental harm, the principle will not apply; and

Third, where the threatened harm is of a serious or irreversible nature. Where threatened damage is trivial or easily reversible, the principle will not be relevant.

[…]

To apply the precautionary principle effectively:

A. ESTABLISH THE FRAMEWORK

Guideline 1: INCORPORATE

Incorporate the Precautionary Principle explicitly into appropriate legal, institutional and policy frameworks for biodiversity conservation and natural resource management.

[...]

Guideline 2: INTEGRATE

Integrate application of the Precautionary Principle with the application of other relevant principles and rights.

Guideline 3: OPERATIONALISE

Develop clear and context-specific obligations and operational measures for particular sectors and contexts, and with respect to specific conservation or management problems.

[...]

Guideline 5: USE THE BEST INFORMATION AVAILABLE

Base precautionary decision-making on the best available information, including that relating to human drivers of threats, and traditional and indigenous knowledge.

[...]

C. DEVISE THE APPROPRIATE PRECAUTIONARY MEASURES

Guideline 9: BE EXPLICIT

Specify the precautionary measures being taken and be explicit about the uncertainty to which the precautionary measures are responding.

[...]

Guideline 10: BE PROPORTIONATE

In applying the Precautionary Principle adopt measures that are proportionate to the potential threats.

[...]

Guideline 11: BE EQUITABLE

Consider social and economic costs and benefits when applying the Precautionary Principle and where decisions would have negative impacts on the poor or vulnerable explore ways to avoid or mitigate these.

[...]

5.2.2.2 Regional

Bergen ECE Ministerial Declaration on Sustainable Development, 15 May 1990

Article 7

In order to achieve sustainable development, policies must be based on the precautionary principle. Environmental measures must anticipate, prevent and attack the causes of environmental degradation. Where there are threats of serious or irreversible damage, lack of full scientific certainty should not be used as a reason for postponing measures to prevent environmental degradation.

5.3   CASE LAW

5.3.1   International Court of Justice

CASE
ICJ, *Request for an Examination of the Situation in Accordance with Paragraph 63 of the Court's Judgment of 20 December 1974 in the Nuclear Tests (New Zealand v. France)*, Case, ICJ Reports 288 (1995)

DISS OP JUDGE WEERAMANTRY

THE PRECAUTIONARY PRINCIPLE

Where a party complains to the Court of possible environmental damage of an irreversible nature which another party is committing or threatening to commit, the proof or disproof of the matter alleged may present difficulty to the claimant as the necessary information may largely be in the hands of the party causing or threatening the damage.

The law cannot function in protection of the environment unless a legal principle is evolved to meet this evidentiary difficulty, and environmental law has responded with what has come to be described as the precautionary principle – a principle which is gaining increasing support as part of the international law of the environment [citation omitted].

[...]

New Zealand has placed materials before the Court to the best of its ability, but France is in possession of the actual information. The principle then springs into operation to give the Court the basic rationale for considering New Zealand's request and not postponing the application of such means as are available to the Court to prevent, on a provisional basis, the threatened environmental degradation, until such time as the full scientific evidence becomes available in refutation of the New Zealand contention.

DISS OP OF JUDGE AD HOC SIR GEOFFREY PALMER

91. What those principles of international law establish in my view are the following propositions:

   (a) international environmental law has developed rapidly and is tending to develop in a way that provides comprehensive protection for the natural environment;

   (b) international law has taken an increasingly restrictive approach to the regulation of nuclear radiation;

   (c) customary international law may have developed a norm of requiring environmental impact assessment where activities may have a significant effect on the environment;

   (d) the norm involved in the precautionary principle has developed rapidly and may now be a principle of customary international law relating to the environment;

   (e) there are obligations based on Conventions that may be applicable here requiring environmental impact assessment and the precautionary principle to be observed.

CASE
ICJ, *Gabčíkovo-Nagymaros Project (Hungary v. Slovakia)*, ICJ Reports 7 (1997)

97. Finally, Hungary argued that subsequently imposed requirements of international law in relation to the protection of the environment precluded performance of the Treaty. The previously existing obligation not to cause substantive damage to the territory of another State had, Hungary claimed, evolved into an erga omnes obligation of prevention of damage pursuant to the "precautionary principle". On this basis, Hungary argued, its termination was "forced by the other party's refusal to suspend work on Variant C".

   [...]

112. Neither of the Parties contended that new peremptory norms of environmental law had emerged since the conclusion of the 1977 Treaty, and the Court will consequently not be required to examine the scope of Article 64 of the Vienna Convention on the Law of Treaties. On the other hand, the Court wishes to point out that newly developed norms of environmental law are relevant for the implementation of the Treaty and that the parties could, by agreement, incorporate them through the application of Articles 15, 19 and 20 of the Treaty. These articles do not contain specific obligations of performance but require the parties, in carrying out their obligations to ensure that the quality of water in the Danube is not impaired and that nature is protected, to take new environmental norms into consideration when agreeing upon the means to be specified in the Joint Contractual Plan.

By inserting these evolving provisions in the Treaty, the parties recognized the potential necessity to adapt the Project. Consequently, the Treaty is not static, and is open to adapt to emerging norms of international law. By means of Articles 15 and 19, new environmental norms can be incorporated in the Joint Contractual Plan.

The responsibility to do this was a joint responsibility. The obligations contained in Articles 15, 19 and 20 are, by definition, general and have to be transformed into specific obligations of performance through a process of consultation and negotiation. Their implementation thus requires a mutual willingness to discuss in good faith actual and potential environmental risks.

It is all the more important to do this because as the Court recalled in its Advisory Opinion on the Legality of the Threat or Use of Nuclear Weapons, "the environment is not an abstraction but represents the living space, the quality of life and the very health of human beings, including generations unborn" (ICJ Reports 1996, p. 241, para. 29; see also paragraph 53 above).

The awareness of the vulnerability of the environment and the recognition that environmental risks have to be assessed on a continuous basis have become much stronger in the years since the Treaty's conclusion. These new concerns have enhanced the relevance of Articles 15, 19 and 20.

113. The Court recognizes that both Parties agree on the need to take environmental concerns seriously and to take the required precautionary measures, but they fundamentally disagree on the consequences this has for the joint Project. In such a case, third-party involvement may be helpful and instrumental in finding a solution, provided each of the Parties is flexible in its position.

SEP OP JUDGE KOROMA

152: The importance of the River Danube for both Hungary and Slovakia cannot be overstated. Both countries, by means of the 1977 Treaty, had agreed to co-operate in the exploitation of its resources for their mutual benefit. That Treaty, in spite of the period in which it was concluded, would seem to have incorporated most of the environmental imperatives of today, including the precautionary principle, the principle of equitable and reasonable utilization and the no-harm rule. None of these principles was proved to have been violated to an extent sufficient to have warranted the unilateral termination of the Treaty.

CASE
ICJ, *Pulp Mills on the River Uruguay (Argentina v. Uruguay)*, **ICJ Reports 14**
(2010)

A. BURDEN OF PROOF AND EXPERT EVIDENCE

[...]

162. To begin with, the Court considers that, in accordance with the well-established principle of onus probandi incumbit actori, it is the duty of the party which asserts certain facts to establish the existence of such facts. This principle which has been consistently upheld by the Court [...] applies to the assertions of fact both by the Applicant and the Respondent.

163. It is of course to be expected that the Applicant should, in the first instance, submit the relevant evidence to substantiate its claims. This does not, however, mean that the Respondent should not co-operate in the provision of such evidence as may be in its possession that could assist the Court in resolving the dispute submitted to it.

164. Regarding the arguments put forward by Argentina on the reversal of the burden of proof and on the existence, vis-à-vis each Party, of an equal onus to prove under the 1975 Statute, the Court considers that while a precautionary approach may be relevant in the interpretation and application of the provisions of the Statute, it does not follow that it operates as a reversal of the burden of proof. The Court is also of the view that there is nothing in the 1975 Statute itself to indicate that it places the burden of proof equally on both Parties.

SEP OP JUDGE CANÇADO TRINDADE

2. Precautionary Principle

62. We have before us two key elements which account for this evolution, namely, the awareness of the existence or persistence of risks, and the awareness of scientific uncertainties surrounding the issue at stake. These two elements have occupied a central position in the configuration of the precautionary principle. In the light of the principle of prevention, one is facing threat or dangers to the environment, whilst in the light of the precautionary principle, one is rather before likely of potential threats and dangers to the environment. In these distinct circumstances, both principles are intended to guide or orient initiatives to avoid harm or probable harm to the environment.

[...]

69. The last decades have indeed witnessed a growing awareness of the vulnerability of human beings and of the environment, requiring care and due diligence in face of surrounding risks, incurred by man himself. That vulnerability has led to

the acknowledgement of the need to take initiatives and decisions, even without a thorough knowledge of the relevant factors in a given situation, so as to protect human life and the environment. Prevention envisaged risks, but assumed they were certain. Precaution thus emerged, as an ineluctable principle, to face also uncertain risks, given the uncertainties of life itself, and the intuition of surrounding death.

5.3.2 ITLOS

CASE
ITLOS, *Southern Bluefin Tuna (New Zealand v. Japan; Australia v. Japan)*, Provisional Measures, Case Nos 3–4, ITLOS Reports 280 (27 August 1999)

77. Considering that, in the view of the Tribunal, the parties should in the circumstances act with prudence and caution to ensure that effective conservation measures are taken to prevent serious harm to the stock of southern bluefin tuna;
78. Considering that the parties should intensify their efforts to cooperate with other participants in the fishery for southern bluefin tuna with a view to ensuring conservation and promoting the objective of optimum utilization of the stock;
79. Considering that there is scientific uncertainty regarding measures to be taken to conserve the stock of southern bluefin tuna and that there is no agreement among the parties as to whether the conservation measures taken so far have led to the improvement in the stock of southern bluefin tuna;
80. Considering that, although the Tribunal cannot conclusively assess the scientific evidence presented by the parties, it finds that measures should be taken as a matter of urgency to preserve the rights of the parties and to avert further deterioration of the southern bluefin tuna stock;

CASE
ITLOS, *MOX Plant (Ireland v. United Kingdom)*, Provisional Measures, Case No. 10, ITLOS Reports 95 (3 December 2001)

84. Considering that, in the view of the Tribunal, prudence and caution require that Ireland and the United Kingdom cooperate in exchanging information concerning risks or effects of the operation of the MOX plant and in devising ways to deal with them, as appropriate;

SEP OP JUDGE WOLFRUM

Nevertheless, Ireland could not, for several reasons, rely on the precautionary principle or approach in this case, even it were to be accepted that it is part of customary international law. If the Tribunal had prescribed provisional measures for the preservation of the marine environment under the jurisdiction of Ireland, it could have done so only after a summary assessment of the radioactivity of the Irish Sea, the potential impact the MOX plant might have and whether such impact prejudiced the rights of Ireland. This, however, is an issue to be dealt with under the merits by the Annex VII arbitral tribunal. It should not be forgotten that provisional measures should not anticipate a judgment on the merits.

[...] In my view there was, under the present circumstances, no room for applying the precautionary principle to the prescription of provisional measures for the preservation of the substantive rights of Ireland or the protection of the marine environment.

[...] I fully endorse, however, paragraphs 82 to 84 of the Order, considering that the obligation to cooperate is the overriding principle of international environmental law, in particular when the interests of neighbouring States are at stake. The duty to cooperate denotes an important shift in the general orientation of the international legal order. It balances the principle of sovereignty of States and thus ensures that community interests are taken into account vis-à-vis individualistic State interests. It is a matter of prudence and caution as well as in keeping with the overriding nature of the obligation to co-operate that the parties should engage therein as prescribed in paragraph 89 of the Order.

ADVISORY OPINION
ITLOS, Responsibilities and Obligations of States Sponsoring Persons and Entities with Respect to Activities in the Area, Advisory Opinion, Case No. 17, ITLOS Reports 10 (Seabed Dispute Chamber) (1 February 2011)

131. Having established that under the Nodules Regulations and the Sulphides Regulations, both sponsoring States and the Authority are under an obligation to apply the precautionary approach in respect of activities in the Area, it is appropriate to point out that the precautionary approach is also an integral part of the general obligation of due diligence of sponsoring States, which is applicable even outside the scope of the Regulations. The due diligence obligation of the sponsoring States requires them to take all appropriate measures to prevent damage that might result from the activities of contractors that they sponsor. This obligation applies in situations where scientific evidence concerning the scope and potential negative impact of the activity in question is insufficient but where there are plausible indications of potential risks. A sponsoring State would not meet its obligation of due diligence if it disregarded those risks. Such disregard would amount to a failure to comply with the precautionary approach.

[...]

135. The Chamber observes that the precautionary approach has been incorporated into a growing number of international treaties and other instruments, many of which reflect the formulation of Principle 15 of the Rio Declaration. In the view of the Chamber, this has initiated a trend towards making this approach part of customary international law. This trend is clearly reinforced by the inclusion of the precautionary approach in the Regulations and in the "standard clause" contained in Annex 4, section 5.1, of the Sulphides Regulations. So does the following statement in paragraph 164 of the ICJ Judgment in *Pulp Mills on the River Uruguay* that

"a precautionary approach may be relevant in the interpretation and application of the provisions of the Statute" (i.e., the environmental bilateral treaty whose interpretation was the main bone of contention between the parties). This statement may be read in light of article 31, paragraph 3(c), of the Vienna Convention, according to which the interpretation of a treaty should take into account not only the context but "any relevant rules of international law applicable in the relations between the parties".

5.3.3   WTO

CASE
EC, *Measures Concerning Meat and Meat Products (Hormones)*, WT/DS26/AB/R WT/DS48/AB/R (16 January 1998) (*'Beef Hormones'*)

123. The status of the precautionary principle in international law continues to be the subject of debate among academics, law practitioners, regulators and judges. The precautionary principle is regarded by some as having crystallised into a general principle of customary international *environmental* law. Whether it has been widely accepted by Members as a principle of *general* or *customary international law*. We consider, however, that it is unnecessary, and probably imprudent, for the Appellate Body in this appeal to take a position on this important, but abstract, question.

124. It appears to us important, nevertheless, to note some aspects of the relationship of the precautionary principle to the SPS Agreement. First, the principle has not been written into the SPS Agreement as a ground for justifying SPS measures that are otherwise inconsistent with the obligations of Members set out in particular provisions of that Agreement. Secondly, the precautionary principle indeed finds reflection in Article 5.7 of the SPS Agreement. We agree, at the same time, with the European Communities, that there is no need to assume that Article 5.7 exhausts the relevance of a precautionary principle. It is also reflected in the sixth paragraph of the preamble and in Article 3.3. These explicitly recognise the right of Members to establish their own appropriate level of sanitary protection, which may be higher (i.e. more cautious) that that implied in existing international standards, guidelines, and recommendations Thirdly, a panel charged with determining, for instance, whether "sufficient scientific evidence" exists to warrant the maintenance by a Member of a particular SPS measure may, of course, and should, bear in mind that responsible, representative governments commonly act from perspectives of prudence and precaution where risks of irreversible, e.g. life-terminating, damage to human health are concerned. Lastly, however, the precautionary principle does not, by itself, and without a clear textual directive to that effect, relieve a panel from the duty of applying the normal (i.e. customary international law) principles of treaty interpretation in reading the provisions of the SPS Agreement.

125. We accordingly agree with the findings of the Panel that the precautionary principle does not override the provisions of Article 5.1 and 5.2 of the SPS Agreement.

CASE
EC, *Measures Affecting the Approval and Marketing of Biotech Products*, WT/
DS291/R WT/DS292/R WT/DS293/R (29 September 2006)

7.88   ... It appears to us from the Parties' arguments and other available materials that
        the legal debate over whether the precautionary principle constitutes a recog-
        nized principle of general or customary international law is still ongoing. Notably,
        there has, to date, been no authoritative decision by an international court or
        tribunal which recognizes the precautionary principle as a principle of general or
        customary international law.[262] It is correct that provisions explicitly or implic-
        itly applying the precautionary principle have been incorporated into numerous
        international conventions and declarations, although, for the most part, they
        are environmental conventions and declarations.[263] Also, the principle has been
        referred to and applied by States at the domestic level, again mostly in domestic
        environmental law.[264] On the other hand, there remain questions regarding the
        precise definition and content of the precautionary principle.[265] Finally, regarding
        doctrine, we note that many authors have expressed the view that the precau-
        tionary principle exists as a general principle in international law.[266] At the same
        time, as already noted by the Appellate Body, others have expressed scepticism
        and consider that the precautionary principle has not yet attained the status of
        a general principle in international law.[267]

7.89   Since the legal status of the precautionary principle remains unsettled, like
        the Appellate Body before us, we consider that prudence suggests that we not
        attempt to resolve this complex issue, particularly if it is not necessary to do so.
        Our analysis below makes clear that for the purposes of disposing of the legal
        claims before us, we need not take a position on whether or not the precaution-
        ary principle is a recognized principle of general or customary international law.
        Therefore, we refrain from expressing a view on this issue.

...

7.1521 The European Communities observes that, in view of the fact that the underly-
        ing science is still in a great state of flux, it has chosen to apply a prudent and
        precautionary approach to identifying, assessing and managing risks to human
        health and the environment arising from GMOs and GMO-derived products for
        which marketing approval has been sought.

7.1522 As an initial matter, we note that, in our view, Annex C(1)(a), first clause, does
        not preclude the application of a prudent and precautionary approach to identi-
        fying, assessing and managing risks to human health and the environment arising
        from GMOs and GMO-derived products. As we have said, we consider that
        Annex C(1)(a), first clause, allows a Member to take the time that is reasonably
        needed to determine with adequate confidence whether its relevant SPS require-
        ments are fulfilled. Consistent with this, we consider that a Member which finds
        it appropriate to follow a prudent and precautionary approach in assessing and
        approving applications concerning GMOs and GMO-derived products, might,

for instance, be justified in requesting further information or clarification of an applicant in a situation where another Member considers that the information available is sufficient to carry out its assessment and reach a decision on an application.[1300] Whether a particular request is a reflection of genuine caution and prudence or whether it is a pretext to delay the completion of an approval procedure would need to be determined in the light of all relevant facts and circumstances.

7.1523 It is apparent from the foregoing observations that we perceive no inherent tension between the obligation set out in Annex C(1)(a), first clause, to complete approval procedures without undue delay and the application of a prudent and precautionary approach to assessing and approving GMOs or GMO-derived products. Nevertheless, it is clear that application of a prudent and precautionary approach is, and must be, subject to reasonable limits, lest the precautionary approach swallow the discipline imposed by Annex C(1)(a), first clause. Indeed, if a Member could endlessly defer substantive decisions on the grounds of a perceived need for caution and prudence in the assessment of applications, Annex C(1)(a), first clause, would be devoid of any meaning or effect. In applying the provisions of Annex C(1)(a), first clause, it is therefore important always to bear in mind that Annex C(1)(a), first clause, implies as a core obligation the obligation to come to a decision on an application.

5.3.4   Inter-State Arbitration

CASE
PCA, *Dispute Concerning Access to Information Under Article 9 of the OSPAR Convention (Ireland v. United Kingdom)*, Final Award, PCA Case No. 2001–03 (15 June 2001)

DISS OP SIR GAVAN GRIFFITH QC

72. In my opinion the majority also is in error to assume, and to apply, the burden of proof as falling on Ireland. In this regard, I maintain that the obvious application of the precautionary principle (not considered by the majority) must shift the burden to the United Kingdom.

73. [...] At the least, the precautionary principle, as expressed in Article 2(2)(a), to apply "even when there is no conclusive evidence of a causal relationship between the import and the effects", directs the majority to consider the application of the principle. In my opinion it goes further and explicitly has the effect of transferring the responsibility for providing scientific evidence to the producer of hazardous substances (or, as here, to the Ministers of State as the decision-makers).

[...]

75. The finding by the majority that Ireland "has failed to demonstrate" adverse effect within the second category of information ignores Article 2(2)(a). For this reason, I conclude that the majority has misdirected itself on the question of onus. I regard the precautionary principle so engaged by Article 2(2)(a) as requiring that any finding adverse to Ireland be made in terms inverse to those found by the majority, namely that such a result was and is only open to be made on a finding that in fact there was no such potentially adverse effect. Clearly this was not a matter of fact established on the material before the Tribunal. Nor, as I understand its position, was that contended for by the United Kingdom.

CASE
PCA, *Indus Waters Kishenganga Arbitration (Pakistan v. India)*, Final Award, PCA Case No. 2011-01 (20 December 2013)

112. As the Court held in its Partial Award, "States have 'a duty to prevent, or at least mitigate' significant harm to the environment when pursuing large-scale construction activities."[161] In light of this duty, the Court has no difficulty concluding that the requirement of an environmental flow (without prejudice to the level of such flow) is necessary in the application of the Treaty. At the same time, the Court does not consider it appropriate, and certainly not "necessary," for it to adopt a precautionary approach and assume the role of policymaker in determining the balance between acceptable environmental change and other priorities, or to permit environmental considerations to override the balance of other rights and obligations expressly identified in the Treaty—in particular the entitlement of India to divert the waters of a tributary of the Jhelum. The Court's authority is more limited and extends only to mitigating significant harm.

5.3.5   ECtHR

CASE
ECHR, *Tâtar v. Romania*, Judgment, App No. 67021/01 (27 January 2009)

120. Pour ce qui est des suites de l'accident de janvier 2000, la Cour observe qu'il ressort des éléments du dossier que l'activité industrielle en question n'a pas été arrêtée par les autorités, qui ont continué à utiliser la même technologie (voir le paragraphe 8 ci-dessus, in fine). En ce sens, la Cour rappelle l'importance du principe de précaution (consacré pour la première fois par la Déclaration de Rio), qui « a vocation à s'appliquer en vue d'assurer un niveau de protection élevée de la santé, de la sécurité des consommateurs et de l'environnement, dans l'ensemble des activités de la Communauté ».

5.3.6   IACtHR

ADVISORY OPINION
IACtHR, The Environment and Human Rights, Advisory Opinion, OC-23/17 (15 November 2017), Series A No. 23

180. Notwithstanding the above, the general obligation to ensure the rights to life and to personal integrity means that States must act diligently to prevent harm to these rights (supra para. 118). Also, when interpreting the Convention, as requested in this case, the Court must always seek the "best perspective" for the protection of the individual (supra para. 41). Therefore, the Court understands that States must act in keeping with the precautionary principle in order to protect the rights to life and to personal integrity in cases where there are plausible indications that an activity could result in severe and irreversible damage to the environment, even in the absence of scientific certainty. Consequently, States must act with due caution to prevent possible damage. Thus, in the context of the protection of the rights to life and to personal integrity, the Court considers that States must act in keeping with the precautionary principle. Therefore, even in the absence of scientific certainty, they must take "effective" measures to prevent severe or irreversible damage.

QUESTIONS

1. Do we need the precautionary principle if we have environmental impact assessment?
2. Is the precautionary principle an efficient tool in the protection of the environment?
3. What is the legal status of the precautionary principle?

FURTHER READING

BOOKS

E Fisher, J Jones and R von Schomberg (eds), *Implementing the Precautionary Principle: Perspectives and Prospects* (Edward Elgar 2006)

CE Foster, *Science and the Precautionary Principle in International Courts and Tribunals* (Cambridge University Press 2013)

S Marr, *The Precautionary Principle in the Law of the Sea: Modern Decision Making in International Law* (Kluwer Law Int'l 2003)

J Peel, *Science and Risk Regulation in International Law* (Cambridge University Press 2010)

J Peel, *The Precautionary Principle in Practice* (The Federation Press 2005)

N de Sadeleer, *Environmental Principles: From Political Slogans to Legal Rules* (2nd edn, Oxford University Press 2020)

A Trouwborst, *Evolution and Status of the Precautionary Principle in International Law* (Kluwer The Hague 2002)

CHAPTERS

D Bodansky 'Deconstructing the Precautionary Principle' in DD Caron and HN Scheiber (eds), *Bringing New Law to Ocean Waters* (Nijhoff Leiden 2004)

AA Cançado Trindade, 'Principle 15' in JE Viñuales (ed.), *The Rio Declaration on Environment and Development: A Commentary* (Oxford University Press 2015)

D Freestone, 'International Fisheries Since Rio: The Continued Rise of the Precautionary Principle' in A Boyle and D Freestone (eds), *International Law and Sustainable Development: Past Achievements and Future Challenges* (Oxford University Press 1999)

E Orlando, 'Principles, Standards and Voluntary Commitments in IEL' in E Techera, J Lindley, KN Scott and A Telesetsky (eds), *Routledge Handbook of International Environmental Law* (2nd edn, Routledge 2021)

M Schröder, 'Precautionary Approach/Principle' in *Max Planck Encyclopedia of Public International Law* (2014)

JM Van Dyke 'The Evolution and International Acceptance of the Precautionary Principle' in DD Caron and HN Scheiber (eds) *Bringing New Law to Ocean Waters* (Nijhoff Leiden 2004)

ARTICLES

D Bodansky, 'Scientific Uncertainty and the Precautionary Principle' (1991) 33(4–5) Environment 43

A Fabra, 'The LOSC and the Implementation of the Precautionary Principle' (1999) 10 Yearbook of International Environmental Law 15

A Gillespie, 'The Precautionary Principle and the 21st Century: A Case Study of Noise Pollution in the Ocean' (2007) 22 The International Journal of Marine and Coastal Law 61

E Hey, 'The Precautionary Concept in Environmental Policy and Law: Institutionalizing Caution' (1992) 4 G Int'l Env L Rev 303

S Marr, 'The Southern Bluefin Tuna Cases: The Precautionary Approach and Conservation and Management of Fish Resources' (2000) 11 Eur J Int'l L 815

T Scovazzi, 'Sul principio precauzionale nel diritto internazionale dell'ambiente' (1992) 75 Rivista di diritto internazionale 699

FG Sourgens, 'The Precaution Presumption' (2020) 31(4) European Journal of International Law 1277

JE Viñuales,, 'Legal Techniques for Dealing with Scientific Uncertainty in Environmental Law' (2010) 43 Vanderbilt Journal of Transnational Law 437

6
Polluter-pays principle

6.1   INTRODUCTION

The polluter-pays principle operates as an economic principle for allocating the costs of pollution control. It received its first significant formulation in the 1972 Recommendation on Guiding Principles Concerning International Economic Aspects of Environmental Policies, adopted by the OECD Council, although it was somewhat reflected in earlier instruments such as the 1960 Paris Convention on Third Party Liability in the Field of Nuclear Energy.[1] It has increased in prominence, in particular as environmental law has become more economically sophisticated and with the more general rise of economic awareness embodied, notably in the link between sustainable development and environment.[2]

A central idea underlying the polluter-pays principle is 'cost internalisation'. Economic activity has consequential environmental effects, known as 'environmental externalities'. In principle, such effects may either be to the benefit or detriment of the rest of society. 'Environmental externalities' can be defined as follows:[3]

> Environmental externalities refer to the economic concept of uncompensated environmental effects of production and consumption that affect consumer utility and enterprise cost outside the market mechanism.

As a consequence of negative externalities, private costs of production tend to be lower than its 'social' cost. It is the aim of the 'polluter/user pays' principle to prompt households and enterprises to internalise externalities in their plans and budgets. The polluter-pays principle thus seeks to ensure that the negative costs of production are borne by the producer and not by the rest of society.

---

[1]   See Chapter 17.

[2]   On which see Chapter 2.

[3]   Glossary of Environment Statistics, Studies in Methods, Series F, No. 67, United Nations, New York, 1997, https://stats.oecd.org/glossary/detail.asp?ID=824 accessed 6 June 2021.

The acceptability of 'cost internalisation' is controversial. As Dupuy and Viñuales argue,[4]

> internalisation should only apply to externalities on two strict conditions: namely (i) that the activity producing the externality is socially desirable, and (ii) that the negative externality remains within the bounds of what can be considered as tolerable (less than 'significant') damage. Indeed, beyond the threshold of 'significant damage' it should no longer be a matter of cost internalisation (and hence of market mechanisms) but one of prevention[.]

The polluter-pays principle operates in more than one way, and its scope has evolved over time. According to de Sadeleer,[5]

> the PPP can fulfil a number of functions in embracing the costs of 'remedying pollution', the costs 'arising from the implementation of a policy of prevention', as well as the administrative costs related to the control of the polluting activity. These various functions are at times complementary and at other times mutually exclusive.

The four functions de Sadeleer identifies co-exist within environmental law regimes. The economic integration function has been – and continues to be – important to the relationship between environmental protection and the international economy,[6] since it prevents private economic actors from receiving the benefit of what is in effect the subsidy of having the State pay for the costs of its pollution. The redistribution function, which most reflects the idea of costs internalisation, shifts (or partially shifts) the costs borne by the state in preventing pollution – the costs of monitoring, impact assessment, inspection – back to the polluter. The preventive function is concerned not so much with the shifting costs, but with recalibrating incentives for the polluter – and, moreover, enables the polluter-pays principle to support the broader objective of environmental law of harm prevention.[7] The curative function, which provides a means of allocating liability to compensate for environmental damage arising from pollution, has come to play a significant role in the development of civil liability regimes established under international law.[8]

The principle is now reflected in many domestic laws and in various international and regional instruments. It is generally accepted that it does not reflect a principle of customary international law. In particular, the tribunal in the *Rhine Chlorides* case denied that it is a principle of general international law. Moreover, the principle as it is formulated in Principle 16 of the Rio Declaration is more vague and general than the formulations found in other instruments. According to Sands and Peel, 'This derives, at least in part, from the view held by a number of states, both developed and developing, that the polluter pays principle is applicable at the domestic level but does not govern relations or responsibilities between states at the

---

[4]   P-M Dupuy and J Viñuales, *International Environmental Law* (2nd edn, CUP 2018) 82.

[5]   Nicolas de Sadeleer, *Environmental Principles: From Political Slogans to Legal Rules* (2nd edn, OUP 2020) 42.

[6]   See Chapter 17.

[7]   See Chapter 4.

[8]   See Chapter 17.

international level.'[9] Instead, inter-state responsibility is constructed around the precautionary and preventive principles. Notwithstanding the general view that the polluter-pays principle is not customary international law, in certain instruments, such as the 1990 International Convention on Oil Pollution Preparedness, Response and Cooperation, it is said to be a general principle of international law.

The principle's legal instantiation and role is different in different instruments.[10] In certain treaties it is invoked only in preambular language as part of the interpretive background of the treaty. In other treaties, for instance in the 1992 Helsinki Convention on the Protection and Use of Transboundary Watercourses and International Lakes, states are specifically obliged to take account of the principle to guide the performance of the parties' other obligations under the treaty. In other treaties, the parties are required to apply the polluter-pays principle either generally, as in the 1992 OSPAR Convention, or to underpin 'best endeavours' obligations of states, as in the 1996 Protocol to the 1972 London Convention. The most precise and detailed forms the principle takes are found in civil liability regimes, which seek to fix the liabilities of polluters.

As de Sadeleer makes clear,[11] there are different ways the polluter-pays principle might be applied. The first is a standards-based approach, namely that the polluter is required only to pay for pollution where the pollution exceeds a certain threshold. The second is an impacts-based approach, under which the polluter pays according to the actual effects on the environments caused. These approaches may be combined, and one or other approach may be more appropriate for different functions of the principle. For instance, an impacts-based approach is appropriate for liability regimes, but less suitable for allocating the costs of preventive measures in the context of, e.g., hazardous materials, where the private entity may never cause any pollution.

In general, the polluter-pays principle is enforced by internalising environmental costs through the use of economic instruments. They are implemented through economic incentives, combined with market and non-market mechanisms and private sector pollution and environmental cost-spreading investments. Economic incentives include: emissions charges and taxes; emissions trading; carbon capture and storage mechanisms. A non-market-based incentive system is implemented by way of subsidies, financial assistance, and tax credits or tax breaks. Taxation is, however, a 'a relatively crude way to recoup the external costs of environmentally harmful activities' and 'cannot easily be targeted at accidental damage, nor can they be applied to transboundary polluters'.[12]

Compensation mechanisms, implementing the curative function, tend to involve rigid legal regimes allocating the costs of pollution and preventive measures to particular producers. In the case of liability regimes, it is often seen as requiring strict liability. Neither of these features of the application of the principle necessarily follow from it. Fault-based regimes in which the

[9]   P Sands and J Peel, *Principles of International Environmental Law* (4th edn, CUP 2018) 241.

[10] See below, and further chapter 17.

[11] See de Sadeleer (n 5) 46–50.

[12] A Boyle, 'Polluter pays' in *Max Planck Encyclopedia of International Law* (2009) para. 7.

harmful impacts of pollution are borne by all those causally and morally responsible for it can also be consistent with the polluter-pays principle. Rather the use of fixed allocative regimes that do not depend on direct causation or fault in the application of the polluter-pays principle is a consequence of the need for a simple, effective system to allocative costs in situations where establishing fault is complex and costly. One consequence of this is that civil liability regimes do not, in fact, involve the 'full' internalisation of the costs of environmental harm. Regimes fix limits to the amount of compensation owed, types of damage that may be compensated, and entities from whom compensation may be sought.[13] A fundamental problem that arises is in identifying who is the polluter: who is liable may be difficult to establish in some cases, or may be shared between various actors. Often the 'polluter' is fixed to a certain entity, such as the operator of an installation, who thus assumes the environmental risk of pollution arising from the installation which they operate. In other cases, states may cover part of the costs of environmental damage, in particular where an activity has social value and liability would be too great for a private actor to bear – for instance, in the case of nuclear liability. In such cases, equitable considerations entail that only part of the costs are internalised.

While the particular regimes using the principle may not attain 'full internalisation', the central idea of internalising the costs of environmental harm remains fundamental. The beneficiaries of the externalisation of environmental harms caused by economic activities are not confined to operators of major installations, but include the public more generally, both morally as consumers generating a demand for the harmful activities of such operators and as producers of environmental harm, albeit at relatively low levels individually. As Schwartz writes, the polluter-pays principle should 'influence our conduct: to restrain or reduce our capacity to over-produce, over-consume, over-charge, over-invest, over-innovate, over-trade and over-compete, and so avoid incurring the responsibility to pay, credit or trade the environment'.[14] The principle thus continues to exert a normative influence on environmental law, for example through the creation of 'carbon pricing' in the legal regimes for climate change.

6.2   LEGAL INSTRUMENTS

6.2.1   Legally Binding Instruments

Treaty on the European Union (Consolidated Version) OJ C 325/5

Article 191
(ex Article 174 TEC)
1.   Union policy on the environment shall contribute to pursuit of the following objectives:
  –   preserving, protecting and improving the quality of the environment,

---

[13]   See Chapter 17.

[14]   P Schwartz, 'Polluter pays principle' in L Krämer, E Orlando (eds), *Principles of Environmental Law* (EE 2018) 270–271.

    –   protecting human health,
    –   prudent and rational utilisation of natural resources, promoting measures at international level to deal with regional or worldwide environmental problems, and in particular combating climate change.

2.   Union policy on the environment shall aim at a high level of protection taking into account the diversity of situations in the various regions of the Union. It shall be based on the precautionary principle and on the principles that preventive action should be taken, that environmental damage should as a priority be rectified at source and that the polluter should pay.

1990 International Convention on Oil Pollution Preparedness, Response and Cooperation, 1891 UNTS 78

Preamble

[…]

TAKING ACCOUNT of the "polluter pays" principle as a general principle of international environmental law,

Final Act of the Conference on International Co-Operation Oil Pollution Preparedness and Response (London, 13 November 1990)
CONFERENCE RESOLUTION 5
    ESTABLISHMENT OF OIL POLLUTION COMBATING EQUIPMENT STOCKPILES

[…]

RECOGNIZING ALSO that one of the basic principles used for providing funds following pollution damage is the "polluter pays" principle,

1992 OSPAR Convention

Article 2 General Obligations
[…]

2.   The Contracting Parties shall apply:

[…]

    (b)   the polluter pays principle, by virtue of which the costs of pollution prevention, control and reduction measures are to be borne by the polluter.

1992 Helsinki Convention on the Protection of the Marine Environment of the Baltic Sea Area

Article 3 Fundamental Principles and Obligations
[...]

4.   The Contracting Parties shall apply the polluter-pays principle.

1992 Convention on the Protection and Use of Transboundary Watercourses and International Lakes, 1936 UNTS 269

Article 2 General Provisions
[...]

5.   In taking the measures referred to in paragraphs 1 and 2 of this article, the Parties shall be guided by the following principles:

[...]

      (b)   The polluter-pays principle, by virtue of which costs of pollution prevention, control and reduction measures shall be borne by the polluter;

2003 Kiev Protocol on Civil Liability and Compensation for Damage Caused by the Transboundary Effects of Industrial Accidents on Transboundary Waters to the 1992 Convention on the Protection and Use of Transboundary Watercourses and International Lakes and to the 1992 Convention on the Transboundary Effects of Industrial Accidents

Preamble
[...]

Having in mind the relevant provisions of principles 13 and 16 of the Rio Declaration on Environment and Development,
    Taking into account the polluter pays principle as a general principle of international environmental law, accepted also by the Parties to the above-mentioned Conventions,

1996 Protocol to the London Convention on the Prevention of Marine Pollution by Dumping of Wastes and Other Matter, 1972 (as amended 2006)

Article 3 General Obligations
[...]

2.   Taking into account the approach that the polluter should, in principle, bear the cost of pollution, each Contracting Party shall endeavour to promote practices

whereby those it has authorized to engage in dumping or incineration at sea bear the cost of meeting the pollution prevention and control requirements for the authorized activities, having due regard to the public interest.

2001 Stockholm Convention on Persistent Organic Pollutants, 2256 UNTS 119

Preamble
Reaffirming Principle 16 of the Rio Declaration on Environment and Development which states that national authorities should endeavour to promote the internalization of environmental costs and the use of economic instruments, taking into account the approach that the polluter should, in principle, bear the cost of pollution, with due regard to the public interest and without distorting international trade and investment,

Table 6.1 Other treaties referring to 'polluter-pays principle'

1977 Civil Liability for Pollution Convention Art 6(4)
1991 Alpine Convention
Protocol on Environmental Protection to the Antarctic Treaty (done 4 October 1991, entered into force 14 January 1998) (1991) 30 ILM 1455
1992 UNECE Convention on the Transboundary Effects of Industrial Accidents (as amended 2015)
1994 Danube
1994 Energy Charter Treaty
2003 Carpathians Convention
1996 The International Convention on Liability and Compensation for Damaged in Connection with Hazardous then Carriage of Hazardous and Noxious Substances by Sea (The 'HNS Convention') and the 2010 Protocol
1999 Convention on the Protection of the Rhine (12 April 1999, entered into force 1 January 2003)
1999 Protocol on Water and Health to the 1992 Convention on the Protection and Use of Transboundary Watercourses and International Lakes
International Convention on Civil Liability for Bunker Oil Pollution Damage (adopted 23 March 2001, entered into force 21 November 2008) (2002) OJ L256/9
2002 North-East Pacific Convention Art 5(6)(b)

6.2.2 Non-Binding Instruments

Recommendation on Guiding Principles concerning International Economic Aspects of Environmental Policies as adopted by the OECD Council on 26 May 1972

A. Guiding Principles
   a)   Cost Allocation: the Polluter-Pays Principle

      2.   Environmental resources are in general limited and their use in production and consumption activities may lead to their deterioration. When the cost of this deterioration is not adequately taken into account in the price

system, the market fails to reflect the scarcity of such resources both at the national and international levels. Public measures are thus necessary to reduce pollution and to reach a better allocation of resources by ensuring that prices of goods depending on the quality and/or quantity of environmental resources reflect more closely their relative scarcity and that economic agents concerned react accordingly.

3.   In many circumstances, in order to ensure that the environment is in an acceptable state, the reduction of pollution beyond a certain level will not be practical or even necessary in view of the costs involved.

4.   The principle to be used for allocating costs of pollution prevention and control measures to encourage rational use of scarce environmental resources and to avoid distortions in international trade and investment is the so-called "Polluter-Pays Principle". This principle means that the polluter should bear the expenses of carrying out the above-mentioned measures decided by public authorities to ensure that the environment is in an acceptable state. In other words, the cost of these measures should be reflected in the cost of goods and services which cause pollution in production and/or consumption. Such measures should not be accompanied by subsidies that would create significant distortions in international trade and investment.

5.   This principle should be an objective of Member countries; however, there may be exceptions or special arrangements, particularly for the transitional periods, provided that they do not lead to significant distortions in international trade and investment.

1992 Rio Declaration

Principle 16
National authorities should endeavour to promote the internalization of environmental costs and the use of economic instruments, taking into account the approach that the polluter should, in principle, bear the cost of pollution, with due regard to the public interest and without distorting international trade and investment.

2006 ILC Draft Principles Allocation of Loss

Preamble
The General Assembly,
Reaffirming Principles 13 and 16 of the Rio Declaration on Environment and Development

[...]

Commentary

[...]

2)   [...] The Commission considers the "polluter pays" principle as an essential component in underpinning the present draft principles to ensure that victims that suffer harm as a result of an incident involving a hazardous activity are able to obtain prompt and adequate compensation.

6.3   CASE LAW

CASE
PCA, *Case Concerning the Auditing of Accounts Between the Kingdom of the Netherlands and the French Republic pursuant to the Additional Protocol of 25 September 1991 to the Convention on the Protection of the Rhine Against Pollution by Chlorides of 3 December 1976, (Netherlands v. France)*, Award, PCA Case No. 2002-02 (12 March 2004) (*'Rhine Chlorides'*)

102. In carrying out its task, the Tribunal must also take into account "any relevant rules of international law applicable in the relations between the parties" (Article 31, paragraph 3 (c) of the Vienna Convention).

The Tribunal notes that the Netherlands has referred to the "polluter pays" principle in support of its claim.

103. The Tribunal observes that this principle features in several international instruments, bilateral as well as multilateral, and that it operates at various levels of effectiveness. Without denying its importance in treaty law, the Tribunal does not view this principle as being a part of general international law. The "polluter pays" principle does not appear anywhere in the Convention or the Protocol. The Protocol, furthermore, adopts a different solution. Besides, the Netherlands acknowledges that the Protocol derogates from the "polluter pays" principle. It follows that this principle is of no relevance for the interpretation of point 4.2.1.

CASE
United States – Taxes on Petroleum and Certain Imported Substances, L/6175 – 34S/136, Report of the Panel (17 June 1987)

5.2.5   The Panel wishes to point out,.however, that the Working Part on Border Tax Adjustment agreed that the provisions of the General Agreement on tax adjustment

"set maxima limits for adjustment (compensation) which were not to be exceeded, but below which every contracting party was free to differentiate in the degree of compensation applied, provided that such action WAS in conformity with other provisions of the General Agreement" (BISD 18S/100).

Consequently, if a contracting party wishes to tax the sale of certain domestic products (because their production pollutes the domestic environment) and to impose a lower tax or no tax at all on like imported products (because their consumption or use causes fewer or no environmental problems), it is in principle free to do so. The General Agreement's rules on tax adjustment thus give the contracting party in such a case the possibility to follow the Polluter-Pays Principle, but they do not oblige it to do so.

QUESTIONS

1. Identify the different ways the polluter-pays principle is given effect in international law.
2. Discuss the relationship between the polluter-pays principle and the principles of prevention and precaution.
3. 'The polluter-pays principle promises to be an effective tool in the fight against climate change.' Do you agree?

FURTHER READING

BOOKS

P Birnie, A Boyle and C Redgwell, *International Law and the Environment* (4th edn, Oxford University Press 2021)

P-M Dupuy and J Viñuales, *International Environmental Law* (2nd edn, Cambridge University Press 2018)

A Heyes (ed.), *The Law and Economics of the Environment* (Edward Elgar 2001)

N de Sadeleer, *Environmental Principles: From Political Slogans to Legal Rules* (2nd edn, Oxford University Press 2020)

P Sands and J Peel (eds), *Principles of International Environmental Law* (4th edn, Cambridge University Press 2018)

E Scotford, *Environmental Principles and the Evolution of Environmental Law* (Hart 2017)

CHAPTERS

A Boyle, 'Making the Polluter Pay?' in F Franzioni and T Scovazzi (eds), *International Responsibility for Environmental Harm* (Graham & Trotman 1991)

A Boyle, 'Polluter Pays' in *Max Planck Encyclopedia of International Law* (2009)

H-C Bugge, 'The Principle of Polluter-Pays in Economics and Law' in E Eide and R Van den Bergh (eds), *Law and Economics of the Environment* (Juridisk Forlag 1996)

E Morgera, 'Principle 16' in J Viñuales (ed.), *The Rio Declaration on Environment and Development* (Oxford University Press 2015)

E Orlando, 'Principles, Standards and Voluntary Commitments in IEL' in E Techera, J Lindley, KN Scott and A Telesetsky (eds), *Routledge Handbook of International Environmental Law* (2nd edn, Routledge 2020)

P Schwartz, 'Polluter Pays Principle' in L Krämer and E Orlando (eds), *Principles of Environmental Law* (Edward Elgar 2018)

ARTICLES

J Adshead, 'The Application and Development of the Polluter-Pays Principle across Jurisdictions in Liability for Marine Oil Pollution: The Tales of the "Erika" and the "Prestige"' (2018) 30 Journal of Environmental Law 425

C Foster, 'The ILC Draft Principles on the Allocation of Loss in Case of Transboundary Harm Arising out of Hazardous Activities: Privatizing Risk?' (2005) 14(3) RECIEL 272

S Gaines, 'The Polluter-Pays Principle: From Economic Equity to Environmental Ethos (1991) 26 Texas International Law Journal 463

MR Grossman, 'Agriculture and Polluter Pays Principle: An Introduction' (2006) 59 Oklahoma Law Review 1

M Khan, 'Polluter-Pays-Principle: The Cardinal Instrument for Addressing Climate Change' (2015) 4 Laws 638

J F Pinto-Bazurco 'How to Enforce the Polluter-Pays Principle' (2022) *International Institute for Sustainable Development* https://www.iisd.org/system/files/2022-02/still-one-earth-polluter-pays-principle.pdf

7
Intergenerational equity

7.1   INTRODUCTION

The principle of intergenerational equity (IE) is one of the components of the concept of sustainable development. '*Inter*generational' means between generations present, past and unborn. This relationship was conceptualised by Professor Brown Weiss in her seminal monograph: *Fairness to Future Generations: International Law, Common Patrimony, and Intergenerational Equity* (1989). Her very rich ideas can be summarised as follows. The present generation holds the earth in trust for future generations. At the same time the present generation are the beneficiaries, as the concept of IE requires each generation to pass the planet on in no worse condition than it received it. According to Weiss, each generation is both a trustee for the planet with a duty to care for it and a beneficiary with a right to use it. Weiss distinguishes three basic principles of intergenerational equity: the 'conservation of options', which entails conserving the diversity of the natural and cultural resource base to a level comparable with that enjoyed by the previous generation; the 'conservation of quality', which entails passing on a planet that is comparable in quality with that enjoyed by previous generations; and third, 'the conservation of access', which entails rights of access to past legacies. Furthermore, 'Intergenerational planetary rights may be regarded as group rights... they exist regardless of the number and identity of individuals making up each generation.' A trust is a legal relationship whereby the trustee holds the property and manages it (legal ownership) for the trust's beneficiaries, who enjoy the property and rights under the trust (equitable ownership). Brown Weiss's theory that 'the rights are always associated with obligations' and that 'each generation is both a trustee for the planet with obligations to care for it and a beneficiary with rights to use it' caused controversy, with opposition premised on the view that future generations can only have a moral rather than a legal right, so that there be no *locus standi* in adjudication and therefore no right of legal enforcement. Rawls' egalitarian conception of distributive justice seen in his formulation 'justice as fairness' forms the basis of Weiss's trust theory.[1] Rawls uses the 'original position' to justify his perspective of justice, which operates behind a veil of ignorance and is akin to the Hobbesian social contract. He states: 'we begin with the idea of a state of nature... we then ask under what conditions... persons in such a state

---

[1]   John Rawls, *A Theory of Justice* (Harvard UP 1971).

would be willing to form a contract that establishes a government... justified by unanimous consent.' Rawls notes that

> in justice as fairness the original position of equality corresponds to a state of nature... no one knows his place in society, his class position or social status... his fortune in the distribution of natural assets and abilities, his intelligence, strength and the like... the principles of justice are chosen behind a veil of ignorance. This ensures that no one is advantaged or disadvantaged in the choice of principles.

Additionally and most importantly in the intergenerational context, 'the historical record is closed to them' and so cannot know where precisely they find themselves on the spectrum of time. Weiss's trust is a clear example of distributive justice in that the burdens and benefits of conserving and enjoying the environment respectively are unevenly spread throughout time.

Theories of justice resting on a contractual basis are based on the principle of reciprocity and therefore they cannot establish a basis of an obligation towards future generations based on justice; it equates to mutual exchange. Future generations cannot offer anything to those living. Such criticism makes Weiss's application of Rawls' theory – which rests on the notion of a social contract – to an intergenerational context nonsensical. The theory of Brown Weiss was also subject to much criticism also on the grounds of being overly anthropocentric.

Professor Vaughan Lowe expressed his criticism of the theory of intergenerational equity in rather strong words. Lowe is of the opinion that 'the principle of intergenerational equity... is a chimera', thus attributing to it a mythological, illusory character. He asks, 'Who are the beneficiaries? What are their rights of actions? What are the duties of trustees?' He also notes that it is hard to see what legal content intergenerational equity has and takes the perceived rights of future generations to be merely metaphorical. Lowe further insists that the obligations and duties of trustees, contrary to the opinions of Weiss and Sands, cannot be enforced. He claims 'international law lacks institutions and mechanisms with the authority and ability to make rational choices of this kind', namely, distributive choices concerning the content of such duties.

Lowe's critique deserves further attention. For example, if State A has X coal reserves and State B has X+500 coal reserves, the content of the duty to pass on the planet in no worse condition will differ between different states. If each state handles questions of conservation in isolation and in ignorance of one another's obligations, there is less potential for conflict between different states whose citizens are unaware of the differing burdens amongst them. A planetary trust, however, to achieve intergenerational equity as a response to a communal problem does not agree with state isolation, thereby invoking the problem of common but differentiated responsibilities in climate change, or more broadly speaking intragenerational equity.[2]

Weiss confesses that intragenerational equity 'requires attention' in order to attain intergenerational equity. Intragenerational equity places unequal burdens on the current generations of different states, to bring about a sense of equality between them, and is difficult to achieve

---

2   Vaughan Lowe, 'Sustainable Development and Unsustainable Arguments' in A Boyle and D Freestone (eds), *International Law and Sustainable Development: Past Achievements and Future Challenges* (1999) 27.

in itself. Achieving distributive justice across time, in the form of intergenerational equity amongst generations, when its attainment is an almost formidable task in a space of controlled time, within a generation as intragenerational equity, one might say is almost unworkable.

There are some constitutions that recognise the rights of future generations. The Kenyan Constitution of 2010 explicitly recognises the rights of future generations. The Argentinian Constitution Article 41, clause 1, states, 'All inhabitants are entitled to the right to a healthy and balanced environment... productive activities shall meet present needs without endangering those of future generations; and shall have the duty to preserve it.' The Constitution of Poland Article 74, clause 1, states, 'Public authorities shall pursue policies ensuring the ecological security of current and future generations.'

In Israel, the Commission for Future Generations operated from 2001 until 2006. The Commission regulated matters which were of special interest to future generations, providing parliament with recommendations on bills and secondary legislation. Former Deputy Commissioner Nira Lamay wrote that the 'motto was that while the political world was busy with issues of defence and war, we would prepare for the "day after" peace, when future generations would have clean water to drink and clean air to breathe'.[3] The institution allegedly ceased to exist in 2006 as it alleged that the commission was unnecessary, ineffective and wasted public funds. In Hungary, the Hungarian Parliamentary Commissioner for Future Generations (so-called Green Ombudsman) was established in 2008 in order to reinforce advocacy for the natural environment and to safeguard intergenerational justice. It had a wide range of powers: it served as a consultative body to the parliament regarding environmental legislation; it could initiate proceedings at the Constitutional Court; or it could intervene in court litigations in the interest of future generations and the enforcement of the right to a healthy environment. The basic task of the Commissioner for Future Generations was monitoring 'the enforcement of legal provisions that promote environmental sustainability, to influence local and national legislation as well as to participate in the domestic enforcement of international conventions and even in Hungarian decision-making procedures related to the European Union'.[4] The Ombudsman has ceased to exist and from 1 January 2012 its tasks were overtaken by its legal successor, the Office of the Commissioner for Fundamental Rights.

The principle has mostly been invoked within international treaties in preambles, and thus may, in such cases, have some limited interpretative weight. Two exceptions to this are the 1972 World Heritage Convention and the 1992 UN Framework Convention on Climate Change, in the latter of which its status as a guiding principle is recognised within the operative part of the treaty. Soft law instruments have made reference to it, notably in the Stockholm Declaration and Rio Declaration. The Stockholm Declaration approach is framed in terms of resource management, but, under the influence of the Brundtland Report, intergenerational equity has been integrated with the concept of sustainable development. UNESCO has also

---

[3]   Reem Al-Shareef and Nira Lamay, 'Perspectives: Israelis and Palestinians – Generation 2.0' (Common Ground News Service, 2009) available at http://www.commongroundnews.org/article.php?id=25099&lan=en&sid=1&sp.

[4]   Dr Marcel Szabó, 'The Way Forward: Protecting Future Generations through the Institution of Green Ombudsman', available at http://www.futurejustice.org/blog/guest-contribution/an-example-guest-post/.

issued a declaration elaborating the content of intergenerational equity in greater detail, but it is clear from the declaration's preamble that it is understood as a moral principle only.

International courts have not made great use of the concept of intergenerational equity. The concept can be first seen in the statement of the US Secretary in the *Pacific Fur Seal Arbitration*. Its main appearance before the ICJ is in three individual opinions by Judge Weeramantry in *Revised Nuclear Tests*, *Legality of the Use or Threat of Nuclear Weapons*, and *Gabčikovo-Nagymaros Project*. In these cases, Judge Weeramantry pressed the view that intergenerational equity was part of the fabric of international law, and the Court was thus under a duty in rendering its judicial decisions to have regard to the impacts of its judgments on future generations. His view, however, was a minority one. The rights of future generations have been recognised by the Inter-American Court of Human Rights. Another interesting case in which they have been recognised, with a strong dissent by Judge Feliciano, is the *Minors Oposa*[5] case in the Philippines, in which the minors claimed that they were 'entitled to the full benefit, use and enjoyment of the natural resource treasures that is the country's virgin tropical rainforests'. The claim was filed on behalf of children and generations yet unborn, thereby incorporating intergenerational equity into their suit. Standing was permitted insofar as it accommodated the right to a healthful ecology as embodied in Sections 15 and 16 of Article II of the Philippines Constitution.

With regard to the status of intergenerational equity today, Catherine Redgwell's analysis of the principle in the climate change regime may give an indication of the more general position:[6]

> at best inter-generational equity may be said to constitute a 'guiding principle' in the application of substantive norms, including existing treaty obligations, under international law. Whether this guiding principle has assumed more concrete form in addressing the 'inherently inter-generational issues' raised by climate change, [...] will depend, *inter alia*, on the crucial next steps in the evolution of the climate regime.

---

[5]   *Minors Oposa v. Secretary of The Department of Environment and Natural Resources (DENR), Supreme Court of the Philippines*, ILM 33 (30 July 1993), p. 173

[6]   C Redgwell, 'Principles and Emerging Norms in International Law: Intra- and Inter-generational Equity in Carlarne C.P., Gray K.R., and Tarasofsky R. (eds), *The Oxford Handbook of International Climate Change Law* (OUP 2016) 199.

7.2   LEGAL INSTRUMENTS

7.2.1   Legally Binding Instruments

1946 International Convention for the Regulation of Whaling

Preamble
Recognizing the interest of the nations of the world in safeguarding for future generations the great natural resources represented by the whale stocks;

1972 World Heritage Convention, 1037 UNTS 151

Article 4
Each State Party to this Convention recognizes that the duty of ensuring the identification, protection, conservation, presentation and transmission to future generations of the cultural and natural heritage referred to in Articles 1 and 2 and situated on its territory, belongs primarily to that State. It will do all it can to this end, to the utmost of its own resources and, where appropriate, with any international assistance and co-operation, in particular, financial, artistic, scientific and technical, which it may be able to obtain.

1973 Convention on International Trade in Endangered Species of Wild Fauna and Flora, 993 UNTS 443

Preamble
Recognizing that wild fauna and flora in their many beautiful and varied forms are an irreplaceable part of the natural systems of the earth which must be protected for this and the generations to come;

1979 Bonn Convention on the Conservation of Migratory Species of Wild Animals, 1651 UNTS

Preamble
The Contracting Parties

[...]

AWARE that each generation of man holds the resources of the earth for future generations and has an obligation to ensure that this legacy is conserved and, where utilized, is used wisely.

1992 United Nations Framework Convention on Climate Change, 1771 UNTS 107

Article 3 Principles
In their actions to achieve the objective of the Convention and to implement its provisions, the Parties shall be guided, *inter alia*, by the following:
1.   The Parties should protect the climate system for the benefit of present and future generations of humankind, on the basis of equity and in accordance with their common but differentiated responsibilities and respective capabilities.

Accordingly, the developed country Parties should take the lead in combating climate change and the adverse effects thereof.

2015 Paris Agreement

Preamble

Acknowledging that climate change is a common concern of humankind, Parties should, when taking action to address climate change, respect, promote and consider their respective obligations on human rights, the right to health, the rights of indigenous peoples, local communities, migrants, children, persons with disabilities and people in vulnerable situations and the right to development, as well as gender equality, empowerment of women and intergenerational equity,

7.2.2   Non-Legally Binding Instruments

1972 Stockholm Declaration (Declaration of the United Nations Conference on the Human Environment 1972 (16 June 1972) UN Doc A/CONF.48/14/Rev. 1, 3, reprinted in 11 ILM 1416 (1972))

Principle 1

Man has the fundamental right to freedom, equality and adequate conditions of life, in an environment of a quality that permits a life of dignity and well-being, and he bears a solemn responsibility to protect and improve the environment for present and future generations. In this respect, policies promoting or perpetuating apartheid, racial segregation, discrimination, colonial and other forms of oppression and foreign domination stand condemned and must be eliminated.

Principle 2

The natural resources of the earth, including the air, water, land, flora and fauna and especially representative samples of natural ecosystems, must be safeguarded for the benefit of present and future generations through careful planning or management, as appropriate.

1987 Report of the Brundtland Commission: *Our Common Future*

Overview by the World Commission on Environment and Development

[...]

25.   Many present efforts to guard and maintain human progress, to meet human needs, and to realize human ambitions are simply unsustainable – in both the rich and poor nations. They draw too heavily, too quickly, on already overdrawn environmental resource accounts to be affordable far into the future without bankrupting those accounts. They may show profit on the balance sheets of our generation, but our children will inherit the losses. We borrow environmental capital from future generations with no intention or prospect of repaying. They may damn us for our spendthrift ways, but they can never collect on our debt to them. We act as we do because we can get away with it: future generations do not vote; they have no political or financial power; they cannot challenge our decisions.

26.   But the results of the present profligacy are rapidly closing the options for future generations. Most of today's decision makers will be dead before the planet feels the heavier effects of acid precipitation, global warming, ozone depletion, or widespread desertification and species loss. Most of the young voters of today will still be alive. In the Commission's hearings it was the young, those who have the most to lose, who were the harshest critics of the planet's present management.

3.   Sustainable Development

27.   Humanity has the ability to make development sustainable to ensure that it meets the needs of the present without compromising the ability of future generations to meet their own needs. The concept of sustainable development does imply limits – not absolute limits but limitations imposed by the present state of technology and social organization on environmental resources and by the ability of the biosphere to absorb the effects of human activities.

[...]

Chapter IV Sustainable Development

[...]

1.   Sustainable development is development that meets the needs of the present without compromising the ability of future generations to meet their own needs.

1992 Rio Declaration on Environment and Development 1992 (UN Conference on Environment and Development) (14 June 1992) UN Doc A/CONF.151/126/Rev.1 vol. I, 3

Principle 3
The right to development must be fulfilled so as to equitably meet developmental and environmental needs of present and future generations.

Agenda 21

(d) Adopting a national strategy for sustainable development

8.7.   Governments, in cooperation, where appropriate, with international organizations, should adopt a national strategy for sustainable development based on, *inter alia*, the implementation of decisions taken at the Conference, particularly in respect of Agenda 21. This strategy should build upon and harmonize the various sectoral economic, social and environmental policies and plans that are operating in the country. The experience gained through existing planning exercises such as national reports for the Conference, national conservation strategies and environment action plans should be fully used and incorporated into a country-driven sustainable development strategy. Its goals should be to ensure socially responsible economic development while protecting the resource base and the environment for the benefit of future generations. It should be developed through the widest possible participation. It should be based on a thorough assessment of the current situation and initiatives.

1997 United Nations Educational, Scientific and Cultural Organization (UNESCO) Declaration on the Responsibilities of the Present Generation Towards Future Generations, Resolution 44 adopted by the General Conference at its 29th session, 12 November 1997

The General Conference of the United Nations Educational, Scientific and Cultural Organization, meeting in Paris from 21 October to 12 November 1997 at its 29th session,

Recognizing that the task of protecting the needs and interests of future generations, particularly through education, is fundamental to the ethical mission of UNESCO, whose Constitution enshrines the ideals of 'justice and liberty and peace' founded on 'the intellectual and moral solidarity of mankind',

Bearing in mind that the fate of future generations depends to a great extent on decisions and actions taken today, and that present-day problems, including poverty, technological and material underdevelopment, unemployment, exclusion, discrimination and threats to the environment, must be solved in the interests of both present and future generations,

Convinced that there is a moral obligation to formulate behavioural guidelines for the present generations within a broad, future-oriented perspective,

Solemnly proclaims on this twelfth day of November 1997 this Declaration on the Responsibilities of the Present Generations Towards Future Generations
Article 1 – Needs and interests of future generations
The present generations have the responsibility of ensuring that the needs and interests of present and future generations are fully safeguarded.

Article 2 – Freedom of choice
It is important to make every effort to ensure, with due regard to human rights and fundamental freedoms, that future as well as present generations enjoy full freedom of choice as to their political, economic and social systems and are able to preserve their cultural and religious diversity.

Article 3 – Maintenance and perpetuation of humankind
The present generations should strive to ensure the maintenance and perpetuation of humankind with due respect for the dignity of the human person. Consequently, the nature and form of human life must not be undermined in any way whatsoever.

Article 4 – Preservation of life on Earth
The present generations have the responsibility to bequeath to future generations an Earth which will not one day be irreversibly damaged by human activity. Each generation inheriting the Earth temporarily should take care to use natural resources reasonably and ensure that life is not prejudiced by harmful modifications of the ecosystems and that scientific and technological progress in all fields does not harm life on Earth.

Article 5 – Protection of the environment

1. In order to ensure that future generations benefit from the richness of the Earth's ecosystems, the present generations should strive for sustainable development and preserve living conditions, particularly the quality and integrity of the environment.
2. The present generations should ensure that future generations are not exposed to pollution which may endanger their health or their existence itself.
3. The present generations should preserve for future generations natural resources necessary for sustaining human life and for its development.
4. The present generations should take into account possible consequences for future generations of major projects before these are carried out.

Article 6 – Human genome and biodiversity

The human genome, in full respect of the dignity of the human person and human rights, must be protected and biodiversity safeguarded. Scientific and technological progress should not in any way impair or compromise the preservation of the human and other species.

[…]

Article 8 – Common heritage of humankind

The present generations may use the common heritage of humankind, as defined in international law, provided that this does not entail compromising it irreversibly.

[…]

Article 10 – Development and education

1. The present generations should ensure the conditions of equitable, sustainable and universal socio-economic development of future generations, both in its individual and collective dimensions, in particular through a fair and prudent use of available resources for the purpose of combating poverty.
2. Education is an important instrument for the development of human persons and societies. It should be used to foster peace, justice, understanding, tolerance and equality for the benefit of present and future generations.

'The Future We Want: Outcome Document of the United Nations Conference on Sustainable Development', Rio de Janeiro, Brazil, 20–22 June 2012 (Rio 2012)

I. Our Common Vision

1. We, the Heads of State and Government and high-level representatives, having met at Rio de Janeiro, Brazil, from 20 to 22 June 2012, with the full participation of civil society, renew our commitment to sustainable development and to ensuring the promotion of an economically, socially and environmentally sustainable future for our planet and for present and future generations.

Following the Rio 2012/Rio+20 Conference, the UN Secretary General presented a report to the UN General Assembly on intergenerational equity. The Report focuses on ways to enable the representation of future generations, but looks at the issue broadly, taking into account moral as well as practical considerations. In particular, the Secretary General's report engages with the tension between intergenerational and intra-generational justice.

15.　　The sustainable development agenda is deeply intertwined with issues of intra-generational equity and justice. Not for nothing does the Rio+20 outcome document state that: "Poverty eradication is the greatest global challenge facing the world today and an indispensable requirement for sustainable development."[13] The fair and equitable distribution of benefits and opportunities among the currently living is one of world's most difficult challenges. However, addressing the needs of future generations is not meaningful if delinked from addressing the needs of those living. Poverty eradication is not just about intra-generational equity but also about intergenerational equity given the strong tendency for parent-to-child transmission of poverty – this varies from society to society depending on social mobility, but mobility seems to be on the decline in many developed countries at least in recent decades. The poor are likely to stay poor into the next generation.

16.　　The vision of sustainable development does not endorse the sacrifice of the legitimate aspirations of the poorest in the name of future generations. At the same time, this in no way implies that the needs of present generations always enjoy priority over those of future generations, but at the very least the poorest and most vulnerable should not be called to make sacrifices for the long-term good of humanity.

'Transforming Our World: the 2030 Agenda for Sustainable Development' UNGA Res 70/1 (25 September 2015)

Preamble

[…]

Planet
We are determined to protect the planet from degradation, including through sustainable consumption and production, sustainably managing its natural resources and taking urgent action on climate change, so that it can support the needs of the present and future generations.

[…]

The New Agenda
18.　　[…]We will implement the Agenda for the full benefit of all, for today's generation and for future generations[…]

7.3   CASE LAW

7.3.1   International

CASE
Pacific Fur Seal Arbitration (United States of America v. Great Britain), Award, 1 Moore's International Arbitral Awards 733; RIAA 263 (1893)

[US Secretary of State:]
[p. 781]
...Under these circumstances and in view of the common interest of all nations in preventing indiscriminate killing of seals consequent extermination of an animal which contributes importantly to the commercial wealth and general use of mankind, you are hereby instructed to draw the attention of the government to which you are accredited to the subject, and to invite it to enter into such an arrangement with the Government of the United States as will prevent the citizens of either country from killing seals in the Behring Sea at such times and places, and by such methods as at present are pursued, and which threaten the speedy extermination of those animals and consequent serious loss to mankind.

[p. 783]
Here is valuable fishery, and a large and, if properly managed, permanent industry, the property of nations on whose shores it is carried on. It is proposed by the colony of a foreign nation, in defiance of the joint remonstrance slaughter and extermination of the animals in question, in then open neighbouring sea, during the period of gestation, when common dictates of humanity ought to protect them, were no interest of at all involved.

CASE
ICJ, *Request for an Examination of the Situation in Accordance with Paragraph 63 of the Court's Judgment of 20 December 1974 in the Nuclear Tests (New Zealand v. France)*, Case, ICJ Reports 288 (1995)

DISS OP JUDGE WEERAMANTRY

[pp 341-342]
The case before the Court raises, as no case ever before the Court has done, the principle of intergenerational equity – an important and rapidly developing principle of contemporary environmental law.

Professor Lauterpacht, on behalf of New Zealand, adverted to this aspect when he submitted to the Court that if damage of the kind alleged had been inflicted on the environment by the people of the Stone Age, it would be with us today. Having regard to the information before us that the half-life of a radioactive by-product of nuclear tests can extend to over 20,000 years, this is an important aspect that an international tribunal cannot fail to notice. In a matter of which it is duly seised, this Court must regard itself as a trustee of those rights in the sense that a domestic court is a trustee of the interests of an infant unable to speak for itself. If this Court is charged with administering international law, and if this principle is building itself into the corpus of international law, or has already done so, this principle is one which must inevitably be a concern of this Court. The consideration involved is too serious to be dismissed as lacking in importance merely because there is no precedent on which it rests.

New Zealand's complaint that its rights are affected does not relate only to the rights of people presently in existence. The rights of the people of New Zealand include the rights of unborn posterity. Those are rights which a nation is entitled, and indeed obliged, to protect. In considering whether New Zealand has made out a prima facie case of damage to its interests sufficient to bring the processes of this Court into operation in terms of paragraph 63, this is therefore an important aspect not to be ignored.

In the words of an important recent work on this question:

> "The starting proposition is that each generation is both a custodian and a user of Our common natural and cultural patrimony. As custodians of this planet, we have certain moral obligations to future generations which we can transform into legally enforceable norms." (See E. Brown Weiss, In Fairness to Future Generations: International Law, Common Patrimony and Intergenerational Equity, 1989, p. 21.)

The Stockholm Declaration on the Human Environment adopted by the United Nations Conference on the Environment at Stockholm, 16 June 1972, formulated nearly a quarter century ago the principle of "a solemn responsibility to protect and improve the environment for present and future generations" (Principle 1). This guideline sufficiently spells out the approach to this new principle which is relevant to the problem the Court faces of assessing the likely damage to the people of New Zealand. This Court has not thus far had occasion to make any pronouncement on this developing field. The present case presents it with a pre-eminent opportunity to do so, as it raises in pointed form the possibility of damage to generations yet unborn.

ADVISORY OPINION
ICJ, Legality of the Threat or Use of Nuclear Weapons, Advisory Opinion, ICJ Reports 226 (1996)

29. The Court recognizes that the environment is under daily threat and that the use of nuclear weapons could constitute a catastrophe for the environment. *The Court also recognizes that the environment is not an abstraction but represents the living space, the quality of life and the very health of human beings, including generations unborn.* The existence of the general obligation of States to ensure that activities within their jurisdiction and control respect the environment of other States or of areas beyond national control is now part of the corpus of international law relating to the environment.

[...]

35. In applying this law to the present case, the Court cannot however fail to take into account certain unique characteristics of nuclear weapons.

[...] These characteristics render the nuclear weapon potentially catastrophic. The destructive power of nuclear weapons cannot be contained in either space *or time*. They have the potential to destroy all civilization and the entire ecosystem of the planet.

[...] Further, the use of nuclear weapons would be *a serious danger to future generations*. Ionizing radiation has the potential to damage the future environment, food and marine ecosystem, and to cause genetic defects and illness *in future generations*.

36. In consequence, in order correctly to apply to the present case the Charter law on the use of force and the law applicable in armed conflict, in particular humanitarian law, it is imperative for the Court to take account of the unique characteristics of nuclear weapons, and in particular their destructive capacity, their capacity to cause untold human suffering, and their *ability to cause damage to generations to come*.

DISS OP WEERAMANTRY

[p 455]

This Court, as the principal judicial organ of the United Nations, empowered to state and apply international law with an authority matched by no other tribunal must, in its jurisprudence, pay due recognition to the rights of future generations. If there is any tribunal that can recognize and protect their interests under the law, it is this Court.

It is to be noted in this context that the rights of future generations have passed the stage when they were merely an embryonic right struggling for recognition. They have woven themselves into international law through major treaties, through juristic opinion and through general principles of law recognized by civilized nations.

CASE
ICJ, *Gabcikovo-Nagymaros Project (Hungary v. Slovakia)*, ICJ Reports 7 (1997)

140. [...] Throughout the ages, mankind has, for economic and other reasons, constantly interfered with nature. In the past, this was often done without consideration of the effects upon the environment. Owing to new scientific insights and to a growing awareness of the risks for mankind – for present and future generations – of pursuit of such interventions at an unconsidered and unabated pace, new norms and standards have been developed, set forth in a great number of instruments during the last two decades. Such new norms have to be taken into consideration, and such new standards given proper weight, not only when States contemplate new activities but also when continuing with activities begun in the past. This need to reconcile

economic development with protection of the environment is aptly expressed in the concept of sustainable development.

SEP OP VICE-PRESIDENT WEERAMANTRAY

[p 110]:

As modern environmental law develops, it can, with profit to itself, take account of the perspectives and principles of traditional systems, not merely in a general way, but with reference to specific principles, concepts, and aspirational standards.

Among those which may be extracted from the systems already referred to are such far-reaching principles as the principle of trusteeship of earth resources, the principle of intergenerational rights, and the principle that development and environmental conservation must go hand in hand. Land is to be respected as having a vitality of its own and being integrally linked to the welfare of the community. When it is used by humans, every opportunity should be afforded to it to replenish itself. Since flora and fauna have a niche in the ecological system, they must be expressly protected. There is a duty lying upon all members of the community to preserve the integrity and purity of the environment.

7.3.2   Regional

CASE
IACtHR, *Mayagna (Sumo) Awas Tingni Community v. Nicaragua*, Judgment (31 August 2001), Series C No. 79

The petition before the IACtHR was brought by an indigenous community, the Awas Tingni Community, and claimed that Nicaragua had failed to protect their indigenous rights, including property rights over ancestral lands and natural resources. In reaching its decision, the Court recognised, in the context of indigenous rights, the idea that the environment is something that is for the benefit of future generations.

149. Given the characteristics of the instant case, some specifications are required on the concept of property in indigenous communities. Among indigenous peoples there is a communitarian tradition regarding a communal form of collective property of the land, in the sense that ownership of the land is not centered on an individual but rather on the group and its community. Indigenous groups, by the fact of their very existence, have the right to live freely in their own territory; the close ties of indigenous people with the land must be recognized and understood as the fundamental basis of their cultures, their spiritual life, their integrity, and their economic survival. For indigenous communities, relations to the land are not merely a matter of possession and production but a material and spiritual element which they must fully enjoy, even to preserve their cultural legacy and transmit it to future generations.

ADVISORY OPINION
IACtHR, The Environment and Human Rights, Advisory Opinion, OC-23/17 (15 November 2017), Series A No. 23

59. The human right to a healthy environment has been understood as a right that has both individual and also collective connotations. In its collective dimension, the right to a healthy environment constitutes a universal value that is owed to both present and future generations. That said, the right to a healthy environment also has an individual dimension insofar as its violation may have a direct and an indirect impact on the individual owing to its connectivity to other rights, such as the rights to health, personal integrity, and life. Environmental degradation may cause irreparable harm to human beings; thus, a healthy environment is a fundamental right for the existence of humankind.

7.3.3 National

CASE
ILM, *Minors Oposa v. Secretary of The Department of Environment and Natural Resources (DENR), Supreme Court of the Philippines*, ILM 33 (30 July 1993), p. 173

This case, however, has a special and novel element. Petitioner minors assert that they represent their generation as well as generations yet unborn. We find no difficulty in ruling that they can, for themselves, for others of their generation and for the succeeding generations, file a class suit. Their personality to sue on behalf of the succeeding generations can only be based on the concept of intergenerational responsibility insofar as the right to a balanced and healthful ecology is concerned. Such a right, as hereinafter expounded, considers the "rhythm and harmony of nature." Nature means the created world in its entirety. Such rhythm and harmony indispensably include, *inter alia*, the judicious disposition, utilization, management, renewal and conservation of the country's forest, mineral, land, waters, fisheries, wildlife, off-shore areas and other natural resources to the end that their exploration, development and utilization be equitably accessible to the present as well as future generations. Needless to say, every generation has a responsibility to the next to preserve that rhythm and harmony for the full enjoyment of a balanced and healthful ecology. Put a little differently, the minors' assertion of their right to a sound environment constitutes, at the same time, the performance of their obligation to ensure the protection of that right for the generations to come.

JUDGE FELICIANO, SEPARATE OPINION

The Court explicitly states that petitioners have the locus standi necessary to sustain the bringing and, maintenance of this suit (Decision, pp. 11-12). Locus standi is not a function of petitioners' claim that their suit is properly regarded as a class suit. I understand locus standi to refer to the legal interest which a plaintiff must have in the subject matter of the suit. Because of the very broadness of the concept of "class" here involved — membership in this "class" appears to embrace everyone living in the country whether now or in the future — it appears to me that everyone who may be expected to benefit from the course of action petitioners seek to require public respondents to take, is vested with the necessary locus standi. The Court has also declared that the complaint has alleged and focused upon "one specific fundamental legal right — the right to a balanced and healthful ecology" [...] There is no question that "the right to a balanced and healthful ecology" is "fundamental" and that, accordingly, it has been "constitutionalized." But although it is fundamental in character, I suggest, with very great respect, that it cannot be characterized as "specific," without doing excessive violence to language. It is in fact very difficult to fashion language more comprehensive in scope and generalized in character than a right to "a balanced and healthful ecology." The list of particular claims which can be subsumed under this rubric appears to be entirely open-ended: prevention and control of emission of toxic fumes and smoke from factories and motor vehicles; of discharge of oil, chemical effluents, garbage and raw sewage into rivers, inland and coastal waters by vessels, oil rigs, factories, mines and whole communities; of dumping of organic and inorganic wastes on open land, streets and thoroughfares; failure to rehabilitate land after strip-mining or open-pit mining; *kaingin* or slash-and-burn farming; destruction of fisheries, coral reefs and other living sea resources through the use of dynamite or cyanide and other chemicals; contamination of ground water resources; loss of certain species of fauna and flora; and so on... As a matter of logic, by finding petitioners' cause of action as anchored on a legal right comprised in the constitutional statements above noted, the Court is in effect saying that Section 15 (and Section 16) of Article II of the Constitution are self-executing and judicially enforceable even in their present form. The implications of this doctrine will have to be explored in future cases; those implications are too large and far-reaching in nature even to be hinted at here. My suggestion is simply that petitioners must, before the trial court, show a more specific legal right — a right cast in language of a significantly lower order of generality than Article II (15) of the Constitution — that is or may be violated by the actions, or failures to act, imputed to the public respondent by petitioners so that the trial court can validly render judgment granting all or part of the relief prayed for. To my mind, the Court should be understood as simply saying that such a more specific legal right or rights may well exist in our corpus of law, considering the general policy principles found in the Constitution and the existence of the Philippine Environment Code, and that the trial court should have given petitioners an effective opportunity so to demonstrate, instead of aborting the proceedings on a motion to dismiss. It seems to me important that the legal right which is an essential component of a cause of action be a specific, operable legal right, rather than a constitutional or statutory policy, for at least two (2) reasons. One is that unless the legal right claimed to have been violated or disregarded is given specification in operational terms, defendants may well be unable to defend themselves intelligently and effectively; in other words, there are due process dimensions to this matter.

Table 7.1   Other national cases of note

M Farooque v. Bangladesh and Others
Calcutta v. State of West Bengal
S Jagannath v. Union of India
Vedanta Alumina Ltd. v. Prafulla Samantra & Ors
ND Jayal v. Union of India

QUESTIONS

1. Is intergenerational equity a moral or legal principle?
2. Is the principle of intergenerational equity an effective tool of protection of the rights of future generations?
3. Should we protect the rights of future generations or be more concerned with the rights of present generations?

FURTHER READING

BOOKS

E Agius and S Busuttil (eds), *Future Generations and International Law* (Earthscan 1998)

E Brown Weiss, *In Fairness to Future Generations: International Law, Common Patrimony, and Intergenerational Equity* (Transnational Publishers & United Nations University 1989)

M Fitzmaurice, *Contemporary Issues in International Environmental Law* (Edward Elgar Publishing 2009)

C Redgwell, *Intergenerational Trusts and Environmental Protection* (Manchester University Press 1999)

JC Tremmel (ed.), *Handbook of Intergenerational Justice* (Edward Elgar 2006)

CHAPTERS

E Brown Weiss, 'Intergenerational Equity' in *Max Planck Encyclopedia of International Law* (2021) https://opil.ouplaw.com/view/10.1093/law:epil/9780199231690/law-9780199231690-e1421 (accessed 19 March 2022)

M Fitzmaurice, 'Intergenerational Equity, Ocean Governance and the United Nations' in DJ Attard, M Fitzmaurice and A Ntovas (eds), *The IMLI Treatise on Global Ocean Governance* (Vol. II, Oxford University Press 2018)

M Fitzmaurice, 'Intergenerational Equity Revisited' in I Buffard, J Crawford, A Pellet and S Wittich (eds), *International Law between Universalism and Fragmentation: Festschrift in Honour of Gerhard Hafner* (Brill/Nijhoff 2008)

C Redgwell, 'Principles and Emerging Norms in International Law: Intra- and Inter-generational Equity' in CP Carlarne, KR Gray and R Tarasofsky (eds), *The Oxford Handbook of International Climate Change Law* (Oxford University Press 2016)

ARTICLES

E Brown Weiss, 'Our Rights and Obligations to Future Generations' (1990) 94 AJIL 198

E Brown Weiss, 'Intergenerational Equity in a Kaleidoscopic World' (2019) 49 Envtl Pol'y & L. 3

E Brown Weiss, 'Climate Change, Intergenerational Equity, and International Law' (2008) 9 9 Vt J Envtl L 615

G Davies, 'Climate Change and Reversed Intergenerational Equity: the Problem of Costs Now, for Benefits Later' (2020) 10 Climate Law 266

Z Hadjiagyrou, 'A Conceptual and Practical Evaluation of Intergenerational Equity in International Environmental Law' (2016) 18 International Community Law Review 248

8

The human right to a healthy environment

8.1   INTRODUCTION

Since the link between human rights and the environment was first noted in the 1972 Stockholm Conference on the Human Environment, the implications of the interaction between the two has been extensively researched and analysed.[1] The ways in which the two have developed are, in part, an accident of history. Early human rights instruments, both international and regional, predate the Stockholm Declaration, and therefore do not contain direct references to environmental concerns or environmental human rights. Later human rights instruments, notably the African Charter on Human and Peoples' Rights (1981), have given explicit recognition to specifically environmental human rights, such as the right to a healthy environment, and specific environmental rights are now recognised in a large number of national constitutions. Differences in the structure of the primary rules found in different instruments result in the use of differing methods by human rights bodies to synthesise environmental and human rights problems.

As the two fields of law have become increasingly intertwined, three distinct strands to the interaction can be discerned. The OHCHR Analytical Study (2011) describes the interaction thus:[2]

> 7. In connection with the first issue, namely the nature of the relationship between human rights and the environment, there are three major approaches to explaining this. These approaches are capable of coexisting and do not necessarily exclude one another. The first approach postulates that the environment is a precondition to the enjoyment of human rights. This approach underscores the fact that life and human dignity are only possible where people have access to an environment with certain basic qualities.

---

[1]   See discussion in M Fitzmaurice, 'A Human Right to a Clean Environment: A Reappraisal' in Giuliana Ziccardi Capaldo (ed.), *The Global Community Yearbook of International Law and Jurisprudence* 2015 (OUP 2016).

[2]   Office of the High Commissioner for Human Rights, 'Annual Report: Analytical study on the relationship between human rights and the environment' (2011) A/HRC/19/34.

Environmental degradation, including pollution of air, water and land can affect the realization of particular rights, such as the rights to life, food and health.

8. The second approach submits that human rights are tools to address environmental issues, both procedurally and substantively. This approach emphasizes the possibility of using human rights to achieve adequate levels of environmental protection. From a procedural perspective, rights such as access to information, participation in public affairs and access to justice are central to securing governance structures that enable society to adopt fair decision-making processes with respect to environmental issues. From a substantive perspective, this approach underscores the environmental dimensions of certain protected rights.

9. The third approach proposes the integration of human rights and the environment under the concept of sustainable development. Accordingly, this approach underlines that societal objectives must be treated in an integrated manner and that the integration of economic, environmental and social justice issues is done with a view to the concept of sustainable development.

Together, these three approaches have led to a twin 'greening' of human rights law and 'humanising' of environmental law. The focus of the present chapter is on the substantive aspects of the interaction, while rights to public participation are addressed in Chapter 9.

The substantive dimension of environmental human rights involves the question of the recognition of environmental human rights, notably the right to a healthy environment and also the right to water. In the first place, there is the question of whether such rights exist as a matter of general human rights law. Second, if it exists, what is its content? Third, who has standing to enforce it?

Of the international human rights instruments covered below, only the African Charter of Human and Peoples' Rights (art 24) and San Salvador Protocol to the American Convention on Human Rights recognise a standalone right to a healthy environment (art 11). Other human rights treaties explicitly recognise environmental rights as aspects of other human rights, such as the right to health (International Covenant on Economic, Social and Cultural Rights, art 12; Convention on the Rights of the Child, art 24; Arab Charter, art 39), and right to an adequate standard of living (Convention on the Elimination of Discrimination Against Women, art 14; Convention on the Rights of Persons with Disabilities, art 28; Arab Charter, art 38; ASEAN Declaration, art 28).

Alternatively, environmental rights may, as a result of a purposive interpretation, be implicit in other rights, including the right to life (e.g., European Convention on Human Rights, art 2; International Covenant on Civil and Political Rights, art 6), right to a private life (e.g., ECHR, art 8) and right to health (e.g., European Social Charter, art 12). A different perspective, however, reflecting the second approach identified by the OHCHR, is that a right to a healthy environment is not implicit within other human rights, and environmental degradation is simply a circumstance in which a human right might be violated. In other words, only environmental harm of a certain type or severity is within the scope of human rights.

General recognition of specifically environmental rights is a work in progress. The European Court of Human Rights has stated that the ECHR does not protect environmental rights per se, but has increasingly recognised that rights may be impaired by environmental harm. A somewhat different approach has been taken by the UN human rights treaty bodies. The Committee on Economic, Social and Cultural Rights has recognised the 'right to water', which has also been recognised by the UN General Assembly (2010). The Human Rights Committee has not implied a right to a healthy environment into ICCPR rights, but it has recognised that *severe* environmental degradation would violate the right to life and therefore that the positive measures required of states under environmental law are also positive obligations needed to protect human rights. Unlike the right to water, the right to a healthy environment has not received general recognition by the UN General Assembly. It has gained significant impetus as a result of recent reports of the Special Rapporteur on Human Rights and the Environment, John Knox, and this year the Human Rights Council expressly recognised, for the first time, a human right to a healthy environment.

A different aspect of the growing relationship between human rights and the environment involves the nascent recognition of the relationship in environmental treaties. While the Stockholm Declaration and Rio Declaration both imply the linkage, many environmental treaties have not invoked human rights but rather more general considerations of human welfare or needs. The 2015 Paris Agreement, however, makes the connection to *rights* (and corresponding state obligations) explicit in its preamble.

The connection between human rights and the environment is significant as a potential avenue through which environmental norms might receive judicial consideration. An important, recent trend in tackling climate change has been through the use of human rights litigation.[3] Claims have been brought, but not yet decided, before the European Court of Human Rights in the *Portuguese Youth* case,[4] and a claim brought against Switzerland.[5] A large number of human rights cases, now totalling over 100 cases,[6] have been brought globally, mostly before national courts. The most significant such decision is the *Urgenda* case in the Netherlands, in which the Dutch Supreme Court has upheld the decision of the Court of Appeal that in order to comply with ECHR article 2 (right to life) and article 8 (right to a private and family life) required the Netherlands to reduce greenhouse gas emissions by 25% compared with 1990 levels.

The development of the idea of environmental rights has accompanied the development of legal personality for the environment. In a landmark decision in 2017, the High Court of Uttarakhand declared the Ganges and Yamuna Rivers as having the status of a legal person.[7]

---

[3]   On climate change, see Chapter 16.

[4]   *Duarte Agostinho and Others v. Portugal and 32 Other States*, App No. 39371/20 (13 November 2020).

[5]   *Verein Klima Seniorinnen Schweiz and Others v. Switzerland*, App No. 53600/20 (17 March 2021).

[6]   Joana Setzer and Catherine Higham, *Global Trends in Climate Change Litigation: 2021 Snapshot* (July 2021) Grantham Research Institute on Climate Change and the Environment and Centre for Climate Change https://www.lse.ac.uk/granthaminstitute/wp-content/uploads/2021/07/Global-trends-in-climate-change-litigation_2021-snapshot.pdf accessed 18 August 2021,

[7]   Mohd Salim v. State of Uttarakhand & others, WPPIL 126/2014, High Court of Uttarakhand 19 (2017). See Erin L O'Donnell, 'At the Intersection of the Sacred and the Legal: Rights for Nature in Uttarakhand, India' (2018) 30 J Int'l Environmental Law 135.

Similar recognition of rivers as bearers of legal personality has occurred in Bangladesh, Bolivia, Colombia, Ecuador, New Zealand, and Uganda, either under constitutional law, legislation, or judicial decisions.[8] This nascent area of environmental regulation remains of limited scope both in terms of state participation and objects of protection, and its usefulness remains to be seen. But it represents a potentially significant new direction for the use of rights in environmental law.

8.2   ENVIRONMENTAL LAW

8.2.1   Legally Binding Instruments

1999 Protocol on Water and Health to the 1992 Convention on the Protection and Use of Transboundary Watercourses and International Lakes, 2331 UNTS 202

Preamble
Mindful that water is essential to sustain life and that the availability of water in quantities, and of a quality, sufficient to meet basic human needs is a prerequisite both for improved health and for sustainable development,

Acknowledging the benefits to human health and well-being that accrue from wholesome and clean water and a harmonious and properly functioning water environment,

Aware that surface waters and groundwater are renewable resources with a limited capacity to recover from adverse impacts from human activities on their quantity and quality, that any failure to respect those limits may result in adverse effects, in both the short and long terms, on the health and well-being of those who rely on those resources and their quality, and that in consequence sustainable management of the hydrological cycle is essential for both meeting human needs and protecting the environment,

Aware also of the consequences for public health of shortfalls of water in the quantities, and of the quality, sufficient to meet basic human needs, and of the serious effects of such shortfalls, in particular on the vulnerable, the disadvantaged and the socially excluded,

[…]

Article 6 TARGETS AND TARGET DATES
1.   In order to achieve the objective of this Protocol, the Parties shall pursue the aims of:
(a)   Access to drinking water for everyone;
(b)   Provision of sanitation for everyone;

within a framework of integrated water-management systems aimed at sustainable use of water resources, ambient water quality which does not endanger human health, and protection of water ecosystems.

---

8   On rivers, see generally Chapter 13.

2015 Paris Agreement

Preamble
[...]

Acknowledging that climate change is a common concern of humankind, Parties should, when taking action to address climate change, respect, promote and consider their respective obligations on human rights, the right to health, the rights of indigenous peoples, local communities, migrants, children, persons with disabilities and people in vulnerable situations and the right to development, as well as gender equality, empowerment of women and intergenerational equity,

8.2.2   Non-Binding Instruments

1972 Stockholm Declaration

Principle 1
Man has the fundamental right to freedom, equality and adequate conditions of life, in an environment of a development through the transfer of substantial quantities quality that permits a life of dignity and well-being, and of financial and technological assistance as a supplement he bears a solemn responsibility to protect and improve the environment for present and future generations. In this respect, policies promoting or perpetuating apartheid, racial segregation, discrimination, colonial and other forms of oppression and foreign domination stand condemned and must be eliminated.

1992 Rio Declaration

Principle 1
Human beings are at the centre of concerns for sustainable development. They are entitled to a healthy and productive life in harmony with nature.

8.3   INTERNATIONAL HUMAN RIGHTS LAW

8.3.1   Legally Binding Instruments

1966 International Covenant on Civil and Political Rights, 999 UNTS 171

Article 6
1.   Every human being has the inherent right to life. This right shall be protected by law. No one shall be arbitrarily deprived of his life.

Article 27
In those States in which ethnic, religious or linguistic minorities exist, persons belonging to such minorities shall not be denied the right, in community with the other members of their group, to enjoy their own culture, to profess and practise their own religion, or to use their own language.

1966 International Covenant on Economic, Social and Cultural Rights, 993 UNTS 3

Article 1
[…]

2.   All peoples may, for their own ends, freely dispose of their natural wealth and resources without prejudice to any obligations arising out of international economic co-operation, based upon the principle of mutual benefit, and international law. In no case may a people be deprived of its own means of subsistence.

Article 11
1.   The States Parties to the present Covenant recognize the right of everyone to an adequate standard of living for himself and his family, including adequate food, clothing and housing, and to the continuous improvement of living conditions. The States Parties will take appropriate steps to ensure the realization of this right, recognizing to this effect the essential importance of international co-operation based on free consent.

Article 12
1.   The States Parties to the present Covenant recognize the right of everyone to the enjoyment of the highest attainable standard of physical and mental health.
2.   The steps to be taken by the States Parties to the present Covenant to achieve the full realization of this right shall include those necessary for:

[…]

(b)   The improvement of all aspects of environmental and industrial hygiene;

1977 ILO Working Environment (Air Pollution, Noise and Vibration) Convention, 1977 (No. 148)

Article 3

For the purpose of this Convention–

(a)   the term *air pollution* covers all air contaminated by substances, whatever their physical state, which are harmful to health or otherwise dangerous;

(b)   the term *noise* covers all sound which can result in hearing impairment or be harmful to health or otherwise dangerous;

(c)   the term *vibration* covers any vibration which is transmitted to the human body through solid structures and is harmful to health or otherwise dangerous.

PART II. GENERAL PROVISIONS

Article 4

1.   National laws or regulations shall prescribe that measures be taken for the prevention and control of, and protection against, occupational hazards in the working environment due to air pollution, noise and vibration.

2.   Provisions concerning the practical implementation of the measures so prescribed may be adopted through technical standards, codes of practice and other appropriate methods.

[…]

Article 8

1.   The competent authority shall establish criteria for determining the hazards of exposure to air pollution, noise and vibration in the working environment and, where appropriate, shall specify exposure limits on the basis of these criteria.

1979 Convention on the Elimination of All Forms of Discrimination against Women, 1249 UNTS 13

Article 14

1.   States Parties shall take into account the particular problems faced by rural women and the significant roles which rural women play in the economic survival of their families, including their work in the non-monetized sectors of the economy, and shall take all appropriate measures to ensure the application of the provisions of the present Convention to women in rural areas.

2.   States Parties shall take all appropriate measures to eliminate discrimination against women in rural areas in order to ensure, on a basis of equality of men and women, that they participate in and benefit from rural development and, in particular, shall ensure to such women the right:

[…]

(h)   To enjoy adequate living conditions, particularly in relation to housing, sanitation, electricity and water supply, transport and communications.

1989 Convention on the Rights of the Child, 1577 UNTS 3

Article 24
1.   States Parties recognize the right of the child to the enjoyment of the highest attainable standard of health and to facilities for the treatment of illness and rehabilitation of health. States Parties shall strive to ensure that no child is deprived of his or her right of access to such health care services.
2.   States Parties shall pursue full implementation of this right and, in particular, shall take appropriate measures:

[...]

(c)   To combat disease and malnutrition, including within the framework of primary health care, through, *inter alia*, the application of readily available technology and through the provision of adequate nutritious foods and clean drinking-water, taking into consideration the dangers and risks of environmental pollution;

[...]

(e)   To ensure that all segments of society, in particular parents and children, are informed, have access to education and are supported in the use of basic knowledge of child health and nutrition, the advantages of breastfeeding, hygiene and environmental sanitation and the prevention of accidents;

2006 Convention on the Rights of Persons with Disabilities, 2515 UNTS 3

Article 28 – Adequate standard of living and social protection
1.   States Parties recognize the right of persons with disabilities to an adequate standard of living for themselves and their families, including adequate food, clothing and housing, and to the continuous improvement of living conditions, and shall take appropriate steps to safeguard and promote the realization of this right without discrimination on the basis of disability.
2.   States Parties recognize the right of persons with disabilities to social protection and to the enjoyment of that right without discrimination on the basis of disability, and shall take appropriate steps to safeguard and promote the realization of this right, including measures:
         (a)   To ensure equal access by persons with disabilities to clean water services, and to ensure access to appropriate and affordable services, devices and other assistance for disability-related needs;

8.3.2   Non-Binding Instruments

General Comment No. 14 The right to the highest attainable standard of health (Article 12 of the International Covenant on Economic, Social and Cultural Rights) (2000) E/C.12/2000/4

Article 12.2 (b). The right to healthy natural and workplace environments

4.   In drafting article 12 of the Covenant, the Third Committee of the United Nations General Assembly did not adopt the definition of health contained in the preamble to the Constitution of WHO, which conceptualizes health as "a state of complete physical, mental and social well-being and not merely the absence of disease or infirmity". However, the reference in article 12.1 of the Covenant to "the highest attainable standard of physical and mental health" is not confined to the right to health care. On the contrary, the drafting history and the express wording of article 12.2 acknowledge that the right to health embraces a wide range of socio-economic factors that promote conditions in which people can lead a healthy life, and extends to the underlying determinants of health, such as food and nutrition, housing, access to safe and potable water and adequate sanitation, safe and healthy working conditions, and a healthy environment.

[...]

15.   "The improvement of all aspects of environmental and industrial hygiene" (art. 12.2 (b)) comprises, *inter alia*, preventive measures in respect of occupational accidents and diseases; the requirement to ensure an adequate supply of safe and potable water and basic sanitation; the prevention and reduction of the population's exposure to harmful substances such as radiation and harmful chemicals or other detrimental environmental conditions that directly or indirectly impact upon human health.

CESCR General Comment No. 15: The Right to Water (Arts 11 and 12 of the Covenant) (20 January 2003) E/C.12/2002/11

3.   Article 11, paragraph 1, of the Covenant specifies a number of rights emanating from, and indispensable for, the realization of the right to an adequate standard of living "including adequate food, clothing and housing". The use of the word "including" indicates that this catalogue of rights was not intended to be exhaustive. The right to water clearly falls within the category of guarantees essential for securing an adequate standard of living, particularly since it is one of the most fundamental conditions for survival.

[...]

8.   Environmental hygiene, as an aspect of the right to health under article 12, paragraph 2 (b), of the Covenant, encompasses taking steps on a non-discriminatory

basis to prevent threats to health from unsafe and toxic water conditions. For example, States parties should ensure that natural water resources are protected from contamination by harmful substances and pathogenic microbes. Likewise, States parties should monitor and combat situations where aquatic ecosystems serve as a habitat for vectors of diseases wherever they pose a risk to human living environments.

[...]

12.   While the adequacy of water required for the right to water may vary according to different conditions, the following factors apply in all circumstances:

    (b)   Quality. The water required for each personal or domestic use must be safe, therefore free from micro-organisms, chemical substances and radiological hazards that constitute a threat to a person's health. Furthermore, water should be of an acceptable colour, odour and taste for each personal or domestic use;

[...]

28.   States parties should adopt comprehensive and integrated strategies and programmes to ensure that there is sufficient and safe water for present and future generations. Such strategies and programmes may include: (a) reducing depletion of water resources through unsustainable extraction, diversion and damming; (b) reducing and eliminating contamination of watersheds and water-related ecosystems by substances such as radiation, harmful chemicals and human excreta; (c) monitoring water reserves; (d) ensuring that proposed developments do not interfere with access to adequate water; (e) assessing the impacts of actions that may impinge upon water availability and natural-ecosystems watersheds, such as climate change, desertification and increased soil salinity, deforestation and loss of biodiversity; (f) increasing the efficient use of water by end-users; (g) reducing water wastage in its distribution; (h) response mechanisms for emergency situations; (i) and establishing competent institutions and appropriate institutional arrangements to carry out the strategies and programmes.

UNGA Resolution 64/292 The human right to water and sanitation (adopted on 28 July 2010) A/RES/64/292

1.   Recognizes the right to safe and clean drinking water and sanitation as a human right that is essential for the full enjoyment of life and all human rights;

2.   Calls upon States and international organizations to provide financial resources, capacity-building and technology transfer, through international assistance and cooperation, in particular to developing countries, in order to scale up efforts to provide safe, clean, accessible and affordable drinking water and sanitation for all;

Framework principles on human rights and the environment, in Annex to Report of the Special Rapporteur on the issue of human rights obligations relating to the enjoyment of a safe, clean, healthy and sustainable environment (24 January 2018) A/HRC/37/59

Framework principle 1
States should ensure a safe, clean, healthy and sustainable environment in order to respect, protect and fulfil human rights.

Framework principle 2
States should respect, protect and fulfil human rights in order to ensure a safe, clean, healthy and sustainable environment.

Commentary on framework principles 1 and 2
4.   Human rights and environmental protection are interdependent. A safe, clean, healthy and sustainable environment is necessary for the full enjoyment of human rights, including the rights to life, to the highest attainable standard of physical and mental health, to an adequate standard of living, to adequate food, to safe drinking water and sanitation, to housing, to participation in cultural life and to development, as well as the right to a healthy environment itself, which is recognized in regional agreements and most national constitutions.[...]

5.   The obligations of States to respect human rights, to protect the enjoyment of human rights from harmful interference, and to fulfil human rights by working towards their full realization all apply in the environmental context. States should therefore refrain from violating human rights through causing or allowing environmental harm; protect against harmful environmental interference from other sources, including business enterprises, other private actors and natural causes; and take effective steps to ensure the conservation and sustainable use of the ecosystems and biological diversity on which the full enjoyment of human rights depends. While it may not always be possible to prevent all environmental harm that interferes with the full enjoyment of human rights, States should undertake due diligence to prevent such harm and reduce it to the extent possible, and provide for remedies for any remaining harm.

6.   At the same time, States must fully comply with their obligations in respect of human rights, such as freedom of expression, that are exercised in relation to the environment. Such obligations not only have independent bases in human rights law; they are also required in order to respect, protect and fulfil the human rights whose enjoyment depends on a safe, clean, healthy and sustainable environment.

Human Rights Committee, 'General Comment No 36, Article 6: Right to Life' (3 September 2019) CCPR/C/GC/36
26.   The duty to protect life also implies that States parties should take appropriate measures to address the general conditions in society that may give rise to direct threats to life or prevent individuals from enjoying their right to life with dignity. These general conditions may include high levels of criminal and gun violence, pervasive traffic and industrial accidents, degradation of the environment (see also para. 62 below), deprivation of indigenous peoples' land, territories and resources,

the prevalence of life-threatening diseases, such as AIDS, tuberculosis and malaria, extensive substance abuse, widespread hunger and malnutrition and extreme poverty and homelessness.

[...]

62.   Environmental degradation, climate change and unsustainable development constitute some of the most pressing and serious threats to the ability of present and future generations to enjoy the right to life. The obligations of States parties under international environmental law should thus inform the content of article 6 of the Covenant, and the obligation of States parties to respect and ensure the right to life should also inform their relevant obligations under international environmental law. Implementation of the obligation to respect and ensure the right to life, and in particular life with dignity, depends, *inter alia*, on measures taken by States parties to preserve the environment and protect it against harm, pollution and climate change caused by public and private actors. States parties should therefore ensure sustainable use of natural resources, develop and implement substantive environmental standards, conduct environmental impact assessments and consult with relevant States about activities likely to have a significant impact on the environment, provide notification to other States concerned about natural disasters and emergencies and cooperate with them, provide appropriate access to information on environmental hazards and pay due regard to the precautionary approach.

Human Rights Council, Resolution 48/..., The human right to a clean, healthy and sustainable environment (adopted at 48th session, 13 September–8 October 2021)

[...]

Recognizing that environmental degradation, climate change and unsustainable development constitute some of the most pressing and serious threats to the ability of present and future generations to enjoy human rights, including the right to life,
Recognizing also that the exercise of human rights, including the rights to seek, receive and impart information, to participate effectively in the conduct of government and public affairs and in environmental decision-making and to an effective remedy, is vital to the protection of a safe, clean, healthy and sustainable environment,

[...]

1.   *Recognizes* the right to a safe, clean, healthy and sustainable environment as a human right that is important for the enjoyment of human rights;

8.3.3   Case Law

CASE
ICCPR, *Portillo Cáceres v. Paraguay*, CCPR/C/126/D/2751/2016 (25 July 2019)

7.3 The Committee observes that a narrow interpretation does not adequately convey the full concept of the right to life and that States must take positive action to protect that right. The Committee recalls its general comment No. 36, in which it has established that the right to life also concerns the entitlement of individuals to enjoy a life with dignity and to be free from acts or omissions that would cause their unnatural or premature death. States parties should take all appropriate measures to address the general conditions in society that may give rise to threats to the right to life or prevent individuals from enjoying their right to life with dignity, and these conditions include environmental pollution. In that respect, the Committee observes that the State party is also bound by the Stockholm Convention on Persistent Organic Pollutants. Furthermore, the Committee recalls that States parties may be in violation of article 6 of the Covenant even if such threats and situations do not result in loss of life.

7.4 The Committee also takes note of developments in other international tribunals that have recognized the existence of an undeniable link between the protection of the environment and the realization of human rights and that have established that environmental degradation can adversely affect the effective enjoyment of the right to life. Thus, severe environmental degradation has given rise to findings of a violation of the right to life.

[...]

7.8 The Committee observes that the authors, who are campesinos from the same family engaged in family farming on lands owned by the State and administered by a State entity (para. 2.2), depend on their crops, fruit trees, livestock, fishing and water resources for their livelihoods. This has not been contested by the State party. The Committee recalls that the term "home" is to be understood to indicate the place where a person resides or carries out his or her usual occupation. Further, the Committee considers that the aforementioned elements constitute components of the way of life of the authors, who have a special attachment to and dependency on the land, and that these elements can be considered to fall under the scope of protection of article 17 of the Covenant. In addition, the Committee considers that article 17 should not be understood as being limited to the refraining from arbitrary interference, but rather as also covering the obligation of States parties to adopt positive measures that are needed to ensure the effective exercise of this right, in the light of interference by the State authorities and physical or legal persons. In the present case, the Committee observes that the State party did not place appropriate controls upon illegal activities that were creating pollution. The State party's failure to discharge its duty to protect, as acknowledged in the *amparo* decision (paras. 2.20 and 2.21), made it possible for large-scale fumigations to continue, in contravention of internal regulations, including the use of prohibited agrochemicals, which caused not only the pollution of well water in the authors' homes, as recognized by the Public Prosecution Service, but also the death of fish and livestock and the loss of crops and fruit trees on the land on which the authors live and grow crops, elements that constitute components of the authors' private life, family and home. The Committee observes that the State party has not provided any alternative explanation in that regard. When pollution has direct repercussions on the right to one's private and family life and home, and the adverse consequences of that pollution are serious because of its intensity or duration and the physical or mental harm that it does, then the degradation of the environment may adversely affect the well-being of individuals and constitute violations of private and family life and the home. Consequently, in the light of the information that it has before it, the Committee concludes that the events at issue in the present case disclose a violation of article 17 of the Covenant.

CASE
ICCPR, *Ioane Teitiota v. New Zealand*, CCPR/C/127/D/2728/2016 (24 October 2019)

9.4 The Committee recalls that the right to life cannot be properly understood if it is interpreted in a restrictive manner, and that the protection of that right requires States parties to adopt positive measures. The Committee also recalls its general comment No. 36 (2018) on the right to life, in which it established that the right to life also includes the right of individuals to enjoy a life with dignity and to be free from acts or omissions that would cause their unnatural or premature death (para. 3). The Committee further recalls that the obligation of States parties to respect and ensure the right to life extends to reasonably foreseeable threats and life-threatening situations that can result in loss of life. States parties may be in violation of article 6 of the Covenant even if such threats and situations do not result in the loss of life. Furthermore, the Committee recalls that environmental degradation, climate change and unsustainable development constitute some of the most pressing and serious threats to the ability of present and future generations to enjoy the right to life.

9.5 Moreover, the Committee observes that both it and regional human rights tribunals have established that environmental degradation can compromise effective enjoyment of the right to life, and that severe environmental degradation can adversely affect an individual's well-being and lead to a violation of the right to life.

9.6 In the present case, the Committee recalls that it must assess whether there was clear arbitrariness, error or injustice in the evaluation by the State party's authorities of the author's claim that when he was removed to Kiribati he faced a real risk of a threat to his right to life under article 6 of the Covenant. The Committee observes that the State party thoroughly considered and accepted the author's statements and evidence as credible, and that it examined his claim for protection separately under both the Convention relating to the Status of Refugees and the Covenant. The Committee notes that in their decisions, the Immigration and Protection Tribunal and the Supreme Court both allowed for the possibility that the effects of climate change or other natural disasters could provide a basis for protection. Although the Immigration and Protection Tribunal found the author to be entirely credible and accepted the evidence he presented, it considered that the evidence he provided did not establish that he faced a risk of an imminent, or likely, risk of arbitrary deprivation of life upon return to Kiribati. In particular, the Tribunal found that there was no evidence that: (a) the author had been in any land disputes in the past, or faced a real chance of being physically harmed in such a dispute in the future; (b) the author would be unable to find land to provide accommodation for himself and his family; (c) the author would be unable to grow food or access potable water; (d) the author would face life-threatening environmental conditions; (e) the author's situation was materially different from that of every other resident of Kiribati; or (f) the Government of Kiribati had failed to take programmatic steps to provide for the basic necessities of life, in order to meet its positive obligation to fulfil the author's right to life. The Tribunal observed that the Government of Kiribati had taken steps to address the effects of climate change, according to the 2007 National Adaptation Programme of Action submitted by Kiribati under the United Nations Framework Convention on Climate Change.

[...]

9.11 The Committee takes note of the observation of the Immigration and Protection Tribunal that climate change-induced harm can occur through sudden onset events and slow onset processes. Reports indicate that sudden-onset events are discrete occurrences that have an immediate and obvious impact over a period of hours or days, while slow-onset processes may have a gradual, adverse impact on livelihoods and resources over a period of months or years. Both sudden-onset events, such as intense storms and flooding, and slow-onset processes, such as sea level rise, salinization and land degradation, can propel cross-border movement of individuals seeking protection from climate change-related harm. The Committee is of the view that without robust national and international efforts, the effects of climate change in receiving States may expose individuals to a violation of their rights under articles 6 or 7 of the Covenant, thereby triggering the non-refoulement obligations of sending States. Furthermore, given that the risk of an entire country becoming submerged under water is such an extreme risk, the conditions of life in such a country may become incompatible with the right to life with dignity before the risk is realized.

9.12 In the present case, the Committee accepts the author's claim that sea level rise is likely to render Kiribati uninhabitable. However, it notes that the time frame of 10 to 15 years, as suggested by the author, could allow for intervening acts by Kiribati, with the assistance of the international community, to take affirmative measures to protect and, where necessary, relocate its population. The Committee notes that the State party's authorities thoroughly examined that issue and found that Kiribati was taking adaptive measures to reduce existing vulnerabilities and build resilience to climate change-related harms. Based on the information made available to it, the Committee is not in a position to conclude that the domestic authorities' assessment that the measures taken by Kiribati would suffice to protect the author's right to life under article 6 of the Covenant was clearly arbitrary or erroneous in that regard, or amounted to a denial of justice.

8.4   REGIONAL HUMAN RIGHTS LAW

8.4.1   Legally Binding Instruments

1950 European Convention for the Protection of Human Rights and Fundamental Freedoms, ETS 5

Article 2 – Right to life
1. Everyone's right to life shall be protected by law. No one shall be deprived of his life intentionally save in the execution of a sentence of a court following his conviction of a crime for which this penalty is provided by law.

Article 8 – Right to respect for private and family life
1. Everyone has the right to respect for his private and family life, his home and his correspondence.
2. There shall be no interference by a public authority with the exercise of this right except such as is in accordance with the law and is necessary in a democratic society in the interests of national security, public safety or the economic well-being of the country, for the prevention of disorder or crime, for the protection of health or morals, or for the protection of the rights and freedoms of others.

Protocol 1

Article 1 – Protection of property
Every natural or legal person is entitled to the peaceful enjoyment of his possessions. No one shall be deprived of his possessions except in the public interest and subject to the conditions provided for by law and by the general principles of international law.
The preceding provisions shall not, however, in any way impair the right of a State to enforce such laws as it deems necessary to control the use of property in accordance with the general interest or to secure the payment of taxes or other contributions or penalties.

1961 European Social Charter, ETS 35

Article 11 – The right to protection of health
With a view to ensuring the effective exercise of the right to protection of health, the Parties undertake, either directly or in cooperation with public or private organisations, to take appropriate measures designed *inter alia*:
1.   to remove as far as possible the causes of ill-health;
2.   to provide advisory and educational facilities for the promotion of health and the encouragement of individual responsibility in matters of health;
3.   to prevent as far as possible epidemic, endemic and other diseases, as well as accidents.

1969 American Convention on Human Rights

Article 26. Progressive Development
The States Parties undertake to adopt measures, both internally and through international cooperation, especially those of an economic and technical nature, with a view to achieving progressively, by legislation or other appropriate means, the full realization of the rights implicit in the economic, social, educational, scientific, and cultural standards set forth in the Charter of the Organization of American States as amended by the Protocol of Buenos Aires.

1988 Additional Protocol to the American Convention on Human Rights in the Area of Economic, Social and Cultural Rights "Protocol of San Salvador"

Article 11 Right to a Healthy Environment
1.   Everyone shall have the right to live in a healthy environment and to have access to basic public services.
2.   The States Parties shall promote the protection, preservation, and improvement of the environment.

1981 African Charter on Human and Peoples' Rights, 21 ILM 58

ARTICLE 16
1.   Every individual shall have the right to enjoy the best attainable state of physical and mental health.
2.   State Parties to the present Charter shall take the necessary measures to protect the health of their people and to ensure that they receive medical attention when they are sick.

ARTICLE 24
All peoples shall have the right to a general satisfactory environment favourable to their development.

2004 Arab Charter on Human Rights

Article 38
Everyone shall have the right to an adequate standard of living for himself and his family, ensuring well-being and a decent life, including adequate food, clothing, housing, services and a right to a safe environment. The State Parties shall take appropriate measures within their available resources to ensure the realization of this right.

Article 39
1.   The State Parties shall recognize the right of everyone to the enjoyment of the highest attainable standard of physical and mental health and the right of every citizen to enjoy free and non-discriminatory access to health services and health care centres.

2.   The steps to be taken by the State Parties shall include those necessary to:

[…]

e.   Ensure basic nutrition and clean water for everybody.
f.   Fight environmental pollution and supply sanitation systems.

8.4.2   Non-Binding Instruments

2012 ASEAN Declaration
28.   Every person has the right to an adequate standard of living for himself or herself and his or her family including:

[…]

e.   The right to safe drinking water and sanitation;
f.   The right to a safe, clean and sustainable environment.

8.4.3   Case Law

CASE
ECtHR, *Lopez Ostra v. Spain*, App No. 16798/90, 20 EHRR 277 (19 December 1994)

51. Naturally, severe environmental pollution may affect individuals' well-being and prevent them from enjoying their homes in such a way as to affect their private and family life adversely, without, however, seriously endangering their health.
     Whether the question is analysed in terms of a positive duty on the State – to take reasonable and appropriate measures to secure the applicant's rights under paragraph 1 of Article 8 (art. 8-1), as the applicant wishes in her case, or in terms of an "interference by a public authority" to be justified in accordance with paragraph 2 (art. 8-2), the applicable principles are broadly similar. In both contexts regard must be had to the fair balance that has to be struck between the competing

interests of the individual and of the community as a whole, and in any case the State enjoys a certain margin of appreciation. Furthermore, even in relation to the positive obligations flowing from the first paragraph of Article 8 (art. 8-1), in striking the required balance the aims mentioned in the second paragraph (art. 8-2) may be of a certain relevance (see, in particular, *Rees v. the United Kingdom*, Judgment (17 October 1986), Series A No. 106, p. 15, para. 37, and *Powell and Rayner v. the United Kingdom*, Judgment (21 February 1990), Series A No. 172, p. 18, para. 41).

52. It appears from the evidence that the waste-treatment plant in issue was built by SACURSA in July 1988 to solve a serious pollution problem in Lorca due to the concentration of tanneries. Yet as soon as it started up, the plant caused nuisance and health problems to many local people (see paragraphs 7 and 8 above).

    Admittedly, the Spanish authorities, and in particular the Lorca municipality, were theoretically not directly responsible for the emissions in question. However, as the Commission pointed out, the town allowed the plant to be built on its land and the State subsidised the plant's construction (see paragraph 7 above).

53. The town council reacted promptly by rehousing the residents affected, free of charge, in the town centre for the months of July, August and September 1988 and then by stopping one of the plant's activities from 9 September (see paragraphs 8 and 9 above). However, the council's members could not be unaware that the environmental problems continued after this partial shutdown (see paragraphs 9 and 11 above). This was, moreover, confirmed as early as 19 January 1989 by the regional Environment and Nature Agency's report and then by expert opinions in 1991, 1992 and 1993 (see paragraphs 11 and 18 above).

[...]

56. It has to be noted that the municipality not only failed to take steps to that end after 9 September 1988 but also resisted judicial decisions to that effect. In the ordinary administrative proceedings instituted by Mrs López Ostra's sisters-in-law it appealed against the Murcia High Court's decision of 18 September 1991 ordering temporary closure of the plant, and that measure was suspended as a result (see paragraph 16 above).

    Other State authorities also contributed to prolonging the situation. On 19 November 1991 Crown Counsel appealed against the Lorca investigating judge's decision of 15 November temporarily to close the plant in the prosecution for an environmental health offence (see paragraph 17 above), with the result that the order was not enforced until 27 October 1993 (see paragraph 22 above).

57. The Government drew attention to the fact that the town had borne the expense of renting a flat in the centre of Lorca, in which the applicant and her family lived from 1 February 1992 to February 1993 (see paragraph 21 above).

    The Court notes, however, that the family had to bear the nuisance caused by the plant for over three years before moving house with all the attendant inconveniences. They moved only when it became apparent that the situation could continue indefinitely and when Mrs López Ostra's daughter's paediatrician recommended that they do so (see paragraphs 16, 17 and 19 above). Under these circumstances, the municipality's offer could not afford complete redress for the nuisance and inconveniences to which they had been subjected.

58. Having regard to the foregoing, and despite the margin of appreciation left to the respondent State, the Court considers that the State did not succeed in striking a fair balance between the interest of the town's economic well-being – that of having a waste-treatment plant – and the applicant's effective enjoyment of her right to respect for her home and her private and family life.

   There has accordingly been a violation of Article 8 (art. 8).

CASE
ACHPR, *Social and Economic Rights Action Center and the Center for Economic and Social Rights v. Nigeria* (Communication No. 155/96) (May 27 2002), para. 56

52. The right to a general satisfactory environment, as guaranteed under Article 24 of the African Charter or the right to a healthy environment, as it is widely known, therefore imposes clear obligations upon a government. It requires the state to take reasonable and other measures to prevent pollution and ecological degradation, to promote conservation, and to secure an ecologically sustainable development and use of natural resources. Article 12 of the International Covenant on Economic, Social and Cultural Rights (ICESCR), to which Nigeria is a party, requires governments to take necessary steps for the improvement of all aspects of environmental and industrial hygiene. The right to enjoy the best attainable state of physical and mental health enunciated in Article 16(1) of the African Charter and the right to a general satisfactory environment favourable to development (Article 16 (3)[sic]) already noted obligate governments to desist from directly threatening the health and environment of their citizens. The state is under an obligation to respect the just noted rights and this entails largely non-interventionist conduct from the state for example, not from carrying out, sponsoring or tolerating any practice, policy or legal measures violating the integrity of the individual.

53. Government compliance with the spirit of Article 16 and Article 24 of the African Charter must also include ordering or at least permitting independent scientific monitoring of threatened environments, requiring and publicising environmental and social impact studies prior to any major industrial development, undertaking appropriate monitoring and providing information to those communities exposed to hazardous materials and activities and providing meaningful opportunities for individuals to be heard and to participate in the development decisions affecting their communities.

54. We now examine the conduct of the Government of Nigeria in relation to Article 16 and Article 24 of the African Charter. Undoubtedly and admittedly, the Government of Nigeria, through NNPC has the right to produce oil, the income from which will be used to fulfil the economic and social rights of Nigerians. But the care that should have been taken as outlined in the preceding paragraph and which would have protected the rights of the victims of the violations complained of was not taken. To exacerbate the situation, the security forces of the government engaged in conduct

in violation of the rights of the Ogonis by attacking, burning and destroying several Ogoni villages and homes.

[...]

64. The communication argues that the right to food is implicit in the African Charter, in such provisions as the right to life (Article 4), the right to health (Article 16) and the right to economic, social and cultural development (Article 22). By its violation of these rights, the Nigerian Government trampled upon not only the explicitly protected rights but also upon the right to food implicitly guaranteed.

65. The right to food is inseparably linked to the dignity of human beings and is therefore essential for the enjoyment and fulfilment of such other rights as health, education, work and political participation. The African Charter and international law require and bind Nigeria to protect and improve existing food sources and to ensure access to adequate food for all citizens. Without touching on the duty to improve food production and to guarantee access, the minimum core of the right to food requires that the Nigerian Government should not destroy or contaminate food sources. It should not allow private parties to destroy or contaminate food sources, and prevent peoples' efforts to feed themselves.

66. The government's treatment of the Ogonis has violated all three minimum duties of the right to food. The government has destroyed food sources through its security forces and state oil company; has allowed private oil companies to destroy food sources; and, through terror, has created significant obstacles to Ogoni communities trying to feed themselves. The Nigerian Government has again fallen short of what is expected of it as under the provisions of the African Charter and international human rights standards, and hence, is in violation of the right to food of the Ogonis.

CASE
ECtHR, *Hatton and Others 2003 Grand Chamber*, 37 EHRR 28 (2003)

120. The Court notes at the outset that in previous cases in which environmental questions gave rise to violations of the Convention, the violation was predicated on a failure by the national authorities to comply with some aspect of the domestic regime. Thus, in López Ostra, the waste-treatment plant at issue was illegal in that it operated without the necessary licence, and was eventually closed down (López Ostra, cited above, pp. 46-47, §§ 16-22). In Guerra and Others, the violation was also founded on an irregular position at the domestic level, as the applicants had been unable to obtain information that the State was under a statutory obligation to provide (Guerra and Others, cited above, p. 219, §§ 25-27).

This element of domestic irregularity is wholly absent in the present case. The policy on night flights which was set up in 1993 was challenged by the local authorities, and was found, after a certain amount of amendment, to be compatible with domestic law. The applicants do not suggest that the policy (as amended) was in any way unlawful at a domestic level, and indeed they have not exhausted domestic remedies in respect of any such claim. Further, they do not claim that any of the night flights which disturbed their sleep violated the relevant regulations, and again any such claim could have been pursued in the domestic courts under section 76(1) of the Civil Aviation Act 1982.

121. In order to justify the night flight scheme in the form in which it has operated since 1993, the Government refer not only to the economic interests of the operators of airlines and other enterprises as well as their clients, but also, and above all, to the economic interests of the country as a whole. In their submission these considerations make it necessary to impinge, at least to a certain extent, on the Article 8 rights of the persons affected by the scheme. The Court observes that according to the second paragraph of Article 8 restrictions are permitted, *inter alia*, in the interests of the economic well-being of the country and for the protection of the rights and freedoms of others. It is therefore legitimate for the State to have taken the above economic interests into consideration in the shaping of its policy.

122. The Court must consider whether the State can be said to have struck a fair balance between those interests and the conflicting interests of the persons affected by noise disturbances, including the applicants. Environmental protection should be taken into consideration by States in acting within their margin of appreciation and by the Court in its review of that margin, but it would not be appropriate for the Court to adopt a special approach in this respect by reference to a special status of environmental human rights. In this context the Court must revert to the question of the scope of the margin of appreciation available to the State when taking policy decisions of the kind at issue (see paragraph 103 above).

CASE
ECtHR, *Fadeyeva v. Russia*, Application No. 55723/00 (9 June 2005)

68. Article 8 has been relied on in various cases involving environmental concern, yet it is not violated every time that environmental deterioration occurs: no right to nature preservation is as such included among the rights and freedoms guaranteed by the Convention (see *Kyrtatos v. Greece*, No. 41666/98, § 52, ECHR 2003-VI). Thus, in order to raise an issue under Article 8 the interference must directly affect the applicant's home, family or private life.

69. The Court further points out that the adverse effects of environmental pollution must attain a certain minimum level if they are to fall within the scope of Article 8 (see *López Ostra v. Spain*, Judgment (9 December 1994), Series A No. 303-C, p. 54, § 51; see also, *mutatis mutandis*, *Hatton and Others v. the United Kingdom* [GC], No. 36022/97, § 118, ECHR 2003-VIII). The assessment of that minimum is relative and depends on all the circumstances of the case, such as the intensity and duration of the nuisance, and its physical or mental effects. The general context of the environment should also be taken into account. There would be no arguable claim under Article 8 if the detriment complained of was negligible in comparison to the environmental hazards inherent to life in every modern city.

70. Thus, in order to fall within the scope of Article 8, complaints relating to environ-

mental nuisances have to show, firstly, that there was an actual interference with
the applicant's private sphere, and, secondly, that a level of severity was attained.

[...]

3. "NECESSARY IN A DEMOCRATIC SOCIETY"

(a) General principles

102. The Court reiterates that, in deciding what is necessary for achieving one of the
aims mentioned in Article 8 § 2 of the Convention, a margin of appreciation must be
left to the national authorities, who are in principle better placed than an international court to evaluate local needs and conditions. While it is for the national
authorities to make the initial assessment of necessity, the final evaluation as to
whether the justification given by the State is relevant and sufficient remains subject
to review by the Court (see, among other authorities, *Lustig-Prean and Beckett v. the
United Kingdom*, Nos. 31417/96 and 32377/96, §§ 80–81, 27 September 1999).

103. In recent decades environmental pollution has become a matter of growing public concern. As a consequence, States have adopted various measures in order to
reduce the adverse effects of industrial activities. When assessing these measures
from the standpoint of Article 1 of Protocol No. 1, the Court has, as a rule, accepted that the States have a wide margin of appreciation in the sphere of environmental
protection. Thus, in 1991 in *Fredin v. Sweden (No. 1)*, Judgment (18 February 1991),
Series A No. 192, p. 16, § 48) the Court recognised that "in today's society the
protection of the environment is an increasingly important consideration", and held
that the interference with a private property right (revoking the applicant's licence
to extract gravel from his property on the ground of nature conservation) was not
inappropriate or disproportionate in the context of Article 1 of Protocol No. 1. Later
that year, in *Pine Valley Developments Ltd and Others v. Ireland*, Judgment (29
November 1991), Series A No. 222), the Court confirmed this approach.

104. In another group of cases where the State's failure to act was in issue, the Court has
also preferred to refrain from revising domestic environmental policies. In a recent
Grand Chamber judgment, the Court held that "it would not be appropriate for the
Court to adopt a special approach in this respect by reference to a special status
of environmental human rights" (see *Hatton and Others*, cited above, § 122). In an
earlier case the Court held that "it is certainly not for ... the Court to substitute for
the national authorities any other assessment of what might be best policy in this
difficult technical and social sphere. This is an area where the Contracting Parties
are to be recognised as enjoying a wide margin of appreciation" (see *Powell and
Rayner*, cited above, p. 19, § 44).

105. It remains open to the Court to conclude that there has been a manifest error
of appreciation by the national authorities in striking a fair balance between the
competing interests of different private actors in this sphere. However, the complexity of the issues involved with regard to environmental protection renders the
Court's role primarily a subsidiary one. The Court must first examine whether the
decision-making process was fair and such as to afford due respect to the inter-

ests safeguarded to the individual by Article 8 (see *Buckley v. the United Kingdom*, Judgment (25 September 1996), Reports 1996-IV, pp. 1292–1293, §§ 76–77), and only in exceptional circumstances may it go beyond this line and revise the material conclusions of the domestic authorities (see *Taşkın and Others v. Turkey*, No. 46117/99, § 117, ECHR 2004-X).

CASE
ECtHR, *Budayeva and Others v. Russia*, Case Nos 15339/02, 20 March 2008

128. The Court reiterates that Article 2 does not solely concern deaths resulting from the use of force by agents of the State but also, in the first sentence of its first paragraph, lays down a positive obligation on States to take appropriate steps to safeguard the lives of those within their jurisdiction (see, for example, *L.C.B. v. the United Kingdom*, cited above, p. 1403, § 36, and *Paul and Audrey Edwards v. the United Kingdom*, No. 46477/99, § 54, ECHR 2002-II).

129. This positive obligation entails above all a primary duty on the State to put in place a legislative and administrative framework designed to provide effective deterrence against threats to the right to life (see, for example, *mutatis mutandis*, *Osman v. the United Kingdom*, Judgment (28 October 1998), *Reports* 1998VIII, p. 3159, § 115; *Paul and Audrey Edwards*, cited above, § 54; *İlhan v. Turkey* [GC], No. 22277/93, § 91, ECHR 2000-VII; *Kılıç v. Turkey*, No. 22492/93, § 62, ECHR 2000-III; and *Mahmut Kaya v. Turkey*, No. 22535/93, § 85, ECHR 2000-III).

130. This obligation must be construed as applying in the context of any activity, whether public or not, in which the right to life may be at stake (see *Öneryıldız v. Turkey* [GC], No. 48939/99, § 71, ECHR 2004XII). In particular, it applies to the sphere of industrial risks, or "dangerous activities", such as the operation of waste collection sites in the case of *Öneryıldız* (ibid. §§ 71 and 90).

131. The obligation on the part of the State to safeguard the lives of those within its jurisdiction has been interpreted so as to include both substantive and procedural aspects, notably a positive obligation to take regulatory measures and to adequately inform the public about any life-threatening emergency, and to ensure that any occasion of the deaths caused thereby would be followed by a judicial enquiry (*Öneryıldız*, cited above, §§ 89–118).

132. As regards the substantive aspect, in the particular context of dangerous activities the Court has found that special emphasis must be placed on regulations geared to the special features of the activity in question, particularly with regard to the level of the potential risk to human lives. They must govern the licensing, setting up, operation, security and supervision of the activity and must make it compulsory for all those concerned to take practical measures to ensure the effective protection of citizens whose lives might be endangered by the inherent risks. Among these preventive measures, particular emphasis should be placed on the public's right to information, as established in the case-law of the Convention institutions. The relevant regulations must also provide for appropriate procedures, taking into account the technical aspects of the activity in question, for identifying shortcomings in the

processes concerned and any errors committed by those responsible at different levels (see *Öneryıldız*, cited above, §§ 89–90).

133. It has been recognised that in the context of dangerous activities the scope of the positive obligations under Article 2 of the Convention largely overlap with those under Article 8 (see *Öneryıldız*, cited above, §§ 90 and 160). Consequently, the principles developed in the Court's case-law relating to planning and environmental matters affecting private life and home may also be relied on for the protection of the right to life.

134. As to the choice of particular practical measures, the Court has consistently held that where the State is required to take positive measures, the choice of means is in principle a matter that falls within the Contracting State's margin of appreciation. There are different avenues to ensure Convention rights, and even if the State has failed to apply one particular measure provided by domestic law, it may still fulfil its positive duty by other means (see, among other cases, *Fadeyeva v. Russia*, No. 55723/00, § 96, ECHR 2005IV).

135. In this respect an impossible or disproportionate burden must not be imposed on the authorities without consideration being given, in particular, to the operational choices which they must make in terms of priorities and resources (see *Osman*, cited above, pp. 3159–3160, § 116); this results from the wide margin of appreciation States enjoy, as the Court has previously held, in difficult social and technical spheres (see *Hatton and Others v. the United Kingdom* [GC], No. 36022/97, §§ 100–01, ECHR 2003-VIII, and *Öneryıldız*, cited above, § 107). This consideration must be afforded even greater weight in the sphere of emergency relief in relation to a meteorological event, which is as such beyond human control, than in the sphere of dangerous activities of a man-made nature.

136. In assessing whether the respondent State had complied with the positive obligation, the Court must consider the particular circumstances of the case, regard being had, among other elements, to the domestic legality of the authorities' acts or omissions (see *López Ostra v. Spain*, Judgment (9 December 1994), Series A No. 303C, pp. 46–47, §§ 16–22, and *Guerra and Others v. Italy*, Judgment (19 February 1998), *Reports* 1998I, p. 219, §§ 25–27), the domestic decision-making process, including the appropriate investigations and studies, and the complexity of the issue, especially where conflicting Convention interests are involved (see *Hatton and others*, cited above, § 128, and *Fadeyeva*, cited above, §§ 96–98).

137. In the sphere of emergency relief, where the State is directly involved in the protection of human lives through the mitigation of natural hazards, these considerations should apply in so far as the circumstances of a particular case point to the imminence of a natural hazard that had been clearly identifiable, and especially where it concerned a recurring calamity affecting a distinct area developed for human habitation or use (see, *mutatis mutandis, Murillo Saldías and others*, cited above). The scope of the positive obligations imputable to the State in the particular circumstances would depend on the origin of the threat and the extent to which one or the other risk is susceptible to mitigation.

C) L'APPRÉCIATION DE LA COUR

I. PRINCIPES GÉNÉRAUX

157. La Cour rappelle que des atteintes graves à l'environnement peuvent affecter le bien-être des personnes et les priver de la jouissance de leur domicile de manière à nuire à leur vie privée (*López Ostra c. Espagne*, 9 décembre 1994, série A no 303-C, § 51, et *Guerra et autres c. Italie*, 19 février 1998, § 60, *Recueil* 1998l).

    À cet égard la Cour rappelle également que, dans les affaires où la notion de seuil de gravité a été spécifiquement examinée en matière d'environnement, la Cour a jugé qu'un grief défendable sur le terrain de l'article 8 peut naître si un risque écologique atteint un niveau de gravité diminuant notablement la capacité du requérant à jouir de son domicile ou de sa vie privée ou familiale. L'appréciation de ce niveau minimum dans ce type d'affaires est relative et dépend de l'ensemble des données de la cause, notamment de l'intensité et de la durée des nuisances ainsi que de leurs conséquences physiques ou psychologiques sur la santé ou la qualité de vie de l'intéressé (*Fadeïeva*, précité, §§ 68 et 69, *Dubetska et autres c. Ukraine*, no 30499/03, § 105, 10 février 2011, et *Grimkovskaya c. Ukraine*, no 38182/03, § 58, 21 juillet 2011).

158. L'article 8 ne se borne pas à astreindre l'État à s'abstenir d'ingérences arbitraires : à cet engagement plutôt négatif peuvent s'ajouter des obligations positives inhérentes à un respect effectif de la vie privée. En tout état de cause, que l'on aborde la question sous l'angle de l'obligation positive de l'État d'adopter des mesures raisonnables et adéquates pour protéger les droits de l'individu, en vertu du premier paragraphe de l'article 8, ou sous celui d'une ingérence d'une autorité publique, à justifier selon le second paragraphe, les principes applicables sont assez voisins. Dans les deux cas, il faut avoir égard au juste équilibre à ménager entre les intérêts concurrents de l'individu et de la société dans son ensemble, l'État jouissant en toute hypothèse d'une certaine marge d'appréciation (*López Ostra,* précité, § 51, et *Guerra et autres*, précité, § 58).

159. Les États ont avant tout l'obligation positive, en particulier dans le cas d'une activité dangereuse, de mettre en place une réglementation adaptée aux spécificités de ladite activité, notamment au niveau du risque qui pourrait en résulter. Cette règlementation doit régir l'autorisation, la mise en fonctionnement, l'exploitation, la sécurité et le contrôle de l'activité en question, ainsi qu'imposer à toute personne concernée par celle-ci l'adoption de mesures d'ordre pratique propres à assurer la protection effective des citoyens dont la vie risque d'être exposée aux dangers inhérents au domaine en cause (voir, *mutatis mutandis, Oneryildiz c. Turquie*, [GC], no 48939/99, § 90, CEDH 2004-XII, et *Brincat et autres c. Malte*, nos 60908/11 et 4 autres, §§ 101-102, 24 juillet 2014).

CASE
IACtHR, *Indigenous Communities of the Lhaka Honhat (Our Land) Association v. Argentina* (Merits, Reparations and Costs), Judgment, (6 February 2020), Series C No. 420

224. Furthermore, it should be underlined that, on July 28, 2010, the United Nations General Assembly issued Resolution 64/292 entitled "The human right to water and sanitation, which recognizes the right to safe and clean drinking water and sanitation as a human right that is essential for the full enjoyment of life and all human rights." Likewise, article 9 in Chapter III of the Social Charter of the Americas asserts that "[t]he [...] States recognize that water is fundamental for life and central to socioeconomic development and environmental sustainability" and that they "undertake to continue working to ensure access to safe drinking water and sanitation services for present and future generations." Also, in 2007 and 2012, the OAS General Assembly adopted resolutions 2349/07 and 2760/12, entitled, respectively, "Water, health and human rights" and "The human right to safe drinking water and sanitation." In its articles 1 and 4, the former resolves "to recognize that water is essential for life and health" and "indispensable for a life with human dignity," as well as "to recognize and respect, in accordance with national law, the ancestral use of water by urban, rural and indigenous communities in the framework of their habits and customs on water use." The second, in its first article resolves "to invite" States "to continue working to ensure access to safe drinking water and sanitation services for present and future generations." The right is also established in Article 12 of the Inter-American Convention on Protecting the Human Rights of Older Persons.

[...]

228. When explaining how the right to water is related to other rights, the CESCR noted "the importance of ensuring sustainable access to water resources for agriculture to realize the right to adequate food." It added that "States [...] should ensure that there is adequate access to water for subsistence farming and for securing the livelihoods of indigenous peoples." It asserted that "[e]nvironmental hygiene, as an aspect of the right to health [...], encompasses taking steps on a non-discriminatory basis to prevent threats to health from unsafe and toxic water conditions." Similarly, the Court has already noted that "the right to water" (as also the rights to food and to take part in cultural life) are "among the rights that are especially vulnerable to environmental impact."

[...]

B.1.2 INTERDEPENDENCE BETWEEN THE RIGHTS TO A HEALTHY ENVIRONMENT, ADEQUATE FOOD, WATER AND CULTURAL IDENTITY AND SPECIFICITY IN RELATION TO INDIGENOUS PEOPLES

243. The rights referred to above are closely related, so that some aspects related to the observance of one of them may overlap with the realization of others.

244. Referring to diverse statements made by international bodies, the Court has under-lined the "close" relationship or "interdependence" between the environment and human rights. This is because the latter may be adversely affected by environmental degradation and, in turn, because – as United Nations agencies have indicated – "effective environmental protection often depends on the exercise of human rights."

245. In this context, there are threats to the environment that may have an impact on food. The right to food, and also the right to take part in cultural life and the right to water, are "particularly vulnerable" to "environmental impact" (*supra* para. 228). The CESCR has indicated that the "policies" that should be "adopted" owing to the right to food include "environmental" policies. Likewise, it has indicated that "in economic development and environmental policies and programs" the States should "[r]espect and protect the cultural heritage of all the groups and communities, in particular the most disadvantaged and marginalized individuals and groups."

246. The CESCR has also pointed out that:

> the right to adequate food is [...] indispensable for the fulfilment of other human rights [... and] also inseparable from social justice, requiring the adoption of appropriate economic, environmental and social policies, at both the national and international levels, oriented to the eradication of poverty and the fulfilment of all human rights for all.

It added that the "the precise meaning of 'adequacy' is to a large extent determined by prevailing social, economic, cultural, climatic, ecological and other conditions." The WGPSS has indicated, similarly, that it is "necessary to consider" the "cultural dimension" of the right to adequate food and that "because food is a cultural manifestation of peoples, it is necessary to adopt an integral approach and with a direct interdependence between civil and political rights and economic, social and cultural rights."

[...]

248. Likewise, articles 20(1), 29(1) and 32(1) of the United Nations Declaration on the Rights of Indigenous Peoples indicate the rights of the indigenous peoples "to be secure in the enjoyment of their own means of subsistence and development"; "to the conservation and protection of the environment and the productive capacity of their lands or territories and resources" and "to determine and develop priorities and strategies for the development or use of their lands or territories and other resources." Meanwhile, article XIX of the American Declaration on the Rights of Indigenous Peoples refers to the "the right to protection of a healthy environment," which includes the right of the "indigenous peoples" "to live in harmony with nature and to a healthy, safe, and sustainable environment"; "to conserve, restore, and protect the environment and to manage their lands, territories and resources in a sustainable way," and "to the conservation and protection of the environment and the productive capacity of their lands or territories and resources."

[...]

250. It is also important to emphasize that the management by the indigenous communities of the resources that exist in their territories should be understood in pragmatic terms, favorable to environmental preservation. The Court has considered that:

> In general, indigenous peoples play a significant role in the conservation of nature because certain traditional customs result in sustainable practices and are considered essential for effective conservation strategies. Hence, respect for the rights of indigenous peoples may have a positive effect on environmental conservation. Consequently, the rights of such communities and the international environmental standards should be understood as complementary and non-exclusive rights.

> Principle 22 of the Rio Declaration is very clear in this regard when it indicates that

> > "indigenous people and their communities [...] have a vital role in environmental management and development because of their knowledge and traditional practices. States should recognize and duly support their identity, culture and interests and enable their effective participation in the achievement of sustainable development."

251. Additionally, it is necessary to take into account the indications of the Human Rights Committee that the right of the people to enjoy a particular culture "may consist in a way of life closely associated with territory and the use of its resources" as in the case of members of indigenous communities. The right to cultural identity may be expressed in different ways; in the case of indigenous peoples this includes "a particular way of life associated with the use of land resources [...]. That right may include such traditional activities a fishing or hunting and the right to live in reserves protected by law." In this regard, the Court has had occasion to note that the right to collective ownership of indigenous people is connected to the protection of and access to the natural resources that are on their territories (*supra* para. 94). Likewise, the WGPSS has noted that "the physical, spiritual, and cultural well-being of indigenous communities is closely tied to the quality of the environment where they live."

8.4.4   Advisory Opinions

ADVISORY OPINION
IACtHR, The Environment and Human Rights, Advisory Opinion, OC-23/17 (15 November 2017), Series A No. 23

A. THE INTERRELATIONSHIP BETWEEN HUMAN RIGHTS AND THE ENVIRONMENT

47. This Court has recognized the existence of an undeniable relationship between the protection of the environment and the realization of other human rights, in that environmental degradation and the adverse effects of climate change affect the real

enjoyment of human rights. In addition, the preamble to the Additional Protocol to the American Convention on Human Rights in the Area of Economic, Social and Cultural Rights (hereinafter "Protocol of San Salvador"), emphasizes the close relationship between the exercise of economic, social and cultural rights – which include the right to a healthy environment – and of civil and political rights, and indicates that the different categories of rights constitute an indivisible whole based on the recognition of the dignity of the human being. They therefore require permanent promotion and protection in order to ensure their full applicability; moreover, the violation of some rights in order to ensure the exercise of others can never be justified.

48. Specifically, in cases concerning the territorial rights of indigenous and tribal peoples, the Court has referred to the relationship between a healthy environment and the protection of human rights, considering that these peoples' right to collective ownership is linked to the protection of, and access to, the resources to be found in their territories, because those natural resources are necessary for the very survival, development and continuity of their way of life. The Court has also recognized the close links that exist between the right to a dignified life and the protection of ancestral territory and natural resources. In this regard, the Court has determined that, because indigenous and tribal peoples are in a situation of special vulnerability, States must take positive measures to ensure that the members of these peoples have access to a dignified life – which includes the protection of their close relationship with the land – and to their life project, in both its individual and collective dimension. The Court has also emphasized that the lack of access to the corresponding territories and natural resources may expose indigenous communities to precarious and subhuman living conditions and increased vulnerability to disease and epidemics, and subject them to situations of extreme neglect that may result in various violations of their human rights in addition to causing them suffering and undermining the preservation of their way of life, customs and language.

49. Meanwhile, the Inter-American Commission has stressed that "several fundamental rights require, as a necessary precondition for their enjoyment, a minimum environmental quality, and are profoundly affected by the degradation of natural resources." Likewise, the OAS General Assembly has recognized the close relationship between the protection of the environment and human rights (supra para. 22) and emphasized that "the adverse effects of climate change have a negative impact on the enjoyment of human rights."

[...]

55. Owing to the close connection between environmental protection, sustainable development and human rights (supra paras 47 to 55), currently (i) numerous human rights protection systems recognize the right to a healthy environment as a right in itself, particularly the Inter-American human rights system, while it is evident that (ii) numerous other human rights are vulnerable to environmental degradation, all of which results in a series of environmental obligations for States to comply with their duty to respect and to ensure those rights. Specifically, another consequence of the

interdependence and indivisibility of human rights and environmental protection is that, when determining these State obligations, the Court may avail itself of the principles, rights and obligations of international environmental law, which, as part of the international *corpus iuris* make a decisive contribution to establishing the scope of the obligations under the American Convention in this regard (supra paras 43 to 45).

B. HUMAN RIGHTS AFFECTED BY ENVIRONMENTAL DEGRADATION, INCLUDING THE RIGHT TO A HEALTHY ENVIRONMENT

56. Under the inter-American human rights system, the right to a healthy environment is established expressly in Article 11 of the Protocol of San Salvador: [...]

57. It should also be considered that this right is included among the economic, social and cultural rights protected by Article 26 of the American Convention, because this norm protects the rights derived from the economic, social, educational, scientific and cultural provisions of the OAS Charter, the American Declaration of the Rights and Duties of Man (to the extent that the latter "contains and defines the essential human rights referred to in the Charter") and those resulting from an interpretation of the Convention that accords with the criteria established in its Article 29 (supra para. 42). The Court reiterates the interdependence and indivisibility of the civil and political rights, and the economic, social and cultural rights, because they should be understood integrally and comprehensively as human rights, with no order of precedence, that are enforceable in all cases before the competent authorities.

58. The Court underscores that the right to a healthy environment is recognized explicitly in the domestic laws of several States of the region, as well as in some provisions of the international corpus iuris, in addition to the aforementioned Protocol of San Salvador (supra para. 56), such as the American Declaration on the Rights of Indigenous Peoples; the African Charter on Human and Peoples' Rights; the ASEAN Human Rights Declaration, and the Arab Charter on Human Rights.

59. The human right to a healthy environment has been understood as a right that has both individual and also collective connotations. In its collective dimension, the right to a healthy environment constitutes a universal value that is owed to both present and future generations. That said, the right to a healthy environment also has an individual dimension insofar as its violation may have a direct and an indirect impact on the individual owing to its connectivity to other rights, such as the rights to health, personal integrity, and life. Environmental degradation may cause irreparable harm to human beings; thus, a healthy environment is a fundamental right for the existence of humankind.

[...]

62. The Court considers it important to stress that, as an autonomous right, the right to a healthy environment, unlike other rights, protects the components of the envi-

ronment, such as forests, rivers and seas, as legal interests in themselves, even in the absence of the certainty or evidence of a risk to individuals. This means that it protects nature and the environment, not only because of the benefits they provide to humanity or the effects that their degradation may have on other human rights, such as health, life or personal integrity, but because of their importance to the other living organisms with which we share the planet that also merit protection in their own right. In this regard, the Court notes a tendency, not only in court judgments, but also in, to recognize legal personality and, consequently, rights to nature.

63. Thus, the right to a healthy environment as an autonomous right differs from the environmental content that arises from the protection of other rights, such as the right to life or the right to personal integrity.

64. That said and as previously mentioned, in addition to the right to a healthy environment, damage to the environment may affect all human rights, in the sense that the full enjoyment of all human rights depends on a suitable environment. Nevertheless, some human rights are more susceptible than others to certain types of environmental damage (supra paras. 47 to 55). The rights especially linked to the environment have been classified into two groups: (i) rights whose enjoyment is particularly vulnerable to environmental degradation, also identified as substantive rights (for example, the rights to life, personal integrity, health or property), and (ii) rights whose exercise supports better environmental policymaking, also identified as procedural rights (such as the rights to freedom of expression and association, to information, to participation in decision-making, and to an effective remedy).

[...]

66. The Court considers that the rights that are particularly vulnerable to environmental impact include the rights to life, personal integrity, private life, health, water, food, housing, participation in cultural life, property, and the right to not be forcibly displaced. Without prejudice to the foregoing, according to Article 29 of the Convention, other rights are also vulnerable and their violation may affect the rights to life, liberty and security of the individual, and infringe on the obligation of all persons to conduct themselves fraternally, such as the right to peace, because displacements caused by environmental deterioration frequently unleash violent conflicts between the displaced population and the population settled on the territory to which it is displaced. Some of these conflicts are massive and thus extremely grave.

67. The Court also bears in mind that the effects on these rights may be felt with greater intensity by certain groups in vulnerable situations. It has been recognized that environmental damage "will be experienced with greater force in the sectors of the population that are already in a vulnerable situation"; hence, based on "international human rights law, States are legally obliged to confront these vulnerabilities based on the principle of equality and non-discrimination." Various human rights bodies have recognized that indigenous peoples, children, people living in extreme poverty, minorities, and people with disabilities, among others, are groups that are especially vulnerable to environmental damage, and have also recognized the differentiated impact that it has on women. In addition, the groups that are especially

vulnerable to environmental degradation include communities that, essentially, depend economically or for their survival on environmental resources from the marine environment, forested areas and river basins, or run a special risk of being affected owing to their geographical location, such as coastal and small island communities. In many cases, the special vulnerability of these groups has led to their relocation or internal displacement.

8.4.5   National Courts

State of the Netherlands v. Urgenda, **Number 19/00135 (20 December 2019) ECLI: HR: 2019:2007 (translated from Dutch)**

5.3.1   The protection afforded by Articles 2 and 8 ECHR is not limited to specific persons, but to society or the population as a whole. The latter is for instance the case with environmental hazards. In the case of environmental hazards that endanger an entire region, Articles 2 and 8 ECHR offer protection to the residents of that region.

5.3.2   The obligation to take appropriate steps pursuant to Articles 2 and 8 ECHR also encompasses the duty of the state to take preventive measures to counter the danger, even if the materialisation of that danger is uncertain. This is consistent with the precautionary principle. If it is clear that the real and immediate risk referred to above in paras. 5.2.2 and 5.2.3 exists, states are obliged to take appropriates steps without having a margin of appreciation. The states do have discretion in choosing the steps to be taken, although these must actually be reasonable and suitable.

The obligation pursuant to Articles 2 and 8 ECHR to take appropriate steps to counter an imminent threat may encompass both mitigation measures (measures to prevent the threat from materialising) or adaptation measures (measures to lessen or soften the impact of that materialisation). According to ECtHR case law, which measures are suitable in a given case depends on the circumstances of that case.

[...]

5.7.1   The answer to the question referred to in 5.6.3 above is in the opinion of the Supreme Court, that, under Articles 2 and 8 ECHR, the Netherlands is obliged to do 'its part' in order to prevent dangerous climate change, even if it is a global problem. This is based on the following grounds.

5.7.2   The UNFCCC is based on the idea that climate change is a global problem that needs to be solved globally. Where emissions of greenhouse gases take place from the territories of all countries and all countries are affected, measures will have to be taken by all countries. Therefore, all countries will have to do the necessary. The preamble to this convention states, among other things, the following in this context:

> *Acknowledging that the global nature of climate change calls for the widest possible cooperation by all countries and their participation in an effective*

and appropriate international response, in accordance with their common but differentiated responsibilities and respective capabilities and their social and economic conditions, (...).

Recalling also that States have (...) the responsibility to ensure that activities within their jurisdiction or control do not cause damage to the environment of other States or of areas beyond the limits of national jurisdiction.

5.7.3   The objective of the UNFCCC is to stabilise greenhouse gas concentrations in the atmosphere at a level that would prevent dangerous human induced interference with the climate system (Article 2). Article 3 contains various principles to achieve this objective. For instance, Article 3(1) provides that the parties "should protect the climate system for the benefit of present and future generations of humankind, on the basis of equity and in accordance with their common but differentiated responsibilities and respective capabilities". Article 3(3) provides that the parties "should take precautionary measures to anticipate, prevent or minimize the causes of climate change and mitigate its adverse effects". And Article 4 provides, put succinctly, that all parties will take measures and develop policy in this area. It follows from these provisions that each state has an obligation to take the necessary measures in accordance with its specific responsibilities and possibilities.

5.7.4   At the annual climate change conferences held on the basis of the UNFCCC since 1992, the provisions mentioned above in 5.7.3 have been further developed in various COP decisions. In each case these are based first and foremost on an acknowledgement of the above understanding: all countries will have to do the necessary. Articles 3 et seq. of the 2015 Paris Agreement reiterates this in so many words.

5.7.5   This understanding corresponds to what is commonly referred to as the 'no harm principle', a generally accepted principle of international law which entails that countries must not cause each other harm. This is also referred to in the preamble to the UNFCCC (in the section cited in 5.7.2 above). Countries can be called to account for the duty arising from this principle. Applied to greenhouse gas emissions, this means that they can be called upon to make their contribution to reducing greenhouse gas emissions. This approach justifies partial responsibility: each country is responsible for its part and can therefore be called to account in that respect.

[...]

5.7.7   Partly in view of the serious consequences of dangerous climate change as referred to in 4.2 above, the defence that a state does not have to take responsibility because other countries do not comply with their partial responsibility, cannot be accepted. Nor can the assertion that a country's own share in global greenhouse gas emissions is very small and that reducing emissions from one's own territory makes little difference on a global scale, be accepted as a defence. Indeed, acceptance of these defences would mean that a country could easily evade its partial responsibility by pointing out other countries or its own small share. If, on the other hand, this defence is ruled out, each country can be effectively called to account for its share of emissions and the chance of all countries actually making their contribution will be greatest, in accordance with the principles laid down in the preamble to the UNFCCC cited above in 5.7.2.

5.7.8   Also important in this context is that, as has been considered in 4.6 above about the carbon budget, each reduction of greenhouse gas emissions has a positive effect on combating dangerous climate change, as every reduction means that more room remains in the carbon budget. The defence that a duty to reduce greenhouse gas emissions on the part of the individual states does not help because other countries will continue their emissions cannot be accepted for this reason either: no reduction is negligible.

5.7.9   Climate change threatens human rights, as follows from what has been considered in 5.6.2 above. This is also recognised internationally outside the context of the Council of Europe. In order to ensure adequate protection from the threat to those rights resulting from climate change, it should be possible to invoke those rights against individual states, also with regard to the aforementioned partial responsibility. This is in line with the principle of effective interpretation, referred to in 5.4.1 above, that the ECtHR applies when interpreting the ECHR and also with the right to effective legal protection guaranteed by Article 13 ECHR, referred to 5.5.1–5.5.3 above.

QUESTIONS

1. What is the difference between the substantive and procedural environmental right?
2. Is environmental impact assessment a procedural environmental right?
3. Are all environmental human rights justiciable?

FURTHER READING

BOOKS

D Anton and D Shelton, *Environmental Protection and Human Rights* (Cambridge University Press 2011)

AE Boyle and MR Anderson (eds), *Human Rights Approaches to Environmental Protection* (Oxford University Press 1996)

M Fitzmaurice and A Fijalkowski (eds), *Right of the Child to Clean Environment* (Ashgate 2000)

A Grear and LJ Kotzé (eds), *Research Handbook on Human Rights and the Environment* (Edward Elgar 2015)

L Hajjar Leib, *Human Rights and the Environment: Philosophical, Theoretical and Legal Perspectives* (Martinus Nijhoff 2011)

JH Knox and Ramin Pejan (eds), *The Human Right to a Healthy Environment* (Cambridge University Press 2018)

JR May and E Daly (eds), *Human Rights and the Environment: Legality, Indivisibility, Dignity and Geography* (Edward Elgar 2019)

D Shelton (ed), *Human Rights and the Environment* (Edward Elgar 2011)

SJ Turner, DL Shelton, J Razzaque, O McIntyre and JR May (eds), *Environmental Rights: The Development of Standards* (Cambridge University Press 2019)

A von Arnauld, K von der Decken and M Susi (eds), *The Cambridge Handbook of Human Rights* (Cambridge University Press 2020)

K Woods, *Human Rights and Environmental Sustainability* (Edward Elgar 2010)

CHAPTERS

M Fitzmaurice, 'A Human Right to a Clean Environment: A Reappraisal' in G Ziccardi Capaldo (ed.), *The Global Community Yearbook of International Law and Jurisprudence* 2015 (Oxford University Press 2016)

JG Merrills, 'Environmental Rights' in D Bodansky, J Brunnée and E Hey (eds), *The Oxford Handbook of International Environmental Law* (Oxford University Press 2008)

M Orellana, 'Human Rights and Environmental Law' in E Techera, J Lindley, KN Scott, A Telesetsky (eds), *Routledge Handbook of International Environmental Law* (2nd edn, Routledge 2021)

B Peters, 'Clean and Healthy Environment, Right to, International Protection' in A Peters (ed.), *Max Planck Encyclopedia of Public International Law* (2009)

JE Viñuales, 'A Human Rights Approach to Extraterritorial Environmental Protection? An Assessment' in N Bhuta (ed.), *The Frontiers of Human Rights: Extraterritoriality and its Challenges* (Oxford University Press 2016)

K Wood, 'The State of Play and the Road Ahead: The Environment and Human Rights' in D Akande, J Kuosmanen, H McDermott and D Roser (eds), *Human Rights and 21st Century Challenges: Poverty, Conflict, and the Environment* (Oxford University Press 2020)

ARTICLES

A Boyle, 'Human Rights and the Environment: Where Next?' (2012) 23(3) European Journal of International Law 613

A Boyle, 'Climate Change, the Paris Agreement and Human Rights' (2018) 67 ICLQ 759

P Cullet, 'Definition of an Environmental Right in a Human Rights Context' (1995) 13 Netherlands Quarterly of Human Rights 25

M Fitzmaurice, 'International Protection of the Environment' (2001) 293 RCADI 17

M Fitzmaurice, 'Linking Human Rights and Environment' (2004) 16(3) Journal of Environmental Law 411

M Fitzmaurice, 'The Human Right to Water' (2007) 18 Fordham Environmental Law Review 537

M Fitzmaurice and J Marshall, 'The Human Right to a Clean Environment – Phantom or Reality? The European Court of Human Rights and English Courts' Perspective on Balancing Rights in Environmental Cases' (2007) 76 Nordic Journal of International Law 103

F Francioni, 'International Human Rights in the Environmental Horizon' (2010) 21 EJIL 41

I Hodkova, 'Is There a Right to a Healthy Environment in the International Legal Order?' (1991) 7 Connecticut Journal of International Law 65

JH Knox, 'Linking Human Rights and Climate Change at the United Nations' (2009) 33 Harvard Environmental Law Review 477

JH Knox, 'The Global Pact for the Environment: At the Crossroads of Human Rights and the Environment' (2019) 28 RECIEL 40

B Mayer, 'Human Rights in the Paris Agreement' (2016) 6 Climate Law 109

D Shelton, 'Developing Substantive Environmental Rights' (2010) 1 Journal of Human Rights and the Environment 89

L Sohn, 'The Stockholm Declaration on the Human Environment' (1972) 14 Harvard International Law Journal 423

9
Environmental impact assessment

9.1   INTRODUCTION

Environmental impact assessment (EIA) is a procedure for evaluating the likely environmental impacts of a proposed project or development, taking into account inter-related socio-economic, cultural and human-health impacts, both beneficial and adverse. The UNEP defines environmental impact assessment (EIA) as a tool used to identify the environmental, social and economic impacts of a project *before* a decision with potential impacts on the environment is made. As Neil Craik observes, 'EIAs are clearly one of the central mechanisms used by states to acquire knowledge respecting the environmental consequences of their actions.'[1] The use of EIAs allows decision-makers to ensure that their decisions are based on a proper understanding of their environmental effects. EIAs identify and predict foreseeable environmental impacts at an early stage in project planning and help to find ways to reduce adverse impacts and shape projects to suit the local environment.

EIA has its origins in the US National Environmental Policy Act (NEPA) adopted in 1969, and has since been adopted into the domestic law of other states. Following the 1972 Stockholm Declaration, EIA has been included within international and regional treaties, as well as numerous other soft-law instruments, most notably the 1987 UNEP Goals and Principles of Environmental Impact Assessment, and in Principle 17 of the 1992 Rio Declaration.

EIA is closely associated with the 'no-harm' principle, and the principles of prevention and precaution.[2] The connection is apparent in the codification efforts of the International Law Commission in its 'Draft Articles on the Prevention on Transboundary Harm': article 7. It is also closely related to the duty to cooperate with other states, including obligations to notify and consult prior to decisions being taken. Procedural EIA commitments also constitute a mechanism through which sustainable development can be taken into consideration,[3] particularly through the process of strategic environmental impact assessment (SEA). SEA is a form of environmental impact assessment concerning strategic decisions, rather than at the level of particular projects.

---

[1]   Neil Craik, *The International Law of Environmental Impact Assessment* (CUP 2010) 64.

[2]   See Chapters 4 and 5, respectively.

[3]   See Chapter 2.

Environmental treaties often include references to the need to conduct an EIA. Of universal treaties, UNCLOS provides an early example of an obligation to conduct an EIA. The Espoo Convention is one of the most significant treaties on the obligation to conduct an environmental impact assessment. Unlike other Conventions, it is dedicated to EIA in general, and not limited to any particular type of environmental harm. It provides a detailed framework and set of obligations to conduct EIAs in the context of transboundary environmental impact. The Convention was originally only open to UNECE members, but following an amendment in 2001 (which entered into force in 2014), it is now open to all UN members. It has 30 signatories, including the US and Russian Federation, neither of whom have ratified the Convention, and it now has 45 parties. A second amendment in 2004 (which entered into force in 2014) changed the scope of the covered activities listed in Appendix I, and allows, as appropriate, affected Parties to participate in scoping and requires reviews of compliance. The general obligation to conduct an EIA is set out in article 2, which also makes the link between EIA and the 'no-harm' principle explicit. Under article 2, paragraphs 1 and 3, the threshold for an EIA is where the adverse impact is 'significant'. Paragraph 7 of article 2, above, is important in that it imposes a requirement of EIAs at the project level and also an obligation to endeavour to conduct an SEA 'To the extent appropriate'. The Convention, under article 4, requires that EIA documentation contains certain information, and thus guides, indirectly, the content of an EIA. The required information is set out in Appendix II to the Convention. A significant aspect of the Convention is the requirement for public participation, both for the public of the party of origin and of the affected party. The Kiev Protocol to the Espoo Convention provides a more specific and detailed regime on conducting SEAs. The Kiev Protocol provides a focus on sustainable development, and is concerned with integrating environmental, and human health, considerations into the parties' 'plans and programmes and, to the extent appropriate, policies and legislation': Preamble. As exemplified by the Protocol, SEA has evolved largely as an extension of EIA principles and procedures. The Protocol reflects certain basic principles of SEAs and the actions that need to be taken for its effective application.

The 1991 Antarctic Protocol takes a different approach from the Espoo Convention. The objective of the Convention, specified in article 2, is the 'comprehensive protection of the Antarctic environment and dependent and associated ecosystems', and Antarctica is designated 'as a natural reserve, devoted to peace and science'. The requirement of an EIA is set out in article 8, which differentiates between a range of procedures for an EIA depending on the impact of the activity (art 8(1)).

Recognition of the need to conduct EIAs is found in many declarations and other soft-law instruments. The Stockholm Declaration does not specifically refer to EIA, but, in Principle 14, it describes 'rational planning' as 'an essential tool', and 'the rationale underlying environmental impact assessment can be identified in [that] principle'.[4] The 1978 UNEP Draft Goals and Principles provide, in Principle 5, the first recognition of EIA. The UNEP set out clear guidelines on EIA for the first time in the 1987 Goals and Principles.

---

[4]   P Sands and J Peel, *Principles of International Environmental Law* (4th edn, CUP 2018) 658–659.

EIA is also given a prominent place within the 2001 ILC Articles on Prevention of Transboundary Harm from Hazardous Activities. The article differs from other approaches, insofar as it is concerned with language of risk assessment – 'risk' and 'harm' – rather than 'impact'.[5] Moreover, the risk must reach the threshold of 'significant'. This determination is not absolute but depends on a context.[6] The article does not specify the content of the EIA, and the ILC leaves the determination of content to the domestic law of states. The Commentary provides some indications of what is required: the risk of the activity must be related to the risk of transboundary harm, and the assessment should consider risks to (i) persons, (ii) property and (iii) the environment.

Certain features of EIAs have been recognised by international courts. The first clear discussion of EIA in the ICJ was by Judge Weeramantry in the 1995 *Nuclear Tests (New Zealand v. France)* case, in which he endorsed the 1987 UNEP Goals and Principles. Recognition by the majority of the Court has since occurred in *Pulp Mills*, in which the Court made clear that it was grounded in customary international law. In addition, the Court drew a connection between EIA and the due diligence standard. The features of EIAs recognised by the ICJ include a requirement that EIAs must be conducted prior to any decision: *Pulp Mills*. In addition, the obligation of the EIA is an ongoing obligation, and requires ongoing monitoring. This aspect of the EIA was emphasised by Judge Weermantry in the *Gabčikovo-Nagymaros* case, see above, and *Pulp Mills*. There is, moreover, a duty to consult with other states where the EIA reveals a risk of transboundary harm: *Nicaragua v.Costa Rica* (at 104). Failure, moreover, to conduct an EIA is justiciable and may be reviewed by a court. The tendency, particularly by the ICJ, to leave the content of EIA under customary international law to domestic law is controversial. There are many differences between EIA in domestic systems and the requirements that tend to be recognised in a transboundary context. For example, in a domestic context, post-project monitoring is frequently not mandatory.

A question in connection with the content of EIAs that arouses controversy is whether there is a requirement to consult the affected population. Rights to public participation are recognised under the Espoo Convention as forming part of an environmental impact assessment. In 2006, the Aarhus Convention was adopted, which is dedicated to providing procedural rights of individuals in respect of public participation in general environmental decision-making beyond just EIA. Moreover, it appears to fall within the procedural right to a healthy environment.[7] As Duvic-Paoli writes:[8]

> Effective public participation in decision-making is becoming an element of increasing importance in the exercise of due diligence to prevent environmental harm. Obligations of 'environmental democracy' — right to information, to participate in decision-making and access to justice — are driven by the principle of prevention, in the sense that they are

---

[5]   Ibid., 661.

[6]   Craik (n 1).

[7]   On human rights and the environment, see Chapter 8.

[8]   L-A Duvic-Paoli, *The Prevention Principle in International Environmental Law* (CUP 2018) 228.

an extension of the logic underpinning the obligation to notify, exchange information and consult other States applied to individuals and communities.

However, the ICJ has so far rejected the proposition that public participation in EIA has customary status. The Inter-American Court of Human Rights has, in its 2018 Advisory Opinion on human rights and the environment, held that the right to public participation is an environmental human right, but did not conclude from this that there is an obligation to invite public participation in EIAs, stating merely that public participation in EIAs is 'recommendable'.

9.2   ENVIRONMENTAL IMPACT ASSESSMENT

9.2.1   Legally Binding Instruments

1982 United Nations Convention on the Law of the Sea, 1833 UNTS 3

Article 206 Assessment of potential effects of activities
When States have reasonable grounds for believing that planned activities under their jurisdiction of control may cause substantial pollution of or significant and harmful changes to the marine environment, they shall, as far as practicable, assess the potential effects of such activities on the marine environment and shall communicate reports of the results of such assessments in the manner provided in article 205.

1992 Convention on Biological Diversity, 1760 UNTS 79

Article 7 Identification and Monitoring
Each Contracting Party shall, as far as possible and as appropriate, in particular for the purposes of Articles 8 to 10:
(c) Identify processes and categories of activities which have or are likely to have significant adverse impacts on the conservation and sustainable use of biological diversity, and monitor their effects through sampling and other techniques;

Article 14
1.   Each Contracting Party, as far as possible and as appropriate, shall:
    (a)   Introduce appropriate procedures requiring environmental impact assessment of its proposed projects that are likely to have significant adverse effects on biological diversity with a view to avoiding or minimizing such effects and, where appropriate, allow for public participation in such procedures;
    (b)   Introduce appropriate arrangements to ensure that the environmental consequences of its programmes and policies that are likely to have significant adverse impacts on biological diversity are duly taken into account;
    (c)   Promote, on the basis of reciprocity, notification, exchange of information and consultation on activities under their jurisdiction or control which are likely to significantly affect adversely the biological diversity of other States or areas beyond the limits of national jurisdiction, by encouraging the conclusion of bilateral, regional or multilateral arrangements, as appropriate;

1991 Espoo Convention on Environmental Impact Assessment in a Transboundary Context, 30 ILM 802

Article 1 Definitions

...

(vi) "Environmental impact assessment" means a national procedure for evaluating the likely impact of a proposed activity on the environment;

(vii) "Impact" means any effect caused by a proposed activity on the environment including human health and safety, flora, fauna, soil, air, water, climate, landscape and historical monuments or other physical structures or the interaction among these factors; it also includes effects on cultural heritage or socio-economic conditions resulting from alterations to those factors;

(viii) "Transboundary impact" means any impact, not exclusively of a global nature, within an area under the jurisdiction of a Party caused by a proposed activity the physical origin of which is situated wholly or in part within the area under the jurisdiction of another Party;

Article 2 General Provisions

1. The Parties shall, either individually or jointly, take all appropriate and effective measures to prevent, reduce and control significant adverse transboundary environmental impact from proposed activities.

2. Each Party shall take the necessary legal, administrative or other measures to implement the provisions of this Convention, including, with respect to proposed activities listed in Appendix I that are likely to cause significant adverse transboundary impact, the establishment of an environmental impact assessment procedure that permits public participation and preparation of the environmental impact assessment documentation described in Appendix II.

3. The Party of origin shall ensure that in accordance with the provisions of this Convention an environmental impact assessment is undertaken prior to a decision to authorize or undertake a proposed activity listed in Appendix I that is likely to cause a significant adverse transboundary impact.

4. The Party of origin shall, consistent with the provisions of this Convention, ensure that affected Parties are notified of a proposed activity listed in Appendix I that is likely to cause a significant adverse transboundary impact.

5. Concerned Parties shall, at the initiative of any such Party, enter into discussions on whether one or more proposed activities not listed in Appendix I is or are likely to cause a significant adverse transboundary impact and thus should be treated as if it or they were so listed. Where those Parties so agree, the activity or activities shall be thus treated. General guidance for identifying criteria to determine significant adverse impact is set forth in Appendix III.

6. The Party of origin shall provide, in accordance with the provisions of this Convention, an opportunity to the public in the areas likely to be affected to participate in relevant environmental impact assessment procedures regarding proposed activities and shall ensure that the opportunity provided to the public of the affected Party is equivalent to that provided to the public of the Party of origin.

7.   Environmental impact assessments as required by this Convention shall, as a minimum requirement, be undertaken at the project level of the proposed activity. To the extent appropriate, the Parties shall endeavour to apply the principles of environmental impact assessment to policies, plans and programmes.

[...]

Article 3 Notification

1.   For a proposed activity listed in Appendix I that is likely to cause a significant adverse transboundary impact, the Party of origin shall, for the purposes of ensuring adequate and effective consultations under Article 5, notify any Party which it considers may be an affected Party as early as possible and no later than when informing its own public about that proposed activity.

2.   This notification shall contain, *inter alia*:
   (a)   Information on the proposed activity, including any available information on its possible transboundary impact;
   (b)   The nature of the possible decision; and
   (c)   An indication of a reasonable time within which a response under paragraph 3 of this Article is required, taking into account the nature of the proposed activity and may include the information set out in paragraph 5 of this Article.

3.   The affected Party shall respond to the Party of origin within the time specified in the notification, acknowledging receipt of the notification, and shall indicate whether it intends to participate in the environmental impact assessment procedure.

4.   If the affected Party indicates that it does not intend to participate in the environmental impact assessment procedure, or if it does not respond within the time specified in the notification, the provisions in paragraphs 5, 6, 7 and 8 of this Article and in Articles 4 to 7 will not apply. In such circumstances the right of a Party of origin to determine whether to carry out an environmental impact assessment on the basis of its national law and practice is not prejudiced.

5.   Upon receipt of a response from the affected Party indicating its desire to participate in the environmental impact assessment procedure, the Party of origin shall, if it has not already done so, provide to the affected Party;
   (a)   Relevant information regarding the environmental impact assessment procedure, including an indication of the time schedule for transmittal of comments; and
   (b)   Relevant information on the proposed activity and its possible significant adverse transboundary impact.

6.   An affected Party shall, at the request of the Party of origin, provide the latter with reasonably obtainable information relating to the potentially affected environment under the jurisdiction of the affected Party, where such information is necessary for the preparation of the environmental impact assessment documentation. The information shall be furnished promptly and, as appropriate, through a joint body where one exists.

7.   When a Party considers that it would be affected by a significant adverse transboundary impact of a proposed activity listed in Appendix I, and when no notifica-

tion has taken place in accordance with paragraph 1 of this Article, the concerned Parties shall, at the request of the affected Party, exchange sufficient information for the purposes of holding discussions on whether there is likely to be a significant adverse transboundary impact. If those Parties agree that there is likely to be a significant adverse transboundary impact, the provisions of this Convention shall apply accordingly. If those Parties cannot agree whether there is likely to be a significant adverse transboundary impact, any such Party may submit that question to an inquiry commission in accordance with the provisions of Appendix IV to advise on the likelihood of significant adverse transboundary impact, unless they agree on another method of settling this question.

Article 4 Preparation of the Environmental Impact Assessment Documentation
1. The environmental impact assessment documentation to be submitted to the competent authority of the Party of origin shall contain, as a minimum, the information described in Appendix II.
2. The Party of origin shall furnish the affected Party, as appropriate through a joint body where one exists, with the environmental impact assessment documentation. The concerned Parties shall arrange for distribution of the documentation to the authorities and the public of the affected Party in the areas likely to be affected and for the submission of comments to the competent authority of the Party of origin, either directly to this authority or, where appropriate, through the Party of origin within a reasonable time before the final decision is taken on the proposed activity.

Article 5 Impact Assessment Documentation
The Party of origin shall, after completion of the environmental impact assessment documentation, without undue delay enter into consultations with the affected Party concerning, *inter alia*, the potential transboundary impact of the proposed activity and measures to reduce or eliminate its impact. Consultations may relate to:
(a) Possible alternatives to the proposed activity, including the no-action alternative and possible measures to mitigate significant adverse transboundary impact and to monitor the effects of such measures at the expense of the Party of origin;
(b) Other forms of possible mutual assistance in reducing any significant adverse transboundary impact of the proposed activity; and
(c) Any other appropriate matters relating to the proposed activity.

The Parties shall agree, at the commencement of such consultations, on a reasonable time-frame for the duration of the consultation period. Any such consultations may be conducted through an appropriate joint body, where one exists.

2003 Protocol on Strategic Environmental Assessment to the Convention on Environmental Impact Assessment in a Transboundary Context 2685 UNTS 140

These include the following:
(1) SEAs should be undertaken by the authority responsible for a plan or programme. It should be integrated into the plan- or programme-making process.
(2) SEAs should be applied as early as possible in the decision-making process when all the alternatives and options remain open for consideration.

(3)   SEAs should focus on the key issues that matter in the relevant stages of the plan- or programme-making process. This will facilitate the process being undertaken in a timely, cost-effective and credible manner.

(4)   SEAs should evaluate a reasonable range of alternatives, recognizing that their scope will vary with the level of decision-making. Wherever possible and appropriate, it should identify the best practicable environmental option.

(5)   SEAs should provide appropriate opportunities for the involvement of key stakeholders and the public, beginning at an early stage in the process and carried out through clear procedures. It should employ easy-to-use consultation techniques that are suitable for the target groups.

(6)   SEAs should be carried out with appropriate and cost-effective methods and techniques of analysis. It should achieve its objectives within the limits of the available information, time and resources and should gather information only in the amount and detail necessary for sound decision-making.

The Protocol defines the following key terms:
The Protocol is stated to have the following objective:

Article 1 Objective

The objective of this Protocol is to provide for a high level of protection of the environment, including health, by:

(a)   Ensuring that environmental, including health, considerations are thoroughly taken into account in the development of plans and programmes;

(b)   Contributing to the consideration of environmental, including health, concerns in the preparation of policies and legislation;

(c)   Establishing clear, transparent and effective procedures for strategic environmental assessment;

(d)   Providing for public participation in strategic environmental assessment; and

(e)   Integrating by these means environmental, including health, concerns into measures and instruments designed to further sustainable development.

Article 2 Definitions

6.   "Strategic environmental assessment" means the evaluation of the likely environmental, including health, effects, which comprises the determination of the scope of an environmental report and its preparation, the carrying-out of public participation and consultations, and the taking into account of the environmental report and the results of the public participation and consultations in a plan or programme.

7.   "Environmental, including health, effect" means any effect on the environment, including human health, flora, fauna, biodiversity, soil, climate, air, water, landscape, natural sites, material assets, cultural heritage and the interaction among these factors.

[...]

Article 3 General Provisions

1.   Each Party shall take the necessary legislative, regulatory and other appropriate measures to implement the provisions of this Protocol within a clear, transparent framework.

2.   Each Party shall endeavour to ensure that officials and authorities assist and provide guidance to the public in matters covered by this Protocol.

3.   Each Party shall provide for appropriate recognition of and support to associations, organizations or groups promoting environmental, including health, protection in the context of this Protocol.

4.   The provisions of this Protocol shall not affect the right of a Party to maintain or introduce additional measures in relation to issues covered by this Protocol.

5.   Each Party shall promote the objectives of this Protocol in relevant international decision-making processes and within the framework of relevant international organizations.

6.   Each Party shall ensure that persons exercising their rights in conformity with the provisions of this Protocol shall not be penalized, persecuted or harassed in any way for their involvement. This provision shall not affect the powers of national courts to award reasonable costs in judicial proceedings.

7.   Within the scope of the relevant provisions of this Protocol, the public shall be able to exercise its rights without discrimination as to citizenship, nationality or domicile and, in the case of a legal person, without discrimination as to where it has its registered seat or an effective centre of its activities.

Article 4 Field of Application Concerning Programmes and Plans

1.   Each Party shall ensure that a strategic environmental assessment is carried out for plans and programmes referred to in paragraphs 2, 3 and 4 which are likely to have significant environmental, including health, effects.

2.   The draft plan or programme and the environmental report shall be made available to the authorities referred to in paragraph 1.

3.   Each Party shall ensure that the authorities referred to in paragraph 1 are given, in an early, timely and effective manner, the opportunity to express their opinion on the draft plan or programme and the environmental report.

4.   Each Party shall determine the detailed arrangements for informing and consulting the environmental and health authorities referred to in paragraph 1.

1991 Protocol on Environmental Protection to the Antarctic Treaty, 30 ILM 1455

Article 8 Environmental Impact Assessment

1.   Proposed activities referred to in paragraph 2 below shall be subject to the procedures set out in Annex I for prior assessment of the impacts of those activities on the Antarctic environment or on dependent or associated ecosystems according to whether those activities are identified as having:
        (a)   less than a minor or transitory impact;
        (b)   a minor or transitory impact; or
        (c)   more than a minor or transitory impact.

2.   Each Party shall ensure that the assessment procedures set out in Annex I are applied in the planning processes leading to decisions about any activities undertaken in the Antarctic Treaty area pursuant to scientific research programmes, tourism and all other governmental and non-governmental activities in the Antarctic Treaty area for which advance notice is required under Article VII (5) of the Antarctic Treaty, including associated logistic support activities.

3.   The assessment procedures set out in Annex I shall apply to any change in an activity whether the change arises from an increase or decrease in the intensity of an existing activity, from the addition of an activity, the decommissioning of a facility, or otherwise.

9.2.2 Non-Binding Instruments

1982 World Charter for Nature

II Functions

7.   In the planning and implementation of social and economic development activities, due account shall be taken of the fact that the conservation of nature is an integral part of those activities.

8.   In formulating long-term plans for economic development, population growth and the improvement of standards of living, due account shall be taken of the long-term capacity of natural systems to ensure the subsistence and settlement of the populations concerned, recognizing that this capacity may be enhanced through science and technology.

...

11.   Activities which might have an impact on nature shall be controlled, and the best available technologies that minimize significant risks to nature or other adverse effects shall be used; in particular:

...

(b)   Activities which are likely to pose a significant risk to nature shall be preceded by an exhaustive examination; their proponents shall demonstrate that expected benefits outweigh potential damage to nature, and where potential adverse effects are not fully understood, the activities should not proceed;

(c)   Activities which may disturb nature shall be preceded by assessment of their consequences, and environmental impact studies of development projects shall be conducted sufficiently in advance, and if they are to be undertaken, such activities shall be planned and carried out so as to minimize potential adverse effects;

1987 UNEP Goals and Principles of Environmental Impact Assessment

Goals

1.   To establish that before decisions are taken by the competent authority or authorities to undertake or to authorize activities that are likely to significantly affect the environment, the environmental effects of those activities should be taken fully into account.

2.   To promote the implementation of appropriate procedures in all countries consistent with national laws and decision-making processes, through which the foregoing goal may be realized.

3.   To encourage the development of reciprocal procedures for information exchange, notification and consultation between States when proposed activities are likely to have significant transboundary effects on the environment of those States.

Principles

Principle 1

States (including their competent authorities) should not undertake or authorize activities without prior consideration, at an early stage, of their environmental effects. Where the extent, nature or location of a proposed activity is such that it is likely to significantly affect the environment, a comprehensive environmental impact assessment should be undertaken in accordance with the following principles.

Principle 2

The criteria and procedures for determining whether an activity is likely to significantly affect the environment and is therefore subject to an EIA, should be defined clearly by Legislation, regulation, or other means, so that subject activities can be quickly and surely identified, and EIA can be applied as the activity is being planned.[2]

Principle 3

In the EIA process the relevant significant environmental issues should be identified and studied. Where appropriate, all efforts should be made to identify these issues at an early stage in the process.

Principle 4

An EIA should include, at a minimum:

(a)   A description of the proposed activity;
(b)   A description of the potentially affected environment, including specific information necessary for identifying and assessing the environmental effects of the proposed activity;
(c)   A description of practical alternatives, as appropriate;
(d)   An assessment of the likely or potential environmental impacts of the proposed activity and alternatives, including the direct, indirect, cumulative, short-term and long-term effects;
(e)   An identification and description of measures available to mitigate adverse environmental impacts of the proposed activity and alternatives, and an assessment of those measures;
(f)   An indication of gaps in knowledge and uncertainties which may be encountered in compiling the required information;
(g)   An indication of whether the environment of any other State or areas beyond national jurisdiction is likely to be affected by the proposed activity or alternatives;

(h)   A brief, non-technical summary of the information provided under the above headings.

Principle 5
The environmental effects in an EIA should be assessed with a degree of detail commensurate with their likely environmental significance.

Principle 6
The information provided as part of EIA should be examined impartially prior to the decision.

Principle 7
Before a decision is made on an activity, government agencies, members of the public, experts in relevant disciplines and interested groups should be allowed appropriate opportunity to comment on the EIA.

1992 Rio Declaration

Principle 17
Environmental impact assessment, as a national instrument, shall be undertaken for proposed activities that are likely to have a significant adverse impact on the environment and are subject to a decision of a competent authority.

2001 ILC Draft Articles

Article 7 Assessment of Risk
Any decision in respect of the authorization of an activity within the scope of the present articles shall, in particular, be based on an assessment of the possible transboundary harm caused by that activity, including any environmental impact assessment.
Commentary:
(4)   The practice of requiring an environmental impact assessment has become very prevalent in order to assess whether a particular activity has the potential of causing significant transboundary harm. The legal obligation to conduct an environmental impact assessment under national law was first developed in the United States of America in the 1970s. Later, Canada and Europe adopted the same approach and essentially regulated it by guidelines. In 1985, a European Community directive required member States to conform to a minimum requirement of environmental impact assessment. Since then, many other countries have also made environmental impact assessment a necessary condition under their national law for authorization to be granted for developmental but hazardous industrial activities. According to one United Nations study, the environmental impact assessment has already shown its value for implementing and strengthening sustainable development, as it combines the precautionary principle with the principle of preventing environmental damage and also allows for public participation.
(5)   The question of who should conduct the assessment is left to States. Such assessment is normally conducted by operators observing certain guidelines set by the States. These matters would have to be resolved by the States themselves through their domestic laws or as parties to international instruments. However, it is

presumed that a State of origin will designate an authority, whether or not governmental, to evaluate the assessment on behalf of the Government and will accept responsibility for the conclusions reached by that authority.

(6)   The article does not specify what the content of the risk assessment should be. Obviously, the assessment of risk of an activity can only be meaningfully prepared if it relates the risk to the possible harm to which the risk could lead. This corresponds to the basic duty contained in article 3. Most existing international conventions and legal instruments do not specify the content of assessment. There are exceptions, such as the Convention on Environmental Impact Assessment in a Transboundary Context, which provides in detail the content of such assessment. The 1981 study of the legal aspects concerning the environment related to offshore mining and drilling within the limits of national jurisdiction, prepared by the Working Group of Experts on Environmental Law of UNEP, also provides, in its conclusion No. 8, in detail the content of assessment for offshore mining and drilling.

(7)   The specifics of what ought to be the content of assessment is left to the domestic laws of the State conducting such assessment. For the purposes of article 7, however, such an assessment should contain an evaluation of the possible transboundary harmful impact of the activity. In order for the States likely to be affected to evaluate the risk to which they might be exposed, they need to know what possible harmful effects that activity might have on them.

(8)   The assessment should include the effects of the activity not only on persons and property, but also on the environment of other States. The importance of the protection of the environment, independently of any harm to individual human beings or property, is clearly recognized.

(9)   This article does not oblige the State of origin to require risk assessment for any activity being undertaken within their territory or otherwise under their jurisdiction or control. Activities involving a risk of causing significant transboundary harm have some general characteristics which are identifiable and could provide some indication to States as to which activities might fall within the terms of these articles. For example, the type of the source of energy used in manufacturing, the location of the activity and its proximity to the border area, etc. could all give an indication of whether the activity might fall within the scope of these articles. There are certain substances that are listed in some conventions as dangerous or hazardous and their use in any activity may in itself be an indication that those activities might involve a risk of significant transboundary harm. There are also certain conventions that list the activities that are presumed to be harmful and that might signal that those activities might fall within the scope of these articles.

Article 8 Notification and Information

1.   If the assessment referred to in article indicates a risk of causing significant transboundary harm, the State of origin shall provide the State likely to be affected with timely notification of the risk and the assessment and shall transmit to it the available technical and all other relevant information on which the assessment is based.

2.   The State of origin shall not take any decision on authorization of the activity pending the receipt, within a period not exceeding six months, of the response from the State likely to be affected.

Article 13. Information to the Public

States concerned shall, by such means as are appropriate, provide the public likely to be affected by an activity within the scope of the present articles with relevant information relating to that activity, the risk involved and the harm which might result and ascertain their views.

DECISION ADOPTED BY THE CONFERENCE OF THE PARTIES TO THE CONVENTION ON BIOLOGICAL DIVERSITY AT ITS EIGHTH MEETING VIII/28.
Impact assessment: Voluntary guidelines on biodiversity-inclusive impact assessment
UNEP/CBD/COP/DEC/VIII/28 (15 June 2006)

Environmental impact assessment

3.   Endorses the voluntary guidelines on biodiversity-inclusive environmental impact assessment contained in the annex to the present decision;

4.   Emphasizes that the voluntary guidelines on biodiversity-inclusive environmental impact assessment are intended to serve as guidance for Parties and other Governments, subject to their national legislation, and for regional authorities or international agencies, as appropriate, in the development and implementation of their impact-assessment instruments and procedures;

5.   Urges Parties, other Governments and relevant organizations to apply the voluntary guidelines on biodiversity-inclusive environmental impact assessment as appropriate in the context of their implementation of paragraph 1 (a) of Article 14 of the Convention and of target 5.1 of the provisional framework of goals and targets for assessing progress towards 2010 and to share their experience, *inter alia*, through the clearing-house mechanism and national reporting;

[…]

Strategic environmental assessment

9.   Endorses the draft guidance on biodiversity-inclusive strategic environmental assessment contained in annex II to the note by the Executive Secretary on voluntary guidelines on biodiversity-inclusive impact assessment (UNEP/CBD/COP/8/27/Add.2);

10.   Encourages Parties, other Governments and relevant organizations to take into account as appropriate this guidance in the context of their implementation of paragraph 1 (b) of Article 14 of the Convention and other relevant mandates and to share their experience, *inter alia*, through the clearing-house mechanism;

9.2.3   Case Law

CASE
ICJ, *Request for an Examination of the Situation in Accordance with Paragraph 63 of the Court's Judgment of 20 December 1974 in the Nuclear Tests (New Zealand v. France)*, Case, ICJ Reports 288 (1995)

DISS OP JUDGE WEERAMANTRY

[pp 344–345]
Environmental Impact Assessment (EIA)
This principle is ancillary to the broader principle just discussed. As with the previous principle, this principle is gathering strength and international acceptance, and has reached the level of general recognition at which this Court should take notice of it.

...

This Court, situated as it is at the apex of international tribunals, necessarily enjoys a position of special trust and responsibility in relation to the principles of environmental law, especially those relating to what is described in environmental law as the Global Commons. When a matter is brought before it which raises serious environmental issues of global importance, and a prima facie case is made out of the possibility of environmental damage, the Court is entitled to take into account the Environmental Impact Assessment principle in determining its preliminary approach.

CASE
ICJ, *Gabčíkovo-Nagymaros Project (Hungary v. Slovakia)*, ICJ Reports 7 Sep Op Vice-President Weeramantry

[pp 111–112]
I wish in this opinion to clarify further the scope and extent of the environmental impact principle in the sense that environmental impact assessment means not merely an assessment prior to the commencement of the project, but a continuing assessment and evaluation as long as the project is in operation. This follows from the fact that EIA is a dynamic principle and is not confined to a pre-project evaluation of possible environmental consequences. As long as a project of some magnitude is in operation, EIA must continue, for every such project can have unexpected consequences; and considerations of prudence would point to the need for continuous monitoring.

...

Environmental law in its current state of development would read into treaties which may reasonably be considered to have a significant impact upon the environment, a duty of environmental impact assessment and this means also, whether the treaty expressly so provides or not, a duty of monitoring the environmental impacts of any substantial project during the operation of the scheme.

CASE
ICJ, *Pulp Mills on the River Uruguay (Argentina v. Uruguay)*, ICJ Reports 14 (2010)

204. It is the opinion of the Court that in order for the Parties properly to comply with their obligations under Article 41 (a) and (b) of the 1975 Statute, they must, for the purposes of protecting and preserving the aquatic environment with respect to activities which may be liable to cause transboundary harm, carry out an environmental impact assessment…. In this sense, the obligation to protect and preserve, under Article 41 (a) of the Statute, has to be interpreted in accordance with a practice, which in recent years has gained so much acceptance among States that it may now be considered a requirement under general international law to undertake an environmental impact assessment where there is a risk that the proposed industrial activity may have a significant adverse impact in a transboundary context, in particular, on a shared resource. Moreover, due diligence, and the duty of vigilance and prevention which it implies, would not be considered to have been exercised, if a party planning works liable to affect the régime of the river or the quality of its waters did not undertake an environmental impact assessment on the potential effects of such works.

205. The Court observes that neither the 1975 Statute nor general international law specify the scope and content of an environmental impact assessment. It points out moreover that Argentina and Uruguay are not parties to the Espoo Convention. Finally, the Court notes that the other instrument to which Argentina refers in support of its arguments, namely, the UNEP Goals and Principles, is not binding on the Parties, but, as guidelines issued by an international technical body, has to be taken into account by each Party in accordance with Article 41 (a) in adopting measures within its domestic regulatory framework. Moreover, this instrument provides only that the "environmental effects in an EIA should be assessed with a degree of detail commensurate with their likely environmental significance" (Principle 5) without giving any indication of minimum core components of the assessment. Consequently, it is the view of the Court that it is for each State to determine in its domestic legislation or in the authorization process for the project, the specific content of the environmental impact assessment required in each case, having regard to the nature and magnitude of the proposed development and its likely adverse impact on the environment as well as to the need to exercise due diligence in conducting such an assessment.

ADVISORY OPINION
ITLOS, Responsibilities and Obligations of States Sponsoring Persons and Entities with Respect to Activities in the Area, Advisory Opinion, Case No. 17, ITLOS Reports 10 (Seabed Dispute Chamber) (1 February 2011)

148 ...The Court's reasoning [in *Pulp Mills*] in a transboundary context may also apply to activities with an impact on the environment in an area beyond the limits of national jurisdiction; and the Court's references to "shared resources" may also apply to resources that are the common heritage of mankind. Thus, in light of the customary rule mentioned by the ICJ, it may be considered that environmental impact assessments should be included in the system of consultations and prior notifications set out in article 142 of the Convention with respect to "resource deposits in the Area which lie across limits of national jurisdiction".

CASE
ICJ, *Certain Activities Carried Out by Nicaragua in the Border Area (Costa Rica v. Nicaragua)* and *Construction of a Road in Costa Rica along the San Juan River (Nicaragua v. Costa Rica)*, ICJ Reports 665 (2015)

153. The Court recalls (see paragraph 104 above) that a State's obligation to exercise due diligence in preventing significant transboundary harm requires that State to ascertain whether there is a risk of significant transboundary harm prior to undertaking an activity having the potential adversely to affect the environment of another State. If that is the case, the State concerned must conduct an environmental impact assessment. The obligation in question rests on the State pursuing the activity. Accordingly, in the present case, it fell on Costa Rica, not on Nicaragua, to assess the existence of a risk of significant transboundary harm prior to the construction of the road, on the basis of an objective evaluation of all the relevant circumstances.

154. ...The Court observes that to conduct a preliminary assessment of the risk posed by an activity is one of the ways in which a State can ascertain whether the proposed activity carries a risk of significant transboundary harm. However, Costa Rica has not adduced any evidence that it actually carried out such a preliminary assessment.

155. In evaluating whether, as of the end of 2010, the construction of the road posed a risk of significant transboundary harm, the Court will have regard to the nature and magnitude of the project and the context in which it was to be carried out.

[...]

156. In conclusion, the Court finds that the construction of the road by Costa Rica carried a risk of significant transboundary harm. Therefore, the threshold for triggering the obligation to evaluate the environmental impact of the road project was met.

[...]

159. Having thus concluded that, in the circumstances of this case, there was no emergency justifying the immediate construction of the road, the Court does not need to decide whether there is an emergency exemption from the obligation to carry out an environmental impact assessment in cases where there is a risk of significant transboundary harm.

SEP OP BHANDARI

29. Thus, we see that while the Pulp Mills Judgment elevated the practice of conducting an EIA to an imperative under general international law when certain preconditions are met, at the same time it allowed for a renvoi to domestic law in terms of the procedure and content required when carrying out such an assessment. In view of the paucity of guidance from the Court and other sources of international law, it could plausibly be argued there are presently no minimum binding standards under public international law that nation-States must follow when conducting an EIA.

SEP OP DUGARD

18. In Pulp Mills the Court stated that general international law does not "specify the scope and content of an environmental impact assessment" with the result "that it is for each State to determine in its domestic legislation or in the authorization process for the project, the specific content of the environmental impact assessment required in each case" (ICJ Reports 2010 (I), p. 83, para. 205). This dictum, which is reaffirmed by the Court in the present case (Judgment, para. 104), has on occasion been interpreted as meaning that the environmental impact assessment obligation has no independent content and that there is simply a renvoi to domestic law[4]. This is incorrect. Obviously there are some matters relating to the carrying out of an environmental impact assessment which must be left to domestic law. These include the identity of the authority responsible for conducting the examination, the format of the assessment, the time frame and the procedures to be employed. But there are certain matters inherent in the nature of an environmental impact assessment that must be considered if it is to qualify as an environmental impact assessment and to satisfy the obligation of due diligence in the preparation of an environmental impact assessment. This is made clear by the International Law Commission in its Commentary on Article 7 of its Draft Articles on the Prevention of Transboundary Harm from Hazardous Activities which declares that an environmental impact assessment should relate the risk involved in an activity "to the possible harm to which the risk could lead", contain "an evaluation of the possible transboundary harmful impact of the activity", and include an assessment of the "effects of the activity not only on persons and property, but also on the environment of other States" (YILC, 2001, Vol. II, Part Two, pp. 158-159, paras 6-8).

9.3   PUBLIC PARTICIPATION

9.3.1   Legally Binding Instruments

1991 Espoo Convention

Article 3 Notification
[...]
8.   The concerned Parties shall ensure that the public of the affected Party in the areas likely to be affected be informed of, and be provided with possibilities for making comments or objections on, the proposed activity, and for the transmittal of these comments or objections to the competent authority of the Party of origin, either directly to this authority or, where appropriate, through the Party of origin.

2003 Protocol on Strategic Environmental Assessment to the Convention on Environmental Impact Assessment in a Transboundary Context (the Kiev Protocol) (entered into force in 2013, UNTS vol. 2685 140

Article 8 Public Participation
1.   Each Party shall ensure early, timely and effective opportunities for public participation, when all options are open, in the strategic environmental assessment of plans and programmes.
2.   Each Party, using electronic media or other appropriate means, shall ensure the timely public availability of the draft plan or programme and the environmental report.
3.   Each Party shall ensure that the public concerned, including relevant non-governmental organizations, is identified for the purposes of paragraphs 1 and 4.
4.   Each Party shall ensure that the public referred to in paragraph 3 has the opportunity to express its opinion on the draft plan or programme and the environmental report within a reasonable time frame.
5.   Each Party shall ensure that the detailed arrangements for informing the public and consulting the public concerned are determined and made publicly available. For this purpose, each Party shall take into account to the extent appropriate the elements listed in annex V.

Convention on Access to Information, Public Participation in Decision-making and Access to Justice in Environmental Matters 1998 (adopted 25 June 1998, entered into force 30 October 2001) 2161 UNTS 447 (Aarhus Convention)

Article 1 OBJECTIVE
In order to contribute to the protection of the right of every person of present and future generations to live in an environment adequate to his or her health and well-being, each Party shall guarantee the rights of access to information, public participation in

decision-making, and access to justice in environmental matters in accordance with the provisions of this Convention.

Article 2 DEFINITIONS

For the purposes of this Convention,

1. "Party" means, unless the text otherwise indicates, a Contracting Party to this Convention;
2. "Public authority" means:
    (a) Government at national, regional and other level;
    (b) Natural or legal persons performing public administrative functions under national law, including specific duties, activities or services in relation to the environment;
    (c) Any other natural or legal persons having public responsibilities or functions, or providing public services, in relation to the environment, under the control of a body or person falling within subparagraphs (a) or (b) above;
    (d) The institutions of any regional economic integration organization referred to in article 17 which is a Party to this Convention.

This definition does not include bodies or institutions acting in a judicial or legislative capacity;

3. "Environmental information" means any information in written, visual, aural, electronic or any other material form on:
    (a) The state of elements of the environment, such as air and atmosphere, water, soil, land, landscape and natural sites, biological diversity and its components, including genetically modified organisms, and the interaction among these elements;
    (b) Factors, such as substances, energy, noise and radiation, and activities or measures, including administrative measures, environmental agreements, policies, legislation, plans and programmes, affecting or likely to affect the elements of the environment within the scope of subparagraph (a) above, and cost-benefit and other economic analyses and assumptions used in environmental decision-making;
    (c) The state of human health and safety, conditions of human life, cultural sites and built structures, inasmuch as they are or may be affected by the state of the elements of the environment or, through these elements, by the factors, activities or measures referred to in subparagraph (b) above;
4. "The public" means one or more natural or legal persons, and, in accordance with national legislation or practice, their associations, organizations or groups;
5. "The public concerned" means the public affected or likely to be affected by, or having an interest in, the environmental decision-making — for the purposes of this definition, non-governmental organizations promoting environmental protection and meeting any requirements under national law shall be deemed to have an interest.

Article 3 GENERAL PROVISIONS

1. Each Party shall take the necessary legislative, regulatory and other measures, including measures to achieve compatibility between the provisions implementing the information, public participation and access-to-justice provisions in this Convention, as well as proper enforcement measures, to establish and maintain a clear, transparent and consistent framework to implement the provisions of this Convention.

2. Each Party shall endeavour to ensure that officials and authorities assist and provide guidance to the public in seeking access to information, in facilitating participation in decision-making and in seeking access to justice in environmental matters.

3. Each Party shall promote environmental education and environmental awareness among the public, especially on how to obtain access to information, to participate in decision-making and to obtain access to justice in environmental matters.

4. Each Party shall provide for appropriate recognition of and support to associations, organizations or groups promoting environmental protection and ensure that its national legal system is consistent with this obligation.

5. The provisions of this Convention shall not affect the right of a Party to maintain or introduce measures providing for broader access to information, more extensive public participation in decision-making and wider access to justice in environmental matters than required by this Convention.

6. This Convention shall not require any derogation from existing rights of access to information, public participation in decision-making and access to justice in environmental matters.

7. Each Party shall promote the application of the principles of this Convention in international environmental decision-making processes and within the framework of international organizations in matters relating to the environment.

8. Each Party shall ensure that persons exercising their rights in conformity with the provisions of this Convention shall not be penalized, persecuted or harassed in any way for their involvement. This provision shall not affect the powers of national courts to award reasonable costs in judicial proceedings.

9. Within the scope of the relevant provisions of this Convention, the public shall have access to information, have the possibility to participate in decision-making and have access to justice in environmental matters without discrimination as to citizenship, nationality or domicile and, in the case of a legal person, without discrimination as to where it has its registered seat or an effective centre of its activities.

Article 6
PUBLIC PARTICIPATION IN DECISIONS ON SPECIFIC ACTIVITIES

1. Each Party:
   (a) Shall apply the provisions of this article with respect to decisions on whether to permit proposed activities listed in annex I;
   (b) Shall, in accordance with its national law, also apply the provisions of this article to decisions on proposed activities not listed in annex I which may have a significant effect on the environment. To this end, Parties shall

determine whether such a proposed activity is subject to these provisions; and

(c)   May decide, on a case-by-case basis if so provided under national law, not to apply the provisions of this article to proposed activities serving national defence purposes, if that Party deems that such application would have an adverse effect on these purposes.

2.   The public concerned shall be informed, either by public notice or individually as appropriate, early in an environmental decision-making procedure, and in an adequate, timely and effective manner, *inter alia*, of:

(a)   The proposed activity and the application on which a decision will be taken;

(b)   The nature of possible decisions or the draft decision;

(c)   The public authority responsible for making the decision;

(d)   The envisaged procedure, including, as and when this information can be provided:

   (i)   The commencement of the procedure;

   (ii)   The opportunities for the public to participate;

   (iii)   The time and venue of any envisaged public hearing;

   (iv)   An indication of the public authority from which relevant information can be obtained and where the relevant information has been deposited for examination by the public;

   (v)   An indication of the relevant public authority or any other official body to which comments or questions can be submitted and of the time schedule for transmittal of comments or questions; and

   (vi)   An indication of what environmental information relevant to the proposed activity is available;

(e)   The fact that the activity is subject to a national or transboundary environmental impact assessment procedure.

[...]

Article 7 PUBLIC PARTICIPATION CONCERNING PLANS, PROGRAMMES AND POLICIES RELATING TO THE ENVIRONMENT

Each Party shall make appropriate practical and/or other provisions for the public to participate during the preparation of plans and programmes relating to the environment, within a transparent and fair framework, having provided the necessary information to the public. Within this framework, article 6, paragraphs 3, 4 and 8, shall be applied. The public which may participate shall be identified by the relevant public authority, taking into account the objectives of this Convention. To the extent appropriate, each Party shall endeavour to provide opportunities for public participation in the preparation of policies relating to the environment.

Article 9 ACCESS TO JUSTICE

1.   Each Party shall, within the framework of its national legislation, ensure that any person who considers that his or her request for information under article 4 has been ignored, wrongfully refused, whether in part or in full, inadequately answered, or otherwise not dealt with in accordance with the provisions of that

article, has access to a review procedure before a court of law or another independent and impartial body established by law.

In the circumstances where a Party provides for such a review by a court of law, it shall
ensure that such a person also has access to an expeditious procedure established by law
that is free of charge or inexpensive for reconsideration by a public authority or review by
an independent and impartial body other than a court of law.

Final decisions under this paragraph 1 shall be binding on the public authority holding
the information. Reasons shall be stated in writing, at least where access to information is
refused under this paragraph.

9.3.2   Cases

CASE
ICJ, *Pulp Mills on the River Uruguay (Argentina v. Uruguay)*, ICJ Reports 14
(2010)

(II) CONSULTATION OF THE AFFECTED POPULATIONS

215. The Parties disagree on the extent to which the populations likely to be affected by
the construction of the Orion (Botnia) mill, particularly on the Argentine side of the
river, were consulted in the course of the environmental impact assessment. While
both Parties agree that consultation of the affected populations should form part
of an environmental impact assessment, Argentina asserts that international law
imposes specific obligations on States in this regard. In support of this argument,
Argentina points to Articles 2.6 and 3.8 of the Espoo Convention, Article 13 of the
2001 International Law Commission draft Articles on Prevention of Transboundary
Harm from Hazardous Activities, and Principles 7 and 8 of the UNEP Goals and
Principles. Uruguay considers that the provisions invoked by Argentina cannot serve
as a legal basis for an obligation to consult the affected populations and adds that in
any event the affected populations had indeed been consulted.

216. The Court is of the view that no legal obligation to consult the affected populations
arises for the Parties from the instruments invoked by Argentina.

ADVISORY OPINION
IACtHR, The Environment and Human Rights, Advisory Opinion, OC-23/17 (15
November 2017), Series A No. 23

D. PARTICIPATION OF INTERESTED PARTIES

166. The Court has not ruled on the participation in environmental impact assessments
of interested parties when this is not related to the protection of the rights of indigenous communities. In the case of projects that may affect indigenous and tribal ter-

ritories, the Court has indicated that the community should be allowed to take part in the environmental impact assessment process through consultation. The right to participate in matters that could affect the environment is dealt with, in general, in the section on procedural obligations below (paras 226 to 232).

167. However, regarding the participation of interested parties in environmental impact assessments, the Court notes that in 1987, the United Nations Environmental Programme adopted the Goals and Principles of Environmental Impact Assessments, which established that States should permit experts and interested groups to comment on environmental impact assessments. Even though the principles are not binding, they are recommendations by an international technical body that States should take into account. The Court also notes that the domestic laws of Argentina, Belize, Brazil, Canada, Chile, Colombia, Ecuador, El Salvador, Guatemala, Peru, Dominican Republic, Trinidad and Tobago and Venezuela include provisions that establish public participation in environmental impact assessments while, in general, Bolivia, Costa Rica, Cuba, Honduras and Mexico promote public participation in decisions relating to the environment.

168. The Court considers that, in general, the participation of the interested public allows a more complete assessment of the possible impact of a project or activity and whether it will affect human rights. Thus, it is recommendable that States allow those who could be affected or, in general, any interested person, to have the opportunity to present their opinions or comments on a project or activity before it is approved, while it is being implemented, and after the environmental impact assessment has been issued.

[...]

B.4.B PUBLIC PARTICIPATION

226. Public participation is one of the fundamental pillars of instrumental or procedural rights, because it is through participation that the individual exercises democratic control of the State's activities and is able to question, investigate and assess compliance with public functions. In this regard, public participation allows the individual to become part of the decision-making process and have his or her opinion heard. In particular, public participation enables communities to require accountability from public authorities when taking decisions and, also, improves the efficiency and credibility of government processes. As mentioned on previous occasions, public participation requires implementation of the principles of disclosure and transparency and, above all, should be supported by access to information that permits social control through effective and responsible participation.

227. The right of the public to take part in the management of public affairs is established in Article 23(1)(a) of the American Convention. In the context of indigenous communities, this Court has determined that the State must ensure the rights to consultation and to participation at all stages of the planning and implementation of a project or measure that could have an impact on the territory of an indigenous or

tribal community, or on other rights that are essential for their survival as a people in keeping with their customs and traditions. This means that, in addition to receiving and providing information, the State must make sure that members of the community are aware of the possible risks, including health and environmental risks, so that they can provide a voluntary and informed opinion about any project that could have an impact on their territory within the consultation process. The State must, therefore, create sustained, effective and trustworthy channels for dialogue with the indigenous peoples, through their representative institutions, in the consultation and participation procedures.

228. In the case of environmental matters, participation is a mechanism for integrating public concerns and knowledge into public policy decisions affecting the environment. Moreover, participation in decision-making makes Governments better able to respond promptly to public concerns and demands, build consensus, and secure increased acceptance of and compliance with environmental decisions.

229. The European Court of Human Rights has underlined the importance of public participation in environmental decision-making as a procedural guarantee of the right to private and family life. It has also stressed that an essential element of this procedural guarantee is the ability of individuals to challenge official acts or omissions that affect their rights before an independent authority, and to play an active role in the planning procedures for activities and projects by expressing their opinions.

230. The right of public participation is also reflected in various regional and international instruments relating to the environment and sustainable development, the Declarations of Stockholm and Rio, and the World Charter for Nature which establishes:

All persons, in accordance with their national legislation, shall have the opportunity to participate, individually or with others, in the formulation of decisions of direct concern to their environment, and shall have access to means of redress when their environment has suffered damage or degradation.

231. Therefore, this Court considers that the State obligation to ensure the participation of persons subject to their jurisdiction in decision-making and policies that could affect the environment, without discrimination and in a fair, significant and transparent manner, is derived from the right to participate in public affairs and, to this end, States must have previously ensured access to the necessary information.

232. As regards the moment of the public participation, the State must ensure that there are opportunities for effective participation from the initial stages of the decision-making process, and inform the public about these opportunities for participation. Lastly, different mechanisms exist for public participation in environmental matters including public hearings, notification and consultations, as well as participation in the elaboration and enforcement of laws; there are also mechanisms for judicial review.

QUESTIONS

1. How would you characterise EIA from the point of view usefulness in terms of protection of transboundary watercourses?
2. Do we need EIA if we have the precautionary principle?
3. Identify the core elements of EIA.

FURTHER READING

BOOKS

K Batmeijer and T Koivurova (eds), *Theory and Practice of Transboundary Environmental Impact Assessment* (Martinus Nijhoff 2008)

N Craik, *The International Law of Environmental Impact Assessment* (Cambridge University Press 2010) 64

L-A Duvic-Paoli, *The Prevention Principle in International Environmental Law* (Cambridge University Press 2018)

J Glasson and R Therivel, *Introduction to Environmental Impact Assessment* (5th edn, Routledge 2019)

C Wood, *Environmental Impact Assessment* (2nd edn, Routledge 2002)

CHAPTERS

T Koivurova, 'Transboundary Environmental Impact Assessment in International Law' in S Marsden and T Koivurova (eds), *Transboundary Environmental Impact Assessment in the European Union: The Espoo Convention and its Kiev Protocol on Strategic Environmental Assessment* (Earthscan 2011)

S Marsden, 'Public Participation in Transboundary Environmental Impact Assessment' in B Jessup and K Rubinstein, *Environmental Discourses in Public International Law* (Cambridge University Press 2012)

J Razzaque, 'Information, Public Participation and Access to Justice in Environmental Matters' in E Techera, J Lindley, KN Scott and A Telesetsky (eds), *Routledge Handbook of International Environmental Law* (2nd edn, Routledge 2021)

ARTICLES

P-M Dupuy, 'Soft Law and the International Law of the Environment' (1991) 12 Mich J Int'l L 420

J Ebbeson, 'The Notion of Public Participation in International Environmental Law' (1997) 8 Yearbook of International Environmental Law 51

U Etemire, 'Insights on the UNEP Bali Guidelines and the Development of Environmental Democratic Rights' (2016) 23 Journal of Environmental Law 393

J Knox, 'The Myth and Reality of Transboundary Environmental Impact Assessment' (2002) 96 AJIL 291

L Kong, 'Environmental Impact Assessment under the United Nations Convention on the Law of the Sea' (2011) 10(3) Chinese Journal of International Law 651

P Okowa, 'Procedural Obligations in International Environmental Agreements' (1996) 67 BYBIL 275

B Peters, 'Unpacking the Diversity of Procedural Environmental Rights: The European Convention on Human Rights and the Aarhus Convention' (2018) 30(1) Journal of Environmental Law 1

PART II
SUBSTANTIVE LAW

10
Protection of the marine environment

10.1 INTRODUCTION

The Earth's seas and oceans are of great significance for human beings and the planet. They are essential to the carriage of goods, provide numerous natural resources, and sustain large ecosystems. There is, however, a serious amount of harm done to the oceans, and it is having deleterious consequences. As James Harrison observes,[1]

> In light of the mounting scientific evidence of serious harm to the oceans, the need for action to tackle the problems of marine environmental degradation is now incontestable. [...] The need for collective action is even more obvious in the case of controlling the effects of ships on the marine environment [...]
>   It is for these reasons that the protection of the marine environment should be considered a common concern of humankind, in common with other environmental issues such as the protection of the global atmosphere and the conservation of biological diversity.

Throughout the second half of the 20th century, the international community has sought to limit the harm done to the oceans from human activities. The international legal regimes concerned with protecting marine living resources are addressed in Chapter 11. The focus of the present chapter is on the regulations concerned to limit the impact of pollution on the marine environment.

Although by no means the first international treaty concerned with the protection of the marine environment, the 1982 United Nations Convention on the Law of the Sea (the 'constitution of the oceans') is central to the global governance of the marine environment. As Sands and Peel note, the 'contribution of UNCLOS to the progressive development of international environmental law at the general level cannot be overstated'.[2] The Convention has 168 parties, and provides a comprehensive regime on the law of the sea, including the protection of the

---

[1]   James Harrison, *Saving the Oceans Through Law* (OUP 2017) 2–3.

[2]   P Sands and J Peel, *Principles of International Environmental Law* (4th edn, CUP 2018) 464.

marine environment. Many provisions of UNCLOS are generally regarded to reflect customary international law, and this includes its rules on the marine environment.[3]

The Convention covers the marine environment in general, including a general obligation
incumbent on states to protect and preserve the marine environment, balanced against a recognition of a state's sovereignty over natural resources. Importantly, in complying with measures to prevent pollution, states are obliged not to convert one type of pollution into another
– protection of the oceans is not intended to be attained through the creation of other kinds of
environmental harm. UNCLOS requires global cooperation, in particular in the case of environmental emergencies. The centrepiece of UNCLOS's protection of the marine environment
comes in the form of legal obligations to take steps to prevent, reduce and control pollution.
UNCLOS divides pollution of the marine environment into six categories, according to the
source of the pollution:

(1)   from land-based sources;
(2)   from seabed activities subject to national jurisdiction;
(3)   from activities from the Area;
(4)   by dumping;
(5)   from vessels;
(6)   from or through atmosphere.

UNCLOS regulates the scope of each state party's jurisdiction, both prescriptive and enforcement, in respect of the prevention of each category of pollution. Indeed, Harrison argues that
its most significant legal importance is that it 'establishes the jurisdictional framework that
dictates which States have the power to adopt and enforce rules and standards for maritime
activities in all ocean areas'.[4] It also provides for various other matters, including: scientific
and technical assistance to developing states; monitoring requirements; ice-covered areas;
responsibility and liability; and sovereign immunity.

While UNCLOS provides a global set of rules covering a wide field of regulation, it was
intended to exist alongside various other legal regimes, both those that pre-dated it and
subsequent regimes directed to more particular problems. Indeed, UNCLOS obliges states to
adopt further measures at the international or regional levels. Of these other treaties, they can
be divided into two broad types: (1) regional treaties which provide comprehensive regulation
of marine pollution within a defined geographical area; (2) international or regional treaties
that are 'source specific' – that is, they provide detailed regulation of particular problems of
pollution.[5]

Comprehensive regional treaties are primarily found within UNEP's Regional Seas
Programme ('UNEP RSP'), which began in the 1970s, following the 1972 Stockholm
Conference. It covers 14 geographical areas. The aim of the Programme is to develop various
treaty and soft law norms that are tailored to the particular challenges and circumstances of

---

[3]   Ibid., 462.

[4]   Harrison (n 1) 20.

[5]   Tanaka distinguishes between international source-specific and regional source-specific treaties, and thus sep-
arates them into three categories, see *The International Law of the Sea* (3rd edn, CUP 2019) 331.

each region. Beginning with the adoption of the Mediterranean Action Plan in 1975, 13 of the 14 Regional Seas Programmes have, to date, developed an Action Plan providing a soft law framework for developing protection of the region's marine environment. In addition, 11 regions have adopted treaties governing the local marine environment, of which 10 are currently in force. The form these treaties take is that of a framework convention, supplemented by specific protocols addressing particular, source-specific issues. Of these conventions that exist under the UNEP RSP, some are administered by UNEP, while others are not.

In addition to the UNEP treaties, other comprehensive regional treaties have been concluded in respect of geographical areas outside those covered by UNEP. The two most notable of these treaties are the 1992 OSPAR Convention, for the North-East Atlantic region, and the 1992 Helsinki Convention, for the Baltic region. Both treaties are very detailed and comprehensive, but are perhaps most notable for being progressive in nature and at the forefront of shifts in approach taken to the regulation of various types of pollution.

In terms of sources-based approaches, many sources of pollution are subject to special regulation at the international and regional levels. A notable exception to this is the regulation of land-based sources. Although regional treaties tend to provide rules for land-based pollution, there has yet to be an international treaty on this subject. UNCLOS provides for some very general rules on land-based pollution, but specific detailed regimes equivalent to those governing, e.g., dumping or pollution from vessels have not been concluded. Tanaka provides four explanations for why international regulation is absent from this area: first, land-based pollution arises from various economic activities within the territorial jurisdiction of states, and so it raises a problem of sovereign regulation that states are more hesitant to give up. Second, land-based pollution arises from a greater number of substances and activities than other types of pollution – it arises, in principle, from any activity found on land – and thus is much more complicated to regulate than pollution from other sources. Third, the urgent need for international regulation differs in different geographical areas, and so it is better suited to treatment at a regional level. Fourth, land-based pollution is linked with poverty and development, which is not a problem that can be regulated in the manner that other pollution problems are approached. Instead of hard law at the international level, therefore, there is soft law, most notably in the Global Programme of Action for the Protection of the Marine Environment from Land-Based Activities (1995), which provides a global framework for tackling challenges concerning land-based pollution.

Pollution arising from seabed activities, notably the exploration and extraction of substances from the seabed, are divided into two types by UNCLOS, according to the locus of jurisdictional authority to regulate the activity: activities subject to national jurisdiction and activities in the Area, subject to the authority of the International Seabed Authority, set up under UNCLOS. The International Seabed Authority is empowered under UNCLOS to make regulations to govern activities in the seabed Area, including measures for the protection of the environment. Moreover, the Council of the Seabed Authority is obliged not to approve areas for resource exploitation where 'substantial evidence indicated the rise of serious harm to the marine environment'. In addition to international regulation, offshore activities in connection with seabed exploration and exploitation are subject to several regional treaties, notably OSPAR and the Helsinki Convention.

Pollution as a result of dumping at sea is primarily regulated by the 1972 London Convention and its 1996 Protocol. These instruments constitute the global standards in this area, and are thus implicitly referred to in the UNCLOS provisions on dumping. They are of global application, administered by the IMO, with 87 and 53 parties respectively, accounting for ~58% and 40% of world tonnage. However, they adopt two very different approaches to regulation.

The 1972 Convention adopts what is known as a 'black list'/'grey list' approach. It establishes three categories of waste. The first category of waste, which comprises highly hazardous substances (set out in Annex I), is 'blacklisted', i.e., prohibited from being dumped at sea; the second (substances listed in Annex II) requires a special permit to be granted for dumping ('grey list'); the third category of waste, namely waste not listed in the Annexes, requires a general permit. National authorities are required to comply with certain criteria when granting special and general permits.

The 1996 Protocol was intended to replace the 1972 Convention, and adopts a more restrictive approach, known as 'reverse listing'. The Protocol followed several agreements by the contracting parties restricting permissible waste. In 1985, the parties to the convention agreed to a moratorium on dumping radioactive wastes. In 1993, the parties amended the convention, and incorporated previous resolutions on the prohibition of dumping: industrial wastes, radioactive wastes, other radioactive matter. Under the 'reverse listing' approach adopted in 1996, *all* substances are prohibited *except* for those listed (in Annex I) as permitted. Moreover, where dumping is permitted (because the substance is listed in Annex I, or dumping is due to *force majeure*) the State is required to follow strict procedures to record, monitor and report the incident. Unlike the 1972 Convention, which does not apply to internal waters, the 1996 Protocol also extends to a limited extent to internal waters. More generally, the Protocol is based upon the precautionary principle[6] and the 'polluter pays' principle.[7]

The London Convention regime is supplemented by several regionally specific instruments under both the UNEP RSP and also the OSPAR and Helsinki Conventions.

Pollution from vessels is governed at the international level primarily through the International Convention on Prohibition of Pollution from Ships 1973. Although concluded in 1973, it did not enter into force until 1983, by which time it had already been amended by the 1978 Protocol (which entered into force at the same time). The regime established is generally known as MARPOL. MARPOL is administered by the IMO. It has 156 parties, representing 99.42% of the world's shipping tonnage. The main provisions of the MARPOL Convention are effectively concerned with duties to enforce the Convention, namely by requiring enforcement by state authorities against vessels. The main body of MARPOL comprises six Annexes containing detailed regulations to prevent and control various types of pollution from vessels. The Annexes are regularly amended and new Annexes may also be adopted (and the Appendices may have appendices of their own). The current Annexes cover oil pollution

---

6　　See Chapter 5.
7　　See Chapter 4.

(Annex I); noxious liquid substances in bulk (Appendix II);[8] harmful substances carried by sea in packaged form (Annex III); sewage from ships (Annex IV); garbage from ships (Annex V); air pollution from ships (Annex VI). After MARPOL Annex VI came into force in 2005, the Marine Environment Protection Committee (MEPC) agreed to revise MARPOL Annex VI to strengthen emission limits as a result of technological improvements and implementation experience. Following three years of examination, MEPC 58 (October 2008) adopted the revised MARPOL Annex VI and the associated NOX Technical Code 2008, which came into force on 1 July 2010. The revised Annex VI is aimed at (1) the reduction globally in emissions of sulphur oxide (SOx), (2) reduction of nitrogen oxide (NOx) and particulate matter, and the introduction of emission control areas (ECAs) to further reduce emissions of those air pollutants in designated sea areas.

A feature common to both the London Convention and MARPOL is their ability to be kept up to date by the adoption of amendments. The ease with which they are updated is a result of the use of a tacit amendment procedure. Under one of MARPOL's amendment procedures, the Parties are deemed to have consented to an amendment to one of the Annexes proposed by the IMO where two-thirds of the Parties that are present for the vote are in favour and, following notification by the Secretary-General of the IMO, within a specific period, that must not be less than 10 months, no objection has been received representing either one-third of the states Parties or a number of states comprising not less than 50% of the world's merchant fleet. This enables the IMO to propose effective amendments without the practical difficulties involved in convening all the Parties to the Convention and obtaining their express consent.

The international legal regime for the protection of the marine environment also encompasses several instruments concerned with responding to emergencies. These treaties require states to prepare for and respond to emergencies at sea that would impair the marine environment. The systems these set up for prompt response to emergencies are the complement to the protective regimes discussed above. It is obvious that regimes setting standards in order to pre-empt and prevent harm to the oceans cannot entirely avoid marine disasters, and so other measures are required where such harms occur.[9]

As is apparent from the foregoing, the legal regime for the protection of the marine environment is the subject of a vast amount of detailed and complex regulation. This chapter will, therefore, present only fundamental problems of marine environmental protection. It is organised broadly in line with order of sources of pollution as set out in UNCLOS, although it addresses pollution from seabed activities in areas subject to national jurisdiction and from the Area together, and atmospheric pollution is largely left to Chapters 15 and 16 of this book. This chapter, therefore, commences with the (I) global frameworks, (II) pollution from land-based sources, (III) pollution from seabed activities, (IV) pollution by dumping, (V) pollution from vessels, and (VI) the additional regimes covering emergencies.

---

[8]   These can be found in the International Bulk Chemical Code available at https://www.wartsila.com/encyclopedia/term/international-bulk-chemical-code-(ibc-code) accessed 3 February 2021.

[9]   See further, Harrison (n 1) 160ff.

10.2 GENERAL LEGAL FRAMEWORKS

1982 United Nations Convention on the Law of the Sea, 1833 UNTS 3 ('UNCLOS')

PART I INTRODUCTION
Article 1
Use of terms and scope
1.　　For the purposes of this Convention: […]
　　(4)　　"pollution of the marine environment" means the introduction by man, directly or indirectly, of substances or energy into the marine environment, including estuaries, which results or is likely to result in such deleterious effects as harm to living resources and marine life, hazards to human health, hindrance to marine activities, including fishing and other legitimate uses of the sea, impairment of quality for use of sea water and reduction of amenities;
　　(5) (a)　　"dumping" means:
　　　　(i)　　any deliberate disposal of wastes or other matter from vessels, aircraft, platforms or other man-made structures at sea;
　　　　(ii)　　any deliberate disposal of vessels, aircraft, platforms or other man-made structures at sea;
　　(b)　　"dumping" does not include:
　　　　(i)　　the disposal of wastes or other matter incidental to, or derived from the normal operations of vessels, aircraft, platforms or other man-made structures at sea and their equipment, other than wastes or other matter transported by or to vessels, aircraft, platforms or other man-made structures at sea, operating for the purpose of disposal of such matter or derived from the treatment of such wastes or other matter on such vessels, aircraft, platforms or structures;
　　　　(ii)　　placement of matter for a purpose other than the mere disposal thereof, provided that such placement is not contrary to the aims of this Convention.

PART XII. PROTECTION AND PRESERVATION OF THE MARINE ENVIRONMENT
SECTION 1. GENERAL PROVISIONS

Article 192 General obligation
States have the obligation to protect and preserve the marine environment.

Article 193
Sovereign right of States to exploit their natural resources
States have the sovereign right to exploit their natural resources pursuant to their environmental policies and in accordance with their duty to protect and preserve the marine environment.

Article 194
Measures to prevent, reduce and control pollution of the marine environment
1.   States shall take, individually or jointly as appropriate, all measures consistent with this Convention that are necessary to prevent, reduce and control pollution of the marine environment from any source, using for this purpose the best practicable means at their disposal and in accordance with their capabilities, and they shall endeavour to harmonize their policies in this connection.
2.   States shall take all measures necessary to ensure that activities under their jurisdiction or control are so conducted as not to cause damage by pollution to other States and their environment, and that pollution arising from incidents or activities under their jurisdiction or control does not spread beyond the areas where they exercise sovereign rights in accordance with this Convention.
3.   The measures taken pursuant to this Part shall deal with all sources of pollution of the marine environment. These measures shall include, *inter alia*, those designed to minimize to the fullest possible extent:
(a)   the release of toxic, harmful or noxious substances, especially those which are persistent, from land-based sources, from or through the atmosphere or by dumping;
(b)   pollution from vessels, in particular measures for preventing accidents and dealing with emergencies, ensuring the safety of operations at sea, preventing intentional and unintentional discharges, and regulating the design, construction, equipment, operation and manning of vessels;
(c)   pollution from installations and devices used in exploration or exploitation of the natural resources of the seabed and subsoil, in particular measures for preventing accidents and dealing with emergencies, ensuring the safety of operations at sea, and regulating the design, construction, equipment, operation and manning of such installations or devices;
(d)   pollution from other installations and devices operating in the marine environment, in particular measures for preventing accidents and dealing with emergencies, ensuring the safety of operations at sea, and regulating the design, construction, equipment, operation and manning of such installations or devices.
4.   In taking measures to prevent, reduce or control pollution of the marine environment, States shall refrain from unjustifiable interference with activities carried out by other States in the exercise of their rights and in pursuance of their duties in conformity with this Convention.
5.   The measures taken in accordance with this Part shall include those necessary to protect and preserve rare or fragile ecosystems as well as the habitat of depleted, threatened or endangered species and other forms of marine life.

Article 195
Duty not to transfer damage or hazards or transform one type of pollution into another
In taking measures to prevent, reduce and control pollution of the marine environment, States shall act so as not to transfer, directly or indirectly, damage or hazards from one area to another or transform one type of pollution into another.

[...]

SECTION 5. INTERNATIONAL RULES AND NATIONAL LEGISLATION TO PREVENT, REDUCE AND CONTROL POLLUTION OF THE MARINE ENVIRONMENT

Article 207
Pollution from land-based sources
1.   States shall adopt laws and regulations to prevent, reduce and control pollution of the marine environment from land-based sources, including rivers, estuaries, pipelines and outfall structures, taking into account internationally agreed rules, standards and recommended practices and procedures.
2.   States shall take other measures as may be necessary to prevent, reduce and control such pollution.
3.   States shall endeavour to harmonize their policies in this connection at the appropriate regional level.
4.   States, acting especially through competent international organizations or diplomatic conference, shall endeavour to establish global and regional rules, standards and recommended practices and procedures to prevent, reduce and control pollution of the marine environment from land-based sources, taking into account characteristic regional features, the economic capacity of developing States and their need for economic development. Such rules, standards and recommended practices and procedures shall be re-examined from time to time as necessary.
5.   Laws, regulations, measures, rules, standards and recommended practices and procedures referred to in paragraphs 1, 2 and 4 shall include those designed to minimize, to the fullest extent possible, the release of toxic, harmful or noxious substances, especially those which are persistent, into the marine environment.

Article 208
Pollution from seabed activities subject to national jurisdiction
1   Coastal States shall adopt laws and regulations to prevent, reduce and control pollution of the marine environment arising from or in connection with seabed activities subject to their jurisdiction and from artificial islands, installations and structures under their jurisdiction, pursuant to articles 60 and 80.

[...]

Article 209
Pollution from activities in the Area
1.   International rules, regulations and procedures shall be established in accordance with Part XI to prevent, reduce and control pollution of the marine environment from activities in the Area. Such rules, regulations and procedures shall be re-examined from time to time as necessary.
2.   Subject to the relevant provisions of this section, States shall adopt laws and regulations to prevent, reduce and control pollution of the marine environment from activities in the Area undertaken by vessels, installations, structures and other devices flying their flag or of their registry or operating under their authority, as

the case may be. The requirements of such laws and regulations shall be no less effective than the international rules, regulations and procedures referred to in paragraph 1.

Article 210 Pollution by dumping

1. States shall adopt laws and regulations to prevent, reduce and control pollution of the marine environment by dumping.
2. States shall take other measures as may be necessary to prevent, reduce and control such pollution.
3. Such laws, regulations and measures shall ensure that dumping is not carried out without the permission of the competent authorities of States.
4. States, acting especially through competent international organizations or diplomatic conference, shall endeavour to establish global and regional rules, standards and recommended practices and procedures to prevent, reduce and control such pollution. Such rules, standards and recommended practices and procedures shall be re-examined from time to time as necessary.
5. Dumping within the territorial sea and the exclusive economic zone or onto the continental shelf shall not be carried out without the express prior approval of the coastal State, which has the right to permit, regulate and control such dumping after due consideration of the matter with other States which by reason of their geographical situation may be adversely affected thereby.
6. National laws, regulations and measures shall be no less effective in preventing, reducing and controlling such pollution than the global rules and standards.

Article 211 Pollution from vessels

1. States, acting through the competent international organization or general diplomatic conference, shall establish international rules and standards to prevent, reduce and control pollution of the marine environment from vessels and promote the adoption, in the same manner, wherever appropriate, of routeing systems designed to minimize the threat of accidents which might cause pollution of the marine environment, including the coastline, and pollution damage to the related interests of coastal States. Such rules and standards shall, in the same manner, be re-examined from time to time as necessary.
2. States shall adopt laws and regulations for the prevention, reduction and control of pollution of the marine environment from vessels flying their flag or of their registry. Such laws and regulations shall at least have the same effect as that of generally accepted international rules and standards established through the competent international organization or general diplomatic conference.
3. States which establish particular requirements for the prevention, reduction and control of pollution of the marine environment as a condition for the entry of foreign vessels into their ports or internal waters or for a call at their off-shore terminals shall give due publicity to such requirements and shall communicate them to the competent international organization. Whenever such requirements are established in identical form by two or more coastal States in an endeavour to harmonize policy, the communication shall indicate which States are participating in such cooperative arrangements. Every State shall require the master of a vessel flying its flag or of its registry, when navigating within the territorial sea of a State

participating in such cooperative arrangements, to furnish, upon the request of that State, information as to whether it is proceeding to a State of the same region participating in such cooperative arrangements and, if so, to indicate whether it complies with the port entry requirements of that State. This article is without prejudice to the continued exercise by a vessel of its right of innocent passage or to the application of article 25, paragraph 2.

4.   Coastal States may, in the exercise of their sovereignty within their territorial sea, adopt laws and regulations for the prevention, reduction and control of marine pollution from foreign vessels, including vessels exercising the right of innocent passage. Such laws and regulations shall, in accordance with Part II, section 3, not hamper innocent passage of foreign vessels.

5.   Coastal States, for the purpose of enforcement as provided for in section 6, may in respect of their exclusive economic zones adopt laws and regulations for the prevention, reduction and control of pollution from vessels conforming to and giving effect to generally accepted international rules and standards established through the competent international organization or general diplomatic conference.

6.

(a)   Where the international rules and standards referred to in paragraph 1 are inadequate to meet special circumstances and coastal States have reasonable grounds for believing that a particular, clearly defined area of their respective exclusive economic zones is an area where the adoption of special mandatory measures for the prevention of pollution from vessels is required for recognized technical reasons in relation to its oceanographical and ecological conditions, as well as its utilization or the protection of its resources and the particular character of its traffic, the coastal States, after appropriate consultations through the competent international organization with any other States concerned, may, for that area, direct a communication to that organization, submitting scientific and technical evidence in support and information on necessary reception facilities. Within 12 months after receiving such a communication, the organization shall determine whether the conditions in that area correspond to the requirements set out above. If the organization so determines, the coastal States may, for that area, adopt laws and regulations for the prevention, reduction and control of pollution from vessels implementing such international rules and standards or navigational practices as are made applicable, through the organization, for special areas. These laws and regulations shall not become applicable to foreign vessels until 15 months after the submission of the communication to the organization.

(b)   The coastal States shall publish the limits of any such particular, clearly defined area.

(c)   If the coastal States intend to adopt additional laws and regulations for the same area for the prevention, reduction and control of pollution from vessels, they shall, when submitting the aforesaid communication, at the same time notify the organization thereof. Such additional laws and regulations may relate to discharges or navigational practices but shall not require foreign vessels to observe design, construction, manning or equipment standards other than generally accepted international rules and standards;

they shall become applicable to foreign vessels 15 months after the submission of the communication to the organization, provided that the organization agrees within 12 months after the submission of the communication.

7. The international rules and standards referred to in this article should include *inter alia* those relating to prompt notification to coastal States, whose coastline or related interests may be affected by incidents, including maritime casualties, which involve discharges or probability of discharges.

Article 212
Pollution from or through the atmosphere

1. States shall adopt laws and regulations to prevent, reduce and control pollution of the marine environment from or through the atmosphere, applicable to the air space under their sovereignty and to vessels flying their flag or vessels or aircraft of their registry, taking into account internationally agreed rules, standards and recommended practices and procedures and the safety of air navigation.

[…]

3. States, acting especially through competent international organizations or diplomatic conference, shall endeavour to establish global and regional rules, standards and recommended practices and procedures to prevent, reduce and control such pollution.

SECTION 6. ENFORCEMENT

Article 213 Enforcement with respect to pollution from land-based sources
States shall enforce their laws and regulations adopted in accordance with article 207 and shall adopt laws and regulations and take other measures necessary to implement applicable international rules and standards established through competent international organizations or diplomatic conference to prevent, reduce and control pollution of the marine environment from land-based sources.

Article 214 Enforcement with respect to pollution from seabed activities
States shall enforce their laws and regulations adopted in accordance with article 208 and shall adopt laws and regulations and take other measures necessary to implement applicable international rules and standards established through competent international organizations or diplomatic conference to prevent, reduce and control pollution of the marine environment arising from or in connection with seabed activities subject to their jurisdiction and from artificial islands, installations and structures under their jurisdiction, pursuant to articles 60 and 80.

Article 215 Enforcement with respect to pollution from activities in the Area
Enforcement of international rules, regulations and procedures established in accordance with Part XI to prevent, reduce and control pollution of the marine environment from activities in the Area shall be governed by that Part.

Article 216 Enforcement with respect to pollution by dumping

1.   Laws and regulations adopted in accordance with this Convention and applicable international rules and standards established through competent international organizations or diplomatic conference for the prevention, reduction and control of pollution of the marine environment by dumping shall be enforced:

(a)   by the coastal State with regard to dumping within its territorial sea or its exclusive economic zone or onto its continental shelf;

(b)   by the flag State with regard to vessels flying its flag or vessels or aircraft of its registry;

(c)   by any State with regard to acts of loading of wastes or other matter occurring within its territory or at its off-shore terminals.

2.   No State shall be obliged by virtue of this article to institute proceedings when another State has already instituted proceedings in accordance with this article.

Article 217 Enforcement by flag States

1.   States shall ensure compliance by vessels flying their flag or of their registry with applicable international rules and standards, established through the competent international organization or general diplomatic conference, and with their laws and regulations adopted in accordance with this Convention for the prevention, reduction and control of pollution of the marine environment from vessels and shall accordingly adopt laws and regulations and take other measures necessary for their implementation. Flag States shall provide for the effective enforcement of such rules, standards, laws and regulations, irrespective of where a violation occurs. [...]

Article 218 Enforcement by port States

1.   When a vessel is voluntarily within a port or at an off-shore terminal of a State, that State may undertake investigations and, where the evidence so warrants, institute proceedings in respect of any discharge from that vessel outside the internal waters, territorial sea or exclusive economic zone of that State in violation of applicable international rules and standards established through the competent international organization or general diplomatic conference. [...]

Article 220 Enforcement by coastal States

1.   When a vessel is voluntarily within a port or at an off-shore terminal of a State, that State may, subject to section 7, institute proceedings in respect of any violation of its laws and regulations adopted in accordance with this Convention or applicable international rules and standards for the prevention, reduction and control of pollution from vessels when the violation has occurred within the territorial sea or the exclusive economic zone of that State.

2.   Where there are clear grounds for believing that a vessel navigating in the territorial sea of a State has, during its passage therein, violated laws and regulations of that State adopted in accordance with this Convention or applicable international rules and standards for the prevention, reduction and control of pollution from vessels, that State, without prejudice to the application of the relevant provisions of Part II, section 3, may undertake physical inspection of the vessel relating to the violation

and may, where the evidence so warrants, institute proceedings, including detention of the vessel, in accordance with its laws, subject to the provisions of section 7.

3. Where there are clear grounds for believing that a vessel navigating in the exclusive economic zone or the territorial sea of a State has, in the exclusive economic zone, committed a violation of applicable international rules and standards for the prevention, reduction and control of pollution from vessels or laws and regulations of that State conforming and giving effect to such rules and standards, that State may require the vessel to give information regarding its identity and port of registry, its last and its next port of call and other relevant information required to establish whether a violation has occurred.

[…]

6. Where there is clear objective evidence that a vessel navigating in the exclusive economic zone or the territorial sea of a State has, in the exclusive economic zone, committed a violation referred to in paragraph 3 resulting in a discharge causing major damage or threat of major damage to the coastline or related interests of the coastal State, or to any resources of its territorial sea or exclusive economic zone, that State may, subject to section 7, provided that the evidence so warrants, institute proceedings, including detention of the vessel, in accordance with its laws.

7. Notwithstanding the provisions of paragraph 6, whenever appropriate procedures have been established, either through the competent international organization or as otherwise agreed, whereby compliance with requirements for bonding or other appropriate financial security has been assured, the coastal State if bound by such procedures shall allow the vessel to proceed.

[…]

SECTION 11. OBLIGATIONS UNDER OTHER CONVENTIONS ON THE PROTECTION AND PRESERVATION OF THE MARINE ENVIRONMENT

Article 237
Obligations under other conventions on the protection and preservation of the marine environment

- The provisions of this Part are without prejudice to the specific obligations assumed by States under special conventions and agreements concluded previously which relate to the protection and preservation of the marine environment and to agreements which may be concluded in furtherance of the general principles set forth in this Convention.

2. Specific obligations assumed by States under special conventions, with respect to the protection and preservation of the marine environment, should be carried out in a manner consistent with the general principles and objectives of this Convention.

10.3   LAND-BASED SOURCES

10.3.1   Legally Binding Instruments

1992 OSPAR Convention

Article 3

The Contracting Parties shall take, individually and jointly, all possible steps to prevent and eliminate pollution from land-based sources in accordance with the provisions of the Convention, in particular as provided for in Annex I.

1992 Helsinki Convention

Article 6

1.   The Contracting Parties undertake to prevent and eliminate pollution of the Baltic Sea Area from land-based sources by using, *inter alia*, Best Environmental Practice for all sources and Best Available Technology for point sources. The relevant measures to this end shall be taken by each Contracting Party in the catchment area of the Baltic Sea without prejudice to its sovereignty.

2.   The Contracting Parties shall implement the procedures and measures set out in Annex III. To this end they shall, *inter alia*, as appropriate co-operate in the development and adoption of specific programmes, guidelines, standards or regulations concerning emissions and inputs to water and air, environmental quality, and products containing harmful substances and materials and the use thereof.

3.   Harmful substances from point sources shall not, except in negligible quantities, be introduced directly or indirectly into the marine environment of the Baltic Sea Area, without a prior special permit, which may be periodically reviewed, issued by the appropriate national authority in accordance with the principles contained in Annex III, Regulation 3. The Contracting Parties shall ensure that authorized emissions to water and air are monitored and controlled.

4.   If the input from a watercourse, flowing through the territories of two or more Contracting Parties or forming a boundary between them, is liable to cause pollution of the marine environment of the Baltic Sea Area, the Contracting Parties concerned shall jointly and, if possible, in co-operation with a third state interested or concerned, take appropriate measures in order to prevent and eliminate such pollution.

10.3.2   Non-Legally Binding Instruments

Table 10.1 Pollution from land-based sources: main non-binding instruments

Montreal Guidelines for the Protection of the Marine Environment Against Pollution from Land-Based Sources (1985)
Agenda 21 (1992)
Washington Declaration on the Protection of the Marine Environment from Land-Based Activities (1993)
Global Programme of Action for the Protection of the Marine Environment from Land-Based Activities (1995)
Montreal Declaration on the Protection of the Marine Environment from Land-Based Activities (2001)
Manila Declaration on Furthering the Implementation of the Global Programme of Action for the Protection of the Marine Environment from Land-Based Activities (2012)

10.4   SEABED ACTIVITIES

10.4.1   Legally Binding Instruments

10.4.1.1 International

UNCLOS

Article 145 Protection of the marine environment

Necessary measures shall be taken in accordance with this Convention with respect to activities in the Area to ensure effective protection for the marine environment from harmful effects which may arise from such activities. To this end the Authority shall adopt appropriate rules, regulations and procedures for *inter alia*:

(a)   the prevention, reduction and control of pollution and other hazards to the marine environment, including the coastline, and of interference with the ecological balance of the marine environment, particular attention being paid to the need for protection from harmful effects of such activities as drilling, dredging, excavation, disposal of waste, construction and operation or maintenance of installations, pipelines and other devices related to such activities;

(b)   the protection and conservation of the natural resources of the Area and the prevention of damage to the flora and fauna of the marine environment.

Article 162 Powers and functions

1.   The Council is the executive organ of the Authority. The Council shall have the power to establish, in conformity with this Convention and the general policies established by the Assembly, the specific policies to be pursued by the Authority on any question or matter within the competence of the Authority.

2.   In addition, the Council shall:

[…]

(w)   issue emergency orders, which may include orders for the suspension or adjustment of operations, to prevent serious harm to the marine environment arising out of activities in the Area;

(x)   disapprove areas for exploitation by contractors or the Enterprise in cases where substantial evidence indicates the risk of serious harm to the marine environment;

10.4.1.2 Regional

1992 OSPAR Convention

Article 5 POLLUTION FROM OFFSHORE SOURCES
The Contracting Parties shall take, individually and jointly, all possible steps to prevent and eliminate pollution from offshore sources in accordance with the provisions of the Convention, in particular as provided for in Annex III.

ANNEX III ON THE PREVENTION AND ELIMINATION OF POLLUTION FROM OFFSHORE SOURCES

ARTICLE 3
1.   Any dumping of wastes or other matter from offshore installations is prohibited.
2.   This prohibition does not relate to discharges or emissions from offshore sources.
3.   The prohibition referred to in paragraph 1 of this Article does not apply to carbon dioxide streams from carbon dioxide capture processes for storage, provided
    (a)   disposal is into a sub-soil geological formation;
    (b)   the streams consist overwhelmingly of carbon dioxide. They may contain incidental associated substances derived from the source material and the capture, transport and storage processes used;
    (c)   no wastes or other matter are added for the purpose of disposing of those wastes or other matter;
    (d)   they are intended to be retained in these formations permanently and will not lead to significant adverse consequences for the marine environment, human health and other legitimate uses of the maritime area.
4.   The Contracting Parties shall ensure that no streams referred to in paragraph 3 shall be disposed of in sub-soil geological formations without authorisation or regulation by their competent authorities. Such authorisation or regulation shall, in particular, implement the relevant applicable decisions, recommendations and all other agreements adopted under the Convention.

ARTICLE 4
1.   The use on, or the discharge or emission from, offshore sources of substances which may reach and affect the maritime area shall be strictly subject to authorisation or regulation by the competent authorities of the Contracting Parties. Such authorisation or regulation shall, in particular, implement the relevant applicable decisions, recommendations and all other agreements adopted under the Convention.

2.   The competent authorities of the Contracting Parties shall provide for a system of monitoring and inspection to assess compliance with authorisation or regulation as provided for in paragraph 1 of Article 4 of this Annex.

[...]

ARTICLE 6

Articles 3 and 5 of this Annex shall not apply in case of force majeure, due to stress of weather or any other cause, when the safety of human life or of an offshore installation is threatened. Such dumping shall be so conducted as to minimise the likelihood of damage to human or marine life and shall immediately be reported to the Commission, together with full details of the circumstances and of the nature and quantities of the matter dumped.

10.5   DUMPING

10.5.1   Legal Instruments

10.5.1.1 International

1972 London Convention on the Prevention of Marine Pollution by Dumping of Wastes and Other Matter, 1046 UNTS 120

[Preamble:]
THE CONTRACTING PARTIES TO THIS CONVENTION,

RECOGNIZING that the marine environment and the living organisms which it supports are of vital importance to humanity, and all people have an interest in assuring that it is so managed that its quality and resources are not impaired;

RECOGNIZING that the capacity of the sea to assimilate wastes and render them harmless, and its ability to regenerate natural resources, is not unlimited;

RECOGNIZING that States have, in accordance with the Charter of the United Nations and the principles of international law, the sovereign right to exploit their own resources pursuant to their own environmental policies, and the responsibility to ensure that activities within their jurisdiction or control do not cause damage to the environment of other States or of areas beyond the limits of national jurisdiction;

RECALLING resolution 2749(XXV) of the General Assembly of the United Nations on the principles governing the sea-bed and the ocean floor and the subsoil thereof, beyond the limits of national jurisdiction;

NOTING that marine pollution originates in many sources, such as dumping and discharges through the atmosphere, rivers, estuaries, outfalls and pipelines, and that it is important that States use the best practicable means to prevent such pollution and develop products and processes which will reduce the amount of harmful wastes to be disposed of;

BEING CONVINCED that international action to control the pollution of the sea by dumping can and must be taken without delay but that this action should not preclude discussion of measures to control other sources of marine pollution as soon as possible; and

WISHING to improve protection of the marine environment by encouraging States with a common interest in particular geographical areas to enter into appropriate agreements supplementary to this Convention;

HAVE AGREED as follows:

Article I
Contracting Parties shall individually and collectively promote the effective control of all sources of pollution of the marine environment, and pledge themselves especially to take all practicable steps to prevent the pollution of the sea by the dumping of waste and other matter that is liable to create hazards to human health, to harm living resources and marine life, to damage amenities or to interfere with other legitimate uses of the sea.

Article II
Contracting Parties shall, as provided for in the following articles, take effective measures individually, according to their scientific, technical and economic capabilities, and collectively, to prevent marine pollution caused by dumping and shall harmonize their policies in this regard.

Article III
For the purposes of this Convention:

1 (a) "Dumping" means:
   (i)   any deliberate disposal at sea of wastes or other matter from vessels, aircraft, platforms or other man-made structures at sea;
   (ii) any deliberate disposal at sea of vessels, aircraft, platforms or other man-made structures at sea.

(b) "Dumping" does not include:
   (i)   the disposal at sea of wastes or other matter incidental to, or derived from the normal operations of vessels, aircraft, platforms or other man-made structures at sea and their equipment, other than wastes or other matter transported by or to vessels, aircraft, platforms or other man-made structures at sea, operating for the purpose of disposal of such matter or derived from the treatment of such wastes or other matter on such vessels, aircraft, platforms or structures;
   (ii) placement of matter for a purpose other than the mere disposal thereof, provided that such placement is not contrary to the aims of this Convention.

(c) The disposal of wastes or other matter directly arising from, or related to the exploration, exploitation and associated off-shore processing of sea-bed mineral resources will not be covered by the provisions of this Convention.

2   "Vessels and aircraft" means waterborne or airborne craft of any type whatsoever. This expression includes air cushioned craft and floating craft, whether self-propelled or not.

3   "Sea" means all marine waters other than the internal waters of States.

4   "Wastes or other matter" means material and substance of any kind, form or description.

5   "Special permit" means permission granted specifically on application in advance and in accordance with Annex II and Annex III.

6   "General permit" means permission granted in advance and in accordance with
        Annex III.
7   "The Organization" means the Organization designated by the Contracting Parties
        in accordance with article XIV(2).

Article IV
1   In accordance with the provisions of this Convention Contracting Parties shall
        prohibit the dumping of any wastes or other matter in whatever form or condition
        except as otherwise specified below:
        (a)   the dumping of wastes or other matter listed in Annex I is prohibited;
        (b)   the dumping of wastes or other matter listed in Annex II requires a prior
                special permit;
        (c)   the dumping of all other wastes or matter requires a prior general permit.
2   Any permit shall be issued only after careful consideration of all the factors set forth
        in Annex III, including prior studies of the characteristics of the dumping site, as
        set forth in sections B and C of that Annex.
3   No provision of this Convention is to be interpreted as preventing a Contracting
        Party from prohibiting, insofar as that Party is concerned, the dumping of wastes
        or other matter not mentioned in Annex I. That Party shall notify such measures to
        the Organization.

1996 Protocol to the Convention on the Prevention of Marine Pollution by Dumping (as amended in 2006)

ARTICLE 1 DEFINITIONS
[…]
4.1   "Dumping" means:

                .1   any deliberate disposal into the sea of wastes or other matter from
                        vessels, aircraft, platforms or other man-made structures at sea;
                .2   any deliberate disposal into the sea of vessels, aircraft, platforms or
                        other man-made structures at sea;
                .3   any storage of wastes or other matter in the seabed and the subsoil
                        thereof from vessels, aircraft, platforms or other man-made struc-
                        tures at sea; and
                .4   any abandonment or toppling at site of platforms or other man-made
                        structures at sea, for the sole purpose of deliberate disposal.

        2
        .2   "Dumping" does not include:
                .1   the disposal into the sea of wastes or other matter incidental to, or
                        derived from the normal operations of vessels, aircraft, platforms
                        or other man-made structures at sea and their equipment, other
                        than wastes or other matter transported by or to vessels, aircraft,
                        platforms or other man-made structures at sea, operating for the
                        purpose of disposal of such matter or derived from the treatment of
                        such wastes or other matter on such vessels, aircraft, platforms or
                        other man-made structures;

      .2   placement of matter for a purpose other than the mere disposal thereof, provided that such placement is not contrary to the aims of this Protocol; and

      .3   notwithstanding paragraph 4.1.4, abandonment in the sea of matter (e.g., cables, pipelines and marine research devices) placed for a purpose other than the mere disposal thereof.

.3   The disposal or storage of wastes or other matter directly arising from, or related to the exploration, exploitation and associated off-shore processing of seabed mineral resources is not covered by the provisions of this Protocol.

5   .1   "Incineration at sea" means the combustion on board a vessel, platform or other man-made structure at sea of wastes or other matter for the purpose of their deliberate disposal by thermal destruction.

      .2   "Incineration at sea" does not include the incineration of wastes or other matter on board a vessel, platform, or other man-made structure at sea if such wastes or other matter were generated during the normal operation of that vessel, platform or other man-made structure at sea.

6   "Vessels and aircraft" means waterborne or airborne craft of any type whatsoever. This expression includes air-cushioned craft and floating craft, whether self-propelled or not.

7   "Sea" means all marine waters other than the internal waters of States, as well as the seabed and the subsoil thereof; it does not include sub-seabed repositories accessed only from land.

8   "Wastes or other matter" means material and substance of any kind, form or description.

9   "Permit" means permission granted in advance and in accordance with relevant measures adopted pursuant to article 4.1.2 or 8.2.

10   "Pollution" means the introduction, directly or indirectly, by human activity, of wastes or other matter into the sea which results or is likely to result in such deleterious effects as harm to living resources and marine ecosystems, hazards to human health, hindrance to marine activities, including fishing and other legitimate uses of the sea, impairment of quality for use of sea water and reduction of amenities.

ARTICLE 2 OBJECTIVES

Contracting Parties shall individually and collectively protect and preserve the marine environment from all sources of pollution and take effective measures, according to their scientific, technical and economic capabilities, to prevent, reduce and where practicable eliminate pollution caused by dumping or incineration at sea of wastes or other matter. Where appropriate, they shall harmonize their policies in this regard.

ARTICLE 3 GENERAL OBLIGATIONS

1   In implementing this Protocol, Contracting Parties shall apply a precautionary approach to environmental protection from dumping of wastes or other matter whereby appropriate preventative measures are taken when there is reason to believe that wastes or other matter introduced into the marine environment are likely to cause harm even when there is no conclusive evidence to prove a causal relation between inputs and their effects.

2   Taking into account the approach that the polluter should, in principle, bear the cost of pollution, each Contracting Party shall endeavour to promote practices whereby those it has authorized to engage in dumping or incineration at sea bear the cost of meeting the pollution prevention and control requirements for the authorized activities, having due regard to the public interest.

3   In implementing the provisions of this Protocol, Contracting Parties shall act so as not to transfer, directly or indirectly, damage or likelihood of damage from one part of the environment to another or transform one type of pollution into another.

4   No provision of this Protocol shall be interpreted as preventing Contracting Parties from taking, individually or jointly, more stringent measures in accordance with international law with respect to the prevention, reduction and where practicable elimination of pollution.

ARTICLE 4 DUMPING OF WASTES OR OTHER MATTER
Contracting Parties shall prohibit the dumping of any wastes or other matter with the exception of those listed in Annex 1.

4
　.2   The dumping of wastes or other matter listed in Annex 1 shall require a permit. Contracting Parties shall adopt administrative or legislative measures to ensure that issuance of permits and permit conditions comply with provisions of Annex 2. Particular attention shall be paid to opportunities to avoid dumping in favour of environmentally preferable alternatives.

2   No provision of this Protocol shall be interpreted as preventing a Contracting Party from prohibiting, insofar as that Contracting Party is concerned, the dumping of wastes or other matter mentioned in Annex 1. That Contracting Party shall notify the Organization of such measures.

10.5.1.2 Regional

1992 OSPAR Convention

Article 4 Pollution by Dumping or Incineration
The Contracting Parties shall take, individually and jointly, all possible steps to prevent and eliminate pollution by dumping or incineration of wastes or other matter in accordance with the provisions of the Convention, in particular as provided for in Annex II.

1992 Helsinki Convention

Article 11 Prevention of Dumping
1.   The Contracting Parties shall, subject to exemptions set forth in paragraphs 2 and 4 of this Article, prohibit dumping in the Baltic Sea Area.

2.   Dumping of dredged material shall be subject to a prior special permit issued by the appropriate national authority in accordance with the provisions of Annex V.

3.   Each Contracting Party undertakes to ensure compliance with the provisions of this Article by ships and aircraft:
    a)   registered in its territory or flying its flag;
    b)   loading, within its territory or territorial sea, matter which is to be dumped; or
    c)   believed to be engaged in dumping within its internal waters and territorial sea.

4.   The provisions of this Article shall not apply when the safety of human life or of a ship or aircraft at sea is threatened by the complete destruction or total loss of the ship or aircraft, or in any case which constitutes a danger to human life, if dumping appears to be the only way of averting the threat and if there is every probability that the damage consequent upon such dumping will be less than would otherwise occur. Such dumping shall be so conducted as to minimize the likelihood of damage to human or marine life.

5.   Dumping made under the provisions of paragraph 4 of this Article shall be reported and dealt with in accordance with Annex VII and shall be reported forthwith to the Commission in accordance with the provisions of Regulation 4 of Annex V.

6.   In case of dumping suspected to be in contravention of the provisions of this Article the Contracting Parties shall co-operate in investigating the matter in accordance with Regulation 2 of Annex IV.

10.6   VESSELS

10.6.1   Legal Instruments

10.6.1.1 International

MARPOL

1973 International Convention for the Prevention of Pollution from Ships

Article 1

General obligations under the Convention

(1)   The Parties to the Convention undertake to give effect to the provisions of the present Convention and those Annexes thereto by which they are bound, in order to prevent the pollution of the marine environment by the discharge of harmful substances or effluents containing such substances in contravention of the Convention.

(2)   Unless expressly provided otherwise, a reference to the present Convention constitutes at the same time a reference to its Protocols and to the Annexes.

Article 2

Definitions

For the purposes of the present Convention, unless expressly provided otherwise:

(1)   Regulation means the regulations contained in the Annexes to the present Convention.

(2)   Harmful substance means any substance which, if introduced into the sea, is liable to create hazards to human health, to harm living resources and marine life, to damage amenities or to interfere with other legitimate uses of the sea, and includes any substance subject to control by the present Convention.

(3)

   (a) Discharge, in relation to harmful substances or effluents containing such substances, means any release howsoever caused from a ship and includes any escape, disposal, spilling, leaking, pumping, emitting or emptying;

   (b) Discharge does not include:

      (i) dumping within the meaning of the Convention on the Prevention of Marine Pollution by Dumping of Wastes and Other Matter, done at London on 13 November 1972; or

      (ii) release of harmful substances directly arising from the exploration, exploitation and associated offshore processing of sea-bed mineral resources; or

      (iii) release of harmful substances for purposes of legitimate scientific research into pollution abatement or control.

(4) Ship means a vessel of any type whatsoever operating in the marine environment and includes hydrofoil boats, air-cushion vehicles, submersibles, floating craft and fixed or floating platforms.

(5) Administration means the Government of the State under whose authority the ship is operating. With respect to a ship entitled to fly a flag of any State, the Administration is the Government of that State. With respect to fixed or floating platforms engaged in exploration and exploitation of the sea-bed and subsoil thereof adjacent to the coast over which the coastal State exercises sovereign rights for the purposes of exploration and exploitation of their natural resources, the Administration is the Government of the coastal State concerned.

(6) Incident means an event involving the actual or probable discharge into the sea of a harmful substance, or effluents containing such a substance.

(7) Organization means the Inter-Governmental Maritime Consultative Organization.

Article 3
Application

(1) The present Convention shall apply to:

   (a) ships entitled to fly the flag of a Party to the Convention; and

   (b) ships not entitled to fly the flag of a Party but which operate under the authority of a Party.

(2) Nothing in the present article shall be construed as derogating from or extending the sovereign rights of the Parties under international law over the sea-bed and subsoil thereof adjacent to their coasts for the purposes of exploration and exploitation of their natural resources.

(3) The present Convention shall not apply to any warship, naval auxiliary or other ship owned or operated by a State and used, for the time being, only on government non-commercial service. However, each Party shall ensure by the adoption of appropriate measures not impairing the operations or operational capabilities of such ships owned or operated by it, that such ships act in a manner consistent, so far as is reasonable and practicable, with the present Convention.

Article 4
Violation
(1) Any violation of the requirements of the present Convention shall be prohibited and sanctions shall be established therefor under the law of the Administration of the ship concerned wherever the violation occurs. If the Administration is informed of such a violation and is satisfied that sufficient evidence is available to enable proceedings to be brought in respect of the alleged violation, it shall cause such proceedings to be taken as soon as possible, in accordance with its law.

(2) Any violation of the requirements of the present Convention within the jurisdiction of any Party to the Convention shall be prohibited and sanctions shall be established therefor under the law of that Party. Whenever such a violation occurs, that Party shall either:
  (a) cause proceedings to be taken in accordance with its law; or
  (b) furnish to the Administration of the ship such information and evidence as may be in its possession that a violation has occurred.

(3) Where information or evidence with respect to any violation of the present Convention by a ship is furnished to the Administration of that ship, the Administration shall promptly inform the Party which has furnished the information or evidence, and the Organization, of the action taken.

(4) The penalties specified under the law of a Party pursuant to the present article shall be adequate in severity to discourage violations of the present Convention and shall be equally severe irrespective of where the violations occur.

Article 5
Certificates and special rules on inspection of ships
(1) Subject to the provisions of paragraph (2) of the present article a certificate issued under the authority of a Party to the Convention in accordance with the provisions of the regulations shall be accepted by the other Parties and regarded for all purposes covered by the present Convention as having the same validity as a certificate issued by them.

(2) A ship required to hold a certificate in accordance with the provisions of the regulations is subject, while in the ports or offshore terminals under the jurisdiction of a Party, to inspection by officers duly authorized by that Party. Any such inspection shall be limited to verifying that there is on board a valid certificate, unless there are clear grounds for believing that the condition of the ship or its equipment does not correspond substantially with the particulars of that certificate. In that case, or if the ship does not carry a valid certificate, the Party carrying out the inspection shall take such steps as will ensure that the ship shall not sail until it can proceed to sea without presenting an unreasonable threat of harm to the marine environment. That Party may, however, grant such a ship permission to leave the port or offshore terminal for the purpose of proceeding to the nearest appropriate repair yard available.

(3) If a Party denies a foreign ship entry to the ports or offshore terminals under its jurisdiction or takes any action against such a ship for the reason that the ship does not comply with the provisions of the present Convention, the Party shall immediately inform the consul or diplomatic representative of the Party whose

flag the ship is entitled to fly, or if this is not possible, the Administration of the ship concerned. Before denying entry or taking such action the Party may request consultation with the Administration of the ship concerned.

Article 6
Detection of violations and enforcement of the Convention

(1)	Parties to the Convention shall co-operate in the detection of violations and the enforcement of the provisions of the present Convention, using all appropriate and practicable measures of detection and environmental monitoring, adequate procedures for reporting and accumulation of evidence.

(2)	A ship to which the present Convention applies may, in any port or offshore terminal of a Party, be subject to inspection by officers appointed or authorized by that Party for the purpose of verifying whether the ship has discharged any harmful substances in violation of the provisions of the regulations. If an inspection indicates a violation of the Convention, a report shall be forwarded to the Administration for any appropriate action.

(3)	Any Party shall furnish to the Administration evidence, if any, that the ship has discharged harmful substances or effluents containing such substances in violation of the provisions of the regulations. If it is practicable to do so, the competent authority of the former Party shall notify the master of the ship of the alleged violation.

(4)	Upon receiving such evidence, the Administration so informed shall investigate the matter, and may request the other Party to furnish further or better evidence of the alleged contravention. If the Administration is satisfied that sufficient evidence is available to enable proceedings to be brought in respect of the alleged violation, it shall cause such proceedings to be taken in accordance with its law as soon as possible. The Administration shall promptly inform the Party which has reported the alleged violation, as well as the Organization, of the action taken.

(5)	A Party may also inspect a ship to which the present Convention applies when it enters the ports or offshore terminals under its jurisdiction, if a request for an investigation is received from any Party together with sufficient evidence that the ship has discharged harmful substances or effluents containing such substances in any place. The report of such investigation shall be sent to the Party requesting it and to the Administration so that the appropriate action may be taken under the present Convention.

Article 7
Undue delay to ships

(1)	All possible efforts shall be made to avoid a ship being unduly detained or delayed under articles 4, 5 or 6 of the present Convention.

(2)	When a ship is unduly detained or delayed under articles 4, 5 or 6 of the present Convention, it shall be entitled to compensation for any loss or damage suffered.

Article 8
Reports on incidents involving harmful substances

(1)	A report of an incident shall be made without delay to the fullest extent possible in accordance with the provisions of Protocol I to the present Convention.

(2)   Each Party to the Convention shall:
    (a)   make all arrangements necessary for an appropriate officer or agency to receive and process all reports on incidents; and
    (b)   notify the Organization with complete details of such arrangements for circulation to other Parties and Member States of the Organization.
(3)   Whenever a Party receives a report under the provisions of the present article, that Party shall relay the report without delay to:
    (a)   the Administration of the ship involved; and
    (b)   any other State which may be affected.
(4)   Each Party to the Convention undertakes to issue instructions to its maritime inspection vessels and aircraft and to other appropriate services, to report to its authorities any incident referred to in Protocol I to the present Convention. That Party shall, if it considers it appropriate, report accordingly to the Organization and to any other Party concerned.

Article 9
Other treaties and interpretation
(1)   Upon its entry into force, the present Convention supersedes the International Convention for the Prevention of Pollution of the Sea by Oil, 1954, as amended, as between Parties to that Convention.
(2)   Nothing in the present Convention shall prejudice the codification and development of the law of the sea by the United Nations Conference on the Law of the Sea convened pursuant to resolution 2750 C(XXV) of the General Assembly of the United Nations nor the present or future claims and legal views of any State concerning the law of the sea and the nature and extent of coastal and flag State jurisdiction.
(3)   The term "jurisdiction" in the present Convention shall be construed in the light of international law in force at the time of application or interpretation of the present Convention.

1978 Protocol relating to the International Convention for the Prevention of Pollution from Ships 1973

Article I General obligations
1   The Parties to the present Protocol undertake to give effect to the provisions of:
    (a)   the present Protocol and the Annex hereto which shall constitute an integral part of the present Protocol; and
    (b)   the International Convention for the Prevention of Pollution from Ships, 1973 (hereinafter referred to as "the Convention"), subject to the modifications and additions set out in the present Protocol.
2   The provisions of the Convention and the present Protocol shall be read and interpreted together as one single instrument.
3   Every reference to the present Protocol constitutes at the same time a reference to the Annex hereto.

Article II Implementation of Annex II of the Convention
1   Notwithstanding the provisions of article 14(1) of the Convention, the Parties to the present Protocol agree that they shall not be bound by the provisions of

Annex II of the Convention for a period of three years from the date of entry into force of the present Protocol or for such longer period as may be decided by a two-thirds majority of the Parties to the present Protocol in the Marine Environment Protection Committee (hereinafter referred to as "the Committee") of the Inter-Governmental Maritime Consultative Organization (hereinafter referred to as "the Organization").B

2   During the period specified in paragraph 1 of this article, the Parties to the present Protocol shall not be under any obligations nor entitled to claim any privileges under the Convention in respect of matters relating to Annex II of the Convention and all reference to Parties in the Convention shall not include the Parties to the present Protocol in so far as matters relating to that Annex are concerned.

Protocol I

Article I Duty to report

(1)   The master or other person having charge of any ship involved in an incident referred to in article II of this Protocol shall report the particulars of such incident without delay and to the fullest extent possible in accordance with the provisions of this Protocol.

(2)   In the event of the ship referred to in paragraph (1) of this article being abandoned, or in the event of a report from such a ship being incomplete or unobtainable, the owner, charterer, manager or operator of the ship, or their agent shall, to the fullest extent possible, assume the obligations placed upon the master under the provisions of this Protocol.

Article II When to make reports

(1)   The report shall be made when an incident involves:

    (a)   a discharge above the permitted level or probable discharge of oil or of noxious liquid substances for whatever reason including those for the purpose of securing the safety of the ship or for saving life at sea; or

    (b)   a discharge or probable discharge of harmful substances in packaged form, including those in freight containers, portable tanks, road and rail vehicles and shipborne barges; or

    (c)   damage, failure or breakdown of a ship of 15 metres in length or above which:

        (i)   affects the safety of the ship; including but not limited to collision, grounding, fire, explosion, structural failure, flooding and cargo shifting; or

        (ii)   results in impairment of the safety of navigation; including but not limited to, failure or breakdown of steering gear, propulsion plant, electrical generating system, and essential shipborne navigational aids; or

    (d)   a discharge during the operation of the ship of oil or noxious liquid substances in excess of the quantity or instantaneous rate permitted under the present Convention.

(2)   For the purposes of this Protocol:

    (a)   Oil referred to in subparagraph 1(a) of this article means oil as defined in regulation 1(1) of Annex I of the Convention.

(b)   Noxious liquid substances referred to in subparagraph 1(a) of this article means noxious liquid substances as defined in regulation 1(6) of Annex II of the Convention.

(c)   Harmful substances in packaged form referred to in subparagraph 1(b) of this article means substances which are identified as marine pollutants in the International Maritime Dangerous Goods Code (IMDG Code).

[...]

Article V Reporting Procedures
(1)   Reports shall be made by the fastest telecommunications channels available with the highest possible priority to the nearest coastal State.
(2)   In order to implement the provisions of this Protocol, Parties to the present Convention shall issue, or cause to be issued, regulations or instructions on the procedures to be followed in reporting incidents involving harmful substances, based on guidelines developed by the Organization.

Table 10.2 MARPOL Annexes

Annex I, Regulations for the Prevention of Pollution by Oil
Annex II, Regulations for the Control of Pollution by Noxious Liquid Substances in Bulk
Annex III, Regulations for the Prevention of Pollution by Harmful Substances Carried by Sea in Packaged Form
Annex IV, Regulations for the Prevention of Pollution by Sewage from Ships
Annex V, Regulations for the Prevention of Pollution by Garbage from Ships
Annex VI, Regulations for the Prevention of Air Pollution from Ships

10.7   EMERGENCIES

UNCLOS

Article 198 Notification of imminent or actual damage
When a State becomes aware of cases in which the marine environment is in imminent danger of being damaged or has been damaged by pollution, it shall immediately notify other States it deems likely to be affected by such damage, as well as the competent international organizations.

Article 199 Contingency plans against pollution
In the cases referred to in article 198, States in the area affected, in accordance with their capabilities, and the competent international organizations shall cooperate, to the extent possible, in eliminating the effects of pollution and preventing or minimizing the damage. To this end, States shall jointly develop and promote contingency plans for responding to pollution incidents in the marine environment.

1969 International Intervention Convention

ARTICLE I

1.   Parties to the present Convention may take such measures on the high seas as may be necessary to prevent, mitigate or eliminate grave and imminent danger to their coastline or related interests from pollution or threat of pollution of the sea by oil; following upon a maritime casualty or acts related to such a casualty, which may reasonably be expected to result in major harmful consequences.

2.   However, no measures shall be taken under the present Convention against any warship or other ship owned or operated by a State and used, for the time being, only on government noncommercial services.

ARTICLE II

For the purposes of the present Convention:

1.   "maritime casualty" means a collision of ships, stranding or other incident of navigation, or other occurrence on board a ship or external to it resulting in material damage or imminent threat of material damage to a ship or cargo;

1973 Protocol Relating to Intervention on the High Seas in Cases of Pollution by Substances other than Oil

Article I

1.   Parties to the present Protocol may take such measures on the high seas as may be necessary to prevent, mitigate or eliminate grave and imminent danger to their coastline or related interests from pollution or threat of pollution by substances other than oil following upon a maritime casualty or acts related to such a casualty, which may reasonably be expected to result in major harmful consequences.

2.   "Substances other than oil" as referred to in paragraph 1 shall be:

(a)   those substances enumerated in a list which shall be established by an appropriate body designated by the Organization and which shall be annexed to the present Protocol, and

(b)   those other substances which are liable to create hazards to human health, to harm living resources and marine life, to damage amenities or to interfere with other legitimate uses of the sea.

1989 International Convention on Salvage, 1953 UNTS 165

Chapter III Rights of salvors

Article 12 Conditions for reward

1   Salvage operations which have had a useful result give right to a reward.

2   Except as otherwise provided, no payment is due under this Convention if the Salvage operations have had no useful result.

3   This chapter shall apply, notwithstanding that the salved vessel and the vessel undertaking the salvage operations belong to the same owner.

Article 13 Criteria for fixing the reward

1   The reward shall be fixed with a view to encouraging salvage operations, taking into account the following criteria without regard to the order in which they are presented below:

[...]

(b)   the skill and efforts of the salvors in preventing or minimizing damage to the environment;

Article 14 Special compensation

1   If the salvor has carried out salvage operations in respect of a vessel which by itself or its cargo threatened damage to the environment and has failed to earn a reward under Article 13 at least equivalent to the special compensation assessable in accordance with this Article, he shall be entitled to special compensation from the owner of that vessel equivalent to his expenses as herein defined.

2   If, in the circumstances set out in paragraph 1, the salvor by his salvage operations has prevented or minimized damage to the environment, the special compensation payable by the owner to the salvor under paragraph 1 may be increased up to a maximum of 30% of the expenses incurred by the salvor. However, the tribunal, if it deems it fair and just to do so and bearing in mind the relevant criteria set out in Article 13, paragraph 1, may increase such special compensation further, but in no event shall the total increase be more than 100% of the expenses incurred by the salvor.

[...]

5   If the salvor has been negligent and has thereby failed to prevent or minimize damage to the environment, he may be deprived of the whole or part of any special compensation due under this Article.

1990 International Convention on Oil Pollution Preparedness, Response and Cooperation, 1891 UNTS 78

Preamble

THE PARTIES TO THE PRESENT CONVENTION,

CONSCIOUS of the need to preserve the human environment in general and the marine environment in particular,

RECOGNIZING the serious threat posed to the marine environment by oil pollution incidents involving ships, offshore units, sea ports and oil handling facilities,

MINDFUL of the importance of precautionary measures and prevention in avoiding oil pollution in the first instance, and the need for strict application of existing international instruments dealing with maritime safety and marine pollution prevention, particularly the International Convention for the Safety of Life at Sea, 1974, as amended, and the International Convention for the Prevention of Pollution from Ships, 1973, as modified by the Protocol of 1978 relating thereto, as amended, and also the speedy development of enhanced standards for the design, operation and maintenance of ships carrying oil, and of offshore units,

MINDFUL ALSO that, in the event of an oil pollution incident, prompt and effective action is essential in order to minimize the damage which may result from such an incident,

[...]

TAKING ACCOUNT of the "polluter pays" principle as a general principle of international environmental law,

[...]

HAVE AGREED as follows:

Article 1 General provisions

(1)   Parties undertake, individually or jointly, to take all appropriate measures in accordance with the provisions of this Convention and the Annex thereto to prepare for and respond to an oil pollution incident.

2000 Protocol on Preparedness, Response and Co-operation to Pollution Incidents by Hazardous and Noxious Substances

ARTICLE 1

General provisions

(1)   Parties undertake, individually or jointly, to take all appropriate measures in accordance with the provisions of this Protocol and the Annex thereto to prepare for and respond to a pollution incident by hazardous and noxious substances.

[...]

ARTICLE 2

Definitions

For the purposes of this Protocol:

(1)   *Pollution incident by hazardous and noxious substances* (hereinafter referred to as "pollution incident") means any occurrence or series of occurrences having the same origin, including fire or explosion, which results or may result in a discharge, release or emission of hazardous and noxious substances and which poses or may pose a threat to the marine environment, or to the coastline or related interests of one or more States, and which requires emergency action or immediate response.

(2)   *Hazardous and noxious substances* means any substance other than oil which, if introduced into the marine environment is likely to create hazards to human health, to harm living resources and marine life, to damage amenities or to interfere with other legitimate uses of the sea.

QUESTIONS

1. Identify the sources of marine pollution and the manner in which UNCLOS regulates them.
2. 'MARPOL, along with its Annexes, is sufficiently detailed and comprehensive to achieve its objective of eliminating marine pollution arising from harmful substances, and the fact it has not achieved its goal can be attributed to failures of compliance.' Discuss.
3. In your view, is the regulation of land-source marine pollution adequate?

FURTHER READING

BOOKS

J Harrison, *Saving the Oceans Through Law: The International Legal Framework for the Protection of the Marine Environment* (Oxford University Press 2017)

AL Jaeckel, *The International Seabed Authority and the Precautionary Principle: Balancing Deep Seabed Mineral Mining and Marine Environmental Protection* (Brill/Nijhoff 2017)

N Oral, *Regional Co-operation and Protection of the Marine Environment under International Law: Black Sea* (Brill/Nijhoff 2013)

R Rayfuse (ed.), *Research Handbook on International Marine Environmental Law* (Edward Elgar 2015)

AK-J Tan, *Vessel-Source Marine Pollution* (Cambridge University Press 2005)

Y Tanaka, *The International Law of the Sea* (3rd edn, Cambridge University Press 2019)

R Warner and S Kaye (eds), *Routledge Handbook of Maritime Regulation and Enforcement* (Routledge 2018)

CHAPTERS

M Fitzmaurice, 'Enhanced Marine Environmental Protection: A Case Study of the Baltic Sea' in J Barrett and R Barnes (eds), *Law of the Sea: UNCLOS as a Living Treaty* (BIICL 2016)

M Fitzmaurice, 'The International Convention for the Prevention of Pollution from Ships (MARPOL)' in D Attard, M Fitzmaurice, NA Martínez Gutiérrez and R Hamza (eds), *The IMLI Manual on International Maritime Law – Volume III* (Oxford University Press 2016)

J Harrison, 'Pollution from or through the Marine Environment' in D Attard, M Fitzmaurice, N Martinez and R Hamza (eds), *The IMLI Manual of International Maritime Law Volume III* (Oxford University Press 2016)

J Harrison, 'Resources of the International Seabed Area' in E Morgera and K Kulovesi (eds), *Research Handbook on International Law and Natural Resources* (Edward Elgar 2016)

E Kirk, 'Science and the International Regulation of Marine Pollution' in D Rothwell, AO Elferink, K Scott and T Stephens (eds), *The Oxford Handbook of the Law of the Sea* (Oxford University Press 2015)

TA Mensah, 'The International Legal Regime for the Protection and Preservation of the Marine Environment from Land-based Sources of Pollution' in AE Boyle and D Freestone (eds), *International Law and Sustainable Development* (Oxford University Press 1999)

C Redgwell, 'From Permission to Prohibition: The 1982 Convention on the Law of the Sea and Protection of the Marine Environment' in D Freestone, R Barnes and D One (eds), *The Law of the Sea: Progress and Present* (Oxford University Press 2006)

ARTICLES

A Boyle, 'Marine Pollution under the Law of the Sea Convention' (1985) 79 AJIL 347

A Boyle, 'Land-based Sources of Marine Pollution: Current Legal Regime' (1992) 16 Marine Policy 20

EJ Molenaar, 'The 1996 Protocol to the 1972 London Convention' (1997) 12 IJMCL 396

T Scovazzi, 'The Exploration of Resources of the Deep Seabed and the Protection of the Environment' (2014) 57 GYIL 181

Y Tanaka, 'The South China Sea Arbitration: Environmental Obligations Under the Law of the Sea Convention' (2018) 27 RECIEL 90

11

Conservation of marine living resources

11.1 INTRODUCTION

Marine living resources, broadly speaking, refers to species that are alive in our seas. As observed by Yoshifumi Tanaka, marine living resources 'are of vital importance for mankind because these resources are an essential source of protein and many human communities depend on fishing'.[1] This chapter is structured in three parts. First, the legal framework pertaining to the conservation of marine living resources is set out in 11.2. Sands and Peel suggest 'the main objective of international law for fisheries conservation has been to establish a framework for international cooperation towards the management and conservation of fisheries and marine living resources'.[2] Most regrettably, an issue of global concern is illegal, unreported and unregulated ('IUU') fishing, which undermines the conservation measures taken by states and regional fisheries management organisations ('RFMO'), and is considered in 11.3. Another complex contemporary phenomenon in international law that has recently gained attention is whaling in relation to the conservation of marine mammals, which is considered in 11.4.

11.1.1 Conservation of Marine Living Resources

The current international legal-conservation framework on the conservation of marine living resources, like most areas of the international law of the sea, looks first to the UN Convention on the Law of the Sea 1982 ('UNCLOS'). Notably, UNCLOS does not define (marine) living resources; yet recognises in its preamble the desirability of promoting the conservation of living resources and establishes rights and duties on states with regard to conservation and management of living resources in the exclusive economic zone and high seas respectively.[3] UNCLOS does adopt the nomenclature of 'fisheries' in some provisions while also leaving this undefined. An observation can be made that 'living resources' has connotations of being economically exploitable, and indeed fisheries as an umbrella term has been regarded as such by

---

[1] Yoshifumi Tanaka, *The International Law of the Sea* (3rd edn, CUP 2019) 281.

[2] Philippe Sands and Jacqueline Peel, *Principles of International Environmental Law* (4th edn, CUP Press 2018) 507.

[3] Articles 61–63, Arts 116–119, UN Convention on the Law of the Sea 1982 ('UNCLOS').

states. The nomenclature in UNCLOS which also refers to living resources as 'stocks' further hints to living resources in the sea being regarded as economic resources for states. That said, even in the pre-UNCLOS era, fishing rights has always been very much an issue at the heart of states, both domestically and for international trade. Within the era of UNCLOS, the legal framework on the conservation of marine living resources is premised on the 'maritime zone' approach and 'species-specific' approach. The former is premised on areas within national jurisdiction, i.e., territorial sea and exclusive economic zone, and areas beyond national jurisdiction, i.e., the high seas; whilst the latter governs specific species, i.e., shared fish stocks (Art 63(1); straddling fish stocks (Art 63(2); highly migratory species (Art 64)); marine mammals (Art 65); anadromous stocks (Art 66); catadromous species (Art 67); and sedentary species (Art 68).

The maritime zone approach refers to the rights and duties on states pursuant to the legal framework applicable within the territorial sea (exclusive jurisdiction and absolute sovereignty),[4] exclusive economic zones;[5] and high seas (freedom of fishing on the high seas).[6] With regard to the species-specific approach, conservation measures are premised according to the category of the species. Both approaches have their limitations. Tanaka aptly describes the 'divergence of the law and nature' as one of the limitations associated with the maritime zonal approach:[7]

[…] the ecological interactions between marine spaces as well as the ecological conditions of the physical surroundings are to be ignored. […] the spatial scope of man-made jurisdictional zones does not always correspond to the 'ecologically defined space' which comprises the area where marine ecosystems extend.[8]

The first and rather obvious limitation pertaining to the species-specific approach is that not all species are protected.[9] Further, like most provisions in UNCLOS, broader ecological implications are not considered, which in the specific context of species is particularly noted. To address the limitations in UNCLOS, the Agenda 21 1992 addressed in Chapter 17 the need for the protection of the oceans, all kinds of seas, including enclosed and semi-enclosed seas, and coastal areas and the protection, rational use and development of their living resources.

17.1 stipulates:

The marine environment – including the oceans and all seas and adjacent coastal areas – forms an integrated whole that is an essential component of the global life-support system

---

4   Part II, Section 2, UNCLOS.

5   Part V, UNCLOS.

6   Part VII, UNCLOS.

7   Tanaka (n 1) 288.

8   Ibid., 289.

9   See e.g. Lee Kimball, 'Deep-Sea Fisheries of the High Seas: The Management Impasse' (2004) 2004 The International Journal of Marine and Coastal Law 259.

and a positive asset that presents opportunities for sustainable development. International law, as reflected in the provisions of the United Nations Convention on the Law of the Sea 1/, 2/ referred to in this chapter of Agenda 21, sets forth rights and obligations of States and provides the international basis upon which to pursue the protection and sustainable development of the marine and coastal environment and its resources. This requires new approaches to marine and coastal area management and development, at the national, subregional, regional and global levels, approaches that are integrated in content and are precautionary and anticipatory in ambit, as reflected in the following programme areas: 3/

(a) Integrated management and sustainable development of coastal areas, including exclusive economic zones;
(b) Marine environmental protection;
(c) Sustainable use and conservation of marine living resources of the high seas;
(d) Sustainable use and conservation of marine living resources under national jurisdiction;
(e) Addressing critical uncertainties for the management of the marine environment and climate change;
(f) Strengthening international, including regional, cooperation and coordination;
(g) Sustainable development of small islands.

Eventually this led to a new internationally binding agreement – the United Nations Agreement for the Implementation of the Provisions of the United Nations Convention on the Law of the Sea of 10 December 1982 relating to the Conservation and Management of Straddling Fish Stocks and Highly Migratory Fish Stocks ('Fish Stock Agreement'). Under this instrument, sustainable development,[10] ecosystem approach,[11] and precautionary approach is reflected.[12] The obligations placed by UNCLOS upon states to conserve marine living resources also includes cooperation with other states and appropriate regional and international organisations,[13] thereby serving as a 'framework convention' which provides a legal basis for regional and international organisations to be established by contracting states parties.

11.1.2   IUU Fishing

There is no uniformly agreed upon definition of IUU fishing.[14] Yet, it is globally acknowledged that IUU fishing is a major concern and according to the FAO 'remains one of the greatest

---

[10]   Articles 5(a) and (h), Tanaka (n 1) 301. See also Chapter 17 of Agenda 21 of 1992, 1995 Code of Conduct for Responsibility Fisheries; 1999 Rome Declaration on the Implementation of the Code of Conduct for responsible fisheries; 2001 Reykjavik Declaration on responsible fishers in the marine environment.

[11]   Article 5(g); Article 4(a) of the 2006 Southern Indian Ocean Fisheries Agreement; 2001 Reykjavik Declaration.

[12]   Article 6(1); Annex II; see also Principle 15 of 1992 Rio Declaration on Environment and Development; 2006 Southern Indian Ocean Fisheries Agreement; 2009 Convention on Conservation and Management of High Seas Fisheries.

[13]   Articles 118–119, UNCLOS.

[14]   Oral points out that 'The concept of IUU fishing was predated by Distant Water Fishing (DWF), based on the open access regime of freedom of the high seas. DWF had existed for centuries, but expanded due to technological

threats to marine ecosystems due to its potent ability to undermine national and regional efforts to manage fisheries sustainably as well as its endeavours to conserve marine biodiversity [...] IUU fishing therefore threatens livelihoods, exacerbates poverty, and augments food insecurity.'[15]

The concept of IUU fishing gained recognition in 1997 by CCAMLR.[16] In 1999, the FAO Committee on Fisheries (COFI) considered IUU fishing to be a matter of high priority and adopted on March 2001 the International Plan of Action to Prevent, Deter and Eliminate Illegal, Unreported and Unregulated Fishing (IPOA-IUU), which was elaborated within the framework of the Code of Conduct for Responsible Fisheries. The IPOA-IUU contains the most commonly accepted definition for IUU fishing:

Illegal fishing refers to activities
3.1.1 conducted by national or foreign vessels in waters under the jurisdiction of a State, without the permission of that State, or in contravention of its laws and regulations;
3.1.2 conducted by vessels flying the flag of States that are parties to a relevant regional fisheries management organization but operate in contravention of the conservation and management measures adopted by that organization and by which the States are bound, or relevant provisions of the applicable international law; or
3.1.3 in violation of national laws or international obligations, including those undertaken by cooperating States to a relevant regional fisheries management organization.

Unreported fishing refers to fishing activities
3.2.1 which have not been reported, or have been misreported, to the relevant national authority, in contravention of national laws and regulations; or
3.2.2 undertaken in the area of competence of a relevant regional fisheries management organization which have not been reported or have been misreported, in contravention of the reporting procedures of that organization.

Unregulated fishing refers to fishing activities
3.3.1 in the area of application of a relevant regional fisheries management organization that are conducted by vessels without nationality, or by those flying the flag of a State not party to that organization, or by a fishing entity, in a manner that is not consistent with or contravenes the conservation and management measures of that organization;
3.3.2 in areas or for fish stocks in relation to which there are no applicable conservation or management measures and where such fishing activities are conducted in a manner inconsistent with State responsibilities for the conservation of living marine resources under international law.

---

advancements in years following the Second World War', Nilüfer Oral, 'Reflections on the Past, Present, and Future of IUU Fishing under International Law' (2020) 22 International Community Law Review 368, 368.

[15]   'Illegal, Unreported and Unregulated Fishing'. Available at: http://www.fao.org/iuu-fishing/en/

[16]   'Illegal, Unreported and Unregulated Fishing (IUU)'. Available at: https://www.ccamlr.org/en/compliance/illegal-unreported-and-unregulated-iuu-fishing Sands and Peel (n 2) 543.

The objective of the IPOA-IUU pursuant to Article 8 is 'to prevent, deter and eliminate IUU fishing by providing all States with comprehensive, effective and transparent measures by which to act, including through appropriate regional fisheries management organizations established in accordance with international law'.[17]

According to UNCLOS, primary responsibility for the conservation and management of living resources in the high seas rests with states.[18] This is particularly because Article 94 stipulates that 'every State shall effectively exercise its jurisdiction [...] over ships flying its flag'. However, flags of convenience ships are a serious problem in international law. Tanaka points out 'the effective implementation of the flag State's jurisdiction over fishing vessels is undermined by the practice of flag of convenience States which often lack the will and capability to properly regulate fishing activities by vessels flying its flag'.[19]

The 1993 FAO Compliance Agreement (Arts III(3); III(5)) and the 1995 UN Fish Stocks Agreement (Articles 18–20) are examples of legal instruments that attempt to strengthen flag state responsibility as steps towards preventing IUU fishing. The 1993 FAO Compliance Agreement aims *inter alia* to enhance the role of flag states by noting the special responsibility of flag states to ensure that none of their vessels are fishing on the high seas unless authorised; and to seek to prevent 're-flagging' of vessels fishing on the high seas under flags of states that are unable or unwilling to enforce international fisheries conservation and management measures.[20]

Additionally, port state measures have also been introduced on the global level in the 1995 Fish Stocks Agreement in Article 23, which provides port states with the right and duty to take measures in accordance with international law to promote the effectiveness of [...] conservation and management measures, whereby they may *inter alia* inspect documents, fishing gear and catch on board vessels, when such vessels are voluntarily in its ports or at its offshore terminals.[21]

In 2005, the FAO Committee on Fisheries endorsed the Model Scheme on Port State Measures to combat IUU Fishing, which recommends minimum standards for PSMs, requiring appropriate implementation at the regional or national level; and adopted the 2009 Agreement on Port State Measures to Prevent, Deter and Eliminate Illegal, Unreported and Unregulated Fishing ('2009 Port State Agreement').[22] In its Preamble, the 2009 Agreement recognises that 'port State measures provide a powerful and cost-effective means of preventing, deterring and eliminating illegal, unreported and unregulated fishing'. The agreement is global

---

[17]   Article 8, March 2001 the International Plan of Action to Prevent, Deter and Eliminate Illegal, Unreported and Unregulated Fishing ('IPOA-IUU').

[18]   Arts 91, 92, 94, 192 and 193, UNCLOS.

[19]   Tanaka (n 1) 312.

[20]   'FAO Compliance Agreement', Available at: http://www.fao.org/iuu-fishing/international-framework/fao-compliance-agreement/en/

[21]   Article 23, 1995 Fish Stock Agreement.

[22]   'Benefits of implementing PSMA', Available at: http://www.fao.org/port-state-measures/background/benefits-implementing-psma/en/

in scope [Art 3(5)], and entered into force in July 2016.[23] As pointed out by Oral, 'together with FAO instruments and the management and conservation regimes of different regional fisheries organizations, these agreements comprise the current international law framework to prevent, deter, and eliminate IUU fishing'.[24]

11.1.3   Conservation of Marine Mammals

According to Tanaka, marine mammals are 'warm-blooded animals which are characterized by the production of milk in the female mammary glands and spend the majority of their lives in or close in the sea'.[25] Mammals include cetaceans (whales, dolphins, and porpoises), pinnipeds (walruses, sea lions, eared seals, fur seals and true seals), sirenians (manatees and dugongs), sea otters and polar bears.

Under UNCLOS, marine mammals may also be considered to be highly migratory species in light of Article 64, and states have obligations to conserve marine mammals in their EEZ and high seas.[26] The Convention on International Trade in Endangered Species of Wild Fauna and Flora (CITES) does not expressly mention marine mammals in the text of the convention, but nevertheless controls and prevents international commercial trade in endangered species which include marine mammals or their products,[27] i.e., Article II(1) stipulates that 'Appendix I shall include all species threatened with extinction which are or may be affected by trade. Trade in specimens of these species must be subject to particularly strict regulation in order not to endanger further their survival and must only be authorized in exceptional circumstances.'[28]

On the regional level: There are several regional treaties, as will be listed below, that concern conservation of marine mammals.[29]

Whaling, and more specifically the legality of scientific whaling,[30] remains the most contentious issue related to the conservation of marine mammals. As eloquently put by Malgosia Fitzmaurice:

There is no other object in international law which raises as many emotions and conflicting views as the whale. The whale is both an object of love and a utilitarian object treated as any

---

[23]   'Port State Measures Agreement enters into force as international treaty'. Available at: http://www.fao.org/blogs/blue-growth-blog/port-state-measures-agreement-enters-into-force-as-international-treaty/en/

[24]   Oral (n 14) 371.

[25]   Tanaka (n 1) 292.

[26]   Articles 62 and 120, UNCLOS.

[27]   Appendices to CITES.

[28]   Article II(1), Ibid.

[29]   1971 Agreement on Sealing and the Conservation of the Seal Stocks.

[30]   Article VIII(1) International Convention for the Regulation of Whaling ('CRW'). See also Whaling in the Antarctic (Australia v. Japan: New Zealand intervening), Judgment, ICJ Reports 2014, p. 226; and Malgosia Fitzmaurice, *Whaling and International Law* (CUP 2015) 47–48; Tanaka (n 1) 296–297.

other animal to fulfil the needs of human beings. The international legal regulation of the whale also demonstrates these conflicting aims.[31]

The ICRW is the principal international instrument for the regulation of whaling, which was adopted in 1946;[32] differing from the 1937 International Agreement for the Regulation of Whaling (along with the Final Act) whose preamble reads that the regulation of whaling was to secure 'the prosperity of the whaling industry and, for that purpose, to maintain the stock of whales'.[33] The object and purpose of the ICRW is to:[34]

> establish a system of international regulation for the whale fisheries to ensure proper and effective conservation and development of whale stocks on the basis of the principles embodied in the provisions of the International Agreement for the Regulation of Whaling, signed in London on 8th June, 1937, and the protocols to that Agreement signed in London on 24th June, 1938, and 26th November, 1945; and Having decided to conclude a convention to provide for the proper conservation of whale stocks and thus make possible the orderly development of the whaling industry.[35]

The tension between different interests of states parties is observed by Fitzmaurice:

> The international legal regulation of the whale also demonstrates these conflicting aims. The 1946 International Convention for the Regulation of Whaling ('ICRW' or 'Convention') has the binary object and purpose—i.e. the conservation and management of whale stocks—on the one hand, and the orderly development of the whaling industry on the other, which has resulted in intervening years in disputes between State Parties to the Convention as to which is its dominant objective.[36]

The ICRW comprises the text of the Convention itself, and a Schedule which is an integral part of the Convention text.[37] Notably, the Convention does not define a whale, which Fitzmaurice observes 'has created much confusion as to exactly which cetaceans fall within its scope – in particular whether its provisions cover so called "small" as well as "large" cetaceans'.[38]

---

[31]   Malgosia Fitzmaurice, 'Compliance Mechanism: International Whaling Commission', *Max Planck Encyclopedia of Public International Law* (2018), para.1.

[32]   For an overview of the history and evaluation of whaling see Fitzmaurice (n 30) 16–27.

[33]   Tanaka has observed that 'it may be said that the whale treaties reflected two requirements that are not easily reconciled: the prosperity of the whaling industry and the need for the conservation of whales' at Tanaka (n 1) 294. Fitzmaurice notes that early efforts to regulate whaling were not aimed at the protection of whales, but rather, at securing a high price for whale oil'; Fitzmaurice (n 30) 9.

[34]   See Fitzmaurice (n 30) 44–47.

[35]   *Preamble*, ICRW.

[36]   The tension can be seen in the Preamble to 1946 Convention: 'proper conservation of whale stocks' and 'the orderly development of thee whaling industry'.

[37]   For background, see Fitzmaurice (n 30) 29–37.

[38]   Ibid., 50–51.

The Convention sets out the general regulatory scheme for the management of whale stocks. According to Article V(1), the provisions of the Schedule introduces standards to be followed regarding 'conservation and utilization' of whale resources.[39] The Schedule is an integral part of the Convention, which is legally binding as a central component of the Convention.

'Scientific' whaling pursuant to Article VIII(1) of the ICRW is a special category which is excluded from the operation of the Convention, providing:

> Notwithstanding anything contained in this Convention any Contracting Government may grant to any of its nationals a special permit authorizing that national to kill, take and treat whales for purposes of scientific research subject to such restrictions as to number and subject to such other conditions as the Contracting Government thinks fit, and the killing, taking, and treating of whales in accordance with the provisions of this Article shall be exempt from the operation of this Convention. Each Contracting Government shall report at once to the Commission all such authorizations which it has granted. Each Contracting Government may at any time revoke any such special permit which it has granted.

Whaling by indigenous or aboriginal peoples for their own subsistence purposes is recognised in Article 2 of the Schedule, which states 'it is forbidden to take or kill grey whales or right whales, except when the meat and products of such whales are to be used exclusively for local consumption of the aborigines'. Fitzmaurice submits

> the absence of express positive provisions relating to aboriginal whaling generally is reflected in the absence of any definition of what it comprises in the current treaty provisions. [...] However, the IWC has developed a definition of aboriginal subsistence agriculture so that it must be conducted under the 'needs' and that meat and other whale products are to be used exclusively for the purpose of local consumption by the aboriginal people.

The definition states that the objectives of such whaling are to:[40]

- Ensure that risks of extinction are not seriously increased by whaling;
- Enable native people to hunt whales at levels appropriate to their cultural and nutritional requirements (also called 'needs'); and
- Move populations towards and then maintain them at healthy levels.[41]

---

39   Article V 1. The Commission may amend from time to time the provisions of the Schedule by adopting regulations with respect to the conservation and utilization of whale resources, fixing (a) protected and unprotected species; (b) open and closed seasons; (c) open and closed waters, including the designation of sanctuary areas; (d) size limits for each species; (e) time, methods, and intensity of whaling (including the maximum catch of whales to be taken in any one season); (f) types and specifications of gear and apparatus and appliances which may be used; (g) methods of measurement; and (h) catch returns and other statistical and biological records.

40   'Aboriginal subsistence whaling'. Available at: https://iwc.int/aboriginal.

41   Fitzmaurice (n 30) 49.

The ICRW establishes a treaty body, the International Whaling Commission (IWC), composed of one member from each Contracting Government,[42] which is aimed at the implementation of the ICRW.[43] The functions of the Commission include encouraging, recommending or organising studies and investigations relating to whales and whaling; collecting and analysing statistical information concerning the current condition and trend of the whale stocks and the effects of whaling activities thereon; studying, appraising, and disseminating information concerning methods of maintaining and increasing the populations of whale stocks.[44] The Commission may also amend from time to time the provisions of the Schedule by adopting regulations with respect to the conservation and utilisation of whale resources, fixing (a) protected and unprotected species; (b) open and closed seasons; (c) open and closed waters, including the designation of sanctuary areas; (d) size limits for each species; (e) time, methods, and intensity of whaling (including the maximum catch of whales to be taken in any one season); (f) types and specifications of gear and apparatus and appliances which may be used; (g) methods of measurement; and (h) catch returns and other statistical and biological records.[45]

The IWC has made some amendments to the Schedule, e.g., in 1982, a moratorium on commercial whaling on all whale stocks was adopted in Schedule 10(e).[46] Notably, para 13 of the Schedule exempts aboriginal substance whaling from the moratorium. The IWC has also established the Indian Ocean Sanctuary in 1979,[47] and the Southern Ocean Sanctuary in 1994.[48]

In 2018, at the Florianópolis meeting, the Parties to the Whaling Convention adopted Resolution 2018–5, known as the 'Florianópolis Declaration'.[49] The Declaration states that the IWC's role 'includes ensuring the recovery of cetacean populations to pre-industrial levels (the IWC, therefore, reaffirms the importance of maintaining the moratorium on commercial whaling)'.[50] The Declaration was a direct response to Japan's proposed 'Way Forward' for the

---

[42]   Article III.

[43]   Fitzmaurice (n 30) 57–66.

[44]   Article IV.

[45]   Article V.

[46]   The moratorium was opposed by Japan, Norway, Peru and the USSR. Note that Peru withdrew its objection in 1983; and Japan in 1987 and 1988. See Fitzmaurice (n 30) 66–76.

[47]   Rule 7(a) of the Schedule.

[48]   Rule 7(b) of the Schedule.

[49]   'The Florianópolis Declaration on the Role of the Management of the International Whaling Commission in the Conservation and Management of Whaling in the 21st Century' Resolution 2018–5, 67th Meeting of the IWC (2018) https://www.gov.br/mma/pt-br/centrais-de-conteudo/declaracao-20florianopolis-pdf accessed 27 December 2021.

[50]   Nicola Wheen, '23. International Whaling Commission' (2018) 29 Yearbook of International Environmental Law 495.

IWC involving a scheme for recommencing commercial whaling,[51] which was rejected by the Parties. This Declaration resulted in Japan's withdrawal from the Convention.

11.2   CONSERVATION OF MARINE LIVING RESOURCES

11.2.1   Legal Instruments

11.2.1.1 Legally binding instruments

1982 United Nations Convention on the Law of the Sea, 1833 UNTS 3

Article 55
Specific legal regime of the exclusive economic zone
    The exclusive economic zone is an area beyond and adjacent to the territorial sea, subject to the specific legal regime established in this Part, under which the rights and jurisdiction of the coastal State and the rights and freedoms of other States are governed by the relevant provisions of this Convention.

Article 56
Rights, jurisdiction and duties of the coastal State in the exclusive economic zone
1.   In the exclusive economic zone, the coastal State has:
    (a)   sovereign rights for the purpose of exploring and exploiting, conserving and managing the natural resources, whether living or non-living, of the waters superjacent to the seabed and of the seabed and its subsoil, and with regard to other activities for the economic exploitation and exploration of the zone, such as the production of energy from the water, currents and winds;

Article 57
Breadth of the exclusive economic zone
The exclusive economic zone shall not extend beyond 200 nautical miles from the baselines from which the breadth of the territorial sea is measured.

[...]

Article 61
Conservation of the living resources
1.   The coastal State shall determine the allowable catch of the living resources in its exclusive economic zone.

---

[51]   Government of Japan, 'The Way Forward of the IWC: The Reform Proposal including a draft Resolution and Schedule Amendment' IWC/67/08, Agenda item 6, 7 and 12 (12 July 2018) https://www.jfa.maff.go.jp/e/whale/attach/pdf/index-4.pdf accessed 27 December 2021.

2.   The coastal State, taking into account the best scientific evidence available to it, shall ensure through proper conservation and management measures that the maintenance of the living resources in the exclusive economic zone is not endangered by over-exploitation. As appropriate, the coastal State and competent international organizations, whether subregional, regional or global, shall cooperate to this end.

3.   Such measures shall also be designed to maintain or restore populations of harvested species at levels which can produce the maximum sustainable yield, as qualified by relevant environmental and economic factors, including the economic needs of coastal fishing communities and the special requirements of developing States, and taking into account fishing patterns, the interdependence of stocks and any generally recommended international minimum standards, whether subregional, regional or global.

4.   In taking such measures the coastal State shall take into consideration the effects on species associated with or dependent upon harvested species with a view to maintaining or restoring populations of such associated or dependent species above levels at which their reproduction may become seriously threatened.

5.   Available scientific information, catch and fishing effort statistics, and other data relevant to the conservation of fish stocks shall be contributed and exchanged on a regular basis through competent international organizations, whether subregional, regional or global, where appropriate and with participation by all States concerned, including States whose nationals are allowed to fish in the exclusive economic zone.

Article 62
Utilization of the living resources

1.   The coastal State shall promote the objective of optimum utilization of the living resources in the exclusive economic zone without prejudice to article 61.

2.   The coastal State shall determine its capacity to harvest the living resources of the exclusive economic zone. Where the coastal State does not have the capacity to harvest the entire allowable catch, it shall, through agreements or other arrangements and pursuant to the terms, conditions, laws and regulations referred to in paragraph 4, give other States access to the surplus of the allowable catch, having particular regard to the provisions of articles 69 and 70, especially in relation to the developing States mentioned therein.

Article 63
Stocks occurring within the exclusive economic zones of two or more coastal States or both within the exclusive economic zone and in an area beyond and adjacent to it

1.   Where the same stock or stocks of associated species occur within the exclusive economic zones of two or more coastal States, these States shall seek, either directly or through appropriate subregional or regional organizations, to agree upon the measures necessary to coordinate and ensure the conservation and development of such stocks without prejudice to the other provisions of this Part.

2.   Where the same stock or stocks of associated species occur both within the exclusive economic zone and in an area beyond and adjacent to the zone, the coastal State and the States fishing for such stocks in the adjacent area shall seek, either

directly or through appropriate subregional or regional organizations, to agree upon the measures necessary for the conservation of these stocks in the adjacent area.

Article 64
Highly migratory species

1.   The coastal State and other States whose nationals fish in the region for the highly migratory species listed in Annex I shall cooperate directly or through appropriate international organizations with a view to ensuring conservation and promoting the objective of optimum utilization of such species throughout the region, both within and beyond the exclusive economic zone. In regions for which no appropriate international organization exists, the coastal State and other States whose nationals harvest these species in the region shall cooperate to establish such an organization and participate in its work.

2.   The provisions of paragraph 1 apply in addition to the other provisions of this Part.

[...]

Article 66
Anadromous stocks

1.   States in whose rivers anadromous stocks originate shall have the primary interest in and responsibility for such stocks.

2.   The State of origin of anadromous stocks shall ensure their conservation by the establishment of appropriate regulatory measures for fishing in all waters landward of the outer limits of its exclusive economic zone and for fishing provided for in paragraph 3(b). The State of origin may, after consultations with the other States referred to in paragraphs 3 and 4 fishing these stocks, establish total allowable catches for stocks originating in its rivers.

Article 67
Catadromous species

1.   A coastal State in whose waters catadromous species spend the greater part of their life cycle shall have responsibility for the management of these species and shall ensure the ingress and egress of migrating fish.

2.   Harvesting of catadromous species shall be conducted only in waters landward of the outer limits of exclusive economic zones. When conducted in exclusive economic zones, harvesting shall be subject to this article and the other provisions of this Convention concerning fishing in these zones.

Article 87
Freedom of the high seas

1.   The high seas are open to all States, whether coastal or land-locked. Freedom of the high seas is exercised under the conditions laid down by this Convention and by other rules of international law. It comprises, *inter alia*, both for coastal and land-locked States:

       (e)   freedom of fishing, subject to the conditions laid down in section 2

[...]

Article 116
Right to fish on the high seas
All States have the right for their nationals to engage in fishing on the high seas subject to:
(a)   their treaty obligations;
(b)   the rights and duties as well as the interests of coastal States provided for, *inter alia*, in article 63, paragraph 2, and articles 64 to 67; and
(c)   the provisions of this section.

Article 117
Duty of States to adopt with respect to their nationals measures for the conservation of the living resources of the high seas
   All States have the duty to take, or to cooperate with other States in taking, such measures for their respective nationals as may be necessary for the conservation of the living resources of the high seas.

Article 118
Cooperation of States in the conservation and management of living resources
States shall cooperate with each other in the conservation and management of living resources in the areas of the high seas. States whose nationals exploit identical living resources, or different living resources in the same area, shall enter into negotiations with a view to taking the measures necessary for the conservation of the living resources concerned. They shall, as appropriate, cooperate to establish subregional or regional fisheries organizations to this end.

Article 119
Conservation of the living resources of the high seas
1.   In determining the allowable catch and establishing other conservation measures for the living resources in the high seas, States shall:
      (a)   take measures which are designed, on the best scientific evidence available to the States concerned, to maintain or restore populations of harvested species at levels which can produce the maximum sustainable yield, as qualified by relevant environmental and economic factors, including the special requirements of developing States, and taking into account fishing patterns, the interdependence of stocks and any generally recommended international minimum standards, whether subregional, regional or global;
      (b)   take into consideration the effects on species associated with or dependent upon harvested species with a view to maintaining or restoring populations of such associated or dependent species above levels at which their reproduction may become seriously threatened.
2.   Available scientific information, catch and fishing effort statistics, and other data relevant to the conservation of fish stocks shall be contributed and exchanged on a regular basis through competent international organizations, whether subregional, regional or global, where appropriate and with participation by all States concerned.

3.   States concerned shall ensure that conservation measures and their implementa-
        tion do not discriminate in form or in fact against the fishermen of any State.

1995 Agreement on Straddling Fish Stocks, 2167 UNTS 88

Article 2
The objective of this Agreement is to ensure the long-term conservation and sustainable
use of straddling fish stocks and highly migratory fish stocks through effective implementation of the relevant provisions of the Convention.

[...]

Article 5
In order to conserve and manage straddling fish stocks and highly migratory fish stocks,
coastal States and States fishing on the high seas shall, in giving effect to their duty to cooperate in accordance with the Convention:
(a)   adopt measures to ensure long-term sustainability of straddling fish stocks and
        highly migratory fish stocks and promote the objective of their optimum utilization;
(b)   ensure that such measures are based on the best scientific evidence available and
        are designed to maintain or restore stocks at levels capable of producing maximum
        sustainable yield, as qualified by relevant environmental and economic factors,
        including the special requirements of developing States, and taking into account
        fishing patterns, the interdependence of stocks and any generally recommended
        international minimum standards, whether subregional, regional or global;
(c)   apply the precautionary approach in accordance with article 6;
(d)   assess the impacts of fishing, other human activities and environmental factors on
        target stocks and species belonging to the same ecosystem or associated with or
        dependent upon the target stocks;
(e)   adopt, where necessary, conservation and management measures for species
        belonging to the same ecosystem or associated with or dependent upon the target
        stocks, with a view to maintaining or restoring populations of such species above
        levels at which their reproduction may become seriously threatened;
(f)   minimize pollution, waste, discards, catch by lost or abandoned gear, catch of
        non-target species, both fish and non-fish species, (hereinafter referred to as
        non-target species) and impacts on associated or dependent species, in particular
        endangered species, through measures including, to the extent practicable, the
        development and use of selective, environmentally safe and cost-effective fishing
        gear and techniques;
(g)   protect biodiversity in the marine environment;
(h)   take measures to prevent or eliminate overfishing and excess fishing capacity and
        to ensure that levels of fishing effort do not exceed those commensurate with the
        sustainable use of fishery resources;
(i)   take into account the interests of artisanal and subsistence fishers;
(j)   collect and share, in a timely manner, complete and accurate data concerning
        fishing activities on, *inter alia*, vessel position, catch of target and non-target species
        and fishing effort, as set out in Annex I, as well as information from national and
        international research programmes;

(k)   promote and conduct scientific research and develop appropriate technologies in support of fishery conservation and management; and

(l)   implement and enforce conservation and management measures through effective monitoring, control and surveillance.

Article 6
Application of the precautionary approach

1.   States shall apply the precautionary approach widely to conservation, management and exploitation of straddling fish stocks and highly migratory fish stocks in order to protect the living marine resources and preserve the marine environment.

2.   States shall be more cautious when information is uncertain, unreliable or inadequate. The absence of adequate scientific information shall not be used as a reason for postponing or failing to take conservation and management measures.

Article 7
Compatibility of conservation and management measures

1.   Without prejudice to the sovereign rights of coastal States for the purpose of exploring and exploiting, conserving and managing the living marine resources within areas under national jurisdiction as provided for in the Convention, and the right of all States for their nationals to engage in fishing on the high seas in accordance with the Convention:

    (a)   with respect to straddling fish stocks, the relevant coastal States and the States whose nationals fish for such stocks in the adjacent high seas area shall seek, either directly or through the appropriate mechanisms for cooperation provided for in Part III, to agree upon the measures necessary for the conservation of these stocks in the adjacent high seas area;

    (b)   with respect to highly migratory fish stocks, the relevant coastal States and other States whose nationals fish for such stocks in the region shall cooperate, either directly or through the appropriate mechanisms for cooperation provided for in Part III, with a view to ensuring conservation and promoting the objective of optimum utilization of such stocks throughout the region, both within and beyond the areas under national jurisdiction.

2.   Conservation and management measures established for the high seas and those adopted for areas under national jurisdiction shall be compatible in order to ensure conservation and management of the straddling fish stocks and highly migratory fish stocks in their entirety. To this end, coastal States and States fishing on the high seas have a duty to cooperate for the purpose of achieving compatible measures in respect of such stocks. [...]

11.2.1.2 Non-binding instruments

Resolution adopted by the General Assembly on 27 July 2012
[without reference to a Main Committee (A/66/L.56)] 66/288:
'The future we want' (2012 Rio+20 Summit)

168.   We commit to intensify our efforts to meet the 2015 target as agreed to in the Johannesburg Plan of Implementation to maintain or restore stocks to levels that can produce maximum sustainable yield on an urgent basis. In this regard, we

further commit to urgently take the measures necessary to maintain or restore all stocks at least to levels that can produce the maximum sustainable yield, with the aim of achieving these goals in the shortest time feasible, as determined by their biological characteristics. To achieve this, we commit to urgently develop and implement science-based management plans, including by reducing or suspending fishing catch and fishing effort commensurate with the status of the stock. We further commit to enhance action to manage by-catch, discards and other adverse ecosystem impacts from fisheries, including by eliminating destructive fishing practices. We also commit to enhance actions to protect vulnerable marine ecosystems from significant adverse impacts, including through the effective use of impact assessments. Such actions, including those through competent organizations, should be undertaken consistent with international law, the applicable international instruments and relevant General Assembly resolutions and guidelines of the Food and Agriculture Organization of the United Nations.

Sustainable Development Goal 14:

Conserve and sustainably use the oceans, seas and marine resources for sustainable development.

11.2.2 Case Law

CASE

ICJ, *Fisheries Jurisdiction (Spain v. Canada)*, Judgment, Jurisdiction of the Court, ICJ Reports 432 (1998)

70. According to international law, in order for a measure to be characterized as a "conservation and management measure", it is sufficient that its purpose is to conserve and manage living resources and that, to this end, it satisfies various technical requirements. It is in this sense that the terms "conservation and management measures" have long been understood by States in the treaties which they conclude. Notably, this is the sense in which "conservation and management measures" is used in paragraph 4 of Article 62 of the 1982 United Nations Convention on the Law of the Sea (see also 1923 Convention between the United States of America and Canada for the Preservation of the Halibut Fisheries of the Northern Pacific Ocean, especially Articles 1 and 2; 1930 Convention between the United States of America and Canada for the Preservation of the Halibut Fisheries of the Northern Pacific Ocean and Bering Sea, Arts. 1, 2 and 3; 1949 International Convention for the Northwest Atlantic Fisheries, Art. IV (2) and especially Art. VIII; 1959 North-East Atlantic Fisheries Convention, Art. 7; 1973 Convention on Fishing and Conservation of the Living Resources in the Baltic Sea and the Belts, Art. 1 and especially Art. X. Cf. 1958 Geneva Convention on Fishing and Conservation of the Living Resources of the High Seas, Art. 2). The same usage is to be found in the practice of States. Typically, in their enactments and administrative acts, States describe such measures by reference to such criteria as: the limitation of catches through quotas; the regulation of catches by prescribing periods and zones in which fishing is permitted;

and the setting of limits on the size of fish which may be caught or the types of fishing gear which may be used (see, among very many examples, Algerian Legislative Decree No. 94-13 of 28 May 1994, establishing the general rules relating to fisheries; Argentine Law No. 24922 of 6 January 1998, establishing the Federal Fishing Régime; Malagasy Ordinance No. 93-022 of 1993 regulating fishing and aquaculture; New Zealand Fisheries Act 1996; as well as, for the European Union, the basic texts formed by Regulation (EEC) No. 3760192 of 20 December 1992, establishing a Community system for fisheries and aquaculture, and Regulation (EC) No. 894197 of 29 April 1997, laying down certain technical measures for the conservation of fisheries resources. For NAFO practice, see its document entitled Conservation and Enforcement Measures (NAFO/FC/Doc. 96/1)). International law thus characterizes "conservation and management measures" by reference to factual and scientific criteria.

Agreement on Straddling Stocks of 1995 and the "Agreement to Promote Compliance with International Conservation and Management Measures by Fishing Vessels on the High Seas" (FAO, 1993), neither of which has entered into force) the parties have expressly stipulated, "for purposes of th[e] Agreement", that what is generally understood by "conservation and management measures" must comply with the obligations of international law that they have undertaken pursuant to these agreements, such as, compatibility with maximum sustainable yield, concern for the needs of developing States, the duty to exchange scientific data, effective flag State control of its vessels, and the maintenance of detailed records of fishing vessels. The question of who may take conservation and management measures, and the areas to which they may relate, is neither in international law generally nor in these agreements treated as an element of the definition of conservation and management measures. The authority from which such measures derive, the area affected by them, and the way in which they are to be enforced do not belong to the essential attributes intrinsic to the very concept of conservation and management measures; they are, in contrast, elements to be taken into consideration for the purpose of determining the legality of such measures under international law.

71. Reading the words of the reservation in a "natural and reasonable" manner, there is nothing which permits the Court to conclude that Canada intended to use the expression "conservation and management measures" in a sense different from that generally accepted in international law and practice. Moreover, any other interpretation of that expression would deprive the reservation of its intended effect.

DISSENTING OPINION OF JUDGE BEDJAOUI

50. I therefore regret that the Court did not reject, or even hold null and void, a reservation whose obvious purpose, when read together with a piece of domestic legislation, was to permit encroachment upon an essential freedom of international law, both past and present, without fear of judicial intervention. Canada - admittedly with legitimate concern for the conservation of fishery resources - unfortunately yielded to temptation and took a regrettable legislative initiative with a view to an

operation on the high seas, believing it could escape judicial sanction by simultaneously notifying the international community of a new reservation adopted for purposes it feared might be illegal. Such a reservation could not and should not be accepted by the Court

---

CASE

ITLOS, *Southern Bluefin Tuna (New Zealand v. Japan; Australia v. Japan)*, Provisional Measures, Case Nos 3–4, ITLOS Reports 280 (27 August 1999)

THE TRIBUNAL,

1.   Prescribes, pending a decision of the arbitral tribunal, the following measures:

[...]

   (d)   Australia, Japan and New Zealand shall each refrain from conducting an experimental fishing programme involving the taking of a catch of southern bluefin tuna, except with the agreement of the other parties or unless the experimental catch is counted against its annual national allocation as prescribed in subparagraph (c);

   (e)   Australia, Japan and New Zealand should resume negotiations without delay with a view to reaching agreement on measures for the conservation and management of southern bluefin tuna;

   (f)   Australia, Japan and New Zealand should make further efforts to reach agreement with other States and fishing entities engaged in fishing for southern bluefin tuna, with a view to ensuring conservation and promoting the objective of optimum utilization of the stock;

SEPARATE OPINION OF SIR KENNETH KEITH

8.   The urgency needed in the present case does not, in my opinion, concern the danger of a collapse of the stock in the months which will elapse between the reading of the Order and the time when the arbitral tribunal will be in a position to prescribe provisional measures. This event, in light of scientific evidence, is uncertain and unlikely. The urgency concerns the stopping of a trend towards such collapse. The measures prescribed by the Tribunal aim at stopping the deterioration in the southern bluefin tuna stock. Each step in such deterioration can be seen as "serious harm" because of its cumulative effect towards the collapse of the stock. There is no controversy that such deterioration has been going on for years. However, as there is scientific uncertainty as to whether the situation of the stock has recently improved, the Tribunal must assess the urgency of the prescription of its measures in the light of prudence and caution. This approach, which may be called precautionary, is hinted at in the Order, in particular in paragraph 77. However, that paragraph refers it to the future conduct of the parties. While, of course, a precautionary approach by the parties in their future conduct is necessary, such precautionary approach, in my

opinion, is necessary also in the assessment by the Tribunal of the urgency of the measures it might take. In the present case, it would seem to me that the requirement of urgency is satisfied only in the light of such precautionary approach. I regret that this is not stated explicitly in the Order

9. I fully understand the reluctance of the Tribunal in taking a position as to whether the precautionary approach is a binding principle of customary international law. Other courts and tribunals, recently confronted with this question, have avoided to give an answer. In my opinion, in order to resort to the precautionary approach for assessing the urgency of the measures to be prescribed in the present case, it is not necessary to hold the view that this approach is dictated by a rule of customary international law. The precautionary approach can be seen as a logical consequence of the need to ensure that, when the arbitral tribunal decides on the merits, the factual situation has not changed. In other words, a precautionary approach seems to me inherent in the very notion of provisional measures. It is not by chance that in some languages the very concept of "caution" can be found in the terms used to designate provisional measures: for instance, in Italian, misure cautelari, in Portuguese, medidas cautelares, in Spanish, medidas cautelares or medidas precautorias.

CASE
Southern Bluefin Tuna Case between New Zealand v. Japan; Australia v. Japan, Award on Jurisdiction and Admissibility (4 August 2000)

21. Southern Bluefin Tuna (Thunnus maccoyi, hereafter sometimes designated "SBT") is a migratory species of pelagic fish that is included in the list of highly migratory species set out in Annex I of the United Nations Convention on the Law of the Sea. Southern Bluefin Tuna range widely through the oceans of the Southern Hemisphere, principally the high seas, but they also traverse the exclusive economic zones and territorial waters of some States, notably Australia, New Zealand and South Africa. They spawn in the waters south of Indonesia. The main market for the sale of Southern Bluefin Tuna is in Japan, where the fish is prized as a delicacy for sashimi.

22. It is common ground between the Parties that commercial harvest of Southern Bluefin Tuna began in the early 1950s and that, in 1961, the global catch peaked at 81,000 metric tons ("mt"). By the early 1980s, the SBT stock had been severely overfished; it was estimated that the parental stock had declined to 23-30% of its 1960 level. In 1982, Australia, New Zealand and Japan began informally to manage the catching of SBT. Japan joined with Australia and New Zealand in 1985 to introduce a global total allowable catch (hereafter, "TAC") for SBT, initially set at 38,650 mt. In 1989, a TAC of 11,750 tons was agreed, with national allocations of 6,065 tons to Japan, 5,265 tons to Australia and 420 tons to New Zealand; Japan, as the largest harvester of SBT, sustained the greatest cut. But the SBT stock continued to decline. In 1997, it was estimated to be in the order of 7-15% of its 1960 level. Recruitment of SBT stock - the entry of new fish into the fishery - was estimated in

1998 to be about one third of the 1960 level. The institution of total allowable catch restrictions by Japan, Australia and New Zealand to some extent has been offset by the entry into the SBT fishery of fishermen from the Republic of Korea, Taiwan and Indonesia, and some flag-of-convenience States. Whether, in response to TAC restrictions, the stock has in fact begun to recover is at the core of the dispute between Australia and New Zealand, on the one hand, and Japan, on the other. They differ over the current state and recovery prospects of SBT stock and the means by which scientific uncertainty in respect of those matters can best be reduced.

[...]

71. [...] the Tribunal observes that, when it comes into force, the Agreement for the Implementation of the Provisions of the United Nations Convention on the Law of the Sea of 10 December 1982 Relating to the Conservation and Management of Straddling Fish Stocks and Highly Migratory Fish Stocks, which was adopted on August 4, 1995 and opened for signature December 4, 1995 (and signed by Australia, Japan and New Zealand), should, for States Parties to it, not only go far towards resolving procedural problems that have come before this Tribunal but, if the Convention is faithfully and effectively implemented, ameliorate the substantive problems that have divided the Parties. The substantive provisions of the Straddling Stocks Agreement are more detailed and far-reaching than the pertinent provisions of UNCLOS or even of the CCSBT. The articles relating to peaceful settlement of disputes specify that the provisions relating to the settlement of disputes set out in Part XV of UNCLOS apply mutatis mutandis to any dispute between States Parties to the Agreement concerning its interpretation or application. They further specify that the provisions relating to settlement of disputes set out in Part XV of UNCLOS apply mutatis mutandis to any dispute between States Parties to the Agreement concerning the interpretation or application of a subregional, regional or global fisheries agreement relating to straddling fish stocks or highly migratory fish stocks to which they are parties, including any dispute concerning the conservation and management of such stocks

72. FOR THESE REASONS The Arbitral Tribunal
    1. Decides that it is without jurisdiction to rule on the merits of the dispute; and, Unanimously,

[...]

    2. Decides, in accordance with Article 290(5) of the United Nations Convention on the Law of the Sea, that provisional measures in force by Order of the International Tribunal for the Law of the Sea prescribed on August 27, 1999 are revoked from the day of the signature of this Award.

CASE
PCA, *South China Sea Arbitration (Philippines v. China)*, Final Award, PCA Case
No. 2013–19 (12 July 2016)

735. The Tribunal has held that Mischief Reef and Second Thomas Shoal are low-tide elevations located within areas where only the Philippines possesses possible entitlements to maritime zones under the Convention. The relevant areas can only constitute the exclusive economic zone of the Philippines. Accordingly, the Philippines—and not China—possesses sovereign rights with respect to resources in these areas, and the law relevant to Chinese fishing activities at these reef formations is the law governing fishing by the vessels of one State in the exclusive economic zone of another.

736. In this respect, Article 61(1) of the Convention provides that "[t]he coastal State shall determine the allowable catch of the living resources in its exclusive economic zone." The remainder of Article 61 concerns the process through which the coastal State will determine the allowable catch.

737. Article 62 of the Convention then outlines the circumstances in which vessels of other States will have access to the fisheries of a State's exclusive economic zone. Article 62(2) provides that "[w]here the coastal State does not have the capacity to harvest the entire allowable catch, it shall, through agreements or other arrangements and pursuant to the terms, conditions, laws and regulations referred to in paragraph 4, give other States access to the surplus of the allowable catch…." Article 62(3) then provides guidance on the factors to be considered in according access to other States.

738. These provisions make clear that it is the Philippines that controls the process of granting and regulating access to the fisheries of its exclusive economic zone, subject to the provisions of the Convention in doing so. It is thus for the Philippines to determine the allowable catch for fisheries within its exclusive economic zone. If after determining the allowable catch, the Philippines also determines that it lacks the capacity to fully harvest the allowable catch, it must allow other States access to the fishery.

739. Article 62(4) then imposes an obligation on nationals of other States fishing in the exclusive economic zone to comply with the laws and regulations of the coastal State and sets out an illustrative list of the areas that may be regulated. […]

740. Article 62(4) thus expressly requires Chinese nationals to comply with the licensing and other access procedures of the Philippines within any area forming part of the exclusive economic zone of the Philippines. […]

741. The Convention also imposes obligations on States Parties with respect to activities in the exclusive economic zone of other States. […]

742. The nature of the obligation to have "due regard to the rights and duties" of another State was considered by the tribunal in the Chagos Marine Protected Area Arbitration in the context of Article 56(2) (concerning the reversed situation of the regard owed by the coastal State to the rights and duties of other States within its

exclusive economic zone). The tribunal in that matter reasoned as follows:

> the ordinary meaning of "due regard" calls for the [first State] to have such regard for the rights of [the second State] as is called for by the circumstances and by the nature of those rights. [...]

743. In the context of the duties of a flag State with respect to fishing by its nationals, the International Tribunal for the Law of the Sea interpreted the obligation of due regard, when read in conjunction with the obligations directly imposed upon nationals by Article 62(4), to extend to a duty "to take the necessary measures to ensure that their nationals and vessels flying their flag are not engaged in IUU fishing activities." The Fisheries Advisory Opinion goes on to note that:

> the obligation of a flag State ... to ensure that vessels flying its flag are not involved in IUU fishing is also an obligation "of conduct"... as an obligation "of conduct" this is a "due diligence obligation", not an obligation "of result".... The flag State is under the "due diligence obligation" to take all necessary measures to ensure compliance and to prevent IUU fishing by fishing vessels flying its flag.

744. The Tribunal agrees with the Fisheries Advisory Opinion in this respect. Given the importance of fisheries to the entire concept of the exclusive economic zone, the degree to which the Convention subordinates fishing within the exclusive economic zone to the control of the coastal State, and the obligations expressly placed on the nationals of other States by Article 62(4) of the Convention, the Tribunal considers that anything less than due diligence by a State in preventing its nationals from unlawfully fishing in the exclusive economic zone of another would fall short of the regard due pursuant to Article 58(3) of the Convention.

11.3   (IUU) FISHING

11.3.1   Legal Instruments

11.3.1.1 Internationally legally binding instruments
2009 Port State Measures Agreement

Article 1:

(e)   "illegal, unreported and unregulated fishing" refers to the activities set out in paragraph 3 of the 2001 FAO International Plan of Action to Prevent, Deter and Eliminate Illegal, Unreported and Unregulated Fishing, hereinafter referred to as 'IUU fishing

Article 2

Objective

The objective of this Agreement is to prevent, deter and eliminate IUU fishing through the implementation of effective port State measures, and thereby to ensure the long-term conservation and sustainable use of living marine resources and marine ecosystems.

Article 3

Application

1.   Each Party shall, in its capacity as a port State, apply this Agreement in respect of vessels not entitled to fly its flag that are seeking entry to its ports or are in one of its ports, except for:

(a)   vessels of a neighbouring State that are engaged in artisanal fishing for subsistence, provided that the port State and the flag State cooperate to ensure that such vessels do not engage in IUU fishing or fishing related activities in support of such fishing; and

(b)   container vessels that are not carrying fish or, if carrying fish, only fish that have been previously landed, provided that there are no clear grounds for suspecting that such vessels have engaged in fishing related activities in support of IUU fishing.

2.   A Party may, in its capacity as a port State, decide not to apply this Agreement to vessels chartered by its nationals exclusively for fishing in areas under its national jurisdiction and operating under its authority therein. Such vessels shall be subject to measures by the Party which are as effective as measures applied in relation to vessels entitled to fly its flag.

3.   This Agreement shall apply to fishing conducted in marine areas that is illegal, unreported or unregulated, as defined in Article 1(e) of this Agreement, and to fishing related activities in support of such fishing.

[...]

PART 2 ENTRY INTO PORT

Article 7

Designation of ports

1.   Each Party shall designate and publicize the ports to which vessels may request entry pursuant to this Agreement. Each Party shall provide a list of its designated ports to FAO, which shall give it due publicity. [...]

Article 9

Port entry, authorization or denial

1.   After receiving the relevant information required pursuant to Article 8, as well as such other information as it may require to determine whether the vessel requesting entry into its port has engaged in IUU fishing or fishing related activities in support of such fishing, each Party shall decide whether to authorize or deny the

entry of the vessel into its port and shall communicate this decision to the vessel or to its representative.

[...]

Article 11
Use of ports
1.   Where a vessel has entered one of its ports, a Party shall deny, pursuant to its laws and regulations and consistent with international law, including this Agreement, that vessel the use of the port for landing, transshipping, packaging and processing of fish that have not been previously landed and for other port services, including, *inter alia*, refuelling and resupplying, maintenance and drydocking, if:
   (a)   the Party finds that the vessel does not have a valid and applicable authorization to engage in fishing or fishing related activities required by its flag State;
   (b)   the Party finds that the vessel does not have a valid and applicable authorization to engage in fishing or fishing related activities required by a coastal State in respect of areas under the national jurisdiction of that State;
   (c)   the Party receives clear evidence that the fish on board was taken in contravention of applicable requirements of a coastal State in respect of areas under the national jurisdiction of that State;
   (d)   the flag State does not confirm within a reasonable period of time, on the request of the port State, that the fish on board was taken in accordance with applicable requirements of a relevant regional fisheries management organization taking into due account paragraphs 2 and 3 of Article 4; or
   (e)   the Party has reasonable grounds to believe that the vessel was otherwise engaged in IUU fishing or fishing related activities in support of such fishing, including in support of a vessel referred to in paragraph 4 of Article 9, unless the vessel can establish:
      (i)   that it was acting in a manner consistent with relevant conservation and management measures; or
      (ii)   in the case of provision of personnel, fuel, gear and other supplies at sea, that the vessel that was provisioned was not, at the time of provisioning, a vessel referred to in paragraph 4 of Article 9.

[...]

1993 FAO Agreement to Promote Compliance with International Conservation and Management Measures by Fishing Vessels on the High Seas, 2221 UNTS 91

Article III
FLAG STATE RESPONSIBILITY
1.   (a) Each Party shall take such measures as may be necessary to ensure that fishing vessels entitled to fly its flag do not engage in any activity that undermines the effectiveness of international conservation and management measures. (b) In the event that a Party has, pursuant to paragraph 2 of Article II, granted an exemption for fishing vessels of less than 24 metres in length entitled to fly its flag from the

application of other provisions of this Agreement, such Party shall nevertheless take effective measures in respect of any such fishing vessel that undermines the effectiveness of international conservation and management measures. These measures shall be such as to ensure that the fishing vessel ceases to engage in activities that undermine the effectiveness of the international conservation and management measures.

2.   In particular, no Party shall allow any fishing vessel entitled to fly its flag to be used for fishing on the high seas unless it has been authorized to be so used by the appropriate authority or authorities of that Party. A fishing vessel so authorized shall fish in accordance with the conditions of the authorization.

[...]

11.3.1.2 Non-legally binding instruments
Code of Conduct for Responsible Fisheries 1995

8.2   Flag State duties
    8.2.1   Flag States should maintain records of fishing vessels entitled to fly their flag and authorized to be used for fishing and should indicate in such records details of the vessels, their ownership and authorization to fish.
    8.2.2   Flag States should ensure that no fishing vessels entitled to fly their flag fish on the high seas or in waters under the jurisdiction of other States unless such vessels have been issued with a Certificate of Registry and have been authorized to fish by the competent authorities. Such vessels should carry on board the Certificate of Registry and their authorization to fish.
    8.2.3   Fishing vessels authorized to fish on the high seas or in waters under the jurisdiction of a State other than the flag State, should be marked in accordance with uniform and internationally recognizable vessel marking systems such as the FAO Standard Specifications and Guidelines for Marking and Identification of Fishing Vessels.

[...]

8.3   Port State duties
    8.3.1   Port States should take, through procedures established in their national legislation, in accordance with international law, including applicable international agreements or arrangements, such measures as are necessary to achieve and to assist other States in achieving the objectives of this Code, and should make known to other States details of regulations and measures they have established for this purpose. When taking such measures a port State should not discriminate in form or in fact against the vessels of any other State.
    8.3.2   Port States should provide such assistance to flag States as is appropriate, in accordance with the national laws of the port State and international law, when a fishing vessel is voluntarily in a port or at an offshore terminal of the port State and the flag State of the vessel requests the port State for assistance in respect of non-compliance with subregional, regional or global

conservation and management measures or with internationally agreed minimum standards for the prevention, of pollution and for safety, health and conditions of work on board fishing vessels.

**Resolution adopted by the General Assembly on 27 July 2012
[without reference to a Main Committee (A/66/L.56)] 66/288:
'The future we want' (2012 Rio+20 Summit)**

170.   We acknowledge that illegal, unreported and unregulated fishing deprive many countries of a crucial natural resource and remain a persistent threat to their sustainable development. We recommit to eliminate illegal, unreported and unregulated fishing as advanced in the Johannesburg Plan of Implementation, and to prevent and combat these practices, including through the following: developing and implementing national and regional action plans in accordance with the FAO International Plan of Action to Prevent, Deter and Eliminate Illegal, Unreported and Unregulated Fishing; implementing, in accordance with international law, effective and coordinated measures by coastal States, flag States, port States, chartering nations and the States of nationality of the beneficial owners and others who support or engage in illegal, unreported and unregulated fishing by identifying vessels engaged in such fishing and by depriving offenders of the benefits accruing from it; as well as cooperating with developing countries to systematically identify needs and build capacity, including support for monitoring, control, surveillance, compliance and enforcement systems.

11.3.2   Case Law

ADVISORY OPINION
ITLOS, Request for an Advisory Opinion Submitted by the Sub-Regional Fisheries Commission (SRFC), Advisory Opinion, Case No. 21, ITLOS Reports 4 (2 April 2015)

64. [...] The questions read as follows: 1. What are the obligations of the flag State in cases where illegal, unreported and unregulated (IUU) fishing activities are conducted within the Exclusive Economic Zone of third party States? 2. To what extent shall the flag State be held liable for IUU fishing activities conducted by vessels sailing under its flag? 3. Where a fishing license is issued to a vessel within the framework of an international agreement with the flag State or with an international agency, shall the State or international agency be held liable for the violation of the fisheries legislation of the coastal State by the vessel in question? 4. What are the rights and obligations of the coastal State in ensuring the sustainable management of shared stocks and stocks of common interest, especially the small pelagic species and tuna?

[...]

124. It follows from article 58, paragraph 3, and article 62, paragraph 4, as well as from article 192, of the Convention that flag States are obliged to take the necessary measures to ensure that their nationals and vessels flying their flag are not engaged in IUU fishing activities. In accordance with the MCA Convention and the national legislation of the SRFC Member States, such activities also constitute an infringement of the conservation and management measures adopted by these States within their exclusive economic zones. In other words, while under the Convention the primary responsibility for the conservation and management of living resources in the exclusive economic zone, including the adoption of such measures as may be necessary to ensure compliance with the laws and regulations enacted by the coastal State in this regard, rests with the coastal State, flag States also have the responsibility to ensure that vessels flying their flag do not conduct IUU fishing activities within the exclusive economic zones of the SRFC Member States.

129. In the case of IUU fishing in the exclusive economic zones of the SRFC Member States, the obligation of a flag State not party to the MCA Convention to ensure that vessels flying its flag are not involved in IUU fishing is also an obligation "of conduct". In other words, as stated in the Advisory Opinion of the Seabed Disputes Chamber, this is an obligation "to deploy adequate means, to exercise best possible efforts, to do the utmost" to prevent IUU fishing by ships flying its flag. However, as an obligation "of conduct" this is a "due diligence obligation", not an obligation "of result". This means that this is not an obligation of the flag State to achieve compliance by fishing vessels flying its flag in each case with the requirement not to engage in IUU fishing in the exclusive economic zones of the SRFC Member States. The flag State is under the "due diligence obligation" to take all necessary measures to ensure compliance and to prevent IUU fishing by fishing vessels flying its flag.

[...]

219. For these reasons, THE TRIBUNAL,

[...]

3. [...]: The flag State has the obligation to take necessary measures, including those of enforcement, to ensure compliance by vessels flying its flag with the laws and regulations enacted by the SRFC Member States concerning marine living resources within their exclusive economic zones for purposes of conservation and management of these resources. The flag State is under an obligation, in light of the provisions of article 58, paragraph 3, article 62, paragraph 4, and article 192 of the Convention, to take the necessary measures to ensure that vessels flying its flag are not engaged in IUU fishing activities as defined in the MCA Convention within the exclusive economic zones of the SRFC Member States. The flag State, in fulfilment of its obligation to effectively exercise jurisdiction and control in administrative matters under article 94 of the Convention, has the obligation to adopt the necessary administrative measures to ensure that fishing vessels flying its flag are not involved in activities in the

exclusive economic zones of the SRFC Member States which undermine the flag State's responsibility under article 192 of the Convention for protecting and preserving the marine environment and conserving the marine living resources which are an integral element of the marine environment. The foregoing obligations are obligations of "due diligence". The flag State and the SRFC Member States are under an obligation to cooperate in cases related to IUU fishing by vessels of the flag State in the exclusive economic zones of the SRFC Member States concerned. The flag State, in cases where it receives a report from an SRFC Member State alleging that a vessel or vessels flying its flag have been involved in IUU fishing within the exclusive economic zone of that SRFC Member State, has the obligation to investigate the matter and, if appropriate, take any action necessary to remedy the situation, and to inform the SRFC Member State of that action.

4. [...] The liability of the flag State arises from its failure to comply with its "due diligence" obligations concerning IUU fishing activities conducted by vessels flying its flag in the exclusive economic zones of the SRFC Member States. The SRFC Member States may hold liable the flag State of a vessel conducting IUU fishing activities in their exclusive economic zones for a breach, attributable to the flag State, of its international obligations, referred to in the reply to the first question. The flag State is not liable if it has taken all necessary and appropriate measures to meet its "due diligence" obligations to ensure that vessels flying its flag do not conduct IUU fishing activities in the exclusive economic zones of the SRFC Member States.

[...]

6. [...] Under the Convention, the SRFC Member States have the obligation to ensure the sustainable management of shared stocks while these stocks occur in their exclusive economic zones; this includes the following:

(i) the obligation to cooperate, as appropriate, with the competent international organizations, whether subregional, regional or global, to ensure through proper conservation and management measures that the maintenance of the shared stocks in the exclusive economic zone is not endangered by over-exploitation (see article 61, paragraph 2, of the Convention);

[...]

(iii) in relation to tuna species, the obligation to cooperate directly or through the SRFC with a view to ensuring conservation and promoting the objective of optimum utilization of such species in their exclusive economic zones (see article 64, paragraph 1, of the Convention). The measures taken pursuant to such obligation should be consistent and compatible with those taken by the appropriate regional organization, namely the International Commission for the Conservation of Atlantic Tunas, throughout the region, both within and beyond the exclusive economic zones of the SRFC Member States. To comply with these obligations, the SRFC Member States, pursuant to the Convention, specifically articles 61 and 62, must ensure that:

(i) the maintenance of shared stocks, through conservation and management measures, is not endangered by over-exploitation;

(ii) conservation and management measures are based on the best scientific evidence available to the SRFC Member States and, when such evidence is insufficient, they must apply the precautionary approach, pursuant to article 2, paragraph 2, of the MCA Convention;

(iii) conservation and management measures are designed to maintain or restore stocks at levels which can produce the maximum sustainable yield, as qualified by relevant environmental and economic factors, including the economic needs of coastal fishing communities and the special needs of the SRFC Member States, taking into account fishing patterns, the interdependence of stocks and any generally recommended international minimum standards, whether subregional, regional or global. Such measures shall:

(i) take into consideration the effects on species associated with or dependent upon harvested species with a view to maintaining or restoring populations of such associated or dependent species above levels at which their reproduction may become seriously threatened;

(ii) provide for exchange on a regular basis through competent international organizations, of available scientific information, catch and fishing efforts statistics, and other data relevant to the conservation of shared stocks. The obligation to "seek to agree…" under articles 63, paragraph 1, and the obligation to cooperate under article 64, paragraph 1, of the Convention are "due diligence" obligations which require the States concerned to consult with one another in good faith, pursuant to article 300 of the Convention. The consultations should be meaningful in the sense that substantial effort should be made by all States concerned, with a view to adopting effective measures necessary to coordinate and ensure the conservation and development of shared stocks. The conservation and development of shared stocks in the exclusive economic zone of an SRFC Member State require from that State effective measures aimed at preventing over-exploitation of such stocks that could undermine their sustainable exploitation and the interests of neighbouring Member States. [...]

> **CASE**
> PCA, *South China Sea Arbitration (Philippines v. China)*, Final Award, PCA Case
> No. 2013-19 (12 July 2016)

[...]

743. In the context of the duties of a flag State with respect to fishing by its nationals, the International Tribunal for the Law of the Sea interpreted the obligation of due regard, when read in conjunction with the obligations directly imposed upon nationals by Article 62(4), to extend to a duty "to take the necessary measures to ensure that their nationals and vessels flying their flag are not engaged in IUU fishing activities."[761] The Fisheries Advisory Opinion goes on to note that: the obligation of a flag State ... to ensure that vessels flying its flag are not involved in IUU fishing is also an obligation "of conduct"... as an obligation "of conduct" this is a "due diligence obligation", not an obligation "of result".... The flag State is under the "due diligence obligation" to take all necessary measures to ensure compliance and to prevent IUU fishing by fishing vessels flying its flag.

744. The Tribunal agrees with the Fisheries Advisory Opinion in this respect. Given the importance of fisheries to the entire concept of the exclusive economic zone, the degree to which the Convention subordinates fishing within the exclusive economic zone to the control of the coastal State, and the obligations expressly placed on the nationals of other States by Article 62(4) of the Convention, the Tribunal considers that anything less than due diligence by a State in preventing its nationals from unlawfully fishing in the exclusive economic zone of another would fall short of the regard due pursuant to Article 58(3) of the Convention.

11.4   CONSERVATION OF MARINE MAMMALS

11.4.1   Legal Instruments

11.4.1.1 Legally binding instruments
1946 International Whaling Convention, 161 UNTS 72

Article III
1.   The Contracting Governments agree to establish an International Whaling Commission, hereinafter referred to as the Commission, to be composed of one member from each Contracting Government. Each member shall have one vote and may be accompanied by one or more experts and advisers.

Article V
1.   The Commission may amend from time to time the provisions of the Schedule by adopting regulations with respect to the conservation and utilization of whale resources, fixing
       (a)   protected and unprotected species;

(b)   open and closed seasons;

(c)   open and closed waters, including the designation of sanctuary areas;

(d)   size limits for each species;

(e)   time, methods, and intensity of whaling (including the maximum catch of whales to be taken in any one season);

(f)   types and specifications of gear and apparatus and appliances which may be used;

(g)   methods of measurement; and

(h)   catch returns and other statistical and biological records.

2.   These amendments of the Schedule

(a)   shall be such as are necessary to carry out the objectives and purposes of this Convention and to provide for the conservation, development, and optimum utilization of the whale resources;

(b)   shall be based on scientific findings;

(c)   shall not involve restrictions on the number or nationality of factory ships or land stations, nor allocate specific quotas to any factory ship or land station or to any group of factory ships or land stations; and

(d)   shall take into consideration the interests of the consumers of whale products and the whaling industry.

3.   Each of such amendments shall become effective with respect to the Contracting Governments ninety days following notification of the amendment by the Commission to each of the Contracting Governments, except that (a) if any Government presents to the Commission objection to any amendment prior to the expiration of this ninety-day period, the amendment shall not become effective with respect to any of the Governments for an additional ninety days; (b) thereupon, any other Contracting Government may present objection to the amendment at any time prior to the expiration of the additional ninety-day period, or before the expiration of thirty days from the date of receipt of the last objection received during such additional ninety-day period, whichever date shall be the later; and (c) thereafter, the amendment shall become effective with respect to all Contracting Governments which have not presented objection but shall not become effective with respect to any Government which has so objected until such date as the objection is withdrawn. The Commission shall notify each Contracting Government immediately upon receipt of each objection and withdrawal and each Contracting Government shall acknowledge receipt of all notifications of amendments, objections, and withdrawals.

Article VIII

1.   Notwithstanding anything contained in this Convention any Contracting Government may grant to any of its nationals a special permit authorizing that national to kill, take and treat whales for purposes of scientific research subject to such restrictions as to number and subject to such other conditions as the Contracting Government thinks fit, and the killing, taking, and treating of whales in accordance with the provisions of this Article shall be exempt from the operation of this Convention. Each Contracting Government shall report at once to the Commission all such authorizations which it has granted. Each Contracting Government may at any time revoke any such special permit which it has granted.

2.   Any whales taken under these special permits shall so far as practicable be processed and the proceeds shall be dealt with in accordance with directions issued by the Government by which the permit was granted.

3.   Each Contracting Government shall transmit to such body as may be designated by the Commission, in so far as practicable, and at intervals of not more than one year, scientific information available to that Government with respect to whales and whaling, including the results of research conducted pursuant to paragraph 1 of this Article and to Article IV.

4.   Recognizing that continuous collection and analysis of biological data in connection with the operations of factory ships and land stations are indispensable to sound and constructive management of the whale fisheries, the Contracting Governments will take all practicable measures to obtain such data.

Schedule to the ICRW Convention
Article 10

(d)   Notwithstanding the other provisions of paragraph 10 there shall be a moratorium on the taking, killing or treating of whales, except minke whales, by factory ships or whale catchers attached to factory ships. This moratorium applies to sperm whales, killer whales and baleen whales, except minke whales.

(e)   Notwithstanding the other provisions of paragraph 10, catch limits for the killing for commercial purposes of whales from all stocks for the 1986 coastal and the 1985/86 pelagic seasons and thereafter shall be zero. This provision will be kept under review, based upon the best scientific advice, and by 1990 at the latest the Commission will undertake a comprehensive assessment of the effects of this decision on whale stocks and consider modification of this provision and the establishment of other catch limits.*

UNCLOS

Article 65
Nothing in this Part restricts the right of a coastal State or the competence of an international organization, as appropriate, to prohibit, limit or regulate the exploitation of marine mammals more strictly than provided for in this Part. States shall cooperate with a view to the conservation of marine mammals and in the case of cetaceans shall in particular work through the appropriate international organizations for their conservation, management and study

Art 120
Article 65 also applies to the conservation and management of marine mammals in the high seas.

11.4.1.2 Regional agreements

Table 11.1 Regional agreements on cetaceans and other marine mammals

A. Cetaceans
1991 Agreement on the Conservation of Small Cetaceans of the Baltic and North Seas (1991 ASCOBANS)
1996 Agreement on the Conservation of Cetaceans of the Black Sea, Mediterranean Sea, and Contiguous Atlantic Area (ACCOBAMS)
B. Mammals in General
1992 Agreement Establishing the North Atlantic Marine Mammals Conservation Organization (1992 NAMMCO)
1999 Agreement Concerning the Creation of a Marine Mammal Sanctuary in the Mediterranean, France, Italy and Monaco

11.4.2 Case Law

> **CASE**
> ICJ, *Whaling in the Antarctic (Australia v. Japan: New Zealand intervening)*, Judgment, ICJ Reports 226 (2014)

55. The Court notes that Article VIII is an integral part of the Convention. It therefore has to be interpreted in light of the object and purpose of the Convention and taking into account other provisions of the Convention, including the Schedule. However, since Article VIII, paragraph 1, specifies that "the killing, taking, and treating of whales in accordance with the provisions of this Article shall be exempt from the operation of this Convention", whaling conducted under a special permit which meets the conditions of Article VIII is not subject to the obligations under the Schedule concerning the moratorium on the catching of whales for commercial purposes, the prohibition of commercial whaling in the Southern Ocean Sanctuary and the moratorium relating to factory ships.

B. THE RELATIONSHIP BETWEEN ARTICLE VIII AND THE OBJECT AND PURPOSE OF THE CONVENTION

56. The Preamble of the ICRW indicates that the Convention pursues the purpose of ensuring the conservation of all species of whales while allowing for their sustainable exploitation. Thus, the first preambular paragraph recognizes "the interest of the nations of the world in safeguarding for future generations the great natural resources represented by the whale stocks". In the same vein, the second paragraph of the Preamble expresses the desire "to protect all species of whales from further overfishing", and the fifth paragraph stresses the need "to give an interval for recovery to certain species now depleted in numbers". However, the Preamble also refers to the exploitation of whales, noting in the third paragraph that "increases in the size of whale stocks will permit increases in the number of whales which may be captured without endangering these natural resources", and adding in the fourth

paragraph that "it is in the common interest to achieve the optimum level of whale stocks as rapidly as possible without causing widespread economic and nutritional distress" and in the fifth that "whaling operations should be confined to those species best able to sustain exploitation". The objectives of the ICRW are further indicated in the final paragraph of the Preamble, which states that the Contracting Parties "decided to conclude a convention to provide for the proper conservation of whale stocks and thus make possible the orderly development of the whaling industry". Amendments to the Schedule and recommendations by the IWC may put an emphasis on one or the other objective pursued by the Convention, but cannot alter its object and purpose.

57. In order to buttress their arguments concerning the interpretation of Article VIII, paragraph 1, Australia and Japan have respectively emphasized conservation and sustainable exploitation as the object and purpose of the Convention in the light of which the provision should be interpreted. According to Australia, Article VIII, paragraph 1, should be interpreted restrictively because it allows the taking of whales, thus providing an exception to the general rules of the Convention which give effect to its object and purpose of conservation. New Zealand also calls for "a restrictive rather than an expansive interpretation of the conditions in which a Contracting Government may issue a Special Permit under Article VIII", in order not to undermine "the system of collective regulation under the Convention". This approach is contested by Japan, which argues in particular that the power to authorize the taking of whales for purposes of scientific research should be viewed in the context of the freedom to engage in whaling enjoyed by States under customary international law.

58. Taking into account the Preamble and other relevant provisions of the Convention referred to above, the Court observes that neither a restrictive nor an expansive interpretation of Article VIII is justified. The Court notes that programmes for purposes of scientific research should foster scientific knowledge; they may pursue an aim other than either conservation or sustainable exploitation of whale stocks. This is also reflected in the Guidelines issued by the IWC for the review of scientific permit proposals by the Scientific Committee. In particular, the Guidelines initially applicable to JARPA II, Annex Y, referred not only to programmes that "contribute information essential for rational management of the stock" or those that are relevant for "conduct[ing] the comprehensive assessment" of the moratorium on commercial whaling, but also those responding to "other critically important research needs". The current Guidelines, Annex P, list three broad categories of objectives. Besides programmes aimed at "improv[ing] the conservation and management of whale stocks", they envisage programmes which have as an objective to "improve the conservation and management of other living marine resources or the ecosystem of which the whale stocks are an integral part" and those directed at "test[ing] hypotheses not directly related to the management of living marine resources".

[...]

61. The Court considers that Article VIII gives discretion to a State party to the ICRW to reject the request for a special permit or to specify the conditions under which a permit will be granted. However, whether the killing, taking and treating of whales pursuant to a requested special permit is for purposes of scientific research cannot depend simply on that State's perception.

[...]

223. In light of the standard of review set forth above (see paragraph 67), and having considered the evidence with regard to the design and implementation of JARPA II and the arguments of the Parties, it is now for the Court to conclude whether the killing, taking and treating of whales under the special permits granted in connection with JARPA II is "for purposes of scientific research" under Article VIII of the Convention.

224. The Court finds that the use of lethal sampling per se is not unreasonable in relation to the research objectives of JARPA II. However, as compared to JARPA, the scale of lethal sampling in JARPA II is far more extensive with regard to Antarctic minke whales, and the programme includes the lethal sampling of two additional whale species. Japan states that this expansion is required by the new research objectives of JARPA II, in particular, the objectives relating to ecosystem research and the construction of a model of multi-species competition. In the view of the Court, however, the target sample sizes in JARPA II are not reasonable in relation to achieving the programme's objectives.

225. First, the broad objectives of JARPA and JARPA II overlap considerably. To the extent that the objectives are different, the evidence does not reveal how those differences lead to the considerable increase in the scale of lethal sampling in the JARPA II Research Plan. Secondly, the sample sizes for fin and humpback whales are too small to provide the information that is necessary to pursue the JARPA II research objectives based on Japan's own calculations, and the programme's design appears to prevent random sampling of fin whales. Thirdly, the process used to determine the sample size for minke whales lacks transparency, as the experts called by each of the Parties agreed. In particular, the Court notes the absence of complete explanations in the JARPA II Research Plan for the underlying decisions that led to setting the sample size at 850 minke whales (plus or minus 10 per cent) each year. Fourthly, some evidence suggests that the programme could have been adjusted to achieve a far smaller sample size, and Japan does not explain why this was not done. The evidence before the Court further suggests that little attention was given to the possibility of using non-lethal research methods more extensively to achieve the JARPA II objectives and that funding considerations, rather than strictly scientific criteria, played a role in the programme's design.

227. Taken as a whole, the Court considers that JARPA II involves activities that can broadly be characterized as scientific research (see paragraph 127 above), but that the evidence does not establish that the programme's design and implementation are reasonable in relation to achieving its stated objectives. The Court concludes that the special permits granted by Japan for the killing, taking and treating of

whales in connection with JARPA II are not "for purposes of scientific research" pursuant to Article VIII, paragraph 1, of the Convention.

[...]

230. The Court therefore proceeds on the basis that whaling that falls outside Article VIII, paragraph 1, other than aboriginal subsistence whaling, is subject to the three Schedule provisions invoked by Australia. As this conclusion flows from the interpretation of the Convention and thus applies to any special permit granted for the killing, taking and treating of whales that is not "for purposes of scientific research" in the context of Article VIII, paragraph 1, the Court sees no reason to evaluate the evidence in support of the Parties' competing contentions about whether or not JARPA II has attributes of commercial whaling.

231. The moratorium on commercial whaling, paragraph 10 (e), provides: "Notwithstanding the other provisions of paragraph 10, catch limits for the killing for commercial purposes of whales from all stocks for the 1986 coastal and the 1985–1986 pelagic seasons and thereafter shall be zero. This provision will be kept under review, based upon the best scientific advice, and by 1990 at the latest the Commission will undertake a comprehensive assessment of the effects of this decision on whale stocks and consider modification of this provision and the establishment of other catch limits." From 2005 to the present, Japan, through the issuance of JARPA II permits, has set catch limits above zero for three species — 850 for minke whales, 50 for fin whales and 50 for humpback whales. As stated above (see paragraphs 229-230), the Court considers that all whaling that does not fit within Article VIII of the Convention (other than aboriginal subsistence whaling) is subject to paragraph 10 (e) of the Schedule. It follows that Japan has not acted in conformity with its obligations under paragraph 10 (e) in each of the years in which it has granted permits for JARPA II (2005 to the present) because those permits have set catch limits higher than zero.

232. The factory ship moratorium, paragraph 10 (d), provides: "Notwithstanding the other provisions of paragraph 10, there shall be a moratorium on the taking, killing or treating of whales, except minke whales, by factory ships or whale catchers attached to factory ships. This moratorium applies to sperm whales, killer whales and baleen whales, except minke whales." The Convention defines a "factory ship" as a ship "in which or on which whales are treated either wholly or in part" and defines a "whale catcher" as a ship "used for the purpose of hunting, taking, towing, holding on to, or scouting for whales" (Art. II, paras 1 and 3). The vessel Nisshin Maru, which has been used in JARPA II, is a factory ship, and other JARPA II vessels have served as whale catchers. As stated above (see paragraphs 229-230), the Court considers that all whaling that does not fit within Article VIII of the Convention (other than aboriginal subsistence whaling) is subject to paragraph 10 (d) of the Schedule. It follows that Japan has not acted in conformity with its obligations under paragraph 10 (d) in each of the seasons during which fin whales were taken, killed and treated in JARPA II.

233. Paragraph 7 (b), which establishes the Southern Ocean Sanctuary, provides in pertinent part: "In accordance with Article V (1) (c) of the Convention, commercial whaling, whether by pelagic operations or from land stations, is prohibited in a region designated as the Southern Ocean Sanctuary." As previously noted, JARPA II operates within the Southern Ocean Sanctuary (see paragraph 120). Paragraph 7 (b) does not apply to minke whales in relation to Japan, as a consequence of Japan's objection to the paragraph. As stated above (see paragraphs 229–230), the Court considers that all whaling that does not fit within Article VIII of the Convention (other than aboriginal subsistence whaling) is subject to paragraph 7 (b) of the Schedule. It follows that Japan has not acted in conformity with its obligations under paragraph 7 (b) in each of the seasons of JARPA II during which fin whales have been taken.

The Court,

[...]

Finds that the special permits granted by Japan in connection with JARPA II do not fall within the provisions of Article VIII, paragraph 1, of the International Convention for the Regulation of Whaling;

[...]

Finds that Japan, by granting special permits to kill, take and treat fin, humpback and Antarctic minke whales in pursuance of JARPA II, has not acted in conformity with its obligations under paragraph 10 (e) of the Schedule to the International Convention for the Regulation of Whaling;

[...]

Finds that Japan has not acted in conformity with its obligations under paragraph 10 (d) of the Schedule to the International Convention for the Regulation of Whaling in relation to the killing, taking and treating of fin whales in pursuance of JARPA II;

[...]

Finds that Japan has not acted in conformity with its obligations under paragraph 7 (b) of the Schedule to the International Convention for the Regulation of Whaling in relation to the killing, taking and treating of fin whales in the "Southern Ocean Sanctuary" in pursuance of JARPA II;

QUESTIONS

1. Critically assess the strengths and limitations of UNCLOS in relation to the conservation of marine living resources.
2. How is UNCLOS a framework convention?
3. Discuss the problems of high seas fishing.

FURTHER READING

BOOKS

S Borg, *Conservation on the High Seas: Harmonizing International Regimes for the Sustainable Use of Living Resources* (Edward Elgar Publishing 2012)

WT Burke, *The New International Law of Fisheries: UNCLOS 1982 and Beyond* (Clarendon Press 1994)

R Caddell and EJ Molenaar (eds), *Strengthening International Fisheries Law in an Era of Changing Oceans* (Hart Publishing 2019)

Y-T Chen, *Fishing Entity Enforcement in High Seas Fisheries* (Cambridge Scholars Publishing 2014)

R Churchill and A Lowe, *The Law of the Sea* (3rd edn, Manchester University Press 1999)

M Fitzmaurice, *Whaling and International Law* (Cambridge University Press 2015)

M Fitzmaurice and D Tamada (eds), *Whaling in the Antarctic: Significance and Implications of the ICJ Judgment* (Brill/Nijhoff 2016)

D Freestone, R Barnes and D Ong (eds), *The Law of the Sea: Progress and Prospects* (Oxford University Press 2006)

J Harrison, *Making the Law of the Sea: A Study in the Development of International Law* (Cambridge University Press 2011)

E Hey, *The Regime for the Exploitation of Transboundary Marine Fisheries Resources: The United Nations Law of the Sea Convention* (Martinus Nijhoff 1989)

R Hillborn, *Overfishing: What Everyone Needs to Know* (Oxford University Press 2012)

CSG Jefferies, *Marine Mammal Conservation and the Law of the Sea* (Oxford University Press 2016)

DM Johnson, *The International Law of Fisheries: A Framework for Policy Oriented Enquiries* (Yale University Press 1956)

N Liu and CM Brooks, *Governing Marine Living Resources in the Polar Regions* (Edward Elgar Publishing 2019)

M Markowski, *The International Law of EEZ Fisheries: Principles and Implementation* (Europa Law Publishing 2010)

M H Nordquist, S Rosenne, A Yancov and N Grandy (eds), *United Nations Convention on the Law of the Sea 1982: A Commentary, Vol. IV, Articles 192 to 278, Final Act, Annex VI* (Brill/Nijhoff 1991)

F Orrego Vicuña, *The Changing International Law of High Seas Fisheries* (Cambridge University Press 1999)

DR Rothwell, AO Elferink, K Scott and T Stephens (eds), *The Oxford Handbook on the Law of the Sea* (Oxford University Press 2015)

A Serdy, *The New Entrants Problem in International Fisheries Law* (Cambridge University Press 2016)

Y Takei, *Filling Regulatory Gaps in High Seas Fisheries: Discrete High Seas Fish Stocks, Deep-Sea Fisheries and Vulnerable Marine Ecosystems* (Brill/Nijhoff 2013)

Y Tanaka, *A Dual Approach to Ocean Governance: The Cases of Zonal and Integrated Management in International Law of the Sea* (Ashgate 2008)

M Young, *Trading Fish, Saving Fish: The Interaction Between Regimes in International Law* (Cambridge University Press 2011)

CHAPTERS

K Bangert, 'Fisheries Agreements' in *Max Planck Encyclopedia of Public International Law* (2018)

S Borg, 'The Conservation of Marine Living Resources under International Law' in D Attard, M Fitzmaurice, NA Martínez Gutiérrez and R Hamza (eds), *The IMLI Manual on International Maritime Law – Vol. I* (Oxford University Press 2016)

J Braig, 'Whaling' in *Max Planck Encyclopedia of Public International Law* (2013)

ME Desmond and A Powers, 'Convention for the Protection and Development of the Marine Environment of the Wider Caribbean Region 1983 (Cartagena Convention)' in M Fitzmaurice and A Tanzi (eds), *Multilateral Environmental Treaties* (Edward Elgar 2017)

GM Farnelli, 'Convention for the Protection of the Marine Environment of the Baltic Sea 1992 (Helsinki)' in M Fitzmaurice and A Tanzi (eds), *Multilateral Environmental Treaties* (Edward Elgar 2017)

M Fitzmaurice, 'Compliance Mechanism: International Whaling Commission' in *Max Planck Encyclopedia of Public International Law* (2018)

D Freestone, 'Fisheries, High Seas' in *Max Planck Encyclopedia of Public International Law* (2009)

D Freestone, 'Fisheries, Commissions and Organizations' in *Max Planck Encyclopedia of Public International Law* (2010)

J Fuchs, 'Marine Living Resources, International Protection' in *Max Planck Encyclopedia of Public International Law* (2015)

D Heywood Anderson, 'Straddling and Highly Migratory Fish Stocks' in *Max Planck Encyclopedia of Public International Law* (2008)

M Lewis and A Trouwborst, 'Agreement on the Conservation of Small Cetaceans in the Baltic, North East Atlantic, Irish and North Seas (ASCOBANS), the Agreement on the Conservation of Gorillas and their Habitats (Gorilla Agreement), and the Agreement on the Conservation of African-Eurasian Migratory Waterbirds (AEWA)' in M Fitzmaurice and A Tanzi (eds), *Multilateral Environmental Treaties* (Edward Elgar 2017)

N Matz-Luck and J Fuchs, 'Marine Living Resources' in D Rothwell, AO Elferink, K Scott and T Stephens (eds), *The Oxford Handbook of the Law of the Sea* (Oxford University Press 2015)

R Rayfuse, 'Regional Fisheries Management Organisations' in D Rothwell, AO Elferink, K Scott and T Stephens (eds), *The Oxford Handbook of the Law of the Sea* (Oxford University Press 2015)

RG Rayfuse, 'Article 116 – Right to Fish on the High Seas' in A Proelss (ed.), *United Nations Convention on the Law of the Sea commentary* (Hart 2017)

RG Rayfuse, 'Article 117 – Duty of States to Adopt with respect to Their National Measures for the Conservation of the Living Resources of the High Seas' in A Proelss (ed.), *United Nations Convention on the Law of the Sea commentary* (Hart 2017)

RG Rayfuse, 'Article 118 – Cooperation of States in the Conservation and Management of Living Resources' in A Proelss (ed.), *United Nations Convention on the Law of the Sea: A Commentary* (Hart 2017)

RG Rayfuse, 'Article 119 – Conservation of the Living Resources of the High Seas' in A Proelss (ed.), *United Nations Convention on the Law of the Sea: A Commentary* (Hart 2017)

RG Rayfuse, 'Article 120 – Marine Mammals', in A Proelss (ed.), *United Nations Convention on the Law of the Sea: A Commentary* (Hart 2017)

R Rayfuse, 'Out of Sight, Out of Mind: The Challenge of Regulating High Seas Fisheries' in E Probyn, K Johnston and N Lee (eds), *Sustaining Seas: Oceanic Space and the Politics of Care* (Rowman & Littlefield 2020)

R Rayfuse, 'Taming the Wild North? High Seas Fisheries in the Warming Arctic' in R Barnes and R Long (eds), *Frontiers in International Environmental Law: Oceans and Climate Challenges: Essays in Honour of David Freestone* (Brill 2021)

R Rayfuse, 'Settling Disputes in Regional Fisheries Management Organisations: Dealing with Objections' in HR Fabri, E Franckx, M Benetar and T Meshel (eds), *A Bridge over Troubled Waters: Dispute Resolution in the Law of International Watercourses and the Law of the Sea* (Brill 2021)

KN Scott, 'Integrated Oceans Management: A New Frontier in Marine Environmental Protection' in D Rothwell, AO Elferink, K Scott and T Stephens (eds), *The Oxford Handbook of the Law of the Sea* (Oxford University Press 2015)

K Steenmans, 'International Convention for the Regulation of Whaling 1946' in M Fitzmaurice and A Tanzi (eds), *Multilateral Environmental Treaties* (Edward Elgar 2017)

A Sydenes, 'Regional Fisheries Organisations and International Fisheries Governance' in SA Ebbin, A Hoel and A Sydnes (eds), *A Sea Change: The Exclusive Economic Zone and Governance Institutions for Living Marine Resources* (Springer 2005)

MS Wong, 'OSPAR Convention 1992 – Convention for the Protection of the Marine Environment of the North-East Atlantic (and Annexes I, II, III, IV)' in M Fitzmaurice and A Tanzi (eds), *Multilateral Environmental Treaties* (Edward Elgar 2017)

MS Wong, 'United Nations Convention on the Law of the Sea 1982' in M Fitzmaurice and A Tanzi (eds), *Multilateral Environmental Treaties* (Edward Elgar 2017)

ARTICLES

A Charles, 'Fisheries Management and Governance: Forces of Change and Ineria' (2013) 27 Ocean Yearbook 249

PGG Davies and C Redgwell, 'The International Legal Regulation of Straddling Fish Stocks' (1996) 67(1) British Yearbook of International Law 199

A Dieter, 'From Harbor to High Seas: Argument for Thinking Fishery Management Systems and Multinational Fishing Treaties' (2014) 32 Wisconsin International Law Journal 725

A Fabra and V Gascón, 'The Convention on the Conservation of Antarctic Marine Living Resources (CCAMLR) and the Ecosystem Approach' (2008) 23 The International Journal of Marine and Coastal Law 567

M Fitzmaurice and M Rosello, 'IUU Fishing as a Disputed Concept and Its Application to Vulnerable Groups: A Case Study on Arctic Fisheries' (2020) 22 International Community Law Review 410

E Franckx, 'Regional Marine Environment Protection Regimes in the Context of UNCLOS' (1998) 13 International Journal of Marine and Coastal Law 307

E Franckx, 'Fisheries in the South China Sea: A Centrifugal or Centripetal Force?' (2012) 11(4) Chinese Journal of International Law 727

D Freestone and Z Makuch, 'The New International Environmental Law of Fisheries: The 1995 United Nations Straddling Stocks Agreement' (1995) 7 Yearbook of International Environmental Law 3

J Gao, 'The ITLOS Advisory Opinion for the SRFC' (2015) 14(4) Chinese Journal of International Law 735

M Hayashi, 'The 1995 Agreement on the Conservation and Management of Straddling and Highly Migratory Fish Stocks: Significance for the Law of the Sea Convention' (1995) 29 Ocean and Coastal Management 51

CR Hernández-Salas, 'Seamounts Protection in the Pacific Insular Region of Chile' (2015) 14(1) Chinese Journal of International Law 151

B Hutniczak and F Meere, 'International Co-operation as a Key Tool to Prevent IUU Fishing and Disputes Over It' (2020) 22 International Community Law Review 439

B Kunoy, 'The Ambit of *Pactum de Negotiatum* in the Management of Shared Fish Stocks: A Rumble in the Jungle' (2012) 11 Chinese Journal of International Law 689

M Lando, 'The Advisory Jurisdiction of the International Tribunal for the Law of the Sea: Comments on the *Request for an Advisory Opinion Submitted by the Sub-Regional Fisheries Commission*' (2016) 29(2) Leiden Journal of International Law 441

T Malick Ndiaye, 'Illegal, Unreported and Unregulated Fishing: Responses in General and in West Africa' (2011) 10(2) Chinese Journal of International Law 373

A Proelß, 'Conservation and Management of Shared and Straddling Fish Stocks: The International Trade Regime' (2011) 54 German Yearbook of International Law 421

R Rayfuse and R Waner, 'Securing a Sustainable Future for the Oceans Beyond National Jurisdiction: The Legal Basis for an Integrated Cross-Sectoral Regime for High Seas Governance for the 21st Century' (2008) 23 International Journal of Marine and Coastal Law 399

O Spijkers and N Jevglevskaja, 'Sustainable Development and High Seas Fisheries' (2013) 9 Utrecht Law Review 24

JL Suárez, 'Report on the Exploitation of the Products of the Sea' (1926) 20 AJIL Supplement 235

12
Biodiversity and marine biodiversity

12.1 INTRODUCTION

Biodiversity is essential to humankind and survival and cuts across rights and duties of states and their incumbent obligations pursuant to international environmental agreements and other topics addressed in this book, such as, *inter alia*, climate change, the protection of the marine environment, and freshwater. This chapter focuses specifically on the international legal framework pertaining to the conservation of biological diversity. It is structured in two parts. The first part examines the conservation of biodiversity under international law, whilst the second part examines the conservation of marine biodiversity more specifically.

12.1.1 Biodiversity

As mentioned above, biological diversity is essential to humankind, for evolution and for maintaining life-sustaining systems of the biosphere.[1] Further, biological diversity is of intrinsic value and of ecological, genetic, social, economic, scientific, educational, cultural, recreational and aesthetic value.[2] The term 'biological diversity' itself is not defined in international law, but is generally understood to encompass genetic diversity and species diversity. Biological diversity is defined in Article 2 of the Convention of Biological Diversity 1992 ('CBD') as the 'variability among living organisms from all sources including, *inter alia*, terrestrial, marine and other aquatic ecosystems and ecological complexes of which they are part'.

The decline of biodiversity has given rise to global concern.[3] The threats – or, as identified by the Millennium Ecosystem Assessment as 'drivers affecting biodiversity' – include habitat change, climate change, invasive species, over-exploitation and unsustainable use and pollution.[4]

---

[1]   *Preamble*, Convention on Biological Diversity 1992 ('CBD').

[2]   Ibid.

[3]   See, e.g. Millennium Ecosystem Assessment, 2005. Ecosystems and Human Well-being: Biodiversity Synthesis. World Resources Institute, Washington, DC, pp. 42–50; Global Biodiversity Outlook 3, Convention on Biological Diversity Secretariat, p. 34. Global Forest Resources Assessment 2015: How are the world's forests changing? (2nd ed, FAO), pp. 28–32.

[4]   Ibid 47. Indirect drivers of changes include economic activity, demographic change, sociopolitical factors, cultural and religious factors, and scientific and technological change.

Sands and Peel have provided three reasons for conserving nature and biodiversity:

First, biodiversity provides an actual and potential source of biological resources including, for example, for use as food and feed, as well as pharmaceutical, industrial and other applications. Second, biodiversity contributes to the maintenance of the biosphere in a condition that supports human and other life. This concept of 'ecosystem services' provided by biodiversity has become central to contemporary policy debates on the issue. Third, biodiversity conservation may be based on ethical, intrinsic, aesthetic and cultural considerations.[5]

The starting point of the international community to acknowledge the need for the conservation of biological diversity can be seen in the 1972 Stockholm Declaration,[6] followed by the 1982 World Charter for Nature,[7] and Chapter 15 of Agenda 21, which addresses the conservation of marine biodiversity.[8]

The 1992 Convention on Biodiversity ('CBD') and its two protocols, the 2000 Cartagena Protocol on Biosafety and 2010 Nagoya Protocol, can be seen as the comprehensive framework that addresses biodiversity.[9] In particular, the CBD is the 'only global and comprehensive agreement addressing all different aspects of biological diversity with the objective to conserve its intrinsic value'.[10] The main objectives of the CBD are threefold: the conservation of biological diversity; sustainable use of the components of biological diversity; the fair and equitable sharing of the benefits arising out of the utilisation of genetic resources.[11] The Conference of the Parties (COP) is the CBD's treaty body that meets every two years, or as may be deemed necessary, that *inter alia* keeps under review the implementation of the Convention.[12] The Subsidiary Body on Scientific, Technical, and Technological Advice ('SBSTTA') is established to provide the COP with timely advice relating to the implementation of the Convention, and is open to participation by all parties and is multidisciplinary in nature.[13]

Notably, the COP adopted the Cartagena Protocol on Biosafety on 29 January 2000, and also serves as the Meeting of the Parties to the Protocol (COP-MOP),[14] the governing body of the Protocol. The Protocol's objective is to contribute to 'ensuring an adequate level of protection in the field of the safe transfer, handling and use of living modified organisms resulting from

---

[5]   Philippe Sands and Jacqueline Peel, *Principles of International Environmental Law* (4th edn, Cambridge University Press 2018) 385.

[6]   Articles 2, 3, 4 and 7, Declaration of the United Nations Conference on the Human Environment ('Stockholm Declaration'), A/CONF.48/14/Rev.1.

[7]   Articles 2 and 4, World Charter for Nature 1982.

[8]   https://www.un.org/esa/dsd/agenda21/res_agenda21_15.shtml

[9]   https://www.cbd.int/history/

[10]   Nele Matz-Lück, 'Biological Diversity, International Protection', *Max Planck Encyclopedia of Public International Law* (2008), para. 2.

[11]   Sands and Peel (n 5) 389.

[12]   Article 23, CBD.

[13]   Article 25, CBD.

[14]   Article 29, CBD.

modern biotechnology that may have adverse effects on the conservation and sustainable use of biological diversity, taking into account risks to human health, and specifically focusing on transboundary movements'.[15] A Biosafety Clearing-House is established a part of the clearing-house mechanism to facilitate the exchange of scientific, technical, environmental and legal information on, and experience with, living modified organisms; and to assist parties to implement the Protocol, taking into account the special needs of developing country parties, in particular the least developed and small island developing states among them, and countries with economies in transition as well as countries that are centres of origin and centres of genetic diversity.'[16]

Another notable milestone of the COP is in relation to access to genetic resources and benefit-sharing in 2002, the sixth meeting of the Conference of Parties – 'Bonn Guidelines on Access to Genetic Resources and Fair and equitable sharing of the benefits arising out of their utilization, access and benefit sharing' ('Bonn Guidelines').[17] These Guidelines are voluntary, and are designed to be easy to use, practical, and evolutionary in the sense that the Guidelines are intended to be reviewed and accordingly revised and improved as experience is gained in access and benefit-sharing, flexible and transparent.[18] Further, the Guidelines are intended to assist parties in developing an overall access and benefit-sharing strategy, which may be part of their national biodiversity strategy and action plan, and in identifying the steps involved in the process of obtaining access to genetic resources and sharing benefits.[19]

The Bonn Guidelines were the first step in advancing the international legal framework on access and benefit-sharing. This was followed by the Johannesburg World Summit for Sustainable Development, whereby governments called for the elaboration of an international regime on benefit-sharing.[20] This eventually led to the adoption of the Nagoya Protocol on Access to Genetic Resources and the Fair and Equitable Sharing of Benefits arising from their utilisation ('Nagoya Protocol') in Nagoya in 2010 as a supplementary agreement to the CBD.[21] The objective is 'the fair and equitable sharing of the benefits arising from the utilization of genetic resources, including by appropriate access to genetic resources and by appropriate transfer of relevant technologies, taking into account all rights over those resources and to technologies, and by appropriate funding, thereby contributing to the conservation of biological diversity and the sustainable use of its components'.[22]

In 2010, the COP met from 18–29 October 2010 in Nagoya, Aichi and adopted a revised and updated Strategic Plan for Biodiversity, including the Aichi Biodiversity Targets for the

---

[15]   Article 1, CBD.

[16]   Article 20, CBD.

[17]   COP 6 Decision VI/24 ('Bonn Guidelines').

[18]   Para. 7, Bonn Guidelines.

[19]   Para. 12, Bonn Guidelines.

[20]   Plan of Implementation of the World Summit on Sustainable Development, para. 44(o), A/CONF.199/20/Corr.1.

[21]   For history, see https://www.cbd.int/abs/background.

[22]   Article 1, Nagoya Protocol.

2011–2020 period,[23] in order to take effective and urgent action to halt the loss of biodiversity and improve the resilience of ecosystems. The COP has put in place a process for the development of a new post-2020 global biodiversity framework, and this is due to be adopted by the COP at the resumption of its fifteenth meeting in 2022. In addition to CBD, the legal framework also encompasses other conventions, notably Convention on International Trade in Endangered Species 1973 ('CITES'); the Bonn Convention on Migratory Species 1979 ('CMS'); Ramsar Convention on Wetlands of International Importance 1971; the World Heritage Convention 1972; the International Treaty on Plant Genetic Resources for Food and Agriculture 2001; and the International Plant Protection Convention 1951. To promote coherence and cooperation between these conventions, a mechanism known as the Liaison group of Biodiversity-related Conventions has been established between the heads of the secretariats of the seven biodiversity-related conventions, as mandated by the parties of the CBD.[24]

Harrison writes that:

> the CBD deserves a significant amount of credit for mainstreaming biodiversity protection in modern international law, but it does not entirely overshadow other earlier treaties that were concerned with the protection of specific species, habitats, or other particular aspects of nature conservation. These other treaties can all contribute towards the overarching goals of conserving biodiversity contained in the CBD, even if they do so in a 'piecemeal fashion'. Indeed, the CBD COP itself has recognized the important role of these other treaties and the need to enhance synergies between the biodiversity-related conventions.[25]

12.1.2   Marine Biodiversity

Marine biodiversity is vital and essential for ocean and human life. Indeed, like biodiversity more generally, marine biodiversity is in rapid decline.[26] Tanaka has suggested that given its vital importance for the survival of mankind, [marine] biodiversity is to be considered as a 'community interest of the international community as a whole'.[27] On the tenth anniversary of the entry into force of UNCLOS, the main report of the Secretary-General on Oceans and the Law of the Sea recognized that 'the conservation of marine biodiversity is now at the forefront of international consciousness'.[28] The report points to the main threats to ecosystems and components of biodiversity, and the main anthropogenic pressures that may affect key species and habitats in areas beyond national jurisdiction: *inter alia* pollution, climate change, over-fishing and destructive fishing practices, shipping, seafloor drilling and mining, laying of

---

23   COP 10 Decision X/2.

24   COP 7 Decision VII/26, paras 1 and 2.

25   James Harrison, *Saving the Oceans through Law: The International Legal Framework for the Protection of the Marine Environment* (Oxford University Press 2017) 51.

26   UN Report: Nature's Dangerous Decline 'Unprecedented'; Species Extinction Rates 'Accelerating', last accessed 28 May 2021: https://www.un.org/sustainabledevelopment/blog/2019/05/nature-decline-unprecedented-report/

27   Tanaka Yoshifumi, *The International Law of the Sea* (3rd edn, CUP 2019) 405.

28   Report of the Secretary-General on Oceans and the Law of the Sea, 18 Aug 2004, A/59/62/Add.1, para. 2.

cables and pipelines, marine scientific research and commercially orientated activities relating to genetic resources, tourism, marine debris, land-based activities, climate change and cyclical climate variability, oil and gas exploration and exploitation, and deep seabed mining.[29] The increase in sea surface temperatures poses a threat to coral reefs.[30]

In Johannesburg, South Africa on 26 August to 4 September 2002, the World Summit on Sustainable Development strongly affirmed the full implementation of Agenda 21, the Programme for Further Implementation of Agenda 21 and the Commitments to the Rio principles. Agenda 21 as adopted by UNCED in 1992 contains Chapter 17, which calls for the 'Protection of the Oceans, all kinds of seas, including enclosed and semi-enclosed seas, and coastal areas and the protection, rational use and development of their living resources'. This requires, *inter alia*,

new approaches to marine and coastal area management and development at the national subregional, regional and global levels, approaches that are integrated in content and are precautionary and anticipatory in ambit, as reflected in the following programme areas: [...]

a. Integrated management and sustainable development of coastal areas, including exclusive economic zones;
b. Marine environmental protection;
c. Sustainable use and conservation of marine living resources of the high seas;
d. Sustainable use and conservation of marine living resources under national jurisdiction;
e. Addressing critical uncertainties for the management of the marine environment and climate change;
f. Strengthening international, including regional, cooperation and coordination;
g. Sustainable development of small islands.

Notably, paragraph 32 stipulates:

In accordance with chapter 17 of Agenda 21, promote the conservation and management of the oceans through actions at all levels, giving due regard to the relevant international instruments to:
(a) Maintain the productivity and biodiversity of important and vulnerable marine and coastal areas, including in areas within and beyond national jurisdiction;
(b) Implement the work programme arising from the Jakarta Mandate on the Conservation and Sustainable Use of Marine and Coastal Biological Diversity of the Convention on Biological Diversity, including through the urgent mobilization of financial resources

---

[29] Ibid, paras 205–206.
[30] Report of the Ad Hoc Technical Expert Group on Biodiversity and Climate Change UNEP/CBD/SBSTTA/9/INF/12 30 September 2003, Subsidiary body on Scientific, Technical and Technological Advice Ninth meeting Montreal, 10–14 November 2003, p. 37, para. 63.

and technological assistance and the development of human and institutional capacity, particularly in developing countries;

(c) Develop and facilitate the use of diverse approaches and tools, including the ecosystem approach, the elimination of destructive fishing practices, the establishment of marine protected areas consistent with international law and based on scientific information, including representative networks by 2012 and time/area closures for the protection of nursery grounds and periods, proper coastal land use and watershed planning and the integration of marine and coastal areas management into key sectors;

(d) Develop national, regional and international programmes for halting the loss of marine biodiversity, including in coral reefs and wetlands;

(e) Implement the Ramsar Convention, including its joint work programme with the Convention on Biological Diversity, and the programme of action called for by the International Coral Reef Initiative to strengthen joint management plans and international networking for wetland ecosystems in coastal zones, including coral reefs, mangroves, seaweed beds and tidal mud flats.[31]

The UN Sustainable Development Goals as agreed upon in 2015 comprise Sustainable Development Goal 14, which aims to 'conserve and sustainably use the oceans, seas and marine resources for sustainable development'.

In relation to the international legal framework governing marine biodiversity, the first point of reference is UNCLOS, which, regrettably, only comprises two general provisions under the legal framework for the protection of the marine environment that directly relate to marine biodiversity: Articles 194(5) and 196(1). At present, there is no provision that places obligations on states to conserve or manage marine biodiversity in areas beyond national jurisdiction. The 1995 Fish Stocks Agreement can be said to address the limitations in UNCLOS as Article 5(g) mentions the protection of biodiversity in the marine environment, whilst also incorporating an ecosystem approach and the precautionary principle.

The CBD, as already examined above, also applies to marine biodiversity, although not explicitly so. Nevertheless, marine and coastal biodiversity was a priority for the COP right from the very beginning. At the first COP meeting, the SBSTTA was requested to advise on scientific, technical and technological aspects of the conservation and sustainable use of marine and coastal biological diversity.[32] In 1995, the COP adopted Decision IV/5, also known as the Jakarta Mandate on Marine and Coastal Biological Diversity, which identifies key operational objectives and priority activities within five key programme elements: integrated marine and coastal area management, marine and coastal living resources, marine and coastal protected areas, mariculture, and alien species and genotypes. It also provides a general programme

[31]   Para. 32.

[32]   https://www.cbd.int/decision/cop/?id=7067

element to encompass the coordination role of the Secretariat, the collaborative linkages required and the effective use of experts.[33]

As mentioned above, the Aichi targets were adopted in 2010, setting out objectives that cover both terrestrial and marine biodiversity. The COP has also taken several decisions on ocean-related issues, including a decision relating to conservation and sustainable use of deep seabed genetics resources beyond the limits of national jurisdiction – Decision VIII/21 (2006); implementation of integrated marine and coastal area management, Decision VIII/22 (2006); marine and coastal biodiversity; sustainable fisheries and adverse impacts of human activities, Decision XI/18 (2012).

Harrison has observed a 'large overlap' between the CBD and UNCLOS in relation to the relevant provisions and that 'nevertheless, they can be read in a mutually supportive manner'.[34] He continues that:

the CBD itself stresses it must be read in light of 'the right and obligations of States under the law of the sea' which is a veiled reference to the legal framework established by UNCLOS. The essence of both instruments is that States must take further actions to regulate activities and processes, which may have a detrimental impact on the marine environment. Both treaties also leave it to States to determine, either individually or collectively, the precise measures which must be taken to fulfil these obligations. The CBD, therefore, requires further elaboration and it can thus be considered as an umbrella treaty, like UNCLOS itself.[35]

Marine protected areas (MPAs) are a useful area-based management tool with regard to the protection and conservation of marine biodiversity. There is no accepted definition for an MPA, but broadly speaking, it is understood to be an established protected area in a marine space.[36] The COP to the Convention on Biological Diversity has provided that an MPA is:

any defined area within or adjacent to the marine environment, together with its over-lying waters and associated flora, fauna and historical or cultural features, which has been reserved by legislation or other effective means, including custom, with the effect that its marine and/or coastal biodiversity enjoys a higher level of protection than its surroundings.[37]

The Biodiversity Committee of the OSPAR Convention has defined an MPA as 'an area within the maritime area for which protective, conservation, restorative or precautionary measures,

---

[33]   Decision adopted by the conference of the parties to the Convention on Biological Diversity at its 7th meeting, Annex I, COP 4 Decision IV/5(2004). https://www.cbd.int/sp/targets/; See Targets 6, 10 and 11.

[34]   Harrison (n 25) 47.

[35]   Ibid., 47–48.

[36]   E.g. Article 10 Barcelona Convention; Art 14 Noumea Convention; Art 10 Nairobi Convention; Art 10 Cartagena Protocol; Art 11 Abidjan Convention.

[37]   Decision VII/5, note 11.

consistent with international law have been instituted for the purpose of protecting and conserving species, habitats, ecosystems or ecological processes of the marine environment'.[38]

MPAs can be an effective area-based management tool to protect the marine environment,[39]
recover and maintain ecosystem and habitats, which is directly relevant to marine biodiversity.
Tanaka has observed MPAs that relate directly to conservation of marine biodiversity, which
broadly exist in two sub-categories:[40] MPAs that protect marine life such as marine mammals
in a particular region;[41] and MPAs that seek to protect rare or fragile ecosystems and the
habitat of depleted or endangered species and other marine life in a particular region.[42]

As mentioned above, Chapter 17 of Agenda 21, in promoting the conservation and management of the oceans, gives due regard to the relevant international instruments to establish
MPAs consistent with international law and based on scientific information, including representative networks by 2012.[43] As mentioned above, the COP of the CBD has been working on
marine issues, which also extends towards work on marine protected areas.

---

[38]   OSPAR Recommendation 2003/3 adopted by OSPAR 2003 (OSPAR 03/17/1 Annex 9) amended by OSPAR
Recommendation 2010/2 (OSPAR 10/23/1, Annex 7), para.1.1.

[39]   E.g. Articles 211(6) and 234 of UNCLOS; MARPOL 'special areas'; PSSA : 'an area that needs special protection through action by IMO because of its significance or recognized ecological, socio-economic, or scientific reasons
and because it may be vulnerable to damage by international shipping activities' IMO Resolution A.927(22) Annex 2,
Guidelines for the Identification and Designation of Particularly Sensitive Sea Areas, 15 Jan 2002, para.1.2.

[40]   Tanaka Yoshifumi, *The Peaceful Settlement of International Disputes* (Cambridge University Press 2018) 420.

[41]   E.g. 1990 Agreement on the Conservation of Seals in the Wadden Sea; 1997 Agreement on the Conservation
of Cetaceans of the Black Sea, Mediterranean Sea and Contiguous Atlantic Area (ACCOBAMS), 1999 Agreement
Establishing a Sanctuary for Marine Mammals; Inter-American Convention for the Protection and Conservation of
Sea Turtles.

[42]   E.g. Art II, Convention on the Conservation of nature in the South Pacific 1976; Article 9(2)(g) Convention
on the Conservation of Antarctic Marine Living Resources 1980); Article 11 Convention for Co-operation in the
Protection and Development of the Marine and Coastal Environment of the West and Central African Region 1981;
Article 3(1) Protocol Concerning Mediterranean Specially Protected Areas 1982; Article 10 Convention for the
Protection, Management and Development of the Marine and Coastal Environment of the Eastern African Region
1985; Article 8 Protocol Concerning Protected Areas and Wild Fauna and Flora in the Eastern African Region 1985;
Article 3(3)(a) ASEAN Agreement on the Conservation of Nature and Natural Resources 1985; Article 14, Convention
for the Protection of the Natural Resources and Environment of the South Pacific Region 1986; Articles 2 and 3
Protocol for the Conservation and management of Protected Marine and Coastal Areas of the South-East Pacific
1989; Articles 2 and 3 Protocol for the Conservation and Management of Protected Marine and Coastal Areas of the
South-East Pacific 1989; Article 4 Protocol Concerning specially protected areas and wildlife in the wider Caribbean
region 1990; Annex V Protocol to the Antarctic Treaty on Environmental Protection; Article 8(a) Convention on
Biological Diversity 1992.

[43]   Para 32(c), Chapter 17 of Agenda 21.

In 2006–2012, the UN moved towards considering issues relating to the conservation and sustainable use of marine biological diversity beyond areas of national jurisdiction, where in resolution GA 68/70 (para. 200):

Requests the Secretary-General to convene three meetings of the Ad Hoc Open-ended Informal Working Group, to take place from 1 to 4 April and 16 to 19 June 2014 and from 20 to 23 January 2015, and requests the Secretary-General to make every effort to provide full conference services within existing resources.

In 2015, the GA adopted Resolution 69/292 (2015), which decided to develop 'an international legally binding instrument under the United Nations Convention on the Law of the Sea on the conservation and sustainable use of marine biological diversity of areas beyond national jurisdiction' and to that end:

(a) Decides to establish, prior to holding an intergovernmental conference, a preparatory committee, open to all States Members of the United Nations, members of the special-ized agencies and parties to the Convention, with others invited as observers in accord-ance with past practice of the United Nations, to make substantive recommendations to the General Assembly on the elements of a draft text of an international legally binding instrument under the Convention, taking into account the various reports of the Co-Chairs on the work of the Ad Hoc Open-ended Informal Working Group to study issues relating to the conservation and sustainable use of marine biological diversity beyond areas of national jurisdiction, and that the preparatory committee will start its work in 2016 and, by the end of 2017, report to the Assembly on its progress.[44]

In GA Resolution 72/249 (2017), the GA decided to:

convene an intergovernmental conference, under the auspices of the United Nations, to consider the recommendations of the Preparatory Committee on the elements and to elaborate the text of an international legally binding instrument under the United Nations Convention on the Law of the Sea on the conservation and sustainable use of marine biological diversity of areas beyond national jurisdiction, with a view to developing the instrument as soon as possible.[45]

It was also decided that the negotiations shall address four topics, together and as a whole: (i) marine genetic resources, including questions on the sharing of benefits; (ii) measures such as area-based management tools, including MPAs; (iii) environmental impact assessments; (iv) capacity-building and the transfer of marine technology;[46] and notably, recognises that 'this

---

[44] GA adopted Resolution 69/292 (2015), para. 1.

[45] GA Resolution 72/249 (2017), para. 1.

[46] Ibid, para. 2.

process and its result should not undermine existing relevant legal instruments and frameworks and relevant global, regional and sectoral bodies'.[47] The negotiations are ongoing.

12.2   CONSERVATION OF BIODIVERSITY

12.2.1   Legal instruments

12.2.1.1 International

1971 Ramsar Convention, 996 UNTS 245

Article 1

1.   For the purpose of this Convention wetlands are areas of marsh, fen, peatland or water, whether natural or artificial, permanent or temporary, with water that is static or flowing, fresh, brackish or salt, including areas of marine water the depth of which at low tide does not exceed six metres.

Article 2

1.   Each Contracting Party shall designate suitable wetlands within its territory for inclusion in a List of Wetlands of International Importance, hereinafter referred to as "the List" which is maintained by the bureau established under Article 8. The boundaries of each wetland shall be precisely described and also delimited on a map and they may incorporate riparian and coastal zones adjacent to the wetlands, and islands or bodies of marine water deeper than six metres at low tide lying within the wetlands, especially where these have importance as waterfowl habitat.

2.   Wetlands should be selected for the List on account of their international significance in terms of ecology, botany, zoology, limnology or hydrology. In the first instance wetlands of international importance to waterfowl at any season should be included.

1972 World Heritage Convention, 1037 UNTS 151

Article 1

For the purpose of this Convention, the following shall be considered as "cultural heritage": monuments: architectural works, works of monumental sculpture and painting, elements or structures of an archaeological nature, inscriptions, cave dwellings and combinations of features, which are of outstanding universal value from the point of view of history, art or science; groups of buildings: groups of separate or connected buildings which, because of their architecture, their homogeneity or their place in the landscape, are of outstanding universal value from the point of view of history, art or science; sites: works of man or the combined works of nature and man, and areas including archaeological sites which are of

---

47   Ibid, para. 7.

outstanding universal value from the historical, aesthetic, ethnological or anthropological point of view.

Article 2
For the purposes of this Convention, the following shall be considered as "natural heritage": natural features consisting of physical and biological formations or groups of such formations, which are of outstanding universal value from the aesthetic or scientific point of view; geological and physiographical formations and precisely delineated areas which constitute the habitat of threatened species of animals and plants of outstanding universal value from the point of view of science or conservation; natural sites or precisely delineated natural areas of outstanding universal value from the point of view of science, conservation or natural beauty.

Article 3
It is for each State Party to this Convention to identify and delineate the different properties situated on its territory mentioned in Articles 1 and 2 above.

Article 4
Each State Party to this Convention recognizes that the duty of ensuring the identification, protection, conservation, presentation and transmission to future generations of the cultural and natural heritage referred to in Articles 1 and 2 and situated on its territory, belongs primarily to that State. It will do all it can to this end, to the utmost of its own resources and, where appropriate, with any international assistance and co-operation, in particular, financial, artistic, scientific and technical, which it may be able to obtain.

1992 Convention on Biological Diversity, 1760 UNTS 79

Preamble

Conscious of the intrinsic value of biological diversity and of the ecological, genetic, social, economic, scientific, educational, cultural, recreational and aesthetic values of biological diversity and its components.

Conscious also of the importance of biological diversity for evolution and for maintaining life sustaining systems of the biosphere

Article 1 Objectives
The objectives of this Convention, to be pursued in accordance with its relevant provisions, are the conservation of biological diversity. the sustainable use of its components and the fair and equitable sharing of the benefits arising out of the utilization of genetic resources, including by appropriate access to genetic resources and by appropriate transfer of relevant technologies, taking into account all rights over those resources and to technologies, and by appropriate funding.

Article 2 Use of Terms

For the purposes of this Convention:

"Biological diversity" means the variability among living organisms from all sources including, *inter alia*, terrestrial, marine and other aquatic ecosystems and the ecological complexes of which they are part: this includes diversity within species, between species and of ecosystems.

"Biological resources" includes genetic resources, organisms or parts thereof, populations, or any other biotic component of ecosystems with actual or potential use or value for humanity.

"Biotechnology" means any technological application that uses biological systems, living organisms, or derivatives thereof, to make or modify products or processes for specific use.

"Country of origin of genetic resources" means the country which possesses those genetic resources in in-situ conditions.

"Country providing genetic resources" means the country supplying genetic resources collected from in situ sources, including populations of both wild and domesticated species, or taken from ex-situ sources, which may or may not have originated in that country.

"Domesticated or cultivated species" means species in which the evolutionary process has been influenced by humans to meet their needs.

"Ecosystem" means a dynamic complex of plant, animal and micro-organism communities and their non-living environment interacting as a functional unit.

"Ex-situ conservation" means the conservation of components of biological diversity outside their natural habitats.

"Genetic material" means any material of plant, animal, microbial or other origin containing functional units of heredity.

"Genetic resources" means genetic material of actual or potential value.

"Habitat" means the place or type of site where an organism or population naturally occurs. "In-situ conditions" means conditions where genetic resources exist within ecosystems and natural habitats, and. in the case of domesticated or cultivated species, in the surroundings where they have developed their distinctive properties.

"In-situ conservation" means the conservation of ecosystems and natural habitats and the maintenance and recovery of viable populations of species in their natural surroundings and, in the case of domesticated or cultivated species, in the surroundings where they have developed their distinctive properties.

"Protected area" means a geographically defined area which is designated or regulated and managed to achieve specific conservation objectives. "Regional economic integration organization" means an organization constituted by sovereign States of a given region, to which its member States have transferred competence in respect of matters governed by this Convention and which has been duly authorized, in accordance with its internal procedures, to sign, ratify, accept, approve or accede to it.

"Sustainable use" means the use of components of biological diversity in a way and at a rate that does not lead to the long-term decline of biological diversity, thereby maintaining its potential to meet the needs and aspirations of present and future generations.

[...]

Article 4 Jurisdictional Scope
Subject to the rights of other States, and except as otherwise expressly provided in this Convention, the provisions of this Convention apply, in relation to each Contracting Party:
(a)   In the case of components of biological diversity, in areas within the limits of its national jurisdiction; and
(b)   In the case of processes and activities, regardless of where their effects occur, carried out under its jurisdiction or control, within the area of its national jurisdiction or beyond the limits of national jurisdiction.

[...]

Article 6 General Measures for Conservation and Sustainable Use
Each Contracting Party shall, in accordance with its particular conditions and capabilities:
(a)   Develop national strategies, plans or programmes for the conservation and sustainable use of biological diversity or adapt for this purpose existing strategies, plans or programmes which shall reflect, *inter alia*, the measures set out in this Convention relevant to the Contracting Party concerned; and
(b)   Integrate, as far as possible and as appropriate, the conservation and sustainable use of biological diversity into relevant sectoral or cross-sectoral plans, programmes and policies.

2000 Cartagena Protocol on Biosafety, 2226 UNTS 208

Article 1
Objective
In accordance with the precautionary approach contained in Principle 15 of the Rio Declaration on Environment and Development, the objective of this Protocol is to contribute to ensuring an adequate level of protection in the field of the safe transfer, handling and use of living modified organisms resulting from modern biotechnology that may have adverse effects on the conservation and sustainable use of biological diversity, taking also into account risks to human health, and specifically focusing on transboundary movements.

[...]

Article 4

Scope

This Protocol shall apply to the transboundary movement, transit, handling and use of all living modified organisms that may have adverse effects on the conservation and sustainable use of biological diversity, taking also into account risks to human health.

[...]

Article 20

Information Sharing and the Biosafety Clearing-House

1. A Biosafety Clearing-House is hereby established as part of the clearing-house mechanism under Article 18, paragraph 3, of the Convention, in order to:
    (a) Facilitate the exchange of scientific, technical, environmental and legal information on, and experience with, living modified organisms; and
    (b) Assist Parties to implement the Protocol, taking into account the special needs of developing country Parties, in particular the least developed and small island developing States among them, and countries with economies in transition as well as countries that are centres of origin and centres of genetic diversity.

2. The Biosafety Clearing-House shall serve as a means through which information is made available for the purposes of paragraph 1 above. It shall provide access to information made available by the Parties relevant to the implementation of the Protocol. It shall also provide access, where possible, to other international biosafety information exchange mechanisms.

3. Without prejudice to the protection of confidential information, each Party shall make available to the Biosafety Clearing-House any information required to be made available to the Biosafety Clearing-House under this Protocol, and:
    (a) Any existing laws, regulations and guidelines for implementation of the Protocol, as well as information required by the Parties for the advance informed agreement procedure;
    (b) Any bilateral, regional and multilateral agreements and arrangements;
    (c) Summaries of its risk assessments or environmental reviews of living modified organisms generated by its regulatory process, and carried out in accordance with Article 15, including, where appropriate, relevant information regarding products thereof, namely, processed materials that are of living modified organism origin, containing detectable novel combinations of replicable genetic material obtained through the use of modern biotechnology;
    (d) Its final decisions regarding the importation or release of living modified organisms; and
    (e) Reports submitted by it pursuant to Article 33, including those on implementation of the advance informed agreement procedure.

4. The modalities of the operation of the Biosafety Clearing-House, including reports on its activities, shall be considered and decided upon by the Conference of the

Parties serving as the meeting of the Parties to this Protocol at its first meeting, and kept under review thereafter.

2010 Nagoya-Kuala Lumpur Supplementary Protocol on Liability and Redress to the Cartagena Protocol on Biosafety

Article 1 OBJECTIVE

The objective of this Protocol is the fair and equitable sharing of the benefits arising from the utilization of genetic resources, including by appropriate access to genetic resources and by appropriate transfer of relevant technologies, taking into account all rights over those resources and to technologies, and by appropriate funding, thereby contributing to the conservation of biological diversity and the sustainable use of its components.

[...]

Article 3 SCOPE

This Protocol shall apply to genetic resources within the scope of Article 15 of the Convention and to the benefits arising from the utilization of such resources. This Protocol shall also apply to traditional knowledge associated with genetic resources within the scope of the Convention and to the benefits arising from the utilization of such knowledge.

[...]

Article 5 FAIR AND EQUITABLE BENEFIT-SHARING

1. In accordance with Article 15, paragraphs 3 and 7 of the Convention, benefits arising from the utilization of genetic resources as well as subsequent applications and commercialization shall be shared in a fair and equitable way with the Party providing such resources that is the country of origin of such resources or a Party that has acquired the genetic resources in accordance with the Convention. Such sharing shall be upon mutually agreed terms.
2. Each Party shall take legislative, administrative or policy measures, as appropriate, with the aim of ensuring that benefits arising from the utilization of genetic resources that are held by indigenous and local communities, in accordance with domestic legislation regarding the established rights of these indigenous and local communities over these genetic resources, are shared in a fair and equitable way with the communities concerned, based on mutually agreed terms.
3. To implement paragraph 1 above, each Party shall take legislative, administrative or policy measures, as appropriate.
4. Benefits may include monetary and non-monetary benefits, including but not limited to those listed in the Annex.
5. Each Party shall take legislative, administrative or policy measures, as appropriate, in order that the benefits arising from the utilization of traditional knowledge associated with genetic resources are shared in a fair and equitable way with indigenous and local communities holding such knowledge. Such sharing shall be upon mutually agreed terms.

Article 6 ACCESS TO GENETIC RESOURCES

1. In the exercise of sovereign rights over natural resources, and subject to domestic access and benefit-sharing legislation or regulatory requirements, access to genetic resources for their utilization shall be subject to the prior informed consent of the Party providing such resources that is the country of origin of such resources or a Party that has acquired the genetic resources in accordance with the Convention, unless otherwise determined by that Party.

2. In accordance with domestic law, each Party shall take measures, as appropriate, with the aim of ensuring that the prior informed consent or approval and involvement of indigenous and local communities is obtained for access to genetic resources where they have the established right to grant access to such resources.

3. Pursuant to paragraph 1 above, each Party requiring prior informed consent shall take the necessary legislative, administrative or policy measures, as appropriate, to:

    (a) Provide for legal certainty, clarity and transparency of their domestic access and benefit-sharing legislation or regulatory requirements;

    (b) Provide for fair and non-arbitrary rules and procedures on accessing genetic resources;

    (c) Provide information on how to apply for prior informed consent;

    (d) Provide for a clear and transparent written decision by a competent national authority, in a cost-effective manner and within a reasonable period of time;

    (e) Provide for the issuance at the time of access of a permit or its equivalent as evidence of the decision to grant prior informed consent and of the establishment of mutually agreed terms, and notify the Access and Benefitsharing Clearing-House accordingly;

    (f) Where applicable, and subject to domestic legislation, set out criteria and/ or processes for obtaining prior informed consent or approval and involvement of indigenous and local communities for access to genetic resources; and

    (g) Establish clear rules and procedures for requiring and establishing mutually agreed terms. Such terms shall be set out in writing and may include, *inter alia*:

        (i)   A dispute settlement clause;

        (ii) Terms on benefit-sharing, including in relation to intellectual property rights;

        (iii) Terms on subsequent third-party use, if any; and

        (iv) Terms on changes of intent, where applicable.

Article 7 ACCESS TO TRADITIONAL KNOWLEDGE ASSOCIATED WITH GENETIC RESOURCES

In accordance with domestic law, each Party shall take measures, as appropriate, with the aim of ensuring that traditional knowledge associated with genetic resources that is held by indigenous and local communities is accessed with the prior and informed consent or approval and involvement of these indigenous and local communities, and that mutually agreed terms have been established.

[...]

Article 23 TECHNOLOGY TRANSFER, COLLABORATION AND COOPERATION
In accordance with Articles 15, 16, 18 and 19 of the Convention, the Parties shall collaborate and cooperate in technical and scientific research and development programmes, including biotechnological research activities, as a means to achieve the objective of this Protocol. The Parties undertake to promote and encourage access to technology by, and transfer of technology to, developing country Parties, in particular the least developed countries and small island developing States among them, and Parties with economies in transition, in order to enable the development and strengthening of a sound and viable technological and scientific base for the attainment of the objectives of the Convention and this Protocol. Where possible and appropriate such collaborative activities shall take place in and with a Party or the Parties providing genetic resources that is the country or are the countries of origin of such resources or a Party or Parties that have acquired the genetic resources in accordance with the Convention.

Table 12.1 Other global biodiversity-related conventions

1950 International Convention for the Protection of Birds (1950 Birds Convention)
1951 International Plant Protection Convention
1970 Benelux Convention on the Hunting and Protection of Birds (1970 Benelux Convention)
1973 Agreement on Conservation of Polar Bears (1973 Polar Bear Agreement)

1973 Convention on International Trade and Endangered Species (CITES)

Article I
Definitions For the purpose of the present Convention, unless the context otherwise requires:
(a)   "Species" means any species, subspecies, or geographically separate population thereof;
(b)   "Specimen" means:
    (i)   any animal or plant, whether alive or dead;
    (ii)   in the case of an animal: for species included in Appendices I and II, any readily recognizable part or derivative thereof; and for species included in Appendix III, any readily recognizable part or derivative thereof specified in Appendix III in relation to the species; and
    (iii)   in the case of a plant: for species included in Appendix I, any readily recognizable part or derivative thereof; and for species included in Appendices II and III, any readily recognizable part or derivative thereof specified in Appendices II and III in relation to the species;

(c)   "Trade" means export, re-export, import and introduction from the sea;
(d)   "Re-export" means export of any specimen that has previously been imported;
(e)   "Introduction from the sea" means transportation into a State of specimens of any species which were taken in the marine environment not under the jurisdiction of any State;

Article II Fundamental principles

1.   Appendix I shall include all species threatened with extinction which are or may be affected by trade. Trade in specimens of these species must be subject to particularly strict regulation in order not to endanger further their survival and must only be authorized in exceptional circumstances.
2.   Appendix II shall include:
       (a)   all species which although not necessarily now threatened with extinction may become so unless trade in specimens of such species is subject to strict regulation in order to avoid utilization incompatible with their survival; and
       (b)   other species which must be subject to regulation in order that trade in specimens of certain species referred to in sub-paragraph (a) of this paragraph may be brought under effective control.
3.   Appendix III shall include all species which any Party identifies as being subject to regulation within its jurisdiction for the purpose of preventing or restricting exploitation, and as needing the co-operation of other Parties in the control of trade.
4.   The Parties shall not allow trade in specimens of species included in Appendices I, II and III except in accordance with the provisions of the present Convention.

1979 Bonn Convention on the Conservation of Migratory Species of Wild Animals, 1651 UNTS

Article I Interpretation

1.   For the purpose of this Convention:
       a)   "Migratory species" means the entire population or any geographically separate part of the population of any species or lower taxon of wild animals, a significant proportion of whose members cyclically and predictably cross one or more national jurisdictional boundaries;
       b)   "Conservation status of a migratory species" means the sum of the influences acting on the migratory species that may affect its long-term distribution and abundance;
       c)   "Conservation status" will be taken as "favourable" when:
              (1)   population dynamics data indicate that the migratory species is maintaining itself on a long-term basis as a viable component of its ecosystems;
              (2)   the range of the migratory species is neither currently being reduced, nor is likely to be reduced, on a long-term basis;
              (3)   there is, and will be in the foreseeable future, sufficient habitat to maintain the population of the migratory species on a long-term basis; and

(4)   the distribution and abundance of the migratory species approach historic coverage and levels to the extent that potentially suitable ecosystems exist and to the extent consistent with wise wildlife management;

d)   "Conservation status" will be taken as "unfavourable" if any of the conditions set out in sub-paragraph (c) of this paragraph is not met;

e)   "Endangered" in relation to a particular migratory species means that the migratory species is in danger of extinction throughout all or a significant portion of its range;

f)   "Range" means all the areas of land or water that a migratory species inhabits, stays in temporarily, crosses or overflies at any time on its normal migration route;

g)   "Habitat" means any area in the range of a migratory species which contains suitable living conditions for that species;

h)   "Range State" in relation to a particular migratory species means any State (and where appropriate any other Party referred to under sub-paragraph (k) of this paragraph) that exercises jurisdiction over any part of the range of that migratory species, or a State, flag vessels of which are engaged outside national jurisdictional limits in taking that migratory species;

i)   "Taking" means taking, hunting, fishing, capturing, harassing, deliberate killing, or attempting to engage in any such conduct;

j)   "AGREEMENT" means an international agreement relating to the conservation of one or more migratory species as provided for in Articles IV and V of this Convention; and

k)   "Party" means a State or any regional economic integration organization constituted by sovereign States which has competence in respect of the negotiation, conclusion and application of international agreements in matters covered by this Convention for which this Convention is in force.

Article II Fundamental Principles

1.   The Parties acknowledge the importance of migratory species being conserved and of Range States agreeing to take action to this end whenever possible and appropriate, paying special attention to migratory species the conservation status of which is unfavourable, and taking individually or in co-operation appropriate and necessary steps to conserve such species and their habitat.

2.   The Parties acknowledge the need to take action to avoid any migratory species becoming endangered.

Article III Endangered Migratory Species:

Appendix I

1.   Appendix I shall list migratory species which are endangered.

2.   A migratory species may be listed in Appendix I provided that reliable evidence, including the best scientific evidence available, indicates that the species is endangered.

Article IV Migratory Species to Be the Subject of AGREEMENTS: Appendix II

1.   Appendix II shall list migratory species which have an unfavourable conservation status and which require international agreements for their conservation and management, as well as those which have a conservation status which would significantly benefit from the international co-operation that could be achieved by an international agreement.
2.   If the circumstances so warrant, a migratory species may be listed both in Appendix I and Appendix II.
3.   Parties that are Range States of migratory species listed in Appendix II shall endeavour to conclude AGREEMENTS where these would benefit the species and should give priority to those species in an unfavourable conservation status.

Article V Guidelines for AGREEMENTS

1.   The object of each AGREEMENT shall be to restore the migratory species concerned to a favourable conservation status or to maintain it in such a status. Each AGREEMENT should deal with those aspects of the conservation and management of the migratory species concerned which serve to achieve that object.
2.   Each AGREEMENT should cover the whole of the range of the migratory species concerned and should be open to accession by all Range States of that species, whether or not they are Parties to this Convention.
3.   An AGREEMENT should, wherever possible, deal with more than one migratory species.

Table 12.2 Examples of species-specific conventions

1979 Convention for the Conservation and Management of the Vicuna (1979 Vicuna Convention)
1990 Agreement on the Conservation of Seals in the Wadden Sea Area
1991 Agreement on the Conservation of Populations of European Bats (EUROBATS)
1991 Agreement on the Conservation of Small Cetaceans of the Baltic, North East Atlantic, Irish and North Seas (ASCOBANS)
1995 Agreement on the Conservation of African-Eurasian Migratory Waterbirds (AEWA)
1996 Agreement on the Conservation of Cetaceans of the Black Sea, Mediterranean Sea and Contiguous Atlantic Sea (ACCOBAMS)
2001 Agreement on the Conservation of Albatrosses and Petrels (ACAP)
2007 Agreement on the Conservation of Gorillas and Their Habitats

2006 International Tropical Timber Agreement

Article 1 OBJECTIVES

The objectives of the International Tropical Timber Agreement, 2006 (hereinafter referred to as "this Agreement") are to promote the expansion and diversification of international trade in tropical timber from sustainably managed and legally harvested forests and to promote the sustainable management of tropical timber producing forests by:

(a)   Providing an effective framework for consultation, international cooperation and policy development among all members with regard to all relevant aspects of the world timber economy;

(b)   Providing a forum for consultation to promote non-discriminatory timber trade practices;

(c)   Contributing to sustainable development and to poverty alleviation;

[...]

2001 International treaty on plant genetic resources for food and agriculture

Article 1 – Objectives

1.1   The objectives of this Treaty are the conservation and sustainable use of plant genetic resources for food and agriculture and the fair and equitable sharing of the benefits arising out of their use, in harmony with the Convention on Biological Diversity, for sustainable agriculture and food security.

1.2   These objectives will be attained by closely linking this Treaty to the Food and Agriculture Organization of the United Nations and to the Convention on Biological Diversity

Article 2 – Use of Terms

For the purpose of this Treaty, the following terms shall have the meanings hereunder assigned to them. These definitions are not intended to cover trade in commodities:

"In situ conservation" means the conservation of ecosystems and natural habitats and the maintenance and recovery of viable populations of species in their natural surroundings and, in the case of domesticated or cultivated plant species, in the surroundings where they have developed their distinctive properties.

"Ex situ conservation" means the conservation of plant genetic resources for food and agriculture outside their natural habitat.

"Plant genetic resources for food and agriculture" means any genetic material of plant origin of actual or potential value for food and agriculture.

"Genetic material" means any material of plant origin, including reproductive and vegetative propagating material, containing functional units of heredity.

"Variety" means a plant grouping, within a single botanical taxon of the lowest known rank, defined by the reproducible expression of its distinguishing and other genetic characteristics.

"Ex situ collection" means a collection of plant genetic resources for food and agriculture maintained outside their natural habitat.

"Centre of origin" means a geographical area where a plant species, either domesticated or wild, first developed its distinctive properties.

"Centre of crop diversity" means a geographic area containing a high level of genetic diversity for crop species in in situ conditions.

[...]

Article 5 – Conservation, Exploration, Collection, Characterization, Evaluation and Documentation of Plant Genetic Resources for Food and Agriculture

5.1   Each Contracting Party shall, subject to national legislation, and in cooperation with other Contracting Parties where appropriate, promote an integrated approach to the exploration, conservation and sustainable use of plant genetic resources for food and agriculture and shall in particular, as appropriate:

    a)   Survey and inventory plant genetic resources for food and agriculture, taking into account the status and degree of variation in existing populations, including those that are of potential use and, as feasible, assess any threats to them;

    b)   Promote the collection of plant genetic resources for food and agriculture and relevant associated information on those plant genetic resources that are under threat or are of potential use;

    c)   Promote or support, as appropriate, farmers and local communities' efforts to manage and conserve on-farm their plant genetic resources for food and agriculture;

    d)   Promote in situ conservation of wild crop relatives and wild plants for food production, including in protected areas, by supporting, *inter alia*, the efforts of indigenous and local communities;

    e)   Cooperate to promote the development of an efficient and sustainable system of ex situ conservation, giving due attention to the need for adequate documentation, characterization, regeneration and evaluation, and promote the development and transfer of appropriate technologies for this purpose with a view to improving the sustainable use of plant genetic resources for food and agriculture;

    f)   Monitor the maintenance of the viability, degree of variation, and the genetic integrity of collections of plant genetic resources for food and agriculture.

5.2   The Contracting Parties shall, as appropriate, take steps to minimize or, if possible, eliminate threats to plant genetic resources for food and agriculture.

Article 6 – Sustainable Use of Plant Genetic Resources

6.1   The Contracting Parties shall develop and maintain appropriate policy and legal measures that promote the sustainable use of plant genetic resources for food and agriculture.

12.2.1.2 Regional

Table 12.3 Examples of regional instruments

1968 African Nature Convention on the Conservation of Nature and Natural Resources – 2003 Revised African Nature Convention
1976 Convention on the Conservation of Nature in the South Pacific (1976 APIA Convention)
1978 Treaty for Amazonian Cooperation
1979 Berne Convention
1982 Benelux Convention on the Nature Conservation and Landscape Protection
1991 Alpine Convention on the Protection of the Alps
1994 Lusaka Agreement on the Co-operative Enforcement Operations Directed at Illegal Trade in Wild Fauna and Flora
2003 Framework Convention on the Protection and Sustainable Development of the Carpathians

12.2.2   Non-Binding Instruments

Table 12.4 Instruments that relate to forests

United Nations Conference on Environment & Development, Rio de Janeiro, Brazil 1992 – AGENDA 21, Chapter 11
Non-legally binding authoritative Statement of Principles for a Global Consensus on the Management, Conservation and Sustainable Development of All Types of Forests ('1992 Forest Principles')
2007 United Nations Forest Instrument

12.2.3   Case Law

> **CASE**
> ICJ, *Certain Activities Carried Out by Nicaragua in the Border Area (Costa Rica v. Nicaragua)* and *Construction of a Road in Costa Rica along the San Juan River (Nicaragua v. Costa Rica)*, ICJ Reports 665 (2015)

109. As to the alleged existence of an obligation to notify and consult in treaties binding on the Parties, the Court observes that both Costa Rica and Nicaragua are parties to the Ramsar Convention and the Convention for the Conservation of the Biodiversity and Protection of Priority Wilderness Areas in Central America. The Court recalls that Article 3, paragraph 2, of the Ramsar Convention provides that: "Each Contracting Party shall arrange to be informed at the earliest possible time if the ecological character of any wetland in its territory and included in the List [of wetlands of international importance] has changed, is changing or is likely to change as the result of technological developments, pollution or other human interference. Information on such changes shall be passed without delay to the [Ramsar Secretariat]." While this provision contains an obligation to notify, that obligation is limited to notifying the Ramsar Secretariat of changes or likely changes in the "ecological character of any wetland" in the territory of the notifying State. In the present case, the evidence before the Court does not indicate that Nicaragua's dredging programme has brought about any changes in the ecological character of the wetland, or that it was likely to do so unless it were to be expanded. Thus the Court finds that no obligation to inform the Ramsar Secretariat arose for Nicaragua.

110. The Court further recalls that Article 5 of the Ramsar Convention provides that: "The Contracting Parties shall consult with each other about implementing obligations arising from the Convention especially in the case of a wetland extending over the territories of more than one Contracting Party or where a water system is shared by Contracting Parties. They shall at the same time endeavour to co-ordinate and support present and future policies and regulations concerning the conservation of wetlands and their flora and fauna." While this provision contains a general obligation to consult "about implementing obligations arising from the Convention", it does not create an obligation on Nicaragua to consult with Costa Rica concerning a particular project that it is undertaking, in this case the dredging of the Lower

San Juan River. In light of the above, Nicaragua was not required under the Ramsar Convention to notify, or consult with, Costa Rica prior to commencing its dredging project.

111. As to the Convention for the Conservation of the Biodiversity and Protection of Priority Wilderness Areas in Central America, the Court sees no need to take its enquiry further, as neither of the two provisions invoked by Costa Rica contains a binding obligation to notify or consult.

112. In light of the above, the Court concludes that it has not been established that Nicaragua breached any procedural obligations owed to Costa Rica under treaties or the customary international law of the environment. The Court takes note of Nicaragua's commitment, made in the course of the oral proceedings, to carry out a new Environmental Impact Study before any substantial expansion of its current dredging programme. The Court further notes that Nicaragua stated that such a study would include an assessment of the risk of transboundary harm, and that it would notify, and consult with, Costa Rica as part of that process.

[...]

163. Nicaragua submits that Costa Rica was required to carry out an environmental impact assessment by Article 14 of the Convention on Biological Diversity. Costa Rica responds that the provision at issue concerns the introduction of appropriate procedures with respect to projects that are likely to have a significant adverse effect on biological diversity. It claims that it had such procedures in place and that, in any event, they do not apply to the construction of the road, as it was not likely to have a significant adverse effect on biological diversity.

164. The Court recalls that the provision reads, in relevant part: "Each Contracting Party, as far as possible and as appropriate, shall: (a) Introduce appropriate procedures requiring environmental impact assessment of its proposed projects that are likely to have significant adverse effects on biological diversity with a view to avoiding or minimizing such effects and, where appropriate, allow for public participation in such procedures." The Court considers that the provision at issue does not create an obligation to carry out an environmental impact assessment before undertaking an activity that may have significant adverse effects on biological diversity. Therefore, it has not been established that Costa Rica breached Article 14 of the Convention on Biological Diversity by failing to conduct an environmental impact assessment for its road project.

12.3 CONSERVATION OF MARINE BIODIVERSITY

12.3.1 Legal Instruments

12.3.1.1 International

1972 World Heritage Convention, 1037 UNTS 151

Article 2
For the purposes of this Convention, the following shall be considered as "natural heritage": natural features consisting of physical and biological formations or groups of such formations, which are of outstanding universal value from the aesthetic or scientific point of view; geological and physiographical formations and precisely delineated areas which constitute the habitat of threatened species of animals and plants of outstanding universal value from the point of view of science or conservation; natural sites or precisely delineated natural areas of outstanding universal value from the point of view of science, conservation or natural beauty.

1982 United Nations Convention on the Law of the Sea, 1833 UNTS 3

194
[...]

5.   The measures taken in accordance with this Part shall include those necessary to protect and preserve rare or fragile ecosystems as well as the habitat of depleted, threatened or endangered species and other forms of marine life.

1995 Agreement on Straddling Fish Stocks, 2167 UNTS 88

Article 5:
In order to conserve and manage straddling fish stocks and highly migratory fish stocks, coastal States and States fishing on the high seas shall, in giving effect to their duty to cooperate in accordance with the Convention:

(g)   protect biodiversity in the marine environment.

1992 Convention on Biological Diversity

Article 3.
States have, in accordance with the Charter of the United Nations and the principles of international law, the sovereign right to exploit their own resources pursuant to their own environmental policies, and the responsibility to ensure that activities within their jurisdiction or control do not cause damage to the environment of other States or of areas beyond the limits of national jurisdiction.

12.3.1.2   Regional

Table 12.5 Regional agreements on marine biodiversity

1982 Geneva Protocol Concerning Mediterranean Specially Protected Areas (1982 Geneva SPA Protocol)
1985 Nairobi Protocol Concerning Protected Areas and Wild Fauna and Flora (1985 Nairobi Fauna and Floral Protocol)
1989 Paipa Protocol for the Conservation and management of Marine and Coastal Areas of the South-East Pacific (1989 Paipa SPA Protocol)
1990 Kingston Protocol concerning Specially Protected Areas and Wildlife in the Wider Caribbean Region (1990 Kingston SPA Protocol)
2002 Black Sea Biodiversity and Landscape Conservation Protocol
2005 Protocol Concerning the Conservation of Biological Diversity and the Establishment of a Network of Protected Areas in the Red Sea and Gulf of Aden
2008 Protocol on Integrated Coastal Zone Management in the Mediterranean
2014 Protocol for the Conservation of Biological Diversity to the Framework Convention for the Protection of Marine Environment of the Caspian Sea.

12.3.2   Non-Binding Instruments

Transforming Our World: the 2030 Agenda for Sustainable Development (2015)

Goal 14. Conserve and sustainably use the oceans, seas and marine resources for sustainable development
[...]
Target 14.2: By 2020, sustainably manage and protect marine and coastal ecosystems to avoid significant adverse impacts, including by strengthening their resilience, and take action for their restoration in order to achieve healthy and productive oceans
Target 14.3: Minimize and address the impacts of ocean acidification, including through enhanced scientific cooperation at all levels
Target 14.4: By 2020, effectively regulate harvesting and end overfishing, illegal, unreported and unregulated fishing and destructive fishing practices and implement science-based management plans, in order to restore fish stocks in the shortest time feasible, at least to levels that can produce maximum sustainable yield as determined by their biological characteristics

GA Resolution 61/105 (2006):

This resolution, adopted by consensus, sets objectives for States and RFMOS with competence to regulate bottom fisheries:

5.   Calls upon all States, directly or through regional fisheries management organizations and arrangements, to apply widely, in accordance with international law and the Code,[4] the precautionary approach and an ecosystem approach to the conservation, management and exploitation of fish stocks, including straddling fish stocks, highly migratory fish stocks and discrete high seas fish stocks, and also calls upon

States parties to the Agreement to implement fully the provisions of article 6 of the Agreement as a matter of priority.

83.   Calls upon regional fisheries management organizations or arrangements with the competence to regulate bottom fisheries to adopt and implement measures, in accordance with the precautionary approach, ecosystem approaches and international law, for their respective regulatory areas as a matter of priority, but not later than 31 December 2008:

(a)   To assess, on the basis of the best available scientific information, whether individual bottom fishing activities would have significant adverse impacts on vulnerable marine ecosystems, and to ensure that if it is assessed that these activities would have significant adverse impacts, they are managed to prevent such impacts, or not authorized to proceed;

(b)   To identify vulnerable marine ecosystems and determine whether bottom fishing activities would cause significant adverse impacts to such ecosystems and the long-term sustainability of deep sea fish stocks, *inter alia*, by improving scientific research and data collection and sharing, and through new and exploratory fisheries;

(c)   In respect of areas where vulnerable marine ecosystems, including seamounts, hydrothermal vents and cold water corals, are known to occur or are likely to occur based on the best available scientific information, to close such areas to bottom fishing and ensure that such activities do not proceed unless conservation and management measures have been established to prevent significant adverse impacts on vulnerable marine ecosystems;

(d)   To require members of the regional fisheries management organizations or arrangements to require vessels flying their flag to cease bottom fishing activities in areas where, in the course of fishing operations, vulnerable marine ecosystems are encountered, and to report the encounter so that appropriate measures can be adopted in respect of the relevant site.

GA Resolution 64/72 (2009):

119.   Considers that, on the basis of the review carried out in accordance with paragraph 91 of resolution 61/105, further actions in accordance with the precautionary approach, ecosystem approaches and international law are needed to strengthen the implementation of paragraphs 80 and 83 to 87 of resolution 61/105, and in this regard calls upon regional fisheries management organizations or arrangements with the competence to regulate bottom fisheries, States participating in negotiations to establish such organizations or arrangements, and flag States to take the following urgent actions in areas beyond national jurisdiction:

(a)   Conduct the assessments called for in paragraph 83 (a) of resolution 61/105, consistent with the Guidelines, and ensure that vessels do not engage in bottom fishing until such assessments have been carried out;

(b)   Conduct further marine scientific research and use the best scientific and technical information available to identify where vulnerable marine ecosystems are known to occur or are likely to occur and adopt conservation and management measures to prevent significant adverse impacts on such ecosystems consistent with the Guidelines, or close such areas to bottom fishing until conservation and management measures have been established, as called for in paragraph 83 (c) of resolution 61/105;

(c)   Establish and implement appropriate protocols for the implementation of paragraph 83 (d) of resolution 61/105, including definitions of what constitutes evidence of an encounter with a vulnerable marine ecosystem, in particular threshold levels and indicator species, based on the best available scientific information and consistent with the Guidelines, and taking into account any other conservation and management measures to prevent significant adverse impacts on vulnerable marine ecosystems, including those based on the results of assessments carried out pursuant to paragraph 83 (a) of resolution 61/105 and paragraph 119 (a) of the present resolution;

(d)   Adopt conservation and management measures, including monitoring, control and surveillance measures, on the basis of stock assessments and the best available scientific information, to ensure the long-term sustainability of deep sea fish stocks and non-target species, and the rebuilding of depleted stocks, consistent with the Guidelines; and, where scientific information is uncertain, unreliable, or inadequate, ensure that conservation and management measures are established consistent with the precautionary approach, including measures to ensure that fishing effort, fishing capacity and catch limits, as appropriate, are at levels commensurate with the long-term sustainability of such stocks;

120.   Calls upon flag States, members of regional fisheries management organizations or arrangements with the competence to regulate bottom fisheries and States participating in negotiations to establish such organizations or arrangements to adopt and implement measures in accordance with paragraphs 83, 85 and 86 of resolution 61/105, paragraph 119 of the present resolution, and international law, and consistent with the Guidelines, and not to authorize bottom fishing activities until such measures have been adopted and implemented

12.3.3   Case Law

CASE
PCA, *Chagos Marine Protected Area Arbitration (Mauritius v. United Kingdom)*, Final Award, ICGJ 486 (18 March 2015)

320. In reaching this conclusion, the Tribunal rejects the suggestion that either Article 297(1)(c) or Part XII of the Convention (relating to the protection and preservation of the marine environment) are limited to measures aimed at controlling marine pollution. While the control of pollution is certainly an important aspect of environmental protection, it is by no means the only one. Far from equating the preservation of the marine environment with pollution control, the Tribunal notes that Article 194(5) expressly provides that – The measures taken in accordance with this Part shall include those necessary to protect and preserve rare or fragile ecosystems as well as the habitat of depleted, threatened or endangered species and other forms of marine life. Notably, in the Tribunal's view, this provision offers a far better fit with the MPA as presented by the United Kingdom than its characterization as a fisheries measure.

[...]

538. In the Tribunal's view, the Parties' disagreement regarding the scope of Article 194 is answered by the fifth provision of that Article, which expressly provides that – the measures taken in accordance with this Part shall include those necessary to protect and preserve rare or fragile ecosystems as well as the habitat of depleted, threatened or endangered species and other forms of marine life. Article 194 is accordingly not limited to measures aimed strictly at controlling pollution and extends to measures focused primarily on conservation and the preservation of ecosystems. As repeatedly justified by the United Kingdom, the MPA is such a measure.

CASE
PCA, *South China Sea Arbitration (Philippines v. China)*, Final Award, PCA Case No. 2013–19 (12 July 2016)

[...]

823. The South China Sea includes highly productive fisheries and extensive coral reef ecosystems, which are among the most biodiverse in the world. The marine environment around Scarborough Shoal and the Spratly Islands has an extremely high level of biodiversity of species, including fishes, corals, echinoderms, mangroves, seagrasses, giant clams, and marine turtles, some of which are recognised as vulnerable or endangered.
824. While coral reefs are amongst the most biodiverse and socioeconomically important ecosystems, they are also fragile and degrade under human pressures. Threats to coral reefs include overfishing, destructive fishing, pollution, human habitation, and construction.
825. In the South China Sea, ocean currents and the life cycles of marine species create a high degree of connectivity between the different ecosystems.

[...]

880. This means that the impact of any environmental harm occurring at Scarborough Shoal and in the Spratly Islands may not be limited to the immediate area, but can affect the health and viability of ecosystems elsewhere in the South China Sea.

[...]

906. In connection with the marine environment, the Philippines alleges China has breached Articles 123, 192, 194, 197, 205, and 206 of the Convention.
907. The Philippines recalls that the general obligation on States under Article 192 to "protect and preserve the marine environment"—which it considers to form part of customary international law—covers areas within national jurisdiction as well as areas beyond national jurisdiction. According to the Philippines, this requires States

to take "active measures" to prevent harm, to "conserve marine living resources," and to "preserve the ecological balance of the oceans as a whole."

908. The Philippines notes that the interpretation of Article 192 may be guided by reference to standards in other multilateral environmental instruments, such as CITES and the CBD. 1035 Likewise those instruments provide content for the obligation under Article 194(5) with respect to measures necessary to protect and preserve "rare or fragile ecosystems" and "places that provide habitats for ... endangered species."

909. The Philippines notes that States are only required to take appropriate measures and act with due diligence. In this case, however, the Philippines argues that the clear evidence of deliberate and irreparable ecological destruction cannot be squared with China's own laws on environmental protection. While China's island-building activities at the seven reefs were unquestionably within the control and jurisdiction of China, the Philippines acknowledges that the unlawful harvesting was carried out by non-government Chinese fishing vessels and that "China is not responsible for the actions of its fishermen." China is, however, "responsible for its own failure to control their illegal and damaging activities." The Philippines argues that China has "not even attempted to do so" but rather has actively "supported, protected and facilitate[ed] their harmful practices." The Philippines also observes that as the flag State, China is obliged to monitor and enforce compliance with its laws by all ships flying its flag.

910. The Philippines highlights five obligations that it considers applicable to States under Part XII of the Convention and relevant in the context of this case:

(a) To protect and preserve marine ecosystems: The Philippines observes that coral reefs are a fragile and vitally important part of the marine ecosystem and argues that "creating artificial islands out of coral reefs is the worst possible way to treat these fundamental ecological building blocks."

(b) To ensure sustainable use of biological resources: The Philippines notes that this reflects a long-recognised duty to conserve living resources. Blast fishing and the use of cyanide are wasteful and unsustainable, and violate Articles 192 and 194 (including as marine pollution), whether the methods are used in the territorial sea or beyond.

(c) To protect and preserve endangered species: The Philippines argues that this is implicit in Article 194(5). According to the Philippines, the harvesting of giant clams in April 2012 under the protection of Chinese authorities constitutes a clear violation of Articles 192 and 194.

(d) To apply a precautionary approach in all of these respects: The Philippines considers this obligation applicable to China, but argues this is not necessary to the Tribunal's findings in the current case because the risks to the marine environment are obvious and there can be no uncertainty.

(e) To consult and cooperate with the relevant coastal States: The Philippines draws this obligation from Articles 197 and 123 of the Convention, the latter of which takes into account the "characteristic regional features" which would include the fundamental biological and ecological importance and fragile nature of the coral reef ecosystem of the South China Sea. The Philippines submits that there is very little evidence of genuine Chinese cooperation on matters of environmental protection in the South China Sea. The Philippines considers China's behaviour towards the Philippines and other States bordering the South China Sea to be aggressive rather than cooperative.

950. Based on contemporaneous reports of naval, coastguard and fisheries authorities, diplomatic exchanges and photographic evidence presented in the record, the Tribunal is satisfied that Chinese fishing vessels have been involved in harvesting of threatened or endangered species on the following occasions at or in the waters of Scarborough Shoal:

(a) In January and March 1998, Chinese fishermen were found in possession of corals and marine turtles.

(b) In April 2000, Chinese fishing vessels were found with four tons of corals on board.

(c) In January 2001, Chinese fishing vessels were found with endangered sea turtles, sharks, and corals.

(d) Tons of corals as well as clams were confiscated from Chinese fishing vessels in February, March and September of 2002.

(e) In October 2004, Chinese fishing vessels loaded and photographed with giant clams were intercepted by the Philippine Navy.

(f) In December 2005, four Chinese fishing vessels were found and photographed in possession of "assorted corals and live clamshells weighing about 16 tons."

(g) In April 2006, Chinese fishing vessels were found and photographed with corals.

(h) On 10 April 2012, large amounts of corals and giant claims were found and photographed on board Chinese fishing vessels that were later joined by Chinese Government vessels.

(i) On 23 and 26 April 2012, at least two Chinese fishing vessels, operating under the protection of CMS vessels were observed to have giant clams inside the cargo hold.

951. In addition to the above events at Scarborough Shoal, the Tribunal has reviewed reports of an incident in the vicinity of Second Thomas Shoal in May 2013, in which fishing vessels from Hainan, accompanied by a Chinese naval ship and two CMS ships, were sighted by Philippine armed forces and "believed to be gathering corals and clams and dredging in the shoal." Photographs from the incident show the harvesting of giant claims.

952. Recent evidence also indicates the large-scale harvest of endangered hawksbill sea turtles by Chinese fishermen, whose arrest by Philippine authorities led to protests by China.

953. Finally, in addition to the occurrence of the above events recounted in the Philippines' Memorial, the Tribunal is satisfied based on its review of satellite imagery, photographic and video evidence, contemporaneous press reports, scientific studies and the materials from Professor McManus, that in recent years, Chinese fishing vessels have been engaged in widespread harvesting of giant clams through the use of boat propellers to break through the coral substrate in search of buried clam shells.

954. The Tribunal turns now to the harmful impact of the above-described activities and then addresses the extent to which China may be held responsible for breach of the Convention in connection with those activities.

955. Many of the above-listed incidents involved the harvesting of coral species. The Ferse Report describes the impact on the marine environment from the harvesting of coral as follows: stony corals are frequently harvested as construction material, or for sale in the curio trade, e.g. to tourists. The repeated, targeted removal of coral colonies can modify the community structure – branching species are preferably targeted for the curio trade, and their removal leads to an overall loss of structural complexity. Decreased live coral cover and structural complexity severely affects the reef fish community, as a large proportion of the species on the reef utilise live corals at some point in their life history.

956. All of the sea turtles (Cheloniidae) found on board Chinese fishing vessels are listed under Appendix I to the CITES Convention as species threatened with extinction and subject to the strictest level of international controls on trade. 1122 CITES is the subject of nearly universal adherence, including by the Philippines and China, and in the Tribunal's view forms part of the general corpus of international law that informs the content of Article 192 and 194(5) of the Convention.

"[T]he conservation of the living resources of the sea is an element in the protection and preservation of the marine environment," and the Tribunal considers that the general obligation to "protect and preserve the marine environment" in Article 192 includes a due diligence obligation to prevent the harvesting of species that are recognised internationally as being at risk of extinction and requiring international protection.

The Tribunal is particularly troubled by the evidence with respect to giant clams, tons of which were harvested by Chinese fishing vessels from Scarborough Shoal, and in recent years, elsewhere in the Spratly Islands. Giant clams (Tridacnidae) and many of the corals found in the Spratly Islands are listed in Appendix II to CITES and are unequivocally threatened, even if they are not subject to the same level of international controls as Appendix I species. Equally important, however, giant clams play a significant role in the overall growth and maintenance of the reef structure.

The Ferse Report describes the effects of harvesting them as follows: Giant clams have historically been harvested widely throughout Southeast Asia and beyond, both for their meat and their shells. The larger species can reach considerable sizes (the largest species, Tridacna gigas, can reach almost 1.5m in size and a weight of over 300kg), but they grow slowly. Thus, large individuals have become rare on most reefs. As their shells are highly coveted, collectors have begun to target fossil shells buried in the reef flat (the shallow, extensive habitat on top of reefs). Excavation is highly destructive, with early reports showing a drop in coral cover by 95% from its original value. More recently, fishermen in the South China Sea are reported to utilise the propellers of their boats to excavate shells from reef flats in the Spratly Islands on an industrial scale, leading to near complete destruction of the affected reef areas.

958. The Tribunal recalls in particular the very recent examinations conducted by Professor McManus, which led him to estimate that China is responsible for almost 70 square kilometres of coral reef damage from giant clam harvesting using pro- pellers, a practice he described as more thoroughly damaging to marine life than anything he had seen in four decades of investigating coral reef degradation.

959. The Tribunal has noted that it considers the duty to prevent the harvest of en- dangered species follows from Article 192, read against the background of other applicable international law. The Tribunal considers that this general obligation is given particular shape in the context of fragile ecosystems by Article 194(5). Read in this context, the Tribunal thus considers that Article 192 imposes a due diligence obligation to take those measures "necessary to protect and preserve rare or fragile ecosystems as well as the habitat of depleted, threatened or endangered species and other forms of marine life." Therefore, in addition to preventing the direct harvesting of species recognised internationally as being threatened with extinction, Article 192 extends to the prevention of harms that would affect depleted, threat- ened, or endangered species indirectly through the destruction of their habitat.

960. The Tribunal thus considers the harvesting of sea turtles, species threatened with extinction, to constitute a harm to the marine environment as such. The Tribunal further has no doubt that the harvesting of corals and giant clams from the waters surrounding Scarborough Shoal and features in the Spratly Islands, on the scale that appears in the record before it, has a harmful impact on the fragile marine environment. The Tribunal therefore considers that a failure to take measures to prevent these practices would constitute a breach of Articles 192 and 194(5) of the Convention, and turns now to consider China's responsibility for such breaches.

961. The vessels involved in the incidents described above were all Chinese flag vessels, under the jurisdiction and control of China. In the Tribunal's view, where a State is aware that vessels flying its flag are engaged in the harvest of species recognised in- ternationally as being threatened with extinction or are inflicting significant damage on rare or fragile ecosystems or the habitat of depleted, threatened, or endangered species, its obligations under the Convention include a duty to adopt rules and measures to prevent such acts and to maintain a level of vigilance in enforcing those rules and measures.

962. On the question of awareness, it is clear from the record that the Philippines had brought its concerns about poaching of endangered species to the attention of China as early as January 2000, when it stated to the Chinese Embassy that unlawful harvesting "disturbed the tranquillity of the ecosystem and habitat of important species of marine life and ... caused irreparable damage to the marine environment of the area."

The Philippines also recalled that the gathering and trade of corals violates the provisions of three international conventions to which China is a signatory, including the CBD and CITES. In 2001, China assured the Philippines that it "attaches great importance to environmental protection and violators are dealt with in accordance with Chinese laws and regulations." After finding 16 tons of clams and corals aboard Chinese fishing vessels in 2005, the Philippines expressed its grave concern to China over the "rampant trading of endangered corals and marine species in the South China Sea."[1130]

963. China was therefore, certainly by 2005, on notice of poaching practices of Chinese fishing vessels in Scarborough Shoal and aware of the Philippines' concerns. The poaching, however, has persisted, despite (a) China's earlier statements that it would deal with violators, (b) China being party to CITES since 1981, and (c) China having enacted in 1989 a Law of the Protection of Wildlife, which prohibits the catching or killing of two classes of special state protected wildlife,[1131] and specifically lists among them sea turtles and giant clams.

964. As the Tribunal has noted above, adopting appropriate rules and measures to prohibit a harmful practice is only one component of the due diligence required by States pursuant to the general obligation of Article 192, read in the context of Article 194(5) and the international law applicable to endangered species. There is no evidence in the record that would indicate that China has taken any steps to enforce those rules and measures against fishermen engaged in poaching of endangered species. Indeed, at least with respect to the April 2012 incidents, the evidence points directly to the contrary. China was aware of the harvesting of giant clams. It did not merely turn a blind eye to this practice. Rather, it provided armed government vessels to protect the fishing boats. The Chinese Ministry of Foreign Affairs Spokesperson confirmed on 12 April 2012 that it had "dispatched administrative vessels ... to protect the safety and legitimate fishing activities of Chinese fishermen and fishing vessels."

Despite the reference to "legitimate fishing activities", the photographic evidence of endangered species, including giant clams and sharks, on board the vessels in question indicates China must have known of, and deliberately tolerated, and protected the harmful acts. Similarly, with respect to the May 2013 incident in the vicinity of Second Thomas Shoal, the Tribunal accepts, on the basis of the photographic and contemporaneous documentary evidence, that Chinese naval and CMS vessels were escorting Chinese fishing vessels in gathering clams. The Tribunal therefore has no hesitation in finding that China breached its obligations under Articles 192 and 194(5) of the Convention, to take necessary measures to protect and preserve the marine environment, with respect to the harvesting of endangered species from the fragile ecosystems at Scarborough Shoal and Second Thomas Shoal.

965. There remains the question of China's responsibility for the more recent and widespread environmental degradation caused by propeller chopping for giant clams across the Spratlys. From satellite imagery showing scarring from this practice, it appears the harvesting took place in areas under control of Chinese authorities, at a time and in locations where Chinese authorities were engaged in planning and implementing China's island-building activities. The Tribunal considers that the small propeller vessels involved in harvesting the giant clams were within China's jurisdiction and control. The Tribunal finds that China, despite its rules on the protection of giant clams, and on the preservation of the coral reef environment generally, was fully aware of the practice and has actively tolerated it as a means to exploit the living resources of the reefs in the months prior to those reefs succumbing to the near permanent destruction brought about by the island-building activities discussed in Section 4.1

966. Accordingly, the Tribunal finds that China has also breached its obligation to protect and preserve the marine environment in respect of its toleration and protection of the harvesting of giant clams by the propeller chopping method.

[...]

(12) FINDS, with respect to the protection and preservation of the marine environment in the South China Sea: a. that fishermen from Chinese flagged vessels have engaged in the harvesting of endangered species on a significant scale; b. that fishermen from Chinese flagged vessels have engaged in the harvesting of giant clams in a manner that is severely destructive of the coral reef ecosystem; and c. that China was aware of, tolerated, protected, and failed to prevent the aforementioned harmful activities; and DECLARES that China has breached its obligations under Articles 192 and 194(5) of the Convention;

(13) FINDS further, with respect to the protection and preservation of the marine environment in the South China Sea: a. that China's land reclamation and construction of artificial islands, installations, and structures at Cuarteron Reef, Fiery Cross Reef, Gaven Reef (North), Johnson Reef, Hughes Reef, Subi Reef, and Mischief Reef has caused severe, irreparable harm to the coral reef ecosystem; b. that China has not cooperated or coordinated with the other States bordering the South China Sea concerning the protection and preservation of the marine environment concerning such activities; and c. that China has failed to communicate an assessment of the potential effects of such activities on the marine environment, within the meaning of Article 206 of the Convention; and DECLARES that China has breached its obligations under Articles 123, 192, 194(1), 194(5), 197, and 206 of the Convention.

QUESTIONS

1. How is the 1992 Convention on Biological Diversity a framework convention?
2. Why is the protection of marine biodiversity inadequate in the 1982 UN Convention on the Law of the Sea?
3. Do you think that the overall international legal framework of biodiversity is inadequate in the rule that it sets out?

FURTHER READING

BOOKS

D Attard, M Fitzmaurice and NA Martinez Gutierrez (eds), *The IMLI Manual on International Maritime Law, Vol.1: The Law of the Sea* (Oxford University Press 2014)

E Couzens, S Riley and Y Fristikawati (eds), *Protecting Forest and Marine Biodiversity: The Role of Law* (Edward Elgar 2019)

EJ Goodwin, *International Environmental Law and the Conservation of Coral Reefs* (Routledge 2011)

J Harrison, *Saving the Oceans through Law: The International Legal Framework for the Protection of the Marine Environment* (Oxford University Press 2017)

DK Leary, *International Law and the Genetic Resources of the Deep Sea* (Martinus Nijhoff 2007)

E Morgera and J Razzaque (eds), *Biodiversity and Nature Protection Law* (Edward Elgar 2017)

R Warner, *Protecting the Oceans Beyond National Jurisdiction: Strengthening the International Law Framework* (Martnius Nijhoff 2009)

W Wijnstekers, *The Evolution of CITES* (9th edn, Cites Secretariat 2011)

CHAPTERS

BH Desai, 'Forests, International Protection' in *Max Planck Encyclopedia of Public International Law* (2011)

ME Desmond and A Powers, 'Protocol Concerning Specially Protected Areas and Wildlife Protocol to the Convention for the Protection and Development of the Marine Environment of the Wider Caribbean Region 1983 (Cartagena Protocol)' in M Fitzmaurice and A Tanzi, *Multilateral Environmental Treaties* (Edward Elgar 2017)

A Dizdarevic, 'Convention on International Trade in Endangered Species of Wild Fauna and Flora 1973' in M Fitzmaurice and A Tanzi, *Multilateral Environmental Treaties* (Edward Elgar 2017)

EJ Goodwin, 'Threatened Species and Vulnerable Marine Ecosystems' in DR Rothwell, AG Elferink, KN Scott and T Stephens (eds), *The Oxford Handbook of the Law of the Sea* (Oxford University Press 2015)

M Lewis and A Trouwborst, 'Bonn Convention on the Conservation of Migratory Species of Wild Animals 1979 (CMS)' in M Fitzmaurice and A Tanzi, *Multilateral Environmental Treaties* (Edward Elgar 2017)

N Matz-Lück, 'Biological Diversity, International Protection' in *Max Planck Encyclopedia of Public International Law* (2008)

R Pavoni and D Piselli, 'Access to Genetic Resources and Benefit-sharing' in E Morgera and J Razzaque (eds), *Biodiversity and Nature Protection Law* (Edward Elgar 2017)

GA Oanta, 'The Black Sea Biodiversity and Landscape Conservation Protocol to the Convention on the Protection of the Black Sea Against Pollution 2002' in M Fitzmaurice and A Tanzi, *Multilateral Environmental Treaties* (Edward Elgar 2017)

N Oral, 'The Institutional Schizophrenia of Ocean Governance through the Lens of the Conservation of Biological Diversity in Areas Beyond National Jurisdiction' in RR Holst, S Trevisanut and N Giannopoulos (eds), *Regime International in Ocean Governance* (Brill 2020)

N Oral, 'The Oceans in the 21st Century' in M Ribeiro and W Menezes (eds), *Direito do Mar Regulamentação Normativa dos Espaços Marítimos* (2020)

N Oral, 'Forty Years of the UNEP Regional Seas Programme: From Past to Future' in R Rayfuse (ed.), *Research Manual on International Marine Environment Law* (Edward Elgar 2015)

N Oral, 'Protection of Vulnerable Marine Ecosystems in Areas Beyond National Jurisdiction: Can International Law Meet the Challenge?' in A Strati, M Gavouneli and N Skourtos (eds), *Time Before and Time After Unresolved Issues and New Challenges to the Law of the Sea* (Martinus Nijhoff 2006)

RM Warner, 'Conserving Marine Biodiversity in Areas Beyond National Jurisdiction: Co-Evolution and Interaction with the Law of the Sea' in DR Rothwell, AG Elferink, KN Scott and T Stephens (eds), *The Oxford Handbook of the Law of the Sea* (Oxford University Press 2015)

S Wolf and JA Bischoff, 'Marine Protected Areas' in *Max Planck Encyclopedia of Public International Law* (2013)

M Yzquierdo, 'Convention on Biological Diversity 1992' in M Fitzmaurice and A Tanzi, *Multilateral Environmental Treaties* (Edward Elgar 2017)

ARTICLES

R Barnes, 'The Proposed LOSC Implementation Agreement on Areas Beyond National Jurisdiction and its Impact on International Fisheries' (2016) 31 International Journal of Marine and Coastal Law 583

C Grilo, 'Impact of Maritime Boundaries on Cooperation in the Creation of Transboundary Marine Protected Areas: Insights from Three Cases' (2014) 24 Ocean Yearbook 115

LA de la Fayette, 'A New Regime for the Conservation and Sustainable Use of Marine Biodiversity and Genetic Resources Beyond the Limits of National Jurisdiction' (2009) 24 International Journal of Marine and Coastal Law 221

GJ Edgar, 'Does the Global Network of Marine Protected Areas Provide an Adequate Safety Net for Marine Biodiversity?' (2011) 21 Aquatic Conservation: Marine and Freshwater Ecosystems 313

KM Gjerde, 'Challenges to Protecting the Marine Environment beyond National Jurisdiction' (2012) 27 International Journal of Marine and Coastal Law 839

KM Gjerde, D Currie, K Wowk and KSack, 'Ocean in Peril: Reforming the Management of Global Ocean Living Resources in Areas Beyond National Jurisdiction' (2013) 74 Marine Pollution Bulletin 540

Y Kagami, 'The Exploitation of Resources in the High Seas Fisheries: Discreet High Seas Fish Stocks, Deep-Sea Fisheries and Vulnerable Marine Ecosystems' (2015) 58 Japanese Yearbook of International Law 427

M Lockwood et al., 'Marine Biodiversity Conservation Governance and Management: Regime Requirements for Global Environmental Change' (2012) 69 Ocean & Coastal Management 160

EJ Molenaar, 'Managing Biodiversity in Areas Beyond National Jurisdiction: Strengthening the International Law Framework' (2007) 22 International Journal of Marine and Costal Law 89

EJ Molenaar and AG Elferink, 'Marine Protected Areas in Areas Beyond National Jurisdiction: The Pioneering Efforts under the OSPAR Convention' (2009) 5(1) Utrecht Law Review 5

EJ Molenaar, 'Multilateral Creeping Coastal State Jurisdiction and the BBNJ Negotiations' (2021) 36 International Journal of Marine and Coastal Law 5

N Oral, 'The Legal Framework of Cooperation for Protection of Marine Biodiversity in the Black Sea' (2012) 37 Revue Juridique de L'Environnement 255

MJ Ortiz, 'Aichi Biodiversity Targets on Direct and Indirect Drivers of Biodiversity Loss' (2011) 13 Environmental Law Review 100

RG Rayfuse, 'Protecting Marine Biodiversity in Polar Areas Beyond National Jurisdiction' (2008) 17 Review of European Community and International Environmental Law 3

RG Rayfuse, 'Precaution and the Protection of Marine Biodiversity in Areas Beyond National Jurisdiction' (2012) 27 International Journal of Marine and Coastal Law 773

J Rochette et al., 'The Regional Approach to the Conservation and Sustainable Use of Marine Biodiversity in Areas Beyond National Jurisdiction' (2014) 49 Marine Policy 109

D Rodríguez-Rodríguez, J Rodríguez, D Abdul Malak, A Nastasia and P Hernández, 'Marine Protected Areas and Fisheries Restricted Areas in the Mediterranean: Assessing "Actual" Marine Biodiversity Protection Coverage at Multiple Scales' (2016) 64 Marine Policy 24

T Scovazzi, 'Marine Protected Areas on the High Seas: Some Legal and Policy Considerations' (2004) 19 International Journal of Marine and Coastal Law 1

T Scovazzi, 'The Exploitation of Resources of the Deep Seabed and the Protection of the Environment' (2014) 52 German Yearbook of International Law 181

Y Tanaka, 'Reflections on High Seas Marine Protected Areas: A Comparative Analysis of the Mediterranean and the North-East Atlantic Models' (2012) 81 Nordic Journal of International Law 295

Y Tanaka, 'Reflections on the Implications of Environmental Norms for Fishing: The Link Between the Regulation of Fishing and the Protection of Marine Biological Diversity' (2020) 22 International Community Law Review 389

R Warner, 'Tools to Conserve Ocean Biodiversity: Developing the Legal Framework for Environmental Impact Assessment in Marine Areas Beyond National Jurisdiction' (2012) 26 Ocean Yearbook 317

13
The law of international watercourses

13.1   INTRODUCTION

Water is fundamental to human survival and is needed in all aspects of life. As acknowledged in Agenda 21, Chapter 18:

> Freshwater resources are an essential component of the Earth's hydrosphere and an indispensable part of all terrestrial ecosystems. The freshwater environment is characterized by the hydrological cycle, including floods and droughts, which in some regions have become more extreme and dramatic in their consequences. Global climate change and atmospheric pollution could also have an impact on freshwater resources and their availability and, through sea-level rise, threaten low-lying coastal areas and small island ecosystems.[1]
> [...]
> Transboundary water resources and their use are of great importance to riparian States.[2]

Watercourses is defined in the 1997 Convention on the Law of Non-navigational uses of international watercourses (1997 International Watercourses Convention) as 'a system of surface waters and groundwaters constituting by virtue of their physical relationship a unitary whole and normally flowing into a common terminus'[3] and an international watercourse as 'a watercourse, parts of which are situated in different States'.[4]

Broadly speaking, watercourses can be divided into surface water and groundwater. The former would include rivers, lakes, ponds, glaciers in solid form, as well as canals and reservoirs; while the latter is water below the Earth's surface, which constitutes approximately 97% of freshwater on Earth, the former, i.e., groundwater, has received far less attention than

---

[1]   Agenda 21, Chapter 18: Protection of the Quality and Supply of Freshwater Resources: Application of Integrated Approaches to the Development, Management and Use of Water Resources, paragraph 1.

[2]   Ibid, paragraph 4.

[3]   Article 2(a), 1997 Convention on the Law of Non-navigational uses of international watercourses ('1997 International Watercourses Convention').

[4]   Ibid., Article 2(b).

surface water.[5] In relation to the former, the legal framework is broadly considered in two categories: navigation and non-navigation. The focus of this chapter will be on non-navigational uses of freshwater.

Four theories concerning the theoretical basis of the law of the non-navigational uses of international watercourses have been identified: absolute territorial sovereignty;[6] absolute territorial integrity;[7] limited territorial sovereignty;[8] and community of interests[9] – which was reflected in the 1957 arbitral award in the *Lac Lanoux Arbitration*.[10] McCaffrey comments:

> the foregoing discussion of the four theories concerning the theoretical basis of the law of the non-navigational uses of international watercourses yields several conclusions. These may be briefly stated as follows: Second, the doctrine of limited territorial sovereignty—when the expression is properly understood—appears to come closest of the four theories to describing the actual situation produced by state practice. Finally, the community of interest theory has much to recommend it as a theoretical context for the law of international watercourses.[11]

The legal framework on international watercourses, and the protection of international watercourses, comprises customary international law, international treaties, i.e., global conventions, regional conventions and bilateral treaties. There are global conventions that pertain to freshwater. There are two global conventions: the 1992 UN Economic Commission for Europe Convention on the Protection and Use of Transboundary Watercourses and International Lakes ('1992 Water Convention'); and the 1997 International Watercourses Convention. The Institut de Droit International (Institute of International Law) and the International Law Association have played a role in the development of the law of shared freshwater resources.[12]

The 1992 Water Convention was initially a regional convention which was concluded between member states of the UN Economic Commission for Europe (UNECE) at Helsinki in 1992 and entered into force in October 1996; but in 2003, parties adopted amendments to Articles 25 and 26, which opened the Convention to accession by UN member States outside of the UNECE region. These amendments entered into force on 6 February 2013 and, subject to decision VI/3 of the Meeting of the Parties to the Water Convention, only became operational when all parties (state and organizations) ratify the amendments. As such, states outside of

---

[5] Stephen McCaffrey, *The Law of International Watercourses: Non-navigational Uses* (3rd edn, OUP 2019) 544.

[6] Ibid., 99–116.

[7] Ibid., 116–125.

[8] Ibid., 125–138.

[9] Ibid., 138–151.

[10] *Lake Lanoux Arbitration (France v. Spain)*, Arbitral Tribunal, 12 RIAA 281; 24 ILR 101 (16 November 1957).

[11] McCaffrey (n 5) 157.

[12] Institut de droit International Resolutions: 1911 Madrid Resolution on International Regulations regarding the Use of International Watercourses, 1961 Salzburg Resolution on the Use of International Non-Maritime Waters, 1979 Athens Resolution on the Pollution of Rivers and Lakes and International Law; International Law Association Resolutions: 1966 Helsinki Rules on the Uses of the Waters of International Rivers.

the UNECE region were able to join the Convention after 1 March 2016. The Convention is a framework convention, which governs obligations in relation to the protection and ecologically sound management of transboundary waters. It requires, *inter alia*, parties to prevent, control and reduce transboundary impact; to ensure ecologically sound and rational water management; reasonable and equitable use of transboundary waters; conservation and, where necessary, restoration of ecosystems.[13]

The 1997 International Watercourses Convention is seen to a large extent as a 'codification, of the fundamental rights and obligations that form the basis of the law of international watercourses'.[14] It 'represents an effort by the international community to reflect the general principles and rules of international law governing the use by states of shared freshwater resources, except for principles and rules concerning navigation';[15] and that this Convention 'reflects in large measure rules and principles of customary international law on international courses'.[16] It was referred to by the ICJ in the *Gabčíkovo-Nagymaros Project* case.[17] The Convention is a framework convention,[18] and upholds the cornerstone principle of the 1997 Watercourses Convention that it is equitable and reasonable utilisation, i.e., that watercourse states shall in their respective territories utilise an international watercourse in an equitable and reasonable manner.[19]

McCaffrey observes:

> The Watercourses Convention bears the hallmarks of a codification in the simplicity and relative brevity of its provisions. The Water Convention, on the other hand, is far more detailed, with long paragraphs and some articles that are more than a page long. But the agreements fit together neatly and are mutually supportive.[20]

Both global conventions can be seen to supplement – rather than act as an alternative – to each other.[21] He does point out two differences: first, the 1992 Water Convention contains institutional provisions, while the 1997 International Watercourses Convention does not; second, the 1997 International Watercourses Convention contains a form of compulsory dispute set-

---

[13]   Article 2, 1992 Water Convention.

[14]   McCaffrey (n 5) 409.

[15]   Ibid., 421.

[16]   Ibid., 422.

[17]   *Gabčíkovo-Nagymaros Project (Hungary/Slovakia)*, Judgment, ICJ Reports 1997, p. 7.

[18]   Preamble ('expressing the conviction that a framework convention will ensure the utilization, development, conservation, management and protection of international watercourses and the promotion of the optimal and sustainable utilization thereof for present and future generations'); Stéphane Doumbé-Billé and Françoise Paccaud, 'The Choice of a Framework Convention' in Laurence Boisson de Chazournes and others (eds), *The UN Convention on the Law of the Non-Navigational Uses of International Watercourses: A Commentary* (Cambridge University Press 2018) 20–21.

[19]   Article 5; see also Article 6.; *Gabčíkovo-Nagymaros Project* (n 17) at 78.

[20]   McCaffrey (n 5) 415.

[21]   Ibid.

tlement, while the 1992 Water Convention provides for compulsory arbitration if the parties to the dispute declare acceptance.[22]

In relation to the environmental protection of international watercourses, according to McCaffrey, 'environmental protection' may be taken to 'refer to the protection of those watercourses and their ecosystems, including surrounding areas, from pollution and other adverse effects such as the introduction of alien species. As such, the concept would extend to the protection of so-called "environmental flows", ie, the volumes of water necessary to sustain watercourse ecosystems'.[23] Sands and Peel observe that 'the rules of international environmental law to protect freshwater resources, including international watercourses, from pollution and overuse, have developed primarily as piecemeal and ad hoc responses to problems with particular rivers, lakes and freshwater ecosystems',[24] and that 'states are subject to a customary obligation to negotiate, consult and cooperate to reach an equitable solution to the problems posed by activities that may affect international rivers providing a shared natural resource, including water pollution and excessive use'.[25]

As mentioned above, groundwater constitutes approximately 97% of freshwater on Earth.[26] This includes aquifers, which, broadly speaking, is understood as permeable water-bearing geological formation underlain by a less permeable layer and the water contained in the saturated zone of the formation.[27] Attila Tanzi observes:

> Traditionally, international water law and diplomacy have been concerned with the regulation of surface water, moving from navigation to the non-navigational uses of transboundary watercourses. There is general agreement that groundwater has long been neglected by international water law.[28]

As the definitions of international watercourses in the 1997 Convention includes groundwater that is related to surface water systems, McCaffrey observes that 'the discussion of fundamental obligations in respect of international watercourses has assumed that the same rules apply to surface water and groundwater alike'[29] and that 'this has resulted in a legal regime for groundwater that is rather crude and is in dire need of development given groundwater's abundance

---

[22] Ibid., 419. See also, 420–421.

[23] Stephen McCaffrey, 'International Watercourses, Environmental Protection' (2011) *Max Planck Encyclopedia of Public International Law*.

[24] Philippe Sands and Jacqueline Peel, *Principles of International Environmental Law* (4th edn, Cambridge University Press 2018) 339.

[25] Ibid., 341.

[26] McCaffrey (n 5) 32–39.

[27] Article 2(a) ILC Articles on the Law of Transboundary Aquifers 2008.

[28] Attila Tanzi, 'Furthering International Water Law or Making a New Body of Law on Transboundary Aquifers? An Introduction' (2011) 13 International Community Law Review 193, 193.

[29] McCaffrey (n 5) 544.

and vulnerability relative to surface water. This need has been abated only somewhat by the ILC's adoption of draft articles on the Law of Transboundary Aquifers in 2008'.[30]

With regard to non-legally binding instruments, the 1966 ILA Helsinki Rules defined 'international draining basin' as being 'determined by the watershed limits of the system of waters, including surface and underground waters, flowing into a common terminus', while the ILA's Rules on International Groundwaters adopted in Seoul in 1986 (the 'Seoul Rules') deal specifically with aquifers that are intersected by international boundaries as these fall outside the scope of the 1996 ILA Helsinki Rules. Tanzi comments that 'the Seoul Rules have inaugurated an international law-making trend to the effect that groundwater deserves separate specification of general international water law rules'.[31] Notably the 1966 ILA Helsinki Rules have been replaced by the 2004 ILA Berlin Rules on Water Resources.

In 2002 the ILC decided to include the topic of Shared Natural Resources in its programme of work and appointed Mr Chusei Yamada as Special Rapporteur.[32] The ILC began its work on Shared Natural Resources and focused upon transboundary groundwater. The ILC adopted the final set of articles on the Law of Transboundary Aquifers in 2008 and was annexed in GA Resolution 68/118 (2013).[33]

13.2   LEGAL INSTRUMENTS

13.2.1   International Instruments

1992 Convention on the Protection and Use of Transboundary Watercourses and International Lakes, 1936 UNTS 269 (as amended, along with decision VI/3 clarifying the accession procedure)

Article 1 DEFINITIONS
For the purposes of this Convention,

1.   "Transboundary waters" means any surface or ground waters which mark, cross or are located on boundaries between two or more States; wherever transboundary waters flow directly into the sea, these transboundary waters end at a straight line across their respective mouths between points on the low-water line of their banks;

2.   "Transboundary impact" means any significant adverse effect on the environment resulting from a change in the conditions of transboundary waters caused by a human activity, the physical origin of which is situated wholly or in part within an area under the jurisdiction of a Party, within an area under the jurisdiction of another Party. Such effects on the environment include effects on human health and safety, flora, fauna, soil, air, water, climate, landscape and historical monu-

---

[30]   Ibid., 545–546.

[31]   Tanzi (n 31) 197. See also 1989 Draft Agreement Concerning the Use of Transboundary Groundwaters ('the Bellagio Draft Treaty').

[32]   ILC Report, A/57/10, 2002, chap II, para. 20.

[33]   GA Resolution 68/118 (2013).

ments or other physical structures or the interaction among these factors; they also include effects on the cultural heritage or socio-economic conditions resulting from alterations to those factors;

3. "Party" means, unless the text otherwise indicates, a Contracting Party to this Convention;

4. "Riparian Parties" means the Parties bordering the same transboundary waters;

5. "Joint body" means any bilateral or multilateral commission or other appropriate institutional arrangements for cooperation between the Riparian Parties;

6. "Hazardous substances" means substances which are toxic, carcinogenic, muta-genic, teratogenic or bio-accumulative, especially when they are persistent;

7. "Best available technology" (the definition is contained in annex I to this Convention).

Article 2 GENERAL PROVISIONS

1. The Parties shall take all appropriate measures to prevent, control and reduce any transboundary impact.

2. The Parties shall, in particular, take all appropriate measures:

   (a) To prevent, control and reduce pollution of waters causing or likely to cause transboundary impact;

   (b) To ensure that transboundary waters are used with the aim of ecologically sound and rational water management, conservation of water resources and environmental protection;

   (c) To ensure that transboundary waters are used in a reasonable and equitable way, taking into particular account their transboundary character, in the case of activities which cause or are likely to cause transboundary impact;

   (d) To ensure conservation and, where necessary, restoration of ecosystems.

3. Measures for the prevention, control and reduction of water pollution shall be taken, where possible, at source.

4. These measures shall not directly or indirectly result in a transfer of pollution to other parts of the environment.

5. In taking the measures referred to in paragraphs 1 and 2 of this article, the Parties shall be guided by the following principles:

   (a) The precautionary principle, by virtue of which action to avoid the poten-tial transboundary impact of the release of hazardous substances shall not be postponed on the ground that scientific research has not fully proved a causal link between those substances, on the one hand, and the potential transboundary impact, on the other hand;

   (b) The polluter-pays principle, by virtue of which costs of pollution preven-tion, control and reduction measures shall be borne by the polluter;

   (c) Water resources shall be managed so that the needs of the present gener-ation are met without compromising the ability of future generations to meet their own needs.

6. The Riparian Parties shall cooperate on the basis of equality and reciprocity, in par-ticular through bilateral and multilateral agreements, in order to develop harmo-nized policies, programmes and strategies covering the relevant catchment areas,

or parts thereof, aimed at the prevention, control and reduction of transboundary impact and aimed at the protection of the environment of transboundary waters or the environment influenced by such waters, including the marine environment.

7. The application of this Convention shall not lead to the deterioration of environmental conditions nor lead to increased transboundary impact.

8. The provisions of this Convention shall not affect the right of Parties individually or jointly to adopt and implement more stringent measures than those set down in this Convention.

Article 3 PREVENTION, CONTROL AND REDUCTION

1. To prevent, control and reduce transboundary impact, the Parties shall develop, adopt, implement and, as far as possible, render compatible relevant legal, administrative, economic, financial and technical measures, in order to ensure, *inter alia*, that:

    (a) The emission of pollutants is prevented, controlled and reduced at source through the application of, *inter alia*, low- and non-waste technology;

    (b) Transboundary waters are protected against pollution from point sources through the prior licensing of waste-water discharges by the competent national authorities, and that the authorized discharges are monitored and controlled;

    (c) Limits for waste-water discharges stated in permits are based on the best available technology for discharges of hazardous substances;

    (d) Stricter requirements, even leading to prohibition in individual cases, are imposed when the quality of the receiving water or the ecosystem so requires;

    (e) At least biological treatment or equivalent processes are applied to municipal waste water, where necessary in a step-by-step approach;

    (f) Appropriate measures are taken, such as the application of the best available technology, in order to reduce nutrient inputs from industrial and municipal sources;

    (g) Appropriate measures and best environmental practices are developed and implemented for the reduction of inputs of nutrients and hazardous substances from diffuse sources, especially where the main sources are from agriculture (guidelines for developing best environmental practices are given in annex II to this Convention);

    (h) Environmental impact assessment and other means of assessment are applied;

    (i) Sustainable water-resources management, including the application of the ecosystems approach, is promoted;

    (j) Contingency planning is developed;

    (k) Additional specific measures are taken to prevent the pollution of groundwaters;

    (l) The risk of accidental pollution is minimized.

2. To this end, each Party shall set emission limits for discharges from point sources into surface waters based on the best available technology, which are specifically applicable to individual industrial sectors or industries from which hazardous substances derive. The appropriate measures mentioned in paragraph 1 of this article

to prevent, control and reduce the input of hazardous substances from point and diffuse sources into waters, may, *inter alia*, include total or partial prohibition of the production or use of such substances. Existing lists of such industrial sectors or industries and of such hazardous substances in international conventions or regulations, which are applicable in the area covered by this Convention, shall be taken into account.

3.   In addition, each Party shall define, where appropriate, water-quality objectives and adopt water-quality criteria for the purpose of preventing, controlling and reducing transboundary impact. General guidance for developing such objectives and criteria is given in annex III to this Convention. When necessary, the Parties shall endeavour to update this annex.

Article 4 MONITORING
The Parties shall establish programmes for monitoring the conditions of transboundary waters.

[…]

Article 22 SETTLEMENT OF DISPUTES
1. If a dispute arises between two or more Parties about the interpretation or application of this Convention, they shall seek a solution by negotiation or by any other means of dispute settlement acceptable to the parties to the dispute.
2. When signing, ratifying, accepting, approving or acceding to this Convention, or at any time thereafter, a Party may declare in writing to the Depositary that, for a dispute not resolved in accordance with paragraph 1 of this article, it accepts one or both of the following means of dispute settlement as compulsory in relation to any Party accepting the same obligation:
    (a)   Submission of the dispute to the International Court of Justice;
    (b)   Arbitration in accordance with the procedure set out in annex IV.
3. If the parties to the dispute have accepted both means of dispute settlement referred to in paragraph 2 of this article, the dispute may be submitted only to the International Court of Justice, unless the parties agree otherwise.

1999 Protocol on Water and Health to the 1992 Convention on the Protection and Use of Transboundary Watercourses and International Lakes, 2331 UNTS 202

Article 1 OBJECTIVE
The objective of this Protocol is to promote at all appropriate levels, nationally as well as in transboundary and international contexts, the protection of human health and well-being, both individual and collective, within a framework of sustainable development, through improving water management, including the protection of water ecosystems, and through preventing, controlling and reducing water-related disease.

Article 3 SCOPE
The provisions of this Protocol shall apply to: (a) Surface freshwater; (b) Groundwater; (c) Estuaries; (d) Coastal waters which are used for recreation or for the production of fish by aquaculture or for the production or harvesting of shellfish; (e) Enclosed waters generally

available for bathing; (f) Water in the course of abstraction, transport, treatment or supply; (g) Waste water throughout the course of collection, transport, treatment and discharge or reuse.

Article 4 GENERAL PROVISIONS

1. The Parties shall take all appropriate measures to prevent, control and reduce water-related disease within a framework of integrated water-management systems aimed at sustainable use of water resources, ambient water quality which does not endanger human health, and protection of water ecosystems.

2. The Parties shall, in particular, take all appropriate measures for the purpose of ensuring:
    (a) Adequate supplies of wholesome drinking water which is free from any micro-organisms, parasites and substances which, owing to their numbers or concentration, constitute a potential danger to human health. This shall include the protection of water resources which are used as sources of drinking water, treatment of water and the establishment, improvement and maintenance of collective systems;
    (b) Adequate sanitation of a standard which sufficiently protects human health and the environment. This shall in particular be done through the establishment, improvement and maintenance of collective systems;
    (c) Effective protection of water resources used as sources of drinking water, and their related water ecosystems, from pollution from other causes, including agriculture, industry and other discharges and emissions of hazardous substances. This shall aim at the effective reduction and elimination of discharges and emissions of substances judged to be hazardous to human health and water ecosystems;
    (d) Sufficient safeguards for human health against water-related disease arising from the use of water for recreational purposes, from the use of water for aquaculture, from the water in which shellfish are produced or from which they are harvested, from the use of waste water for irrigation or from the use of sewage sludge in agriculture or aquaculture;
    (e) Effective systems for monitoring situations likely to result in outbreaks or incidents of water-related disease and for responding to such outbreaks and incidents and to the risk of them.

3. Subsequent references in this Protocol to "drinking water" and "sanitation" are to drinking water and sanitation that are required to meet the requirements of paragraph 2 of this article.

4. The Parties shall base all such measures upon an assessment of any proposed measure in respect of all its implications, including the benefits, disadvantages and costs, for:
    (a) Human health;
    (b) Water resources; and
    (c) Sustainable development, which takes account of the differing new impacts of any proposed measure on the different environmental mediums.

5.   The Parties shall take all appropriate action to create legal, administrative and economic frameworks which are stable and enabling and within which the public, private and voluntary sectors can each make its contribution to improving water management for the purpose of preventing, controlling and reducing water-related disease.

6.   The Parties shall require public authorities which are considering taking action, or approving the taking by others of action, that may have a significant impact on the environment of any waters within the scope of this Protocol to take due account of any potential impact of that action on public health.

1997 United Nations Convention on Non-Navigational Uses of Watercourses, 2999 UNTS, A/51/869

Preamble
The Parties to the present Convention,
[…]
Expressing the conviction that a framework convention will ensure the utilization, development, conservation, management and protection of international watercourses and the promotion of the optimal and sustainable utilization thereof for present and future generations

Article 1 Scope of the present Convention
1.   The present Convention applies to uses of international watercourses and of their waters for purposes other than navigation and to measures of protection, preservation and management related to the uses of those watercourses and their waters.
2.   The uses of international watercourses for navigation is not within the scope of the present Convention except insofar as other uses affect navigation or are affected by navigation.

Article 2 Use of terms
For the purposes of the present Convention:
(a)   "Watercourse" means a system of surface waters and groundwaters constituting by virtue of their physical relationship a unitary whole and normally flowing into a common terminus;
(b)   "International watercourse" means a watercourse, parts of which are situated in different States;
(c)   "Watercourse State" means a State Party to the present Convention in whose territory part of an international watercourse is situated, or a Party that is a regional economic integration organization, in the territory of one or more of whose Member States part of an international watercourse is situated;
(d)   "Regional economic integration organization" means an organization constituted by sovereign States of a given region, to which its member States have transferred competence in respect of matters governed by this Convention and which has been duly authorized in accordance with its internal procedures, to sign, ratify, accept, approve or accede to it.

Article 3 Watercourse agreements
1.   In the absence of an agreement to the contrary, nothing in the present Convention shall affect the rights or obligations of a watercourse State arising from agreements in force for it on the date on which it became a party to the present Convention.
2.   Notwithstanding the provisions of paragraph 1, parties to agreements referred to in paragraph 1 may, where necessary, consider harmonizing such agreements with the basic principles of the present Convention.
3.   Watercourse States may enter into one or more agreements, hereinafter referred to as "watercourse agreements", which apply and adjust the provisions of the present Convention to the characteristics and uses of a particular international watercourse or part thereof.
4.   Where a watercourse agreement is concluded between two or more watercourse States, it shall define the waters to which it applies. Such an agreement may be entered into with respect to an entire international watercourse or any part thereof or a particular project, programme or use except insofar as the agreement adversely affects, to a significant extent, the use by one or more other watercourse States of the waters of the watercourse, without their express consent.
5.   Where a watercourse State considers that adjustment and application of the provisions of the present Convention is required because of the characteristics and uses of a particular international watercourse, watercourse States shall consult with a view to negotiating in good faith for the purpose of concluding a watercourse agreement or agreements.
6.   Where some but not all watercourse States to a particular international watercourse are parties to an agreement, nothing in such agreement shall affect the rights or obligations under the present Convention of watercourse States that are not parties to such an agreement.

Article 4 Parties to watercourse agreements
1.   Every watercourse State is entitled to participate in the negotiation of and to become a party to any watercourse agreement that applies to the entire international watercourse, as well as to participate in any relevant consultations.
2.   A watercourse State whose use of an international watercourse may be affected to a significant extent by the implementation of a proposed watercourse agreement that applies only to a part of the watercourse or to a particular project, programme or use is entitled to participate in consultations on such an agreement and, where appropriate, in the negotiation thereof in good faith with a view to becoming a party thereto, to the extent that its use is thereby affected.

PART II. GENERAL PRINCIPLES

Article 5 Equitable and reasonable utilization and participation
1.   Watercourse States shall in their respective territories utilize an international watercourse in an equitable and reasonable manner. In particular, an international watercourse shall be used and developed by watercourse States with a view to attaining optimal and sustainable utilization thereof and benefits therefrom, taking

into account the interests of the watercourse States concerned, consistent with adequate protection of the watercourse.

2. Watercourse States shall participate in the use, development and protection of an international watercourse in an equitable and reasonable manner. Such participation includes both the right to utilize the watercourse and the duty to cooperate in the protection and development thereof, as provided in the present Convention.

Article 6 Factors relevant to equitable and reasonable utilization

1. Utilization of an international watercourse in an equitable and reasonable manner within the meaning of article 5 requires taking into account all relevant factors and circumstances, including:

    (a) Geographic, hydrographic, hydrological, climatic, ecological and other factors of a natural character;

    (b) The social and economic needs of the watercourse States concerned;

    (c) The population dependent on the watercourse in each watercourse State;

    (d) The effects of the use or uses of the watercourses in one watercourse State on other watercourse States;

    (e) Existing and potential uses of the watercourse;

    (f) Conservation, protection, development and economy of use of the water resources of the watercourse and the costs of measures taken to that effect;

    (g) The availability of alternatives, of comparable value, to a particular planned or existing use.

2. In the application of article 5 or paragraph 1 of this article, watercourse States concerned shall, when the need arises, enter into consultations in a spirit of cooperation.

3. The weight to be given to each factor is to be determined by its importance in comparison with that of other relevant factors. In determining what is a reasonable and equitable use , all relevant factors are to be considered together and a conclusion reached on the basis of the whole.

Article 7 Obligation not to cause significant harm

1. Watercourse States shall, in utilizing an international watercourse in their territories, take all appropriate measures to prevent the causing of significant harm to other watercourse States.

2. Where significant harm nevertheless is caused to another watercourse State, the States whose use causes such harm shall, in the absence of agreement to such use, take all appropriate measures, having due regard for the provisions of articles 5 and 6, in consultation with the affected State, to eliminate or mitigate such harm and, where appropriate, to discuss the question of compensation.

Article 8 General obligation to cooperate

1. Watercourse States shall cooperate on the basis of sovereign equality, territorial integrity, mutual benefit and good faith in order to attain optimal utilization and adequate protection of an international watercourse.

2. In determining the manner of such cooperation, watercourse States may consider the establishment of joint mechanisms or commissions, as deemed necessary by them, to facilitate cooperation on relevant measures and procedures in the light of

experience gained th rough cooperation in existing joint mechanisms and commissions in various regions.

Article 9 Regular exchange of data and information

1.   Pursuant to article 8, watercourse States shall on a regular basis exchange readily
      available data and information on the condition of the watercourse, in particular
      that of a hydrological, meteorological, hydrogeological and ecological nature and
      related to the water quality as well as related forecasts.
2.   If a watercourse State is requested by another watercourse State to provide data or
      information that is not readily available, it shall employ its best efforts to comply
      with the request but may condition its compliance upon payment by the requesting
      State of the reasonable costs of collecting and, where appropriate, processing such
      data or information.
3.   Watercourse States shall employ their best efforts to collect and, where appropriate,
      to process data and information in a manner which facilitates its utilization by the
      other watercourse States to which it is communicated.

PART III. PLANNED MEASURES

Article 11 Information concerning planned measures
Watercourse States shall exchange information and consult each other and, if necessary,
negotiate on the possible effects of planned measures on the condition of an international
watercourse.

PART IV. PROTECTION, PRESERVATION AND MANAGEMENT

Article 12 Notification concerning planned measures with possible adverse effects
Before a watercourse State implements or permits the implementation of planned measures which may have a significant adverse effect upon other watercourse States, it shall
provide those States with timely notification thereof. Such notification shall be accompanied by available technical data and information, including the results of any environmental impact assessment, in order to enable the notified States to evaluate the possible effects
of the planned measures.

[...]

Article 20 Protection and preservation of ecosystems
Watercourse States shall, individually and, where appropriate, jointly, protect and preserve
the ecosystems of international watercourses.

Article 21 Prevention, reduction and control of pollution

1.   For the purpose of this article, "pollution of an international watercourse" means
      any detrimental alteration in the composition or quality of the waters of an inter-
      national watercourse which results directly or indirectly from human conduct.
2.   Watercourse States shall, individually and, where appropriate, jointly, prevent,
      reduce and control the pollution of an international watercourse that may cause
      significant harm to other watercourse States or to their environment, including

harm to human health or safety, to the use of the waters for any beneficial purpose or to the living resources of the watercourse. Watercourse States shall take steps to harmonize their policies in this connection.

3. Watercourse States shall, at the request of any of them, consult with a view to arriving at mutually agreeable measures and methods to prevent, reduce and control pollution of an international watercourse, such as:

(a) Setting joint water quality objectives and criteria;

(b) Establishing techniques and practices to address pollution from point and non -point sources;

(c) Establishing lists of substances the introduction of which into the waters of an international watercourse is to be prohibited, limited, investigated or monitored.

13.2.2 Regional Instruments

Table 13.1 Regional treaties

A. Europe
1869 Berne Convention establishing Uniform Regulations concerning fishing in the Rhine between Constance and Basel
1950 Protocol to Establish a Tripartite Standing Committee on Polluted Waters
1960 Convention on the Protection of Lake Constance against Pollution
1961 Protocol Concerning the Constitution of an International Commission for the Protection of the Mosel against Pollution
1962 Convention Concerning the Protection of the Waters of Lake Geneva against Pollution
1963 Berne Agreement on the International Commission for the Protection of the Rhine Against Pollution
1976 Convention for the Protection of the River Rhine Against Chemical Pollution
1976 Convention for the Protection of the Rhine River against Pollution by Chlorides
1990 Convention for the International Commission for the Protection of the Elbe
1994 Convention on Cooperation for the Protection and Sustainable Use of the River Danube
2002 Agreement on the Protection of the River Meuse
2004 Agreement for the Protection and Sustainable Development of Lake Ohrid and its Watershed
B. Americas
1978 Great Lakes Water Quality Agreement
1990 Boundary Waters Treaty
C. Africa
1963 Act Regarding Navigation and Economic Co-operation between the States of the Niger Basin
1987 Agreement on the Action Plan for the Environmentally Sound Management of the Common Zambezi River System
D. Asia
Agreement on the Co-operation for the Sustainable Development of the Mekong River Basin 1995
The Bangladesh-India Treaty on Sharing the Waters of the Ganges River
India-Nepal Treaty on Sharing the Waters of the Mahakali River

13.2.3   Non-Binding Instruments

2004 Berlin Rules on Water Resources

Article 7 establishes the obligation to use watercourse sustainably and article 8 an obligation not to cause harm. Importantly Article 12 supports the principle of equitable utilisation and provides that:

1.   Basin States shall in their respective territories manage the waters of an international drainage basin in an equitable and reasonable manner having due regard for the obligation not to cause significant harm to other basin States.

2.   In particular, basin States shall develop and use the waters of the basin in order to attain the optimal and sustainable use thereof and benefits therefrom, taking into account the interests of other basin States, consistent with adequate protection of the waters.

In terms of determining a reasonable and equitable use, Article 13 details the following factors that may be considered:

1.   Equitable and reasonable use within the meaning of Article 12 is to be determined through consideration of all relevant factors in each particular case.

2.   Relevant factors to be considered include, but are not limited to:

  1.   Geographic, hydrographic, hydrological, hydrogeological, climatic, ecological, and other natural features;

  2.   The social and economic needs of the basin States concerned;

  3.   The population dependent on the waters of the international drainage basin in each basin State;

  4.   The effects of the use or uses of the waters of the international drainage basin in one basin State upon other basin States;

  5.   Existing and potential uses of the waters of the international drainage basin;

  6.   Conservation, protection, development, and economy of use of the water resources of the international drainage basin and the costs of measures taken to achieve these purposes;

  7.   The availability of alternatives, of comparable value, to the particular planned or existing use;

  8.   The sustainability of proposed or existing uses; and

  9.   The minimization of environmental harm.

3.   The weight of each factor is to be determined by its importance in comparison with other relevant factors. In determining what is a reasonable and equitable use, all relevant factors are to be considered together and a conclusion reached on the basis of the whole.

ILC 2008 Articles on Transboundary Aquifers Resolution adopted by the General Assembly on 16 December 2013 [on the report of the Sixth Committee (A/68/470)] 68/118. The law of transboundary aquifers

The General Assembly,
[…]

Noting the major importance of the subject of the law of transboundary aquifers in the relations of States and the need for reasonable and proper management of transboundary aquifers, a vitally important natural resource, through international cooperation for present and future generations,

Noting also that the provisions of the draft articles on the law of transboundary aquifers have been taken into account in relevant instruments such as the Guarani Aquifer Agreement signed by Argentina, Brazil, Paraguay and Uruguay on 2 August 2010, and the Model Provisions on Transboundary Groundwaters adopted by the sixth Meeting of the Parties to the Convention on the Protection and Use of Transboundary Watercourses and International Lakes on 29 November 2012,

Emphasizing the continuing importance of the codification and progressive development of international law, as referred to in Article 13, paragraph 1 (a), of the Charter of the United Nations,

1. Commends to the attention of Governments the draft articles on the law of transboundary aquifers annexed to the present resolution as guidance for bilateral or regional agreements and arrangements for the proper management of transboundary aquifers;

2. Encourages the International Hydrological Programme of the United Nations Educational, Scientific and Cultural Organization to continue its contribution by offering further scientific and technical assistance to the States concerned;

ILC 2008 Articles on Transboundary Aquifers

Part one Introduction
Article 1 Scope
The present articles apply to:
(a) Utilization of transboundary aquifers or aquifer systems;
(b) Other activities that have or are likely to have an impact upon such aquifers or aquifer systems; and
(c) Measures for the protection, preservation and management of such aquifers or aquifer systems.

Article 2 Use of terms
For the purposes of the present articles:
(a) "aquifer" means a permeable water-bearing geological formation underlain by a less permeable layer and the water contained in the saturated zone of the formation;
(b) "aquifer system" means a series of two or more aquifers that are hydraulically connected;

(c)   "transboundary aquifer" or "transboundary aquifer system" means, respectively, an aquifer or aquifer system, parts of which are situated in different States;

(d)   "aquifer State" means a State in whose territory any part of a transboundary aquifer or aquifer system is situated;

(e)   "utilization of transboundary aquifers or aquifer systems" includes extraction of water, heat and minerals, and storage and disposal of any substance;

(f)   "recharging aquifer" means an aquifer that receives a non-negligible amount of contemporary water recharge;

(g)   "recharge zone" means the zone which contributes water to an aquifer, consisting of the catchment area of rainfall water and the area where such water flows to an aquifer by run-off on the ground and infiltration through soil;

(h)   "discharge zone" means the zone where water originating from an aquifer flows to its outlets, such as a watercourse, a lake, an oasis, a wetland or an ocean.

Part two General principles

Article 3 Sovereignty of aquifer States
Each aquifer State has sovereignty over the portion of a transboundary aquifer or aquifer system located within its territory. It shall exercise its sovereignty in accordance with international law and the present articles.

Article 4 Equitable and reasonable utilization
Aquifer States shall utilize transboundary aquifers or aquifer systems according to the principle of equitable and reasonable utilization, as follows:

(a)   They shall utilize transboundary aquifers or aquifer systems in a manner that is consistent with the equitable and reasonable accrual of benefits therefrom to the aquifer States concerned;

(b)   They shall aim at maximizing the long-term benefits derived from the use of water contained therein;

(c)   They shall establish individually or jointly a comprehensive utilization plan, taking into account present and future needs of, and alternative water sources for, the aquifer States; and

(d)   They shall not utilize a recharging transboundary aquifer or aquifer system at a level that would prevent continuance of its effective functioning.

Article 5 Factors relevant to equitable and reasonable utilization

1.   Utilization of a transboundary aquifer or aquifer system in an equitable and reasonable manner within the meaning of article 4 requires taking into account all relevant factors, including:

    (a)   The population dependent on the aquifer or aquifer system in each aquifer State;

    (b)   The social, economic and other needs, present and future, of the aquifer States concerned;

    (c)   The natural characteristics of the aquifer or aquifer system;

    (d)   The contribution to the formation and recharge of the aquifer or aquifer system;

(e)   The existing and potential utilization of the aquifer or aquifer system;
(f)   The actual and potential effects of the utilization of the aquifer or aquifer system in one aquifer State on other aquifer States concerned;
(g)   The availability of alternatives to a particular existing and planned utilization of the aquifer or aquifer system;
(h)   The development, protection and conservation of the aquifer or aquifer system and the costs of measures to be taken to that effect;
(i)   The role of the aquifer or aquifer system in the related ecosystem.

2.   The weight to be given to each factor is to be determined by its importance with regard to a specific transboundary aquifer or aquifer system in comparison with that of other relevant factors. In determining what is equitable and reasonable utilization, all relevant factors are to be considered together and a conclusion reached on the basis of all the factors. However, in weighing different kinds of utilization of a transboundary aquifer or aquifer system, special regard shall be given to vital human needs.

Article 6 Obligation not to cause significant harm

1.   Aquifer States shall, in utilizing transboundary aquifers or aquifer systems in their territories, take all appropriate measures to prevent the causing of significant harm to other aquifer States or other States in whose territory a discharge zone is located.
2.   Aquifer States shall, in undertaking activities other than utilization of a transboundary aquifer or aquifer system that have, or are likely to have, an impact upon that transboundary aquifer or aquifer system, take all appropriate measures to prevent the causing of significant harm through that aquifer or aquifer system to other aquifer States or other States in whose territory a discharge zone is located.
3.   Where significant harm nevertheless is caused to another aquifer State or a State in whose territory a discharge zone is located, the aquifer State whose activities cause such harm shall take, in consultation with the affected State, all appropriate response measures to eliminate or mitigate such harm, having due regard for the provisions of articles 4 and 5.

Article 7 General obligation to cooperate

1.   Aquifer States shall cooperate on the basis of sovereign equality, territorial integrity, sustainable development, mutual benefit and good faith in order to attain equitable and reasonable utilization and appropriate protection of their transboundary aquifers or aquifer systems.
2.   For the purpose of paragraph 1, aquifer States should establish joint mechanisms of cooperation

Article 8 Regular exchange of data and information

1.   Pursuant to article 7, aquifer States shall, on a regular basis, exchange readily available data and information on the condition of their transboundary aquifers or aquifer systems, in particular of a geological, hydrogeological, hydrological, meteorological and ecological nature and related to the hydrochemistry of the aquifers or aquifer systems, as well as related forecasts.
2.   Where knowledge about the nature and extent of a transboundary aquifer or aquifer system is inadequate, aquifer States concerned shall employ their best

efforts to collect and generate more complete data and information relating to such aquifer or aquifer system, taking into account current practices and standards. They shall take such action individually or jointly and, where appropriate, together with or through international organizations.

3. If an aquifer State is requested by another aquifer State to provide data and information relating to an aquifer or aquifer system that are not readily available, it shall employ its best efforts to comply with the request. The requested State may condition its compliance upon payment by the requesting State of the reasonable costs of collecting and, where appropriate, processing such data or information.

4. Aquifer States shall, where appropriate, employ their best efforts to collect and process data and information in a manner that facilitates their utilization by the other aquifer States to which such data and information are communicated.

13.3   CASES

CASE
PCIJ, *Territorial Jurisdiction of Int'l Comm'n of River Oder (U.K. v. Pol.)*, Judgment, PCIJ No. 16 (10 September 1929), Series A No. 23

[74] [...] "the community of interests in a navigable river [which] becomes the basis of a common legal right, the essential features of which are the perfect equality of all riparian states in the use of the whole course of the river and the exclusion of any preferential privilege of any one riparian in relation to others."

CASE
RIAA, *Lake Lanoux Arbitration (France v. Spain)*, Arbitral Tribunal, 12 RIAA 281; 24 ILR 101 (16 November 1957)

13. But international practice does not so far permit more than the following conclusion: the rule that States may utilize the hydraulic power of international watercourses only on condition of a prior agreement between the interested States cannot be established as a custom, even less as a general principle of law. (p.130).

23. In the present case, the Spanish Government reproaches the French Government for not having based the development scheme for the waters of Lake Lanoux on a foundation of absolute equality: this is a double reproach. It attacks simultaneously form and substance. As to form, it is said that the French Government has imposed its scheme unilaterally without associating the Spanish Government with it in a common search for an acceptable solution. Substantively, it is alleged that the French scheme does not maintain a just balance between French interests and Spanish interests. The French scheme, in the Spanish view, would serve perfectly French interests, especially those related to the production of electric energy, but would not take into sufficient consideration Spanish interests in connection with irrigation. According to the Spanish Government, the French Government refused to take into consideration schemes which, in the opinion of the Spanish Government,

would have involved a very small sacrifice of French interests and great advantages for the Spanish rural economy. Spain bases its arguments on the following facts in particular. In the course of the work of the Special Mixed Commission at Madrid (September 12-17, 1955), the French delegation compared three schemes for the development of Lake Lanoux and remarked on the considerable advantages which the first scheme (which was similar to the final scheme) presented, in its view, over the other two. The Spanish delegation having no special objection in regard to the latter schemes, declared itself ready to accept either of the two. The French delegation did not feel itself able to depart from the execution of scheme No. 1, which was more favourable to French interests and was founded, according to the delegation, on French rights (French Memorial, pp. 117 et seq., 127)

[...]

"France is entitled to exercise her rights; she cannot ignore Spanish interests. Spain is entitled to demand that her rights be respected and that her interests be taken into consideration." (140).

"As a matter of form, the upstream State has, procedurally, a right of initiative; it is not obliged to associate the downstream State in the elaboration of its schemes. If, in the course of discussions, the downstream State submits schemes to it, the upstream State must examine them, but it has the right to give preference to the solution contained in its own scheme provided that it takes into consideration in a reasonable manner the interests of the State."

CASE
ICJ, *Gabčíkovo-Nagymaros Project (Hungary v. Slovakia)*, ICJ Reports 7 (1997)

51. The Court considers, first of all, that the state of necessity is a ground recognized by customary international law for precluding the wrongfulness of an act not in conformity with an international obligation. It observes moreover that such ground for precluding wrongfulness can only be accepted on an exceptional basis. The International Law Commission was of the same opinion when it explained that it had opted for a negative form of words in Article 33 of its Draft "in order to show, by this formal means also, that the case of invocation of a state of necessity as a justification must be considered as really constituting an exception – and one even more rarely admissible than is the case with the other circumstances precluding wrongfulness ..." (ibid., p. 51, para. 40). Thus, according to the Commission, the state of necessity can only be invoked under certain strictly defined conditions which must be cumulatively satisfied; and the State concerned is not the sole judge of whether those conditions have been met.

52. In the present case, the following basic conditions set forth in Draft Article 33 are relevant: it must have been occasioned by an "essential interest" of the State which is the author of the act conflicting with one of its international obligations; that interest must have been threatened by a "grave and imminent peril"; the act being

challenged must have been the "only means" of safeguarding that interest; that act must not have "seriously impair[ed] an essential interest" of the State towards which the obligation existed; and the State which is the author of that act must not have "contributed to the occurrence of the state of necessity". Those conditions reflect customary international law.

The Court will now endeavour to ascertain whether those conditions had been met at the time of the suspension and abandonment, by Hungary, of the works that it was to carry out in accordance with the 1977 Treaty.

53. The Court has no difficulty in acknowledging that the concerns expressed by Hungary for its natural environment in the region affected by the *Gabčíkovo-Nagymaros Project* related to an "essential interest" of that State, within the meaning given to that expression in Article 33 of the Draft of the International Law Commission. The Commission, in its Commentary, indicated that one should not, in that context, reduce an "essential interest" to a matter only of the "existence" of the State, and that the whole question was, ultimately, to be judged in the light of the particular case (see Yearbook of the International Law Commission, 1980, Vol. II, Part 2, p. 49, para. 32); at the same time, it included among the situations that could occasion a state of necessity, "a grave danger to ... the ecological preservation of all or some of [the] territory [of a State]" (ibid., p. 35, para. 3); and specified, with reference to State practice, that "It is primarily in the last two decades that safeguarding the ecological balance has come to be considered an 'essential interest' of all States" (Ibid., p. 39, para. 14).

[...]

54. The verification of the existence, in 1989, of the "peril" invoked by Hungary, of its "grave and imminent" nature, as well as of the absence of any "means" to respond to it, other than the measures taken by Hungary to suspend and abandon the works, are all complex processes.

As the Court has already indicated (see paragraphs 33 et seq.), Hungary on several occasions expressed, in 1989, its "uncertainties" as to the ecological impact of putting in place the Gabčikovo-Nagymaros barrage system, which is why it asked insistently for new scientific studies to be carried out.

The Court considers, however, that, serious though these uncertainties might have been they could not, alone, establish the objective existence of a "peril" in the sense of a component element of a state of necessity. The word "peril" certainly evokes the idea of "risk": that is precisely what distinguishes "peril" from material damage. But a state of necessity could not exist without a "peril" duly established at the relevant point in time: the mere apprehension of a possible "peril" could not suffice in that respect. It could moreover hardly be otherwise. when the "peril" constituting the state of necessity has at the same time to be "grave" and "imminent". "Imminence" is synonymous with "immediacy" or "proximity" and goes far beyond the concept of "possibility". As the International Law Commission emphasized in its commentary, the "extremely, grave and imminent" peril must "have been a threat to the interest at the actual time" (Yearbook of the International Law Commission,

1980, Vol. II, Part 2, p. 49, para. 33). That does not exclude, in the view of the Court, that a "peril" appearing in the long term might be held to be "imminent" as soon as it is established, at the relevant point in time, that the realization of that peril, however far off it might be, is not thereby any less certain and inevitable. The Hungarian argument on the state of necessity could not convince the Court unless it was at least proven that a real, "grave" and "imminent" "peril" existed in 1989 and that the measures taken by Hungary were the only possible response to it. Both Parties have placed on record an impressive amount of scientific material aimed at reinforcing their respective arguments. The Court has given most careful attention to this material, in which the Parties have developed their opposing views as to the ecological consequences of the Project. It concludes, however, that, as will be shown below, it is not necessary in order to respond to the questions put to it in the Special Agreement for it to determine which of those points of view is scientifically better founded.

[...]

57. The Court concludes from the foregoing that, with respect to both Nagymaros and Gabčikovo, the perils invoked by Hungary, without prejudging their possible gravity, were not sufficiently established in 1989, nor were they "imminent"; and that Hungary had available to it at that time means of responding to these perceived perils other than the suspension and abandonment of works with which it had been entrusted. What is more, negotiations were under way which might have led to a review of the Project and the extension of some of its time-limits, without there being need to abandon it. The Court infers from this that the respect by Hungary, in 1989, of its obligations under the terms of the 1977 Treaty would not have resulted in a situation "characterized so aptly by the maxim summum jus summa injuria" (Yearbook of the International Law Commission, 1980, Vol. II, Part 2, p. 49, para. 31).

Moreover, the Court notes that Hungary decided to conclude the 1977 Treaty, a Treaty which – whatever the political circumstances prevailing at the time of its conclusion – was treated by Hungary as valid and in force until the date declared for its termination in May 1992. As can be seen from the material before the Court, a great many studies of a scientific and technical nature had been conducted at an earlier time, both by Hungary and by Czechoslovakia. Hungary was, then, presumably aware of the situation as then known, when it assumed its obligations under the Treaty. Hungary contended before the Court that those studies had been inadequate and that the state of knowledge at that time was not such as to make possible a complete evaluation of the ecological implications of the Gabčikovo-Nagymaros Project. It is nonetheless the case that although the principal object of the 1977 Treaty was the construction of a System of Locks for the production of electricity, improvement of navigation on the Danube and protection against flooding, the need to ensure the protection of the environment had not escaped the parties, as can be seen from Articles 15, 19 and 20 of the Treaty.

What is more, the Court cannot fail to note the positions taken by Hungary after the entry into force of the 1977 Treaty. In 1983, Hungary asked that the works under the Treaty should go forward more slowly, for reasons that were essentially economic but also, subsidiarily, related to ecological concerns. In 1989, when, according to Hungary itself, the state of scientific knowledge had undergone a significant development, it asked for the works to be speeded up, and then decided, three months later, to suspend them and subsequently to abandon them. The Court is not however unaware that profound changes were taking place in Hungary in 1989, and that, during that transitory phase, it might have been more than usually difficult to co-ordinate the different points of view prevailing from time to time. The Court infers from all these elements that, in the present case, even if it had been established that there was. in 1989, a state of necessity linked to the performance of the 1977 Treaty, Hungary would not have been permitted to rely upon that state of necessity in order to justify its failure to comply with its treaty obligations, as it had helped, by act or omission to bring it about.

[...]

78. Moreover, in practice, the operation of Variant C led Czechoslovakia to appropriate, essentially for its use and benefit, between 80 and 90 per cent of the waters of the Danube before returning them to the main bed of the river, despite the fact that the Danube is not only a shared international watercourse but also an international boundary river. Czechoslovakia submitted that Variant C was essentially no more than what Hungary had already agreed to and that the only modifications made were those which had become necessary by virtue of Hungary's decision not to implement its treaty obligations. It is true that Hungary, in concluding the 1977 Treaty, had agreed to the damming of the Danube and the diversion of its waters into the bypass canal. But it was only in the context of a joint operation and a sharing of its benefits that Hungary had given its consent. The suspension and withdrawal of that consent constituted a violation of Hungary's legal obligations, demonstrating, as it did, the refusal by Hungary of joint operation; but that cannot mean that Hungary forfeited its basic right to an equitable and reasonable sharing of the resources of an international watercourse. The Court accordingly concludes that Czechoslovakia, in putting Variant C into operation, was not applying the 1977 Treaty but, on the contrary, violated certain of its express provisions, and, in so doing, committed an internationally wrongful act.

79. The Court notes that between November 1991 and October 1992, Czechoslovakia confined itself to the execution, on its own territory, of the works which were necessary for the implementation of Variant C, but which could have been abandoned if an agreement had been reached between the parties and did not therefore predetermine the final decision to be taken. For as long as the Danube had not been unilaterally dammed, Variant C had not in fact been applied. Such a situation is not unusual in international law or, for that matter, in domestic law. A wrongful act or offence is frequently preceded by preparatory actions which are not to be confused with the act or offence itself. It is as well to distinguish between the actual commission of a wrongful act (whether instantaneous or continuous) and the conduct

prior to that act which is of a preparatory character and which "does not qualify as a wrongful act" (see for example the Commentary on Article 41 of the Draft Articles on State Responsibility, "Report of the International Law Commission on the work of its forty-eighth session, 6 May-26 July 1996", Official Records of the General Assembly, Fifty-first Session, Supplement No. 10 (A/51/10), p. 141, and Yearbook of the International Law Commission, 1993, Vol. II, Part 2, p. 57, para. 14).

85. In the view of the Court, an important consideration is that the effects of a counter-measure must be commensurate with the injury suffered, taking account of the rights in question. In 1929, the Permanent Court of International Justice, with regard to navigation on the River Oder, stated as follows: "[the] community of interest in a navigable river becomes the basis of a common legal right, the essential features of which are the perfect equality of all riparian States in the user of the whole course of the river and the exclusion of any preferential privilege of any one riparian State in relation to the others" (Territorial Jurisdiction of the International Commission of the River Oder, Judgment No. 16, 1929, P. C. I. J., Series A, No. 23, p. 27). Modern development of international law has strengthened this principle for non-navigational uses of international watercourses as well, as evidenced by the adoption of the Convention of 21 May 1997 on the Law of the Non-Navigational Uses of International Watercourses by the United Nations General Assembly. The Court considers that Czechoslovakia, by unilaterally assuming control of a shared resource, and thereby depriving Hungary of its right to an equitable and reasonable share of the natural resources of the Danube – with the continuing effects of the diversion of these waters on the ecology of the riparian area of the Szigetkoz – failed to respect the proportionality which is required by international law.

[...]

112. Neither of the Parties contended that new peremptory norms of environmental law had emerged since the conclusion of the 1977 Treaty, and the Court will consequently not be required to examine the scope of Article 64 of the Vienna Convention on the Law of Treaties. On the other hand, the Court wishes to point out that newly developed norms of environmental law are relevant for the implementation of the Treaty and that the parties could, by agreement, incorporate them through the application of Articles 15, 19 and 20 of the Treaty. These articles do not contain specific obligations of performance but require the parties, in carrying out their obligations to ensure that the quality of water in the Danube is not impaired and that nature is protected, to take new environmental norms into consideration when agreeing upon the means to be specified in the Joint Contractual Plan.

By inserting these evolving provisions in the Treaty, the parties recognized the potential necessity to adapt the Project. Consequently, the Treaty is not static, and is open to adapt to emerging norms of international law. By means of Articles 15 and 19, new environmental norms can be incorporated in the Joint Contractual Plan.

The responsibility to do this was a joint responsibility. The obligations contained in Articles 15, 19 and 20 are, by definition, general and have to be transformed into specific obligations of performance through a process of consultation and negotiation. Their implementation thus requires a mutual willingness to discuss in good faith actual and potential environmental risks. It is all the more important to do this because as the Court recalled in its Advisory Opinion on the Legality of the Threat or Use of Nuclear Weapons, "the environment is not an abstraction but represents the living space, the quality of life and the very health of human beings, including generations unborn" (ICJ Reports 1996, p. 241, para. 29; see also paragraph 53 above). The awareness of the vulnerability of the environment and the recognition that environmental risks have to be assessed on a continuous basis have become much stronger in the years since the Treaty's conclusion. These new concerns have enhanced the relevance of Articles 15, 19 and 20.

113. The Court recognizes that both Parties agree on the need to take environmental concerns seriously and to take the required precautionary measures, but they fundamentally disagree on the consequences this has for the joint Project. In such a case, third-party involvement may be helpful and instrumental in finding a solution, provided each of the Parties is flexible in its position.

114. Finally, Hungary maintained that by their conduct both parties had repudiated the Treaty and that a bilateral treaty repudiated by both parties cannot survive. The Court is of the view, however, that although it has found that both Hungary and Czechoslovakia failed to comply with their obligations under the 1977 Treaty, this reciprocal wrongful conduct did not bring the Treaty to an end nor justify its termination. The Court would set a precedent with disturbing implications for treaty relations and the integrity of the rule puctu sunt servunda if it were to conclude that a treaty in force between States, which the parties have implemented in considerable measure and at great cost over a period of years, might be unilaterally set aside on grounds of reciprocal noncompliance. It would be otherwise, of course, if the parties decided to terminate the Treaty by mutual consent. But in this case, while Hungary purported to terminate the Treaty, Czechoslovakia consistently resisted this act and declared it to be without legal effect.

[...]

140. It is clear that the Project's impact upon, and its implications for, the environment are of necessity a key issue. The numerous scientific reports which have been presented to the Court by the Parties – even if their conclusions are often contradictory – provide abundant evidence that this impact and these implications are considerable.

In order to evaluate the environmental risks, current standards must be taken into consideration. This is not only allowed by the wording of Articles 15 and 19, but even prescribed, to the extent that these articles impose a continuing – and thus necessarily evolving – obligation on the parties to maintain the quality of the water of the Danube and to protect nature. The Court is mindful that, in the field of environmental protection, vigilance and prevention are required on account of the often irreversible character of damage to the environment and of the limitations inherent in the very mechanism of reparation of this type of damage.

Throughout the ages, mankind has, for economic and other reasons, constantly interfered with nature. In the past, this was often done without consideration of the effects upon the environment. Owing to new scientific insights and to a growing awareness of the risks for mankind – for present and future generations – of pursuit of such interventions at an unconsidered and unabated pace, new norms and standards have been developed, set forth in a great number of instruments during the last two decades. Such new norms have to be taken into consideration, and such new standards given proper weight, not only when States contemplate new activities but also when continuing with activities begun in the past. This need to reconcile economic development with protection of the environment is aptly expressed in the concept of sustainable development.

For the purposes of the present case, this means that the Parties together should look afresh at the effects on the environment of the operation of the Gabčikovo power plant. In particular they must find a satisfactory solution for the volume of water to be released into the old bed of the Danube and into the side-arms on both sides of the river.

141. It is not for the Court to determine what shall be the final result of these negotiations to be conducted by the Parties. It is for the Parties themselves to find an agreed solution that takes account of the objectives of the Treaty, which must be pursued in a joint and integrated way, as well as the norms of international environmental law and the principles of the law of international watercourses. The Court will recall in this context that, as it said in the North Sea Continental Shelf cases: "[the Parties] are under an obligation so to conduct themselves that the negotiations are meaningful, which will not be the case when either of them insists upon its own position without contemplating any modification of it" (ICJ Reports 1969, p. 47, para. 85).

CASE
ICJ, *Pulp Mills on the River Uruguay (Argentina v. Uruguay)*, ICJ Reports 14 (2010)

187. The Court considers that the obligation laid down in Article 36 is addressed to both Parties and prescribes the specific conduct of co-ordinating the necessary measures through the Commission to avoid changes to the ecological balance. An obligation to adopt regulatory or administrative measures either individually or jointly and to enforce them is an obligation of conduct. Both Parties are therefore called upon, under Article 36, to exercise due diligence in acting through the Commission for the necessary measures to preserve the ecological balance of the river.

188. This vigilance and prevention is all the more important in the preservation of the ecological balance, since the negative impact of human activities on the waters of the river may affect other components of the ecosystem of the watercourse such as its flora, fauna, and soil. The obligation to co-ordinate, through the Commission, the adoption of the necessary measures, as well as their enforcement and observance, assumes, in this context, a central role in the overall system of protection of

the River Uruguay established by the 1975 Statute. It is therefore of crucial importance that the Parties respect this obligation.

189. In light of the above, the Court is of the view that Argentina has not convincingly
demonstrated that Uruguay has refused to engage in such co-ordination as envisaged by Article 36, in breach of that provision.

[...]

195. In view of the central role of this provision in the dispute between the Parties in the
present case and their profound differences as to its interpretation and application,
the Court will make a few remarks of a general character on the normative content
of Article 41 before addressing the specific arguments of the Parties. First, in the
view of the Court, Article 41 makes a clear distinction between regulatory functions
entrusted to CARU under the 1975 Statute, which are dealt with in Article 56 of the
Statute, and the obligation it imposes on the Parties to adopt rules and measures
individually to "protect and preserve the aquatic environment and, in particular, to
prevent its pollution". Thus, the obligation assumed by the Parties under Article 41,
which is distinct from those under Articles 36 and 56 of the 1975 Statute, is to adopt
appropriate rules and measures within the framework of their respective domestic
legal systems to protect and preserve the aquatic environment and to prevent pollution. This conclusion is supported by the wording of paragraphs (b) and (c) of Article
41, which refer to the need not to reduce the technical requirements and severity
of the penalties already in force in the respective legislation of the Parties as well
as the need to inform each other of the rules to be promulgated so as to establish
equivalent rules in their legal systems.

196. Secondly, it is the opinion of the Court that a simple reading of the text of Article 41
indicates that it is the rules and measures that are to be prescribed by the Parties
in their respective legal systems which must be "in accordance with applicable
international agreements" and "in keeping, where relevant, with the guidelines and
recommendations of international technical bodies".

197. Thirdly, the obligation to "preserve the aquatic environment, and in particular to
prevent pollution by prescribing appropriate rules and measures" is an obligation to
act with due diligence in respect of all activities which take place under the jurisdiction and control of each party. It is an obligation which entails not only the adoption
of appropriate rules and measures, but also a certain level of vigilance in their enforcement and the exercise of administrative control applicable to public and private
operators, such as the monitoring of activities undertaken by such operators, to
safeguard the rights of the other party. The responsibility of a party to the 1975
Statute would therefore be engaged if it was shown that it had failed to act diligently
and thus take all appropriate measures to enforce its relevant regulations on a public or private operator under its jurisdiction. The obligation of due diligence under
Article 41 (a) in the adoption and enforcement of appropriate rules and measures is
further reinforced by the requirement that such rules and measures must be "in accordance with applicable international agreements" and "in keeping, where relevant,
with the guidelines and recommendations of international technical bodies". This

requirement has the advantage of ensuring that the rules and measures adopted by the parties both have to conform to applicable international agreements and to take account of internationally agreed technical standards.

198. Finally, the scope of the obligation to prevent pollution must be determined in light of the definition of pollution given in Article 40 of the 1975 Statute. Article 40 provides that: "For the purposes of this Statute, pollution shall mean the direct or indirect introduction by man into the aquatic environment of substances or energy which have harmful effects." The term "harmful effects" is defined in the CARU Digest as: "any alteration of the water quality that prevents or hinders any legitimate use of the water, that causes deleterious effects or harm to living resources, risks to human health, or a threat to water activities including fishing or reduction of recreational activities" (Title I, Chapter 1, Section 2, Article 1 (c) of the Digest (E3)).

199. The Digest expresses the will of the Parties and their interpretation of the provisions of the 1975 Statute. Article 41, not unlike many other provisions of the 1975 Statute, lays down broad obligations agreed to by the Parties to regulate and limit their use of the river and to protect its environment. These broad obligations are given more specific content through the co-ordinated rule-making action of CARU as established under Article 56 of the 1975 Statute or through the regulatory action of each of the parties, or by both means. The two regulatory actions are meant to complement each other. As discussed below (see paragraphs 201 to 202, and 214), CARU standards concern mainly water quality. The CARU Digest sets only general limits on certain discharges or effluents from industrial plants such as: "hydrocarbons", "sedimentable solids", and "oils and greases". As the Digest makes explicit, those matters are left to each party to regulate. The Digest provides that, as regards effluents within its jurisdiction, each party shall take the appropriate "corrective measures" in order to assure compliance with water quality standards (CARU Digest, Sec. E3: Pollution, Title 2, Chapter 5, Section 1, Article 3). Uruguay has taken that action in its Regulation on Water Quality (Decree No. 253/79) and in relation to the Orion (Botnia) mill in the conditions stipulated in the authorization issued by MVOTMA. In Argentina, the Entre Ríos Province, which borders the river opposite the plant, has regulated industrial discharges in a decree that also recognizes the binding effect of the CARU Digest (Regulatory Decree No. 5837, Government of Entre Ríos, 26 December 1991, and Regulatory Decree No. 5394, Government of Entre Ríos, 7 April 1997).

[...]

209. The Court will now consider, first, whether Uruguay failed to exercise due diligence in conducting the environmental impact assessment, particularly with respect to the choice of the location of the plant and, secondly, whether the particular location chosen for the siting of the plant, in this case Fray Bentos, was unsuitable for the construction of a plant discharging industrial effluent of this nature and on this scale, or could have a harmful impact on the river.

210. Regarding the first point, the Court has already indicated that the Espoo Convention is not applicable to the present case (see paragraph 205 above); while with re-

spect to the UNEP Goals and Principles to which Argentina has referred, whose legal character has been described in paragraph 205 above, the Court recalls that Principle 4 (c) simply provides that an environmental impact assessment should include, at a minimum, "[a] description of practical alternatives, as appropriate". It is also to be recalled that Uruguay has repeatedly indicated that the suitability of the Fray Bentos location was comprehensively assessed and that other possible sites were considered. The Court further notes that the IFC's Final Cumulative Impact Study of September 2006 (hereinafter "CIS") shows that in 2003 Botnia evaluated four locations in total at La Paloma, at Paso de los Toros, at Nueva Palmira, and at Fray Bentos, before choosing Fray Bentos. The evaluations concluded that the limited amount of fresh water in La Paloma and its importance as a habitat for birds rendered it unsuitable, while for Nueva Palmira its consideration was discouraged by its proximity to residential, recreational, and culturally important areas, and with respect to Paso de los Toros insufficient flow of water during the dry season and potential conflict with competing water uses, as well as a lack of infrastructure, led to its exclusion. Consequently, the Court is not convinced by Argentina's argument that an assessment of possible sites was not carried out prior to the determination of the final site.

211. Regarding the second point, the Court cannot fail to note that any decision on the actual location of such a plant along the River Uruguay should take into account the capacity of the waters of the river to receive, dilute and disperse discharges of effluent from a plant of this nature and scale.

213. The Court sees no need to go into a detailed examination of the scientific and technical validity of the different kinds of modelling, calibration and validation undertaken by the Parties to characterize the rate and direction of flow of the waters of the river in the relevant area. The Court notes however that both Parties agree that reverse flows occur frequently and that phenomena of low flow and stagnation may be observed in the concerned area, but that they disagree on the implications of this for the discharges from the Orion (Botnia) mill into this area of the river.

214. The Court considers that in establishing its water quality standards in accordance with Articles 36 and 56 of the 1975 Statute, CARU must have taken into account the receiving capacity and sensitivity of the waters of the river, including in the areas of the river adjacent to Fray Bentos. Consequently, in so far as it is not established that the discharges of effluent of the Orion (Botnia) mill have exceeded the limits set by those standards, in terms of the level of concentrations, the Court finds itself unable to conclude that Uruguay has violated its obligations under the 1975 Statute. Moreover, neither of the Parties has argued before the Court that the water quality standards established by CARU have not adequately taken into consideration the geomorphological and hydrological characteristics of the river and the capacity of its waters to disperse and dilute different types of discharges. The Court is of the opinion that, should such inadequacy be detected, particularly with respect to certain areas of the river such as at Fray Bentos, the Parties should initiate a review of the water quality standards set by CARU and ensure that such standards clearly reflect the characteristics of the river and are capable of protecting its waters and its ecosystem.

216. The Court is of the view that no legal obligation to consult the affected populations arises for the Parties from the instruments invoked by Argentina.

[...]

262. The Court is of the opinion that as part of their obligation to preserve the aquatic environment, the Parties have a duty to protect the fauna and flora of the river. The rules and measures which they have to adopt under Article 41 should also reflect their international undertakings in respect of biodiversity and habitat protection, in addition to the other standards on water quality and discharges of effluent. The Court has not, however, found sufficient evidence to conclude that Uruguay breached its obligation to preserve the aquatic environment including the protection of its fauna and flora. The record rather shows that a clear relationship has not been established between the discharges from the Orion (Botnia) mill and the malformations of rotifers, or the dioxin found in the sábalo fish or the loss of fat by clams reported in the findings of the Argentine River Uruguay Environmental Surveillance (URES) programme.

[...]

281. Lastly, the Court points out that the 1975 Statute places the Parties under a duty to co-operate with each other, on the terms therein set out, to ensure the achievement of its object and purpose. This obligation to co-operate encompasses ongoing monitoring of an industrial facility, such as the Orion (Botnia) mill. In that regard the Court notes that the Parties have a long-standing and effective tradition of co-operation and co-ordination through CARU. By acting jointly through CARU, the Parties have established a real community of interests and rights in the management of the River Uruguay and in the protection of its environment. They have also co-ordinated their actions through the joint mechanism of CARU, in conformity with the provisions of the 1975 Statute, and found appropriate solutions to their differences within its framework without feeling the need to resort to the judicial settlement of disputes provided for in Article 60 of the Statute until the present case was brought before the Court.

CASE
PCA, *Indus Waters Kishenganga Arbitration (Pakistan v. India)*, Final Award, PCA Case No. 2011-01 (20 December 2013)

PARTIAL AWARD

II. BACKGROUND

126. This arbitration marks the first instance that a court of arbitration has been constituted since the Indus Waters Treaty was concluded over half a century ago. The

proceedings have arisen out of a dispute between Pakistan and India concerning the interpretation and implementation of the Treaty in relation to the construction and operation of the Kishenganga Hydro-Electric Project. The Treaty sets forth the rights and obligations of the Parties on the use of the waters of the Indus system of rivers. The KHEP is an Indian hydro-electric project located on one such river— known as the "Kishenganga" in India-administered Jammu and Kashmir and as the "Neelum" in Pakistan-administered Jammu and Kashmir (the "Kishenganga/Neelum River," "Kishenganga/Neelum," or "River").

127. The KHEP is designed to generate power by diverting water from a dam site on the Kishenganga/Neelum River (within the Gurez valley, an area of higher elevation) to another river of the Indus system (lower in elevation and located near Wular Lake) through a system of tunnels, with the water powering turbines having a capacity of up to 330 megawatts. In essence, the Parties disagree as to whether the planned diversion of water and other technical design features of the KHEP are in conformity with the provisions of the Treaty. The Parties also disagree over the permissibility under the Treaty of the use of the technique of drawdown flushing for sediment control in Run-of-River Plants.

128. The Indus system of rivers is composed of six main rivers: the Indus, the Jhelum and the Chenab (together with their tributaries, the "Western Rivers"), and the Sutlej, the Beas and the Ravi (together with their tributaries, the "Eastern Rivers"). These rivers and their tributaries rise primarily in the Himalayas and course through Afghanistan, China, India and Pakistan before merging into the Indus river and draining into the Arabian Sea south-east of the port of Karachi in Pakistan [...].

[...]

366. [...] the Court finds that the rights and obligations of the Parties under the Treaty extend to their use of those waters of the Indus system that flow through Pakistan and India, including those waters flowing through either Pakistan-administered or India-administered Jammu and Kashmir. Pakistan is therefore entitled to invoke the Treaty, as it does here, to object to the construction of the KHEP as a hydro-electric project located in India-administered territory, by arguing that it will impermissibly affect the flow of the river and uses of the waters thereof (including future uses by the NJHEP) in Pakistan-administered territory

[...]

398. The Court has little difficulty in holding that the delivery of water from the Kishenganga/Neelum to another tributary is required to achieve the purpose of generating hydro-electricity through the KHEP. If, as the Court has decided, the Treaty confers a right on a Party (in this case, India's right to the use of the waters for the purpose of generating hydroelectricity in conformity with Annexure D), it must be taken to be a right that can meaningfully be exercised. It is true that some hydro-electricity can be generated from the natural flow of the Kishenganga/Neelum at Gurez, but in the Court's understanding, no Run-of-River Plant operat-

ing without making use of the difference in elevation between the two tributaries of the Jhelum would begin to approach the power-generating capacity of the KHEP. Therefore, diversion is necessary for any attempt to generate hydro-electric power on the scale contemplated by India, and Annexure D imposes no limit on the amount of electric power that India may generate through Run-of-River Plants.

[...]

399. The Court's conclusion on this matter should not be taken to mean that potential downstream harm is irrelevant to the analysis. On the contrary, the Court considers that adverse effects on downstream uses are a central element of Paragraph 15(iii), but one that operates in a different manner from the proportionality test advanced by Pakistan. Where necessity is invoked under customary international law as a circumstance precluding the international wrongfulness of State action, proportionality may properly be considered. In that case, the claim being made is not simply that the acts in question were necessary to protect an essential State interest, but also that such interest is of paramount importance—and therefore sufficient to override the rights and interests of the State that would otherwise be wronged. Viewed in terms of its ordinary meaning, however, "necessary" lacks this additional connotation. As a matter of common sense, it is apparent that certain actions may be necessary to accomplish even very modest purposes, and that such actions do not become any less necessary to their intended purpose if it happens that they also inflict ancillary harm.

[...]

445. India's right under the Treaty to divert the waters of the Kishenganga/Neelum to operate the KHEP is subject to the constraints specified by the Treaty, including Paragraph 15(iii) of Annexure D as discussed above and, in addition, by the relevant principles of customary international law to be applied by the Court pursuant to Paragraph 29 of Annexure G when interpreting the Treaty. As discussed in the following paragraphs, both of these limitations require India to operate the KHEP in a manner that ensures a minimum flow of water in the riverbed of the Kishenganga/ Neelum downstream of the Plant.

[...]

449. There is no doubt that States are required under contemporary customary international law to take environmental protection into consideration when planning and developing projects that may cause injury to a bordering State. Since the time of Trail Smelter, a series of international conventions, declarations and judicial and arbitral decisions have addressed the need to manage natural resources in a sustainable manner. In particular, the International Court of Justice expounded upon the principle of "sustainable development" in Gabčíkovo-Nagymaros, referring to the "need to reconcile economic development with protection of the environment."

FINAL AWARD

109. In balancing India's right to operate the KHEP effectively with the needs of the downstream environment, the Court has decided that, on the basis of the evidence currently available, India should have access to at least half of the average flow at the KHEP site during the driest months. In the Court's view, it would not be in conformity with the Treaty to fix a minimum release above half the minimum monthly average flow for the purpose of avoiding adverse effects on the NJHEP.

[...]

113. The Court has also examined India's flow estimates, and has noted (see above at paragraph 103) the extreme sensitivity of low flows at the Line of Control to the release from the KHEP. The most severe winter in the 34-year record used by both India and Pakistan to assess impacts was 1974–75. The Court notes that, based on India's data, a minimum flow criterion of 9 cumecs at KHEP is a relatively severe criterion with respect to environmental flow, but would nevertheless be sufficient to maintain the natural flows through the December, January, February period of that winter.

[...]

115. The Court therefore concludes that a minimum flow criterion of 9 cumecs is consistent with Pakistan's analysis of environmental flows, given the need to balance power generation with environmental and other downstream uses, and, based on India's data, would maintain the natural flow regime in the most severe winter conditions.

[...]

117. As the Court noted in its discussion of Pakistan's environmental submission, a degree of uncertainty is inherent in any attempt to predict environmental responses to changing conditions. In addition, flows at the Line of Control are un-gauged, and understandably subject to estimates which differ between the Parties, at least for the lowest flows. Uncertainty is also present in attempts to predict future flow conditions, and the Court is cognizant that flows in the Kishenganga/Neelum may come to differ, perhaps significantly, from the historical record as a result of factors beyond the control of either Party, including climate change.

118. In its Partial Award, the Court stated that "stability and predictability in the availability of the waters of the Kishenganga/Neelum for each Party's use are vitally important for the effective utilization of rights accorded to each Party by the Treaty (including its incorporation of customary international environmental law)." This remains true. Indeed, the Court rejected a fully ambulatory interpretation of Paragraph 15(iii) of the Treaty for this reason. At the same time, the Court considers it important not to permit the doctrine of res judicata to extend the life of this Award into circumstances in which its reasoning no longer accords with reality along the

Kishenganga/Neelum. The minimum flow will therefore be open to reconsideration as laid down in the following paragraph.

119. The KHEP should be completed in such a fashion as to accommodate possible future variations in the minimum flow requirement. If, beginning seven years after the diversion of the Kishenganga/Neelum through the KHEP, either Party considers that reconsideration of the Court's determination of the minimum flow is necessary, it will be entitled to seek such reconsideration through the Permanent Indus Commission and the mechanisms of the Treaty.

CASE
ICJ, *Certain Activities Carried Out by Nicaragua in the Border Area (Costa Rica v. Nicaragua)* and *Construction of a Road in Costa Rica along the San Juan River (Nicaragua v. Costa Rica)*, ICJ Reports 665 (2015)

192. In the Court's view, Nicaragua's submission that any detrimental impact on the river that is susceptible of being measured constitutes significant harm is unfounded. Sediment is naturally present in the river in large quantities, and Nicaragua has not shown that the river's sediment levels are such that additional sediment eroded from the road passes a sort of critical level in terms of its detrimental effects. Moreover, the Court finds that, contrary to Nicaragua's submissions, the present case does not concern a situation where sediment contributed by the road exceeds maximum allowable limits, which have not been determined for the San Juan River. Thus, the Court is not convinced by Nicaragua's argument that the absolute quantity of sediment in the river due to the construction of the road caused significant harm per se.

[...]

196. In light of the above, the Court concludes that Nicaragua has not established that the fact that sediment concentrations in the river increased as a result of the construction of the road in and of itself caused significant transboundary harm.

QUESTIONS

1. Critically assess and analyse substantive and procedure principles underlying the 1997 Watercourse Convention including existing case law.
2. Assess the relationship with both global treaties on international watercourses law.
3. Explain the judgments of the ICJ in the *Pulp Mills* and *Costa Rica v. Nicaragua* cases in relation to substantive/procedural requirements concerning water cooperation.

FURTHER READING

BOOKS

R Baxter, *The Law of International Waterways* (Harvard University Press 1964)

L Boisson de Chazournes, *Fresh Water in International Law* (2nd edn, Oxford University Press 2021)

L Boisson de Chazournes and S Salman (eds), *Water Resources and International Law* (Martinus Nijhoff 2005)

J Lammers, *Pollution of International Watercourses: A Search for Substantive Rules and Principles* (Martinus Nijhoff 1984)

FV Loures, *The UN Watercourses Convention in Force: Strengthening International Law for Transboundary Water Management* (Routledge 2013)

S McCaffrey, *The Law of International Watercourses* (3rd edn, Oxford University Press 2019)

P Sands and J Peel (eds), *Principles of International Environmental Law* (4th edn, Cambridge University Press 2018)

A Tanzi and M Arcari, *The UN Convention on the Law of International Watercourses* (Kluwer 2001)

A Tanzi, O McIntyre, A Kolliopolous, A Rieu-Clarke and R Kinna (eds), *The UNECE Convention on the Protection and Use of Transboundary Watercourses and International Lakes: Its Contribution to International Water Cooperation* (Brill 2015)

CHAPTERS

L Chiussi, 'United Nations Convention on the Law of the Non-Navigational Uses of International Watercourses 1997' in M Fitzmaurice and A Tanzi (eds), *Multilateral Environmental Treaties* (Edward Elgar 2017)

C Contartese, 'Convention on the Protection and the Use of Transboundary Watercourses and International Lakes 1992 (The UNECE Helsinki Convention)' in M Fitzmaurice and A Tanzi (eds), *Multilateral Environmental Treaties* (Edward Elgar 2017)

SC McCaffrey, 'International Watercourses' in *Max Planck Encyclopedia of Public International Law* (2009)

SC McCaffrey, 'International Watercourses, Environmental Protection' in *Max Planck Encyclopedia of Public International Law* (2011)

K Mechlem, 'Groundwater Protection' in *Max Planck Encyclopedia of Public International Law* (2010)

A Tanzi, 'The Global Water Treaties and Their Relationship' in S McCaffrey, C Leb and R Denoon (eds), *Research Handbook on International Water Law* (Edward Elgar 2019)

A Tanzi, 'Substantialising the Procedural Obligations of International Water Law between Compensatory and Distributive Justice' in H Ruiz Fabri, E Franckx, M Benatar and T Meshel (eds), *A Bridge over Troubled Waters: Dispute Resolution in the Law of International Watercourses and the Law of the Sea* (Brill 2020)

ARTICLES

E Benvenisti, 'Collective Action in the Utilization of Shared Freshwater: The Challenges of International Water Resource Law' (1996) 90 American Journal of International Law 384

C Bourne, 'The Primacy of the Principle of Equitable Utilization in the 1997 Watercourses Convention' (1997) 35 Canadian Yearbook of International Law 222

C Bourne, 'The Primacy of the Principle of Equitable Utilization in the 1997 Watercourse Convention' (1998) 35 The Canadian Yearbook of International Law 215

E Brown Weiss, 'The Evolution of International Water Law' (2007) 331 Recueil des cours de L'Académie de droit international 161

M Fitzmaurice, 'General Principles Governing the Cooperation between States in Relation to Non-Navigational Uses of International Watercourses' (2003) 14 Yearbook of International Environmental Law

X Fuentes, 'The Criteria for the Equitable Utilization of International Rivers' (1997) 67 British Yearbook of International Law 337

X Fuentes 'Sustainable Development and the Equitable Utilization of International Watercourse' (1999) 69 British Yearbook of International Law 119

M Gavounelli, 'A Human Right to Groundwater' (2011) 13 International Community Law Review 305

S McCaffrey, C Stephen and M Sinjela, 'The 1997 United Nations Convention on International Watercourses' (1998) 92 American Journal of International Law 97

P Sands, 'Water and International Law: Science and Evidence in International Litigation' (2010) 22 Environmental Law and Management 151

J Sette-Camara, 'Pollution of International Rivers' (1984) 186 Recueil des Cours 117

A Tanzi, 'Furthering International Water Law or Making a New Body of Law on Transboundary Aquifers? An Introduction' (2011) 13 International Community Law Review 193

S Toope and J Brunée, 'Environmental Security and Freshwater Resources: Ecosystem Regime Building' (1997) 91 American Journal of International Law 26

P Wouters, 'The Legal Response to International Water Conflicts: the UN Water Convention and Beyond' (1999) 42 German Yearbook of International Law 293

P Wouters, 'National and International Water Law: Achieving Equitable and Sustainable Use of Water Resources' (2000) 25 Water International 499

14
Management of hazardous waste

14.1   INTRODUCTION

The need for international regulation on the management of hazardous waste is corollary of the potential long-term transnational danger that the latter poses both to people's health and to the protection of the environment. In particular, the 'management' of hazardous waste relates to the problems posed by prevention and treatment, recycling and reuse, and international movement, including trade, disposal and storage.

It is important to note that there is no global instrument on the management of hazardous waste. On the contrary, these issues are addressed, in a more or less articulated way, in different legal instruments, often in relation to the production of particular waste and, moreover, usually in delimited geographical areas or, in any case, within sectoral or regional organizations, such as the OECD or the EU.[1] In addition, some states have favoured a bilateral approach. The United States, for instance, has concluded a number of bilateral agreements on

---

[1]   See, for instance, OECD Decision-Recommendation of the Council on the Reduction of Transfrontier Movements of Wastes, OECD/LEGAL/0260 (1991) (as last amended by OECD Doc. C(2001)208) and Directive 2008/98/EC of the European Parliament and of the Council of 19 November 2008 on Waste and Repealing Certain Directives, OJEL L 312/3 (2008).

the management of hazardous waste.[2] This clearly raises concerns in terms of fragmentation of the discipline, as is also apparent from the lack of a common definition of 'waste'.[3]

Nevertheless, it is possible to make some common patterns out from this fragmented regulation, especially with respect to transboundary movement and disposal of hazardous waste. The main piece of the puzzle is the Basel Convention of 1989.[4] Negotiated and adopted under the auspices of the United Nations Environmental Programme (UNEP) following the discovery and public exposure of illegal deposits of toxic waste in developing states during the 1980s, the Basel Convention is pivoted on a substantial principle and a procedural requirement: the first one is the principle of the environmentally sound management (ESM) of hazardous waste, which entails 'taking all practicable steps to ensure that hazardous wastes or other wastes are managed in a manner which will protect human health and the environment against the adverse effects which may result from such wastes'.[5] The second one is the so-called prior informed consent (PIC), which requires that, before any exports of hazardous waste take place, the exporting state should notify the authorities of the states of transit and import and provide them with detailed information on the proposed transboundary movement.[6] The movement may only proceed upon the written consent of the states involved.[7] Notably, the Basel Convention also provides for cooperation obligations, especially under the form of exchange of information,[8] and the establishment of a Secretariat to back the cooperation and implementation efforts.[9]

The Basel Convention has represented a reference model for the subsequent binding international instruments on the topic. For instance, the ESM principle and the PIC require-

---

[2]   See: Agreement between the Government of Canada and the Government of the United States concerning the Transboundary Movement of Hazardous Waste (1986); Agreement between Mexico and the United States Regarding the Transboundary Shipments of Hazardous Wastes and Hazardous Substances (1986); Agreement between the Government of America and the Government of Malaysia Concerning the Transboundary Movement of Hazardous Wastes from Malaysia to the United States (1995); Agreement on the Transboundary Movement of Hazardous Waste from Costa Rica to the United States (1997); Agreement between the Government of the United States of America and the Government of the Republic of the Philippines Concerning the Transboundary Movement of Hazardous Wastes from the Philippines to the United States (2001). See also United States-Russian Federation: Agreement between the Government of the United States of America and the Government of the Russian Federation on Scientific and Technical Cooperation in the Management of Plutonium that has been withdrawn from Nuclear Military Programs (1998).

[3]   Philippe Sands et al., Hazardous Substances and Activities, and Waste, in P Sands and J Peel (eds), *Principles of International Environmental Law* (4th edn, CUP 2018), p. 610 ff.

[4]   Convention on the Control of Transboundary Movements of Hazardous Wastes and Their Disposal (1989).

[5]   See Article 2, para. 8.

[6]   See Article 6, para.1.

[7]   Ibid., para. 2.

[8]   See Article 13.

[9]   See Article 16.

ment feature in the Bamako Convention,[10] the Waigani Convention[11] and the Rotterdam Convention.[12] Likewise, these conventions provide for cooperation obligations and set up implementation and compliance mechanisms.

Other aspects of the management of hazardous waste are less developed. For example, in terms of waste prevention and treatment, a few binding international instruments establish targets or timetables, and the quantitative restrictions are substantially limited to atmospheric pollution,[13] more recently in the broader framework of the fight against climate change.[14] Similarly, with the exception of OECD and EU regulation, international law appears deficient both in terms of recycling and reuse[15] and storage of hazardous waste.[16]

It is worth stressing that the various aspects of the management of hazardous waste are also dealt with in the context of international regulation on specific type of pollution, such as marine,[17] freshwater[18] and atmospheric pollution,[19] or on specific hazardous substances or activities. In this last regard, the Convention on the Safe Management of Radioactive Waste,[20] the Stockholm Convention[21] and the Minamata Convention[22] provide good examples.

Finally, over the last 25 years, the issue of the management of hazardous waste has been under the lens of the Human Rights Council as the core part of the mandate on the examination of human rights implications of exposure to hazardous substances and toxic waste.[23] It has also been incidentally touched upon in international case law, in connection both with the protection of human rights, especially under the ECHR, the right to respect for private life and

---

[10]   Convention on the Ban of the Import into Africa and the Control of Transboundary Movement and Management of Hazardous Wastes Within Africa (1991).

[11]   Convention to Ban the Importation into Forum Island Countries of Hazardous and Radioactive Wastes and to Control the Transboundary Movement and Management of Hazardous Wastes within the South Pacific Region (1995).

[12]   Convention on the Prior Informed Consent Procedure for Certain Hazardous Chemicals and Pesticides in International Trade (1998).

[13]   See Chapter 15.

[14]   See Chapter 16.

[15]   On this aspect, the Hong Kong International Convention for the Safe and Environmentally Sound Recycling of Ships (2009) stands out.

[16]   On this aspect, on a regional level, the Convention for the Protection of the Natural Resources and Environment of the South Pacific Region (1986) stands out.

[17]   See Chapter 10.

[18]   See Chapter 13.

[19]   See Chapter 15.

[20]   Joint Convention on the Safety of Spent Fuel Management and on the Safety of Radioactive Waste Management (1997).

[21]   Convention on Persistent Organic Pollutants (2001).

[22]   Minamata Convention on Mercury (2013).

[23]   See, for instance, Human Rights Council, Legal Framework Related to the Release of Toxic and Dangerous Products During Armed Conflict, Report of the Special Rapporteur, Okechukwu Ibeanu, (A/HRC/5/5), 5 May 2007.

family,[24] and to trade and investment-related activities.[25] However, in the absence of any ad hoc judicial, or quasi-judicial mechanisms at the international level, and save for the unfortunate occurrence of a transboundary accident involving hazardous waste, the international (and supranational) law on the management of hazardous waste seems more likely to be applied within domestic jurisdiction, as the infamous *Trafigura* case shows.[26]

14.2 LEGAL INSTRUMENTS

14.2.1 Legally Binding Instruments

14.2.1.1 International

1989 Basel Convention on the Control of Transboundary Movements of Hazardous Wastes and their Disposal (adopted 22 March 1989, entered into force 5 May 1992) 1673 UNTS 57

Article 1 (*Scope of the Convention*)
1. The following wastes that are subject to transboundary movement shall be "hazardous wastes" for the purposes of this Convention:
    (a) Wastes that belong to any category contained in Annex I, unless they do not possess any of the characteristics contained in Annex III; and
    (b) Wastes that are not covered under paragraph (a) but are defined as, or are considered to be, hazardous wastes by the domestic legislation of the Party of export, import or transit.
2. Wastes that belong to any category contained in Annex II that are subject to transboundary movement shall be "other wastes" for the purposes of this Convention.
3. Wastes which, as a result of being radioactive, are subject to other international control systems, including international instruments, applying specifically to radioactive materials, are excluded from the scope of this Convention.
4. Wastes which derive from the normal operations of a ship, the discharge of which is covered by another international instrument, are excluded from the scope of this Convention.

Article 2 (*Definitions*)
For the purposes of this Convention:
1. "Wastes" are substances or objects which are disposed of or are intended to be disposed of or are required to be disposed of by the provisions of national law;

---

[24] See, for instance, *Guerra and Others v. Italy*, Judgment, 116/1996/735/932 (19 February 1998), para. 57 ff.

[25] See, for instance, United States — Standards for reformulated and conventional gasoline, Appellate Body and Panel Report (WT/DS2/9), 20 May 1996, para. 6.21; *S.D. Myers, Inc. v. Government of Canada*, Partial Award (13 November 2000), UNCITRAL, para. 105 ff.

[26] *Trafigura*, Court of District, Amsterdam, Judgment, Case No. 13/846003-06 (23 July 2010).

2.   "Management" means the collection, transport and disposal of hazardous wastes or other wastes, including after-care of disposal sites;

3.   "Transboundary movement" means any movement of hazardous wastes or other wastes from an area under the national jurisdiction of one State to or through an area under the national jurisdiction of another State or to or through an area not under the national jurisdiction of any State, provided at least two States are involved in the movement;

4.   "Disposal" means any operation specified in Annex IV to this Convention;

5.   "Approved site or facility" means a site or facility for the disposal of hazardous wastes or other wastes which is authorized or permitted to operate for this purpose by a relevant authority of the State where the site or facility is located;

6.   "Competent authority" means one governmental authority designated by a Party to be responsible, within such geographical areas as the Party may think fit, for receiving the notification of a transboundary movement of hazardous wastes or other wastes, and any information related to it, and for responding to such a notification, as provided in Article 6;

7.   "Focal point" means the entity of a Party referred to in Article 5 responsible for receiving and submitting information as provided for in Articles 13 and 16;

8.   "Environmentally sound management of hazardous wastes or other wastes" means taking all practicable steps to ensure that hazardous wastes or other wastes are managed in a manner which will protect human health and the environment against the adverse effects which may result from such wastes;

9.   "Area under the national jurisdiction of a State" means any land, marine area or airspace within which a State exercises administrative and regulatory responsibility in accordance with international law in regard to the protection of human health or the environment;

10.   "State of export" means a Party from which a transboundary movement of hazardous wastes or other wastes is planned to be initiated or is initiated;

11.   "State of import" means a Party to which a transboundary movement of hazardous wastes or other wastes is planned or takes place for the purpose of disposal therein or for the purpose of loading prior to disposal in an area not under the national jurisdiction of any State;

12.   "State of transit" means any State, other than the State of export or import, through which a movement of hazardous wastes or other wastes is planned or takes place.

Article 3 (*National Definitions of Hazardous Waste*)

1.   Each Party shall, within six months of becoming a Party to this Convention, inform the Secretariat of the Convention of the wastes, other than those listed in Annexes I and II, considered or defined as hazardous under its national legislation and of any requirements concerning transboundary movement procedures applicable to such wastes.

2.   Each Party shall subsequently inform the Secretariat of any significant changes to the information it has provided pursuant to paragraph 1.

3.   The Secretariat shall forthwith inform all Parties of the information it has received pursuant to paragraphs 1 and 2.

4.   Parties shall be responsible for making the information transmitted to them by the Secretariat under paragraph 3 available to their exporters.

Article 4 (*General Obligations*)

1.

(a)   Parties exercising their right to prohibit the import of hazardous wastes or other wastes for disposal shall inform the other Parties of their decision pursuant to Article 13.

(b)   Parties shall prohibit or shall not permit the export of hazardous wastes and other wastes to the Parties which have prohibited the import of such wastes, when notified pursuant to subparagraph (a) above.

(c)   Parties shall prohibit or shall not permit the export of hazardous wastes and other wastes if the State of import does not consent in writing to the specific import, in the case where that State of import has not prohibited the import of such wastes.

2.   Each Party shall take the appropriate measures to:

(a)   Ensure that the generation of hazardous wastes and other wastes within it is reduced to a minimum, taking into account social, technological and economic aspects;

(b)   Ensure the availability of adequate disposal facilities, for the environmentally sound management of hazardous wastes and other wastes, that shall be located, to the extent possible, within it, whatever the place of their disposal;

(c)   Ensure that persons involved in the management of hazardous wastes or other wastes within it take such steps as are necessary to prevent pollution due to hazardous wastes and other wastes arising from such management and, if such pollution occurs, to minimize the consequences thereof for human health and the environment;

(d)   Ensure that the transboundary movement of hazardous wastes and other wastes is reduced to the minimum consistent with the environmentally sound and efficient management of such wastes, and is conducted in a manner which will protect human health and the environment against the adverse effects which may result from such movement;

(e)   Not allow the export of hazardous wastes or other wastes to a State or group of States belonging to an economic and/or political integration organization that are Parties, particularly developing countries, which have prohibited by their legislation all imports, or if it has reason to believe that the wastes in question will not be managed in an environmentally sound manner, according to criteria to be decided on by the Parties at their first meeting;

(f)   Require that information about a proposed transboundary movement of hazardous wastes and other wastes be provided to the States concerned, according to Annex V A, to state clearly the effects of the proposed movement on human health and the environment;

(g)   Prevent the import of hazardous wastes and other wastes if it has reason to believe that the wastes in question will not be managed in an environmentally sound manner;

(h)   Co-operate in activities with other Parties and interested organizations, directly and through the Secretariat, including the dissemination of information on the transboundary movement of hazardous wastes and other wastes, in order to improve the environmentally sound management of such wastes and to achieve the prevention of illegal traffic.

3.   The Parties consider that illegal traffic in hazardous wastes or other wastes is criminal.

4.   Each Party shall take appropriate legal, administrative and other measures to implement and enforce the provisions of this Convention, including measures to prevent and punish conduct in contravention of the Convention.

5.   A Party shall not permit hazardous wastes or other wastes to be exported to a non-Party or to be imported from a non-Party.

6.   The Parties agree not to allow the export of hazardous wastes or other wastes for disposal within the area south of 60° South latitude, whether or not such wastes are subject to transboundary movement.

7.   Furthermore, each Party shall:

(a)   Prohibit all persons under its national jurisdiction from transporting or disposing of hazardous wastes or other wastes unless such persons are authorized or allowed to perform such types of operations;

(b)   Require that hazardous wastes and other wastes that are to be the subject of a transboundary movement be packaged, labelled, and transported in conformity with generally accepted and recognized international rules and standards in the field of packaging, labelling, and transport, and that due account is taken of relevant internationally recognized practices;

(c)   Require that hazardous wastes and other wastes be accompanied by a movement document from the point at which a transboundary movement commences to the point of disposal.

8.   Each Party shall require that hazardous wastes or other wastes, to be exported, are managed in an environmentally sound manner in the State of import or elsewhere. Technical guidelines for the environmentally sound management of wastes subject to this Convention shall be decided by the Parties at their first meeting.

9.   Parties shall take the appropriate measures to ensure that the transboundary movement of hazardous wastes and other wastes only be allowed if:

(a)   The State of export does not have the technical capacity and the necessary facilities, capacity or suitable disposal sites in order to dispose of the wastes in question in an environmentally sound and efficient manner; or

(b)   The wastes in question are required as a raw material for recycling or recovery industries in the State of import; or

(c)   The transboundary movement in question is in accordance with other criteria to be decided by the Parties, provided those criteria do not differ from the objectives of this Convention.

10.   The obligation under this Convention of States in which hazardous wastes and other wastes are generated to require that those wastes are managed in an environmentally sound manner may not under any circumstances be transferred to the States of import or transit.

11. Nothing in this Convention shall prevent a Party from imposing additional requirements that are consistent with the provisions of this Convention, and are in accordance with the rules of international law, in order better to protect human health and the environment.

12. Nothing in this Convention shall affect in any way the sovereignty of States over their territorial sea established in accordance with international law, and the sovereign rights and the jurisdiction which States have in their exclusive economic zones and their continental shelves in accordance with international law, and the exercise by ships and aircraft of all States of navigational rights and freedoms as provided for in international law and as reflected in relevant international instruments.

13. Parties shall undertake to review periodically the possibilities for the reduction of the amount and/or the pollution potential of hazardous wastes and other wastes which are exported to other States, in particular to developing countries.

Article 5 (*Designation of Competent Authorities and Focal Point*)
To facilitate the implementation of this Convention, the Parties shall:

1. Designate or establish one or more competent authorities and one focal point. One competent authority shall be designated to receive the notification in case of a State of transit.

2. Inform the Secretariat, within three months of the date of the entry into force of this Convention for them, which agencies they have designated as their focal point and their competent authorities.

3. Inform the Secretariat, within one month of the date of decision, of any changes regarding the designation made by them under paragraph 2 above.

Article 6 (*Transboundary Movements Between the Parties*)

1. The State of export shall notify, or shall require the generator or exporter to notify, in writing, through the channel of the competent authority of the State of export, the competent authority of the States concerned of any proposed transboundary movement of hazardous wastes or other wastes. Such notification shall contain the declarations and information specified in Annex V A, written in a language acceptable to the State of import. Only one notification needs to be sent to each State concerned.

2. The State of import shall respond to the notifier in writing, consenting to the movement with or without conditions, denying permission for the movement, or requesting additional information. A copy of the final response of the State of import shall be sent to the competent authorities of the States concerned which are Parties.

3. The State of export shall not allow the generator or exporter to commence the transboundary movement until it has received written confirmation that:
   (a) The notifier has received the written consent of the State of import; and
   (b) The notifier has received from the State of import confirmation of the existence of a contract between the exporter and the disposer specifying environmentally sound management of the wastes in question.

4. Each State of transit which is a Party shall promptly acknowledge to the notifier receipt of the notification. It may subsequently respond to the notifier in writing, within 60 days, consenting to the movement with or without conditions, denying

permission for the movement, or requesting additional information. The State of export shall not allow the transboundary movement to commence until it has received the written consent of the State of transit. However, if at any time a Party decides not to require prior written consent, either generally or under specific conditions, for transit transboundary movements of hazardous wastes or other wastes, or modifies its requirements in this respect, it shall forthwith inform the other Parties of its decision pursuant to Article 13. In this latter case, if no response is received by the State of export within 60 days of the receipt of a given notification by the State of transit, the State of export may allow the export to proceed through the State of transit.

5. In the case of a transboundary movement of wastes where the wastes are legally defined as or considered to be hazardous wastes only:

(a) By the State of export, the requirements of paragraph 9 of this Article that apply to the importer or disposer and the State of import shall apply mutatis mutandis to the exporter and State of export, respectively;

(b) By the State of import, or by the States of import and transit which are Parties, the requirements of paragraphs 1, 3, 4 and 6 of this Article that apply to the exporter and State of export shall apply mutatis mutandis to the importer or disposer and State of import, respectively; or

(c) By any State of transit which is a Party, the provisions of paragraph 4 shall apply to such State.

6. The State of export may, subject to the written consent of the States concerned, allow the generator or the exporter to use a general notification where hazardous wastes or other wastes having the same physical and chemical characteristics are shipped regularly to the same disposer via the same customs office of exit of the State of export via the same customs office of entry of the State of import, and, in the case of transit, via the same customs office of entry and exit of the State or States of transit.

7. The States concerned may make their written consent to the use of the general notification referred to in paragraph 6 subject to the supply of certain information, such as the exact quantities or periodical lists of hazardous wastes or other wastes to be shipped.

8. The general notification and written consent referred to in paragraphs 6 and 7 may cover multiple shipments of hazardous wastes or other wastes during a maximum period of 12 months.

9. The Parties shall require that each person who takes charge of a transboundary movement of hazardous wastes or other wastes sign the movement document either upon delivery or receipt of the wastes in question. They shall also require that the disposer inform both the exporter and the competent authority of the State of export of receipt by the disposer of the wastes in question and, in due course, of the completion of disposal as specified in the notification. If no such information is received within the State of export, the competent authority of the State of export or the exporter shall so notify the State of import.

10. The notification and response required by this Article shall be transmitted to the competent authority of the Parties concerned or to such governmental authority as may be appropriate in the case of non-Parties.

11.   Any transboundary movement of hazardous wastes or other wastes shall be covered by insurance, bond or other guarantee as may be required by the State of import or any State of transit which is a Party.

1991 Bamako Convention on the Ban of the Import into Africa and the Control of Transboundary Movement and Management of Hazardous Wastes Within Africa, 2101 UNTS 177

Article 1 (*Definitions for the Purpose of this Convention*)

1.   "Wastes" are substances or materials which are disposed of, or are intended to be disposed of, or are required to be disposed of by the provisions of national law;

2.   "Hazardous wastes" shall mean wastes as specified in Article 2 of this Convention;

3.   "Management" means the prevention and reduction of hazardous wastes and the collection, transport, storage, treatment either for re-use or disposal of hazardous wastes including after-care of disposal sites;

4.   "Transboundary movement" means any movement of hazardous wastes from an area under the national jurisdiction of any state to or through an area under the national jurisdiction of another State, or to or through an area not under the national jurisdiction of another State, provided at least two States are involved in the movement;

5.   "Clean production methods" means production or industrial systems which avoid or eliminate the generation of hazardous wastes and hazardous products in conformity with Article 4, Section 3 (f) and (g) of this Convention;

6.   "Disposal" means any operation specified in Annex III to this Convention;

7.   "Approved site or facility" means a site or facility for the disposal of hazardous wastes which is authorized or permitted to operate for this purpose by a relevant authority of the State where the site or facility is located;

8.   "Competent authority" means one governmental authority designated by a Party to be responsible, within such geographical areas as the Party may think fit, for receiving the notification of a transboundary movement of hazardous wastes and any information related to it, and for responding to such a notification, as provided in Article 6;

9.   "Focal point" means the entity of a Party referred to in Article 5 responsible for receiving and submitting information as provided for in Articles 13 and 16;

10.   "Environmentally sound management of hazardous wastes" means taking all practicable steps to ensure that hazardous wastes are managed in a manner which will protect human health and environment against the adverse effects which may result from such wastes;

11.   "Area under the national jurisdiction of a State" means any land, marine area or airspace within which a State exercises administrative and regulatory responsibility in accordance with international law in regard to the protection of human health or the environment;

12.   "State of export" means a State from which a transboundary movement of hazardous wastes is planned to be initiated or is initiated;

13.   "State of import" means a State to which a transboundary movement is planned or takes place for the purpose of disposal therein or for the purpose of loading prior to disposal in an area not under the national jurisdiction of any State;

14. "State of transition" means any State, other than the State of export or import, through which a movement of hazardous wastes is planned or takes place;

15. "States concerned" means Parties which are States of export or import, or transit States whether or not Parties;

16. "Person" means any natural or legal person;

17. "Exporter" means any person under the jurisdiction of the State export who arranges for hazardous wastes to be exported;

18. "Importer" means any person under the jurisdiction of the State of import who arranges for hazardous wastes to be imported;

19. "Carrier" means any person who carries out the transport of hazardous wastes;

20. "Generator" means any person whose activity produces hazardous wastes, or, if that person is not known, the person who is in possession and/or control of those wastes;

21. "Disposer" means any person to whom hazardous wastes are shipped and who carries out the disposal of such wastes;

22. "Illegal traffic" means any transboundary movement of hazardous wastes as specified in Article 9;

23. "Dumping at sea" means the deliberate disposal of hazardous wastes at sea from vessels, aircraft, platforms or other man-made structures at sea, and includes ocean incineration and disposal into the seabed and sub-seabed.

Article 2 (*Scope of the Convention*)

1. The following substances shall be "hazardous wastes" for the purposes of this convention:

    (a) Wastes that belong to any category contained in Annex I of this Convention;

    (b) Wastes that are not covered under paragraph (a) above but are defined as, or are considered to be, hazardous wastes by the domestic legislation of the State of export, import or transit;

    (c) Wastes which possess any of the characteristics contained in Annex II of this Convention;

    (d) Hazardous substances which have been banned, cancelled or refused registration by government regulatory action, or voluntarily withdrawn from registration, in the country of manufacture, for human health and environmental reasons.

2. Wastes which, as a result of being radioactive, are subject to any international control systems, including international instruments, applying specifically to radioactive materials, are included in the scope of this Convention.

3. Wastes which derive from the normal operations of a ship, the discharge of which is covered by another international instrument, shall not fall within the scope of this Convention.

Article 3 (*National Definitions of Hazardous Wastes*)

1. Each State shall, within six months of becoming a Party to this Convention, inform the Secretariat of the Convention of the wastes, other than those listed in Annex I of this Convention, considered or defined as hazardous under its national legislation and of any requirements concerning transboundary movement procedures applicable to such wastes.

2. Each Party shall subsequently inform the Secretariat of any significant changes to the information it has provided pursuant to Paragraph 1 of this Convention.

3. The Secretariat shall forthwith inform all Parties of the information it has received pursuant to Paragraphs 1 and 2 of this Article.

4. Parties shall be responsible for making the information transmitted to them by the Secretariat under Paragraph 3 of this Article, available to their exporters and other appropriate bodies.

Article 4 (*General Obligations*)

1. Hazardous Waste Import Ban
   All Parties shall take appropriate legal, administrative and other measures within the area under their jurisdiction to prohibit the import of all hazardous wastes, for any reason, into Africa from non-Contracting Parties. Such import shall be deemed illegal and a criminal act. All Parties shall:
   (a) Forward as soon as possible, all information relating to such illegal hazardous waste import activity to the Secretariat who shall distribute the information to all Contracting Parties;
   (b) Co-operate to ensure that no imports of hazardous wastes from a non-Party enter a Party to this Convention. To this end, the Parties shall, at the Conference of the Contracting Parties, consider other enforcement mechanisms.

2. Ban on Dumping of Hazardous Wastes at Sea, Internal Waters and Waterways
   (a) Parties in conformity with related international conventions and instruments shall, in the exercise of their jurisdiction within their internal waters, territorial seas, exclusive economic zones and continental shelf, adopt legal, administrative and other appropriate measures to control all carriers from non-Parties, and prohibit the dumping at sea of hazardous wastes, including their incineration at sea and their disposal in the seabed and sub-seabed; any dumping of hazardous wastes at sea, including incineration at sea as well as seabed and sub-seabed disposal, by Contracting Parties, whether in internal waters, territorial seas, exclusive economic zones or high seas shall be deemed to be illegal;
   (b) Parties shall forward, as soon as possible, all information relating to dumping of hazardous wastes to the Secretariat which shall distribute the information to all Contracting Parties.

3. Waste Generation in Africa Each Party shall:
   (a) Ensure that hazardous waste generators submit to the Secretariat reports regarding the wastes that they generate in order to enable the Secretariat of the Convention to produce a complete hazardous waste audit;
   (b) Impose unlimited liability as well as joint and several liability on hazardous waste generators;
   (c) Ensure that the generation of hazardous wastes within the area under its jurisdiction is reduced to a minimum taking into account social, technological and economic aspects;
   (d) Ensure the availability of adequate treatment and/or disposal facilities, for the environmentally sound management of hazardous wastes which shall be located, to the extent possible, within its jurisdiction;

(e)   Ensure that persons involved in the management of hazardous wastes within its jurisdiction take such steps as are necessary to prevent pollution arising from such wastes and, if such pollution occurs, to minimize the consequence thereof for human health and environment;

The Adoption of Precautionary Measures;

(f)   Each Party shall strive to adopt and implement the preventive, precautionary approach to pollution problems which entails *inter alia* preventing the release into the environment of substances which may cause harm to humans or the environment without waiting for scientific proof regarding such harm. The Parties shall co-operate with each other in taking the appropriate measures to implement the precautionary principle to pollution prevention through the application of clean production methods, rather than the pursuit of a permissible emissions approach based on assimilative capacity assumptions;

(g)   In this respect Parties shall promote clean production methods applicable to entire product life cycles including: Raw material selection, extraction and processing; Product conceptualization, design, manufacture and assemblage; Materials transport during all phases; Industrial and household usage; Reintroduction of the product into industrial systems or nature when it no longer serves a useful function; Clean production shall not include "end-of-pipe" pollution controls such as filters and scrubbers, or chemical, physical or biological treatment. Measures which reduce the volume of waste by incineration or concentration, mask the hazard by dilution, or transfer pollutants from one environmental medium to another, are also excluded;

(h)   The issue of the transfer to Africa of polluting technologies shall be kept under systematic review by the Secretariat of the Conference and periodic reports made to the Conference of the Parties; Obligations in the Transport and Transboundary Movement of Hazardous Wastes from Contracting Parties;

(i)   Each Party shall prevent the export of hazardous wastes to States which have prohibited by their legislation or international agreements all such imports, or if it has reason to believe that the wastes in question will not be managed in an environmentally sound manner, according to criteria to be decided on by the Parties at their first meeting;

(j)   A Party shall not permit hazardous wastes to be exported to a State which does not have the facilities for disposing of them in an environmentally sound manner;

(k)   Each Party shall ensure that hazardous wastes to be exported are managed in an environmentally sound manner in the State of import and of transit. Technical guidelines for the environmentally sound management of wastes subject to this convention shall be decided by the Parties at their first meeting;

(l)   The Parties agree not to allow the export of hazardous wastes for disposal within the area South of 60 degrees South Latitude, whether or not such wastes are subject to transboundary movement;

(m)   Furthermore, each Party shall:

    (i)   Prohibit all persons under its national jurisdiction from transporting or disposing of hazardous wastes unless such persons are authorized or allowed to perform such operations;

    (ii)   Ensure that hazardous wastes that are to be the subject of a transboundary movement are packaged, labelled, and transported in conformity with generally accepted and recognized international rules and standards in the field of packaging, labelling and transport, and that due account is taken of relevant internationally recognized practices;

    (iii)   Ensure that hazardous wastes be accompanied by a movement document, containing information specified in Annex IV B, from the point at which a transboundary movement commences to the point of disposal.

(n)   Parties shall take the appropriate measures to ensure that the transboundary movements of hazardous wastes only are allowed if:

    (i)   The State of export does not have the technical capacity and the necessary facilities, capacity or suitable disposal sites in order to dispose of the wastes in question in an environmentally sound and efficient manner, or

    (ii)   The transboundary movement in question is in accordance with other criteria to be decided by the Parties, provided those criteria do not differ from the objectives of this Convention.

(o)   Under this Convention, the obligation of States in which hazardous wastes are generated, requiring that those wastes are managed in an environmentally sound manner, may not under any circumstances be transferred to the States of import or transit;

(p)   Parties shall undertake to review periodically the possibilities for the reduction of the amount and/or the pollution potential of hazardous wastes which are exported to other States;

(q)   Parties exercising their right to prohibit the import of hazardous wastes for disposal shall inform the other Parties of their decision pursuant to Article 13;

(r)   Parties shall prohibit or shall not permit the export of hazardous wastes to States which have prohibited the import of such wastes when notified by the Secretariat or any competent authority pursuant to sub-paragraph (q) above;

(s)   Parties shall prohibit or shall not permit the export of hazardous wastes if the State of import does not consent in writing to the specific import, in the case where that State of import has not prohibited the import of such wastes;

(t)   Parties shall ensure that the transboundary movement of hazardous wastes is reduced to the minimum consistent with the environmentally sound and efficient management of such wastes, and is conducted in a manner which will protect human health and the environment against the adverse effects which may result from such movements;

(u)   Parties shall require that information about a proposed transboundary movement of hazardous wastes be provided to the States concerned, according to Annex IV A, and clearly state the potential effects of the proposed movement on human health and the environment.

4.   Furthermore:

(a)   Parties shall undertake to enforce the obligation of this Convention against offenders and infringements according to relevant national laws and/or order to better protect human health and the environment;

(b)   Nothing in this Convention shall prevent a Party from imposing additional requirements that are consistent with the provisions of this Convention, and are in accordance with the rules of international law, in order to better protect human health and the environment;

(c)   This Convention recognizes the sovereignty of States over their territorial sea, waterways and air space established in accordance with international law, and jurisdiction which States have in their exclusive economic zone and their continental shelves in accordance with international law, and the exercise by ships and aircraft of all States of navigation rights and freedoms as provided for in international law and as reflected in relevant international instruments.

Article 5 (*Designation of Competent Authorities, Focal Point and Dumpwatch*)

To facilitate the implementation of this Convention, the Parties shall

1.   Designate or establish one or more competent authorities and one focal point. One competent authority shall be designated to receive the notification in case of a State of transit.

2.   Inform the Secretariat, within three months of the date of the entry into force of this Convention for them, which agencies they have designated as their focal point and their competent authorities.

3.   Inform the Secretariat, within one month of the date of decision, of any changes regarding the designations made by them under paragraph 2 above.

4.   Appoint a national body to act as a Dumpwatch. In such capacity as a dumpwatch, the designated national body only will be required to co-ordinate with the concerned governmental and non-governmental bodies.

Article 6 (*Transboundary Movement and Notification Procedures*)

1.   The State of export shall notify, or shall require the generator or exporter to notify, in writing, through the channel of the competent authority of the State of export, the competent authority of the State concerned of any proposed transboundary movement of hazardous wastes. Such notification shall contain the declaration and information specified in Annex IV A of this Convention, written in a language acceptable to the State of import. Only one notification needs to be sent to each State concerned.

2.   The State of import shall respond to the notifier in writing consenting to the movement with or without conditions, denying permission for the movement, or requesting additional information. A copy of the final response of the State of

import shall be sent to the competent authorities of the States concerned that are Parties to this Convention.

3.   The State of export shall not allow the transboundary movement until it has received:

(a)   Written consent of the State of import, and

(b)   From the State of import written confirmation of the existence of a contract between the exporter and the disposer specifying environmentally sound management of the wastes in question.

4.   Each State of transit which is a Party to this Convention shall promptly acknowledge to the notifier receipt of the notification. It may subsequently respond to the notifier in writing within 60 days consenting to the movement with or without conditions, denying permission for the movement, or requesting additional information. The State of export shall not allow the transboundary movement to commence until it has received the written consent of the State of transit.

5.   In the case of a transboundary movement of hazardous wastes where the wastes are legally defined as or considered to be hazardous wastes only:

(a)   By the State of export, the requirements of paragraph 8 of this Article that apply to the importer or disposer and the State of import shall apply mutatis mutandis to the exporter and State of export, respectively;

(b)   By the State of import or by the States of import and transit which are Parties to this Convention, the requirements of paragraph 1, 3, 4 and 6 of this Article that apply to the exporter and State of export shall apply mutatis mutandis to the importer or disposer and State of import, respectively; or

(c)   By any State of transit which is Party to this Convention, the provisions of paragraph 4 shall apply to such State.

6.   The State shall use a specific notification even where hazardous wastes having the same physical and chemical characteristics are shipped regularly to the same disposer via the same customs office of entry of the State of import, and in the case of transit via the same customs office of entry and exit of the State or States of transit; specific notification of each and every shipment shall be required and contain the information in Annex IVA of this Convention.

7.   Each Party to this Convention shall meet their points or ports of entry and notify the Secretariat to this effect for distribution to all Contracting Parties. Such points and ports shall be the only ones permitted for the transboundary movement of hazardous wastes.

8.   The Parties to this Convention shall require that each person who takes charge of a transboundary movement of hazardous wastes sign the movement document either upon delivery or receipt of the wastes in question. They shall also require that the disposer inform both the exporter and the competent authority of the State of export of receipt by the disposer of the wastes in question and, in due course, of the completion of disposal as specified in the notification. If no such information is received within the State of export, the competent authority of the State of export or the exporter shall so notify the State of import.

9.   The notification and response by this Article shall be transmitted to the competent authority of the States concerned.

10.   Any transboundary movement of hazardous wastes shall be covered by insurance, bond or other guarantee as may be required by the State of import or any State of transit which is a Party to this Convention.

1995 Waigani Convention to Ban the Importation into Forum Island Countries of Hazardous and Radioactive Wastes and to Control the Transboundary Movement and Management of Hazardous Wastes within the South Pacific Region, 2161 UNTS 91

Article 2 (*Scope of the Convention and Area of Coverage Scope of the Convention*)

1.   The following substances shall be "hazardous wastes" for the purposes of this Convention:

   (a)   Wastes that belong to any category contained in Annex I of this Convention, unless they do not possess any of the characteristics contained in Annex II of this Convention; and

   (b)   Wastes that are not covered under sub-paragraph (a) above, but which are defined as, or are considered to be, hazardous wastes by the national legislation of the exporting, importing or transit Party to, from or through which such wastes are to be sent.

2.   Radioactive wastes are excluded from the scope of this Convention except as specifically provided for in Articles 4.1, 4.2, 4.3, and 4.5 of this Convention.

3.   Wastes which derive from the normal operations of a vessel, the discharge of which is covered by another international instrument, shall not fall within the scope of this Convention.

4.   Nothing in this Convention shall affect in any way the sovereignty of States over their territorial sea, the sovereign rights and jurisdiction that States have in their exclusive economic zones and continental shelves, and the exercise by vessels and aircraft of all States of navigational rights and freedoms, as provided for in international law and as reflected in the 1982 United Nations Convention on the Law of the Sea and other relevant international instruments.

5.   Nothing in this Convention shall affect in any way the rights and obligations of any Party under international law including under other international agreements in force. Such agreements include the London Convention as amended; the 1982 United Nations Convention on the Law of the Sea, including in particular Articles 31, 210 and 236 thereof; the South Pacific Nuclear Free Zone Treaty, 1985, including in particular Article 7 thereof; and the International Convention for the Prevention of Pollution from Ships, 1973.

Area of Coverage

6.   A Party may add areas under its jurisdiction within the Pacific Ocean between the Tropic of Cancer and 60 degrees South latitude and between 130 degrees East longitude and 120 degrees West longitude to the Convention Area. Such addition shall be notified to the Depositary who shall promptly notify the other Parties and the Secretariat. Such areas shall be incorporated within the Convention Area ninety days after notification to the Parties by the Depositary, provided there has been no objection to the proposal to add new areas by any Party. If there is any such objection the Parties concerned will consult with a view to resolving the matter.

Article 3 (*National Definitions of Hazardous Wastes*)

1. Each Party shall, within six months of becoming a Party to this Convention, inform the Secretariat of the wastes, other than those listed in Annex I of this Convention, considered or defined as hazardous under its national legislation and of any requirements concerning transboundary movement procedures applicable to such wastes.

2. Each Party shall subsequently inform the Secretariat of any significant changes to the information it has provided pursuant to paragraph 1 of this Article.

3. The Secretariat shall forthwith inform all Parties of the information it has received pursuant to paragraphs 1 and 2 of this Article. 4. Parties shall be responsible for making the information transmitted to them by the Secretariat under paragraph 3 of this Article available to their exporters, importers and other appropriate bodies.

Article 4 (*General Obligations*)

1. Hazardous Wastes and Radioactive Wastes Import and Export Ban

    (a) Each Pacific Island Developing Party shall take appropriate legal, administrative and other measures within the area under its jurisdiction to ban the import of all hazardous wastes and radioactive wastes from outside the Convention Area. Such import shall be deemed an illegal and criminal act; and

    (b) Each Other Party shall take appropriate legal, administrative and other measures within the area under its jurisdiction to ban the export of all hazardous wastes and radioactive wastes to all Forum Island Countries, or to territories located in the Convention Area with the exception of those that have the status of Other Parties in accordance with Annex IV. Such export shall be deemed an illegal and criminal act.

2. To facilitate compliance with paragraph 1 of this Article, all Parties:

    (a) Shall forward in a timely manner all information relating to illegal hazardous wastes and radioactive wastes import activity within the area under its jurisdiction to the Secretariat who shall distribute the information as soon as possible to all Parties; and

    (b) Shall cooperate to ensure that no illegal import of hazardous wastes and radioactive wastes from a non-Party enters areas under the jurisdiction of a Party to this Convention.

3. Ban on Dumping of Hazardous Wastes and Radioactive Wastes at Sea

    (a) Each Party which is a Party to the London Convention, the South Pacific Nuclear Free Zone Treaty, 1985, the 1982 United Nations Convention on the Law of the Sea or the Protocol for the Prevention of Pollution of the South Pacific Region by Dumping, 1986, reaffirms the commitments under those instruments which require it to prohibit dumping of hazardous wastes and radioactive wastes at sea; and

    (b) Each Party which is not a Party either to the London Convention or the Protocol for the Prevention of Pollution of the South Pacific Region by Dumping, 1986, should consider becoming a Party to both of those instruments.

4. Wastes Located in the Convention Area Each Party shall:

(a)   Ensure that within the area under its jurisdiction, the generation of hazard-
        ous wastes is reduced at its source to a minimum taking into account social,
        technological and economic needs;

(b)   Take appropriate legal, administrative and other measures to ensure that
        within the area under its jurisdiction, all transboundary movements of
        hazardous wastes generated within the Convention Area are carried out in
        accordance with the provisions of this Convention;

(c)   Ensure the availability of adequate treatment and disposal facilities for the
        environmentally sound management of hazardous wastes, which shall be
        located, to the extent practicable, within areas under its jurisdiction, taking
        into account social, technological and economic considerations. However,
        where Parties are for geographic, social or economic reasons unable to
        dispose safely of hazardous wastes within those areas, cooperation should
        take place as provided for under Article 10 of this Convention;

(d)   In cooperation with SPREP, participate in the development of programmes
        to manage and simplify the transboundary movement of hazardous wastes
        which cannot be disposed of in an environmentally sound manner in the
        countries in which they are located. Provided that such programmes do
        not derogate from the environmentally sound management of hazardous
        wastes as required by this Convention, they may be registered as arrange-
        ments under Article 11 of this Convention;

(e)   Develop a national hazardous wastes management strategy which is com-
        patible with the SPREP South Pacific Regional Pollution Prevention, Waste
        Minimization and Management Programme;

(f)   Submit to the Secretariat such reports as the Conference of the Parties may
        require regarding the hazardous wastes generated in the area under its
        jurisdiction in order to enable the Secretariat to produce a regular hazard-
        ous wastes report;

(g)   Subject to Article 11 of this Convention, prohibit within the area under its
        jurisdiction hazardous wastes from being exported to or imported from
        non-Parties within the Convention Area; and

(h)   Take appropriate legal, administrative and other measures to prohibit
        vessels flying its flag or aircraft registered in its territory from carrying out
        activities in contravention of this Convention.

5.   Radioactive Wastes

(a)   Parties shall give active consideration to the implementation of the IAEA
        Code of Practice on the International Transboundary Movement of
        Radioactive Wastes and such other international and national standards
        which are at least as stringent; and

(b)   Subject to available resources, Parties shall actively participate in the devel-
        opment of the Convention on the Safe Management of Nuclear Waste.

6.   Domestically Prohibited Goods:

(a)   Subject to available resources, Parties shall endeavour to participate in
        relevant international fora to find an appropriate global solution to the
        problems associated with the international trade of domestically prohibited
        goods; and

(b)   Nothing in this Convention shall be interpreted as limiting the sovereign right of Parties to act individually or collectively, consistent with their international obligations, to ban the importation of domestically prohibited goods into areas under their jurisdiction.

Article 5 (*Competent Authorities and Focal Points*)

1. To facilitate the implementation of this Convention, each Party shall designate or establish one competent authority and one focal point. A Party need not designate or establish new or separate authorities to perform the functions of the competent authority and the focal point.

2. The competent authority shall be responsible for the implementation of notification procedures for transboundary movement of hazardous wastes in accordance with the provisions of Article 6 of this Convention.

3. The focal point shall be responsible for transmitting and receiving information in accordance with the provisions of Article 7 of this Convention.

4. The Parties shall inform the Secretariat, within three months of the date of the entry into force of this Convention for them, which authorities they have designated or established as the competent authority and the focal point.

Article 6 (*Notification Procedures for Transboundary Movements of Hazardous Wastes between Parties*)

1. The exporting Party shall notify, or shall require the generator or exporter to notify, in writing, through its competent authority, the competent authority of the countries concerned of any proposed transboundary movement of hazardous wastes. Such notification shall contain the declarations and information specified in Annex VI A of this Convention, written in a language acceptable to the importing Party. Only one notification needs to be sent to each country concerned.

2. The importing Party shall acknowledge within reasonable time, which in the case of Other Parties shall not exceed fourteen working days, the receipt of the notification referred to in paragraph 1 of this Article. The importing Party shall have sixty days after issuing the acknowledgement to inform the notifier that it is consenting to the movement, with or without conditions, denying permission for the movement or requesting additional information. In the event that additional information has been sought, a new period of twenty one days recommences from the time of receipt of the additional information.

3. The exporting Party shall not allow the transboundary movement until it has received:

   (a)   Written consent of the importing Party;

   (b)   Written consent from every transit Party;

   (c)   Written consent of every non-Party country of transit;

   (d)   Written confirmation from the importing Party of the existence of a contract between the exporter and the disposer specifying the environmentally sound management of the wastes in question; and

   (e)   Written confirmation from the exporter of the existence of adequate insurance, bond or other guarantee satisfactory to the exporting Party.

4.   Each transit Party shall acknowledge within reasonable time, which in the case of Other Parties shall not exceed fourteen working days, the receipt of the notification referred to in paragraph 1 of this Article. Each transit Party shall have sixty days after issuing the acknowledgement to inform the notifier that it is consenting to the movement, with or without conditions, denying permission for the movement or requesting additional information. In the event that additional information has been sought, a new period of twenty one days recommences from the time of receipt of the additional information.

5.   In the case of a transboundary movement of hazardous wastes, where the wastes are legally defined as or are considered to be hazardous wastes only:

(a)   By the exporting Party, the requirement at paragraph 10 of this Article, that any transboundary movement shall be covered by insurance, bond or other guarantee shall be as required by the exporting Party; or

(b)   By the importing Party, or the transit Party, the requirements of paragraphs 1, 3, 4, and 6 of this Article that apply to the exporter and exporting Party, shall apply mutatis mutandis to the importer or disposer and importing Party, respectively; or

(c)   By any transit Party, the provisions of paragraph 4 of this Article shall apply to such Party.

6.   The exporting Party may, subject to the written consent of the countries concerned, allow the generator or the exporter to use a general notification where hazardous wastes having the same physical and chemical characteristics are shipped regularly to the same disposer via the same customs office of exit of the exporting Party, via the same customs office of entry of the importing Party, and, in the case of transit, via the same customs office of entry and exit of the Party or Parties of transit.

7.   The countries concerned may make their written consent to the use of the general notification referred to in paragraph 6 of this Article subject to the supply of certain information, such as the exact quantities or periodical lists of hazardous wastes to be shipped.

8.   The general notification and written consent referred to in paragraphs 6 and 7 of this Article may cover multiple shipments of hazardous wastes during a maximum period of twelve months.

9.   Each transboundary movement of hazardous wastes shall be accompanied by a movement document which includes the information listed in Annex VI B. The Parties to this Convention shall require that each person who takes charge of a transboundary movement of hazardous wastes sign the movement document either upon delivery or receipt of the wastes in question. They shall also require the disposer to inform both the exporter and the competent authority of the exporting Party of receipt by the disposer of the wastes in question and, in due course, of the completion of disposal as specified in the notification. If no such information is received by the exporting Party, the competent authority of the exporting Party or the exporter shall so notify the importing Party.

10.   Any transboundary movement of hazardous wastes shall be covered by insurance, bond or other guarantee as may be required or agreed to by the importing Party or any transit Party.

1998 Rotterdam Convention on the Prior Informed Consent Procedure for Certain Hazardous Chemicals and Pesticides in International Trade, 2244 UNTS 337

Article 1 (*Objective*)

The objective of this Convention is to promote shared responsibility and cooperative efforts among Parties in the international trade of certain hazardous chemicals in order to protect human health and the environment from potential harm and to contribute to their environmentally sound use, by facilitating information exchange about their characteristics, by providing for a national decision-making process on their import and export and by disseminating these decisions to Parties.

Article 2 (*Definitions*)

For the purposes of this Convention:

(a) "Chemical" means a substance whether by itself or in a mixture or preparation and whether manufactured or obtained from nature, but does not include any living organism. It consists of the following categories: pesticide (including severely hazardous pesticide formulations) and industrial;

(b) "Banned chemical" means a chemical all uses of which within one or more categories have been prohibited by final regulatory action, in order to protect human health or the environment. It includes a chemical that has been refused approval for first-time use or has been withdrawn by industry either from the domestic market or from further consideration in the domestic approval process and where there is clear evidence that such action has been taken in order to protect human health or the environment;

(c) "Severely restricted chemical" means a chemical virtually all use of which within one or more categories has been prohibited by final regulatory action in order to protect human health or the environment, but for which certain specific uses remain allowed. It includes a chemical that has, for virtually all use, been refused for approval or been withdrawn by industry either from the domestic market or from further consideration in the domestic approval process, and where there is clear evidence that such action has been taken in order to protect human health or the environment;

(d) "Severely hazardous pesticide formulation" means a chemical formulated for pesticidal use that produces severe health or environmental effects observable within a short period of time after single or multiple exposure, under conditions of use;

(e) "Final regulatory action" means an action taken by a Party, that does not require subsequent regulatory action by that Party, the purpose of which is to ban or severely restrict a chemical;

(f) "Export" and "import" mean, in their respective connotations, the movement of a chemical from one Party to another Party, but exclude mere transit operations;

(g) "Party" means a State or regional economic integration organization that has consented to be bound by this Convention and for which the Convention is in force;

(h) "Regional economic integration organization" means an organization constituted by sovereign States of a given region to which its member States have transferred competence in respect of matters governed by this Convention and which has been duly authorized, in accordance with its internal procedures, to sign, ratify, accept, approve or accede to this Convention;

(i)   "Chemical Review Committee" means the subsidiary body referred to in paragraph 6 of Article 18.

Article 3 (*Scope of the Convention*)
1.   This Convention applies to:
        (a)   Banned or severely restricted chemicals; and
        (b)   Severely hazardous pesticide formulations.

2.   This Convention does not apply to:
        (a)   Narcotic drugs and psychotropic substances;
        (b)   Radioactive materials;
        (c)   Wastes;
        (d)   Chemical weapons;
        (e)   Pharmaceuticals, including human and veterinary drugs;
        (f)   Chemicals used as food additives;
        (g)   Food;
        (h)   Chemicals in quantities not likely to affect human health or the environment provided they are imported:
                (i)   For the purpose of research or analysis; or
                (ii)   By an individual for his or her own personal use in quantities reasonable for such use.

[...]

Article 5 (*Procedures for Banned or Severely Restricted Chemicals*)
1.   Each Party that has adopted a final regulatory action shall notify the Secretariat in writing of such action. Such notification shall be made as soon as possible, and in any event no later than ninety days after the date on which the final regulatory action has taken effect, and shall contain the information required by Annex I, where available.
2.   Each Party shall, at the date of entry into force of this Convention for it, notify the Secretariat in writing of its final regulatory actions in effect at that time, except that each Party that has submitted notifications of final regulatory actions under the Amended London Guidelines or the International Code of Conduct need not resubmit those notifications.
3.   The Secretariat shall, as soon as possible, and in any event no later than six months after receipt of a notification under paragraphs 1 and 2, verify whether the notification contains the information required by Annex I. If the notification contains the information required, the Secretariat shall forthwith forward to all Parties a summary of the information received. If the notification does not contain the information required, it shall inform the notifying Party accordingly.
4.   The Secretariat shall every six months communicate to the Parties a synopsis of the information received pursuant to paragraphs 1 and 2, including information regarding those notifications which do not contain all the information required by Annex I.
5.   When the Secretariat has received at least one notification from each of two Prior Informed Consent regions regarding a particular chemical that it has verified

meet the requirements of Annex I, it shall forward them to the Chemical Review Committee. The composition of the Prior Informed Consent regions shall be defined in a decision to be adopted by consensus at the first meeting of the Conference of the Parties.

6.   The Chemical Review Committee shall review the information provided in such notifications and, in accordance with the criteria set out in Annex II, recommend to the Conference of the Parties whether the chemical in question should be made subject to the Prior Informed Consent procedure and, accordingly, be listed in Annex III.

Article 6 (*Procedures for Severely Hazardous Pesticide Formulations*)

1.   Any Party that is a developing country or a country with an economy in transition and that is experiencing problems caused by a severely hazardous pesticide formulation under conditions of use in its territory, may propose to the Secretariat the listing of the severely hazardous pesticide formulation in Annex III. In developing a proposal, the Party may draw upon technical expertise from any relevant source. The proposal shall contain the information required by part 1 of Annex IV.

2.   The Secretariat shall, as soon as possible, and in any event no later than six months after receipt of a proposal under paragraph 1, verify whether the proposal contains the information required by part 1 of Annex IV. If the proposal contains the information required, the Secretariat shall forthwith forward to all Parties a summary of the information received. If the proposal does not contain the information required, it shall inform the proposing Party accordingly.

3.   The Secretariat shall collect the additional information set out in part 2 of Annex IV regarding the proposal forwarded under paragraph 2.

4.   When the requirements of paragraphs 2 and 3 above have been fulfilled with regard to a particular severely hazardous pesticide formulation, the Secretariat shall forward the proposal and the related information to the Chemical Review Committee.

5.   The Chemical Review Committee shall review the information provided in the proposal and the additional information collected and, in accordance with the criteria set out in part 3 of Annex IV, recommend to the Conference of the Parties whether the severely hazardous pesticide formulation in question should be made subject to the Prior Informed Consent procedure and, accordingly, be listed in Annex III.

2001 Stockholm Convention on Persistent Organic Pollutants, 2256 UNTS 119

Article 1 (*Objective*)

Mindful of the precautionary approach as set forth in Principle 15 of the Rio Declaration on Environment and Development, the objective of this Convention is to protect human health and the environment from persistent organic pollutants.

Article 2 (*Definitions*)

For the purposes of this Convention:

(a)   "Party" means a State or regional economic integration organization that has consented to be bound by this Convention and for which the Convention is in force;

(b)   "Regional economic integration organization" means an organization constituted by sovereign States of a given region to which its member States have transferred competence in respect of matters governed by this Convention and which has been duly authorized, in accordance with its internal procedures, to sign, ratify, accept, approve or accede to this Convention;

(c)   "Parties present and voting" means Parties present and casting an affirmative or negative vote.

Article 3 (*Measures to Reduce or Eliminate Releases from Intentional Production and Use*)

1.   Each Party shall:

    (a)   Prohibit and/or take the legal and administrative measures necessary to eliminate:

        (i)   Its production and use of the chemicals listed in Annex A subject to the provisions of that Annex; and

        (ii)   Its import and export of the chemicals listed in Annex A in accordance with the provisions of paragraph 2; and

    (b)   Restrict its production and use of the chemicals listed in Annex B in accordance with the provisions of that Annex.

2.   Each Party shall take measures to ensure:

    (a)   That a chemical listed in Annex A or Annex B is imported only:

        (i)   For the purpose of environmentally sound disposal as set forth in paragraph 1 (d) of Article 6; or

        (ii)   For a use or purpose which is permitted for that Party under Annex A or Annex B;

    (b)   That a chemical listed in Annex A for which any production or use specific exemption is in effect or a chemical listed in Annex B for which any production or use specific exemption or acceptable purpose is in effect, taking into account any relevant provisions in existing international prior informed consent instruments, is exported only:

        (i)   For the purpose of environmentally sound disposal as set forth in paragraph 1 (d) of Article 6;

        (ii)   To a Party which is permitted to use that chemical under Annex A or Annex B; or

        (iii)   To a State not Party to this Convention which has provided an annual certification to the exporting Party. Such certification shall specify the intended use of the chemical and include a statement that, with respect to that chemical, the importing State is committed to:

        a. Protect human health and the environment by taking the necessary measures to minimize or prevent releases;

        b. Comply with the provisions of paragraph 1 of Article 6; and

        c. Comply, where appropriate, with the provisions of paragraph 2 of Part II of Annex B. The certification shall also include any appropriate supporting documentation, such as legislation, regulatory instruments, or administrative or policy guidelines. The exporting Party shall transmit the certification to the Secretariat within sixty days of receipt.

(c)   That a chemical listed in Annex A, for which production and use specific exemptions are no longer in effect for any Party, is not exported from it except for the purpose of environmentally sound disposal as set forth in paragraph 1 (d) of Article 6;

(d)   For the purposes of this paragraph, the term "State not Party to this Convention" shall include, with respect to a particular chemical, a State or regional economic integration organization that has not agreed to be bound by the Convention with respect to that chemical.

3.   Each Party that has one or more regulatory and assessment schemes for new pesticides or new industrial chemicals shall take measures to regulate with the aim of preventing the production and use of new pesticides or new industrial chemicals which, taking into consideration the criteria in paragraph 1 of Annex D, exhibit the characteristics of persistent organic pollutants.

4.   Each Party that has one or more regulatory and assessment schemes for pesticides or industrial chemicals shall, where appropriate, take into consideration within these schemes the criteria in paragraph 1 of Annex D when conducting assessments of pesticides or industrial chemicals currently in use.

5.   Except as otherwise provided in this Convention, paragraphs 1 and 2 shall not apply to quantities of a chemical to be used for laboratory-scale research or as a reference standard.

6.   Any Party that has a specific exemption in accordance with Annex A or a specific exemption or an acceptable purpose in accordance with Annex B shall take appropriate measures to ensure that any production or use under such exemption or purpose is carried out in a manner that prevents or minimizes human exposure and release into the environment. For exempted uses or acceptable purposes that involve intentional release into the environment under conditions of normal use, such release shall be to the minimum extent necessary, taking into account any applicable standards and guidelines.

Table 14.1   Other Conventions addressing hazardous waste

Antarctic Treaty, 402 UNTS 71 (1959), including the Protocol on Environmental Protection to the Antarctic Treaty ('Madrid Protocol'), 30 ILM 1455 (1991)
South Pacific Nuclear Free Zone Treaty, 1445 UNTS 177 (1985)
Convention for the Protection of the Natural Resources and Environment of the South Pacific Region ('Noumea' or 'SPREP Convention'), 26 ILM 38 (1986)
Agreement between the Government of Canada and the Government of the United States concerning the Transboundary Movement of Hazardous Waste, Canada Treaty Series 1986/39 (1986)
Agreement between Mexico and the United States Regarding the Transboundary Shipments of Hazardous Wastes and Hazardous Substances (1986)
EEC–ACP Convention of Lomé ('Lomé IV Convention'), 29 ILM 783 (1989)
1994 Convention on Nuclear Safety, 1963 UNTS 293
Agreement between the Government of America and the Government of Malaysia Concerning the Transboundary Movement of Hazardous Wastes from Malaysia to the United States (1995)
Protocol on the Prevention of Pollution of the Mediterranean Sea by Transboundary Movements of Hazardous Wastes and their Disposal ('Izmir Protocol') 2942 UNTS (1996)

International Convention on Liability and Compensation for Damage in Connection with the Carriage of Hazardous and Noxious Substances by Sea ('HNS Convention'), 25 ILM 1406 (1996), including the Protocol to the International Convention on Liability and Compensation for Damage in Connection with the Carriage of Hazardous and Noxious Substances by Sea (2010)

Joint Convention on the Safety of Spent Fuel Management and on the Safety of Radioactive Waste Management, 2153 UNTS 303 (1997)

Agreement on the Transboundary Movement of Hazardous Waste from Costa Rica to the United States (1997)

United States-Russian Federation: Agreement between the Government of the United States of America and the Government of the Russian Federation on Scientific and Technical Cooperation in the Management of Plutonium that has been withdrawn from Nuclear Military Programs, 37 ILM 1296 (1998)

Agreement between the Government of the United States of America and the Government of the Republic of the Philippines Concerning the Transboundary Movement of Hazardous Wastes from the Philippines to the United States (2001)

Framework Agreement on a Multilateral Nuclear Environmental Programme in the Russian Federation, 2265 UNTS 5 (2003)

Hong Kong International Convention for the Safe and Environmentally Sound Recycling of Ships (2009)

Minamata Convention on Mercury, 55 ILM 582 (2013)

Protocol on Amendments to the Protocol on the Statute of the African Court of Justice and Human Rights (2014)

Kyoto-Varanasi Partner City Agreement (2014)

14.2.1.2 Regional

Table 14.2 OECD Decisions

OECD Decision concerning the Mutual Acceptance of Data in the Assessment of Chemicals, OECD Doc. C(81)30 (1981) (as last amended by OECD Doc. C(2019)12)

OECD Decision-Recommendation of the Council on Compliance with Principles of Good Laboratory Practice, OECD/LEGAL/0252 (1989) (as last amended by OECD Doc. C(95)8/FINAL)

OECD Decision-Recommendation of the Council on the Reduction of Transfrontier Movements of Wastes, OECD/LEGAL/0260 (1991) (as last amended by OECD Doc. C(2001)208)

OECD Decision concerning the Adherence of Non-Member Countries to the Council Acts Related to the Mutual Acceptance of Data in the Assessment of Chemicals, OECD Doc. C(97)114 (1998)

OECD Decision of the Council concerning the Revision of Decision C(92)39/FINAL on the Control of Transboundary Movements of Wastes Destined for Recovery Operations, C(2001)107FINAL (2002)

14.2.2 Non-Binding Instruments

14.2.2.1 International

Table 14.3 Examples of non-binding international instruments

Cairo Guidelines and Principles for the Environmentally Sound Management of Hazardous Wastes, UNEP(092)/ E5 (1987)
International Atomic Energy Agency: General Conference Resolution on Code of Practice on the International Transboundary Movement of Radioactive Waste, 30 ILM 556 (1991)
United Nations Conference on Environment and Development: Rio Declaration on Environment and Development, 31 ILM 874 (1992)
Report of the United Nations Conference on Environment and Development, Rio de Janeiro, 3–14 June 1992 ('Agenda 21'), Volume II (*Proceedings of the Conference*) (A/CONF.151/26/ver.1 (Vol. II))
Report of the Global Conference on the Sustainable Development of Small Island Developing States, Bridgetown, Barbados, 25 April–6 May 1994 (including 'Declaration of Barbados' (Annex I) and Program of Action for the Sustainable Development of Small Island Developing States (Annex II)) (A/CONF.167/9)
Basel Declaration on Environmentally Sound Management (1999)
World Summit on Sustainable Development, Johannesburg, South Africa, 26 August–4 September 2002, Draft Plan on the Implementation of the World Summit on Sustainable Development (A./CONF.199/L.1)
Ministerial Statement on Partnership for Meeting the Global Waste Challenge (2004)
International Meeting to Review the Implementation of the Program of Action for the Sustainable Development of Small Island Developing States, Port Louis, Mauritius, 10–14 January 2005, Mauritius Declaration (A/ CONF.207/L.6)
Nairobi Declaration on the Environmentally Sound Management of Electrical and Electronic Waste, Eighth Meeting of the Conference of the Parties to the Basel Convention on the Control of Transboundary Movements of Hazardous Wastes and their Disposal (2006)
Bali Declaration on Waste Management for Human Health and Livelihood, Ninth Meeting of the Conference of the Parties to the Basel Convention on the Control of Transboundary Movements of Hazardous Wastes and their Disposal (2008)
Cartagena Declaration on the Prevention, Minimization a Recovery of Hazardous Wastes and Other Waste, Tenth meeting of the Conference of the Parties to the Basel Convention on the Control of Transboundary Movements of Hazardous Wastes and their Disposal (2011)

14.2.2.2 Regional

Table 14.4 OECD Instruments

OECD Recommendation of the Council on the Environmentally Sound Management (ESM) of Waste, OECD/ LEGAL/0329 (2004) (as last amended by OECD Doc. C(2007)97)
OECD (2007), *Guidance Manual on Environmentally Sound Management of Waste*, OECD Publishing, Paris
OECD (2009), *Guidance Manual for the Control of Transboundary Movements of Recoverable Wastes*, OECD Publishing, Paris
OECD Report by the Environment Policy Committee on the Implementation of the Council Recommendation on Environmentally Sound Management of Waste, OECD Doc. C(2009)123 (2009)

14.3   CASE LAW

14.3.1   International

CASE
United States, *Standards for reformulated and conventional gasoline, Appellate Body and Panel Report*, WT/DS2/9 (20 May 1996)

(6.21) The Panel noted the United States argument that air pollution, in particular ground-level ozone and toxic substances, presented health risks to humans, animals and plants. The United States argued that, since about one-half of such pollution was caused by vehicle emissions, and the Gasoline Rule reduced these, the Gasoline Rule was within the range of policy goals described in Article XX(b). Venezuela and Brazil did not disagree with this view. The Panel agreed with the parties that a policy to reduce air pollution resulting from the consumption of gasoline was a policy within the range of those concerning the protection of human, animal and plant life or health mentioned in Article XX(b).

CASE
UNCITRAL, *S.D. Myers, Inc. v. Government of Canada*, Partial Award (13 November 2000)

(105) In March 1989 a number of countries including CANADA signed the Basel Convention. This convention deals with international traffic in PCBs and other hazardous wastes. It was developed under the auspices of the United Nations Environment Programme. Although the USA signed the Basel Convention it had not ratified it by the time of the events under review in this arbitration.

(106) State parties to the Basel Convention accept the obligation to ensure that hazardous wastes are managed in an environmentally sound manner. The Basel Convention establishes rules and procedures to govern the transboundary movement of hazardous wastes and their disposal. Amongst other things, it prohibits the export and import of hazardous wastes from and to states that are not party to the Basel Convention (Article 4(5)), unless such movement is subject to bilateral, multilateral or regional agreements or arrangements whose provisions are not less stringent that those of the Basel Convention (Article 11).

(107) The Basel Convention also requires appropriate measures to ensure the availability of adequate disposal facilities for the environmentally sound management of hazardous wastes that are located within it (Article 4(2)(b)). It also requires that the transboundary movement of hazardous wastes be reduced to the minimum consistent with the environmentally sound and efficient management of such wastes and be conducted in a manner that will protect human health and the environment (Article 4(2)(d)).

[...]

(212)   The Basel Convention is not as explicit as the Transboundary Agreement in emphasizing the potential benefits of cross-border movement of toxic wastes in achieving economies and better protecting the environment. Article 4(2)(d) of the Basel Convention acknowledges that the environmentally sound and efficient management of waste is not necessarily accomplished by avoiding cross-border shipments.

(213)   Article 11 [of the Transboundary Agreement] expressly allows parties to enter into bilateral or multilateral agreements for the cross-border movement of waste, provided that these agreements do not undermine the Basel Convention's own insistence on environmentally sound management. So far as CANADA and the USA were concerned, Article 11 clearly permitted the continuation of the Transboundary Agreement with its emphasis on including cross-border movements as a means to be considered in achieving the most cost-effective and environmentally sound solution to hazardous waste management.

(214)   The drafters of the NAFTA evidentially considered which earlier environmental treaties would prevail over the specific rules of the NAFTA in case of conflict. Annex 104 provided that the Basel Convention would have priority if and when it was ratified by the NAFTA Parties.

14.3.2   Regional

CASE
ECtHR, *Lopez Ostra v. Spain*, App no. 16798/90, 20 EHRR 277 (19 December 1994)

(51) Naturally, severe environmental pollution may affect individuals' well-being and prevent them from enjoying their homes in such a way as to affect their private and family life adversely, without, however, seriously endangering their health.

CASE
ECtHR, *Guerra and Others v. Italy*, Judgment, 116/1996/735/932 (19 February 1998)

(57) The Court's task is to determine whether Article 8 is applicable and, if so, whether it has been infringed. The Court notes, firstly, that all the applicants live at Manfredonia, approximately a kilometre away from the factory [...] In the course of its production cycle the factory released large quantities of inflammable gas and other toxic substances, including arsenic trioxide. [T]he direct effect of the toxic emissions on the applicants' right to respect for their private and family life means that Article 8 is applicable.

(58) [A]lthough the object of Article 8 is essentially that of protecting the individual against arbitrary interference by the public authorities, it does not merely compel

the State to abstain from such interference: in addition to this primarily negative undertaking, there may be positive obligations inherent in effective respect for private or family life [...]. In the present case it need only be ascertained whether the national authorities took the necessary steps to ensure effective protection of the applicants' right to respect for their private and family life as guaranteed by Article 8 [...].

[...]

(60). The Court reiterates that severe environmental pollution may affect individuals' well-being and prevent them from enjoying their homes in such a way as to affect their private and family life adversely [...].

CASE
ECtHR, *Öneryildiz v. Turkey*, Judgment, Application no. 48939/99 (18 June 2002)

(54) [P]rimary responsibility for the treatment of urban waste falls on local authorities, which the Governments are obliged to provide with financial and technical assistance. The operation by the public authorities of a site for the storage of waste is described as a "dangerous activity" and a "death" resulting from the deposit of waste on a site for the permanent deposit of waste is considered to be "damage" incurring the liability of the public authorities [...].

(55) In that connection, the Strasbourg Convention calls on the Parties to adopt such appropriate measures as may be necessary to establish as criminal offences the unlawful storage of hazardous waste which causes or is likely to cause death or serious injury to any person, specifying that this offence can also be committed with "negligence" (Articles 2 to 4). Article 6 of that Convention requires further that such appropriate measures as may be necessary also be taken to make those offences punishable by criminal sanctions which take into account the serious nature of those offences and include imprisonment of the perpetrators.

(56) With regard to such hazardous activities, public access to clear and full information is deemed to be a basic human right [which] must not be deemed to be limited to the risks associated with the use of nuclear energy in the civil sector.

CASE
ECtHR, *Taşkin and Others v. Turkey*, Judgment, Application No. 46117/99 (10 November 2004)

(113)   The Court points out that Article 8 applies to severe environmental pollution which may affect individuals' well-being and prevent them from enjoying their homes in such a way as to affect their private and family life adversely, without, however, seriously endangering their health [...]. The same is true where the dangerous effects of an activity to which the individuals concerned are likely to be exposed have been determined as part of an environmental impact assessment procedure in such a way as to establish a sufficiently close link with private and family life for the purposes of Article 8 of the Convention.

CASE
ECtHR, *Öneryildiz v. Turkey*, Judgment, Application no. 48939/99 (18 June 2002)

(65)   [T]he Chamber emphasised that the protection of the right to life, as required by Article 2 of the Convention, could be relied on in connection with the operation of waste-collection sites, on account of the potential risks inherent in that activity. It accordingly held that the positive obligation on States to take appropriate steps to safeguard the lives of those within their jurisdiction, for the purposes of Article 2, applied in the instant case.

CASE
ECtHR, *Di Sarno and Others v. Italy*, Case, Judgment, Application No. 30765/08 (10 January 2012)

(108)   The Court has already noted ... that the municipality of Somma Vesuviana, where the applicants live or work, was affected by the "waste crisis". [...] The Court considers that this situation may have led to a deterioration of the applicants' quality of life and, in particular, adversely affected their right to respect for their homes and their family life. Article 8 therefore applies in the present case. [A]rticle 8 may be relied on even in the absence of any evidence of a serious danger to people's health [...].

[...]

(109)   The collection, treatment and disposal of waste are without a doubt dangerous activities [...]. That being so, the State was under a positive obligation to take reasonable and adequate steps to protect the right of the people concerned to respect for their homes and their private life and, more generally, to live in a safe and healthy environment [...].

ADVISORY OPINION
IACtHR, The Environment and Human Rights, Advisory Opinion, OC-23/17 (15 November 2017), Series A No. 23

(54). Numerous points of interconnection arise from this relationship of interdependence and indivisibility between human rights, the environment, and sustainable development owing to which, as indicated by the Independent Expert, "all human rights are vulnerable to environmental degradation, in that the full enjoyment of all human rights depends on a supportive environment." In this regard, the Human Rights Council has identified environmental threats that may affect, directly or indirectly, the effective enjoyment of specific human rights, affirming that: (i) illicit traffic in, and improper management and disposal of, hazardous substances and wastes constitute a serious threat to a range of rights, including the rights to life and health.

QUESTIONS

1. In which sense might international law on the management of hazardous waste be regarded as a fragmented regulation area?
2. What does the principle of environmentally sound management entail? And what is the 'prior informed consent' requirement?
3. Which aspects of the 'management' of hazardous waste are more developed at the international level? Which less so?

FURTHER READING

BOOKS

K Kummer, *International Management of Hazardous Wastes* (Oxford University Press 1995)
B Kwiatkowska, AHA Soons and MK Tolba (eds), *Transboundary Movements and Disposal of Hazardous Wastes in International Law: Basic Documents* (Martinus Nijhoff 1993)
P Sands, and J Peel (eds), *Principles of International Environmental Law* (4th edn, Cambridge University Press 2018)

CHAPTERS

A Daniel, 'Hazardous Substances, Transboundary Impacts' in *Max Planck Encyclopedia of Public International Law* (2009)
A Daniel, 'Hazardous Waste, Transboundary Impacts' in R Wolfrum et al. (eds), *Max Planck Encyclopedia of Public International Law* (2011)
K Kummer Peiry, 'International Chemicals and Waste Management' in M Fitzmaurice, D Ong and P Merkouris (eds), *Research Handbook on International Environmental Law* (Edward Elgar 2010)
K Kummer Peiry, 'Transboundary Movement of Hazardous Waste and Chemicals' in A Nollkaemper and I Plakokefalos (eds), *The Practice of Shared Responsibility in International Law* (Cambridge University Press 2017)
Z Lipman, 'Trade in Hazardous Waste' in S Alam et al. (eds), *International Environmental Law and the Global South* (Cambridge University Press 2015)
Z Lipman, 'Pollution Control and the Regulation of Chemical and E-Waste' in S Alam et al. (eds), *Routledge Handbook of International Environmental Law* (Routledge 2013)

TG Puthucherril, 'Two Decades of the Basel Convention' in S Alam et al. (eds), *Routledge Handbook of International Environmental Law* (Routledge 2013)

G Rose, 'Persistent Organic Pollutants (POPs)' in *Max Planck Encylopedia of Public International Law* (2014)

B Sievers, 'Nuclear Waste Disposal' in R Wolfrum et al. (eds), *Max Planck Encyclopedia of Public International Law* (2011)

ARTICLES

AA Agbor, 'The Ineffectiveness and Inadequacies of International Instruments in Combatting and Ending the Transboundary Movement of Hazardous Wastes and Environmental Degradation in Africa' (2016) 9 African Journal of Legal Studies 235

O Barsalou and MH Picard, 'International Environmental Law in an Era of Globalized Waste' (2018) 17 Chinese Journal of International Law 887

K Dawson, 'Wag the Dog: Towards a Harmonization of the International Hazardous Waste Transfer Regime' (2004) 19(1) Canadian Journal of Law and Society 31

SD Murphy, 'Prospective Liability Regimes for the Transboundary Movement of Hazardous Wastes' (1994) 88(1) American Journal of International Law 24

W Onzivu, '(Re)invigorating the Health Protection Objective of the Basel Convention on Transboundary Movement of Hazardous Wastes and their Disposal' (2013) 33 Legal Studies 621

15
Atmospheric protection

15.1   INTRODUCTION

The protection of the atmosphere encompasses a broad range of legal regimes whose objectives concern protection of the atmosphere from some particular harm. Atmospheric protection is piecemeal in nature. International legal regulation of environmental harm to the atmosphere is predominantly treaty-based. These treaties were invariably adopted as responses to specific problems. The topic can be divided into three areas. First, atmospheric protection concerns control of substances emitted into the atmosphere that cause transboundary pollution harmful to humans, animals or plants. Examples of this are the emission of substances, like sulphur dioxide, that cause acid rain. Second, the emission of certain substances can damage the atmosphere itself, and thereby cause harm to the global environment. The most notable example of this is the emission of hydrofluorocarbons causing depletion of the ozone layer. The third sort of negative environmental consequence arising from emissions into the atmosphere is climate change, namely global environmental harms due to changes in the Earth's atmosphere. The first two of these are considered within this chapter, but climate change is increasingly treated as a separate field of law. Notably, despite some calls for the two regimes to remain connected, climate change was excluded from the ILC's remit for examining atmospheric protection.[1] Climate change is addressed in Chapter 16.

The most significant early engagement by international law with problems concerning the atmosphere was in the *Trail Smelter Arbitration* case. The case was a straightforward instance of transboundary air pollution. Smelting conducted at a Canadian plant released sulphur dioxide into the atmosphere, which was carried over the USA, where it caused acid rain and damage to the environment. The Tribunal held that:[2]

> under the principles of international law, as well as of the law of the United States, no State has the right to use or permit the use of its territory in such a manner as to cause injury by fumes in or to the territory of another or the properties or persons therein, when the case is of serious consequence and the injury is established by clear and convincing evidence.

---

[1]   In line with this, climate change is considered separately in Chapter 16.

[2]   *Trail Smelter Arbitration (United States v. Canada)*, 3 RIAA 1905 (1938 and 1941)

While some other international cases have touched upon atmospheric protection, international courts have had little directly to say upon the topic.[3] The ICJ *Aerial Spraying* case would have provided major judicial consideration of it, but the case was discontinued in 2013.[4]

There is, as of yet, no general international law specific to atmospheric protection. Aspects of air pollution, especially in the form of transboundary harm, have customary status. The International Law Commission, however, has, in its recent work, sought to provide a unified account of the protection of the atmosphere as a discrete field. The outcome so far of this work is the '2021 Draft Guidelines and Preamble on the Protection of the Atmosphere' adopted by the Drafting Committee of the ILC at its Seventy-Second Session. The scope of the project, however, is not to lay down principles and rules of customary international law, and the Preamble makes clear that 'the present draft guidelines were elaborated on the understanding that they were not intended to interfere with relevant political negotiations or to impose on current treaty regimes rules or principles not already contained therein'. In short, the guidelines – even where they use the language of obligation – do not impose any constraints beyond those found in international treaties.

The first, and main, multilateral treaty devoted to transboundary air pollution is the 1979 Convention on Long-Range Transboundary Air Pollution (LRTAP), which entered into force in 1983. The Convention has over 50 states parties from Europe, North America and Central Asia. The catalyst for the Convention was the problem posed by acid rain in the 1960s and 1970s. Acidification caused by emissions of sulphur and nitrogen was observed to cause harm to water sources, soil, vegetation and also to buildings. Other pollutants cause harm to human health. The LRTAP Convention creates a framework for the Europe and North America region to regulate harmful air pollutants. It sets out general commitments and cooperative methods, such as the exchange of information and review of policies, scientific activities and technical measures, to limit, gradually reduce and prevent air pollution. The Convention has eight protocols, which provide for a range of more specific, technical matters directed to particular issues. The majority of the protocols regulate the emissions of a particular substance, and limit emissions to a specified amount, e.g., a percentage reduction compared with a particular baseline. The protocols have also evolved over time. This is most noticeable in the two Sulphur Protocols. The 1985 Protocol lasted until 1993 and was replaced by the 1994 Protocol. The biggest difference to be found is in how the Protocols define emissions reduction targets. The 1985 Protocol adopts a flat rate of 30% compared with 1980 levels for all parties. The 1994 Protocol, informed by different methods adopted in other treaties, including the 1988 NOx Protocol, adopts a more varied approach with a long-term limit on emissions within the 'criti-

---

[3]   *Nuclear Tests (Australia v. France)*, ICJ Reports 253 (1974); *Request for an Examination of the Situation in Accordance with Paragraph 63 of the Court's Judgment of 20 December 1974 in the Nuclear Tests (New Zealand v. France)*, Case, ICJ Reports 288 (1995); Legality of the Threat or Use of Nuclear Weapons, Advisory Opinion, ICJ Reports 226 (1996); *Gabcikovo-Nagymaros Project (Hungary v. Slovakia)*, ICJ Reports 7 (1997); *Pulp Mills on the River Uruguay (Argentina v. Uruguay)*, ICJ Reports 14 (2010)

[4]   *Aerial Herbicide Spraying (Ecuador v. Colombia)*, ICJ Reports 278 (13 September 2013).

cal loads' designated in Annex I of the Protocol, and a shorter-term set of emissions reduction targets with emission ceilings differentiated between parties.

In Asia, in the 1990s, haze caused by air pollution, in particular forest fires, became a major issue of transboundary air pollution. In 2002, members of ASEAN signed an Agreement on Transboundary Haze Pollution. The objective of the Agreement is to prevent and monitor transboundary haze pollution as a result of land or forest fires. The Convention provides for several principles that guide the implementation of the objective, including the precautionary principle and stakeholder participation. The Agreement creates numerous requirements for monitoring, data sharing, prevention, emergency response and technical cooperation.

The 2013 Minamata Mercury Convention is, to date, the only global treaty to address air pollution. It entered into force in 2017 and has over 100 parties. The treaty addresses pollution caused by anthropogenic use of mercury and related compounds. It is not limited in scope to atmospheric emissions, and covers the release of mercury into water sources, storage of waste mercury, and management of contaminated mercury sites.

Regulation of the second type of atmospheric protection, namely ozone protection, is governed by the 1985 Vienna Convention for the Protection of the Ozone Layer and the 1987 Montreal Protocol, which accompanies it.[5] Both treaties are subject to universal ratification (197 parties, including the European Union). The ozone regime has proved remarkably successful. The regime was devised in response to serious concerns arising in the 1960s over the 'hole' in the ozone layer caused by the emission of certain substances, most notably chlorofluorocarbons, which were commonly used as a refrigerant and aerosol propellant. Negotiated under the UNEP, the 1985 Convention creates a framework for international cooperation and to adopt appropriate legislative or administrative measures to control, limit, reduce or prevent human activities that are likely to have adverse effects on the ozone layer.

The 1987 Protocol has proved both greatly successful and also influential on subsequent international environmental law – notably the climate regime and Kyoto Protocol was consciously modelled on the Montreal Protocol. Given its success and popularity, it is easy to overlook the difficulties faced in concluding the Protocol:[6] although the 'hole' in the ozone had been identified, scientific understanding of the causal processes involved and measurement of the problem was still in its early stages. The Protocol creates, at its core, technically complex obligations controlling the emissions (and trade) of certain substances known to contribute to ozone depletion, and new regulations for substances are added by amendments to the Protocol as knowledge develops. In addition, it provides for technical assistance, reporting and institutional arrangements. A significant innovation was the inclusion of a financial mechanism for the purposes of providing financial and technical cooperation to developing countries. This provides for technology transfer and also the creation of a financial body, called the

---

[5]   To date, the 1987 Protocol has been the subject of five amendments: London 29 June 1990, entered into force 10 August 1992; Copenhagen, 25 November 1992, entered into force 14 June 1994; Montreal, 25 September 1997, entered into force 10 November 1999; Beijing, 17 December 1999, entered into force 25 February 2002; and Kigali, 15 October 2016, entered into force 1 January 2019.

[6]   For an account of the negotiations, see R Benedick, *Ozone Diplomacy* (Harvard UP 1991).

Multilateral Fund, to provide funding support to developing countries in order to help them meet their commitments.

15.2   AIR POLLUTION

1979 Convention on Long-Range Transboundary Air Pollution, 1302 UNTS 217

Article 1: DEFINITIONS
For the purposes of the present Convention:
(a)   "Air Pollution" means the introduction by man, directly or indirectly, of substances or energy into the air resulting in deleterious effects of such a nature as to endanger human health, harm living resources and ecosystems and material property and impair or interfere with amenities and other legitimate uses of the environment, and "air pollutants" shall be construed accordingly;
(b)   "Long-range transboundary air pollution" means air pollution whose physical origin is situated wholly or in part within the area under the national jurisdiction of one State and which has adverse effects in the area under the jurisdiction of another State at such a distance that it is not generally possible to distinguish the contribution of individual emission sources or groups of sources.

Article 2: FUNDAMENTAL PRINCIPLES
The Contracting Parties, taking due account of the facts and problems involved, are determined to protect man and his environment against air pollution and shall endeavour to limit and, as far as possible, gradually reduce and prevent air pollution including long-range transboundary air pollution.

Article 3:
The Contracting Parties, within the framework of the present Convention, shall by means of exchanges of information, consultation, research and monitoring, develop without undue delay policies and strategies which shall serve as a means of combating the discharge of air pollutants, taking into account efforts already made at national and international levels.

Article 4:
The Contracting Parties shall exchange information on and review their policies, scientific activities and technical measures aimed at combating, as far as possible, the discharge of air pollutants which may have adverse effects, thereby contributing to the reduction of air pollution including long- range transboundary air pollution.

Article 5:
Consultations shall be held, upon request, at an early stage between, on the one hand, Contracting Parties which are actually affected by or exposed to a significant risk of long-range transboundary air pollution and, on the other hand, Contracting Parties within which and subject to whose jurisdiction a significant contribution to long-range trans-

boundary air pollution originates, or could originate, in connection with activities carried on or contemplated therein.

Article 6: AIR QUALITY MANAGEMENT

Taking into account articles 2 to 5, the ongoing research, exchange of information and monitoring and the results thereof, the cost and effectiveness of local and other remedies and, in order to combat air pollution, in particular that originating from new or rebuilt installations, each Contracting Party undertakes to develop the best policies and strategies including air quality management systems and, as part of them, control measures compatible with balanced development, in particular by using the best available technology which is economically feasible and low- and non-waste technology.

Article 7: RESEARCH AND DEVELOPMENT

The Contracting Parties, as appropriate to their needs, shall initiate and co-operate in the conduct of research into and/or development of:

(a)   Existing and proposed technologies for reducing emissions of sulphur compounds and other major air pollutants, including technical and economic feasibility, and environmental consequences;

(b)   Instrumentation and other techniques for monitoring and measuring emission rates and ambient concentrations of air pollutants;

(c)   Improved models for a better understanding of the transmission of long-range transboundary air pollutants;

(d)   The effects of sulphur compounds and other major air pollutants on human health and the environment, including agriculture, forestry, materials, aquatic and other natural ecosystems and visibility, with a view to establishing a scientific basis for dose/effect relationships designed to protect the environment;

(e)   The economic, social and environmental assessment of alternative measures for attaining environmental objectives including the reduction of long-range transboundary air pollution;

(f)   Education and training programmes related to the environmental aspects of pollution by sulphur compounds and other major air pollutants.

Article 8: EXCHANGE OF INFORMATION

The Contracting Parties, within the framework of the Executive Body referred to in article 10 and bilaterally, shall, in their common interests, exchange available information on:

(a)   Data on emissions at periods of time to be agreed upon, of agreed air pollutants, starting with sulphur dioxide, coming from grid-units of agreed size; or on the fluxes of agreed air pollutants, starting with sulphur dioxide, across national borders, at distances and at periods of time to be agreed upon;

(b)   Major changes in national policies and in general industrial development, and their potential impact, which would be likely to cause significant changes in long-range transboundary air pollution;

(c)   Control technologies for reducing air pollution relevant to long-range transboundary air pollution;

(d)   The projected cost of the emission control of sulphur compounds and other major air pollutants on a national scale;

(e)   Meteorological and physico-chemical data relating to the processes during transmission;

(f)   Physico-chemical and biological data relating to the effects of long-range trans-boundary air pollution and the extent of the damage 1/ which these data indicate can be attributed to long-range transboundary air pollution;

(g)   National, sub-regional and regional policies and strategies for the control of sulphur compounds and other major air pollutants.

Article 9: IMPLEMENTATION AND FURTHER DEVELOPMENT OF THE COOPERATIVE PROGRAMME FOR THE MONITORING AND EVALUATION OF THE LONG-RANGE TRANSMISSION OF AIR POLLUTANTS IN EUROPE

The Contracting Parties stress the need for the implementation of the existing "Cooperative programme for the monitoring and evaluation of the long-range transmission of air pollut-ants in Europe" (hereinafter referred to as EMEP) and, with regard to the further develop-ment of this programme, agree to emphasize:

(a)   The desirability of Contracting Parties joining in and fully implementing EMEP which, as a first step, is based on the monitoring of sulphur dioxide and related substances;

(b)   The need to use comparable or standardized procedures for monitoring whenever possible;

(c)   The desirability of basing the monitoring programme on the framework of both national and international programmes. The establishment of monitoring stations and the collection of data shall be carried out under the national jurisdiction of the country in which the monitoring stations are located;

(d)   The desirability of establishing a framework for a cooperative environmental mon-itoring programme, based on and taking into account present and future national, sub-regional, regional and other international programmes;

(e)   The need to exchange data on emissions at periods of time to be agreed upon, of agreed air pollutants, starting with sulphur dioxide, coming from grid-units of agreed size; or on the fluxes of agreed air pollutants, starting with sulphur dioxide, across national borders, at distances and at periods of time to be agreed upon. The method, including the model, used to determine the fluxes, as well as the method, including the model used to determine the transmission of air pollutants based on the emissions per grid-unit, shall be made available and periodically reviewed, in order to improve the methods and the models;

(f)   Their willingness to continue the exchange and periodic updating of national data on total emissions of agreed air pollutants, starting with sulphur dioxide;

    1   The present Convention does not contain a rule on State liability as to damage.

(g)   the need to provide meteorological and physico-chemical data relating to processes during transmission;

(h)   the need to monitor chemical components in other media such as water, soil and vegetation, as well as a similar monitoring programme to record effects on health and environment;

(i)   the desirability of extending the national EMEP networks to make them opera-tional for control and surveillance purposes.

1984 Protocol to the 1979 Convention on Long-range Transboundary Air Pollution on Long-term Financing of the Co-operative Programme for Monitoring and Evaluation of the Long-range Transmission of Air Pollutants in Europe (28 September 1984, entered into force 28 January 1988) 1491 UNTS 167

Article 2
The financing of BHBP shall cover the annual costs of the international centres co-operating within BHBP for the activities appearing in the work progress of the Steering Body of BHEP.

Article 3
Contributions
1. In accordance with the provisions of this article the financing of BHBP shall consist of mandatory contributions, supplemented by voluntary contributions. Contributions may be made in convertible currency, non-convertible currency, or in kind.
2. Mandatory contributions shall be made on an annual basis by all Contracting Parties to the present Protocol which are within the geographical scope of BHBP.
3. Voluntary contributions may be made by the Contracting Parties or Signatories to the present Protocol, even if their territory lies outside the geographical scope of BHBP, as well as, subject to approval by the Executive Body, on the recommendation of the steering Body of BHBP, by any other country, organization or individual which wishes to contribute to the work programme.

1985 Helsinki Protocol to the 1979 Convention on Long-Range Transboundary Air Pollution on the Reduction of Sulphur Emissions or their Transboundary Fluxes by at least 30 per cent, 1480 UNTS 215

Article 2
BASIC PROVISIONS
The Parties shall reduce their national annual sulphur emissions or their transboundary fluxes by at least 30 per cent as soon as possible and at the latest by 1993, using 1980 levels as the basis for calculation of reductions.

Article 3
FURTHER REDUCTIONS
The Parties recognize the need for each of them to study at the national level the necessity for further reductions, beyond those referred to in article 2, of sulphur emissions or their transboundary fluxes when environmental conditions warrant.

[...]

1988 Sofia Protocol to the 1979 Convention on Long-Range Transboundary Air Pollution concerning the Control of Emissions of Nitrogen Oxides or their Transboundary Fluxes, 1593 UNTS 287

Article 2
BASIC OBLIGATIONS

1. The Parties shall, as soon as possible and as a first step, take effective measures to control and/or reduce their national annual emissions of nitrogen oxides or their transboundary fluxes so that these, at the latest by 31 December 1994, do not exceed their national annual emissions of nitrogen oxides or transboundary fluxes of such emissions for the calendar year 1987 or any previous year to be specified upon signature of, or accession to, the Protocol, provided that in addition, with respect to any Party specifying such a previous year, its national average annual transboundary fluxes or national average annual emissions of nitrogen oxides for the period from 1 January 1987 to 1 January 1996 do not exceed its transboundary fluxes or national emissions for the calendar year 1987.

1991 Protocol to the 1979 Convention on Long-Range Transboundary Air Pollution concerning the Control of Emissions of Volatile Organic Compounds or their Transboundary Fluxes, 2001 UNTS 187

Article 1
DEFINITIONS For the purposes of the present Protocol,

...

9. "Volatile organic compounds", or "VOCs", means, unless otherwise specified, all organic compounds of anthropogenic nature, other than methane, that are capable of producing photochemical oxidants by reactions with nitrogen oxides in the presence of sunlight;

...

13. "Photochemical ozone creation potential" (POCP) means the potential of an individual VOC, relative to that of other VOCs, to form ozone by reaction with oxides of nitrogen in the presence of sunlight, as described in annex IV.

Article 2
BASIC OBLIGATIONS

1. The Parties shall control and reduce their emissions of VOCs in order to reduce their transboundary fluxes and the fluxes of the resulting secondary photochemical oxidant products so as to protect human health and the environment from adverse effects.

2. Each Party shall, in order to meet the requirements of paragraph 1 above, control and reduce its national annual emissions of VOCs or their transboundary fluxes in any one of the following ways to be specified upon signature:

(a)   It shall, as soon as possible and as a first step, take effective measures to reduce its national annual emissions of VOCs by at least 30 per cent by the year 1999, using 1988 levels as a basis or any other annual level during the period 1984 to 1990, which it may specify upon signature of or accession to the present Protocol; or

(b)   Where its annual emissions contribute to tropospheric ozone concentrations in areas under the jurisdiction of one or more other Parties, and such emissions originate only from areas under its jurisdiction that are specified as TOMAs in annex I, it shall, as soon as possible and as a first step, take effective measures to:

     (i)   Reduce its annual emissions of VOCs from the areas so specified by at least 30 per cent by the year 1999, using 1988 levels as a basis or any other annual level during the period 1984–1990, which it may specify upon signature of or accession to the present Protocol; and

     (ii)   Ensure that its total national annual emissions of VOCs by the year 1999 do not exceed the 1988 levels; or

(c)   Where its national annual emissions of VOCs were in 1988 lower than 500,000 tonnes and 20 kg/inhabitant and 5 tonnes/km2, it shall, as soon as possible and as a first step, take effective measures to ensure at least that at the latest by the year 1999 its national annual emissions of VOCs do not exceed the 1988 levels.

[…]

4.   In carrying out their obligations under this article, Parties are invited to give highest priority to reduction and control of emissions of substances with the greatest POCP, taking into consideration the information contained in annex IV.

5.   In implementing the present Protocol, and in particular any product substitution measures, Parties shall take appropriate steps to ensure that toxic and carcinogenic VOCs, and those that harm the stratospheric ozone layer, are not substituted for other VOCs.

1994 Oslo Protocol to the 1979 Convention on Long-Range Transboundary Air Pollution on Further Reduction of Sulphur Emissions, 2030 UNTS 122

Article 2
BASIC OBLIGATIONS

1.   The Parties shall control and reduce their sulphur emissions in order to protect human health and the environment from adverse effects, in particular acidifying effects, and to ensure, as far as possible, without entailing excessive costs, that depositions of oxidized sulphur compounds in the long term do not exceed critical loads for sulphur given, in annex I, as critical sulphur depositions, in accordance with present scientific knowledge.

2.   As a first step, the Parties shall, as a minimum, reduce and maintain their annual sulphur emissions in accordance with the timing and levels specified in annex II.

3.   In addition, any Party:

(a)   Whose total land area is greater than 2 million square kilometres;

(b)   Which has committed itself under paragraph 2 above to a national sulphur emission ceiling no greater than the lesser of its 1990 emissions or its obligation in the 1985 Helsinki Protocol on the Reduction of Sulphur Emissions or Their Transboundary Fluxes by at least 30 per cent, as indicated in annex II;

(c)   Whose annual sulphur emissions that contribute to acidification in areas under the jurisdiction of one or more other Parties originate only from within areas under its jurisdiction that are listed as SOMAs in annex III, and has presented documentation to this effect; and

(d)   Which has specified upon signature of, or accession to, the present Protocol its intention to act in accordance with this paragraph, shall, as a minimum, reduce and maintain its annual sulphur emissions in the area so listed in accordance with the timing and levels specified in annex II.

[...]

5.   Each Party, except those Parties subject to the United States/Canada Air Quality Agreement of 1991, shall as a minimum:

(a)   Apply emission limit values at least as stringent as those specified in annex V to all major new stationary combustion sources;

(b)   No later than 1 July 2004 apply, as far as possible without entailing excessive costs, emission limit values at least as stringent as those specified in annex V to those major existing stationary combustion sources the thermal input of which is above 500 MWth taking into account the remaining lifetime of a plant, calculated from the date of entry into force of the present Protocol, or apply equivalent emission limitations or other appropriate provisions, provided that these achieve the sulphur emission ceilings specified in annex II and, subsequently, further approach the critical loads as given in annex I; and no later than 1 July 2004 apply emission limit values or emission limitations to those major existing stationary combustion sources the thermal input of which is between 50 and 500 MWth using annex V as guidance;

(c)   No later than two years after the date of entry into force of the present Protocol apply national standards for the sulphur content of gas oil at least as stringent as those specified in annex V. In cases where the supply of gas oil cannot otherwise be ensured, a State may extend the time period given in this subparagraph to a period of to ten years. In this case it shall specify, in a declaration to be deposited together with the instrument of ratification, acceptance, approval or accession, its intention to extend the time period.

6.   The Parties may, in addition, apply economic instruments to encourage the adoption of cost-effective approaches to the reduction of sulphur emissions.

1998 Aarhus Protocol to the 1979 Convention on Long-Range Transboundary Air Pollution on Heavy Metals, 2237 UNTS 4

Article 2
OBJECTIVE

The objective of the present Protocol is to control emissions of heavy metals caused by anthropogenic activities that are subject to long-range transboundary atmospheric transport and are likely to have significant adverse effects on human health or the environment, in accordance with the provisions of the following articles.

Article 3
BASIC OBLIGATIONS

1.   Each Party shall reduce its total annual emissions into the atmosphere of each of the heavy metals listed in annex I from the level of the emission in the reference year set in accordance with that annex by taking effective measures, appropriate to its particular circumstances.

2.   Each Party shall, no later than the timescales specified in annex IV, apply:

   (a)   The best available techniques, taking into consideration annex III, to each new stationary source within a major stationary source category for which annex III identifies best available techniques;

   (b)   The limit values specified in annex V to each new stationary source within a major stationary source category. A Party may, as an alternative, apply different emission reduction strategies that achieve equivalent overall emission levels;

   (c)   The best available techniques, taking into consideration annex III, to each existing stationary source within a major stationary source category for which annex III identifies best available techniques. A Party may, as an alternative, apply different emission reduction strategies that achieve equivalent overall emission reductions;

   (d)   The limit values specified in annex V to each existing stationary source within a major stationary source category, insofar as this is technically and economically feasible. A Party may, as an alternative, apply different emission reduction strategies that achieve equivalent overall emission reductions.

3.   Each Party shall apply product control measures in accordance with the conditions and timescales specified in annex VI.

1998 Aarhus Protocol to the 1979 Convention on Long-Range Transboundary Air Pollution on Persistent Organic Pollutants, 2230 UNTS 79

Article 2
OBJECTIVE

The objective of the present Protocol is to control, reduce or eliminate discharges, emissions and losses of persistent organic pollutants.

Article 3

BASIC OBLIGATIONS

1. Except where specifically exempted in accordance with article 4, each Party shall take effective measures:

    (a) To eliminate the production and use of the substances listed in annex I in accordance with the implementation requirements specified therein;

    (b)

        (i) To ensure that, when the substances listed in annex I are destroyed or disposed of, such destruction or disposal is undertaken in an environmentally sound manner, taking into account relevant subregional, regional and global regimes governing the management of hazardous wastes and their disposal, in particular the Basel Convention on the Control of Transboundary Movements of Hazardous Wastes and their Disposal;

        (ii) To endeavour to ensure that the disposal of substances listed in annex I is carried out domestically, taking into account pertinent environmental considerations;

        (iii) To ensure that the transboundary movement of the substances listed in annex I is conducted in an environmentally sound manner, taking into consideration applicable subregional, regional, and global regimes governing the transboundary movement of hazardous wastes, in particular the Basel Convention on the Control of Transboundary Movements of Hazardous Wastes and their Disposal;

    (c) To restrict the substances listed in annex II to the uses described, in accordance with the implementation requirements specified therein.

2. The requirements specified in paragraph 1 (b) above shall become effective for each substance upon the date that production or use of that substance is eliminated, whichever is later.

3. For substances listed in annex I, II, or III, each Party should develop appropriate strategies for identifying articles still in use and wastes containing such substances, and shall take appropriate measures to ensure that such wastes and such articles, upon becoming wastes, are destroyed or disposed of in an environmentally sound manner.

4. For the purposes of paragraphs 1 to 3 above, the terms waste, disposal, and environmentally sound shall be interpreted in a manner consistent with the use of those terms under the Basel Convention on the Control of Transboundary Movements of Hazardous Wastes and their Disposal.

5. Each Party shall:

    (a) Reduce its total annual emissions of each of the substances listed in annex III from the level of the emission in a reference year set in accordance with that annex by taking effective measures, appropriate in its particular circumstances;

    (b) No later than the timescales specified in annex VI, apply:

        (i) The best available techniques, taking into consideration annex V, to each new stationary source within a major stationary source category for which annex V identifies best available techniques;

(ii)   Limit values at least as stringent as those specified in annex IV to each new stationary source within a category mentioned in that annex, taking into consideration annex V. A Party may, as an alternative, apply different emission reduction strategies that achieve equivalent overall emission levels;

(iii)   The best available techniques, taking into consideration annex V, to each existing stationary source within a major stationary source category for which annex V identifies best available techniques, insofar as this is technically and economically feasible. A Party may, as an alternative, apply different emission reduction strategies that achieve equivalent overall emission reductions;

(iv)   Limit values at least as stringent as those specified in annex IV to each existing stationary source within a category mentioned in that annex, insofar as this is technically and economically feasible, taking into consideration annex V. A Party may, as an alternative, apply different emission reduction strategies that achieve equivalent overall emission reductions;

(v)   Effective measures to control emissions from mobile sources, taking into consideration annex VII.

6.   In the case of residential combustion sources, the obligations set out in paragraph 5 (b) (i) and (iii) above shall refer to all stationary sources in that category taken together.

1999 Gothenburg Protocol to the 1979 Convention on Long-range Transboundary Air Pollution to Abate Acidification, Eutrophication and Ground-level Ozone, 2319 UNTS 81

Article 2
OBJECTIVE

The objective of the present Protocol is to control and reduce emissions of sulphur, nitrogen oxides, ammonia and volatile organic compounds that are caused by anthropogenic activities and are likely to cause adverse effects on human health, natural ecosystems, materials and crops, due to acidification, eutrophication or ground-level ozone as a result of long-range transboundary atmospheric transport, and to ensure, as far as possible, that in the long term and in a stepwise approach, taking into account advances in scientific knowledge, atmospheric depositions or concentrations do not exceed:

(a)   For Parties within the geographical scope of EMEP and Canada, the critical loads of acidity, as described in annex I;

(b)   For Parties within the geographical scope of EMEP, the critical loads of nutrient nitrogen, as described in annex I; and

(c)   For ozone:

(i)   For Parties within the geographical scope of EMEP, the critical levels of ozone, as given in annex I;

(ii)   For Canada, the Canada-wide Standard for ozone; and

(iii)   For the United States of America, the National Ambient Air Quality Standard for ozone.

Article 3

BASIC OBLIGATIONS

1.   Each Party having an emission ceiling in any table in annex II shall reduce and maintain the reduction in its annual emissions in accordance with that ceiling and the timescales specified in that annex. Each Party shall, as a minimum, control its annual emissions of polluting compounds in accordance with the obligations in annex II.

2.   Each Party shall apply the limit values specified in annexes IV, V and VI to each new stationary source within a stationary source category as identified in those annexes, no later than the timescales specified in annex VII. As an alternative, a Party may apply different emission reduction strategies that achieve equivalent overall emission levels for all source categories together.

3.   Each Party shall, in so far as it is technically and economically feasible and taking into consideration the costs and advantages, apply the limit values specified in annexes IV, V and VI to each existing stationary source within a stationary source category as identified in those annexes, no later than the timescales specified in annex VII. As an alternative, a Party may apply different emission reduction strategies that achieve equivalent overall emission levels for all source categories together or, for Parties outside the geographical scope of EMEP, that are necessary to achieve national or regional goals for acidification abatement and to meet national air quality standards.

2002 ASEAN Agreement on Transboundary Haze Pollution

Article 2 Objective

The objective of this Agreement is to prevent and monitor transboundary haze pollution as a result of land and/or forest fires which should be mitigated, through concerted national efforts and intensified regional and international co-operation. This should be pursued in the overall context of sustainable development and in accordance with the provisions of this Agreement.

Article 3 Principles

The Parties shall be guided by the following principles in the implementation of this Agreement:

1.   The Parties have, in accordance with the Charter of the United Nations and the principles of international law, the sovereign right to exploit their own resources pursuant to their own environmental and developmental policies, and the responsibility to ensure that activities within their jurisdiction or control do not cause damage to the environment and harm to human health of other States or of areas beyond the limits of national jurisdiction.

2.   The Parties shall, in the spirit of solidarity and partnership and in accordance with their respective needs, capabilities and situations, strengthen co-operation and co-ordination to prevent and monitor transboundary haze pollution as a result of land and/or forest fires which should be mitigated.

3.   The Parties should take precautionary measures to anticipate, prevent and monitor transboundary haze pollution as a result of land and/or forest fires which should be mitigated, to minimise its adverse effects. Where there are threats of serious or

irreversible damage from transboundary haze pollution, even without full scientific certainty, precautionary measures shall be taken by Parties concerned.

4.   The Parties should manage and use their natural resources, including forest and land resources, in an ecologically sound and sustainable manner.

5.   The Parties, in addressing transboundary haze pollution, should involve, as appropriate, all stakeholders, including local communities, non-governmental organisations, farmers and private enterprises.

Article 4 General Obligations

In pursuing the objective of this Agreement, the Parties shall:

1.   Co-operate in developing and implementing measures to prevent and monitor transboundary haze pollution as a result of land and/or forest fires which should be mitigated, and to control sources of fires, including by the identification of fires, development of monitoring, assessment and early warning systems, exchange of information and technology, and the provision of mutual assistance.

2.   When the transboundary haze pollution originates from within their territories, respond promptly to a request for relevant information or consultations sought by a State or States that are or may be affected by such transboundary haze pollution, with a view to minimising the consequences of the transboundary haze pollution.

3.   Take legislative, administrative and/or other measures to implement their obligations under this Agreement.

[...]

Article 9 Prevention

Each Party shall undertake measures to prevent and control activities related to land and/ or forest fires that may lead to transboundary haze pollution, which include:

a.   Developing and implementing legislative and other regulatory measures, as well as programmes and strategies to promote zero burning policy to deal with land and/ or forest fires resulting in transboundary haze pollution;

b.   Developing other appropriate policies to curb activities that may lead to land and/ or forest fires;

c.   Identifying and monitoring areas prone to occurrence of land and/or forest fires;

d.   Strengthening local fire management and firefighting capability and co-ordination to prevent the occurrence of land and/or forest fires;

e.   Promoting public education and awareness-building campaigns and strengthening community participation in fire management to prevent land and/or forest fires and haze pollution arising from such fires;

f.   Promoting and utilising indigenous knowledge and practices in fire prevention and management; and

g.   Ensuring that legislative, administrative and/or other relevant measures are taken to control open burning and to prevent land clearing using fire.

Article 10 Preparedness

1.   The Parties shall, jointly or individually, develop strategies and response plans to identify, manage and control risks to human health and the environment arising from land and/or forest fires and related haze pollution arising from such fires.

2.   The Parties shall, as appropriate, prepare standard operating procedures for regional co-operation and national action required under this Agreement.

2013 Minamata Convention on Mercury

Article 1
Objective
The objective of this Convention is to protect the human health and the environment from anthropogenic emissions and releases of mercury and mercury compounds.

[…]

Article 8
Emissions
1.   This Article concerns controlling and, where feasible, reducing emissions of mercury and mercury compounds, often expressed as "total mercury", to the atmosphere through measures to control emissions from the point sources falling within the source categories listed in Annex D.
2.   For the purposes of this Article:
   (a)   "Emissions" means emissions of mercury or mercury compounds to the atmosphere;
   (b)   "Relevant source" means a source falling within one of the source categories listed in Annex D. A Party may, if it chooses, establish criteria to identify the sources covered within a source category listed in Annex D so long as those criteria for any category include at least 75 per cent of the emissions from that category;
   (c)   "New source" means any relevant source within a category listed in Annex D, the construction or substantial modification of which is commenced at least one year after the date of:
      (i)   Entry into force of this Convention for the Party concerned; or
      (ii)   Entry into force for the Party concerned of an amendment to Annex D where the source becomes subject to the provisions of this Convention only by virtue of that amendment;
   (d)   "Substantial modification" means modification of a relevant source that results in a significant increase in emissions, excluding any change in emissions resulting from by-product recovery. It shall be a matter for the Party to decide whether a modification is substantial or not;
   (e)   "Existing source" means any relevant source that is not a new source;
   (f)   "Emission limit value" means a limit on the concentration, mass or emission rate of mercury or mercury compounds, often expressed as "total mercury", emitted from a point source.
3.   A Party with relevant sources shall take measures to control emissions and may prepare a national plan setting out the measures to be taken to control emissions and its expected targets, goals and outcomes. Any plan shall be submitted to the Conference of the Parties within four years of the date of entry into force of the Convention for that Party. If a Party develops an implementation plan in accord-

ance with Article 20, the Party may include in it the plan prepared pursuant to this paragraph.

4.   For its new sources, each Party shall require the use of best available techniques and best environmental practices to control and, where feasible, reduce emissions, as soon as practicable but no later than five years after the date of entry into force of the Convention for that Party. A Party may use emission limit values that are consistent with the application of best available techniques.

5.   For its existing sources, each Party shall include in any national plan, and shall implement, one or more of the following measures, taking into account its national circumstances, and the economic and technical feasibility and affordability of the measures, as soon as practicable but no more than ten years after the date of entry into force of the Convention for it:

(a)   A quantified goal for controlling and, where feasible, reducing emissions from relevant sources;

(b)   Emission limit values for controlling and, where feasible, reducing emissions from relevant sources;

(c)   The use of best available techniques and best environmental practices to control emissions from relevant sources;

(d)   A multi-pollutant control strategy that would deliver co-benefits for control of mercury emissions;

(e)   Alternative measures to reduce emissions from relevant sources.

6.   Parties may apply the same measures to all relevant existing sources or may adopt different measures in respect of different source categories. The objective shall be for those measures applied by a Party to achieve reasonable progress in reducing emissions over time.

7.   Each Party shall establish, as soon as practicable and no later than five years after the date of entry into force of the Convention for it, and maintain thereafter, an inventory of emissions from relevant sources.

8.   The Conference of the Parties shall, at its first meeting, adopt guidance on:

(a)   Best available techniques and on best environmental practices, taking into account any difference between new and existing sources and the need to minimize cross-media effects; and

(b)   Support for Parties in implementing the measures set out in paragraph 5, in particular in determining goals and in setting emission limit values.

9.   The Conference of the Parties shall, as soon as practicable, adopt guidance on:

(a)   Criteria that Parties may develop pursuant to paragraph 2 (b);

(b)   The methodology for preparing inventories of emissions.

10.   The Conference of the Parties shall keep under review, and update as appropriate, the guidance developed pursuant to paragraphs 8 and 9. Parties shall take the guidance into account in implementing the relevant provisions of this Article.

11.   Each Party shall include information on its implementation of this Article in its reports submitted pursuant to Article 21, in particular information concerning the measures it has taken in accordance with paragraphs 4 to 7 and the effectiveness of the measures.

15.3   OZONE DEPLETION

1985 Vienna Convention for the Protection of the Ozone Layer, 1513 UNTS 293

Article 1: Definitions

For the purposes of this Convention:

1.   "The ozone layer" means the layer of atmospheric ozone above the planetary boundary layer.
2.   "Adverse effects" means changes in the physical environment or biota, including changes in climate, which have significant deleterious effects on human health or on the composition, resilience and productivity of natural and managed ecosystems, or on materials useful to mankind.
3.   "Alternative technologies or equipment" means technologies or equipment the use of which makes it possible to reduce or effectively eliminate emissions of substances which have or are likely to have adverse effects on the ozone layer.
4.   "Alternative substances" means substances which reduce, eliminate or avoid adverse effects on the ozone layer.
5.   "Parties" means, unless the text otherwise indicates, Parties to this Convention.
6.   "Regional economic integration organization" means an organization constituted by sovereign States of a given region which has competence in respect of matters governed by this Convention or its protocols and has been duly authorized, in accordance with its internal procedures, to sign, ratify, accept, approve or accede to the instruments concerned.
7.   "Protocols" means protocols to this Convention.

Article 2: General obligations

1.   The Parties shall take appropriate measures in accordance with the provisions of this Convention and of those protocols in force to which they are party to protect human health and the environment against adverse effects resulting or likely to result from human activities which modify or are likely to modify the ozone layer.
2.   To this end the Parties shall, in accordance with the means at their disposal and their capabilities:
     (a)   Co-operate by means of systematic observations, research and information exchange in order to better understand and assess the effects of human activities on the ozone layer and the effects on human health and the environment from modification of the ozone layer;
     (b)   Adopt appropriate legislative or administrative measures and co-operate in harmonizing appropriate policies to control, limit, reduce or prevent human activities under their jurisdiction or control should it be found that these activities have or are likely to have adverse effects resulting from modification or likely modification of the ozone layer;
     (c)   Co-operate in the formulation of agreed measures, procedures and standards for the implementation of this Convention, with a view to the adoption of protocols and annexes;
     (d)   Co-operate with competent international bodies to implement effectively this Convention and protocols to which they are party.

3.   The provisions of this Convention shall in no way affect the right of Parties to adopt, in accordance with international law, domestic measures additional to those referred to in paragraphs 1 and 2 above, nor shall they affect additional domestic measures already taken by a Party, provided that these measures are not incompatible with their obligations under this Convention.

4.   The application of this article shall be based on relevant scientific and technical considerations.

Article 3: Research and systematic observations and as further elaborated in annexes I and II.

1.   The Parties undertake, as appropriate, to initiate and co-operate in, directly or through competent international bodies, the conduct of research and scientific assessments on:

(a)   The physical and chemical processes that may affect the ozone layer;

(b)   The human health and other biological effects deriving from any modifications of the ozone layer, particularly those resulting from changes in ultra-violet solar radiation having biological effects (UV-B);

(c)   Climatic effects deriving from any modifications of the ozone layer;

(d)   Effects deriving from any modifications of the ozone layer and any consequent change in UV-B radiation on natural and synthetic materials useful to mankind;

(e)   Substances, practices, processes and activities that may affect the ozone layer, and their cumulative effects;

(f)   Alternative substances and technologies;

(g)   Related socio-economic matters;

2.   The Parties undertake to promote or establish, as appropriate, directly or through competent international bodies and taking fully into account national legislation and relevant ongoing activities at both the national and international levels, joint or complementary programmes for systematic observation of the state of the ozone layer and other relevant parameters, as elaborated in annex I.

3.   The Parties undertake to co-operate, directly or through competent international bodies, in ensuring the collection, validation and transmission of research and observational data through appropriate world data centres in a regular and timely fashion.

Article 4: Co-operation in the legal, scientific and technical fields

1.   The Parties shall facilitate and encourage the exchange of scientific, technical, socio-economic, commercial and legal information relevant to this Convention as further elaborated in annex II. Such information shall be supplied to bodies agreed upon by the Parties. Any such body receiving information regarded as confidential by the supplying Party shall ensure that such information is not disclosed and shall aggregate it to protect its confidentiality before it is made available to all Parties.

2.   The Parties shall co-operate, consistent with their national laws, regulations and practices and taking into account in particular the needs of the developing countries, in promoting, directly or through competent international bodies, the development and transfer of technology and knowledge. Such co-operation shall be carried out particularly through:

(a)   Facilitation of the acquisition of alternative technologies by other Parties;
(b)   Provision of information on alternative technologies and equipment, and supply of special manuals or guides to them;
(c)   The supply of necessary equipment and facilities for research and systematic observations;
(d)   Appropriate training of scientific and technical personnel.

1987 Montreal Protocol on Substances that Deplete the Ozone Layer, 1522 UNTS 3

Article 1: Definitions
For the purposes of this Protocol:
1.   "Convention" means the Vienna Convention for the Protection of the Ozone Layer, adopted on 22 March 1985.
2.   "Parties" means, unless the text otherwise indicates, Parties to this Protocol.
3.   "Secretariat" means the Secretariat of the Convention.
4.   "Controlled substance" means a substance in Annex A, Annex B, Annex C, Annex E or Annex F to this Protocol, whether existing alone or in a mixture. It includes the isomers of any such substance, except as specified in the relevant Annex, but excludes any controlled substance or mixture which is in a manufactured product other than a container used for the transportation or storage of that substance.
5.   "Production" means the amount of controlled substances produced, minus the amount destroyed by technologies to be approved by the Parties and minus the amount entirely used as feedstock in the manufacture of other chemicals. The amount recycled and reused is not to be considered as "production".
6.   "Consumption" means production plus imports minus exports of controlled substances.
7.   "Calculated levels" of production, imports, exports and consumption means levels determined in accordance with Article 3.
8.   "Industrial rationalization" means the transfer of all or a portion of the calculated level of production of one Party to another, for the purpose of achieving economic efficiencies or responding to anticipated shortfalls in supply as a result of plant closures.

Article 2: Control Measures
1.   Incorporated in Article 2A.
2.   Replaced by Article 2B.
3.   Replaced by Article 2A.
4.   Replaced by Article 2A.
5.   Any Party may, for one or more control periods, transfer to another Party any portion of its calculated level of production set out in Articles 2A to 2F, Articles 2H and 2J, provided that the total combined calculated levels of production of the Parties concerned for any group of controlled substances do not exceed the production limits set out in those Articles for that group. Such transfer of production shall be notified to the Secretariat by each of the Parties concerned, stating the terms of such transfer and the period for which it is to apply.
5. *bis.* Any Party not operating under paragraph 1 of Article 5 may, for one or more control periods, transfer to another such Party any portion of its calculated level of

consumption set out in Article 2F, provided that the calculated level of consumption of controlled substances in Group I of Annex A of the Party transferring the portion of its calculated level of consumption did not exceed 0.25 kilograms per capita in 1989 and that the total combined calculated levels of consumption of the Parties concerned do not exceed the consumption limits set out in Article 2F. Such transfer of consumption shall be notified to the Secretariat by each of the Parties concerned, stating the terms of such transfer and the period for which it is to apply.

6. Any Party not operating under Article 5, that has facilities for the production of Annex A or Annex B controlled substances under construction, or contracted for, prior to 16 September 1987, and provided for in national legislation prior to 1 January 1987, may add the production from such facilities to its 1986 production of such substances for the purposes of determining its calculated level of production for 1986, provided that such facilities are completed by 31 December 1990 and that such production does not raise that Party's annual calculated level of consumption of the controlled substances above 0.5 kilograms per capita.

7. Any transfer of production pursuant to paragraph 5 or any addition of production pursuant to paragraph 6 shall be notified to the Secretariat, no later than the time of the transfer or addition.

8. (a) Any Parties which are Member States of a regional economic integration organization as defined in Article 1 (6) of the Convention may agree that they shall jointly fulfil their obligations respecting consumption under this Article and Articles 2A to 2J provided that their total combined calculated level of consumption does not exceed the levels required by this Article and Articles 2A to 2J. Any such agreement may be extended to include obligations respecting consumption or production under Article 2J provided that the total combined calculated level of consumption or production of the Parties concerned does not exceed the levels required by Article 2J.

(b) The Parties to any such agreement shall inform the Secretariat of the terms of the agreement before the date of the reduction in consumption with which the agreement is concerned.

(c) Such agreement will become operative only if all Member States of the regional economic integration organization and the organization concerned are Parties to the Protocol and have notified the Secretariat of their manner of implementation.

9. (a) Based on the assessments made pursuant to Article 6, the Parties may decide whether:

(i) Adjustments to the ozone depleting potentials specified in Annex A, Annex B, Annex C and/or Annex E should be made and, if so, what the adjustments should be;

(ii) Adjustments to the global warming potentials specified in Group I of Annex A, Annex C and Annex F should be made and, if so, what the adjustments should be; and

(iii) Further adjustments and reductions of production or consumption of the controlled substances should be undertaken and, if so, what the scope, amount and timing of any such adjustments and reductions should be;

(b)   Proposals for such adjustments shall be communicated to the Parties by the Secretariat at least six months before the meeting of the Parties at which they are proposed for adoption;

(c)   In taking such decisions, the Parties shall make every effort to reach agreement by consensus. If all efforts at consensus have been exhausted, and no agreement reached, such decisions shall, as a last resort, be adopted by a two-thirds majority vote of the Parties present and voting representing a majority of the Parties operating under Paragraph 1 of Article 5 present and voting and a majority of the Parties not so operating present and voting;

(d)   The decisions, which shall be binding on all Parties, shall forthwith be communicated to the Parties by the Depositary. Unless otherwise provided in the decisions, they shall enter into force on the expiry of six months from the date of the circulation of the communication by the Depositary.

10.   Based on the assessments made pursuant to Article 6 of this Protocol and in accordance with the procedure set out in Article 9 of the Convention, the Parties may decide:

(a)   whether any substances, and if so which, should be added to or removed from any annex to this Protocol, and

(b)   the mechanism, scope and timing of the control measures that should apply to those substances;

11.   Notwithstanding the provisions contained in this Article and Articles 2A to 2J Parties may take more stringent measures than those required by this Article and Articles 2A to 2J.

Article 2A: CFCs
[…]

8.   Each Party shall ensure that for the twelve-month period commencing on 1 January 2010 and in each twelve-month period thereafter, its calculated level of production of the controlled substances in Group I of Annex A for the basic domestic needs of the Parties operating under paragraph 1 of Article 5 does not exceed zero.

9.   For the purposes of calculating basic domestic needs under paragraphs 4 to 8 of this Article, the calculation of the annual average of production by a Party includes any production entitlements that it has transferred in accordance with paragraph 5 of Article 2, and excludes any production entitlements that it has acquired in accordance with paragraph 5 of Article 2.

Article 2B: Halons
[…]

4.   Each Party shall ensure that for the twelve-month period commencing on 1 January 2010 and in each twelve-month period thereafter, its calculated level of production of the controlled substances in Group II of Annex A for the basic domestic needs of the Parties operating under paragraph 1 of Article 5 does not exceed zero.

Article 2C: Other fully halogenated CFCs

[...]

5.   Each Party shall ensure that for the twelve-month period commencing on 1 January 2010 and in each twelve-month period thereafter, its calculated level of production of the controlled substances in Group I of Annex B for the basic domestic needs of the Parties operating under paragraph 1 of Article 5 does not exceed zero.

Article 2D: Carbon tetrachloride

[...]

2.   Each Party shall ensure that for the twelve-month period commencing on 1 January 1996, and in each twelve-month period thereafter, its calculated level of consumption of the controlled substance in Group II of Annex B does not exceed zero. Each Party producing the substance shall, for the same periods, ensure that its calculated level of production of the substance does not exceed zero. However, in order to satisfy the basic domestic needs of the Parties operating under paragraph 1 of Article 5, its calculated level of production may exceed that limit by up to fifteen per cent of its calculated level of production in 1989. This paragraph will apply save to the extent that the Parties decide to permit the level of production or consumption that is necessary to satisfy uses agreed by them to be essential.

Article 2E: 1,1,1-Trichloroethane (Methyl chloroform)

[...]

3.   Each Party shall ensure that for the twelve-month period commencing on 1 January 1996, and in each twelve-month period thereafter, its calculated level of consumption of the controlled substance in Group III of Annex B does not exceed zero. Each Party producing the substance shall, for the same periods, ensure that its calculated level of production of the substance does not exceed zero. However, in order to satisfy the basic domestic needs of the Parties operating under paragraph 1 of Article 5, its calculated level of production may exceed that limit by up to fifteen per cent of its calculated level of production for 1989. This paragraph will apply save to the extent that the Parties decide to permit the level of production or consumption that is necessary to satisfy uses agreed by them to be essential.

Article 2F: Hydrochlorofluorocarbons

1.   Each Party shall ensure that for the twelve-month period commencing on 1 January 1996, and in each twelve-month period thereafter, its calculated level of consumption of the controlled substances in Group I of Annex C does not exceed, annually, the sum of:

    (a)   Two point eight per cent of its calculated level of consumption in 1989 of the controlled substances in Group I of Annex A; and

    (b)   Its calculated level of consumption in 1989 of the controlled substances in Group I of Annex C.

[...]

6.   Each Party shall ensure that for the twelve-month period commencing on 1 January 2020, and in each twelve-month period thereafter, its calculated level of consumption of the controlled substances in Group I of Annex C does not exceed zero. Each Party producing one or more of these substances shall, for the same periods, ensure that its calculated level of production of the controlled substances in Group I of Annex C does not exceed zero. This paragraph will apply save to the extent that the Parties decide to permit the level of production or consumption that is necessary to satisfy uses agreed by them to be essential. However:

(a)   Each Party may exceed that limit on consumption by up to zero point five per cent of the sum referred to in paragraph 1 of this Article in any such twelve-month period ending before 1 January 2030, provided that such consumption shall be restricted to:

(i)   The servicing of refrigeration and air-conditioning equipment existing on 1 January 2020;

(ii)   The servicing of fire suppression and fire protection equipment existing on 1 January 2020;

(iii)   Solvent applications in rocket engine manufacturing; and

(iv)   Topical medical aerosol applications for the specialised treatment of burns.

(b)   Each Party may exceed that limit on production by up to zero point five per cent of the average referred to in paragraph 2 of this Article in any such twelve-month period ending before 1 January 2030, provided that such production shall be restricted to:

(i)   The servicing of refrigeration and air-conditioning equipment existing on 1 January 2020;

(ii)   The servicing of fire suppression and fire protection equipment existing on 1 January 2020;

(iii)   Solvent applications in rocket engine manufacturing; and

(iv)   Topical medical aerosol applications for the specialised treatment of burns.

7.   As of 1 January 1996, each Party shall endeavour to ensure that:

(a)   The use of controlled substances in Group I of Annex C is limited to those applications where other more environmentally suitable alternative substances or technologies are not available;

(b)   The use of controlled substances in Group I of Annex C is not outside the areas of application currently met by controlled substances in Annexes A, B and C, except in rare cases for the protection of human life or human health; and

(c)   Controlled substances in Group I of Annex C are selected for use in a manner that minimizes ozone depletion, in addition to meeting other environmental, safety and economic considerations.

Article 2G: Hydrobromofluorocarbons

Each Party shall ensure that for the twelve-month period commencing on 1 January 1996, and in each twelve-month period thereafter, its calculated level of consumption of the controlled substances in Group II of Annex C does not exceed zero. Each Party producing the substances shall, for the same periods, ensure that its calculated level of production of the substances does not exceed zero. This paragraph will apply save to the extent that the Parties decide to permit the level of production or consumption that is necessary to satisfy uses agreed by them to be essential.

Article 2H: Methyl bromide

[...]

5. *ter.* Each Party shall ensure that for the twelve-month period commencing on 1 January 2015 and in each twelve-month period thereafter, its calculated level of production of the controlled substance in Annex E for the basic domestic needs of the Parties operating under paragraph 1 of Article 5 does not exceed zero.

6. The calculated levels of consumption and production under this Article shall not include the amounts used by the Party for quarantine and pre-shipment applications.

Article 2I: Bromochloromethane

Each Party shall ensure that for the twelve-month period commencing on 1 January 2002, and in each twelve-month period thereafter, its calculated level of consumption and production of the controlled substance in Group III of Annex C does not exceed zero. This paragraph will apply save to the extent that the Parties decide to permit the level of production or consumption that is necessary to satisfy uses agreed by them to be essential.

Article 2J: Hydrofluorocarbons

1. Each Party shall ensure that for the twelve-month period commencing on 1 January 2019, and in each twelve-month period thereafter, its calculated level of consumption of the controlled substances in Annex F, expressed in CO_2 equivalents, does not exceed the percentage, set out for the respective range of years specified in subparagraphs (a) to (e) below, of the annual average of its calculated levels of consumption of Annex F controlled substances for the years 2011, 2012 and 2013, plus fifteen per cent of its calculated level of consumption of Annex C, Group I, controlled substances as set out in paragraph 1 of Article 2F, expressed in CO_2 equivalents:

   (a)   2019 to 2023: 90 per cent
   (b)   2024 to 2028: 60 per cent
   (c)   2029 to 2033: 30 per cent
   (d)   2034 to 2035: 20 per cent
   (e)   2036 and thereafter: 15 per cent

2. Notwithstanding paragraph 1 of this Article, the Parties may decide that a Party shall ensure that, for the twelve-month period commencing on 1 January 2020, and in each twelve-month period thereafter, its calculated level of consumption of the controlled substances in Annex F, expressed in CO_2 equivalents, does not exceed the percentage, set out for the respective range of years specified in subparagraphs (a) to (e) below, of the annual average of its calculated levels of consumption of Annex F controlled substances for the years 2011, 2012 and 2013, plus twenty-five per cent of its calculated level of consumption of Annex C, Group I, controlled substances as set out in paragraph 1 of Article 2F, expressed in CO_2 equivalents:

   (a)   2020 to 2024: 95 per cent

(b)   2025 to 2028: 65 per cent
(c)   2029 to 2033: 30 per cent
(d)   2034 to 2035: 20 per cent
(e)   2036 and thereafter: 15 per cent

[...]

3.   Each Party producing the controlled substances in Annex F shall ensure that for the twelve-month period commencing on 1 January 2019, and in each twelve-month period thereafter, its calculated level of production of the controlled substances in Annex F, expressed in CO_2 equivalents, does not exceed the percentage, set out for the respective range of years specified in subparagraphs (a) to (e) below, of the annual average of its calculated levels of production of Annex F controlled substances for the years 2011, 2012 and 2013, plus fifteen per cent of its calculated level of production of Annex C, Group I, controlled substances as set out in paragraph 2 of Article 2F, expressed in CO_2 equivalents:
(a)   2019 to 2023: 90 per cent
(b)   2024 to 2028: 60 per cent
(c)   2029 to 2033: 30 per cent
(d)   2034 to 2035: 20 per cent
(e)   2036 and thereafter: 15 per cent

4.   Notwithstanding paragraph 3 of this Article, the Parties may decide that a Party producing the controlled substances in Annex F shall ensure that for the twelve-month period commencing on 1 January 2020, and in each twelve-month period thereafter, its calculated level of production of the controlled substances in Annex F, expressed in CO_2 equivalents, does not exceed the percentage, set out for the respective range of years specified in subparagraphs (a) to (e) below, of the annual average of its calculated levels of production of Annex F controlled substances for the years 2011, 2012 and 2013, plus twenty-five per cent of its calculated level of production of Annex C, Group I, controlled substances as set out in paragraph 2 of Article 2F, expressed in CO_2 equivalents:
(a)   2020 to 2024: 95 per cent
(b)   2025 to 2028: 65 per cent
(c)   2029 to 2033: 30 per cent
(d)   2034 to 2035: 20 per cent
(e)   2036 and thereafter: 15 per cent

5.   Paragraphs 1 to 4 of this Article will apply save to the extent that the Parties decide to permit the level of production or consumption that is necessary to satisfy uses agreed by the Parties to be exempted uses.

6.   Each Party manufacturing Annex C, Group I, or Annex F substances shall ensure that for the twelve-month period commencing on 1 January 2020, and in each twelve-month period thereafter, its emissions of Annex F, Group II, substances generated in each production facility that manufactures Annex C, Group I, or Annex F substances are destroyed to the extent practicable using technology approved by the Parties in the same twelve-month period.

7.   Each Party shall ensure that any destruction of Annex F, Group II, substances generated by facilities that produce Annex C, Group I, or Annex F substances shall occur only by technologies approved by the Parties.

Article 3: Calculation of control levels

1.   For the purposes of Articles 2, 2A to 2J and 5, each Party shall, for each group of substances in Annex A, Annex B, Annex C, Annex E or Annex F, determine its calculated levels of:

(a)   Production by:

(i)   multiplying its annual production of each controlled substance by the ozone depleting potential specified in respect of it in Annex A, Annex B, Annex C or Annex E, except as otherwise specified in paragraph 2;

(ii)   adding together, for each such Group, the resulting figures;

(b)   Imports and exports, respectively, by following, *mutatis mutandis*, the procedure set out in subparagraph (a); and

(c)   Consumption by adding together its calculated levels of production and imports and subtracting its calculated level of exports as determined in accordance with subparagraphs (a) and (b). However, beginning on 1 January 1993, any export of controlled substances to non-Parties shall not be subtracted in calculating the consumption level of the exporting Party; and

(d)   Emissions of Annex F, Group II, substances generated in each facility that generates Annex C, Group I, or Annex F substances by including, among other things, amounts emitted from equipment leaks, process vents and destruction devices, but excluding amounts captured for use, destruction or storage.

2.   When calculating levels, expressed in CO_2 equivalents, of production, consumption, imports, exports and emissions of Annex F and Annex C, Group I, substances for the purposes of Article 2J, paragraph 5 of Article 2 and paragraph 1 (d) of Article 3, each Party shall use the global warming potentials of those substances specified in Group I of Annex A, Annex C and Annex F.

[...]

Article 5: Special situation of developing countries

1.   Any Party that is a developing country and whose annual calculated level of consumption of the controlled substances in Annex A is less than 0.3 kilograms per capita on the date of the entry into force of the Protocol for it, or any time thereafter until 1 January 1999, shall, in order to meet its basic domestic needs, be entitled to delay for ten years its compliance with the control measures set out in Articles 2A to 2E, provided that any further amendments to the adjustments or Amendment adopted at the Second Meeting of the Parties in London, 29 June 1990, shall apply to the Parties operating under this paragraph after the review provided for in paragraph 8 of this Article has taken place and shall be based on the conclusions of that review.

...

2.   However, any Party operating under paragraph 1 of this Article shall exceed neither an annual calculated level of consumption of the controlled substances in Annex A of 0.3 kilograms per capita nor an annual calculated level of consumption of controlled substances of Annex B of 0.2 kilograms per capita.

Article 6: Assessment and review of control measures

Beginning in 1990, and at least every four years thereafter, the Parties shall assess the control measures provided for in Article 2 and Articles 2A to 2J on the basis of available scientific, environmental, technical and economic information. At least one year before each assessment, the Parties shall convene appropriate panels of experts qualified in the fields mentioned and determine the composition and terms of reference of any such panels. Within one year of being convened, the panels will report their conclusions, through the Secretariat, to the Parties.

Article 7: Reporting of data

1.   Each Party shall provide to the Secretariat, within three months of becoming a Party, statistical data on its production, imports and exports of each of the controlled substances in Annex A for the year 1986, or the best possible estimates of such data where actual data are not available.

[...]

Article 9: Research, development, public awareness and exchange of information

1.   The Parties shall co-operate, consistent with their national laws, regulations and practices and taking into account in particular the needs of developing countries, in promoting, directly or through competent international bodies, research, development and exchange of information on:

    (a)   best technologies for improving the containment, recovery, recycling, or destruction of controlled substances or otherwise reducing their emissions;

    (b)   possible alternatives to controlled substances, to products containing such substances, and to products manufactured with them; and

    (c)   costs and benefits of relevant control strategies.

2.   The Parties, individually, jointly or through competent international bodies, shall co-operate in promoting public awareness of the environmental effects of the emissions of controlled substances and other substances that deplete the ozone layer.

3.   Within two years of the entry into force of this Protocol and every two years thereafter, each Party shall submit to the Secretariat a summary of the activities it has conducted pursuant to this Article.

Article 10: Financial mechanism

1.   The Parties shall establish a mechanism for the purposes of providing financial and technical co-operation, including the transfer of technologies, to Parties operating under paragraph 1 of Article 5 of this Protocol to enable their compliance with the control measures set out in Articles 2A to 2E, Article 2I and Article 2J, and any control measures in Articles 2F to 2H that are decided pursuant to paragraph 1 *bis* of Article 5 of the Protocol. The mechanism, contributions to which shall be additional to other financial transfers to Parties operating under that paragraph, shall meet all agreed incremental costs of such Parties in order to enable their compliance with the control measures of the Protocol. An indicative list of the categories

of incremental costs shall be decided by the meeting of the Parties. Where a Party operating under paragraph 1 of Article 5 chooses to avail itself of funding from any other financial mechanism that could result in meeting any part of its agreed incremental costs, that part shall not be met by the financial mechanism under Article 10 of this Protocol.

2.   The mechanism established under paragraph 1 shall include a Multilateral Fund. It may also include other means of multilateral, regional and bilateral co-operation.

3.   The Multilateral Fund shall:

(a)   Meet, on a grant or concessional basis as appropriate, and according to criteria to be decided upon by the Parties, the agreed incremental costs;

(b)   Finance clearing-house functions to:

(i)   Assist Parties operating under paragraph 1 of Article 5, through country specific studies and other technical co-operation, to identify their needs for co-operation;

(ii)   Facilitate technical co-operation to meet these identified needs;

(iii)   Distribute, as provided for in Article 9, information and relevant materials, and hold workshops, training sessions, and other related activities, for the benefit of Parties that are developing countries; and

(iv)   Facilitate and monitor other multilateral, regional and bilateral co-operation available to Parties that are developing countries;

(c)   Finance the secretarial services of the Multilateral Fund and related support costs.

4.   The Multilateral Fund shall operate under the authority of the Parties who shall decide on its overall policies.

[...]

Article 10A: Transfer of technology

Each Party shall take every practicable step, consistent with the programmes supported by the financial mechanism, to ensure:

(a)   that the best available, environmentally safe substitutes and related technologies are expeditiously transferred to Parties operating under paragraph 1 of Article 5; and

(b)   that the transfers referred to in subparagraph (a) occur under fair and most favourable conditions.

QUESTIONS

1. Describe the key features of the treaty regime governing long-range transboundary air pollution.
2. Should the whole of the law on the protection of the atmosphere be integrated into a single regime?
3. 'The LRTAP and Ozone Regimes are great successes.' Are they? Give reasons for your answer.

FURTHER READING

BOOKS

S Barrett, *Environment and Statecraft: The Strategy of Environmental Treaty-Making* (Oxford University Press 2005)

S Jayakumar et al. (eds), *Transboundary Pollution: Evolving Issues of International Law and Policy* (Edward Elgar 2015)

S Murase, *International Law: An Integrated Perspective on Transboundary Issues* (Sophia University Press 2011)

P Okowa, *State Responsibility for Transboundary Air Pollution in International Law* (Oxford University Press 2000)

UNEP, *Handbook for the Montreal Protocol on Substances that Deplete the Ozone Layer* (13th edn, 2019)

O Yoshida, *The International Regime for the Protection of the Stratospheric Ozone Layer* (Kluwer 2001)

CHAPTERS

IH Rowlands, 'Atmosphere and Outer Space' in D Bodansky, J Brunée and E Hey (eds), *The Oxford Handbook of International Environmental Law* (Oxford University Press 2007)

ARTICLES

S Alam and L Nurhidayah, 'The International Law on Transboundary Haze Pollution: What Can We Learn from the Southeast Asia Region?' (2017) 26(3) Review of European Comparative & Environmental Law 243

A Byrne, 'The 1979 Convention on Long-Range Transboundary Air Pollution: Assessing its Effectiveness After 35 Years' (2015) 4 Transnational Environmental Law 37

A Byrne, 'Trouble in the Air: Recent Developments under the 1979 Convention on Long-Range Transboundary Air Pollution' (2017) 26(3) Review of European Comparative & Environmental Law 210

DD Caron, 'Protection of the Stratospheric Ozone Layer and the Structure of International Environmental Lawmaking' (1991) 14 Hastings International and Comparative Law Review 755

M Koskenniemi, 'Breach of Treaty or Non-Compliance? Reflections on the Enforcement of the Montreal Protocol' (1992) 3 Yearbook of International Environmental Law 123

B Lode, P Schönberger and P Toussaint, 'Clean Air for All by 2030? Air Quality in the 2030 Agenda and in International Law' (2016) 25(1) Review of European Comparative & Environmental Law 27

MW Roberts, 'Finishing the Job: The Montreal Protocol Moves to Phase Down Hydrofluorocarbons' (2017) 26(3) Review of European Comparative & Environmental Law 220

PH Sand, 'The Discourse on "Protection of the Atmosphere" in the International Law Commission' (2017) 26(3) Review of European Comparative & Environmental Law 201

PH Sand and JB Wiener, 'Towards a New International Law of the Atmosphere' (2015) 7 Göttingen Journal of International Law 2

J Tripp, 'The UNEP Montreal Protocol: Industrialised and Developing Countries Sharing the Responsibility for Protecting Atmospheric Protection' (1988) 20 New York University Journal of International Law and Policy 733

Y Yamineva and S Romppanen, 'Is Law Failing to Address Air Pollution? Reflections on International and EU Developments' (2017) 26(3) Review of European Comparative & Environmental Law 189

16
Climate change

16.1 INTRODUCTION

Few subjects of international law confront problems of the scale and urgency of climate change. As an area of legal regulation, it is comparatively recent, but it has developed into a complex field. Climate change raises two distinct challenges. First, there is the scientific challenge. Although the theoretical possibility of man-made global warming through the use of greenhouse gases has been recognised since the 19th century, scientific analysis of evidence about climate change has mainly developed in the second half of the 20th century,[1] and is a continually developing field of scientific research. In order to provide international policymakers with a clear understanding of the scientific consensus on climate change, the UNEP and WMO created a joint initiative that led to the creation of the Intergovernmental Panel on Climate Change in 1988. The IPCC was subsequently endorsed by the UN General Assembly.[2] The IPCC has, since 1990, periodically produced scientific assessments. Its most recent, the Fifth Assessment Reports (AR5), were in 2014, and its next are due to be completed in 2021–22. In AR5, the IPCC made the following observations on the mitigation efforts required by states:[3]

> Without additional mitigation efforts beyond those in place today, and even with adaptation, warming by the end of the 21st century will lead to high to very high risk of severe, widespread and irreversible impacts globally (high confidence).... Some risks of climate change, such as risks to unique and threatened systems and risks associated with extreme weather events, are moderate to high at temperatures 1°C to 2°C above pre-industrial levels. Substantial cuts in GHG emissions over the next few decades can substantially reduce risks of climate change by limiting warming in the second half of the 21st century and beyond.... Such a limit would require that global net emissions of CO_2 eventually decrease to zero and would constrain annual emissions over the next few decades (Figure SPM.10) (high confidence). But some risks from climate damages are unavoidable, even with mitigation and adaptation. {2.2.5, 3.2, 3.4}

---

[1] S Weart, *The Discovery of Global Warming* (HUP 2008).

[2] UNGA Resolution 43/53, 70th Plenary Meeting, 6 December 1988.

[3] IPCC, Summary for Policy Maker in 'Climate Change 2014: The Synthesis Report' in *Fifth Assessment Report: Climate Change 2014*, 17–19, SPM 3.2.

The IPCC has, following AR5, addressed the question of the differences in likely impact of climate change policies designed to limit global warming by either 1.5°C or 2°C. In its Special Report on the issue, the IPCC advised that there are 'robust differences' between the two thresholds with significantly reduced risks associated with the lower threshold.[4]

The second challenge is that tackling climate change creates serious policy problems for states, individually and collectively.[5] It is not limited either geographically or to a particular substance. It is global, implicating all states, and covers a range of different GHGs that contribute to climate change. The most significant GHG, CO_2, is central to the provision of energy in every part of every state's economy. It is essential to the economies of developed countries, and provides a cheap and readily available fuel source for the economic development of developing countries. Measures to reduce emissions of GHGs require major economic upheaval and, at least in the short term, pose a serious risk of economic harm. Unlike the costs of reducing emissions, the benefits of reducing emissions are global rather than local, and long term rather than immediate. There is, therefore, little self-interested incentive for a country to take action to reduce emissions. Another incentive problem for developed countries is that major emitters in Europe and North America are not likely to be the most severely adversely affected by climate change, with most of the harm falling on developing nations. Moreover, because the reduction of emissions required to limit the impact of climate change is a global reduction in emissions, there is a need for all states to coordinate their policies, making climate change a paradigm case of a cooperation problem. A different problem is that of 'climate justice'. Most historic and current carbon emissions are produced by developed countries, who have largely been the beneficiaries of the carbon economy. To reduce carbon emissions, therefore, raises problems of fairness to developing countries who may be deprived the same economic benefits, at least in the short term. The invasiveness of climate change policy into domestic economic affairs, the lack of immediate incentives for individual states, the need for universal participation, and different positions of developed and developing countries make climate change an almost intractable political problem, both domestically and internationally.

The challenge for the international legal regime for regulating climate change is to navigate these various challenges. In the first place, it requires drastic action over the short and medium term to prevent, mitigate and adapt to climate change. Second, it must be responsive to new information, in particular but not limited to scientific information from the IPCC. Third, to be effective the legal regime requires widespread participation, and in particular the participation of major emitters of GHGs. Which countries fall into this category changes over time – China and India, for example, have, since 1990, become major emitters of GHGs. At the same time, demands for climate justice militate against placing burdens on developing countries that impede their economic development by restricting their access to affordable energy sources. The difficulty this has produced is in managing all three together.

---

[4]   IPCC, Summary for Policy Makers in 'Special Report: Global Warming of 1.5°C' (2016) https://www.ipcc.ch/sr15/chapter/spm/ accessed 1 February 2021.

[5]   See D Bodansky, J Brunée and L Rajamani (eds), *International Climate Change Law* (OUP 2017) Chapter 1.

The international treaty regime developed to address climate change is modelled on the Ozone Regime, which had itself already prohibited the use of certain greenhouse gases.[6] Following the 1990 Ministerial Declaration of the Second World Climate Conference,[7] states commenced negotiations for a framework convention to tackle climate change. The United Nations Framework Convention on Climate Change was signed in 1992. It had 155 initial signatories, including the EU, and now has 197 parties. The Convention goes beyond the skeleton framework adopted in the 1985 Vienna Framework Convention, which was the model advocated by states such as the USA, but falls a long way short of a substantive regime, for which other states had argued. The UNFCCC covers three areas: (1) it provides a general set of purposes and principles for the climate change regime, (2) it creates certain commitments for tackling climate change, and (3) it establishes an institutional framework for future international cooperation.

The first session of the Conference of the Parties at Berlin, in 1995, sought to establish stronger commitments than those found in art 4, in particular art 4(2) of the UNFCCC. The commitment, known as the 'Berlin Mandate', laid the foundations for the adoption of the Kyoto Protocol in 1997, at the third session of the COP, by identifying the strengthening commitments of Annex I (i.e., developed) countries.[8] The Kyoto Protocol's main achievement was to create binding commitments to restrict GHG emissions to specified levels for Annex I countries. Achieving this goal, however, proved difficult and extremely controversial. Although concluded in 1997, many details for the implementation of the Kyoto Protocol were not resolved until 2001 in the Marrakesh Accords. Compromises in the subsequent rounds of negotiations were required to obtain the ratification of many states, but these were unable to retain the support of the USA, which withdrew its participation from the Protocol. Kyoto entered into force in 2005. Its specific commitments were, from the outset, time limited to only the period between 2008 and 2012, with subsequent commitments to be agreed through amendments to Annex B of the Protocol (art 3(9)). Negotiations for a subsequent commitment period proved more difficult still, and, while parties managed to negotiate a second commitment period from 2013–2020 through the 2011 Doha Amendment to the Protocol, it failed to achieve a sufficient number of ratifications prior to 2013, and only entered into force on 31 December 2020, namely one day prior to the expiry of the commitment period. The Kyoto approach was, instead, dispensed with in favour of the different model of international climate regulation in the Paris Agreement 2015. There remains the possibility of further commitment periods, although at present this is not on the agenda.

Under Kyoto, each Annex I state was required to limit emissions in accordance with assigned amounts, representing different proportionate limitations compared with 1990 levels. At one end of the spectrum, the EU agreed to an 8% reduction compared with 1990 levels, and on the other, Iceland agreed to limit increases in emissions to 10% above 1990 levels. Such reductions

---

[6]   See Chapter 15.

[7]   UN Doc A/45/696/Add.1, Annex III.

[8]   Decision 1/CP.1, Report of the Conference of the Parties on its First Sessions, Held at Berlin from 28 March to 7 April 1995, FCCC/CP/1995/7/Add.1, 4 ('Berlin Mandate').

could be achieved both by reducing emissions directly or by increasing biospheric sources and sinks through revegetation, forest management, cropland management, and grazing land management. Among the main innovations of Kyoto are its flexibility mechanisms for achieving reductions in assigned amounts. These are essentially methods of transferring credit for emissions reductions between different parties. The three main mechanisms in the Protocol are a Joint Implementation Mechanism, a Clean Development Mechanism, and Emissions Trading.

Alongside negotiations for a second commitment period, there was a desire to develop a different form of strengthening of the UNFCCC by including commitments for non-Annex I countries. This process culminated in the Paris Agreement, which was adopted at COP21 on 12 December 2015 by consensus in an annex to Decision 1/CP.21. It entered into force on 4 November 2016 and, as of 2021, has 195 signatories and 191 parties, comprising nearly all global greenhouse gas emissions. Despite much contention, it was agreed that the Agreement is legally binding. Second, although it is not immediately apparent on its face, the Agreement is a 'related legal instrument' for the purposes of the UNFCCC and thus operates within the Convention's framework. However, even if the legal status of the Agreement as a whole is clear, it makes use of many 'soft' or flexible norms.

The objectives of the Paris Agreement, taking into account the latest information on the requisite temperature goals, identifies holding the increase in the global average temperature to well below 2°C above pre-industrial levels and pursuing efforts to limit the temperature increase to 1.5°C above pre-industrial levels as necessary to combat climate change. Unlike Kyoto, the Paris Agreement does not define emissions targets. Instead, it creates a more flexible system in which Parties determine contributions to the reduction in global emissions at the national level. Another major development of the Paris Agreement is the promotion of market-based approaches, building upon those already adopted at Kyoto. Clearer content to the obligations set out in the Paris Agreement has been provided by the Conference of the Parties, notably in the so-called 'Katowice Rulebook' agreed at COP24 providing guidance on the requirements for nationally determined contributions. Further developments have occurred at COP26 in Glasgow, in particular in the Glasgow Climate Pact, which reaffirms the 1.5°C target and makes specific efforts to target the use of coal,[9] and also important initiatives on climate finance and deforestation, but issues with the implementation of the Paris Agreement remain outstanding.

It should be noted that this chapter does not cover climate change litigation. This is a novel but potentially very significant development in climate change law, although few cases have been brought so far. To date, cases have not been decided by international courts and tribunals, and the few successful claims have been before national courts. The decision in *Urgenda*, decided by the Dutch Supreme Court in 2019, indicates a potential impact of the treaties and instruments covered in this chapter as providing standards against which national courts can judge the lawfulness of government climate policy. Of particular interest in that decision was

---

9   The text of the decision is not yet official at the time of writing, see Decision -/CP.26 Glasgow Climate Pact (13 November 2021) https://unfccc.int/documents/310475 accessed 27 November 2021.

the synthesis of climate change standards and human rights, and this may well be a recurring theme in future cases.[10]

16.2   LEGAL INSTRUMENTS

16.2.1   Legally Binding Instruments

1992 United Nations Framework Convention on Climate Change, 1771 UNTS 107

Article 1
DEFINITIONS
For the purposes of this Convention:

1.   "Adverse effects of climate change" means changes in the physical environment or biota resulting from climate change which have significant deleterious effects on the composition, resilience or productivity of natural and managed ecosystems or on the operation of socio-economic systems or on human health and welfare.

2.   "Climate change" means a change of climate which is attributed directly or indirectly to human activity that alters the composition of the global atmosphere and which is in addition to natural climate variability observed over comparable time periods.

3.   "Climate system" means the totality of the atmosphere, hydrosphere, biosphere and geosphere and their interactions.

4.   "Emissions" means the release of greenhouse gases and/or their precursors into the atmosphere over a specified area and period of time.

5.   "Greenhouse gases" means those gaseous constituents of the atmosphere, both natural and anthropogenic, that absorb and re-emit infrared radiation.

6.   "Regional economic integration organization" means an organization constituted by sovereign States of a given region which has competence in respect of matters governed by this Convention or its protocols and has been duly authorized, in accordance with its internal procedures, to sign, ratify, accept, approve or accede to the instruments concerned.

7.   "Reservoir" means a component or components of the climate system where a greenhouse gas or a precursor of a greenhouse gas is stored.

8.   "Sink" means any process, activity or mechanism which removes a greenhouse gas, an aerosol or a precursor of a greenhouse gas from the atmosphere.

9.   "Source" means any process or activity which releases a greenhouse gas, an aerosol or a precursor of a greenhouse gas into the atmosphere.

Article 2
OBJECTIVE
The ultimate objective of this Convention and any related legal instruments that the Conference of the Parties may adopt is to achieve, in accordance with the relevant provi-

---

[10]   There is pending litigation before the European Court of Human Rights, including a claim against 33 Member States. On human rights and the environment, see further Chapter 15.

sions of the Convention, stabilization of greenhouse gas concentrations in the atmosphere at a level that would prevent dangerous anthropogenic interference with the climate system. Such a level should be achieved within a time frame sufficient to allow ecosystems to adapt naturally to climate change, to ensure that food production is not threatened and to enable economic development to proceed in a sustainable manner.

Article 3
PRINCIPLES

In their actions to achieve the objective of the Convention and to implement its provisions, the Parties shall be guided, *inter alia*, by the following:

1.	The Parties should protect the climate system for the benefit of present and future generations of humankind, on the basis of equity and in accordance with their common but differentiated responsibilities and respective capabilities. Accordingly, the developed country Parties should take the lead in combating climate change and the adverse effects thereof.
2.	The specific needs and special circumstances of developing country Parties, especially those that are particularly vulnerable to the adverse effects of climate change, and of those Parties, especially developing country Parties, that would have to bear a disproportionate or abnormal burden under the Convention, should be given full consideration.
3.	The Parties should take precautionary measures to anticipate, prevent or minimize the causes of climate change and mitigate its adverse effects. Where there are threats of serious or irreversible damage, lack of full scientific certainty should not be used as a reason for postponing such measures, taking into account that policies and measures to deal with climate change should be cost-effective so as to ensure global benefits at the lowest possible cost. To achieve this, such policies and measures should take into account different socio-economic contexts, be comprehensive, cover all relevant sources, sinks and reservoirs of greenhouse gases and adaptation, and comprise all economic sectors. Efforts to address climate change may be carried out cooperatively by interested Parties.
4.	The Parties have a right to, and should, promote sustainable development. Policies and measures to protect the climate system against human-induced change should be appropriate for the specific conditions of each Party and should be integrated with national development programmes, taking into account that economic development is essential for adopting measures to address climate change.
5.	The Parties should cooperate to promote a supportive and open international economic system that would lead to sustainable economic growth and development in all Parties, particularly developing country Parties, thus enabling them better to address the problems of climate change. Measures taken to combat climate change, including unilateral ones, should not constitute a means of arbitrary or unjustifiable discrimination or a disguised restriction on international trade.

Article 4
COMMITMENTS

1.	All Parties, taking into account their common but differentiated responsibilities and their specific national and regional development priorities, objectives and circumstances, shall:

(a)   Develop, periodically update, publish and make available to the Conference of the Parties, in accordance with Article 12, national inventories of anthropogenic emissions by sources and removals by sinks of all greenhouse gases not controlled by the Montreal Protocol, using comparable methodologies to be agreed upon by the Conference of the Parties;

(b)   Formulate, implement, publish and regularly update national and, where appropriate, regional programmes containing measures to mitigate climate change by addressing anthropogenic emissions by sources and removals by sinks of all greenhouse gases not controlled by the Montreal Protocol, and measures to facilitate adequate adaptation to climate change;

(c)   Promote and cooperate in the development, application and diffusion, including transfer, of technologies, practices and processes that control, reduce or prevent anthropogenic emissions of greenhouse gases not controlled by the Montreal Protocol in all relevant sectors, including the energy, transport, industry, agriculture, forestry and waste management sectors;

(d)   Promote sustainable management, and promote and cooperate in the conservation and enhancement, as appropriate, of sinks and reservoirs of all greenhouse gases not controlled by the Montreal Protocol, including biomass, forests and oceans as well as other terrestrial, coastal and marine ecosystems;

(e)   Cooperate in preparing for adaptation to the impacts of climate change; develop and elaborate appropriate and integrated plans for coastal zone management, water resources and agriculture, and for the protection and rehabilitation of areas, particularly in Africa, affected by drought and desertification, as well as floods;

(f)   Take climate change considerations into account, to the extent feasible, in their relevant social, economic and environmental policies and actions, and employ appropriate methods, for example impact assessments, formulated and determined nationally, with a view to minimizing adverse effects on the economy, on public health and on the quality of the environment, of projects or measures undertaken by them to mitigate or adapt to climate change;

(g)   Promote and cooperate in scientific, technological, technical, socio-economic and other research, systematic observation and development of data archives related to the climate system and intended to further the understanding and to reduce or eliminate the remaining uncertainties regarding the causes, effects, magnitude and timing of climate change and the economic and social consequences of various response strategies;

(h)   Promote and cooperate in the full, open and prompt exchange of relevant scientific, technological, technical, socio-economic and legal information related to the climate system and climate change, and to the economic and social consequences of various response strategies;

(i)   Promote and cooperate in education, training and public awareness related to climate change and encourage the widest participation in this process, including that of non-governmental organizations; and

(j)   Communicate to the Conference of the Parties information related to implementation, in accordance with Article 12.

2.   The developed country Parties and other Parties included in Annex I commit themselves specifically as provided for in the following:

(a)   Each of these Parties shall adopt national policies and take corresponding measures on the mitigation of climate change, by limiting its anthropogenic emissions of greenhouse gases and protecting and enhancing its greenhouse gas sinks and reservoirs. These policies and measures will demonstrate that developed countries are taking the lead in modifying longer-term trends in anthropogenic emissions consistent with the objective of the Convention, recognizing that the return by the end of the present decade to earlier levels of anthropogenic emissions of carbon dioxide and other greenhouse gases not controlled by the Montreal Protocol would contribute to such modification, and taking into account the differences in these Parties' starting points and approaches, economic structures and resource bases, the need to maintain strong and sustainable economic growth, available technologies and other individual circumstances, as well as the need for equitable and appropriate contributions by each of these Parties to the global effort regarding that objective. These Parties may implement such policies and measures jointly with other Parties and may assist other Parties in contributing to the achievement of the objective of the Convention and, in particular, that of this subparagraph;

(b)   In order to promote progress to this end, each of these Parties shall communicate, within six months of the entry into force of the Convention for it and periodically thereafter, and in accordance with Article 12, detailed information on its policies and measures referred to in subparagraph (a) above, as well as on its resulting projected anthropogenic emissions by sources and removals by sinks of greenhouse gases not controlled by the Montreal Protocol for the period referred to in subparagraph (a), with the aim of returning individually or jointly to their 1990 levels these anthropogenic emissions of carbon dioxide and other greenhouse gases not controlled by the Montreal Protocol. This information will be reviewed by the Conference of the Parties, at its first session and periodically thereafter, in accordance with Article 7;

(c)   Calculations of emissions by sources and removals by sinks of greenhouse gases for the purposes of subparagraph (b) above should take into account the best available scientific knowledge, including of the effective capacity of sinks and the respective contributions of such gases to climate change. The Conference of the Parties shall consider and agree regional economic integration organizations. This includes policies and measures adopted by on methodologies for these calculations at its first session and review them regularly thereafter;

(d)   The Conference of the Parties shall, at its first session, review the adequacy of subparagraphs (a) and (b) above. Such review shall be carried out in the light of the best available scientific information and assessment on climate change and its impacts, as well as relevant technical, social and economic information. Based on this review, the Conference of the Parties shall take appropriate action, which may include the adoption of amendments to the commitments in subparagraphs (a) and (b) above. The Conference of the Parties, at its first session, shall also take decisions regarding criteria for joint implementation as indicated in subparagraph (a) above. A second review of subparagraphs (a) and (b) shall take place not later than 31 December 1998, and thereafter at regular intervals determined by the Conference of the Parties, until the objective of the Convention is met;

(e)   Each of these Parties shall:

(i)   Coordinate as appropriate with other such Parties, relevant economic and administrative instruments developed to achieve the objective of the Convention; and

(ii)   Identify and periodically review its own policies and practices which encourage activities that lead to greater levels of anthropogenic emissions of greenhouse gases not controlled by the Montreal Protocol than would otherwise occur;

3.   The developed country Parties and other developed Parties included in Annex II shall provide new and additional financial resources to meet the agreed full costs incurred by developing country Parties in complying with their obligations under Article 12, paragraph 1. They shall also provide such financial resources, including for the transfer of technology, needed by the developing country Parties to meet the agreed full incremental costs of implementing measures that are covered by paragraph 1 of this Article and that are agreed between a developing country Party and the international entity or entities referred to in Article 11, in accordance with that Article. The implementation of these commitments shall take into account the need for adequacy and predictability in the flow of funds and the importance of appropriate burden sharing among the developed country Parties.

4.   The developed country Parties and other developed Parties included in Annex II shall also assist the developing country Parties that are particularly vulnerable to the adverse effects of climate change in meeting costs of adaptation to those adverse effects.

5.   The developed country Parties and other developed Parties included in Annex II shall take all practicable steps to promote, facilitate and finance, as appropriate, the transfer of, or access to, environmentally sound technologies and know-how to other Parties, particularly developing country Parties, to enable them to implement the provisions of the Convention. In this process, the developed country Parties shall support the development and enhancement of endogenous capacities and technologies of developing country Parties. Other Parties and organizations in a position to do so may also assist in facilitating the transfer of such technologies.

[...]

8.   In the implementation of the commitments in this Article, the Parties shall give full consideration to what actions are necessary under the Convention...to meet the specific needs and concerns of developing country Parties arising from the adverse effects of climate change and/or the impact of the implementation of response measures, especially on:

(a)   Small island countries,

(b)   Countries with low-lying coastal areas,

(c)   Countries with arid and semi-arid areas, forest areas and areas liable to forest decay,

(d)   Countries with areas prone to natural disasters,

(e)   Countries with areas liable to drought and desertification,

(f)   Countries with areas of high urban atmospheric pollution,

(g)   Countries with fragile ecosystems, including mountainous ecosystems,

(h)   Countries whose economies are highly dependent on income generated from the production, processing and export, and/or on consumption of fossil fuels and associated energy-intensive products, and

(i)   Landlocked and transit countries.

9.   The Parties shall take full account of the specific needs and special situations of the least developed countries in their actions with regard to funding and transfer of technology.

10.   The Parties shall, in accordance with Article 10, take into consideration in the implementation of the commitments of the Convention the situation of Parties, particularly developing country Parties, with economies that are vulnerable to the adverse effects of the implementation of measures to respond to climate change. This applies notably to Parties with economies that are highly dependent on income generated from the production, processing and export, and/or consumption of fossil fuels and associated energy-intensive products and/or the use of fossil fuels for which such Parties have serious difficulties in switching to alternatives.

Article 7

CONFERENCE OF THE PARTIES

1.   A Conference of the Parties is hereby established.

2.   The Conference of the Parties, as the supreme body of this Convention, shall keep under regular review the implementation of the Convention and any related legal instruments that the Conference of the Parties may adopt, and shall make, within its mandate, the decisions necessary to promote the effective implementation of the Convention. To this end, it shall:

(a)   Periodically examine the obligations of the Parties and the institutional arrangements under the Convention, in the light of the objective of the Convention, the experience gained in its implementation and the evolution of scientific and technological knowledge;

(b)   Promote and facilitate the exchange of information on measures adopted by the Parties to address climate change and its effects, taking into account the differing circumstances, responsibilities and capabilities of the Parties and their respective commitments under the Convention;

(c)   Facilitate, at the request of two or more Parties, the coordination of measures adopted by them to address climate change and its effects, taking into account the differing circumstances, responsibilities and capabilities of the Parties and their respective commitments under the Convention;

(d)   Promote and guide, in accordance with the objective and provisions of the Convention, the development and periodic refinement of comparable methodologies, to be agreed on by the Conference of the Parties, *inter alia,* for preparing inventories of greenhouse gas emissions by sources and removals by sinks, and for evaluating the effectiveness of measures to limit the emissions and enhance the removals of these gases;

(e) Assess, on the basis of all information made available to it in accordance with the provisions of the Convention, the implementation of the Convention by the Parties, the overall effects of the measures taken pursuant to the Convention, in particular environmental, economic and social effects as well as their cumulative impacts and the extent to which progress towards the objective of the Convention is being achieved;

(f) Consider and adopt regular reports on the implementation of the Convention and ensure their publication;

(g) Make recommendations on any matters necessary for the implementation of the Convention;

(h) Seek to mobilize financial resources in accordance with Article 4, paragraphs 3, 4 and 5, and Article 11;

(i) Establish such subsidiary bodies as are deemed necessary for the implementation of the Convention;

(j) Review reports submitted by its subsidiary bodies and provide guidance to them;

(k) Agree upon and adopt, by consensus, rules of procedure and financial rules for itself and for any subsidiary bodies;

(l) Seek and utilize, where appropriate, the services and cooperation of, and information provided by, competent international organizations and inter-governmental and non-governmental bodies; and

(m) Exercise such other functions as are required for the achievement of the objective of the Convention as well as all other functions assigned to it under the Convention.

3. The Conference of the Parties shall, at its first session, adopt its own rules of procedure as well as those of the subsidiary bodies established by the Convention, which shall include decision-making procedures for matters not already covered by decision-making procedures stipulated in the Convention. Such procedures may include specified majorities required for the adoption of particular decisions.

[...]

6. The United Nations, its specialized agencies and the International Atomic Energy Agency, as well as any State member thereof or observers thereto not Party to the Convention, may be represented at sessions of the Conference of the Parties as observers. Any body or agency, whether national or international, governmental or non-governmental, which is qualified in matters covered by the Convention, and which has informed the secretariat of its wish to be represented at a session of the Conference of the Parties as an observer, may be so admitted unless at least one third of the Parties present object. The admission and participation of observers shall be subject to the rules of procedure adopted by the Conference of the Parties.

Article 8
SECRETARIAT
1.   A secretariat is hereby established.
2.   The functions of the secretariat shall be:
   (a)   To make arrangements for sessions of the Conference of the Parties and its subsidiary bodies established under the Convention and to provide them with services as required;
   (b)   To compile and transmit reports submitted to it;
   (c)   To facilitate assistance to the Parties, particularly developing country Parties, on request, in the compilation and communication of information required in accordance with the provisions of the Convention;
   (d)   To prepare reports on its activities and present them to the Conference of the Parties;
   (e)   To ensure the necessary coordination with the secretariats of other relevant international bodies;
   (f)   To enter, under the overall guidance of the Conference of the Parties, into such administrative and contractual arrangements as may be required for the effective discharge of its functions; and
   (g)   To perform the other secretariat functions specified in the Convention and in any of its protocols and such other functions as may be determined by the Conference of the Parties.
3.   The Conference of the Parties, at its first session, shall designate a permanent secretariat and make arrangements for its functioning.

Article 9
SUBSIDIARY BODY FOR SCIENTIFIC AND TECHNOLOGICAL ADVICE.
1.   A subsidiary body for scientific and technological advice is hereby established to provide the Conference of the Parties and, as appropriate, its other subsidiary bodies with timely information and advice on scientific and technological matters relating to the Convention. This body shall be open to participation by all Parties and shall be multidisciplinary. It shall comprise government representatives competent in the relevant field of expertise. It shall report regularly to the Conference of the Parties on all aspects of its work.
2.   Under the guidance of the Conference of the Parties, and drawing upon existing competent international bodies, this body shall:
   (a)   Provide assessments of the state of scientific knowledge relating to climate change and its effects;
   (b)   Prepare scientific assessments on the effects of measures taken in the implementation of the Convention;
   (c)   Identify innovative, efficient and state-of-the-art technologies and know-how and advise on the ways and means of promoting development and/or transferring such technologies;
   (d)   Provide advice on scientific programmes, international cooperation in research and development related to climate change, as well as on ways and means of supporting endogenous capacity-building in developing countries; and

(e)   Respond to scientific, technological and methodological questions that the Conference of the Parties and its subsidiary bodies may put to the body.

[...]

Article 11
FINANCIAL MECHANISM

1.   A mechanism for the provision of financial resources on a grant or concessional basis, including for the transfer of technology, is hereby defined. It shall function under the guidance of and be accountable to the Conference of the Parties, which shall decide on its policies, programme priorities and eligibility criteria related to this Convention. Its operation shall be entrusted to one or more existing international entities.

2.   The financial mechanism shall have an equitable and balanced representation of all Parties within a transparent system of governance.

[...]

5.   The developed country Parties may also provide and developing country Parties avail themselves of, financial resources related to the implementation of the Convention through bilateral, regional and other multilateral channels.

Article 12
COMMUNICATION OF INFORMATION RELATED TO IMPLEMENTATION

1.   In accordance with Article 4, paragraph 1, each Party shall communicate to the Conference of the Parties, through the secretariat, the following elements of information:

(a)   A national inventory of anthropogenic emissions by sources and removals by sinks of all greenhouse gases not controlled by the Montreal Protocol, to the extent its capacities permit, using comparable methodologies to be promoted and agreed upon by the Conference of the Parties;

(b)   A general description of steps taken or envisaged by the Party to implement the Convention; and

(c)   Any other information that the Party considers relevant to the achievement of the objective of the Convention and suitable for inclusion in its communication, including, if feasible, material relevant for calculations of global emission trends.

2.   Each developed country Party and each other Party included in Annex I shall incorporate in its communication the following elements of information:

(a)   A detailed description of the policies and measures that it has adopted to implement its commitment under Article 4, paragraphs 2(a) and 2(b); and

(b)   A specific estimate of the effects that the policies and measures referred to in subparagraph (a) immediately above will have on anthropogenic emissions by its sources and removals by its sinks of greenhouse gases during the period referred to in Article 4, paragraph 2(a).

3.   In addition, each developed country Party and each other developed Party included in Annex II shall incorporate details of measures taken in accordance with Article 4, paragraphs 3, 4 and 5.

4.   Developing country Parties may, on a voluntary basis, propose projects for financing, including specific technologies, materials, equipment, techniques or practices that would be needed to implement such projects, along with, if possible, an estimate of all incremental costs, of the reductions of emissions and increments of removals of greenhouse gases, as well as an estimate of the consequent benefits.

[...]

Article 17
PROTOCOLS

1.   The Conference of the Parties may, at any ordinary session, adopt protocols to the Convention.

2.   The text of any proposed protocol shall be communicated to the Parties by the secretariat at least six months before such a session.

3.   The requirements for the entry into force of any protocol shall be established by that instrument.

4.   Only Parties to the Convention may be Parties to a protocol.

5.   Decisions under any protocol shall be taken only by the Parties to the protocol concerned.

**1997 Kyoto Protocol to the United Nations Framework Convention on
Climate Change, 2303 UNTS 162**

SPECIFIC EMISSIONS REDUCTIONS
Article 3

1.   The Parties included in Annex I shall, individually or jointly, ensure that their aggregate anthropogenic carbon dioxide equivalent emissions of the greenhouse gases listed in Annex A do not exceed their assigned amounts, calculated pursuant to their quantified emission limitation and reduction commitments inscribed in Annex B and in accordance with the provisions of this Article, with a view to reducing their overall emissions of such gases by at least 5 per cent below 1990 levels in the commitment period 2008 to 2012.

[...]

3.   The net changes in greenhouse gas emissions by sources and removals by sinks resulting from direct human-induced land-use change and forestry activities, limited to afforestation, reforestation and deforestation since 1990, measured as verifiable changes in carbon stocks in each commitment period, shall be used to meet the commitments under this Article of each Party included in Annex I. The greenhouse gas emissions by sources and removals by sinks associated with those

activities shall be reported in a transparent and verifiable manner and reviewed in accordance with Articles 7 and 8.

POLICIES AND MEASURES

Article 2

1.   Each Party included in Annex I, in achieving its quantified emission limitation and reduction commitments under Article 3, in order to promote sustainable development, shall:

    (a)   Implement and/or further elaborate policies and measures in accordance with its national circumstances, such as:

        (i)   Enhancement of energy efficiency in relevant sectors of the national economy;

        (ii)   Protection and enhancement of sinks and reservoirs of greenhouse gases not controlled by the Montreal Protocol, taking into account its commitments under relevant international environmental agreements; promotion of sustainable forest management practices, afforestation and reforestation;

        (iii)   Promotion of sustainable forms of agriculture in light of climate change considerations;

        (iv)   Research on, and promotion, development and increased use of, new and renewable forms of energy, of carbon dioxide sequestration technologies and of advanced and innovative environmentally sound technologies;

        (v)   Progressive reduction or phasing out of market imperfections, fiscal incentives, tax and duty exemptions and subsidies in all greenhouse gas emitting sectors that run counter to the objective of the Convention and application of market instruments;

        (vi)   Encouragement of appropriate reforms in relevant sectors aimed at promoting policies and measures which limit or reduce emissions of greenhouse gases not controlled by the Montreal Protocol;

        (vii)   Measures to limit and/or reduce emissions of greenhouse gases not controlled by the Montreal Protocol in the transport sector;

        (viii)   Limitation and/or reduction of methane emissions through recovery and use in waste management, as well as in the production, transport and distribution of energy;

    (b)   Cooperate with other such Parties to enhance the individual and combined effectiveness of their policies and measures adopted under this Article, pursuant to Article 4, paragraph 2 (e) (i), of the Convention. To this end, these Parties shall take steps to share their experience and exchange information on such policies and measures, including developing ways of improving their comparability, transparency and effectiveness. The Conference of the Parties serving as the meeting of the Parties to this Protocol shall, at its first session or as soon as practicable thereafter, consider ways to facilitate such cooperation, taking into account all relevant information.

2.   The Parties included in Annex I shall pursue limitation or reduction of emissions of greenhouse gases not controlled by the Montreal Protocol from aviation

and marine bunker fuels, working through the International Civil Aviation Organization and the International Maritime Organization, respectively.

MECHANISMS

Joint Implementation Mechanism:

Article 6

1.   For the purpose of meeting its commitments under Article 3, any Party included in Annex I may transfer to, or acquire from, any other such Party emission reduction units resulting from projects aimed at reducing anthropogenic emissions by sources or enhancing anthropogenic removals by sinks of greenhouse gases in any sector of the economy, provided that:

(a)   Any such project has the approval of the Parties involved;

(b)   Any such project provides a reduction in emissions by sources, or an enhancement of removals by sinks, that is additional to any that would otherwise occur;

(c)   It does not acquire any emission reduction units if it is not in compliance with its obligations under Articles 5 and 7; and

(d)   The acquisition of emission reduction units shall be supplemental to domestic actions for the purposes of meeting commitments under Article 3.

[...]

3.   A Party included in Annex I may authorize legal entities to participate, under its responsibility, in actions leading to the generation, transfer or acquisition under this Article of emission reduction units.

Clean Development Mechanism ('CDM'):

Article 12

1.   A clean development mechanism is hereby defined.

2.   The purpose of the clean development mechanism shall be to assist Parties not included in Annex I in achieving sustainable development and in contributing to the ultimate objective of the Convention, and to assist Parties included in Annex I in achieving compliance with their quantified emission limitation and reduction commitments under Article 3.

3.   Under the clean development mechanism:

(a)   Parties not included in Annex I will benefit from project activities resulting in certified emission reductions; and

(b)   Parties included in Annex I may use the certified emission reductions accruing from such project activities to contribute to compliance with part of their quantified emission limitation and reduction commitments under Article 3, as determined by the Conference of the Parties serving as the meeting of the Parties to this Protocol.

4.   The clean development mechanism shall be subject to the authority and guidance of the Conference of the Parties serving as the meeting of the Parties to this Protocol and be supervised by an executive board of the clean development mechanism.

5.   Emission reductions resulting from each project activity shall be certified by operational entities to be designated by the Conference of the Parties serving as the meeting of the Parties to this Protocol, on the basis of:

     (a)   Voluntary participation approved by each Party involved;

     (b)   Real, measurable, and long-term benefits related to the mitigation of climate change; and

     (c)   Reductions in emissions that are additional to any that would occur in the absence of the certified project activity.

6.   The clean development mechanism shall assist in arranging funding of certified project activities as necessary.

[…]

9.   Participation under the clean development mechanism, including in activities mentioned in paragraph 3 (a) above and in the acquisition of certified emission reductions, may involve private and/or public entities, and is to be subject to whatever guidance may be provided by the executive board of the clean development mechanism.

Emissions Trading:

Article 17

The Conference of the Parties shall define the relevant principles, modalities, rules and guidelines, in particular for verification, reporting and accountability for emissions trading. The Parties included in Annex B may participate in emissions trading for the purposes of fulfilling their commitments under Article 3. Any such trading shall be supplemental to domestic actions for the purpose of meeting quantified emission limitation and reduction commitments under that Article.

Article 3

[…]

10.   Any emission reduction units, or any part of an assigned amount, which a Party acquires from another Party in accordance with the provisions of Article 6 or of Article 17 shall be added to the assigned amount for the acquiring Party.

11.   Any emission reduction units, or any part of an assigned amount, which a Party transfers to another Party in accordance with the provisions of Article 6 or of Article 17 shall be subtracted from the assigned amount for the transferring Party.

12.   Any certified emission reductions which a Party acquires from another Party in accordance with the provisions of Article 12 shall be added to the assigned amount for the acquiring Party.

DIFFERENTIATION

Article 10

All Parties, taking into account their common but differentiated responsibilities and their specific national and regional development priorities, objectives and circumstances, without introducing any new commitments for Parties not included in Annex I, but reaffirming existing commitments under Article 4, paragraph 1, of the Convention, and continuing to advance the implementation of these commitments in order to achieve sustainable development, taking into account Article 4, paragraphs 3, 5 and 7, of the Convention, shall:

(a) Formulate, where relevant and to the extent possible, cost-effective national and, where appropriate, regional programmes to improve the quality of local emission factors, activity data and/or models which reflect the socio-economic conditions of each Party for the preparation and periodic updating of national inventories of anthropogenic emissions by sources and removals by sinks of all greenhouse gases not controlled by the Montreal Protocol, using comparable methodologies to be agreed upon by the Conference of the Parties, and consistent with the guidelines for the preparation of national communications adopted by the Conference of the Parties;

(b) Formulate, implement, publish and regularly update national and, where appropriate, regional programmes containing measures to mitigate climate change and measures to facilitate adequate adaptation to climate change:

    (i) Such programmes would, *inter alia*, concern the energy, transport and industry sectors as well as agriculture, forestry and waste management. Furthermore, adaptation technologies and methods for improving spatial planning would improve adaptation to climate change; and

    (ii) Parties included in Annex I shall submit information on action under this Protocol, including national programmes, in accordance with Article 7; and other Parties shall seek to include in their national communications, as appropriate, information on programmes which contain measures that the Party believes contribute to addressing climate change and its adverse impacts, including the abatement of increases in greenhouse gas emissions, and enhancement of and removals by sinks, capacity building and adaptation measures;

(c) Cooperate in the promotion of effective modalities for the development, application and diffusion of, and take all practicable steps to promote, facilitate and finance, as appropriate, the transfer of, or access to, environmentally sound technologies, know-how, practices and processes pertinent to climate change, in particular to developing countries, including the formulation of policies and programmes for the effective transfer of environmentally sound technologies that are publicly owned or in the public domain and the creation of an enabling environment for the private sector, to promote and enhance the transfer of, and access to, environmentally sound technologies;

(d) Cooperate in scientific and technical research and promote the maintenance and the development of systematic observation systems and development of data archives to reduce uncertainties related to the climate system, the adverse impacts of climate change and the economic and social consequences of various response strategies, and promote the development and strengthening of endogenous capacities and capabilities to participate in international and intergovernmental efforts, programmes and networks on research and systematic observation, taking into account Article 5 of the Convention;

(e) Cooperate in and promote at the international level, and, where appropriate, using existing bodies, the development and implementation of education and training programmes, including the strengthening of national capacity building, in particular human and institutional capacities and the exchange or secondment of personnel to train experts in this field, in particular for developing countries, and facilitate at the national level public awareness of, and public access to information on, climate change. Suitable modalities should be developed to implement these activities through the relevant bodies of the Convention, taking into account Article 6 of the Convention;

(f)   Include in their national communications information on programmes and activities undertaken pursuant to this Article in accordance with relevant decisions of the Conference of the Parties; and

(g)   Give full consideration, in implementing the commitments under this Article, to Article 4, paragraph 8, of the Convention.

2015 Paris Agreement, FCCC/CP/2015/10/Add.1

Preamble

Acknowledging that climate change is a common concern of humankind, Parties should, when taking action to address climate change, respect, promote and consider their respective obligations on human rights, the right to health, the rights of indigenous peoples, local communities, migrants, children, persons with disabilities and people in vulnerable situations and the right to development, as well as gender equality, empowerment of women and intergenerational equity,

[...]

Emphasizing the intrinsic relationship that climate change actions, responses and impacts have with equitable access to sustainable development and eradication of poverty,

Recognizing the fundamental priority of safeguarding food security and ending hunger, and the particular vulnerabilities of food production systems to the adverse impacts of climate change,

[...]

Taking into account the imperatives of a just transition of the workforce and the creation of decent work and quality jobs in accordance with nationally defined development priorities,

[...]

Recognizing the importance of the engagements of all levels of government and various actors, in accordance with respective national legislations of Parties, in addressing climate change,

Also recognizing that sustainable lifestyles and sustainable patterns of consumption and production, with developed country Parties taking the lead, play an important role in addressing climate change,

OBJECTIVES
Article 2
1.   This Agreement, in enhancing the implementation of the Convention, including its objective, aims to strengthen the global response to the threat of climate change, in the context of sustainable development and efforts to eradicate poverty, including by:

(a)   Holding the increase in the global average temperature to well below 2°C above pre-industrial levels and pursuing efforts to limit the temperature increase to 1.5°C above pre-industrial levels, recognizing that this would significantly reduce the risks and impacts of climate change;

    (b)   Increasing the ability to adapt to the adverse impacts of climate change and foster climate resilience and low greenhouse gas emissions development, in a manner that does not threaten food production; and

    (c)   Making finance flows consistent with a pathway towards low greenhouse gas emissions and climate-resilient development.

2.   This Agreement will be implemented to reflect equity and the principle of common but differentiated responsibilities and respective capabilities, in the light of different national circumstances.

Article 3

As nationally determined contributions to the global response to climate change, all Parties are to undertake and communicate ambitious efforts as defined in Articles 4, 7, 9, 10, 11 and 13 with the view to achieving the purpose of this Agreement as set out in Article 2. The efforts of all Parties will represent a progression over time, while recognizing the need to support developing country Parties for the effective implementation of this Agreement.

Article 4

1.   In order to achieve the long-term temperature goal set out in Article 2, Parties aim to reach global peaking of greenhouse gas emissions as soon as possible, recognizing that peaking will take longer for developing country Parties, and to undertake rapid reductions thereafter in accordance with best available science, so as to achieve a balance between anthropogenic emissions by sources and removals by sinks of greenhouse gases in the second half of this century, on the basis of equity, and in the context of sustainable development and efforts to eradicate poverty.

2.   Each Party shall prepare, communicate and maintain successive nationally determined contributions that it intends to achieve. Parties shall pursue domestic mitigation measures, with the aim of achieving the objectives of such contributions.

3.   Each Party's successive nationally determined contribution will represent a progression beyond the Party's then current nationally determined contribution and reflect its highest possible ambition, reflecting its common but differentiated responsibilities and respective capabilities, in the light of different national circumstances.

[MARKET-BASED APPROACHES]
Article 6

1.   Parties recognize that some Parties choose to pursue voluntary cooperation in the implementation of their nationally determined contributions to allow for higher ambition in their mitigation and adaptation actions and to promote sustainable development and environmental integrity.

2.   Parties shall, where engaging on a voluntary basis in cooperative approaches that involve the use of internationally transferred mitigation outcomes towards nationally determined contributions, promote sustainable development and ensure environmental integrity and transparency, including in governance, and shall apply robust accounting to ensure, *inter alia*, the avoidance of double counting, consistent with guidance adopted by the Conference of the Parties serving as the meeting of the Parties to this Agreement.

3.   The use of internationally transferred mitigation outcomes to achieve nationally determined contributions under this Agreement shall be voluntary and authorized by participating Parties.

4.   A mechanism to contribute to the mitigation of greenhouse gas emissions and support sustainable development is hereby established under the authority and guidance of the Conference of the Parties serving as the meeting of the Parties to this Agreement for use by Parties on a voluntary basis. It shall be supervised by a body designated by the Conference of the Parties serving as the meeting of the Parties to this Agreement, and shall aim:

(a)   To promote the mitigation of greenhouse gas emissions while fostering sustainable development;

(b)   To incentivize and facilitate participation in the mitigation of greenhouse gas emissions by public and private entities authorized by a Party;

(c)   To contribute to the reduction of emission levels in the host Party, which will benefit from mitigation activities resulting in emission reductions that can also be used by another Party to fulfil its nationally determined contribution; and

(d)   To deliver an overall mitigation in global emissions.

5.   Emission reductions resulting from the mechanism referred to in paragraph 4 of this Article shall not be used to demonstrate achievement of the host Party's nationally determined contribution if used by another Party to demonstrate achievement of its nationally determined contribution.

6.   The Conference of the Parties serving as the meeting of the Parties to this Agreement shall ensure that a share of the proceeds from activities under the mechanism referred to in paragraph 4 of this Article is used to cover administrative expenses as well as to assist developing country Parties that are particularly vulnerable to the adverse effects of climate change to meet the costs of adaptation.

7.   The Conference of the Parties serving as the meeting of the Parties to this Agreement shall adopt rules, modalities and procedures for the mechanism referred to in paragraph 4 of this Article at its first session.

8.   Parties recognize the importance of integrated, holistic and balanced non-market approaches being available to Parties to assist in the implementation of their nationally determined contributions, in the context of sustainable development and poverty eradication, in a coordinated and effective manner, including through, *inter alia*, mitigation, adaptation, finance, technology transfer and capacity- building, as appropriate. These approaches shall aim to:

(a)   Promote mitigation and adaptation ambition;

(b)   Enhance public and private sector participation in the implementation of nationally determined contributions; and

(c)   Enable opportunities for coordination across instruments and relevant institutional arrangements.

9.   A framework for non-market approaches to sustainable development is hereby defined to promote the non-market approaches referred to in paragraph 8 of this Article.

[ADAPTATION]
Article 7
1. Parties hereby establish the global goal on adaptation of enhancing adaptive capacity, strengthening resilience and reducing vulnerability to climate change, with a view to contributing to sustainable development and ensuring an adequate adaptation response in the context of the temperature goal referred to in Article 2.
2. Parties recognize that adaptation is a global challenge faced by all with local, subnational, national, regional and international dimensions, and that it is a key component of and makes a contribution to the long-term global response to climate change to protect people, livelihoods and ecosystems, taking into account the urgent and immediate needs of those developing country Parties that are particularly vulnerable to the adverse effects of climate change.
3. The adaptation efforts of developing country Parties shall be recognized, in accordance with the modalities to be adopted by the Conference of the Parties serving as the meeting of the Parties to this Agreement at its first session.
4. Parties recognize that the current need for adaptation is significant and that greater levels of mitigation can reduce the need for additional adaptation efforts, and that greater adaptation needs can involve greater adaptation costs.
5. Parties acknowledge that adaptation action should follow a country-driven, gender-responsive, participatory and fully transparent approach, taking into consideration vulnerable groups, communities and ecosystems, and should be based on and guided by the best available science and, as appropriate, traditional knowledge, knowledge of indigenous peoples and local knowledge systems, with a view to integrating adaptation into relevant socioeconomic and environmental policies and actions, where appropriate.
6. Parties recognize the importance of support for and international cooperation on adaptation efforts and the importance of taking into account the needs of developing country Parties, especially those that are particularly vulnerable to the adverse effects of climate change.
7. Parties should strengthen their cooperation on enhancing action on adaptation, taking into account the Cancun Adaptation Framework, including with regard to:
    (a) Sharing information, good practices, experiences and lessons learned, including, as appropriate, as these relate to science, planning, policies and implementation in relation to adaptation actions;
    (b) Strengthening institutional arrangements, including those under the Convention that serve this Agreement, to support the synthesis of relevant information and knowledge, and the provision of technical support and guidance to Parties;
    (c) Strengthening scientific knowledge on climate, including research, systematic observation of the climate system and early warning systems, in a manner that informs climate services and supports decision-making;
    (d) Assisting developing country Parties in identifying effective adaptation practices, adaptation needs, priorities, support provided and received for adaptation actions and efforts, and challenges and gaps, in a manner consistent with encouraging good practices; and
    (e) Improving the effectiveness and durability of adaptation actions.

8. United Nations specialized organizations and agencies are encouraged to support the efforts of Parties to implement the actions referred to in paragraph 7 of this Article, taking into account the provisions of paragraph 5 of this Article.

9. Each Party shall, as appropriate, engage in adaptation planning processes and the implementation of actions, including the development or enhancement of relevant plans, policies and/or contributions, which may include:
    (a) The implementation of adaptation actions, undertakings and/or efforts;
    (b) The process to formulate and implement national adaptation plans;
    (c) The assessment of climate change impacts and vulnerability, with a view to formulating nationally determined prioritized actions, taking into account vulnerable people, places and ecosystems;
    (d) Monitoring and evaluating and learning from adaptation plans, policies, programmes and actions; and
    (e) Building the resilience of socioeconomic and ecological systems, including through economic diversification and sustainable management of natural resources.

10. Each Party should, as appropriate, submit and update periodically an adaptation communication, which may include its priorities, implementation and support needs, plans and actions, without creating any additional burden for developing country Parties.

11. The adaptation communication referred to in paragraph 10 of this Article shall be, as appropriate, submitted and updated periodically, as a component of or in conjunction with other communications or documents, including a national adaptation plan, a nationally determined contribution as referred to in Article 4, paragraph 2, and/or a national communication.

12. The adaptation communications referred to in paragraph 10 of this Article shall be recorded in a public registry maintained by the secretariat.

13. Continuous and enhanced international support shall be provided to developing country Parties for the implementation of paragraphs 7, 9, 10 and 11 of this Article, in accordance with the provisions of Articles 9, 10 and 11.

14. The global stocktake referred to in Article 14 shall, *inter alia*:
    (a) Recognize adaptation efforts of developing country Parties;
    (b) Enhance the implementation of adaptation action taking into account the adaptation communication referred to in paragraph 10 of this Article;
    (c) Review the adequacy and effectiveness of adaptation and support provided for adaptation; and
    (d) Review the overall progress made in achieving the global goal on adaptation referred to in paragraph 1 of this Article.

LOSS AND DAMAGE
Article 8
1. Parties recognize the importance of averting, minimizing and addressing loss and damage associated with the adverse effects of climate change, including extreme weather events and slow onset events, and the role of sustainable development in reducing the risk of loss and damage.

2.   The Warsaw International Mechanism for Loss and Damage associated with Climate Change Impacts shall be subject to the authority and guidance of the Conference of the Parties serving as the meeting of the Parties to this Agreement and may be enhanced and strengthened, as determined by the Conference of the Parties serving as the meeting of the Parties to this Agreement.

3.   Parties should enhance understanding, action and support, including through the Warsaw International Mechanism, as appropriate, on a cooperative and facilitative basis with respect to loss and damage associated with the adverse effects of climate change.

4.   Accordingly, areas of cooperation and facilitation to enhance understanding, action and support may include:
        (a)   Early warning systems;
        (b)   Emergency preparedness;
        (c)   Slow onset events;
        (d)   Events that may involve irreversible and permanent loss and damage;
        (e)   Comprehensive risk assessment and management;
        (f)   Risk insurance facilities, climate risk pooling and other insurance solutions;
        (g)   Non-economic losses; and
        (h)   Resilience of communities, livelihoods and ecosystems.

5.   The Warsaw International Mechanism shall collaborate with existing bodies and expert groups under the Agreement, as well as relevant organizations and expert bodies outside the Agreement.

SUPPORT MECHANISMS
Article 9

1.   Developed country Parties shall provide financial resources to assist developing country Parties with respect to both mitigation and adaptation in continuation of their existing obligations under the Convention.

2.   Other Parties are encouraged to provide or continue to provide such support voluntarily.

3.   As part of a global effort, developed country Parties should continue to take the lead in mobilizing climate finance from a wide variety of sources, instruments and channels, noting the significant role of public funds, through a variety of actions, including supporting country-driven strategies, and taking into account the needs and priorities of developing country Parties. Such mobilization of climate finance should represent a progression beyond previous efforts.

4.   The provision of scaled-up financial resources should aim to achieve a balance between adaptation and mitigation, taking into account country-driven strategies, and the priorities and needs of developing country Parties, especially those that are particularly vulnerable to the adverse effects of climate change and have significant capacity constraints, such as the least developed countries and small island developing States, considering the need for public and grant-based resources for [...]

8.   The Financial Mechanism of the Convention, including its operating entities, shall serve as the financial mechanism of this Agreement.

9.   The institutions serving this Agreement, including the operating entities of the Financial Mechanism of the Convention, shall aim to ensure efficient access to financial resources through simplified approval procedures and enhanced readi-

ness support for developing country Parties, in particular for the least developed countries and small island developing States, in the context of their national climate strategies and plans.

Article 10

1. Parties share a long-term vision on the importance of fully realizing technology development and transfer in order to improve resilience to climate change and to reduce greenhouse gas emissions.

2. Parties, noting the importance of technology for the implementation of mitigation and adaptation actions under this Agreement and recognizing existing technology deployment and dissemination efforts, shall strengthen cooperative action on technology development and transfer.

3. The Technology Mechanism established under the Convention shall serve this Agreement.

4. A technology framework is hereby established to provide overarching guidance to the work of the Technology Mechanism in promoting and facilitating enhanced action on technology development and transfer in order to support the implementation of this Agreement, in pursuit of the long-term vision referred to in paragraph 1 of this Article.

5. Accelerating, encouraging and enabling innovation is critical for an effective, long-term global response to climate change and promoting economic growth and sustainable development. Such effort shall be, as appropriate, supported, including by the Technology Mechanism and, through financial means, by the Financial Mechanism of the Convention, for collaborative approaches to research and development, and facilitating access to technology, in particular for early stages of the technology cycle, to developing country Parties.

6. Support, including financial support, shall be provided to developing country Parties for the implementation of this Article, including for strengthening cooperative action on technology development and transfer at different stages of the technology cycle, with a view to achieving a balance between support for mitigation and adaptation. The global stocktake referred to in Article 14 shall take into account available information on efforts related to support on technology development and transfer for developing country Parties.

Article 11

1. Capacity-building under this Agreement should enhance the capacity and ability of developing country Parties, in particular countries with the least capacity, such as the least developed countries, and those that are particularly vulnerable to the adverse effects of climate change, such as small island developing States, to take effective climate change action, including, *inter alia*, to implement adaptation and mitigation actions, and should facilitate technology development, dissemination and deployment, access to climate finance, relevant aspects of education, training and public awareness, and the transparent, timely and accurate communication of information.

2. Capacity-building should be country-driven, based on and responsive to national needs, and foster country ownership of Parties, in particular, for developing country Parties, including at the national, subnational and local levels. Capacity-building

should be guided by lessons learned, including those from capacity-building activities under the Convention, and should be an effective, iterative process that is participatory, cross-cutting and gender-responsive.

3. All Parties should cooperate to enhance the capacity of developing country Parties to implement this Agreement. Developed country Parties should enhance support for capacity-building actions in developing country Parties.

4. All Parties enhancing the capacity of developing country Parties to implement this Agreement, including through regional, bilateral and multilateral approaches, shall regularly communicate on these actions or measures on capacity- building. Developing country Parties should regularly communicate progress made on implementing capacity-building plans, policies, actions or measures to implement this Agreement.

5. Capacity-building activities shall be enhanced through appropriate institutional arrangements to support the implementation of this Agreement, including the appropriate institutional arrangements established under the Convention that serve this Agreement. The Conference of the Parties serving as the meeting of the Parties to this Agreement shall, at its first session, consider and adopt a decision on the initial institutional arrangements for capacity-building.

Article 14

1. The Conference of the Parties serving as the meeting of the Parties to this Agreement shall periodically take stock of the implementation of this Agreement to assess the collective progress towards achieving the purpose of this Agreement and its long-term goals (referred to as the "global stocktake"). It shall do so in a comprehensive and facilitative manner, considering mitigation, adaptation and the means of implementation and support, and in the light of equity and the best available science.

[...]

16.2.2 Other Instruments

Table 16.1 List of important climate change instruments

United Nations General Assembly Resolution 45/212, 'Protection of global climate for present and future generations of mankind' (21 December 1990) UN Doc A/RES/45/212
Second World Climate Conference Ministerial Declaration 1990
Berlin Mandate, Decision 1/CP.1 (6 June 1995) FCCC/CP/1995/7/Add.1, 4
Marrakesh Accords, Decisions 2-24/CP.7 (21 January 2002) FCCC/CP/2001/13/Add.1-3
Bali Action Plan, Decision 1/CP.13 (14 March 2008) FCCC/CP/2007/6/Add.1, 3
Copenhagen Accord, Decision 2/CP.15 (30 March 2010) FCCC/CP/2009/11/Add.1, 4
Cancun Agreements Decision 1/CP.16 (15 March 2011) FCCC/CP/2010/7/Add.1, 2
Durban Platform Decision, 1/CP.17 (11 December 2011) FCCC/CP/2011/9/Add.1, 2
Doha Amendment, Decision 1/CMP.8 (28 February 2013) FCCC/KP/CMP/2012/13/Add.1, 2
Warsaw international mechanism for loss and damage, Decision 2/CP.19 (31 January 2014) FCCC/CP/2013/10/Add.1, 6
Lima Call for Climate Action, Decision 1/CP.20 (2 February 2015) FCCC/CP/2014/10/Add.1, 2

The Katowice Rulebook, Decision 4/CMA.1
(15 December 2018) FCCC/PA/CMA/2018/3/Add.1, 6

Further guidance for information to facilitate clarity, transparency and understanding of nationally determined contributions, referred to in decision 1/CP.21, paragraph 28

6.   Further recalls Article 4, paragraph 8, of the Paris Agreement, which provides that, in communicating their nationally determined contributions, all Parties shall provide the information necessary for clarity, transparency and understanding in accordance with decision 1/CP.21 and any relevant decisions of the Conference of the Parties serving as the meeting of the Parties to the Paris Agreement;

7.   Decides that, in communicating their second and subsequent nationally determined contributions, Parties shall provide the information necessary for clarity, transparency and understanding contained in annex I as applicable to their nationally determined contributions, and strongly encourages Parties to provide this information in relation to their first nationally determined contribution, including when communicating or updating it by 2020;

8.   Emphasizes that the guidance on information necessary for clarity, transparency and understanding is without prejudice to the inclusion of components other than mitigation in a nationally determined contribution, notes that Parties may provide other information when submitting their nationally determined contributions, and in particular that, as provided in Article 7, paragraph 11, of the Paris Agreement, an adaptation communication referred to in Article 7, paragraph 10, of the Paris Agreement may be submitted as a component of or in conjunction with a nationally determined contribution as referred to in Article 4, paragraph 2, of the Paris Agreement, and also notes the further guidance in relation to the adaptation communication contained in decision 9/CMA.1;

9.   Recalls decision 1/CP.21, paragraph 27, applicable to Parties' first nationally determined contributions, including those communicated or updated by 2020, pursuant to paragraph 24 of the same decision, in which the Conference of the Parties agreed that the information to be provided by Parties communicating their nationally determined contributions, in order to facilitate clarity, transparency and understanding, may include, as appropriate, *inter alia*, quantifiable information on the reference point (including, as appropriate, a base year), time frames and/or periods for implementation, scope and coverage, planning processes, assumptions and methodological approaches, including those for estimating and accounting for anthropogenic greenhouse gas emissions and, as appropriate, removals, and how the Party considers that its nationally determined contribution is fair and ambitious, in the light of its national circumstances, and how it contributes towards achieving the objective of the Convention as set out in its Article 2;

10.   Recognizes that each Party with a nationally determined contribution under Article 4 of the Paris Agreement that consists of mitigation co-benefits resulting from its adaptation action and/or economic diversification plans consistent with Article 4, paragraph 7, of the Paris Agreement shall provide the information referred to in annex I as applicable to its nationally determined contribution and as it relates to such mitigation co-benefits;

Guidance for accounting for Parties' nationally determined contributions, referred to in decision 1/CP.21, paragraph 31

11.   Recalls Article 4, paragraph 13, of the Paris Agreement, which provides that Parties shall account for their nationally determined contributions, and that, in accounting for anthropogenic emissions and removals corresponding to their nationally determined contributions, Parties shall promote environmental integrity, transparency, accuracy, completeness, comparability and consistency, and ensure the avoidance of double counting, in accordance with guidance adopted by the Conference of the Parties serving as the meeting of the Parties to the Paris Agreement;

12.   Also recalls decision 1/CP.21, paragraph 31, in which the Ad Hoc Working Group on the Paris Agreement was requested to elaborate, drawing on approaches established under the Convention and its related legal instruments, as appropriate, guidance for accounting for Parties' nationally determined contributions, as referred to in Article 4, paragraph 13, of the Paris Agreement, for consideration and adoption by the Conference of the Parties serving as the meeting of the Parties to the Paris Agreement at its first session, which ensures that:

(a)   Parties account for anthropogenic emissions and removals in accordance with methodologies and common metrics assessed by the Intergovernmental Panel on Climate Change and adopted by the Conference of the Parties serving as the meeting of the Parties to the Paris Agreement;

(b)   Parties ensure methodological consistency, including on baselines, between the communication and implementation of nationally determined contributions;

(c)   Parties strive to include all categories of anthropogenic emissions or removals in their nationally determined contributions and, once a source, sink or activity is included, continue to include it;

(d)   Parties shall provide an explanation of why any categories of anthropogenic emissions or removals are excluded;

13.   Decides that, in accounting for anthropogenic emissions and removals corresponding to their nationally determined contributions under Article 4, paragraph 13, of the Paris Agreement, Parties shall account for their nationally determined contributions in accordance with the guidance contained in annex II;

Annex I
Information to facilitate clarity, transparency and understanding of nationally determined contributions, referred to in decision 1/CP.21, paragraph 28

1.   Quantifiable information on the reference point (including, as appropriate, a base year): [...]

2.   Time frames and/or periods for implementation: [...]

3.   Scope and coverage: [...]

4.   Planning processes: [...]

5.   Assumptions and methodological approaches, including those for estimating and accounting for anthropogenic greenhouse gas emissions and, as appropriate, removals: [...]

6.   How the Party considers that its nationally determined contribution is fair and ambitious in the light of its national circumstances: [...]

7.   How the nationally determined contribution contributes towards achieving the objective of the Convention as set out in its Article 2: [...]

Annex II
Accounting for Parties' nationally determined contributions, referred to in decision 1/CP.21, paragraph 31

1.   Accounting for anthropogenic emissions and removals in accordance with methodologies and common metrics assessed by the Intergovernmental Panel on Climate Change (IPCC) and adopted by the Conference of the Parties serving as the meeting of the Parties to the Paris Agreement: [...]
2.   Ensuring methodological consistency, including on baselines, between the communication and implementation of nationally determined contributions: [...]

[...]

3.   Striving to include all categories of anthropogenic emissions or removals in the nationally determined contribution and, once a source, sink or activity is included, continuing to include it:
       (a)   Parties account for all categories of anthropogenic emissions and removals corresponding to their nationally determined contribution;
       (b)   Parties strive to include all categories of anthropogenic emissions and removals in their nationally determined contribution, and, once a source, sink or activity is included, continue to include it.
4.   Providing an explanation of why any categories of anthropogenic emissions or removals are excluded.

ILA, Declaration of Legal Principles Relating to Climate Change, Resolution 2/2014, adopted at the 76th Conference of the ILA (Washington, 7–11 April 2014)

Draft Article 2. Objectives
The purpose of the present draft Articles is to set out legal principles applicable to States in addressing climate change and its adverse effects, bearing in mind that change in the Earth's climate and its adverse effects are a common concern of humankind.

Draft Article 3. Sustainable Development
1.   States shall protect the climate system as a common natural resource for the benefit of present and future generations, within the broader context of the international community's commitment to sustainable development.

[...]

3.   In the context of addressing climate change and its adverse effects, sustainable development requires States to balance economic and social development and the protection of the climate system and supports the realisation of the right of all human beings to an adequate living standard and the equitable distribution of the

benefits thereof. To that extent, policies and measures taken in response to climate change must integrate environmental, economic and social matters.

[...]

Draft Article 4. Equity
1.   States shall protect the climate system on the basis of equity, of which the principle of common but differentiated responsibilities and respective capabilities, laid out in draft Article 5, is a major expression.
2.   States shall protect the climate system in a manner that equitably balances the needs of present and future generations of humankind, keeping in mind that:
    (a)   Present generations in developing States have a legitimate expectation of equitable access to sustainable development. This recognises that to the extent that per capita emissions in developing countries are still low, these will grow, within reason and in a sustainable manner, to meet their social and development needs.
    (b)   Future generations in all States have a legitimate expectation of equitable access to the Earth's resources. This requires that current generations hold the increase in global average temperature to the multilaterally agreed global goal.

[...]

Draft Article 5. Common but Differentiated Responsibilities and Respective Capabilities
1.   States shall protect the climate system in accordance with their common but differentiated responsibilities and respective capabilities.

[...]

Draft Article 6. Special Circumstances and Vulnerability
1.   States shall take full account of the special circumstances and needs of developing countries particularly vulnerable to the effects of climate change, specifically but not limited to the Least Developed Countries and Small Island Developing States.

[...]

Draft Article 7. Prevention & Precaution
Draft Article 7A. Obligation of prevention
1.   States have an obligation to ensure that activities within their jurisdiction or control do not cause damage to the environment of other States or of areas beyond the limits of national jurisdiction, including damage through climate change.
2.   States shall exercise due diligence to avoid, minimise and reduce environmental and other damage through climate change, as described in draft Article 7A.1. In exercising due diligence, States shall take all appropriate measures to anticipate, prevent or minimise the causes of climate change, especially through effective measures to reduce greenhouse gas emissions, and to minimise the adverse effects of climate change through the adoption of suitable adaptation measures.

3.   In determining whether a State has exercised due diligence in accordance with draft Article 7A.2, economic development and available resources, scientific knowledge, the risks involved in an action, and the vulnerability of affected states shall be taken into account. Measures taken by States to anticipate, prevent or minimise the causes and adverse effects of climate change must be proportionate.

Draft Article 7B. Precautionary principle
1.   Where there is a reasonably foreseeable threat of serious or irreversible damage, including serious or irreversible damage to States vulnerable to the impacts of climate change, measures to anticipate, prevent or adapt to climate change shall be taken by States without waiting for conclusive scientific proof of that damage.
2.   Precautionary measures for the purposes of draft Article 7B.1 shall include proactive and cost-effective measures which enable sustainable development, maintain the stability of the climate system and protect the climate system against human-induced change.
3.   As new scientific knowledge relating to the causes or effects of climate change becomes available, States must continuously assess their obligation of prevention and the necessity for precautionary measures. Where scientific knowledge about damage from climate change improves sufficiently, protective measures shall be continued by States pursuant to their obligation to prevent environmental damage, as described in draft Article 7A.1 above.
4.   In light of new scientific knowledge, States must strengthen their emission reduction standards and other preventative and adaptation measures, taking into account the factors listed in draft Article 7A.3.

[…]

Draft Article 8. International Cooperation
1.   States shall cooperate with each other and competent international organisations in good faith to address climate change and its adverse effects.

[…]

Draft Article 9. Good Faith
1.   States commit themselves to act in good faith in addressing climate change and its adverse effects and to achieve internationally agreed objectives. This includes their good faith commitment to engage in constant monitoring and supervision both at the domestic and international levels to ensure that these objectives are met.

[…]

Draft Article 10. Inter-Relationship
1.   In order to effectively address climate change and its adverse effects, States shall formulate, elaborate and implement international law relating to climate change in a mutually supportive manner with other relevant international law.

[…]

QUESTIONS

1. Identify the main themes and legal concepts within the various climate change treaties. Which, if any, would you change, and why?
2. 'Compared with the Kyoto Protocol, the flexibility of the Paris Agreement is a strength, not a weakness.' Discuss.
3. 'International efforts to regulate climate change represent a triumph of diplomatic skill, but not of effective policy.' Do you agree? Give reasons for your answer.

FURTHER READING

BOOKS

I Algona, C Bakker and J-P Gauci (eds), *Climate Change Litigation: Global Perspectives* (Brill/Nijohff 2021)

D Bodansky, J Brunée and L Rajamani (eds), *International Climate Change Law* (Oxford University Press 2017)

CP Carlarne, KR Gray and R Tarasofsky (eds), *The Oxford Handbook of International Climate Change Law* (Oxford University Press 2016)

M Doelle and S Seck (eds), *Research Handbook on Climate Change Loss and Damage* (Edward Elgar 2021)

DA Farber and M Peeters (eds), *Climate Change Law* (Edward Elgar 2016)

D Klein, MP Carazo, M Doelle, J Bulmer and A Higham (eds), *The Paris Agreement on Climate Change: Analysis and Commentary* (Oxford University Press 2017)

B Mayer, *The International Law on Climate Change* (Cambridge University Press 2018)

B Mayer and A Zahar (eds), *Debating Climate Law* (Cambridge University Press 2021)

IR Mintzer and JA Leonard (eds), *Negotiating Climate Change: The Inside Story of the Rio Convention* (Cambridge University Press 1994)

G van Calster and L Reins (eds), *The Paris Agreement on Climate Change: A Commentary* (Edward Elgar 2021)

CHAPTERS

JH Knox, 'The Paris Agreement as a Human Rights Treaty' in D Akande, J Kuosmanen, H McDermott and D Roser (eds), *Human Rights and 21st Century Challenges: Poverty, Conflict, and the Environment* (Oxford University Press 2020)

ARTICLES

HP Aust, 'The Shifting Role of Cities in the Global Climate Change Regime: From Paris to Pittsburgh and Back?' (2019) 28 Review of European Comparative & Environmental Law 57

D Bodansky, 'The United Nations Framework Convention on Climate Change: A Commentary' (1993) 18(2) Yale Journal of International Law 451

D Bodansky, 'The Legal Character of the Paris Agreement' (2016) 25(2) Review of European Comparative & Environmental Law 142

K Bouwer, 'The Unsexy Future of Climate Change Litigation' (2018) 30 Journal of Environmental Law 483

C Breidenich et al., 'The Kyoto Protocol to the United Nations Framework Convention on Climate Change' (1998) 92(2) American Journal of International Law 315

M Burkett, 'Reading Between the Red Lines: Loss and Damage and the Paris Outcome' (2016) 6(1–2) Climate Law 118

M Doelle, 'The Paris Agreement: Historic Breakthrough or High Stakes Experiment?' (2016) 6(1–2) Climate Law Special Issue 1

D French, '1997 Kyoto Protocol to the 1992 UN Framework Convention on Climate Change' (1998) 10(2) Journal of Environmental Law 227

J Lin and A Zahar, 'Special Issue on the Paris Rulebook' (2019) 9 Climate Law 3

MJ Mace, 'Mitigation Commitments Under the Paris Agreement and the Way Forward' (2016) 6 Climate Law 21

B Mayer, 'Obligations of Conduct in the International Law on Climate Change: A Defence' (2018) 27 Review of European Comparative & Environmental Law 130

B Preston, 'The Influence of the Paris Agreement on Climate Litigation: Legal Obligations and Norms (Part I)' (2021) 33 Journal of Environmental Law 1

L Rajamani, 'From Berlin to Bali and Beyond: Killing Kyoto Softly' (2008) 57(4) International and Comparative Law Quarterly 909

L Rajamani, 'The Durban Platform for Enhanced Action and the Future of the Climate Regime' (2012) 61(2) International and Comparative Law Quarterly 501

L Rajamani, 'The Devilish Details: Key Legal Issues in the 2015 Climate Negotiations' (2015) 78(5) Modern Law Review 826

L Rajamani, 'Innovation and Experimentation in the International Climate Change Regime' (2020) 404 RCADI

P Sands, 'Climate Change and International Law: Adjudicating the Future in International Law' (2016) 28 Journal of Environmental Law 1

JE Viñuales, 'The Paris Agreement on Climate Change: Less is More' (2016) 59 German Yearbook of International Law 1

C Voigt and F Ferriera, 'Differentiation in the Paris Agreement' (2016) 6(1–2) Climate Law Special Issue 58

PART III
IMPLEMENTATION AND ENFORCEMENT

17
Responsibility and liability for environmental damage

17.1 INTRODUCTION

A usual consequence of the 'no harm' principle[1] is for the harm to be repaired. This is, as Alena Douhan observes, not a new phenomenon, and the principle of compensation for damage resulting from environmentally harmful activities is well established.[2] Principle 22 of the 1972 Stockholm Declaration states:

> States shall cooperate to develop further the international law regarding liability and compensation for the victims of pollution and other environmental damage caused by activities within the jurisdiction or control of such States to areas beyond their jurisdiction.

Similarly, Principle 13 of the 1992 Rio Declaration states:

> States shall develop national law regarding liability and compensation for the victims of pollution and other environmental damage. States shall also cooperate in an expeditious and more determined manner to develop further international law regarding liability and compensation for adverse effects of environmental damage caused by activities within their jurisdiction or control to areas beyond their jurisdiction.

The implementation, however, of a regime for reparation of environmental harm can be complex. Environmental harm may involve a large amount of damage affecting a variety of entities, potentially involving very large sums in compensation and a large number of claimants, both individuals and States. The harm may be hard to quantify, especially since the effects of the damage may continue for a long period of time. Within the sphere of traditional inter-state relations, it is hard to regulate because the cause of the harm will very often be private actors. Moreover, the cause of the harm may well be accidental, or involve no obvious breach of any particular obligation. In this connection, it is worth noting that many obligations

---

[1] See Chapter 4.

[2] Alena Douhan, 'Liability for Environmental Damage' in R Wolfrum, *Max Planck Encyclopedia of Public International Law* (2019).

to prevent, e.g., in the protection of the marine environment, were concluded only *after* the occurrence of a major environmental incident had highlighted the regulatory gap that needed to be addressed.[3] Furthermore, various actors may bear some causal responsibility,[4] while problems of causation can be highly technical and difficult to establish.

The approach to reparations taken under general international law in the inter-state context exists under the rubric of international responsibility. This is authoritatively contained in the ILC's 2001 Articles on Responsibility of State for International Wrongful Acts. Reparation under state responsibility arises as a consequence of the breach of an international obligation – it requires the state seeking reparations to establish that another state injured them. This approach may be contrasted with a liability model of reparation, in which an entity is strictly liable to compensate for environmental damage arising from an incident, irrespective of whether the operator's conduct breached any relevant legal norms. This model of compensation is found, primarily, in national legal systems and in international regimes for the establishment of civil liability (i.e., for the liability of private actors) in respect of environmental harm. Inter-state liability regimes can, however, be found, exceptionally, in the 1972 Space Liability Convention. A proposal by the ILC in its 1996 draft Articles on International Liability that state liability should operate such that they should be liable for all transboundary harm was not included in the final 2006 Draft Principles on the allocation of loss in the case of transboundary harm arising out of hazardous activities.

When it comes to the legal implementation of any regime for environmental damage, a preliminary and difficult question is what constitutes compensable damage? The particular development of note, here, is the recognition of compensation for pure environmental damage. Traditionally, damage was understood to refer to damage to people or property rather than the environment *per se*. Insofar as damage to the environment was compensable, the ground for compensation was the cost incurred in preventing or responding to the harm. This is reflected in several of the current civil liability regimes that do not provide for pure environmental harm as a head of compensable damage. Many instruments have now recognised a head of pure environmental damage, in which impairment of the environment is itself compensable. Nonetheless the scope of pure environmental damage varies according to the definition employed by each particular regime.

A second issue that arises from the attempt at defining compensable damage is whether damage is equivalent to harm or impairment or whether a further threshold of severity must be met before such harm rises to 'damage'. The general position is that a minimum threshold must be met for impairment to constitute damage, but there is a degree of vagueness about where the line is drawn. According to the ILC in the commentary to the 2006 Draft Principles on the allocation of loss in the case of transboundary harm arising out of hazardous activi-

---

[3]   See Chapter 8 on protection of marine environment.

[4]   See e.g. report into *Deepwater Horizon*: National Commission on the BP Deepwater Horizon Oil Spill and Offshore Drilling, 'Report to the President: Deep Water: The Gulf Oil Disaster and the Future of Offshore Drilling' (2011) https://www.govinfo.gov/content/pkg/GPO-OILCOMMISSION/pdf/GPO-OILCOMMISSION.pdf accessed 4 June 2021.

ties, the harm must be 'significant'. This does not, however, mean that the harm must reach a degree of severity, but instead must be real, in the sense of measurable by objective standards. Other instruments provide for a stricter gravity threshold, such as that the impairment must be above a minimum level or be long term or irreparable.

Two related matters arise in connection with the problem of defining damage: the standard of liability and reparation. Under general international law, state responsibility for environmental harm is fault-based and operates on the principle of full reparation. The standard of fault within environmental law is typically that of due diligence. In international liability regimes, strict liability tends to apply and liability tends to be limited to a specified amount. One particular difficulty arising in the inter-state context is whether environmental norms incumbent on states give rise to any duty of reparation at all. In *Pulp Mills*, the ICJ held that breaches of procedural obligations – such as duties to consult – did not, in themselves, give rise to international responsibility to make reparation. The difficulty for inter-state responsibility that this line of reasoning creates is that many environmental obligations are of this form and would thus not be compensable in practice. Under general international law, however, if a compensable norm is breached, it is clear from *Costa Rica v. Nicaragua* that full reparation is required, and in valuing the amount of compensation, an amount approximately reflecting the value of the damage is possible even if the actual value is not clear.

The responsibility and liability of states for environmental damage is determined largely under the customary international law rules on state responsibility contained within the 2001 ARSIWA. The 1972 Space Liability Convention provides an example of an inter-state liability regime, but it is almost unique in this regard. Where international agreements do refer specifically to reparative obligations, this is done by reference to general custom. A novel approach can be found in the climate change regime, under the Warsaw international mechanism for loss and damage supported by a provision on loss and damage in the 2015 Paris Agreement. The Warsaw International Mechanism and Paris Agreement are not concerned with the allocation of liability to individual states, and it was made clear at the decision of the Conference of the Parties when adopting the Paris Agreement that 'Article 8 of the Agreement does not involve or provide a basis for any liability or compensation'.[5] Instead, the approach taken towards loss and damage is collective and involves coordinating responses, mitigation and adaptation, including the power to address loss and damage, including to the financial mechanism of the Convention.[6]

Civil liability regimes established under international treaties provide for specific liability regimes for certain entities in respect of certain types of environmental harm.[7] For example, the 1963 Vienna Convention on Civil Liability for Nuclear Damage makes the operator of a nuclear installation strictly liable for nuclear damage caused by a nuclear incident. Other treaties create liability for damage arising from oil pollution, hazardous waste, or the carriage

---

[5]   Decision 1/Cp.21, para. 52.

[6]   See discussion in Morten Broberg, 'State of Climate Law' The Third Pillar of International Climate Change Law: Explaining "Loss and Damage" after the Paris Agreement' (2020) 10 Climate Law 211.

[7]   See P Sands and J Peel, *Principles of International Environmental Law* (4th edn, CUP 2018) 771–803.

of dangerous goods. The treaties oblige states to impose the regime within their domestic legal system and allocates jurisdiction between the domestic courts of the Parties for adjudicating claims. The treaties tend to have two main dimensions. First, they establish liability, the scope of any exceptions to the liability, and limits to liability. Second, they prescribe that in the event of a specified incident or event, the relevant entity must ensure the availability of a fund up to a certain amount in order to meet claims for compensation for damage. This can also require mandatory insurance. International treaties also establish funds, such as the International Oil Pollution Compensation Fund 1992, which operators are required to contribute to in order to meet claims exceeding the maximum limit of compensation by the liable entity. These features of the regime, liability and financial security, can be distributed across different instruments. For instance, the current regime for civil liability for oil pollution is to be found in the 1992 Civil Liability Convention and the 1992 Fund Convention, each addressing one feature of the regime. In addition, excess claims may be required to be met by state parties themselves.

The chapter is structured as follows: first, it covers certain fundamental, general problems concerning responsibility and liability for environmental damage. Second, it examines responsibility and liability between states, specifically under the general regime for state responsibility and specific treaty regimes. Third, it examines the regimes for civil liability, with a particular focus on liabilities in respect of damage from oil, nuclear material and hazardous waste. These are selected because they are well-established, detailed regimes, indicative of the general approach towards civil liability found also in other conventions.

17.2   GENERAL ISSUES

17.2.1   Responsibility vs Liability

Institut de Droit International, 'Responsibility and Liability under International Law for Environmental Damage' (Strasbourg, 1997)

Basic Distinction on Responsibility and Liability
Article 1
The breach of an obligation of environmental protection established under international law engages responsibility of the State (international responsibility), entailing as a consequence the obligation to reestablish the original position or to pay compensation.
The latter obligation may also arise from a rule of international law providing for strict responsibility on the basis of harm or injury alone, particularly in case of ultra-hazardous activities (responsibility for harm alone).
Civil liability of operators can be engaged under domestic law or the governing rules of international law regardless of the lawfulness of the activity concerned if it results in environmental damage.
The foregoing is without prejudice to the question of criminal responsibility of natural or juridical persons.

17.2.2   Meaning of 'Damage'

17.2.2.1 Legally binding instruments

UNSC Res 687 (1991)

16.   Reaffirms that Iraq, without prejudice to the debts and obligations of Iraq prior to 2 August 1990, is liable under international law for any direct loss, damage, including environmental damage and the depletion of natural resources, or injury to foreign Governments, nationals and corporations, as a result of Iraq's unlawful invasion of Kuwait;

1993 Lugano Convention on Civil Liability for Damage resulting from Activities Dangerous to the Environment, ETS 150

7   "Damage" means:

a   loss of life or personal injury;

b   loss of or damage to property other than to the installation itself or property held under the control of the operator, at the site of the dangerous activity;

c   loss or damage by impairment of the environment in so far as this is not considered to be damage within the meaning of sub-paragraphs a or b above provided that compensation for impairment of the environment, other than for loss of profit from such impairment, shall be limited to the costs of measures of reinstatement actually undertaken or to be undertaken;

d   the costs of preventive measures and any loss or damage caused by preventive measures, to the extent that the loss or damage referred to in sub-paragraphs a to c of this paragraph arises out of or results from the hazardous properties of the dangerous substances, genetically modified organisms or micro-organisms or arises or results from waste.

2010 Nagoya-Kuala Lumpur Supplementary Protocol on Liability and Redress to the Cartagena Protocol on Biosafety

Article 2 Use of Terms

[...]

(b)   "Damage" means an adverse effect on the conservation and sustainable use of biological diversity, taking also into account risks to human health, that:

(i)   Is measurable or otherwise observable taking into account, wherever available, scientifically-established baselines recognized by a competent authority that takes into account any other human induced variation and natural variation; and

(ii)   Is significant as set out in paragraph 3 below;

[...]

3.   A "significant" adverse effect is to be determined on the basis of factors, such as:

(a)   The long-term or permanent change, to be understood as change that will not be redressed through natural recovery within a reasonable period of time;

(b)   The extent of the qualitative or quantitative changes that adversely affect the components of biological diversity;

(c)   The reduction of the ability of components of biological diversity to provide goods and services;

(d)   The extent of any adverse effects on human health in the context of the Protocol.

17.2.2.2 Non-legally binding instruments
2006 Draft principles on the allocation of loss in the case of transboundary harm arising out of hazardous activities, with commentaries, Yearbook ILC, vol II

Principle 2 Use of Terms

For the purposes of the present draft articles:

(a)   "damage" means significant damage caused to persons, property or the environment; and includes:

(i)   loss of life or personal injury;

(ii)   loss of, or damage to, property, including property which forms part of the cultural heritage;

(iii)   loss or damage by impairment of the environment;

(iv)   the costs of reasonable measures of reinstatement of the property, or environment, including natural resources;

(v)   the cost of reasonable response measures;

(b)   "environment" includes: natural resources, both abiotic and biotic, such as air, water, soil, fauna and flora and the interaction between the same factors; and the characteristic aspects of the landscape.

UNEP GUIDELINES Decision IG 17/4: Guidelines for the Determination of Liability and Compensation for Damage resulting from Pollution of the Marine Environment in the Mediterranean Sea Area (15th Meeting of the Parties)

9.   For the purpose of these Guidelines, "environmental damage" means a measurable adverse change in a natural or biological resource or measurable impairment of a natural or biological resource service which may occur directly or indirectly.

[…]

14.   For the purpose of these Guidelines, "traditional damage" means:

(a)   loss of life or personal injury;

(b)   loss of or damage to property other than property held by the person liable;

(c)   loss of income directly deriving from an impairment of a legally protected interest in any use of the marine environment for economic purposes, incurred as a result of impairment of the environment, taking into account savings and costs;

(d)   any loss or damage caused by preventive measures taken to avoid damage referred to under sub-paragraphs (a), (b) and (c).

15.   These Guidelines also apply to damage caused by pollution of a diffuse character provided that it is possible to establish a causal link between the damage and the activities of individual operators.

17.2.2.3 Cases

> **CASE**
> RIAA, *Trail Smelter Arbitration (United States v. Canada)*, 3 RIAA 1905 (1938 and 1941)
>
> (p. 1965)
> The Tribunal, therefore, finds that the above decisions, taken as a whole, constitute an adequate basis for its conclusions, namely, that, under the principles of international law, as well as of the law of the United States, no State has the right to use or permit the use of its territory in such a manner as to cause injury by fumes in or to the territory of another or the properties or persons therein, when the case is of serious consequence and the injury is established by clear and convincing evidence.

> **CASE**
> *UN Compensation Commission, Report and Recommendations Made by the Panel of Commissioners Concerning the Second Instalment of "F4" Claims*, S/AC.26/2002/26 (3 October 2002)
>
> 23. In the view of the Panel, the term "environmental damage" in paragraph 16 of Security Council resolution 687 (1991) is not limited to losses or expenses resulting from the activities and events listed in paragraph 35 of Governing Council decision 7, but can also cover direct losses or expenses resulting from other activities and events. A loss or expense may be compensable even if does not arise under any of the specific subparagraphs of paragraph 35 of Governing Council decision 7. For example, expenses of measures undertaken to prevent or abate harmful impacts of airborne contaminants on property or human health could qualify as environmental damage, provided that the losses or expenses are a direct result of Iraq's invasion and occupation of Kuwait.

> **CASE**
> *UN Compensation Commission, Report and Recommendations Made by the Panel of Commissioners Concerning the Fifth Instalment of "F4" Claims*, S/AC.26/2005/10 (30 June 2005)
>
> 55. [...] As the Panel stated in the fourth "F4" report, part one, Security Council resolution 687 (1991) and Governing Council decision 7 establish the general principle that Iraq is liable for all damage and losses that result directly from its invasion and occupation of Kuwait. In the opinion of the Panel this means that any loss of or damage to natural resources that can be demonstrated to have resulted directly from Iraq's invasion and occupation of Kuwait must be deemed to be encompassed in the concept of "environmental damage and the depletion of natural resources" within the meaning of Security Council resolution 687 (1991). The Panel does not consider that there is anything in the language or context of Security Council

resolution 687 (1991) or Governing Council decision 7 that mandates or suggests an interpretation that would restrict the term "environmental damage" to damage to natural resources which have commercial value.

56. Furthermore, the Panel does not consider that the fact that the effects of the loss of or damage to natural resources might be for a temporary duration should have any relevance to the issue of the compensability of the damage or loss, although it might affect the nature and quantum of compensation that may be appropriate. In the view of the Panel, it is not reasonable to suggest that a loss that is documented to have occurred, and is shown to have resulted from the invasion and occupation of Kuwait, should nevertheless be denied compensation solely on the grounds that the effects of the loss were not permanent. As the Panel sees it, the critical issue to be determined in each claim is whether the evidence provided is sufficient to show that there has been a loss of or damage to natural resources as alleged and, if so, whether such loss or damage resulted directly from Iraq's invasion and occupation of Kuwait.

57. The Panel, therefore, finds that a loss due to depletion of or damage to natural resources, including resources that may not have a commercial value is, in principle, compensable in accordance with Security Council resolution 687 (1991) and Governing Council decision 7 if such loss was a direct result of Iraq's invasion and occupation of Kuwait. It follows, therefore, that temporary loss of the use of such resources is compensable if it is proved that the loss resulted directly from Iraq's invasion and occupation of Kuwait.

58. The Panel does not consider that this finding is inconsistent with any principle or rule of general international law. In the view of the Panel, there is no justification for the contention that general international law precludes compensation for pure environmental damage. In particular, the Panel does not consider that the exclusion of compensation for pure environmental damage in some international conventions on civil liability and compensation16 is a valid basis for asserting that international law, in general, prohibits compensation for such damage in all cases, even where the damage results from an internationally wrongful act.

ADVISORY OPINION
ITLOS, Responsibilities and Obligations of States Sponsoring Persons and Entities with Respect to Activities in the Area, Advisory Opinion, Case No. 17, ITLOS Reports 10 (Seabed Dispute Chamber) (1 February 2011)

178. As stated above, according to the first sentence of article 139, paragraph 2, of the Convention, the failure of a sponsoring State to carry out its responsibilities entails liability only if there is damage. [...]
179. Neither the Convention nor the relevant Regulations (regulation 30 of the Nodules Regulations and regulation 32 of the Sulphides Regulations) specifies what constitutes compensable damage, or which subjects may be entitled to claim compensation. It may be envisaged that the damage in question would include damage to the Area and its resources constituting the common heritage of mankind, and damage to the marine environment. Subjects entitled to claim compensation may include the Authority, entities engaged in deep seabed mining, other users of the sea, and coastal States.

17.2.3   Inter-State Legal Standards: Due Diligence

17.2.3.1 Legally binding instruments
1997 United Nations Convention on Non-Navigational Uses of Watercourses, 2999 UNTS, A/51/869

Article 7
Obligation not to cause significant harm
1.   Watercourse States shall, in utilizing an international watercourse in their territories, take all appropriate measures to prevent the causing of significant harm to other watercourse States.
2.   Where significant harm nevertheless is caused to another watercourse State, the States whose use causes such harm shall, in the absence of agreement to such use, take all appropriate measures, having due regard for the provisions of articles 5 and 6, in consultation with the affected State, to eliminate or mitigate such harm and, where appropriate, to discuss the question of compensation.

17.2.3.2 Non-legally binding instruments
2001 ILC Draft Articles on Prevention of Transboundary Harm from Hazardous Activities

Article 3
The State of origin shall take all appropriate measures to prevent significant transboundary harm or at any event to minimize the risk thereof.

17.2.3.3 Cases

CASE
ICJ, *Gabčíkovo-Nagymaros Project (Hungary v. Slovakia)*, ICJ Reports 7 (1997)

140 ...in the field of environmental protection, vigilance and prevention are required on account of the often irreversible character of damage to the environment and of the limitations inherent in the very mechanism of reparation of this type of damage.

CASE
ICJ, *Pulp Mills on the River Uruguay (Argentina v. Uruguay)*, ICJ Reports 14 (2010)

187. The Court considers that the obligation laid down in Article 36 is addressed to both Parties and prescribes the specific conduct of co-ordinating the necessary measures through the Commission to avoid changes to the ecological balance. An obligation to adopt regulatory or administrative measures either individually or jointly and to enforce them is an obligation of conduct. Both Parties are therefore called upon, under Article 36, to exercise due diligence in acting through the Commission for the necessary measures to preserve the ecological balance of the river.

ADVISORY OPINION
ITLOS, Responsibilities and Obligations of States Sponsoring Persons and Entities with Respect to Activities in the Area, Advisory Opinion, Case No. 17, ITLOS Reports 10 (Seabed Dispute Chamber) (1 February 2011)

110. The sponsoring State's obligation "to ensure" is not an obligation to achieve, in each and every case, the result that the sponsored contractor complies with the aforementioned obligations. Rather, it is an obligation to deploy adequate means, to exercise best possible efforts, to do the utmost, to obtain this result. To utilize the terminology current in international law, this obligation may be characterized as an obligation "of conduct" and not "of result", and as an obligation of "due diligence".
[...]

112. The expression "to ensure" is often used in international legal instruments to refer to obligations in respect of which, while it is not considered reasonable to make a State liable for each and every violation committed by persons under its jurisdiction, it is equally not considered satisfactory to rely on mere application of the principle that the conduct of private persons or entities is not attributable to the State under international law (see ILC Articles on State Responsibility, Commentary to article 8, paragraph 1).
[...]

117. The content of "due diligence" obligations may not easily be described in precise terms. Among the factors that make such a description difficult is the fact that "due diligence"

is a variable concept. It may change over time as measures considered sufficiently diligent at a certain moment may become not diligent enough in light, for instance, of new scientific or technological knowledge. It may also change in relation to the risks involved in the activity. As regards activities in the Area, it seems reasonable to state that prospecting is, generally speaking, less risky than exploration activities which, in turn, entail less risk than exploitation. Moreover, activities in the Area concerning different kinds of minerals, for example, polymetallic nodules on the one hand and polymetallic sulphides or cobalt rich ferromanganese crusts on the other, may require different standards of diligence. The standard of due diligence has to be more severe for the riskier activities.

17.2.4   Civil Legal Standard: Strict Liability

17.2.4.1 Legally binding instruments

1989 Convention on Civil Liability for Damage Caused During Carriage of Dangerous Goods By Road, Rail and Inland Navigation Vessels

Article 5
1.   Except as provided in paragraphs 4 and 5 of this article and in article 6, the carrier at the time of an incident shall be liable for damage caused by any dangerous goods during their carriage by road, rail or inland navigation vessel.

17.2.4.2 Non-legally binding instruments

2006 Draft principles on the allocation of loss in the case of transboundary harm arising out of hazardous activities, with commentaries, Yearbook ILC, vol II

Principle 4 Prompt and Adequate Compensation
1.   Each State shall take all necessary measures to ensure prompt and adequate compensation is available to victims of transboundary damage caused by hazardous activities located within its territory or otherwise within its jurisdiction or control.
2.   These measures should include the imposition of liability on the operator or, where appropriate, other person or entity. *Such liability should not require proof of fault.* Any conditions, limitations or exceptions to such liability shall be consistent with draft principle 3. [emphasis added]

UNEP GUIDELINES Decision IG 17/4: Guidelines for the Determination of Liability and Compensation for Damage resulting from Pollution of the Marine Environment in the Mediterranean Sea Area (15th Meeting of the Parties)

G. Standard of Liability
19.   The basic standard of liability will be strict liability, that is liability dependent on the establishment of a causal link between the incident and the damage, without it being necessary to establish the fault or negligence of the operator.
20.   In cases of damage resulting from activities not covered by any of the Protocols to the Barcelona Convention, the Contracting Parties may apply fault-based liability.

17.2.5   Reparation

CASE
PCIJ, *Factory at Chorzów* **(Merits), PCIJ Reports 47 (1928), Series A No. 17**

The essential principle contained in the actual notion of an illegal act – a principle which seems to be established by international practice and in particular by the decisions of arbitral tribunals – is that reparation must, as far as possible, wipe out all the consequences of the illegal act and reestablish the situation which would, in all probability, have existed if that act had not been committed. Restitution in kind, or, if this is not possible, payment of a sum corresponding to the value which a restitution in kind would bear; the award, if need be, of damages for loss sustained which would not be covered by restitution in kind or payment in place of it—such are the principles which should serve to determine the amount of compensation due for an act contrary to international law.

CASE
ICJ, *Pulp Mills on the River Uruguay (Argentina v. Uruguay)*, **ICJ Reports 14 (2010)**

275. As the Court has pointed out (see paragraphs 154 to 157 above), the procedural obligations under the 1975 Statute did not entail any ensuing prohibition on Uruguay's building of the Orion (Botnia) mill, failing consent by Argentina, after the expiration of the period for negotiation. The Court has however observed that construction of that mill began before negotiations had come to an end, in breach of the procedural obligations laid down in the 1975 Statute. Further, as the Court has found, on the evidence submitted to it, the operation of the Orion (Botnia) mill has not resulted in the breach of substantive obligations laid down in the 1975 Statute (paragraphs 180, 189 and 265 above). As Uruguay was not barred from proceeding with the construction and operation of the Orion (Botnia) mill after the expiration of the period for negotiation and as it breached no substantive obligation under the 1975 Statute, ordering the dismantling of the mill would not, in the view of the Court, constitute an appropriate remedy for the breach of procedural obligations.

276. As Uruguay has not breached substantive obligations arising under the 1975 Statute, the Court is likewise unable, for the same reasons, to uphold Argentina's claim in respect of compensation for alleged injuries suffered in various economic sectors, specifically tourism and agriculture.

CASE
ICJ, *Certain Activities Carried Out by Nicaragua in the Border Area (Costa Rica v. Nicaragua)*, Compensation, ICJ Reports 15 (2018)

30. The obligation to make full reparation for the damage caused by a wrongful act has been recognized by the Court in other cases (see for example, *Ahmadou Sadio Diallo (Republic of Guinea v. Democratic Republic of the Congo)*, Merits, Judgment, ICJ Reports 691 (2010) (II), para. 161; *Avena and Other Mexican Nationals (Mexico v. United States of America)*, Judgment, ICJ Reports 2004 (I), p. 59, para. 119; *Gabčíkovo-Nagymaros Project (Hungary v. Slovakia)*, ICJ Reports 80 (1997), para. 150).

31. The Court has held that compensation may be an appropriate form of reparation, particularly in those cases where restitution is materially impossible or unduly burdensome (*Pulp Mills on the River Uruguay (Argentina v. Uruguay)*, ICJ Reports 103–104 (2010), para. 273). Compensation should not, however, have a punitive or exemplary character.

[...]

34. In cases of alleged environmental damage, particular issues may arise with respect to the existence of damage and causation. The damage may be due to several concurrent causes, or the state of science regarding the causal link between the wrongful act and the damage may be uncertain. These are difficulties that must be addressed as and when they arise in light of the facts of the case at hand and the evidence presented to the Court. Ultimately, it is for the Court to decide whether there is a sufficient causal nexus between the wrongful act and the injury suffered.

35. In respect of the valuation of damage, the Court recalls that the absence of adequate evidence as to the extent of material damage will not, in all situations, preclude an award of compensation for that damage. For example, in the Ahmadou Sadio Diallo case, the Court determined the amount of compensation due on the basis of equitable considerations (see Ahmadou Sadio Diallo (*Ahmadou Sadio Diallo (Republic of Guinea v. Democratic Republic of the Congo)*, Merits, Judgment, ICJ Reports 337 (2010) (II), para. 33). A similar approach was adopted by the Tribunal in the Trail Smelter case, which, quoting the *Supreme Court of the United States of America in Story Parchment Company v. Paterson Parchment Paper Company*, United States Reports Vol. 282 (1931), p. 555, stated:

> "Where the tort itself is of such a nature as to preclude the ascertainment of the amount of damages with certainty, it would be a perversion of fundamental principles of justice to deny all relief to the injured person, and thereby relieve the wrongdoer from making any amend for his acts. In such case, while the damages may not be determined by mere speculation or guess, it will be enough if the evidence show the extent of the damages as a matter of just and reasonable inference, although the result be only approximate." (*Trail Smelter* case (United States, Canada), 16 April 1938 and 11 March 1941, United Nations, Reports of International Arbitral Awards (RIAA), Vol. III, p. 1920.)

[...]

41. The Court has not previously adjudicated a claim for compensation for environ-mental damage. However, it is consistent with the principles of international law governing the consequences of internationally wrongful acts, including the princi-ple of full reparation, to hold that compensation is due for damage caused to the environment, in and of itself, in addition to expenses incurred by an injured State as a consequence of such damage. The Parties also agree on this point.

42. The Court is therefore of the view that damage to the environment, and the con-sequent impairment or loss of the ability of the environment to provide goods and services, is compensable under international law. Such compensation may include indemnification for the impairment or loss of environmental goods and services in the period prior to recovery and payment for the restoration of the damaged environment.

43. Payment for restoration accounts for the fact that natural recovery may not always suffice to return an environment to the state in which it was before the damage occurred. In such instances, active restoration measures may be required in order to return the environment to its prior condition, in so far as that is possible.

[...]

52. The Court notes that the valuation methods proposed by the Parties are sometimes used for environmental damage valuation in the practice of national and international bodies, and are not therefore devoid of relevance to the task at hand. However, they are not the only methods used by such bodies for that purpose, nor is their use limited to valuation of damage since they may also be used to carry out cost/benefit analysis of environmental projects and programmes for the purpose of public policy setting (see for example UNEP, "Guidance Manual on Valuation and Accounting of Ecosystem Services for Small Island Developing States" (2014), p. 4). The Court will not therefore choose between them or use either of them exclusively for the purpose of valuation of the damage caused to the protected wetland in Costa Rica. Wherever certain elements of either method offer a reasonable basis for valuation, the Court will nonetheless take them into account. This approach is dictated by two factors: first, international law does not prescribe any specific method of valuation for the purposes of compensation for environmental damage; secondly, it is necessary, in the view of the Court, to take into account the specific circumstances and characteristics of each case.

[...]

78. The Court considers, for the reasons specified below, that it is appropriate to approach the valuation of environmental damage from the perspective of the eco-system as a whole, by adopting an overall assessment of the impairment or loss of environmental goods and services prior to recovery, rather than attributing values to specific categories of environmental goods and services and estimating recovery periods for each of them.

79. First, the Court observes, in relation to the environmental goods and services that have been impaired or lost, that the most significant damage to the area, from which other harms to the environment arise, is the removal of trees by Nicaragua during the excavation of the *caños*. An overall valuation can account for the correlation between the removal of the trees and the harm caused to other environmental goods and services (such as other raw materials, gas regulation and air quality services, and biodiversity in terms of habitat and nursery).

80. Secondly, an overall valuation approach is dictated by the specific characteristics of the area affected by the activities of Nicaragua, which is situated in the Northeast Caribbean Wetland, a wetland protected under the Ramsar Convention, where there are various environmental goods and services that are closely interlinked. Wetlands are among the most diverse and productive ecosystems in the world. The interaction of the physical, biological and chemical components of a wetland enable it to perform many vital functions, including supporting rich biological diversity, regulating water régimes, and acting as a sink for sediments and pollutants.

81. Thirdly, such an overall valuation will allow the Court to take into account the capacity of the damaged area for natural regeneration. As stated by the Secretariat of the Ramsar Convention, the area in the vicinity of the 2010 *caño* demonstrates a "high capability for natural regeneration of the vegetation ... provided the physical conditions of the area are maintained".

CASE
IACtHR, *Indigenous Communities of the Lhaka Honhat (Our Land) Association v. Argentina* (Merits, Reparations and Costs), Judgment, (6 February 2020), Series C No. 420

332. Notwithstanding any actions that the State may take to respond to urgent situations, the Court orders the State, within six months of notification of this judgment, to submit a report to the Court identifying, from among all the individuals who are members of the indigenous communities victims, critical situations of lack of access to drinking water or to food that could endanger their health or their life, and to draw up an action plan establishing the actions that the State will take, which must be appropriate to respond adequately to such critical situations, indicating the implementation timetable. The State must begin to implement the actions set out in the action plan as soon as this has been submitted to the Court. The Court will transmit the said report to the Commission and the representatives so that they may forward any comments they deem pertinent. Based on the opinions of the parties and the Commission, the Court will evaluate whether this report and action plan are adequate and meet the terms of this judgment, and may require that they be completed or expanded. The Court will monitor the implementation of the respective actions until it considers that it has sufficient information to consider that this measure of reparation has been completed.

17.3   STATE RESPONSIBILITY

17.3.1   In General

2001 ILC Articles on Responsibility of States for International Wrongful Acts, adopted by UNGA res 56/83 of 12 December 2001, Yearbook ILC, vol II,

Article 2. Elements of an internationally wrongful act of a State
There is an internationally wrongful act of a State when conduct consisting of an action or omission:
(a)   is attributable to the State under international law; and
(b)   constitutes a breach of an international obligation of the State.

Article 23. Force majeure
1.   The wrongfulness of an act of a State not in conformity with an international obligation of that State is precluded if the act is due to force majeure, that is the occurrence of an irresistible force or of an unforeseen event, beyond the control of the State, making it materially impossible in the circumstances to perform the obligation.
2.   Paragraph 1 does not apply if:
    (a)   the situation of force majeure is due, either alone or in combination with other factors, to the conduct of the State invoking it; or
    (b)   the State has assumed the risk of that situation occurring.

Article 24. Distress
1.   The wrongfulness of an act of a State not in conformity with an international obligation of that State is precluded if the author of the act in question has no other reasonable way, in a situation of distress, of saving the author's life or the lives of other persons entrusted to the author's care.
2.   Paragraph 1 does not apply if:
    (a)   the situation of distress is due, either alone or in combination with other factors, to the conduct of the State invoking it; or
    (b)   the act in question is likely to create a comparable or greater peril.

Article 25. Necessity
1.   Necessity may not be invoked by a State as a ground for precluding the wrongfulness of an act not in conformity with an international obligation of that State unless the act:
    (a)   is the only way for the State to safeguard an essential interest against a grave and imminent peril; and
    (b)   does not seriously impair an essential interest of the State or States towards which the obligation exists, or of the international community as a whole.
2.   In any case, necessity may not be invoked by a State as a ground for precluding wrongfulness if:
    (a)   the international obligation in question excludes the possibility of invoking necessity; or
    (b)   the State has contributed to the situation of necessity.

Article 27. Consequences of invoking a circumstance precluding wrongfulness
The invocation of a circumstance precluding wrongfulness in accordance with this chapter is without prejudice to:
(a)　compliance with the obligation in question, if and to the extent that the circumstance precluding wrongfulness no longer exists;
(b)　the question of compensation for any material loss caused by the act in question.

[...]

Article 30. Cessation and non-repetition
The State responsible for the internationally wrongful act is under an obligation:
(a)　to cease that act, if it is continuing;
(b)　to offer appropriate assurances and guarantees of non-repetition, if circumstances so require.

Article 31. Reparation
1.　The responsible State is under an obligation to make full reparation for the injury caused by the internationally wrongful act.
2.　Injury includes any damage, whether material or moral, caused by the internationally wrongful act of a State.

Article 34. Forms of reparation
Full reparation for the injury caused by the internationally wrongful act shall take the form of restitution, compensation and satisfaction, either singly or in combination, in accordance with the provisions of this chapter.

Article 35. Restitution
A State responsible for an internationally wrongful act is under an obligation to make restitution, that is, to re-establish the situation which existed before the wrongful act was committed, provided and to the extent that restitution:
(a)　is not materially impossible;
(b)　does not involve a burden out of all proportion to the benefit deriving from restitution instead of compensation.

Article 36. Compensation
1.　The State responsible for an internationally wrongful act is under an obligation to compensate for the damage caused thereby, insofar as such damage is not made good by restitution.
2.　The compensation shall cover any financially assessable damage including loss of profits insofar as it is established.

Article 37. Satisfaction
1.　The State responsible for an internationally wrongful act is under an obligation to give satisfaction for the injury caused by that act insofar as it cannot be made good by restitution or compensation.
2.　Satisfaction may consist in an acknowledgement of the breach, an expression of regret, a formal apology or another appropriate modality.

3.   Satisfaction shall not be out of proportion to the injury and may not take a form humiliating to the responsible State.

[…]

Article 42. Invocation of responsibility by an injured State
A State is entitled as an injured State to invoke the responsibility of another State if the obligation breached is owed to:
(a)   that State individually; or
(b)   a group of States including that State, or the international community as a whole, and the breach of the obligation:
      (i)   specially affects that State; or
      (ii)   is of such a character as radically to change the position of all the other States to which the obligation is owed with respect to the further performance of the obligation.

[…]

Article 48. Invocation of responsibility by a State other than an injured State
1.   Any State other than an injured State is entitled to invoke the responsibility of another State in accordance with paragraph 2 if:
      (a)   the obligation breached is owed to a group of States including that State, and is established for the protection of a collective interest of the group; or
      (b)   the obligation breached is owed to the international community as a whole.
2.   Any State entitled to invoke responsibility under paragraph 1 may claim from the responsible State:
      (a)   cessation of the internationally wrongful act, and assurances and guarantees of non-repetition in accordance with article 30; and
      (b)   performance of the obligation of reparation in accordance with the preceding articles, in the interest of the injured State or of the beneficiaries of the obligation breached.
3.   The requirements for the invocation of responsibility by an injured State under articles 43, 44 and 45 apply to an invocation of responsibility by a State entitled to do so under paragraph 1.

Article 49. Object and limits of countermeasures
1.   An injured State may only take countermeasures against a State which is responsible for an internationally wrongful act in order to induce that State to comply with its obligations under Part Two.
2.   Countermeasures are limited to the non-performance for the time being of international obligations of the State taking the measures towards the responsible State.
3.   Countermeasures shall, as far as possible, be taken in such a way as to permit the resumption of performance of the obligations in question.

17.3.2   Specific International Regimes

1972 Space Liability Convention, 961 UNTS 187

Article I.

For the purposes of this Convention:

(a)   The term "damage" means loss of life, personal injury or other impairment of health; or loss of or damage to property of States or of persons, natural or juridical, or property of international intergovernmental organisations;

(b)   The term "launching" includes attempted launching;

(c)   The term "launching State" means:

(i)   a state which launches or procures the launching of a space object;

(ii)   a State from whose territory or facility a space object is launched;

(d)   The term "space object" includes component parts of a space object as well as its launch vehicle and parts thereof.

Article II.

A launching State shall be absolutely liable to pay compensation for damage caused by its space object on the surface of the earth or to aircraft in flight.

Article III.

In the event of damage being caused elsewhere than on the surface of the earth to a space object of one launching State or to persons or property on board such a space object by a space object of another launching State, the latter shall be liable only if the damage is due to its fault or the fault of persons for whom it is responsible.

Article IV.

1.   In the event of damage being caused elsewhere than on the surface of the earth to a space object of one launching State or to persons or property on board such a space object by a space object of another launching State, and of damage thereby being caused to a third State or to its natural or juridical persons, the first two States shall be jointly and severally liable to the third State, to the extent indicated by the following:

(a)   If the damage has been caused to the third State on the surface of the earth or to aircraft in flight, their liability to the third State shall be absolute;

(b)   If the damage has been caused to a space object of the third State or to persons or property on board that space object elsewhere than on the surface of the earth, their liability to the third State shall be based on the fault of either of the first two States or on the fault of persons for whom either is responsible.

2.   In all cases of joint and several liability referred to in paragraph 1 of this Article, the burden of compensation for the damage shall be apportioned between the first two States in accordance with the extent to which they were at fault; if the extent of the fault of each of these States cannot be established, the burden of compensation shall be apportioned equally between them. Such apportionment shall be without prejudice to the right of the third State to seek the entire compensation due under this Convention from any or all of the launching States which are jointly and severally liable.

Article V.

1.   Whenever two or more States jointly launch a space object, they shall be jointly and severally liable for any damage caused.

2.   A launching State which has paid compensation for damage shall have the right to present a claim for indemnification to other participants in the joint launching. The participants in a joint launching may conclude agreements regarding the apportioning among themselves of the financial obligation in respect of which they are jointly and severally liable. Such agreements shall be without prejudice to the right of a State sustaining damage to seek the entire compensation due under this Convention from any or all of the launching States which are jointly and severally liable.

3.   A State from whose territory or facility a space object is launched shall be regarded as a participant in a joint launching.

Article VI.

1.   Subject to the provisions of paragraph 2 of this Article, exoneration from absolute liability shall be granted to the extent that a launching State establishes that the damage has resulted either wholly or partially from gross negligence or from an act or omission done with intent to cause damage on the part of a claimant State or of natural or juridical persons it represents.

2.   No exoneration whatever shall be granted in cases where the damage has resulted from activities conducted by a launching State which are not in conformity with international law including, in particular, the Charter of the United Nations and the Treaty on Principles Governing the Activities of States in the Exploration and Use of Outer Space, including the Moon and Other Celestial Bodies.

[…]

Article XII.

The compensation which the launching State shall be liable to pay for damage under this Convention shall be determined in accordance with international law and the principles of justice and equity, in order to provide such reparation in respect of the damage as will restore the person, natural or juridical, State or international organisation on whose behalf the claim is presented to the condition which would have existed if the damage had not occurred.

1982 United Nations Convention on the Law of the Sea, 1833 UNTS 3

Article 235 Responsibility and liability

1.   States are responsible for the fulfilment of their international obligations concerning the protection and preservation of the marine environment. They shall be liable in accordance with international law.

2.   States shall ensure that recourse is available in accordance with their legal systems for prompt and adequate compensation or other relief in respect of damage caused by pollution of the marine environment by natural or juridical persons under their jurisdiction.

3.   With the objective of assuring prompt and adequate compensation in respect of all damage caused by pollution of the marine environment, States shall cooperate in the implementation of existing international law and the further development of international law relating to responsibility and liability for the assessment of and compensation for damage and the settlement of related disputes, as well as, where appropriate, development of criteria and procedures for payment of adequate compensation, such as compulsory insurance or compensation funds.

[...]

Article 263 Responsibility and liability
1.   States and competent international organizations shall be responsible for ensuring that marine scientific research, whether undertaken by them or on their behalf, is conducted in accordance with this Convention.
2.   States and competent international organizations shall be responsible and liable for the measures they take in contravention of this Convention in respect of marine scientific research conducted by other States, their natural or juridical persons or by competent international organizations, and shall provide compensation for damage resulting from such measures.
3.   States and competent international organizations shall be responsible and liable pursuant to article 235 for damage caused by pollution of the marine environment arising out of marine scientific research undertaken by them or on their behalf.

[...]

Article 304 Responsibility and liability for damage
The provisions of this Convention regarding responsibility and liability for damage are without prejudice to the application of existing rules and the development of further rules regarding responsibility and liability under international law.

Decision 2/CP.19 to 1992 UN Framework Convention on Climate Change

Warsaw international mechanism for loss and damage associated with climate change impacts
    [...]
Also acknowledging that loss and damage associated with the adverse effects of climate change includes, and in some cases involves more than, that which can be reduced by adaptation,
Recalling its decision to establish, at its nineteenth session, institutional arrangements, such as an international mechanism, including functions and modalities, to address loss and damage associated with the impacts of climate change in developing countries that are particularly vulnerable to the adverse effects of climate change,

1.   *Establishes* the Warsaw international mechanism for loss and damage, under the Cancun Adaptation Framework, subject to review at the twenty-second session of the Conference of the Parties (November–December 2016) pursuant to paragraph 15 below, to address loss and damage associated with impacts of climate change, including extreme events and slow onset events, in developing countries that are

particularly vulnerable to the adverse effects of climate change (hereinafter referred to as the Warsaw international mechanism), and in line with the provisions contained in paragraphs 2–15 below;

2015 Paris Agreement, FCCC/CP/2015/10/Add.1

Article 8

1. Parties recognize the importance of averting, minimizing and addressing loss and damage associated with the adverse effects of climate change, including extreme weather events and slow onset events, and the role of sustainable development in reducing the risk of loss and damage.

2. The Warsaw International Mechanism for Loss and Damage associated with Climate Change Impacts shall be subject to the authority and guidance of the Conference of the Parties serving as the meeting of the Parties to this Agreement and may be enhanced and strengthened, as determined by the Conference of the Parties serving as the meeting of the Parties to this Agreement.

3. Parties should enhance understanding, action and support, including through the Warsaw International Mechanism, as appropriate, on a cooperative and facilitative basis with respect to loss and damage associated with the adverse effects of climate change.

4. Accordingly, areas of cooperation and facilitation to enhance understanding, action and support may include:

    (a)   Early warning systems;

    (b)   Emergency preparedness;

    (c)   Slow onset events;

    (d)   Events that may involve irreversible and permanent loss and damage;

    (e)   Comprehensive risk assessment and management;

    (f)   Risk insurance facilities, climate risk pooling and other insurance solutions;

    (g)   Non-economic losses; and

    (h)   Resilience of communities, livelihoods and ecosystems.

5. The Warsaw International Mechanism shall collaborate with existing bodies and expert groups under the Agreement, as well as relevant organizations and expert bodies outside the Agreement.

17.4   CIVIL LIABILITY

17.4.1   General

2006 Draft principles on the allocation of loss in the case of transboundary harm arising out of hazardous activities, with commentaries, Yearbook ILC, vol II

Principle 3 Purposes
The purposes of the present draft articles are:
(a)   to ensure prompt and adequate compensation; and

(b)   to preserve and protect the environment in the event of transboundary damage, especially with respect to mitigation of damage to the environment and its restoration.

Principle 4 Prompt and Adequate Compensation
1.   Each State shall take all necessary measures to ensure prompt and adequate compensation is available to victims of transboundary damage caused by hazardous activities located within its territory or otherwise within its jurisdiction or control.
2.   These measures should include the imposition of liability on the operator or, where appropriate, other person or entity. Such liability should not require proof of fault. Any conditions, limitations or exceptions to such liability shall be consistent with draft principle 3.
3.   These measures should also include the requirement on the operator or, where appropriate, other person or entity, to establish and maintain financial security such as insurance, bonds or other financial guarantees to cover claims of compensation.
4.   In appropriate cases, these measures should include the requirement for the establishment of industry-wide funds at the national level.
5.   In the event that the measures under the preceding paragraphs are insufficient to provide adequate compensation, the State of origin should also ensure that additional resources are made available.

[...]

Principle 7 Development of Specific International Regimes
1.   Where, in respect of particular categories of hazardous activities, specific global, regional or bilateral agreements would provide effective arrangements concerning compensation, response measures and international and domestic remedies, all efforts should be made to conclude such agreements.
2.   Such agreements should, as appropriate, include arrangements for industry and/or State funds to provide supplementary compensation in the event that the financial resources of the operator, including financial security measures, are insufficient to cover the damage suffered as a result of an incident. Any such funds may be designed to supplement or replace national industry-based funds.

17.4.2   Specific Convention on Civil Liability

17.4.2.1 Oil

1992 Civil Liability Convention, 1956 UNTS 255

Article I
[...]
3.   "Owner" means the person or persons registered as the owner of the ship or, in the absence of registration, the person or persons owning the ship. However in the

case of a ship owned by a State and operated by a company which in that State is registered as the ship's operator, "owner" shall mean such company.

[...]

5.   "Oil" means any persistent hydrocarbon mineral oil such as crude oil, fuel oil, heavy diesel oil and lubricating oil, whether carried on board a ship as cargo or in the bunkers of such a ship.

6.   "Pollution damage" means:

(a)   loss or damage caused outside the ship by contamination resulting from the escape or discharge of oil from the ship, wherever such escape or discharge may occur, provided that compensation for impairment of the environment other than loss of profit from such impairment shall be limited to costs of reasonable measures of reinstatement actually undertaken or to be undertaken;

(b)   the costs of preventive measures and further loss or damage caused by preventive measures.

[...]

8.   "Incident" means any occurrence, or series of occurrences having the same origin, which causes pollution damage or creates a grave and imminent threat of causing such damage.

Article II

This Convention shall apply exclusively:

(a)   to pollution damage caused:

(i)   in the territory, including the territorial sea, of a Contracting State, and

(ii)   in the exclusive economic zone of a Contracting State, established in accordance with international law, or, if a Contracting State has not established such a zone, in an area beyond and adjacent to the territorial sea of that State determined by that State in accordance with international law and extending not more than 200 nautical miles from the baselines from which the breadth of its territorial sea is measured;

(b)   to preventive measures, wherever taken, to prevent or minimize such damage.

Article III

1.   Except as provided in paragraphs 2 and 3 of this Article, the owner of a ship at the time of an incident, or, where the incident consists of a series of occurrences, at the time of the first such occurrence, shall be liable for any pollution damage caused by the ship as a result of the incident.

2.   No liability for pollution damage shall attach to the owner if he proves that the damage:

(a)   resulted from an act of war, hostilities, civil war, insurrection or a natural phenomenon of an exceptional, inevitable and irresistible character, or

(b)   was wholly caused by an act or omission done with intent to cause damage by a third party, or

(c)   was wholly caused by the negligence or other wrongful act of any Government or other authority responsible for the maintenance of lights or other navigational aids in the exercise of that function.

3.   If the owner proves that the pollution damage resulted wholly or partially either from an act or omission done with intent to cause damage by the person who suffered the damage or from the negligence of that person, the owner may be exonerated wholly or partially from his liability to such person.

4.   No claim for compensation for pollution damage may be made against the owner otherwise than in accordance with this Convention. Subject to paragraph 5 of this Article, no claim for compensation for pollution damage under this Convention or otherwise may be made against:

(a)   the servants or agents of the owner or the members of the crew;
(b)   the pilot or any other person who, without being a member of the crew, performs services for the ship;
(c)   any charterer (how so ever described, including a bareboat charterer), manager or operator of the ship;
(d)   any person performing salvage operations with the consent of the owner or on the instructions of a competent public authority;
(e)   any person taking preventive measures;
(f)   all servants or agents of persons mentioned in subparagraphs (c), (d) and (e);

unless the damage resulted from their personal act or omission, committed with the intent to cause such damage, or recklessly and with knowledge that such damage would probably result.

5.   Nothing in this Convention shall prejudice any right of recourse of the owner against third parties.

Article V

1.   The owner of a ship shall be entitled to limit his liability under this Convention in respect of any one incident to an aggregate amount calculated as follows:

(a)   4,510,000 units of account[2] for a ship not exceeding 5,000 units of tonnage;
(b)   for a ship with a tonnage in excess there of, for each additional unit of tonnage, 631 units of account[2] in addition to the amount mentioned in sub-paragraph (a);

provided, however, that this aggregate amount shall not in any event exceed 89,770,000 units of account.[2]

2.   The owner shall not be entitled to limit his liability under this Convention if it is proved that the pollution damage resulted from his personal act or omission, committed with the intent to cause such damage, or recklessly and with knowledge that such damage would probably result.

3.   For the purpose of availing himself of the benefit of limitation provided for in paragraph 1 of this Article the owner shall constitute a fund for the total sum representing the limit of his liability with the Court or other competent authority of any one of the Contracting States in which action is brought under Article IX or, if no action is brought, with any Court or other competent authority in any one of the Contracting States in which an action can be brought under Article IX. [...]

4.   The fund shall be distributed among the claimants in proportion to the amounts of their established claims.

[...]

Article VII

1.   The owner of a ship registered in a Contracting State and carrying more than 2,000 tons of oil in bulk as cargo shall be required to maintain insurance or other financial security, such as the guarantee of a bank or a certificate delivered by an international compensation fund, in the sums fixed by applying the limits of liability prescribed in Article V, paragraph 1 to cover his liability for pollution damage under this Convention.

1992 Fund Convention, 1110 UNTS 58

Article 1

[...]

2.   "Ship", "Person", "Owner", "Oil", "Pollution Damage", "Preventive Measures", "Incident", and "Organization" have the same meaning as in Article I of the 1992 Liability Convention.

3.   "Contributing Oil" means crude oil and fuel oil as defined in sub-paragraphs (a) and (b) below:

(a)   "Crude Oil" means any liquid hydrocarbon mixture occurring naturally in the earth whether or not treated to render it suitable for transportation. It also includes crude oils from which certain distillate fractions have been removed (sometimes referred to as "topped crudes") or to which certain distillate fractions have been added (sometimes referred to as "spiked" or "reconstituted" crudes).

(b)   "Fuel Oil" means heavy distillates or residues from crude oil or blends of such materials intended for use as a fuel for the production of heat or power of a quality equivalent to the "American Society for Testing and Materials' Specification for Number Four Fuel Oil (Designation D 396–69)", or heavier.

Article 2

1.   An International Fund for compensation for pollution damage, to be named "The International Oil Pollution Compensation Fund 1992" and hereinafter referred to as "the Fund", is hereby established with the following aims:

(a)   to provide compensation for pollution damage to the extent that the protection afforded by the 1992 Liability Convention is inadequate;

(b)   to give effect to the related purposes set out in this Convention.

2.   The Fund shall in each Contracting State be recognized as a legal person capable under the laws of that State of assuming rights and obligations and of being a party in legal proceedings before the courts of that State. Each Contracting State shall recognize the Director of the Fund (hereinafter referred to as "The Director") as the legal representative of the Fund.

Article 4

1.   For the purpose of fulfilling its function under Article 2, paragraph 1(a), the Fund shall pay compensation to any person suffering pollution damage if such person has been unable to obtain full and adequate compensation for the damage under the terms of the 1992 Liability Convention,

(a)   because no liability for the damage arises under the 1992 Liability Convention;

(b)   because the owner liable for the damage under the 1992 Liability Convention is financially incapable of meeting his obligations in full and any financial security that may be provided under Article VII of that Convention does not cover or is insufficient to satisfy the claims for compensation for the damage; an owner being treated as financially incapable of meeting his obligations and a financial security being treated as insufficient if the person suffering the damage has been unable to obtain full satisfaction of the amount of compensation due under the 1992 Liability Convention after having taken all reasonable steps to pursue the legal remedies available to him;

(c)   because the damage exceeds the owner's liability under the 1992 Liability Convention as limited pursuant to Article V, paragraph 1, of that Convention or under the terms of any other international Convention in force or open for signature, ratification or accession at the date of this Convention.

Expenses reasonably incurred or sacrifices reasonably made by the owner voluntarily to prevent or minimize pollution damage shall be treated as pollution damage for the purposes of this Article.

2.   The Fund shall incur no obligation under the preceding paragraph if:

(a)   it proves that the pollution damage resulted from an act of war, hostilities, civil war or insurrection or was caused by oil which has escaped or been discharged from a warship or other ship owned or operated by a State and used, at the time of the incident, only on Government non-commercial service; or

(b)   the claimant cannot prove that the damage resulted from an incident involving one or more ships.

3.   If the Fund proves that the pollution damage resulted wholly or partially either from an act or omission done with the intent to cause damage by the person who suffered the damage or from the negligence of that person, the Fund may be exonerated wholly or partially from its obligation to pay compensation to such person. The Fund shall in any event be exonerated to the extent that the shipowner may have been exonerated under Article III, paragraph 3, of the 1992 Liability Convention. However, there shall be no such exoneration of the Fund with regard to preventive measures.

4.

(a)   Except as otherwise provided in sub-paragraphs (b) and (c) of this paragraph, the aggregate amount of compensation payable by the Fund under this Article shall in respect of any one incident be limited, so that the total sum of that amount and the amount of compensation actually paid under the 1992 Liability Convention for pollution damage within the scope of application of this Convention as defined in Article 3 shall not exceed 203,000,000 units of account.

(b) Except as otherwise provided in sub-paragraph (c), the aggregate amount of compensation payable by the Fund under this Article for pollution damage resulting from a natural phenomenon of an exceptional, inevitable and irresistible character shall not exceed 203,000,000 units of account[5].

(c) The maximum amount of compensation referred to in sub-paragraphs (a) and (b) shall be 300,740,000 units of account[5] with respect to any incident occurring during any period when there are three Parties to this Convention in respect of which the combined relevant quantity of contributing oil received by persons in the territories of such Parties, during the preceding calendar year, equalled or exceeded 600 million tons.

[...]

2006 Small Tanker Oil Pollution Indemnification Agreement (as amended 2017)

II. GENERAL
[...]

(B) The Owner of any Relevant Ship shall be eligible to become a Party and shall do so when made a Party by the Club insuring that Ship as the Rules of that Club may provide.

III. THE STOPIA 2006 (as amended 2017) SCHEME
(A) This Agreement is made to establish STOPIA 2006 (as amended 2017) for payment of Indemnification to the 1992 Fund on the terms set out herein.
(B) A Ship shall be eligible for Entry in the scheme if:
   (1) it is of not more than 29,548 Tons;
   (2) it is insured by a Club; and
   (3) it is reinsured through the Pooling arrangements of the International Group.

Such a ship is referred to herein as a "Relevant Ship".

[...]

IV. INDEMNIFICATION OF THE 1992 FUND
(A) Where, as a result of an Incident, an Entered Ship causes Pollution Damage in respect of which (i) liability is incurred under the Liability Convention by the Participating Owner of that Ship and (ii) the 1992 Fund has paid or expects to pay compensation under the 1992 Fund Convention, the said Owner shall indemnify the 1992 Fund in an amount calculated in accordance with this Clause. [...]

2006 Tanker Oil Pollution Indemnification Agreement (as amended 2017)

II. GENERAL

[...]

(B)   The Owner of any Relevant Ship shall be eligible to become a Party and shall do so when made a Party by the Club insuring that Ship as the Rules of that Club may provide.

III. THE TOPIA 2006 (as amended 2017) SCHEME

(A)   This Agreement is made to establish TOPIA for payment of Indemnification to the Supplementary Fund on the terms set out herein.

(B)   A Ship shall be eligible for Entry in the scheme if:

    (1)   it is insured by a Club; and

    (2)   it is reinsured through the Pooling arrangements of the International Group.

Such a Ship is referred to herein as a "Relevant Ship".

[...]

IV. INDEMNIFICATION OF THE SUPPLEMENTARY FUND

(A)   Where, as a result of an Incident, an Entered Ship causes Pollution Damage in respect of which (1) liability is incurred under the Liability Convention by the Participating Owner of that Ship and (2) the Supplementary Fund has paid or expects to pay compensation under the Protocol, the said Owner shall indemnify the Supplementary Fund in an amount calculated in accordance with this Clause.

2001 International Convention on Civil Liability for Bunker Oil Pollution Damage

ARTICLE 3

Liability of the shipowner

1.   Except as provided in paragraphs 3 and 4, the shipowner at the time of an incident shall be liable for pollution damage caused by any bunker oil on board or originating from the ship, provided that, if an incident consists of a series of occurrences having the same origin, the liability shall attach to the shipowner at the time of the first of such occurrences.

2.   Where more than one person is liable in accordance with paragraph 1, their liability shall be joint and several.

3.   No liability for pollution damage shall attach to the shipowner if the shipowner proves that:

    (a)   the damage resulted from an act of war, hostilities, civil war, insurrection or a natural phenomenon of an exceptional, inevitable and irresistible character; or

    (b)   the damage was wholly caused by an act or omission done with the intent to cause damage by a third party; or

(c)   the damage was wholly caused by the negligence or other wrongful act of any Government or other authority responsible for the maintenance of lights or other navigational aids in the exercise of that function.

4.   If the shipowner proves that the pollution damage resulted wholly or partially either from an act or omission done with intent to cause damage by the person who suffered the damage or from the negligence of that person, the shipowner may be exonerated wholly or partially from liability to such person.

5.   No claim for compensation for pollution damage shall be made against the shipowner otherwise than in accordance with this Convention.

6.   Nothing in this Convention shall prejudice any right of recourse of the shipowner which exists independently of this Convention.

ARTICLE 4
Exclusions

1.   This Convention shall not apply to pollution damage as defined in the Civil Liability Convention, whether or not compensation is payable in respect of it under that Convention.

2.   Except as provided in paragraph 3, the provisions of this Convention shall not apply to warships, naval auxiliary or other ships owned or operated by a State and used, for the time being, only on Government non-commercial service.

3.   A State Party may decide to apply this Convention to its warships or other ships described in paragraph 2, in which case it shall notify the Secretary-General thereof specifying the terms and conditions of such application.

4.   With respect to ships owned by a State Party and used for commercial purposes, each State shall be subject to suit in the jurisdictions set forth in article 9 and shall waive all defences based on its status as a sovereign State.

[…]

ARTICLE 7
Compulsory insurance or financial security

1.   The registered owner of a ship having a gross tonnage greater than 1000 registered in a State Party shall be required to maintain insurance or other financial security, such as the guarantee of a bank or similar financial institution, to cover the liability of the registered owner for pollution damage in an amount equal to the limits of liability under the applicable national or international limitation regime, but in all cases, not exceeding an amount calculated in accordance with the Convention on Limitation of Liability for Maritime Claims, 1976, as amended.

17.4.2.2 Nuclear

1960 Paris Convention on Third Party Liability in the Field of Nuclear Energy, 1519 UNTS 329

Article 1

a.   For the purposes of this Convention:

    i.   "A nuclear incident" means any occurrence or succession of occurrences having the same origin which causes damage, provided that such occurrence or succession of occurrences, or any of the damage caused, arises out of or results either from the radioactive properties, or a combination of radioactive properties with toxic, explosive, or other hazardous properties of nuclear fuel or radioactive products or waste or with any of them, or from ionizing radiations emitted by any source of radiation inside a nuclear installation.

[...]

vi.   "Operator" in relation to a nuclear installation means the person designated or recognised by the competent public authority as the operator of that installation.

[...]

Article 2

This Convention does not apply to nuclear incidents occurring in the territory of non-Contracting States or to damage suffered in such territory, unless otherwise provided by the legislation of the Contracting Party in whose territory the nuclear installation of the operator liable is situated, and except in regard to rights referred to in Article 6(e).

Article 3

a.   The operator of a nuclear installation shall be liable, in accordance with this Convention, for:

     i.   damage to or loss of life of any person; and

     ii.   damage to or loss of any property other than

         1.   the nuclear installation itself and any other nuclear installation, including a nuclear installation under construction, on the site where that installation is located; and

         2.   any property on that same site which is used or to be used in connection with any such installation,

         3.   upon proof that such damage or loss (hereinafter referred to as "damage") was caused by a nuclear incident in such installation or involving nuclear substances coming from such installation, except as otherwise provided for in Article 4.

b.   Where the damage or loss is caused jointly by a nuclear incident and by an incident other than a nuclear incident, that part of the damage or loss which is caused by such other incident, shall, to the extent that it is not reasonably separable from the damage or loss caused by the nuclear incident, be considered to be damage caused by the nuclear incident. Where the damage or loss is caused jointly by a nuclear incident and by an emission of ionizing radiation not covered by this Convention, nothing in this Convention shall limit or otherwise affect the liability of any person in connection with that emission of ionizing radiation.

Article 4

In the case of carriage of nuclear substances, including storage incidental thereto, without prejudice to Article 2:

a. The operator of a nuclear installation shall be liable, in accordance with this Convention, for damage upon proof that it was caused by a nuclear incident outside that installation and involving nuclear substances in the course of carriage therefrom, only if the incident occurs:

   i. before liability with regard to nuclear incidents involving the nuclear substances has been assumed, pursuant to the express terms of a contract in writing, by the operator of another nuclear installation;

   ii. in the absence of such express terms, before the operator of another nuclear installation has taken charge of the nuclear substances; or

   iii. where the nuclear substances are intended to be used in a reactor comprised in a means of transport, before the person duly authorized to operate that reactor has taken charge of the nuclear substances; but

   iv. where the nuclear substances have been sent to a person within the territory of a non-Contracting State, before they have been unloaded from the means of transport by which they have arrived in the territory of that non-Contracting State.

b. The operator of a nuclear installation shall be liable, in accordance with this Convention, for damage upon proof that it was caused by a nuclear incident outside that installation and involving nuclear substances in the course of carriage thereto, only if the incident occurs:

   i. after liability with regard to nuclear incidents involving the nuclear substances has been assumed by him, pursuant to the express terms of a contract in writing, from the operator of another nuclear installation;

   ii. in the absence of such express terms, after he has taken charge of the nuclear substances; or

   iii. after he has taken charge of the nuclear substances from a person operating a reactor comprised in a means of transport; but

   iv. where the nuclear substances have, with the written consent of the operator, been sent from a person within the territory of a non-Contracting State, after they have been loaded on the means of transport by which they are to be carried from the territory of that State.

[...]

Article 10

a. To cover the liability under this Convention, the operator shall be required to have and maintain insurance or other financial security of the amount established pursuant to Article 7 and of such type and terms as the competent public authority shall specify.

1963 Brussels Supplementary Convention

Article 3

a.   Under the conditions established by this Convention, the Contracting Parties undertake that compensation in respect of the damage referred to in Article 2 shall be provided up to the amount of 300 million Special Drawing Rights per incident.

[...]

g.   For the purposes of this Convention, "Special Drawing Right" means the Special Drawing Right as it is defined by the International Monetary Fund. The amounts mentioned in this Convention shall be converted into the national currency of a Contracting Party in accordance with the value of that currency at the date of the incident, unless another date is fixed for a given incident by agreement between the Contracting Parties. The equivalent in Special Drawing Rights of the national currency of a Contracting Party shall be calculated in accordance with the method of valuation applied at the date in question by the International Monetary Fund for its own operations and transactions.

Article 8

Any person who is entitled to benefit from the provisions of this Convention shall have the right to full compensation in accordance with national law for damage suffered, provided that, where the amount of damage exceeds or is likely to exceed:

i.   300 million Special Drawing Rights; or
ii.   if there is aggregate liability under Article 5(d) of the Paris Convention and a higher sum results therefrom, such higher sum,

any Contracting Party may establish equitable criteria for apportionment. Such criteria shall be applied whatever the origin of the funds and, subject to the provisions of Article 2, without discrimination based on the nationality, domicile or residence of the person suffering the damage.

2004 Protocol to Amend the Brussels Supplementary Convention

Article 3

a)   Under the conditions established by this Convention, the Contracting Parties undertake that compensation in respect of nuclear damage referred to in Article 2 shall be provided up to the amount of 1 500 million euro per nuclear incident, subject to the application of Article 12bis.

1963 Vienna Convention on Civil Liability for Nuclear Damage, 1063 UNTS 266

ARTICLE II

1.   The operator of a nuclear installation shall be liable for nuclear damage upon proof that such damage has been caused by a nuclear incident –
       (a)   in his nuclear installation; or
       (b)   involving nuclear material coming from or originating in his nuclear installation, and occurring –

(i)   before liability with regard to nuclear incidents involving the nuclear material has been assumed, pursuant to the express terms of a contract in writing, by the operator of another nuclear installation;

(ii)   in the absence of such express terms, before the operator of another nuclear installation has taken charge of the nuclear material; or

(iii)   where the nuclear material is intended to be used in a nuclear reactor with which a means of transport is equipped for use as a source of power, whether for propulsion thereof or for any other purpose, before the person duly authorized to operate such reactor has taken charge of the nuclear material; but

(iv)   where the nuclear material has been sent to a person within the territory of a non-Contracting State, before it has been unloaded from the means of transport by which it has arrived in the territory of that non-Contracting State;

(c)   involving nuclear material sent to his nuclear installation, and occurring –

(i)   after liability with regard to nuclear incidents involving the nuclear material has been assumed by him, pursuant to the express terms of a contract in writing, from the operator of another nuclear installation;

(ii)   in the absence of such express terms, after he has taken charge of the nuclear material; or

(iii)   after he has taken charge of the nuclear material from a person operating a nuclear reactor with which a means of transport is equipped for use as a source of power, whether for propulsion thereof or for any other purpose; but

(iv)   where the nuclear material has, with the written consent of the operator, been sent from a person within the territory of a non-Contracting State, only after it has been loaded on the means of transport by which it is to be carried from the territory of that State;

provided that, if nuclear damage is caused by a nuclear incident occurring in a nuclear installation and involving nuclear material stored therein incidentally to the carriage of such material, the provisions of sub-paragraph (a) of this paragraph shall not apply where another operator or person is solely liable pursuant to the provisions of sub-paragraph (b) or (c) of this paragraph.

[…]

ARTICLE IV

1.   The liability of the operator for nuclear damage under this Convention shall be absolute.

2.   If the operator proves that the nuclear damage resulted wholly or partly either from the gross negligence of the person suffering the damage or from an act or omission of such person done with intent to cause damage, the competent court may, if its law so provides, relieve the operator wholly or partly from his obligation to pay compensation in respect of the damage suffered by such person.

3.   (a)   No liability under this Convention shall attach to an operator for nuclear damage caused by a nuclear incident directly due to an act of armed conflict, hostilities, civil war or insurrection.

(b)   Except in so far as the law of the Installation State may provide io the contrary, the operator shall not be liable for nuclear damage caused by a nuclear incident directly due to a grave natural disaster of an exceptional character.

4.   Whenever both nuclear damage and damage other than nuclear damage have been caused by a nuclear incident or jointly by a nuclear incident and one or more other occurrences, such other damage shall, to the extent that it is not reasonably separable from the nuclear damage, be deemed, for the purposes of this Convention, to be nuclear damage caused by that nuclear incident. Where, however, damage is caused jointly by a nuclear incident covered by this Convention and by an emission of ionizing radiation not covered by it, nothing in this Convention shall limit or otherwise affect the liability, either as regards any person suffering nuclear damage or by way of recourse or contribution, of any person who may be held liable in connection with that emission of ionizing radiation.

5.   The operator shall not be liable under this Convention for nuclear damage –

(a)   to the nuclear installation itself or to any property on the site of that installation which is used or to be used in connection with that installation; or

(b)   to the means of transport upon which the nuclear material involved was at the time of the nuclear incident.

[...]

7.   Nothing in this Convention shall affect –

(a)   the liability of any individual for nuclear damage for which the operator, by virtue of paragraph 3 or 5 of this Article, is not liable under this Convention and which that individual caused by an act or omission done with intent to cause damage; or

(b)   the liability outside this Convention of the operator for nuclear damage for which, by virtue of sub-paragraph (b) of paragraph 5 of this Article, he is not liable under this Convention.

ARTICLE VII

1.   The operator shall be required to maintain insurance or other financial security covering his liability for nuclear damage in such amount, of such type and in such terms as the Installation State shall specify. The Installation State shall ensure the payment of claims for compensation for nuclear damage which have been established against the operator by providing the necessary funds to the extent that the yield of insurance or other financial security is inadequate to satisfy such claims, but not in excess of the limit, if any, established pursuant to Article V.

[...]

ARTICLE XI

1. Except as otherwise provided in this Article, jurisdiction over actions under Article II shall lie only with the courts of the Contracting Party within whose territory the nuclear incident occurred.

2. Where the nuclear incident occurred outside the territory of any Contracting Party, or where the place of the nuclear incident cannot be determined with certainty, jurisdiction over such actions shall lie with the courts of the Installation State of the operator liable.

3. Where under paragraph 1 or 2 of this Article, jurisdiction would lie with the courts of more than one Contracting Party, jurisdiction shall lie –

    (a) if the nuclear incident occurred partly outside the territory of any Contracting Party, and partly within the territory of a single Contracting Party, with the courts of the latter; and

    (b) in any other case, with the courts of that Contracting Party which is determined by agreement between the Contracting Parties whose courts would be competent under paragraph 1 or 2 of this Article.

1988 Joint Protocol Relating to the Application of the Vienna Convention and the Paris Convention

Article II

For the purpose of this Protocol:

(a) The operator of a nuclear installation situated in the territory of a Party to the Vienna Convention shall be liable in accordance with that Convention for nuclear damage suffered in the territory of a Party to both the Paris Convention and this Protocol;

(b) The operator of a nuclear installation situated in the territory of a Party to the Paris Convention shall be liable in accordance with that Convention for nuclear damage suffered in the territory of a Party to both the Vienna Convention and this Protocol.

Article III

1. Either the Vienna Convention or the Paris Convention shall apply to a nuclear incident to the exclusion of the other.

2. In the case of a nuclear incident occurring in a nuclear installation, the applicable Convention shall be that to which the State is a Party within whose territory that installation is situated.

3. In the case of a nuclear incident outside a nuclear installation and involving nuclear material in the course of carriage, the applicable Convention shall be that to which the State is a Party within whose territory the nuclear installation is situated whose operator is liable pursuant to either Article II.1(b) and (c) of the Vienna Convention or Article 4(a) and (b) of the Paris Convention.

Article IV

1. Articles I to XV of the Vienna Convention shall be applied, with respect to the Contracting Parties to this Protocol which are Parties to the Paris Convention, in the same manner as between Parties to the Vienna Convention.

2.   Articles 1 to 14 of the Paris Convention shall be applied, with respect to the
        Contracting Parties to this Protocol which are Parties to the Vienna Convention, in
        the same manner as between Parties to the Paris Convention.

1997 Vienna Convention on Supplementary Compensation for Nuclear Damage

Article I
Definitions
[...]

(f)   "Nuclear Damage" means:
        (i)   loss of life or personal injury;
        (ii)   loss of or damage to property;

and each of the following to the extent determined by the law of the competent court:

        (iii)   economic loss arising from loss or damage referred to in sub-paragraph
                (i) or (ii), insofar as not included in those sub-paragraphs, if incurred by
                a person entitled to claim in respect of such loss or damage;
        (iv)   the costs of measures of reinstatement of impaired environment, unless
                such impairment is insignificant, if such measures are actually taken or to
                be taken, and insofar as not included in sub-paragraph (ii);
        (v)   loss of income deriving from an economic interest in any use or enjoyment
                of the environment, incurred as a result of a significant impairment of that
                environment, and insofar as not included in sub-paragraph (ii);
        (vi)   the costs of preventive measures, and further loss or damage caused by such
                measures;
        (vii)   any other economic loss, other than any caused by the impairment of the
                environment, if permitted by the general law on civil liability of the compe-
                tent court,

in the case of sub-paragraphs (i) to (v) and (vii) above, to the extent that the loss or
damage arises out of or results from ionizing radiation emitted by any source of radiation inside a nuclear installation, or emitted from nuclear fuel or radioactive products
or waste in, or of nuclear material coming from, originating in, or sent to, a nuclear
installation, whether so arising from the radioactive properties of such matter, or
from a combination of radioactive properties with toxic, explosive or other hazardous
properties of such matter.

[...]

(i)   "Nuclear incident" means any occurrence or series of occurrences having the same
        origin which causes nuclear damage or, but only with respect to preventive meas-
        ures, creates a grave and imminent threat of causing such damage.

Article II Purpose and Application
1.   The purpose of this Convention is to supplement the system of compensation
        provided pursuant to national law which:

(a)   implements one of the instruments referred to in Article I (a) and (b); or

(b)   complies with the provisions of the Annex to this Convention.

2.   The system of this Convention shall apply to nuclear damage for which an operator of a nuclear installation used for peaceful purposes situated in the territory of a Contracting Party is liable under either one of the Conventions referred to in Article I or national law mentioned in paragraph 1(b) of this Article.

3.   The Annex referred to in paragraph 1(b) shall constitute an integral part of this Convention.

Article III
Undertaking

1.   Compensation in respect of nuclear damage per nuclear incident shall be ensured by the following means:

(a)(i) the Installation State shall ensure the availability of 300 million SDRs or a greater amount that it may have specified to the Depositary at any time prior to the nuclear incident, or a transitional amount pursuant to sub-paragraph (ii);

(ii)   a Contracting Party may establish for the maximum of 10 years from the date of the opening for signature of this Convention, a transitional amount of at least 150 million SDRs in respect of a nuclear incident occurring within that period.

(b)   beyond the amount made available under sub-paragraph (a), the Contracting Parties shall make available public funds according to the formula specified in Article IV.

[...]

17.4.2.3 Waste

1996 International Convention on Liability and Compensation for Damage in Connection with the Carriage of Hazardous and Noxious Substances by Sea (and the 2010 Protocol)

Article 1
[...]

5.   Hazardous and noxious substances (HNS) means:

(a)   any substances, materials and articles carried on board a ship as cargo, referred to in (i) to (vii) below:

(i)   oils, carried in bulk, as defined in regulation 1 of Annex I to the International Convention for the Prevention of Pollution from Ships, 1973, as modified by the Protocol of 1978 relating thereto, as amended;

(ii)   noxious liquid substances, carried in bulk, as defined in regulation 1.10 of Annex II to the International Convention for the Prevention of Pollution from Ships, 1973, as modified by the Protocol of 1978 relating thereto, as amended, and those substances and mixtures provisionally categorized as falling in pollution category X, Y or Z in accordance with regulation 6.3 of the said Annex II;

(iii)   dangerous liquid substances carried in bulk listed in chapter 17 of the International Code for the Construction and Equipment of Ships Carrying Dangerous Chemicals in Bulk, as amended, and the dangerous products for which the preliminary suitable conditions for the carriage have been prescribed by the Administration and port administrations involved in accordance with paragraph 1.1.6 of the Code;

(iv)   dangerous, hazardous and harmful substances, materials and articles in packaged form covered by the International Maritime Dangerous Goods Code, as amended;

(v)   liquefied gases as listed in chapter 19 of the International Code for the Construction and Equipment of Ships Carrying Liquefied Gases in Bulk, as amended, and the products for which preliminary suitable conditions for the carriage have been prescribed by the Administration and port administrations involved in accordance with paragraph 1.1.6 of the Code;

(vi)   liquid substances carried in bulk with a flashpoint not exceeding 60°C (measured by a closed-cup test);

(vii)   solid bulk materials possessing chemical hazards covered by the International Maritime Solid Bulk Cargoes Code, as amended, to the extent that these substances are also subject to the provisions of the International Maritime Dangerous Goods Code in effect in 1996, when carried in packaged form; and

(b)   residues from the previous carriage in bulk of substances referred to in (a) (i) to (iii) and (v) to (vii) above.

5bis   Bulk HNS means any hazardous and noxious substances referred to in article 1, paragraph 5(a)(i) to (iii) and (v) to (vii) and paragraph 5(b).

5ter   Packaged HNS means any hazardous and noxious substances referred to in article 1, paragraph 5(a)(iv)

[...]

Article 4

1   This Convention shall apply to claims, other than claims arising out of any contract for the carriage of goods and passengers, for damage arising from the carriage of hazardous and noxious substances by sea.

2   This Convention shall not apply to the extent that its provisions are incompatible with those of the applicable law relating to workers' compensation or social security schemes.

3   This Convention shall not apply:

(a)   to pollution damage as defined in the International Convention on Civil Liability for Oil Pollution Damage, 1969, as amended, whether or not compensation is payable in respect of it under that Convention; and

(b) to damage caused by a radioactive material of class 7 either in the International Maritime Dangerous Goods Code, as amended, or in the International Maritime Solid Bulk Cargoes Code, as amended.

4 Except as provided in paragraph 5, the provisions of this Convention shall not apply to warships, naval auxiliary or other ships owned or operated by a State and used, for the time being, only on Government non-commercial service.

5 A State Party may decide to apply this Convention to its warships or other vessels described in paragraph 4, in which case it shall notify the Secretary-General thereof specifying the terms and conditions of such application.

6 With respect to ships owned by a State Party and used for commercial purposes, each State shall be subject to suit in the jurisdictions set forth in article 38 and shall waive all defences based on its status as a sovereign State.

Liability of the owner
Article 7

1 Except as provided in paragraphs 2 and 3, the owner at the time of an incident shall be liable for damage caused by any hazardous and noxious substances in connection with their carriage by sea on board the ship, provided that if an incident consists of a series of occurrences having the same origin the liability shall attach to the owner at the time of the first of such occurrences.

2 No liability shall attach to the owner if the owner proves that:

(a) the damage resulted from an act of war, hostilities, civil war, insurrection or a natural phenomenon of an exceptional, inevitable and irresistible character; or

(b) the damage was wholly caused by an act or omission done with the intent to cause damage by a third party; or

(c) the damage was wholly caused by the negligence or other wrongful act of any Government or other authority responsible for the maintenance of lights or other navigational aids in the exercise of that function; or

(d) the failure of the shipper or any other person to furnish information concerning the hazardous and noxious nature of the substances shipped either

(i) has caused the damage, wholly or partly; or

(ii) has led the owner not to obtain insurance in accordance with article 12;

provided that neither the owner nor its servants or agents knew or ought reasonably to have known of the hazardous and noxious nature of the substances shipped.

3 If the owner proves that the damage resulted wholly or partly either from an act or omission done with intent to cause damage by the person who suffered the damage or from the negligence of that person, the owner may be exonerated wholly or partially from liability to such person.

4 No claim for compensation for damage shall be made against the owner otherwise than in accordance with this Convention.

5 Subject to paragraph 6, no claim for compensation for damage under this Convention or otherwise may be made against:

(a) the servants or agents of the owner or the members of the crew;

(b) the pilot or any other person who, without being a member of the crew, performs services for the ship;

(c)   any charterer (howsoever described, including a bareboat charterer), manager or operator of the ship;

(d)   any person performing salvage operations with the consent of the owner or on the instructions of a competent public authority;

(e)   any person taking preventive measures; and

(f)   the servants or agents of persons mentioned in (c), (d) and (e);

unless the damage resulted from their personal act or omission, committed with the intent to cause such damage, or recklessly and with knowledge that such damage would probably result.

[…]

Limitation of liability
Article 9

1   The owner of a ship shall be entitled to limit liability under this Convention in respect of any one incident to an aggregate amount calculated as follows:

(a)   Where the damage has been caused by bulk HNS:

(i)   10 million units of account for a ship not exceeding 2,000 units of tonnage; and

(ii)   for a ship with a tonnage in excess thereof, the following amount in addition to that mentioned in (i):

for each unit of tonnage from 2,001 to 50,000 units of tonnage, 1,500 units of account;

for each unit of tonnage in excess of 50,000 units of tonnage, 360 units of account;

provided, however, that this aggregate amount shall not in any event exceed 100 million units of account.

(b)   Where the damage has been caused by packaged HNS, or where the damage has been caused by both bulk HNS and packaged HNS, or where it is not possible to determine whether the damage originating from that ship has been caused by bulk HNS or by packaged HNS:

(i)   11.5 million units of account for a ship not exceeding 2,000 units of tonnage; and

(ii)   for a ship with a tonnage in excess thereof, the following amount in addition to that mentioned in (i):

for each unit of tonnage from 2,001 to 50,000 units of tonnage, 1,725 units of account;

for each unit of tonnage in excess of 50,000 units of tonnage, 414 units of account;

provided, however, that this aggregate amount shall not in any event exceed 115 million units of account.

2   The owner shall not be entitled to limit liability under this Convention if it is proved that the damage resulted from the personal act or omission of the owner, committed with the intent to cause such damage, or recklessly and with knowledge that such damage would probably result.

3   The owner shall, for the purpose of benefitting from the limitation provided for in paragraph 1, constitute a fund for the total sum representing the limit of liability

established in accordance with paragraph 1 with the court or other competent authority of any one of the States Parties in which action is brought under article 38 or, if no action is brought, with any court or other competent authority in any one of the States Parties in which an action can be brought under article 38. The fund can be constituted either by depositing the sum or by producing a bank guarantee or other guarantee, acceptable under the law of the State Party where the fund is constituted, and considered to be adequate by the court or other competent authority.

4 Subject to the provisions of article 11, the fund shall be distributed among the claimants in proportion to the amounts of their established claims.

[...]

11 The insurer or other person providing financial security shall be entitled to constitute a fund in accordance with this article on the same conditions and having the same effect as if it were constituted by the owner. Such a fund may be constituted even if, under the provisions of paragraph 2, the owner is not entitled to limitation of liability, but its constitution shall in that case not prejudice the rights of any claimant against the owner.

Compulsory insurance of the owner
Article 12
1 The owner of a ship registered in a State Party and actually carrying hazardous and noxious substances shall be required to maintain insurance or other financial security, such as the guarantee of a bank or similar financial institution, in the sums fixed by applying the limits of liability prescribed in article 9, paragraph 1, to cover liability for damage under this Convention.

Establishment of the HNS Fund
Article 13
1 The International Hazardous and Noxious Substances Fund (HNS Fund) is hereby established with the following aims:
   (a)   to provide compensation for damage in connection with the carriage of hazardous and noxious substances by sea, to the extent that the protection afforded by chapter II is inadequate or not available; and
   (b)   to give effect to the related tasks set out in article 15.
2 The HNS Fund shall in each State Party be recognized as a legal person capable under the laws of that State of assuming rights and obligations and of being a party in legal proceedings before the courts of that State. Each State Party shall recognize the Director as the legal representative of the HNS Fund.

Table 17.1 Primary treaties and protocols establishing civil liability regimes

1. Oil
Brussels Convention on Civil Liability for Oil Pollution Damage
1992 Oil Fund Convention and 2003 Protocol
Bunker Convention 2001
STOPIA 2006 and TOPIA 2006
2. Nuclear
1960 Paris Convention
1963 Brussels Convention
1963 Supplementary Convention
2004 Protocol to the Paris Convention
1997 Protocol to Vienna Convention
1988 Joint Protocol
1997 Convention on Supplementary Compensation
3. Marine Environment
1978 Kuwait Convention
1982 UNCLOS
1982 Jeddah Convention
1983 Cartagena Convention
1986 Noumea Convention
1992 Baltic Convention
1992 Black Sea Convention
1996 Protocol to the London Convention
2003 Tehran Convention
2010 Amended Nairobi Convention
5. Biodiversity
2010 Nagoya Protocol
6. Waste
1999 Protocol to the 1989 Basel Convention on Liability and Compensation for Damage Resulting from Transboundary Movements of Hazardous Wastes and Their Disposal
7. Transport
1989 Geneva Convention on Civil Liability for Damage Caused During Carriage of Dangerous Goods By Road, Rail and Inland Navigations Vessels
2010 Protocol to the International Convention on Liability and Compensation for Damage in Connection with the Carriage of Hazardous and Noxious Substances by Sea (2010 HNS Protocol
8. Dangerous Goods
1993 Lugano Convention
2003 Civil Liability Protocol to UNESE 1992 Watercourse Convention and 1991 Industrial Accidents Convention
9. Antarctic
1988 CRAMRA
1991 Antarctic Environmental Protocol

QUESTIONS

1. What are the differences between the regimes for state responsibility and civil liability for environmental harm?
2. Critically assess the *Nicaragua v. Costa Rica* decision as it concerns state responsibility for environmental damage.
3. Identify the main principles underlying civil liability regimes.

FURTHER READING

BOOKS

JA Barboza, *The Environment, Risk and Liability in International Law* (Martinus Nijhoff 2011)

M Bowman and A Boyle (eds), *Environmental Damage in International and Comparative Law* (Oxford University Press 2002)

M Goranson, 'Liability for Damage to the Marine Environment' in A Boyle and D Freestone (eds), *International Law and Sustainable Development* (Oxford University Press 1999)

X Hanqin, *Transboundary Damage in International Law* (Cambridge University Press 2009)

A Nollkaemper and I Plakokefalos (eds), *The Practice of Shared Responsibility in International Law* (Cambridge University Press 2017)

P Okowa, *State Responsibility for Transboundary Air Pollution in International Law* (Oxford University Press 2000)

P Sands and J Peel, *Principles of International Environmental Law* (4th edn, Cambridge University Press 2018)

CHAPTERS

A Douhan, 'Liability for Environmental Damage' in R Wolfrum, *Max Planck Encyclopedia of Public International Law* (2019)

M Fitzmaurice, 'International Responsibility and Liability' in D Bodansky, J Brunnée and E Hey (eds), *The Oxford Handbook of International Environmental Law* (Oxford University Press 2008)

M Jacobsson, 'Liability and Compensation for Ship Source Pollution' in D Attard, M Fitzmaurice, N Martinez, and R Hamza (eds), *The IMLI Manual of International Maritime Law Volume III* (Oxford University Press 2016)

C Voigt, 'State Responsibility for Damages Associated with Climate Change' in M Doelle and S Seck (eds), *Research Handbook on Climate Change Loss and Damage* (Edward Elgar 2021)

D Wirth, 'Hazardous Substances and Activities' in D Bodansky, J Brunnée and E Hey (eds), *The Oxford Handbook of International Environmental Law* (Oxford University Press 2007)

ARTICLES

JA Barboza, 'International Liability for the Injurious Consequences of Acts Not Prohibited by International Law and the Protection of the Environment' (1994) 247 RCADI 293

M Broberg, 'State of Climate Law: The Third Pillar of International Climate Change Law: Explaining "Loss and Damage" after the Paris Agreement' (2020) 10 Climate Law 211

J Brunnée, 'Of Sense and Sensibility: Reflections on International Liability Regimes as Tools for Environmental Protection' (2004) 53 Int'l & Comp LQ 351

R Churchill, 'Facilitating Transnational Civil Liability Litigation for Environmental Damage by Means of Treaties: Progress, Problems, and Prospects' (2001) 13 YB Int'l Envt'l L 3

S Maljean-Dubois and B Mayer, 'Liability and Compensation for Marine Plastic Pollution: Conceptual Issues and Possible Ways Forward' (2020) 114 AJIL Unbound 206

LFE Goldie, 'Liability for Damage and the Progressive Development of International Law' (1965) 14 Int'l & Comp LQ 1189

G Handl, 'International Liability of States for Marine Pollution' (1983) 21 Canadian Yearbook of International Law 85

MJL Hardy, 'Nuclear Liability: The General Principles of Law and Further Proposals' (1960) 36 BYBIL 223

RJ Heffron, SF Ashley and WJ Nuttall, 'The Global Nuclear Liability Regime Post Fukushima Daiichi' (2016) 90 Progress in Nuclear Energy 1

W Jenks, 'Liability for Ultra-Hazardous Activities in International Law' (1966) 117 RCADI 99

J Juste-Ruiz, 'Compensation for Pollution Damage Caused by Oil Tanker Accidents: From "Erica" to "Prestige"' (2010) 1 Aegean Review of the Law of the Sea and Maritime Law 37

P Sands and R Stewart, 'Valuation of Environmental Damage—US and International Law Approaches' (1996) 5 Review of European Community and International Environmental Law 290

T Scovazzi, 'State Responsibility for Environmental Harm' (2001) 13 YB Int'l Envt'l L 43

C Voigt, 'International Environmental Responsibility and Liability' (2021) SSRN available at https://ssrn.com/abstract=3791419

C Von Bar, 'Environmental Damage in Private International Law' (1997) 268 RCADI 291

R Wolfrum, 'Means of Ensuring Compliance with and Enforcement of International Environmental Law' (1998) 272 RCADI 9

18
Non-compliance procedures

18.1   INTRODUCTION

Non-compliance procedures ('NCP') play a significant role in the compliance and/or implementation of multilateral environmental agreements ('MEAs'). It is well known that there is no authoritative definition of compliance or implementation, although these terms appear frequently in MEAs. 'Generally from a law of treaties perspective, the obligation of compliance suggests the '"effective implementation of a treaty" of a treaty, i.e. the adoption of relevant measures both at international and national levels, according to Article 26 of the 1969 Vienna Convention on the Law of Treaties, which is based on the principle pacta sunt servanda'.[1] Wolfrum has defined compliance to mean that 'commitments entered into by a State are fully effectuated in practice',[2] and whether a state has implemented treaty obligations 'requires only the assessment of existing laws and regulations of that State'.[3] Fitzmaurice suggests that compliance exceeds implementation as it requires that the state is 'well obliged to provide the necessary administrative procedures for the enforcement of the relevant rules'.[4] Indeed, Wolfrum has also said that 'to ensure compliance, it is necessary to establish whether the factual situation of the State actions or policies are commensurate with the international obligation'.[5] The UNEP Guidelines on Compliance and Enforcement of Multilateral Environmental Agreements ('UNEP Guidelines') have defined compliance as 'fulfilment by the contracting parties of their obligations under a multilateral environmental agreement and any amendments to the multilateral environmental agreement';[6] and implementation as '*inter alia*, all relevant laws, regulations, policies, and other measures and initiatives, that contracting parties

---

[1]   Malgosia Fitzmaurice, 'The Potential of Inter-State Conciliation within the Framework of Environmental Treaties' in Christian Tomuschat and Marcelo Kohen (eds), *Flexibility in International Dispute Settlement: Conciliation Revisited* (2020) 96.

[2]   Rüdiger Wolfrum, 'Means of Ensuring Compliance with and Enforcement of International Environmental Law' (1999) 272 Recueil des cours de l'Académie de droit international 13, 29.

[3]   Ibid.

[4]   Fitzmaurice (n 1) 96–97.

[5]   Wolfrum (n 2) 30.

[6]   Article 9(a) The UNEP Guidelines on Compliance and Enforcement of Multilateral Environmental Agreements ('UNEP Guidelines').

adopt and/or take to meet their obligations under a multilateral environmental agreement and its amendments, if any'.[7]

As the nature of MEAs is special in the sense that while non-compliance of treaty obligations would more generally entail consequences under the law of treaties, i.e., material breach under Article 60 of the 1969 Vienna Convention on the Law of Treaties or content of responsibility under international responsibility, or result in a dispute, the purpose of environmental treaties is better served by ensuring States Parties comply with their obligations. As put by Fitzmaurice:

> Generally, it may be said NCPs were designed to respond to a breach of environmental obligations in a multilateral, not a bilateral context, which is 'capable of accommodating community interests in a truly satisfactory manner'. Environmental obligations, in particular those relating to global issues, are not reciprocal in nature. Therefore, the classical settlement of dispute procedures as envisaged in Article 33 of the UN Charter, bilateral in nature, are not suitable for addressing non-compliance within a multilateral context and therefore remedying non-compliance relating to global issues such as climate change, protection of biodiversity or ozone layer. Classic settlement of dispute procedures were considered too confrontational, thereby capable of undermining the spirit of international cooperation. These procedures have less stringent effects; the decisions of non-compliance bodies are not final in the form of res judicata, may be 'seen as less intrusive on State sovereignty' and do not apply de facto as settlement of dispute mechanisms, i.e., after damage to the environment was done, thereby emphasizing the preventative character of NCPs, which distinguishes this system from settlement of dispute procedures. This approach, favouring prevention, follows the general trend in international environmental law, relying to a greater degree on such means as reporting or verification processes rather than having recourse to settlement of disputes procedures. In fact, national reporting by States Parties to MEAs and their verification form the elements of the NCPs.[8]

The legal basis for most NCPs is premised on 'enabling clauses' in MEAs, often implemented by decisions of Conferences of the Parties or Meetings of the Parties. The exception to this is the 1989 Basel Convention on the Control of Transboundary movements of hazardous wastes and their disposal ('Basel Convention'), where the NCP was enacted by a decision of the COP.[9]

As there is no authoritative definition of an NCP, it is perhaps more useful to understand NCPs in terms of their underlying characteristics. Fitzmaurice observes '[i]t is the underlying characteristic of NCPs that they are intended to provide a non-confrontational procedure the objective of which is to facilitate compliance by Parties in difficulties and to promote the overarching objectives of MEAs'.[10] Dupuy and Viñuales point out that 'the primary objective

---

[7]   Article 9(b) UNEP Guidelines.

[8]   Fitzmaurice (n 1) 97.

[9]   Sixth meeting of the Conference of Parties to the Basel Convention (Decision VI/12), Geneva, 9–13 December 2002.

[10]   Malgosia Fitzmaurice, 'Environmental Compliance Control', *Max Planck Encyclopedia of Public International Law* (2010) para. 55.

of NCPs is to determine the reasons for non-compliance and to provide financial and technical assistance. This is reflected in the measures they are entitled to adopt'.[11]

NCPs are broadly seen to be a mechanism which serves as an alternative to dispute settlement procedures, particularly adversarial mechanisms such as inter-state adjudication. Tanzi and Pitea comment that 'the establishment of non-compliance mechanisms is firmly rooted in the need to foster the effectiveness of MEAs, upon consideration of the fact that traditional means for the enforcement of international law, including dispute settlement, have not proved fully appropriate in this particular field'.[12] Boyle and Harrison aptly observe 'NCPs are unlike litigation in several respects. They are designed to facilitate multilateral solutions to questions of treaty interpretation and allegations of breach or non-compliance with the treaty'.[13]

The UNEP Guidelines have broadly identified two different types of NCPs:

Non-compliance mechanisms:[14]

States can consider the inclusion of non-compliance provisions in a multilateral environmental agreement, with a view to assisting parties having compliance problems and addressing individual cases of non-compliance, taking into account the importance of tailoring compliance provisions and mechanisms to the agreement's specific obligations. The following considerations could be kept in view:

(i)   The parties can consider the establishment of a body, such as a compliance committee, to address compliance issues. Members of such a body could be party representatives or party nominated experts, with appropriate expertise on the relevant subject matter;

(ii) Non-compliance mechanisms could be used by the contracting parties to provide a vehicle to identify possible situations of non-compliance at an early stage and the causes of non-compliance, and to formulate appropriate responses including, addressing and/or correcting the state of non-compliance without delay. These responses can be adjusted to meet varying requirements of cases of non-compliance, and may include both facilitative and stronger measures as appropriate and consistent with applicable international law;

(iii) In order to promote, facilitate and secure compliance, non-compliance mechanisms can be non-adversarial and include procedural safeguards for those involved. In addition, non-compliance mechanisms can provide a means to clarify the content, to

---

[11]   Pierre-Marie Dupuy and Jorge E Viñuales, *International Environmental Law* (2nd edn, CUP 2018) 351.

[12]   Attila Tanzi and Cesare Pitea, 'Non-Compliance Mechanisms: Lessons Learned and the Way Forward' in Tullio Treves and others (eds), *Non-Compliance Procedures and Mechanisms and the Effectiveness of International Environmental Agreements* (Springer 2009) 571.

[13]   Alan Boyle and James Harrison, 'Judicial Settlement of International Environmental Disputes: Current Problems' (2013) 4 Journal of International Dispute Settlement 245, 256.

[14]   Article 14(d), UNEP Guidelines.

promote the application of the provisions of the agreement and thus lead significantly to the prevention of disputes;

(iv) The final determination of non-compliance of a party with respect to an agreement might be made through the conference of the parties of the relevant multilateral environmental agreement or another body under that agreement, if so mandated by the conference of the parties, consistent with the respective multilateral environmental agreement.

[...]

Compliance mechanisms or procedures could be introduced or enhanced after a multilateral environmental agreement has come into effect, provided such mechanisms or procedures have been authorised by the multilateral environmental agreement, subsequent amendment, or conference of the parties decision, as appropriate, and consistent with applicable international law.[15]

Clearly, and understandably, states have discretion when negotiating MEAs to design NCPs which are fitting for the particular treaty setting.

It is well known that the NCP as first introduced under the Montreal Protocol on Substances that Deplete the Ozone Layer ('Montreal Protocol') in the fourth Meeting of the Parties ('MOP') in 1992 has served as a blueprint for other NCPs under MEAs.[16] The legal basis is found in Article 8 of the Montreal Protocol, which stipulates:

The Parties, at their first meeting, shall consider and approve procedures and institutional mechanisms for determining non-compliance with the provisions of this Protocol and for treatment of Parties found to be in non-compliance.

The NCP under the Montreal Protocol established an Implementation Committee, comprising ten Parties elected by the Meeting of the Parties for two years, based on equitable geographical distribution.[17] There are three ways in which a case may be brought before the Implementation Committee: (i) if one or more Parties have reservations regarding another Party's implementation of its obligations under the Protocol, those concerns may be addressed in writing to the Secretariat (such a submission shall be supported by corroborating information);[18] (ii) where the Secretariat becomes aware of possible non-compliance by any Party with its obligations under the Protocol;[19] and (iii) where a Party concludes that, despite its best bona

---

[15]   Ibid., Article 16.

[16]   Philippe Sands and Jacqueline Peel, *Principles of International Environmental Law* (4th edn, CUP 2018) 172; Dupuy and Viñuales (n 11) 344.

[17]   Annex IV: Non-compliance procedure, para. 5.

[18]   Ibid., para. 1.

[19]   Ibid., para. 3.

fide efforts, it is unable to comply fully with its obligations under the Protocol.[20] The functions of the Implementation Committee are:

(a) To receive, consider and report on any submission in accordance with paragraphs 1, 2 and 4;

(b) To receive, consider and report on any information or observations forwarded by the Secretariat in connection with the preparation of the reports referred to in Article 12 (c) of the Protocol and on any other information received and forwarded by the Secretariat concerning compliance with the provisions of the Protocol.

(c) To request, where it considers necessary, through the Secretariat, further information on matters under its consideration;

(d) To undertake, upon the invitation of the Party concerned, information-gathering in the territory of that Party for fulfilling the functions of the Committee;

(e) To maintain, in particular for the purposes of drawing up its recommendations, an exchange of information with the Executive Committee of the Multilateral Fund related to the provision of financial and technical cooperation, including the transfer of technologies to Parties operating under Article 5, paragraph 1, of the Protocol.

The Implementation Committee reports to the Meeting of the Parties and includes any recommendations it considers appropriate; and the Parties may, taking into consideration the circumstances of the matter, decide upon and call for steps to bring about full compliance with the Protocol, including measures to assist the Parties' compliance with the Protocol and to further the Protocol's objectives.[21] The Meeting of the Parties also adopted an 'Indicative List of Measures that might be taken by the Meeting Parties in respect of non-compliance with the Protocol.' These measures include:

A. Appropriate assistance, including assistance for the collection and reporting of data, technical assistance, technology transfer and financial assistance, information transfer and training.

B. Issuing cautions.

C. Suspension, in accordance with the applicable rules of international law concerning the suspension of the operation of a treaty, of specific rights and privileges under the Protocol, whether or not subject to time limits, including those concerned with industrial rationalization, production, consumption, trade, transfer of technology, financial mechanism and institutional arrangements.[22]

---

[20] Ibid., para. 4.

[21] Ibid., para. 9.

[22] Annex V: Indicative list of measures that might be taken by a Meeting of the Parties in respect of non-compliance with the Protocol.

As mentioned, the NCP under the Montreal Protocol is very much a blueprint for non-compliance procedures in other MEAs.[23] The NCP in the Kyoto Protocol, however, notably differs from the NCP in the Montreal Protocol. The objective of the former is 'to facilitate, promote and enforce compliance with the commitments under the Protocol'.[24] Notably, enforcement is not within the functions of the Implementation Committee pursuant to the NCP in the Montreal Protocol, which Fitzmaurice observes is a 'harder' objective in the Kyoto Protocol's compliance procedure than other NCPs.[25]

Under the Kyoto Protocol's NCP, a Compliance Committee is established,[26] which functions through a plenary, a bureau, a Facilitative branch and the Enforcement branch.[27] The Compliance Committee comprises 20 members elected by the Conference of the Parties.[28]

Notably different from the Implementation Committee in the NCP of the Montreal Protocol, members of the Compliance Committee pursuant to the NCP of the Kyoto Protocol, the members of the Committee serve in their individual capacities.[29] Further, the facilitative branch and the enforcement branch shall interact and cooperate in their functioning.[30] The former may provide advice and facilitate Parties in implementing the Protocol, and promoting compliance by Parties with their commitments under the Protocol;[31] and may apply the following consequences, taking into account the principle of common but differentiated responsibilities and respective capabilities:

(a) Provision of advice and facilitation of assistance to individual Parties regarding the implementation of the Protocol;
(b) Facilitation of financial and technical assistance to any Party concerned, including technology transfer and capacity building from sources other than those established under the Convention and the Protocol for the developing countries;
(c) Facilitation of financial and technical assistance, including technology transfer and capacity building [...].[32]

---

[23]   1989 Basel Convention; 1996 Protocol to the 1972 Convention on the Prevention of Marine Pollution by Dumping of Wastes and Other Matter; 1997 Kyoto Protocol; 2000 Cartagena Protocol on Biosafety to the 1992 Convention on Biological Diversity; UNECE for Europe Procedures and Mechanisms for Review of Compliance under the ESPOO Convention.

[24]   Decision 27/CMP.1 Procedures and mechanisms relating to compliance under the Kyoto Protocol FCCC/KP/CMP/2005/8/Add.3, Annex: Procedures and mechanisms relating to compliance under the Kyoto Protocol, Article 1.

[25]   Malgosia Fitzmaurice, 'Environmental Compliance Control', *Max Planck Encyclopedia of Public International Law* (2010) para. 57.

[26]   Article II(1) Ibid.
[27]   Article II(2) Ibid.
[28]   Article II(3) Ibid.
[29]   Article II(6) Ibid.
[30]   Article II(7) Ibid.
[31]   Article IV(4) Ibid.
[32]   Article XIV Ibid.

The Enforcement Branch shall be responsible for determining whether a Party in Annex I (Parties include the industrialized countries that were members of the Organisation for Economic Co-operation and Development in 1992, plus countries with economies in transition including the Russian Federation, the Baltic States, and several Central and Eastern European States) is not in compliance with:

(a) Its quantified emission limitation or reduction commitment under Article 3, paragraph 1, of the Protocol;

(b) The methodological and reporting requirements under Article 5, paragraphs 1 and 2, and Article 7, paragraphs 1 and 4, of the Protocol; and

(c) The eligibility requirements under Articles 6, 12 and 17 of the Protocol.

Consequences applied by the Enforcement Branch, include *inter alia*:

(a) Declaration of non-compliance;

(b) Development of a plan in accordance with paragraphs 2 and 3 below.

2. The Party not in compliance under paragraph 1 above, shall, within three months after the determination of non-compliance, or such longer period that the enforcement branch considers appropriate, submit to the enforcement branch for review and assessment a plan that includes: (a) An analysis of the causes of non-compliance of the Party; (b) Measures that the Party intends to implement in order to remedy the non-compliance; and (c) A timetable for implementing such measures within a time frame not exceeding twelve months which enables the assessment of progress in the implementation.

3. The Party not in compliance under paragraph 1 above shall submit to the enforcement branch progress reports on the implementation of the plan on a regular basis.[33]

Clearly, the Kyoto Protocol Compliance Mechanisms provide different sets of consequences which may be applied, respectively, by the Facilitative and Enforcement Branches. Of further note are the following measures under the Enforcement branch:

Where the enforcement branch has determined that the emissions of a Party have exceeded its assigned amount, calculated pursuant to its quantified emission limitation or reduction commitment inscribed in Annex B to the Protocol and in accordance with the provisions of Article 3 of the Protocol as well as the modalities for the accounting of assigned amounts under Article 7, paragraph 4, of the Protocol, taking into account emission reduction units, certified emission reductions, assigned amount units and removal units the Party has acquired in accordance with section XIII, it shall declare that that Party is not in compliance with its

---

[33] Article XV(1)–(3) Ibid.

commitments under Article 3, paragraph 1, of the Protocol, and shall apply the following consequences:

(a) Deduction from the Party's assigned amount for the second commitment period of a number of tonnes equal to 1.3 times the amount in tonnes of excess emissions;

(b) Development of a compliance action plan in accordance with paragraphs 6 and 7 below; and

(c) Suspension of the eligibility to make transfers under Article 17 of the Protocol until the Party is reinstated in accordance with section X, paragraph 3 or paragraph 4.[34]

The NCP under the 1998 Aarhus Convention was established in 2002 at the first Meeting of the Parties as the Compliance Committee for the review of compliance by the Parties with their obligations under the Convention.[35] The structure of Compliance Committee comprises eight members who serve in their personal capacity.[36] The functions of the Committee are to consider any submission, referral or communication made in accordance with the respective procedures; prepare at the request of the Meeting of the Parties a report on compliance or with implementation of the provisions; monitor, assess and facilitate the implementation of and compliance with the reporting requirements; examine compliance issues and make recommendations if and as appropriate.[37] There are three ways in which a submission may be brought before the Committee: by one or more Parties that have reservations about another Party's compliance with its obligations under the Convention;[38] referrals by the Secretariat;[39] communications brought before the Committee by one or more members of the public concerning the Party's compliance with the Convention.[40] The notable difference with the NCP in the Aarhus Convention and those in the Montreal Protocol and Kyoto Protocol is that the Compliance Committee may receive submissions from members of the public.

The Paris Agreement's NCP – the Paris Agreement Implementation and Compliance Committee – has a 'softer' approach than the Kyoto Protocol's NCP. The emphasis appears to be very heavily centred on promoting compliance. Ms Patricia Espinosa, Executive Secretary of UN Climate Change, has commented:

The Paris Agreement Implementation and Compliance Committee is also important because it builds trust. This trust ensures that each Party honors its commitments to fight

---

[34]   Article XV(5) Ibid.

[35]   Report of the First meeting of the Parties, Decision 1/7 Review of Compliance adopted at the first meeting of the Parties held in Lucca, Italy, on 21–23 October 2002.

[36]   Article 1, *Decision I/7 on review of compliance* (2002).

[37]   Article 13, Ibid.

[38]   Article 15, Ibid.

[39]   Article 17, Ibid.

[40]   Article 18, Ibid.

climate change in accordance with the Paris Agreement. And this, in turn, helps boost the climate ambition of Parties which is what we need in 2020 and well into the future.[41]

The Committee, when considering how to facilitate implementation and promote compliance, shall 'endeavour to constructively engage with and consult the Party concerned at all stages of the process, including by inviting written submissions and providing opportunities to comment'.[42]

Measures that the Paris Agreement Implementation and Compliance Committee may take include the following:

(a) Engage in a dialogue with the Party concerned with the purpose of identifying challenges, making recommendations and sharing information, including in relation to accessing finance, technology and capacity-building support, as appropriate;

(b) Assist the Party concerned in the engagement with the appropriate finance, technology and capacity-building bodies or arrangements under or serving the Paris Agreement in order to identify possible challenges and solutions;

(c) Make recommendations to the Party concerned with regard to challenges and solutions referred to in paragraph 30(b) above and communicate such recommendations, with the consent of the Party concerned, to the relevant bodies or arrangements, as appropriate;

(d) Recommend the development of an action plan and, if so requested, assist the Party concerned in developing the plan;

(e) Issue findings of fact in relation to matters of implementation and compliance referred to in paragraph 22(a) above.[43]

Dupuy and Viñuales have noticed two main features of compliance underlying NCPs: the non-confrontational character of the procedure; and the emphasis on the prevention of environmental damage.[44] They submit:

[t]hese two features are closely related. Failure by a State to comply with an international obligation may not be due to a lack of willingness to comply but rather to certain technical or financial difficulties. In this context, NCPs are intended to help the State to return to a situation of compliance or, at least, to keep non-compliance within reasonable bounds. [...] [O]verall, the approach to compliance underpinning NCPs is clearly focused on prevention and assistance.[45]

---

[41]   https://unfccc.int/news/key-paris-agreement-implementation-and-compliance-work-initiated

[42]   Decision 20/CMA.1 Modalities and procedures for the effective operation of the committee to facilitate implementation and promote compliance referred to in Article 15, paragraph 2, of the Paris Agreement, para. 19(b).

[43]   Decision 20/CMA.1 Modalities and procedures for the effective operation of the committee to facilitate implementation and promote compliance referred to in Article 15, paragraph 2, of the Paris Agreement, para. 30

[44]   Dupuy and Viñuales (n 11) 344.

[45]   Ibid.

This chapter provides an overview of NCPs in MEAs, setting out the institutional framework comprising its legal basis, composition, functions (objectives and purpose) and powers (measures they are entitled to adopt).

18.2   LEGAL INSTRUMENTS

18.2.1   Legally Binding Instruments

1973 Convention on International Trade in Endangered Species of Wild Fauna and Flora, 993 UNTS 243

Conf. 14.3 * CITES compliance procedures (Rev. CoP18)

RECALLING Decision 12.84, whereby the Conference of the Parties instructed the Secretariat to draft a set of guidelines on compliance with implementation of the Convention for consideration by the Standing Committee;

RECALLING FURTHER that the Standing Committee at its 50th meeting (Geneva, March 2004) decided to establish an open-ended working group to draft such guidelines;

THE CONFERENCE OF THE PARTIES TO THE CONVENTION

1.   TAKES NOTE of the Guide to CITES compliance procedures annexed to this Resolution; and

2.   RECOMMENDS that the Guide be referred to, when dealing with compliance matters.

Objective and scope

1.   The objective of this Guide is to inform Parties and others of CITES procedures concerning promoting, facilitating and achieving compliance with obligations under the Convention and, in particular, assisting Parties in meeting their obligations regarding such compliance. Specifically, the Guide describes existing procedures in order to facilitate consistent and effective handling of compliance matters relating to obligations under the Convention, taking into account relevant Resolutions and Decisions, in both specific and general compliance matters. This Guide is non-legally binding.

2.   This Guide addresses compliance matters relating to the obligations under the Convention, taking into account relevant Resolutions and Decisions. Particular attention should be paid to the following: a) designating Management Authority(ies) and Scientific Authority(ies) (Article IX); b) permitting trade in CITES-listed specimens only to the extent consistent with the procedures laid down in the Convention (Articles III, IV, V, VI, VII and XV); c) taking appropriate domestic measures to enforce the provisions of the Convention and prohibit trade in violation thereof (Article VIII, paragraph 1); d) maintaining records of trade and submitting periodic reports (Article VIII, paragraphs 7 and 8); and e) responding as soon as possible to communications of the Secretariat related to information that a species included in Appendix I or II is being adversely affected by trade in specimens of that species or that the provisions of the Convention are not being effectively implemented (Article XIII).

3.   The procedures described in this Guide are without prejudice to any rights and obligations and to any dispute settlement procedure under the Convention.

General principles

4.   A supportive and non-adversarial approach is taken towards compliance matters, with the aim of ensuring long-term compliance.

5.   Compliance matters are handled as quickly as possible. Such matters are considered and ensuing compliance measures are applied in a fair, consistent and transparent manner.

6.   Generally, findings, reports and communications in compliance matters are not treated confidentially. However, communications between the Secretariat and individual Parties on specific compliance matters are generally confidential.

7.   Decisions on whether to close or keep open debates in compliance matters are taken according to the Rules of Procedure of the body considering the matter and generally reasons are given.

8.   The Secretariat communicates compliance-related decisions to the relevant authorities.

The various bodies and their compliance-related tasks

9.   Compliance matters are handled by the following CITES bodies.

Their main compliance-related tasks are listed below.

10.   The Conference of the Parties:
    a)   provides general policy guidance on compliance issues;
    b)   directs and oversees the handling of compliance matters particularly through the identification of key obligations and procedures;
    c)   reviews as needed decisions of the Standing Committee related to specific compliance matters; and
    d)   may delegate certain authority to the Standing Committee or other CITES bodies in accordance with the Convention.

11.   When the Conference of the Parties decides to carry out itself the tasks delegated to the Standing Committee, it follows the same procedures as those described below for the Standing Committee.

12.   The Standing Committee, acting in accordance with instructions from and authority delegated by the Conference of the Parties, handles general and specific compliance matters, including: a) monitoring and assessing overall compliance with obligations under the Convention; b) advising and assisting Parties in complying with obligations under the Convention; c) verifying information; and d) taking compliance measures as described below.

13.   The Animals and Plants Committees, acting in accordance with instructions from and authority delegated by the Conference of the Parties, advise and assist the Standing Committee and the Conference of the Parties with regard to compliance matters, *inter alia*, by undertaking necessary reviews, consultations, assessments and reporting. These Committees are entrusted with specific tasks in the handling of matters related to the Review of Significant Trade.

14.   The Secretariat:
    a)   assists and supports the Animals and Plants Committees, the Standing Committee and the Conference of the Parties in carrying out their func-

tions concerning compliance matters as described in this Guide and, where applicable, according to the procedures set out in relevant Resolutions and Decisions;

b)   receives, assesses and communicates to the Parties information on compliance matters;

c)   advises and assists Parties in complying with obligations under the Convention;

d)   makes recommendations for achieving compliance; and

e)   monitors the implementation of compliance-related decisions.

Handling of specific compliance matters
A. Identification of potential compliance matters

15.   Annual and biennial reports, legislative texts as well as other special reports and responses to information requests, for example within the Review of Significant Trade or the National Legislation Project, provide the primary, but not exclusive, means of monitoring compliance with obligations under the Convention.

16.   The Secretariat provides a Party concerned with information it receives about that Party's compliance, and communicates with the Party regarding this matter.

17.   In response, the Party informs the Secretariat as soon as possible of any relevant facts in so far as its laws permit and, where appropriate, proposes remedial action. Where the Party considers that an inquiry is desirable, such inquiry may be carried out by one or more persons expressly authorized by the Party.

18.   Any Party concerned over matters related to trade in specimens of CITES-listed species by another Party may bring the matter up directly with that Party and/or call upon the Secretariat for assistance.

19.   Parties themselves are encouraged to give the Secretariat early warning of any compliance matter, including the inability to provide information by a certain deadline, and indicate the reasons and any need for assistance.

20.   Where compliance matters are identified, the Parties concerned are given every opportunity to correct them within reasonable time limits, if necessary with the assistance of the Secretariat.

B. Consideration of compliance matters

21.   If the Party fails to take sufficient remedial action within a reasonable time limit, the compliance matter is brought to the attention of the Standing Committee by the Secretariat, in direct contact with the Party concerned.

22.   If a compliance matter is otherwise brought to the attention of the Standing Committee in accordance with the Rules of Procedure, the Standing Committee: a) refers the matter to the Secretariat for action according to the procedure in paragraphs 16–20 above; or b) rejects it as trivial or ill-founded; or c) in exceptional circumstances, after consultation with the Party concerned, follows the procedures as described below.

23.   When compliance matters are brought to the attention of the Standing Committee, it is generally done in writing and includes details as to which specific obligations are concerned and an assessment of the reasons why the Party concerned may be unable to meet those obligations.

24. When a compliance matter is brought to the attention of the Standing Committee, the Secretariat immediately informs the Party or Parties concerned.

25. The Standing Committee rejects compliance matters which it considers are trivial or ill-founded. Where the Standing Committee has decided that the submission is not trivial or ill-founded, the Party concerned is given the opportunity to provide comments within a reasonable time limit.

26. The Standing Committee decides whether to gather or request further information on a compliance matter whenever such information may be found and whether to seek an invitation from the Party concerned to undertake the gathering and verification of information in the territory of that Party or wherever such information may be found.

27. The Party concerned has the right to participate in discussions with respect to its own compliance, in accordance with the Rules of Procedure of the relevant body.

28. If a Party cannot access the financial resources needed to participate in CITES meetings where its own compliance is being considered, it is able to request assistance from the Secretariat or the Standing Committee in identifying such resources.

C. Measures to achieve compliance

29. If a compliance matter has not been resolved, the Standing Committee decides to take one or more of the following measures:

a) provide advice, information and appropriate facilitation of assistance and other capacity-building support to the Party concerned;

b) request special reporting from the Party concerned;

c) issue a written caution, requesting a response and offering assistance;

d) recommend specific capacity-building actions to be undertaken by the Party concerned;

e) provide in-country assistance, technical assessment and a verification mission, upon the invitation of the Party concerned;

f) send a public notification of a compliance matter through the Secretariat to all Parties advising that compliance matters have been brought to the attention of a Party and that, up to that time, there has been no satisfactory response or action;

g) issue a warning to the Party concerned that it is in non-compliance, e.g. in relation to national reporting and/or the National Legislation Project; and

h) request a compliance action plan to be submitted to the Standing Committee by the Party concerned identifying appropriate steps, a timetable for when those steps should be completed and means to assess satisfactory completion.

30. In certain cases, the Standing Committee decides to recommend the suspension of commercial or all trade in specimens of one or more CITES-listed species, consistent with the Convention. Such a recommendation may be made in cases where a Party's compliance matter is unresolved and persistent and the Party is showing no intention to achieve compliance or a State not a Party is not issuing the documentation referred to in Article X of the Convention. Such a recommendation is always specifically and explicitly based on the Convention and on any applicable Resolutions and Decisions of the Conference of the Parties.[1]

31.   The list of measures above is not necessarily an exhaustive list of measures applied to date.

32.   When the Standing Committee decides upon one or more of the measures mentioned above, it takes into account:

   a)   the capacity of the Party concerned, especially developing countries, and in particular the least developed and small island developing States and Parties with economies in transition;

   b)   such factors as the cause, type, degree and frequency of the compliance matters;

   c)   the appropriateness of the measures so that they are commensurate with the gravity of the compliance matter; and

   d)   the possible impact on conservation and sustainable use with a view to avoiding negative results. These considerations are clearly set out in the Standing Committee's recommendations

D. Monitoring and implementation of measures to achieve compliance

33.   The Standing Committee, with the assistance of the Secretariat, monitors the actions taken by the Party concerned to implement measures taken. In this regard, the Standing Committee may, *inter alia*:

   a)   request the Party concerned to submit progress reports in accordance with a schedule; and

   b)   arrange, upon the invitation of the Party concerned, for an in-country technical assessment and for a verification mission. In the light of progress, the Standing Committee decides whether to adjust the measures it has taken, or to take other measures.

34.   Existing recommendations to suspend trade are generally reviewed at each Standing Committee meeting. They are also monitored intersessionally by the Secretariat. A recommendation to suspend trade is withdrawn as soon as the compliance matter has been resolved or sufficient progress has been made. The Secretariat notifies Parties of any such withdrawal as soon as possible.

35.   The general guidelines in paragraphs 33 and 34 above are in some cases supplemented by more precise provisions regarding specific categories of compliance matters, e.g. in the case of significant trade in specimens of Appendix-II species, as laid out in the Resolutions and Decisions related thereto.

1987 Montreal Protocol on Substances that Deplete the Ozone Layer, 1522 UNTS 3

Article 8: Non-compliance

The Parties, at their first meeting, shall consider and approve procedures and institutional mechanisms for determining non-compliance with the provisions of this Protocol and for treatment of Parties found to be in non-compliance.

Montreal Protocol, Non-compliance Procedure, Decision IV/5, 25 Nov 1992

Decision IV/5: Non-compliance procedure
The Fourth Meeting of the Parties decided in Dec. IV/5:

1. to note with appreciation the work of the Ad Hoc Working Group of Legal Experts on Non-Compliance with the Montreal Protocol;

2. to adopt the non-compliance procedure, as set out in Annex IV to the report of the Fourth Meeting of the Parties;

3. to adopt the indicative list of measures that might be taken in respect of non-compliance, as set out in Annex V to the report of the Fourth Meeting of the Parties;

4. to accept the recommendation that there is no need to expedite the amendment procedure under Article 9 of the Vienna Convention for the Protection of the Ozone Layer;

5. to adopt the view that the responsibility for legal interpretation of the Protocol rests ultimately with the Parties themselves.

Annex IV: Non-compliance procedure
The following procedure has been formulated pursuant to Article 8 of the Montreal Protocol. It shall apply without prejudice to the operation of the settlement of disputes procedure laid down in Article 11 of the Vienna Convention.

1. If one or more Parties have reservations regarding another Party's implementation of its obligations under the Protocol, those concerns may be addressed in writing to the Secretariat. Such a submission shall be supported by corroborating information.

2. The Secretariat shall, within two weeks of its receiving a submission, send a copy of that submission to the Party whose implementation of a particular provision of the Protocol is at issue. Any reply and information in support thereof are to be submitted to the Secretariat and to the Parties involved within three months of the date of the despatch or such longer period as the circumstances of any particular case may require. The Secretariat shall then transmit the submission, the reply and the information provided by the Parties to the Implementation Committee referred to in paragraph 5, which shall consider the matter as soon as practicable.

3. Where the Secretariat, during the course of preparing its report, becomes aware of possible non-compliance by any Party with its obligations under the Protocol, it may request the Party concerned to furnish necessary information about the matter. If there is no response from the Party concerned within three months or such longer period as the circumstances of the matter may require or the matter is not resolved through administrative action or through diplomatic contacts, the Secretariat shall include the matter in its report to the Meeting of the Parties pursuant to Article 12 (c) of the Protocol and inform the Implementation Committee accordingly.

4. Where a Party concludes that, despite having made its best, bona fide efforts, it is unable to comply fully with its obligations under the Protocol, it may address to the Secretariat a submission in writing, explaining, in particular, the specific circumstances that it considers to be the cause of its non-compliance. The Secretariat shall transmit such submission to the implementation Committee which shall consider it as soon as practicable.

5. An Implementation Committee is hereby established. It shall consist of 10 Parties elected by the meeting of the Parties for two years, based on equitable geographical distribution. Outgoing Parties may be re-elected for one immediate consecutive

term. The Committee shall elect its own President and Vice-President. Each shall serve for one year at a time. The Vice-President shall, in addition, serve as the rapporteur of the Committee.

6. The Implementation Committee shall, unless it decides otherwise, meet twice a year. The Secretariat shall arrange for and service its meetings.

7. The functions of the Implementation Committee shall be:

(a) To receive, consider and report on any submission in accordance with paragraphs 1, 2 and 4;

(b) To receive, consider and report on any information or observations forwarded by the Secretariat in connection with the preparation of the reports referred to in Article 12 (c) of the Protocol and on any other information received and forwarded by the Secretariat concerning compliance with the provisions of the Protocol.

(c) To request, where it considers necessary, through the Secretariat, further information on matters under its consideration;

(d) To undertake, upon the invitation of the Party concerned, information-gathering in the territory of that Party for fulfilling the functions of the Committee;

(e) To maintain, in particular for the purposes of drawing up its recommendations, an exchange of information with the Executive Committee of the Multilateral Fund related to the provision of financial and technical cooperation, including the transfer of technologies to Parties operating under Article 5, paragraph 1, of the Protocol.

8. The Implementation Committee shall consider the submissions, information and observations referred to in paragraph 7 with a view to securing an amicable solution of the matter on the basis of respect for the provisions of the Protocol.

9. The Implementation Committee shall report to the Meeting of the Parties, including any recommendations it considers appropriate. The report shall be made available to the Parties not later than six weeks before their meeting. After receiving a report by the Committee the Parties may, taking into consideration the circumstances of the matter, decide upon and call for steps to bring about full compliance with the Protocol, including measures to assist the Parties' compliance with the Protocol, and to further the Protocol's objectives.

10. Where a Party that is not a member of the Implementation Committee is identified in a submission under paragraph 1, or itself makes such a submission, it shall be entitled to participate in the consideration by the Committee of that submission.

11. No Party, whether or not a member of the Implementation Committee, involved in a matter under consideration by the Implementation Committee, shall take part in the elaboration and adoption of recommendations on that matter to be included in the report of the Committee.

12. The Parties involved in a matter referred to in paragraphs 1, 3 or 4 shall inform, through the Secretariat, the Meeting of the Parties of the results of proceedings taken under Article 11 of the Convention regarding possible non-compliance, about implementation of those results and about implementation of any decision of the Parties pursuant to paragraph 9.

13. The Meeting of the Parties may, pending completion of proceedings initiated under Article 11 of the Convention, issue an interim call and/or recommendations.

14. The Meeting of the Parties may request the Implementation Committee to make recommendations to assist the Meeting's consideration of matters of possible non-compliance.

15. The members of the Implementation Committee and any Party involved in its deliberations shall protect the confidentiality of information they receive in confidence.

16. The report, which shall not contain any information received in confidence, shall be made available to any person upon request. All information exchanged by or with the Committee that is related to any recommendation by the Committee to the Meeting of the Parties shall be made available by the Secretariat to any Party upon its request; that Party shall ensure the confidentiality of the information it has received in confidence.

Annex V: Indicative list of measures that might be taken by a Meeting of the Parties in respect of non-compliance with the Protocol

A. Appropriate assistance, including assistance for the collection and reporting of data, technical assistance, technology transfer and financial assistance, information transfer and training.

B. Issuing cautions.

C. Suspension, in accordance with the applicable rules of international law concerning the suspension of the operation of a treaty, of specific rights and privileges under the Protocol, whether or not subject to time limits, including those concerned with industrial rationalization, production, consumption, trade, transfer of technology, financial mechanism and institutional arrangements.

1989 Basel Convention on the Control of Transboundary Movements of Hazardous Wastes and their Disposal, 1673 UNTS 57

CONFERENCE OF THE PARTIES TO THE BASEL CONVENTION ON THE CONTROL OF TRANSBOUNDARY MOVEMENTS OF HAZARDOUS WASTES AND THEIR DISPOSAL Sixth meeting Geneva, 9–13 December 2002 UNEP/CHW.6/40 10 February 2003

Appendix
MECHANISM FOR PROMOTING IMPLEMENTATION AND COMPLIANCE
Terms of reference
Objectives

1. The objective of the mechanism is to assist Parties to comply with their obligations under the Convention and to facilitate, promote, monitor and aim to secure the implementation of and compliance with the obligations under the Convention.

Nature of the mechanism

2. The mechanism shall be non-confrontational, transparent, cost-effective and preventive in nature, simple, flexible, non-binding and oriented in the direction of helping parties to implement the provisions of the Basel Convention. It will pay particular attention to the special needs of developing countries and countries with economies in transition, and is intended to promote cooperation between all

Parties. The mechanism should complement work performed by other Convention bodies and by the Basel Convention Regional Centres. Composition and tenure

3.   A Committee for administrating this mechanism ("the Committee") is hereby established. It shall consist of 15 Members nominated by the Parties, serving in accordance with paragraph 4, and based on equitable geographical representation of the five regional groups of the United Nations, elected by the Conference of the Parties.

[...]

Procedures for specific submissions

9.   Submissions may be made to the Committee by:

(a)   A Party that concludes that, despite its best efforts, it is or will be unable to fully implement or comply with its obligations under the Convention;

(b)   A Party that has concerns or is affected by a failure to comply with and/ or implement the Convention's obligations by another Party with whom it is directly involved under the Convention. A Party intending to make a submission under this subparagraph shall inform the Party whose compliance is in question, and both Parties should then try to resolve the matter through consultations;

(c)   The secretariat, if, while acting pursuant to its functions under articles 13 and 16, it becomes aware of possible difficulties of any Party in complying with its reporting obligations under article 13, paragraph 3 of the Convention, provided that the matter has not been resolved within three months by consultation with the Party concerned.

[...]

15.   Where a Party is identified in a submission or itself makes a submission, it shall be invited to participate in the consideration of the submission by the Committee. Such a Party, however, shall not take part in the elaboration and adoption of the conclusions or recommendations by the Committee. Conclusions and recommendations shall be shared with the Party concerned for consideration and an opportunity to comment. Any such comments shall be forwarded with the report of the Committee to the Conference of the Parties.

[...]

Recommendation to the Conference of the Parties on additional measures

20.   If, after undertaking the facilitation procedure in paragraph 19 above and taking into account the cause, type, degree and frequency of compliance difficulties, as well as the capacity of the Party whose compliance is in question, the Committee considers it necessary in the light of paragraphs 1 and 2 to pursue further measures to address a Party's compliance difficulties, it may recommend to the Conference of the Parties that it consider:

(a)   Further support under the Convention for the Party concerned, including prioritization of technical assistance and capacity-building and access to financial resources; or

(b)   Issuing a cautionary statement and providing advice regarding future compliance in order to help Parties to implement the provisions of the Basel Convention and to promote cooperation between all Parties. Any such action shall be consistent with article 15 of the Convention.

1998 Aarhus Convention on Access to Information, Public Participation in Decision-making and Access to Justice in Environmental Matters, 2161 UNTS 447

Article 15 REVIEW OF COMPLIANCE

The Meeting of the Parties shall establish, on a consensus basis, optional arrangements of a non-confrontational, non-judicial and consultative nature for reviewing compliance with the provisions of this Convention. These arrangements shall allow for appropriate public involvement and may include the option of considering communications from members of the public on matters related to this Convention.

'Review of compliance', decision 1/7, 2 April 2004, ECE/MP.PP/2/Add.8

DECISION I/7 REVIEW OF COMPLIANCE adopted at the first meeting of the Parties held in Lucca, Italy, on 21–23 October 2002

I. STRUCTURE

1.   The Committee shall consist of eight members, who shall serve in their personal capacity.

[...]

III. FUNCTIONS OF THE COMMITTEE

13.   The Committee shall

(a)   Consider any submission, referral or communication made in accordance with paragraphs 15 to 24 below;

(b)   Prepare, at the request of the Meeting of the Parties, a report on compliance with or implementation of the provisions of the Convention; and

(c)   Monitor, assess and facilitate the implementation of and compliance with the reporting requirements under article 10, paragraph 2, of the Convention; and act pursuant to paragraphs 36 and 37.

14.   The Committee may examine compliance issues and make recommendations if and as appropriate.

IV. SUBMISSION BY PARTIES

15.   A submission may be brought before the Committee by one or more Parties that have reservations about another Party's compliance with its obligations under the Convention. Such a submission shall be addressed in writing to the secretariat and supported by corroborating information. The secretariat shall, within two weeks of receiving a submission, send a copy of it to the Party whose compliance is at issue. Any reply and supporting information shall be submitted to the secretariat and to the Parties involved within three months or such longer period as the circumstances of a particular case may require but in no case later than six months. The

secretariat shall transmit the submission and the reply, as well as all corroborating and supporting information, to the Committee, which shall consider the matter as soon as practicable.

16.   A submission may be brought before the Committee by a Party that concludes that, despite its best endeavours, it is or will be unable to comply fully with its obligations under the Convention. Such a submission shall be addressed in writing to the secretariat and explain, in particular, the specific circumstances that the Party considers to be the cause of its noncompliance. The secretariat shall transmit the submission to the Committee, which shall consider the matter as soon as practicable

V. REFERRALS BY THE SECRETARIAT

17.   Where the secretariat, in particular upon considering the reports submitted in accordance with the Convention's reporting requirements, becomes aware of possible noncompliance by a Party with its obligations under the Convention, it may request the Party concerned to furnish necessary information about the matter. If there is no response or the matter is not resolved within three months, or such longer period as the circumstances of the matter may require but in no case later than six months, the secretariat shall bring the matter to the attention of the Committee, which shall consider the matter as soon as practicable.

VI. COMMUNICATIONS FROM THE PUBLIC

18.   On the expiry of twelve months from either the date of adoption of this decision or from the date of the entry into force of the Convention with respect to a Party, whichever is the later, communications may be brought before the Committee by one or more members of the public concerning that Party's compliance with the Convention, unless that Party has notified the Depositary in writing by the end of the applicable period that it is unable to accept, for a period of not more than four years, the consideration of such communications by the Committee. The Depositary shall without delay notify all Parties of any such notification received. During the four-year period mentioned above, the Party may revoke its notification thereby accepting that, from that date, communications may be brought before the Committee by one or more members of the public concerning that Party's compliance with the Convention.

19.   The communications referred to in paragraph 18 shall be addressed to the Committee through the secretariat in writing and may be in electronic form. The communications shall be supported by corroborating information.

20.   The Committee shall consider any such communication unless it determines that the communication is:

(a)   Anonymous;

(b)   An abuse of the right to make such communications;

(c)   Manifestly unreasonable;

(d)   Incompatible with the provisions of this decision or with the Convention.

21.   The Committee should at all relevant stages take into account any available domestic remedy unless the application of the remedy is unreasonably prolonged or obviously does not provide an effective and sufficient means of redress.

22.   Subject to the provisions of paragraph 20, the Committee shall as soon as possible bring any communications submitted to it under paragraph 18 to the attention of the Party alleged to be in non-compliance.

23.   A Party shall, as soon as possible but not later than five months after any communication is brought to its attention by the Committee, submit to the Committee written explanations or statements clarifying the matter and describing any response that it may have made.

24.   The Committee shall, as soon as practicable, further consider communications submitted to it pursuant to this chapter and take into account all relevant written information made available to it, and may hold hearings.

IX. ENTITLEMENT TO PARTICIPATE

32.   A Party in respect of which a submission, referral or communication is made or which makes a submission, as well as the member of the public making a communication, shall be entitled to participate in the discussions of the Committee with respect to that submission, referral or communication.

33.   The Party and the member of the public shall not take part in the preparation and adoption of any findings, any measures or any recommendations of the Committee.

34.   The Committee shall send a copy of its draft findings, draft measures and any draft recommendations to the Parties concerned and the member of the public who submitted the communication if applicable, and shall take into account any comments made by them in the finalization of those findings, measures and recommendations.

X. COMMITTEE REPORTS TO THE MEETING OF THE PARTIES

35.   The Committee shall report on its activities at each ordinary meeting of the Parties and make such recommendations as it considers appropriate. Each report shall be finalized by the Committee not later than twelve weeks in advance of the meeting of the Parties at which it is to be considered. Every effort shall be made to adopt the report by consensus. Where this is not possible, the report shall reflect the views of all the Committee members. Committee reports shall be available to the public.

XI. CONSIDERATION BY THE COMPLIANCE COMMITTEE

36.   Pending consideration by the Meeting of the Parties, with a view to addressing compliance issues without delay, the Compliance Committee may:
       (a)   In consultation with the Party concerned, take the measures listed in paragraph 37 (a);
       (b)   Subject to agreement with the Party concerned, take the measures listed in paragraph 37 (b), (c) and (d).

XII. CONSIDERATION BY THE MEETING OF THE PARTIES

37.   The Meeting of the Parties may, upon consideration of a report and any recommendations of the Committee, decide upon appropriate measures to bring about full compliance with the Convention. The Meeting of the Parties may, depending on the particular question before it and taking into account the cause, degree

and frequency of the non-compliance, decide upon one or more of the following measures:

(a)   Provide advice and facilitate assistance to individual Parties regarding the implementation of the Convention;

(b)   Make recommendations to the Party concerned;

(c)   Request the Party concerned to submit a strategy, including a time schedule, to the Compliance Committee regarding the achievement of compliance with the Convention and to report on the implementation of this strategy;

(d)   In cases of communications from the public, make recommendations to the Party concerned on specific measures to address the matter raised by the member of the public;

(e)   Issue declarations of non-compliance;

(f)   Issue cautions;

(g)   Suspend, in accordance with the applicable rules of international law concerning the suspension of the operation of a treaty, the special rights and privileges accorded to the Party concerned under the Convention;

(h)   Take such other non-confrontational, non-judicial and consultative measures as may be appropriate.

XIII. RELATIONSHIP BETWEEN SETTLEMENT OF DISPUTES AND THE COMPLIANCE PROCEDURE

38.   The present compliance procedure shall be without prejudice to article 16 of the Convention on the settlement of disputes.

XIV. ENHANCEMENT OF SYNERGIES

39.   In order to enhance synergies between this compliance procedure and compliance procedures under other agreements, the Meeting of the Parties may request the Compliance Committee to communicate as appropriate with the relevant bodies of those agreements and report back to it, including with recommendations as appropriate. The Compliance Committee may also submit a report to the Meeting of the Parties on relevant developments between the sessions of the Meeting of the Parties.

1998 Rotterdam Convention on the Prior Informed Consent Procedure for Certain Hazardous Chemicals and Pesticides in International Trade, 2244 UNTS 337

ARTICLE 17 Non-Compliance

The Conference of the Parties shall, as soon as practicable, develop and approve procedures and institutional mechanisms for determining non-compliance with the provisions of this Convention and for treatment of Parties found to be in non-compliance.

RC-4/7: Procedures and mechanisms on compliance with the Rotterdam Convention

The Conference of the Parties, Recalling article 17 of the Rotterdam Convention,
Mindful that the procedures and mechanisms called for under article 17 will help address issues of non-compliance, including by facilitating assistance and providing advice to Parties facing compliance issues,

1. Decides to consider further at its next ordinary meeting for adoption the proce-
    dures and institutional mechanisms on non-compliance required under article 17
    of the Convention;

2. Decides also that the draft text contained in the annex to the present decision shall
    be the basis for its further work on the procedures and institutional mechanisms at
    its fifth meeting.

Annex to decision RC-4/7

Procedures and mechanisms on compliance with the Rotterdam Convention: draft text
reflecting the deliberations of the contact group

1. A compliance committee (hereinafter referred to as "the Committee") is hereby
    established.

Members

2. The Committee shall consist of 15 members. Members shall be nominated by
    Parties and elected by the Conference of the Parties on the basis of equitable geo-
    graphical representation of the five regional groups of the United Nations.

[…]

Facilitation

18. The Committee shall consider any submission [or referral] made to it in accord-
    ance with paragraph 12 [or XXX] above with a view to establishing the facts and the
    root causes of the matter of concern, and to assisting in its resolution. To that end,
    the Committee may provide a Party with:

    (a) Advice;
    (b) Non-binding recommendations;
    (c) Any further information required to assist the Party in developing a com-
         pliance plan, including timelines and targets.

Possible measures to address compliance issues

19. If, after undertaking the facilitation procedure set forth in paragraph 18 above and
    taking into account the cause, type, degree and frequency of compliance difficul-
    ties, including financial and technical capacities of the Parties whose compliance is
    in question, the Committee considers it necessary to propose further measures to
    address a Party's compliance problems, it may recommend to the Conference of
    the Parties [, bearing in mind its ability under Article 18 (5) (c) of the Convention,]
    that it consider the following measures, to be taken in accordance with interna-
    tional law, to attain compliance, [including]:

    (a) Further support under the Convention for the Party concerned, including
         facilitation, as appropriate, of access to financial resources, technical assis-
         tance and capacity-building;
    (b) Providing advice regarding future compliance in order to help Parties to
         implement the provisions of the Convention and to promote cooperation
         between all Parties;
    (c) Issuing a statement of concern regarding possible future non-compliance;
    (d) Issuing a statement of concern regarding current non-compliance;

(e)   Requesting the Executive Secretary to make public cases of non-compliance;

[(f)   The Conference of the Parties considers and undertakes any additional action that may be required for the achievement of the objectives of the Convention under Article 18 (5) (c)];

(g)   Recommending that a non-compliant situation be addressed by the non-compliant Party with the aim of resolving the situation.

Monitoring

24.   The Compliance Committee should monitor the consequences of action taken in pursuance of paragraphs 18 or 19 above.

General compliance issues

25.   The Compliance Committee may examine systemic issues of general compliance of interest to all Parties where:

(a)   The Conference of the Parties so requests;

(b)   The Committee, on the basis of information obtained by the secretariat, while acting pursuant to its functions under the Convention, from Parties and submitted to the Committee by the secretariat, decides that there is a need for an issue of general non-compliance to be examined and for a report on it to be made to the Conference of the Parties.

Reports to the Conference of the Parties

26.   The Committee shall submit a report to each ordinary meeting of the Conference of the Parties reflecting:

(a)   The work that the Committee has undertaken;

(b)   The conclusions or recommendations of the Committee;

(c)   The future programme of work of the Committee, including the schedule of expected meetings which it considers necessary for the fulfilment of its programme of work, for the consideration and approval of the Conference of the Parties.

Other subsidiary bodies

27.   Where the activities of the Committee with respect to particular issues overlap with the responsibilities of another Rotterdam Convention body, the Conference of the Parties may direct the Committee to consult with that body.

2001 Stockholm Convention on Persistent Organic Pollutants, 2256 UNTS 119

Article 17 Non-compliance

The Conference of the Parties shall, as soon as practicable, develop and approve procedures and institutional mechanisms for determining non-compliance with the provisions of this Convention and for the treatment of Parties found to be in non-compliance.

SC-7/26: Procedures and mechanisms on compliance with the Stockholm Convention

The Conference of the Parties, Recalling Article 17 of the Stockholm Convention on Persistent Organic Pollutants, Mindful that the procedures and institutional mechanisms called for under Article 17 will help address compliance,

1.   Notes that the negotiations have not yielded a result and that the draft texts contained in the annex to the present decision are entirely bracketed;

2.   Decides to consider further at its eighth meeting, for adoption, the procedures and mechanisms on compliance required under Article 17 of the Convention;

3.   Invites the Bureau of the Conference of the Parties to facilitate intersessional consultations among all parties to promote a policy dialogue on outstanding issues with a view to resolving them in a way that facilitates the possible adoption of the procedures and institutional mechanisms required under Article 17 by the Conference of the Parties at its eighth meeting;

4.   Decides that the draft texts contained in the annex to the present decision shall be the basis for its further work on the procedures and institutional mechanisms at its eighth meeting, bearing in mind that all issues remain outstanding;

5.   Also decides that further work on the procedures and mechanisms on compliance with the Convention shall be placed early on the agenda at its eighth meeting.

Annex to decision SC-7/26 Annex to decision SC-6/24 (version as of 15 May 2015)
[Non-compliance][Compliance]

[P] [p]rocedures and institutional mechanisms under Article 17 of the Stockholm Convention

1 Objective, nature and underlying principles

1.   The objective of the procedures and institutional mechanisms (hereinafter referred to as "the procedures") is to assist Parties to comply with their obligations under the Convention[;] [and] to facilitate, promote, [monitor], assist in, advise on and aim to secure the implementation of and compliance with the obligations under the Convention [and to provide technical assistance, financial resources and transfer of technology].

2.3.4 alt   The mechanism shall be non-confrontational, transparent, cost-effective, preventive and facilitative in nature, simple, flexible, non-binding and oriented in the direction of helping parties to implement the provisions of the Stockholm Convention. It will pay particular attention to the special needs of developing countries and countries with economies in transition, [in line with article 13(4) of the Convention] and is intended to promote cooperation between all Parties. The mechanism should complement work performed by other Convention bodies and by the Stockholm Convention Regional Centres. All obligations under the Convention are subject to the present [non-]compliance procedures and mechanisms [, including Articles 12, 13 and 7.]

Compliance Committee Establishment

5.   A Compliance Committee, hereinafter referred to as the "Committee", is hereby established.

Composition

6.   The Committee shall consist of 15 members. Members shall be experts nominated by Parties and elected by the Conference of the Parties on the basis of equitable geographical representation of the five regional groups of the United Nations.[2]

7.   Members shall have expertise and specific qualifications in the subject matter covered by the Convention. They shall act objectively and in the best interests of the Convention. with due consideration to gender balance.

Election of members

8.   At the meeting at which the present decision is adopted, the Conference of the Parties shall elect half the members for one term and half the members for two terms. The Conference of the Parties shall, at each ordinary meeting thereafter, elect for two full terms new members to replace those members whose period of office has expired or is about to expire. Members shall not serve for more than two consecutive terms. For the purpose of the present procedures and mechanisms, "term" shall mean the period that begins at the end of one ordinary meeting of the Conference of the Parties and ends at the end of the next ordinary meeting of the Conference of the Parties.

9.   If a member of the Committee resigns or is otherwise unable to complete her or his term of office or to perform her or his functions, the Party who nominated that member shall nominate an alternate to serve for the remainder of the term.

Decision-making

15.   [The Committee shall make every effort to reach agreement on all matters of substance by consensus. If all efforts to reach consensus have been exhausted and no agreement has been reached, any decision shall, as a last resort, be taken by a three-quarters majority of the members present and voting or by nine members, whichever is greater. The report of any meeting of the Committee at which consensus is not reached shall reflect the views of all the Committee members]. [15 alt. The Committee shall take its decisions by consensus.] [15 alt bis3]

16.   Each member of the Committee shall, with respect to any matter that is under consideration by the Committee, avoid direct or indirect conflicts of interest. When a member finds himself or herself faced with a direct or indirect conflict of interest, or is a citizen of a Party whose compliance is in question, that member shall bring the issue to the attention of the Committee before consideration of the matter. The concerned member shall not participate in the elaboration and adoption of a recommendation of the Committee in relation to that matter.]

Procedures for submissions

Submissions

17.   Submissions to the Committee may be made by:

(a)   A Party which decides that, despite its best endeavours, it is, or will be, unable to comply with its obligations under the Convention. Any submission under this subparagraph shall be made in writing, through the Secretariat, and should include details as to which specific obligations are concerned and an assessment of the reason why the Party may be unable to meet those obligations. Where possible, substantiating information, or advice as to where such substantiating information may be found, shall be provided. Any such submission may include suggestions for solutions which the Party considers may be most appropriate to its particular needs;

(b)   A Party that is affected or may be affected by another Party's difficulties in complying with the Convention's obligations. Any Party intending to make a submission under this subparagraph should before so doing undertake consultations with the Party whose compliance is in question. Any submission made under this subparagraph shall be made in writing, through the Secretariat, and is to include details as to which specific obligations are concerned and information substantiating the submission;

(c)   The Secretariat, if, while acting pursuant to paragraph 2 of Article 20 of the Convention, it becomes aware that a Party may face difficulties in complying with its obligations under the Convention on the basis of the reports received pursuant to Article 15[, considering [all their] obligations under the Convention, [(including Articles 3, 12 and 13)]], provided that the matter has not been resolved within ninety days by consultation with the Party concerned. Any submission made under this subparagraph shall be made in writing and shall set out the matter of concern, the relevant provisions of the Convention and the information substantiating the matter of concern.] [Committee trigger 17c alt4 [23 bis / 17 (c) alt bis The Committee [may] [shall] [examine][consider][in a nonintrusive manner] Parties' [national implementation plans pursuant to Article 7 and the] national reports pursuant to Article 15, considering [all their] obligations under the Convention, [(including Articles 12 and 13)] and identify questions [difficulties] relating to Parties' compliance. The Committee shall consider [information] [such questions][difficulties] in accordance with paragraphs 21–23.]]. The Committee in order to assess possible difficulties faced by parties in fulfilling their obligations under the [Articles, 7, [12, 13] and [15 (3)] of the] Convention, upon receipt of information from the Secretariat provided by such Parties pursuant to those provisions, [including to the fulfilment of obligations under 12 and 13] shall notify the party in writing regarding the matter of concern. If the matter has not been resolved within 90 days by consultation through the Secretariat with the party concerned and the Committee considers the matter further, it shall do so in accordance with paragraphs [21 to 25].] [The Committee shall certify that all provisions with regard to Articles 12 to 13 have been met for the party in question before proceeding any further.]

18.   The Secretariat shall forward submissions made under subparagraph 17 (a) above, within fifteen days of receipt of such submissions, to the members of the Committee for consideration at the Committee's next meeting.

19.   The Secretariat shall, within fifteen days of receipt of any submission made under subparagraph 17 (b) above, send a copy to the Party whose compliance with the Convention is in question and to the members of the Committee for consideration at the Committee's next meeting.

20.   The Secretariat shall send any submission it makes in accordance with paragraph 17 (c) above directly to the Committee and the Party whose compliance is in ques-

tion within fifteen days of the conclusion of the ninety-day period referred to in paragraph 17 (c) above;][5]

21.   A Party whose compliance is in question may present responses or comments at every step of the proceedings described in the present procedures and mechanisms.

22.   Such a Party shall be entitled to participate in the consideration of the submission by the Committee. For this purpose the Committee shall invite such a Party to participate in the discussions on the submission no later than sixty days before the start of the discussions. Such Party, however, may not take part in the elaboration of a recommendation of the Committee.

23.   Comments or additional information in response to a submission, provided by a Party whose compliance is in question, should be forwarded to the Secretariat within ninety days of the date of receipt of the submission by that Party, unless the Party requests an extension. Such extension may be provided by the Chair, with a reasonable justification, for a period of up to 90 days. Such information shall be immediately transmitted to the members of the Committee for consideration at the Committee's next meeting. Where a submission has been made pursuant to subparagraph 17 (b) above, the information shall be forwarded by the Secretariat to the Party that made the submission.

1999 Protocol on Water and Health to the 1992 Convention on the Protection and Use of Transboundary Watercourses and International Lakes, 2331 UNTS 202

Article 15 REVIEW OF COMPLIANCE

The Parties shall review the compliance of the Parties with the provisions of this Protocol on the basis of the reviews and assessments referred to in article 7. Multilateral arrangements of a non-confrontational, non-judicial and consultative nature for reviewing compliance shall be established by the Parties at their first meeting. These arrangements shall allow for appropriate public involvement.

1999 Gothenburg Protocol to the 1979 Convention on Long-range Transboundary Air Pollution to Abate Acidification, Eutrophication and Ground-level Ozone, 2319 UNTS 81

Article 9 Compliance

Compliance by each Party with its obligations under the present Protocol shall be reviewed regularly. The Implementation Committee established by decision 1997/2 of the Executive Body at its fifteenth session shall carry out such reviews and report to the Parties at a session of the Executive Body in accordance with the terms of the annex to that decision, including any amendments thereto.

2015 Paris Agreement 2015, FCCC/CP/2015/10/Add.1

Article 15

1.   A mechanism to facilitate implementation of and promote compliance with the provisions of this Agreement is hereby established.

2.   The mechanism referred to in paragraph 1 of this Article shall consist of a committee that shall be expert-based and facilitative in nature and function in a manner that is transparent, non-adversarial and non-punitive. The committee shall pay

particular attention to the respective national capabilities and circumstances of Parties.

3. The committee shall operate under the modalities and procedures adopted by the Conference of the Parties serving as the meeting of the Parties to this Agreement at its first session and report annually to the Conference of the Parties serving as the meeting of the Parties to this Agreement.

Decision 1/CP.21 Adoption of the Paris Agreement

Facilitating implementation and compliance

102. Decides that the committee referred to in Article 15, paragraph 2, of the Agreement shall consist of 12 members with recognized competence in relevant scientific, technical, socioeconomic or legal fields, to be elected by the Conference of the Parties serving as the meeting of the Parties to the Paris Agreement on the basis of equitable geographical representation, with two members each from the five regional groups of the United Nations and one member each from the small island developing States and the least developed countries, while taking into account the goal of gender balance;

103. Requests the Ad Hoc Working Group on the Paris Agreement to develop the modalities and procedures for the effective operation of the committee referred to in Article 15, paragraph 2, of the Agreement, with a view to the Ad Hoc Working Group on the Paris Agreement completing its work on such modalities and procedures for consideration and adoption by the Conference of the Parties serving as the meeting of the Parties to the Paris Agreement at its first session.

Annex Modalities and procedures for the effective operation of the committee referred to in Article 15, paragraph 2, of the Paris Agreement

I. Purpose, principles, nature, functions and scope

1. The mechanism to facilitate implementation of and promote compliance with the provisions of the Paris Agreement established under Article 15 of the Agreement consists of a committee (hereinafter referred to as the Committee).

2. The Committee shall be expert-based and facilitative in nature and function in a manner that is transparent, non-adversarial and non-punitive. The Committee shall pay particular attention to the respective national capabilities and circumstances of Parties.

3. The Committee's work shall be guided by the provisions of the Paris Agreement, including its Article 2.

4. In carrying out its work, the Committee shall strive to avoid duplication of effort, shall neither function as an enforcement or dispute settlement mechanism, nor impose penalties or sanctions, and shall respect national sovereignty.

II. Institutional arrangements

5. The Committee shall consist of 12 members with recognized competence in relevant scientific, technical, socioeconomic or legal fields to be elected by the Conference of the Parties serving as the meeting of the Parties to the Paris Agreement (CMA) on the basis of equitable geographical representation, with 2 members each from the five regional groups of the United Nations and 1 member each from the small

island developing States and the least developed countries, taking into account the goal of gender balance.

6.   The CMA shall elect members of the Committee as well as an alternate for each member, taking into account the expert-based nature of the Committee and striving to reflect the diversity of expertise referred to in paragraph 5 above.

7.   Members and alternate members shall be elected to the Committee to serve for a period of three years and for a maximum of two consecutive terms.

8.   At CMA 2 (December 2019), six members and six alternate members shall be elected to the Committee for an initial term of two years and six members and six alternate members for a term of three years. Thereafter, the CMA shall elect at its relevant regular sessions six members and six alternate members for a term of three years. The members and alternate members shall remain in office until their successors are elected.

9.   If a member of the Committee resigns or is otherwise unable to complete the assigned term or to perform the functions in the Committee, an expert from the same Party shall be named by that Party to replace said member for the remainder of the unexpired term.

10.   Members and alternate members of the Committee shall serve in their individual expert capacity.

11.   The Committee shall elect from among its members two Co-Chairs for a period of three years, taking into account the need to ensure equitable geographical representation. The Co-Chairs shall perform the functions to be elaborated in the rules of procedure of the Committee referred to in paragraphs 17 and 18 below.

12.   Unless otherwise decided, the Committee shall meet at least twice a year, beginning in 2020. In scheduling its meetings, the Committee should take into account the desirability of holding its meetings in conjunction with sessions of the subsidiary bodies serving the Paris Agreement, as appropriate.

13.   Only members and alternate members of the Committee and secretariat officials shall be present during the elaboration and adoption of a decision of the Committee.

14.   The Committee, any Party or others involved in the process of the consideration by the Committee shall protect the confidentiality of information received in confidence.

15.   The adoption of decisions by the Committee shall require a quorum of 10 of the members to be present.

16.   The Committee shall make every effort to reach agreement on any decision by consensus. If all efforts at reaching consensus have been exhausted, as a last resort, the decision may be adopted by at least three quarters of the members present and voting.

17.   The Committee shall develop rules of procedure with a view to recommending them to the CMA for consideration and adoption at CMA 3 (November 2020), informed by the principles of transparency, facilitation, the non-adversarial and non-punitive function, and paying particular attention to the respective national capabilities and circumstances of Parties.

18.   The rules of procedure referred to in paragraph 17 above will address any matters necessary for the proper and effective functioning of the Committee, including the role of the Committee Co-Chairs, conflict of interest, any additional time-

lines related to the Committee's work, procedural stages and timelines for the Committee's work, and reasoning in decisions of the Committee.

19. In exercising its functions referred to in paragraphs 20 and 22 below, and subject to these modalities and procedures, the Committee shall apply the relevant rules of procedure to be developed pursuant to paragraphs 17 and 18 above and shall be guided by the following:

(a) Nothing in the work of the Committee may change the legal character of the provisions of the Paris Agreement;

(b) In considering how to facilitate implementation and promote compliance, the Committee shall endeavour to constructively engage with and consult the Party concerned at all stages of the process, including by inviting written submissions and providing opportunities to comment;

(c) The Committee shall pay particular attention to the respective national capabilities and circumstances of Parties, recognizing the special circumstances of the least developed countries and small island developing States, at all stages of the process, in accordance with the provisions of the Paris Agreement, including in determining how to consult with the Party concerned, what assistance can be provided to the Party concerned to support its engagement with the Committee, and what measures are appropriate to facilitate implementation and promote compliance in each situation;

(d) The Committee should take into account the work being undertaken by other bodies and under other arrangements as well as through forums serving or established under the Paris Agreement with a view to avoiding duplication of mandated work;

(e) The Committee should take into account considerations related to the impacts of response measures.

20. The Committee should consider issues related to, as appropriate, a Party's implementation of or compliance with the provisions of the Paris Agreement on the basis of a written submission from that Party with respect to its own implementation of and/or compliance with any provision of the Paris Agreement.

21. The Committee will undertake a preliminary examination of the submission within the timeline to be elaborated in the rules of procedure referred to in paragraphs 17 and 18 above with a view to verifying that the submission contains sufficient information, including on whether the matter relates to the Party's own implementation of or compliance with a provision of the Paris Agreement.

22. The Committee:

(a) Will initiate the consideration of issues in cases where a Party has not:

(i) Communicated or maintained a nationally determined contribution under Article 4 of the Paris Agreement, based on the most up-to-date status of communication in the public registry referred to in Article 4, paragraph 12, of the Paris Agreement;

(ii) Submitted a mandatory report or communication of information under Article 13, paragraphs 7 and 9, or Article 9, paragraph 7, of the Paris Agreement;

(iii) Participated in the facilitative, multilateral consideration of progress, based on information provided by the secretariat;

(iv)   Submitted a mandatory communication of information under Article 9, paragraph 5, of the Paris Agreement;

(b)   May, with the consent of the Party concerned, engage in a facilitative consideration of issues in cases of significant and persistent inconsistencies of the information submitted by a Party pursuant to Article 13, paragraphs 7 and 9, of the Paris Agreement with the modalities, procedures and guidelines referred to in Article 13, paragraph 13, of the Paris Agreement. This consideration will be based on the recommendations made in the final technical expert review reports, prepared under Article 13, paragraphs 11 and 12, of the Agreement, together with any written comments provided by the Party during the review. In its consideration of such matters, the Committee shall take into account Article 13, paragraphs 14 and 15, of the Agreement, as well as the flexibilities provided in the provisions of the modalities, procedures and guidelines under Article 13 of the Paris Agreement for those developing country Parties that need it in the light of their capacities

18.2.2   Non-Legally Binding Instruments

2001 UNECE Guidelines on Compliance with and Enforcement of Multilateral Environmental Agreements

4.   Compliance considerations in multilateral environmental agreements

(d)   Non-compliance mechanisms: States can consider the inclusion of non-compliance provisions in a multilateral environmental agreement, with a view to assisting parties having compliance problems and addressing individual cases of non-compliance, taking into account the importance of tailoring compliance provisions and mechanisms to the agreement's specific obligations. The following considerations could be kept in view:

(i)   The parties can consider the establishment of a body, such as a compliance committee, to address compliance issues. Members of such a body could be party representatives or party-nominated experts, with appropriate expertise on the relevant subject matter;

(ii)   Non-compliance mechanisms could be used by the contracting parties to provide a vehicle to identify possible situations of non-compliance at an early stage and the causes of noncompliance, and to formulate appropriate responses including, addressing and/or correcting the state of non-compliance without delay. These responses can be adjusted to meet varying requirements of cases of non-compliance, and may include both facilitative and stronger measures as appropriate and consistent with applicable international law;

(iii)   In order to promote, facilitate and secure compliance, non-compliance mechanisms can be non-adversarial and include procedural safeguards for those involved. In addition, noncompliance mechanisms can provide a means to clarify the content, to promote the application of the provisions of the agreement and thus lead significantly to the prevention of disputes;

(iv) The final determination of non-compliance of a party with respect to an agreement might be made through the conference of the parties of the relevant multilateral environmental agreement or another body under that agreement, if so mandated by the conference of the parties, consistent with the respective multilateral environmental agreement.

[...]

6. Compliance mechanisms after a multilateral environmental agreement has come into effect.

[...]

16. Compliance mechanisms or procedures could be introduced or enhanced after a multilateral environmental agreement has come into effect, provided such mechanisms or procedures have been authorised by the multilateral environmental agreement, subsequent amendment, or conference of the parties decision, as appropriate, and consistent with applicable international law.

III. Selected practice

Economic Commission for Europe Meeting of the Parties to the Convention on the Protection and Use of Transboundary Watercourses and International Lakes Implementation Committee

Twelfth meeting Geneva, 4 and 5 February 2021 Report of the Implementation Committee on its twelfth meeting, ECE/MP.WAT/IC/2021/1

Requests for advice, submissions and Committee initiatives Advisory procedure WAT/IC/AP/1 (Montenegro and Albania) (closed)

5. The Committee decided to hold the discussions under the item in a closed session.

6. The Chair recalled that advisory procedure WAT/IC/AP/1 had been initiated by the Committee in response to a request from Montenegro related to that country's concerns about the possible transboundary impact of the planned construction of additional small hydropower plants on the Cijevna/Cem River in Albania. The Chair recalled that Albania had subsequently accepted to participate in the advisory procedure by its letter of 31 January 2020.

7. The Chair also recalled that, at its eleventh meeting (Geneva, 31 August–2 September 2020), the Committee had held two separate information-gathering and consultation sessions with the delegations of Montenegro and Albania, respectively, and had subsequently decided to: (a) Send additional questions for clarification to the two countries to complement or clarify information received during the meeting; (b) Continue its involvement in the Cijevna/Cem River-related issues, following a two-track approach under which the Committee would: (i) Stay in contact with the countries to facilitate the exchange of information related to the Cijevna/Cem River basin; (ii) Assist the countries in setting up a joint monitoring and assessment framework for surface waters, groundwaters and ecosystems in the Cijevna/Cem River basin (ECE/MP.WAT/IC/2020/2, para. 14 (a) and (b)).

8. The Chair reported that he had sent letters to the countries on 15 September 2020 to transmit additional questions of the Committee. The replies had subsequently been received from Albania, on 22 October 2020, and from Montenegro, on 8 December 2020.

9. The Chair further recalled the preparatory meeting to the twelfth meeting of the Committee held on 24 November 2020 by videoconference[2] and thanked all members for having subsequently provided written inputs to facilitate preparations for the twelfth meeting.

10. The Committee members discussed and agreed on the proposals to be discussed with the countries during the upcoming consultation sessions, in particular regarding potential steps to be taken by the countries in setting up a harmonized or mutually agreed monitoring and assessment framework and in facilitating the exchange of information.

11. The Committee then held two separate consultation sessions with the delegations of Montenegro and Albania, respectively. During those sessions, held through videoconference, the delegations reported that there had not been any major developments in bilateral cooperation since the previous written communications between the countries and the Committee. In December 2020, Albania had proposed to Montenegro the dates and agenda of the next meeting of the bilateral commission established under the intergovernmental Framework Agreement on Mutual Relations in the Field of Management of Transboundary Waters (2018) but the pandemic situation had negatively affected the process of consultations within Montenegro aimed at preparing that country's reply to Albania. Consequently, no meeting of the bilateral commission had yet been scheduled

12. During the separate consultation sessions with the delegations of Montenegro and Albania, the Committee presented the obligations of the two Parties under the Convention most relevant to the subject matter of advisory procedure WAT/IC/AP/1 and the related obligations under the 2018 Framework Agreement. It also consulted each delegation on the Committee's proposals about potential steps to be taken by the countries in setting up a harmonized or mutually agreed monitoring and assessment framework and in facilitating the exchange of information, as well as the assistance that could be provided by the Committee in that respect.

13. During the separate consultation sessions, both countries expressed appreciation for and accepted the Committee's proposals. With regard to the proposal of the Committee that the bilateral commission should establish a joint technical working group on "Monitoring and assessment", Montenegro noted that it would be appropriate to gradually extend monitoring and assessment activities to other transboundary waters shared by the two countries. Albania emphasized the need to avoid duplication by the proposed joint technical working group of the work of the Expert Working Group on Monitoring and Information Exchange established by the Drin Core Group – a joint body operating under the Memorandum of Understanding for the Management of the Extended Transboundary Drin Basin, concluded by the Drin riparians (Albania, Greece, Montenegro, North Macedonia and Kosovo)[3] in 2011.

14. On the following day, the Committee held a joint consultation session with participation of both countries through videoconference. The Committee further discussed its proposals with both delegations. Albania reiterated the importance of

avoiding overlaps with the work of the Expert Working Group on Monitoring and Information Exchange and recalled the ongoing efforts to establish a commission for the Drin River basin. The Committee recalled that the Expert Working Group on Monitoring and Information Exchange operated in a multilateral framework, bringing together five Drin riparians. The Committee also recalled that its mandate for the purposes of advisory procedure WAT/IC/AP/1 was limited to the Cijevna/ Cem River basin. Accordingly, the Committee's proposals had been anchored in the 2018 intergovernmental Framework Agreement. Therefore, the Committee emphasized the appropriateness of a step-by-step approach in gradually moving from less complex issues towards more comprehensive ones, once the necessary experience had been gained.

15.   During joint consultations facilitated by the Committee, Montenegro and Albania agreed: (a) That the existing bilateral commission established under the 2018 Framework Agreement should establish a joint technical working group on "Monitoring and assessment", define the mandate of the joint technical working group based on pressures in the Cijevna/Cem River basin and ensure its regular meetings; (b) To develop and implement an information-exchange protocol; (c) To use the meetings of the bilateral commission to exchange information, including on existing and planned uses of water and related installations; (d) To convene the next meeting of the bilateral commission in the third week of March 2021, with a view to setting up the joint technical working group; (e) To ensure that the meetings of the bilateral commission were held regularly in the future.

16.   The Committee stated that a member of the Committee, Mr. Cunha Serra, would be available to assist Montenegro and Albania, as appropriate, in the implementation of the technical aspects of the Committee's advice, should such assistance be welcomed by the two countries. Other members of the Committee were available to assist, as appropriate, including with the development of the information-exchange protocol, should such assistance be requested by the countries.

17.   The Committee summarized its legal and technical advice under advisory procedure WAT/IC/AP/1 as presented in the annex to the present document. The Committee requested the Chair to prepare letters to the countries summarizing the Committee's advice and inviting countries to update the Committee on the developments in implementing the Committee's advice at its next meeting.

Legal and technical advice under advisory procedure WAT/IC/AP/1 (Montenegro and Albania)

I. Relevant obligations of the two countries under the Water Convention Obligations under the Water Convention The matter related to Cijevna/Cem River, which is the subject of advisory procedure WAT/IC/AP/1, is related to potential difficulties in implementing such key obligations under the Water Convention as the obligation to prevent, control and reduce transboundary impact (art. 2 (1)), the obligation of cooperation (art. 2 (6)), the obligation to conduct environmental impact assessments (art. 3 (1) (h)), obligations relating to monitoring (arts. 4 and 11), the obligation to exchange information (art. 6), the obligation of Riparian Parties to exchange information between one another (art. 13), and the obligation to exchange information on existing and planned uses of water and related installations through the joint body they have established, which, according to article 9 (2) (h), is to "serve as a forum" for that purpose. Many of the above-mentioned obligations of the Parties to the advisory procedure also follow from customary international law, on which the Water Convention is based and with which it is fully in line.

Based on the information provided by the Parties, and in the absence of sufficient monitoring information and data, the Committee is unable to confirm or deny the likelihood of cumulative transboundary impact of the planned construction of six additional small hydropower plants on the Cijevna/Cem River in Albania within the meaning of article 1 (2).

Nevertheless, the procedural obligations laid down in the Convention are instrumental in operationalizing its substantive obligations, beginning with its core obligation of cooperation (art. 2 (6)), irrespective of the likelihood of the occurrence of transboundary impact arising out of the situation currently under consideration by the Committee. The implementation of the procedural obligations can facilitate the implementation by the countries of the obligation to prevent, control and reduce transboundary impact (art. 2 (1)). Such procedural obligations under the Convention include, among other things, the establishment of joint bodies, conclusion of transboundary water agreements, holding of consultations, joint monitoring and assessment, and exchange of data and information. In line with their obligation to enter into agreements and establish joint bodies (art. 9 (1) and (2)), in 2018, Albania and Montenegro concluded an intergovernmental Framework Agreement on Mutual Relations in the Field of Management of Transboundary Waters to replace a previous bilateral agreement of 2001. The Parties established a bilateral commission, which succeeded the bilateral commission under the 2001 agreement. The first and, to date, only meeting of the bilateral commission under the 2018 agreement took place in September 2019. The 2015 Principles for Effective Joint Bodies for Transboundary Water Cooperation,1 adopted by the seventh session of the Meeting of the Parties to the Water Convention (Budapest, 17–19 November 2015), emphasize the principle of regularity in the work of a joint body. Furthermore, "regular … formal communications between riparian countries in [the] form of meetings" are recognized as a criterion for an arrangement to be considered "operational" within the meaning of indicator 6.5.2 of the Sustainable Development Goals on transboundary water cooperation (ECE/MP.WAT/54/Add.2, decision VIII/1, annex I, para. 6 (b)). Conducting regular meetings of the bilateral commission would therefore be crucial to ensuring the fulfilment of its mandate and the implementation of the Framework Agreement, and would contribute to the implementation by Albania and Montenegro of their obligations under the Water Convention.

The obligation to hold consultations under the Water Convention (art. 10) refers to both the general duty of consultation at the request of any Riparian Party, as well as the obligation of a State to consult its neighbour(s) should it envisage activities likely to cause transboundary impact.[2] The obligation of Riparian Parties to provide prior and timely notification on the activities likely to cause transboundary impact is not explicitly mentioned in the Water Convention but is encompassed under the broader obligation to hold consultations (art. 10). Furthermore, the Water Convention envisages joint bodies as main vehicles for consultations on planned measures, pointing to their task "to serve as a forum for the exchange of information on existing and planned uses of water and related installations that are likely to cause transboundary impact" (art. 9 (2) (h)).

In the matter related to the Cijevna/Cem River basin, Albania and Montenegro have had a few bilateral meetings to consult on the planned construction of additional small hydropower plants. These meetings included a technical meeting in February 2019 and the meeting of the bilateral commission in September 2019. Conducting further bilateral consultations would be crucial to ensuring the implementation of the obligation to hold consultations under the Water Convention and could pave the way for a better understanding of the situation by the Parties.

With regard to the provision of information on the planned construction of six additional small hydropower plants, in June 2019, Albania provided Montenegro with preliminary reports and decisions of environmental impact assessments for three hydropower plants (Vriela, Dobrinje and Murras) and, in October 2019, a map with the planned location of four hydropower plants. It is unclear whether any other information is available in Albania with regard to these and other planned hydropower plants. In turn, Albania reports that it requested Montenegro to provide information on planned developments in the Cijevna/Cem River basin. Exchange of all available information on planned developments between the countries is crucial to their implementation of their duty to cooperate and to the enhancement of cooperation in the Cijevna/Cem River basin in line with the obligations of the Water Convention.

With regard to the obligation to carry out joint monitoring and assessment, the Water Convention requires Riparian Parties to establish joint programmes for monitoring the conditions of transboundary waters and to carry out joint or coordinated assessments of the conditions of transboundary waters (art. 11 (1) and (3)). The term "joint" means that the basic elements of such monitoring and assessment programmes are to be agreed jointly, whereas the sampling, analysis and assessment of data can be, if not agreed otherwise, carried out at the national level on the basis of internationally agreed procedures.

In the matter related to the Cijevna/Cem River basin, the surface water and especially groundwater monitoring data are limited, and no continuous monitoring data are available, except for the data from one monitoring station (Trgaj) reinstalled by Montenegro in 2019. It is therefore advisable that Albania and Montenegro begin cooperation to gradually establish a joint or coordinated monitoring and assessment framework for surface waters, water ecosystems and groundwaters in the Cijevna/Cem River basin, as a prerequisite for gaining a proper understanding of the trends and pressures faced by their transboundary waters.

With regard to the obligation to exchange information and data, the Water Convention requires Riparian Parties to exchange reasonably available data within the framework of relevant agreements on a non-exhaustive list of data categories (art. 13 (1) and (2)) in order to lay down the foundations for cooperation between the riparians. The list of categories of information to be regularly exchanged includes: "measures taken and planned to be taken to prevent, control and reduce transboundary impact" (art. 13 (1) (d)). Such measures should not be confused with the obligation to inform and consult on planned measures, i.e. planned uses, projects, plans or activities that are likely to cause transboundary impact encompassed by the Convention's obligation to hold consultations.

In the matter related to the Cijevna/Cem River basin, Albania and Montenegro do not regularly exchange information and data and do not have any detailed procedures for this purpose. Developing such a practice and related procedures and engaging in such exchanges is a key aspect of the obligation of cooperation in line with the rationale and the provisions of the Water Convention.

Obligations under the intergovernmental Framework Agreement on Mutual Relations in the Field of Management of Transboundary Waters The 2018 Framework Agreement places significant emphasis on the exchange of information and consultations (arts. 5,

10 and 14), monitoring and assessment (arts. 7 and 10) and the implementation of the European Union Water Framework Directive5 (arts. 4, 7 and 9). It provides a good framework for the activities of the bilateral commission in these areas. There are no protocols on data exchange or other protocols on the issue of operational procedures between the countries.

QUESTIONS

1. Please explain why NCP are more efficient than adversarial means of settlement of environmental disputes.
2. Compare and analyse the fundamental principles of non-compliance with legal settlement of environment disputes.
3. Please explain why NCPs are an expression of multilateralism under international environmental law.

FURTHER READING

BOOKS

J Brunée, M Doelle and L Rajamani, *Promoting Compliance in an Evolving Climate Regime* (Cambridge University Press 2012)

J Cameron, J Werksman and P Roderick (eds), *Improving Compliance with International Environmental Law* (Earthscan 1995)

T Treves, A Tanzi, C Pitea, C Ragni and L Pineschi (eds), *Non-Compliance Procedures and Mechanisms and the Effectiveness of International Environmental Agreements* (Cambridge University Press 2009)

CHAPTERS

L Boisson de Chazournes, 'Technical and Financial Assistance' in D Bodanksy, J Brunée and E Hey (eds.) *The Oxford Handbook of International Environmental Law* (Oxford University Press 2007)

M Faure and J Lefevere, 'Compliance with Global Environmental Policy: Climate Change and Ozone Layer Cases' in RS Axelrod and SD VanDeveer (eds), *The Global Environment: Institutions, Law and Policy* (4th edn, CQ Press 2015)

M Fitzmaurice, 'Environmental Compliance Control' in *Max Planck Encyclopedia of Public International Law* (2010)

M Fitzmaurice, 'Environmental Compliance Mechanisms' in *Max Planck Encyclopedia of Public International Law* (2021)

E Hey, 'Compliance Procedure: Aarhus Convention' in *Max Planck Encyclopedia of Public International Law* (2018)

A-S Tabau, 'Climate Change Compliance Procedures' in *Max Planck Encyclopedia of Public International Law* (2019)

A Tanzi, 'Dispute Resolution in the Law of International Watercourses and the Law of the Sea' in HR Fabri, E Franckx, M Benatar and T Meshel (eds), *A Bridge over Troubled Waters: Dispute Resolution in the Law of International Watercourses and the Law of the Sea* (Brill 2020)

A Tanzi and C Pitea, 'Non-Compliance Mechanisms: Lessons Learned and the Way Forward' in T Treves, L Pineschi, A Tanzi, C Pitea, C Ragni and F Romanin Jacur (eds), *Non-Compliance Procedures and Mechanisms and the Effectiveness of International Environmental Agreements* (Asser Press 2009)

ARTICLES

J Brunée, 'COPing with Consent: Law-making under Multilateral Environmental Agreements' (2002) 15 Leiden Journal of International Law 1

T Crossen, 'Multilateral Environmental Agreements and the Compliance Continuum' (2004) 16 Georgetown International Environmental Law Review 473

M Fitzmaurice, 'Compliance with Multilateral Environmental Agreements' (2007) 20 Hague Yearbook of International Law 19

M Fitzmaurice and C Redgwell, 'Environmental Non-Compliance Procedures and International Law' (2000) 31 Netherlands Yearbook of International Law 35

N Goeteyn and F Maes, 'Compliance Mechanisms in Multilateral Environmental Agreements: An Effective Way to Improve Compliance?' (2011) 10 Chinese Journal of International Law 4

G Handl, 'Compliance Control Mechanisms and International Environmental Obligations' (1997) 9 Tulane Journal of International and Comparative Law 29

E Kirk 'Noncompliance and the Development of the Regimes Addressing Marine Pollution from Land-based Activities' (2008) 39 Ocean Development and International Law 235

A Kiss, 'Compliance with International and European Environmental Obligations' (1996) 45 Hague Yearbook of International Environmental Law

M Koskenniemi, 'Breach of Treaty or Non-Compliance: Reflections on the Enforcement of the Montreal Protocol' (1992) 3 Yearbook of International Environmental Law 123

W Lang, 'Compliance Control in International Environmental Law' (1996) 56 ZaöRV 685

A Nollkaemper, 'Compliance Control in International Environmental Law: Traversing the Limits of the National Legal Order' (2002) 13 Yearbook of International Environmental Law 165

K Sachariew, 'Promoting Compliance with International Environmental Legal Standards: Reflections on Monitoring and Reporting Mechanisms' (1991) 2 Yearbook of International Environmental Law 31

P Sands, 'Enforcing Environmental Security: The Challenges of Compliance with International Obligations' (1993) 15 Journal of International Affairs 46

A Tabau and S Maljean-Dubois, 'Non-Compliance Mechanisms: Interaction between the Kyoto Protocol System and the European Union' (2010) 21 European Journal of International Law 749

J Werksman, 'Compliance and the Kyoto Protocol' (1998) 9 Yearbook of International Environmental Law 48

R Wolfrum, 'Means of Ensuring Compliance with and Enforcement of International Environmental Law' (1998) 272 Recueil des Cours 9

19
The settlement of environmental disputes

19.1   INTRODUCTION

The peaceful settlement of disputes is one of the canonical premises of the modern international legal system. As a corollary to the prohibition of the use of force enshrined in Article 2(4) of the UN Charter,[1] member states have an obligation to settle their disputes peacefully pursuant to Article 2(3) of the UN Charter:

> All Members shall settle their international disputes by peaceful means in such a manner that international peace and security, and justice, are not endangered.

Article 33(1) of the UN Charter sets forth the different modalities available for the peaceful settlement of disputes:

> The parties to any dispute, the continuance of which is likely to endanger the maintenance of international peace and security, shall, first of all, seek a solution by negotiation, enquiry, mediation, conciliation, arbitration, judicial settlement, resort to regional agencies or arrangements, or other peaceful means of their own choice.

These modalities can be broadly categorised in two parts: non-legally binding and legally binding measures. The former encompasses negotiation, enquiry, mediation and conciliation; and the latter refers to international arbitration and judicial settlement. Article 33 is not exhaustive, which is reflected in the use of the nomenclature 'peaceful means of their own choice'. Thus, in the event of environmental disputes, states have an obligation to settle their disputes peacefully and have the choice of modality in this regard.

The classical definition of an international dispute is the one in the Mavromatis judgment by the Permanent Court of International Justice (PCIJ), whereby it is a 'disagreement over

---

[1]   Article 2(4) UN Charter: All Members shall refrain in their international relations from the threat or use of force against the territorial integrity or political independence of any state, or in any other manner inconsistent with the Purposes of the United Nations.

a point of law or fact, a conflict of legal views or of interests between two persons'.[2] This was most recently applied and reaffirmed by the Court in *Arbitral Award of 3 October 1899 (Guyana v. Venezuela)*.[3]

An environmental dispute has been difficult to conceptualise – or define.[4] As put by Tanaka, 'in light of the diversity of issues relating to environmental protection, it is difficult and even illusory to define an "international environmental dispute"'.[5] Much of the difficulty stems from conceptualising the framework of international environmental law within the international legal system. Boyle and Harrison aptly point out that 'most "environmental disputes" raise many other legal issues, even if they also involve "environmental" law'.[6] Fitzmaurice reminds that in the *Gabčíkovo-Nagymaros* case, 'the legal questions concerning the environment, the law of treaties and the law of State responsibility were entangled together in a Gordian knot'.[7] For the purposes of this chapter, an environmental dispute will broadly be understood as a dispute which has an environmental element. As mentioned above, there are, broadly speaking, two methods of dispute settlement: diplomatic means and legally binding measures. The former will first be examined, followed by the latter.

Diplomatic means of dispute settlement include negotiation, consultation, mediation, conciliation and good offices. Fitzmaurice observes:

> Negotiations appear to be the means of settlement of disputes to which States have resource most frequently. Negotiations can be conducted at different stages, including the stage when the dispute has not been fully crystallized, as a means of avoiding it. The result of negotiations can be quite varied, providing the negotiating States with flexibility as to the factors taken into consideration and also with regard to the range of suggested solutions which may be accepted.[8]

The ICJ in the *Fisheries Jurisdiction* case outlined conditions establishing negotiations:

> on the basis that each must in good faith pay reasonable regard to the legal rights of the other ... thus bringing about an equitable apportionment of the fishing resources based on the facts of the particular situation, and having regard to the interests of other states which

---

[2] *Mavromatis Palestine Concessions*, Judgment No. 2, 1924, PCIJ, Series A, No. 2, p. 11.

[3] *Arbitral Award of 3 October 1899 (Guyana v. Venezuela)*, Judgment (18 December 2020), para. 64.

[4] James Harrison and Alan Boyle, 'Judicial Settlement of International Environmental Disputes: Current Problems' (2013) 4 Journal of International Dispute Settlement 245, 247–250.

[5] Tanaka Yoshifumi, *The Peaceful Settlement of International Disputes* (CUP 2018) 311.

[6] Harrison and Boyle (n 4) 249.

[7] Malgosia Fitzmaurice, 'The Potential of Inter-State Conciliation within the Framework of Environmental Treaties' in Christian Tomuschat and Marcelo Kohen (eds), *Flexibility in International Dispute Settlement: Conciliation Revisited* (2020) 87.

[8] Ibid., 91.

have established fishing rights in the area. It is not a matter of finding simply an equitable solution, but an equitable solution derived from the applicable law.[9]

Fitzmaurice points out that in some MEAs, 'consultation' is a separate method of dispute settlement from negotiations, e.g., in the 1997 International Watercourses Convention, consultations and negotiations concerning planned measures are listed as two separate courses of action in Article 17 whereby 'the notifying State and the State making the communication shall enter into consultations and, if necessary, negotiations with a view to arriving at an equitable resolution of the situation'. It appears that consultations are the first process, and presumably if unsuccessful, then negotiations would be the next step. Notably, consultations are not included in Article 33 of the UN Charter affirming the earlier point made that the list is not exhaustive. Further, in the *Lake Lanoux* case, the Arbitral Tribunal held that France had an obligation to consult with Spain.[10]

Fitzmaurice also points out that:

> MEAs adopt in relation to the clauses on settlement of disputes a so-called 'integrated approach' which combines legal means (binding) and diplomatic means (non- binding), including conciliation. They provide for a range of procedures: diplomatic means: negotiation/consultation; mediation/good offices; conciliation; legal means: arbitration or judicial settlement – but depending on common agreement of the parties to the dispute to submit it to a relevant organisation. Mediation and good offices are based on the involvement of a third party, which is differently designed in both of these methods for the settlement of disputes. The third-party function in respect of good offices is to bring the parties to a dispute together whilst the role of the third party in mediation is more proactive, suggesting proposals to the parties and evaluating them.[11]

Conciliation is worth noting in more detail, as compulsory conciliation features in many MEAs.[12] This is seen as a form of dispute settlement which comes into play if other means such as negotiation or consultation are not adequate. Fitzmaurice observes that a conciliation commission most likely comprises environmental law experts as well as generalist international lawyers, which would provide an 'optimal approach to an environmental dispute'.[13] Generally,

---

[9]   *Fisheries Jurisdiction (United Kingdom v. Iceland)*, Merits, Judgment, ICJ Reports 3 (1974), para. 78.

[10]   *Lake Lanoux Arbitration (France v. Spain)*, Arbitral Tribunal, 12 RIAA 281; 24 ILR 101 (16 November 1957).

[11]   Fitzmaurice (n 7) 92. See also Philippe Sands and Jacqueline Peel, *Principles of International Environmental Law* (4th edn, CUP 2018) 170–172.

[12]   For example, Article 11, Vienna Convention for the Protection of the Ozone Layer 1985; Article 14, United Nations Framework Climate Change Convention 1992; Article 27, Biological Diversity Convention 1992; Article 32, Convention for the Protection of the Marine Environment of the North-East Atlantic 1992; Article 28 Desertification Convention 1994; Article 33 International Watercourses Convention 1997; Article 20, Rotterdam Convention on the prior informed consent procedure for certain hazardous chemicals and pesticides in international trade; Article 18, Stockholm Convention on Persistent Organic Pollutants 2001.

[13]   Fitzmaurice (n 7) 90.

although the setting up of Conciliation Commissions may be mandatory, the award is not legally binding and is recommendatory.[14]

If parties to a dispute seek a legally binding decision, they would seek arbitration or international adjudication. Notable international arbitration practice of historical significance includes *Pacific Fur Seal Arbitration*,[15] *Trail Smelter Arbitration*,[16] and the *Lake Lanoux Arbitration* (1957).[17] At the Permanent Court of Arbitration (PCA), notable cases include the *Rhine Chlorides (Netherlands v. France)*;[18] *Dispute Concerning Access to Information Under Article 9 of the OSPAR Convention (Ireland v. United Kingdom)*;[19] *Iron Rhine Arbitration (Belgium vs. the Netherlands)*;[20] and *Indus Waters*.[21] Several MEAs refer to the PCA as the appointment authority and/or a forum for settlement (arbitration) of disputes.[22] The PCA adopted the Optional Rules for Arbitration of Disputes Relating to Natural Resources and/or the Environment ('PCA Rules').[23]

---

[14]   Ibid., 93–94.

[15]   *Pacific Fur Seal Arbitration (United States of America v. Great Britain)*, Award, 1 Moore's International Arbitral Awards 733; RIAA 263 (1893).

[16]   *Trail Smelter Arbitration (United States v. Canada)*, 3 RIAA 1905 (1938 and 1941)..

[17]   *Lake Lanoux Arbitration (France v. Spain)*, Arbitral Tribunal, 12 RIAA 281; 24 ILR 101 (16 November 1957).

[18]   *Case Concerning the Auditing of Accounts Between the Kingdom of the Netherlands and the French Republic pursuant to the Additional Protocol of 25 September 1991 to the Convention on the Protection of the Rhine Against Pollution by Chlorides of 3 December 1976, (Netherlands v. France)*, Award, PCA Case No. 2002–02 (12 March 2004) ('*Rhine Chlorides*')

[19]   *Dispute Concerning Access to Information Under Article 9 of the OSPAR Convention (Ireland v. United Kingdom)*, Final Award, PCA Case No. 2001–03 (15 June 2001)

[20]   *Award in the Arbitration regarding the Iron Rhine ('Ijzeren Rijn') Railway between the Kingdom of Belgium and the Kingdom of the Netherlands (Belgium vs. the Netherlands)*, XXVII RIAA 35–125 (24 May 2005).

[21]   *Indus Waters Kishenganga Arbitration (Pakistan v. India)*, Final Award, PCA Case No. 2011–01 (20 December 2013).

[22]   1973 Convention on International Trade in Endangered Species of Wild Fauna and Flora; 1979 Convention on the Conservation of Migratory Species of Wild Animals; 1980 Convention on the Conservation of Antarctic Marine Living Resources; 1991 Protocol to the Antarctic Treaty on Environmental Protection; 1993 Convention for the Conservation of Southern Bluefin Tuna; 1995 Agreement on the Conservation of African-Eurasian Migratory Waterbirds; 2000 Convention on the Conservation and Management of Highly Migratory Fish Stocks in the Western and Central Pacific Ocean; 2000 Protocol to the Convention for the Protection of the Alps; 2002 Treaty on the establishment of the Great Limpopo Transfrontier Park; 2003 Protocol to the Convention on the Protection and Use of Transboundary Watercourses and International Lakes and the Convention on the Transboundary Effects of Industrial Accidents; 2006 Southern Indian Ocean Fisheries Agreement; 2006 Relationship Agreement between the Global Crop Diversity Trust and the Governing Body of the International Treaty on Plant Genetic Resources for Food and Agriculture; 2009 Convention on the Conservation and Management of High Seas Fishery Resources in the South Pacific Ocean.

[23]   Referred to in 2003 Protocol on Civil Liability and Compensation for Damage Caused by the Transboundary Effects of Industrial Accidents on Transboundary Waters.

The 1982 UN Convention on the Law of the Sea provides for compulsory dispute settlement, whereby an arbitration constituted within Annex VII is one of the choices of procedure.[24] There have been a few Annex VII arbitrations which concern the environment, i.e., *Southern Bluefin Tuna*;[25] *MOX Plant*;[26] and more notably and more recently, *Chagos Marine Protected Area Arbitration (Mauritius v. United Kingdom)*[27] and the *South China Sea Arbitration (Philippines v. China)*.[28]

For general observations, Fitzmaurice has commented, '[i]nternational arbitration does not deal with international environmental law in a holistic manner; it is a very piecemeal approach, thus its role in the evolution of environmental principles is rather limited'.[29]

In relation to international adjudication in courts and tribunals, Dupuy and Viñuales have remarked that 'despite its important normative development over the past four decades, international law has not undergone the growing judicialization experienced in other areas'.[30] As mentioned above it is not entirely straightforward to categorise environmental disputes, as issues pertaining to the environment often arise in connection to various international issues in international law. Thus, it is likely that these environmental issues are discussed in multiple judicial forums.[31]

The ICJ has dealt with a few inter-state disputes that concern environmental law. Viñuales has noted the *Corfu Channel* case and the *Nuclear Tests* case and an important obiter dictum made in *Barcelona Traction, Light and Power Company Limited*, as the first trend or 'wave' of cases in ICJ jurisprudence whereby its contribution is 'the confirmation of previous case law on transboundary damages as well as in the introduction of the concept of obligations erga omnes, potentially applicable to some environmental norms',[32] which had set the basis in general international law 'for the protection against environmental damage caused to States and to the environment [...] outside the jurisdiction of any State'.[33] The Certain Phosphate Lands in Nauru and Gačíkovo-Nagymaros Project and Advisory Opinion on the Legality or Threat or Use of Nuclear Weapons is identified as the second wave which confirms that 'not

---

[24]   Article 287, UNCLOS 1982.

[25]   *Southern Bluefin Tuna (New Zealand v. Japan; Australia v. Japan)*, Provisional Measures, Case Nos 3–4, ITLOS Reports (27 August 1999).

[26]   *MOX Plant (Ireland v. United Kingdom)*, Provisional Measures, Case No. 10, ITLOS Reports 95 (3 December 2001).

[27]   *Chagos Marine Protected Area Arbitration (Mauritius v. United Kingdom)*, Final Award, ICGJ 486 (18 March 2015).

[28]   *South China Sea Arbitration (Philippines v. China)*, Final Award, PCA Case No. 2013–19 (12 July 2016).

[29]   Malgosia Fitzmaurice and Catherine Redgwell, 'Environmental Non-Compliance Procedures and International Law' [2000] Netherlands Yearbook of International Law 35, 89.

[30]   Pierre-Marie Dupuy and Jorge E Viñuales, *International Environmental Law* (2nd edn, CUP 2018) 300.

[31]   Yoshifumi (n 5) 312. See also Sands and Peel (n 11) 180–190; Dupuy and Viñuales (n 30) 300–301.

[32]   Jorge E Viñuales, 'The Contribution of the International Court of Justice to the Development of International Environmental Law: A Contemporary Assessment' (2008) 32 Fordham International law Journal 232, 235.

[33]   Dupuy and Viñuales (n 30) 236.

only was the principle asserted in the *Corfu Channel* case expressly acknowledged and formulated specifically with respect to IEL, but in addition the larger component of environmental protection was expressly recognized as part of customary international law'.[34] These two proceedings have also been considered to be a breakthrough for international environmental law at the ICJ as they 'reflected, and affirmed, that environmental law had moved from the margins into the mainstream of international law'.[35] Fitzmaurice, building upon Viñuales' work, expands on the third 'wave',[36] where she observes that 'the Court is beginning to move from general principles to specific norms of international environmental law and to influence their interpretation'.[37] The *Pulp Mills* case was a landmark case for environmental law, as it was environmental concerns that had prompted the application and defined the parties' arguments. The judgment is of significance in relation to procedural aspects of international environmental law.[38]

Other notable cases include *Aerial Herbicide Spraying (Ecuador v. Colombia)*[39] and *Whaling in the Antarctic (Australia v. Japan: New Zealand intervening)*.[40] Regarding the latter, Fitzmaurice submits:

> Because of the general and longstanding public interest in the protection of marine mammals, this case is likely to define the public perception of the Court as a protector of environmental concerns.[41]

She continues:

> The survey of ICJ jurisprudence on environmental issues can perhaps best be seen as a gradual rapprochement: after cautious beginnings, the Court has embraced international environmental law and today can be seen as one of its advocates.[42]

In the more recent *Certain Activities Carried Out by Nicaragua in the Border Area (Costa Rica v. Nicaragua)* and *Construction of a Road in Costa Rica along the San Juan River (Nicaragua v. Costa Rica)* judgment,[43] Fitzmaurice comments that this very important judgment 'has not

---

[34] Viñuales (n 32) 244.

[35] Malgosia Fitzmaurice, 'The International Court of Justice and International Environmental Law' in Christian J Tams and James Sloan (eds), *The Development of International Law by the International Court of Justice* (OUP 2013) 363–364.

[36] Viñuales (n 32) 235, 253–257.

[37] Fitzmaurice (n 35) 373.

[38] Ibid., 370–372.

[39] *Aerial Herbicide Spraying (Ecuador v. Colombia)*, ICJ Reports 278 (13 September 2013).

[40] *Whaling in the Antarctic (Australia v. Japan: New Zealand intervening)*, Judgment, ICJ Reports 226 (2014).

[41] Fitzmaurice (n 35) 373.

[42] Ibid.

[43] *Certain Activities Carried Out by Nicaragua in the Border Area (Costa Rica v. Nicaragua)* and *Construction of a Road in Costa Rica along the San Juan River (Nicaragua v. Costa Rica)*, ICJ Reports 665 (2015)

clarified or developed fundamental principles singular to international environmental law, but rather analyzed a principle of general international law enunciated in the *Factory at Chorzów* case within the framework of international environmental law that a responsible State has to "wipe out all consequences of a wrongful act'".[44]

There have also been some environmental law cases at the International Tribunal for the Law of the Sea (ITLOS): the contentious cases of *Southern Bluefin Tuna (New Zealand v. Japan; Australia v. Japan)* on provisional measures regarding fishing for southern bluefin tuna by Japan;[45] *MOX Plant (Ireland v. United Kingdom)* on provisional measures pending the constitution of an arbitral tribunal to be established under Annex VII UNCLOS;[46] *Land Reclamation By Singapore in and Around the Straits of Johor (Malaysia v. Singapore)* on provisional measures pending the constitution of an arbitral tribunal to be established under Annex VII UNCLOS.[47] The only two Advisory Opinions by the Tribunal pertain to the environment: the Seabed Disputes Chamber of ITLOS gave the Responsibilities and Obligations of States Sponsoring Persons and Entities with Respect to Activities in the Area;[48] and the Tribunal gave the Advisory Opinion submitted by the Sub-Regional Fisheries Commission pursuant to Article 33 of the Convention on the definition of the minimum access conditions and exploitation of fisheries resources within the maritime zones under the jurisdiction of SRFC Member States (MAC Convention).[49]

Indeed, most of the jurisprudence in the inter-state setting relevant to international environmental law is that of the ICJ and ITLOS. That said, it is well known that a proposition has been advanced that there should be a specialised environmental court. Boyle and Harrison question whether there is a need for such a court:

> The reasons for scepticism remain as valid now as they have always been, and despite the problems [...] the existing structure of international courts has much to commend it, including the expertise and authority of the judges, an established reputation, and the ability to look at the law as a coherent whole. [...][50]

It seems better to identify less radical changes that would make the present ad hoc system a better vehicle for the settlement of environmental disputes.

---

[44]   Fitzmaurice (n 7) 85; *Factory at Chorzów* (Merits), PCIJ Reports 47 (1928), Series A No. 17.

[45]   *Southern Bluefin Tuna (New Zealand v. Japan; Australia v. Japan)*, Provisional Measures, Case Nos 3–4, ITLOS Reports 280 (27 August 1999).

[46]   *MOX Plant (Ireland v. United Kingdom)*, Provisional Measures, Case No. 10, ITLOS Reports 95 (3 December 2001)

[47]   *Case Concerning Land Reclamation By Singapore in and Around the Straits of Johor (Malaysia v. Singapore)*, Provisional Measures, Case No. 12, ITLOS Reports 10 (8 October 2003)

[48]   Responsibilities and obligations of States with respect to activities in the Area, Advisory Opinion, 1 February 2011, ITLOS Reports 2011, p. 10.

[49]   Request for Advisory Opinion submitted by the Sub-Regional Fisheries Commission, Advisory Opinion, 2 April 2015, ITLOS Reports 2015, p. 4.

[50]   Harrison and Boyle (n 4) 274.

The debate whether there should be a specialised environmental court exceeds the compass of this chapter.[51] That said, Boyle and Harrison have aptly pointed out that 'it seems better to identify less radical changes that would make the present ad hoc system a better vehicle for the settlement of environmental disputes',[52] and conclude their argument that 'there is significant scope for cross-fertilization in procedural innovations, similar to that taking place between courts and tribunals on substantive rules of international environmental law'.[53]

In a different vein, Fitzmaurice holds the view that:

> judgments of the ICJ, which undoubtedly have dealt with many general underlying principles of international environmental law and even evolved them, cannot even be expected to analyze the in-depth intricate fabric of international environmental law, which would require a more specialist body to deal with it, such as for example a conciliation commission.[54]

It is more generally accepted that non-legally binding methods of dispute settlement are preferable to legally binding methods for environmental disputes. Boyle has pointed out two advantages in relation to the former:

> First, and most importantly, the parties remain in control of the outcome. They can walk away at any time and, until agreement is reached in the form of a treaty, there will be no final or binding determination of rights or obligations. Secondly, there are the added benefits of cheapness, flexibility, privacy, and complete freedom to determine who is involved, what expertise is relevant, and the basis on which any solution will be sought. The solution need not be based on international law.[55]

Fitzmaurice concludes with this view:

> diplomatic means in general appear to be more accessible and suitable for solving environmental disputes. Given the not fully formed and still developing body of environmental law, at times very technical, more flexible means for the settling of disputes appear to more suitable and advantageous to the parties of the dispute.[...][56]

---

[51]   Amedeo Postiglione, 'A More Efficient International Law of the Environmental and Setting up an International Court for the Environment within the United Nations' (1990) 20 321; Robert Jennings, 'Need for Environmental Court?' (1992) 22 Environmental Policy & Law 312; Stuart Bruce, 'The Project for an International Environmental Court' in Christian Tomuschat, Riccardo Pisillo Mazzeschi and Daniel Thürer (eds), *Conciliation in International Law: The OSCE Court of Conciliation and Arbitration* (Brill 2016).

[52]   Harrison and Boyle (n 4) 275.

[53]   Ibid., 276.

[54]   Fitzmaurice (n 7) 85–86.

[55]   Alan Boyle, 'Environmental Dispute Settlement', *Max Planck Encyclopaedia of Public International Law* (2009), para. 21.

[56]   Fitzmaurice (n 7) 90.

On a different note, MEAs increasingly provide for non-compliance procedures (NCPs) which are to provide 'encouragement to States to comply with their treaty obligations and, in the event of non-compliance, to provide a "softer" system to address non-compliance than afforded by traditional dispute procedures under general international law', and 'designed to assist the default State in returning to compliance, not necessarily to incriminate for non-compliance'.[57]

19.2   LEGAL INSTRUMENTS

19.2.1   The Peaceful Settlement of Disputes

1945 Charter of the United Nations, 1 UNTS XVI

Article 2(3) UN Charter:
All Members shall settle their international disputes by peaceful means in such a manner that international peace and security, and justice, are not endangered.
Article 33
1. The parties to any dispute, the continuance of which is likely to endanger the maintenance of international peace and security, shall, first of all, seek a solution by negotiation, enquiry, mediation, conciliation, arbitration, judicial settlement, resort to regional agencies or arrangements, or other peaceful means of their own choice.
2. The Security Council shall, when it deems necessary, call upon the parties to settle their dispute by such means.

Article 96
1. The General Assembly or the Security Council may request the International Court of Justice to give an advisory opinion on any legal question.
2. Other organs of the United Nations and specialized agencies, which may at any time be so authorized by the General Assembly, may also request advisory opinions of the Court on legal questions arising within the scope of their activities.

19.2.2   Non-Adversarial Forms of Dispute Settlement

1968 African Convention on the Conservation of Nature and Natural Resources, 1001 UNTS 3

If so requested by Contracting States, the Organization of African Unity shall organize any meeting which may be necessary to dispose of any matters covered by this Convention. Requests for such meetings must be made by at least three of the Contracting States and be approved by two thirds of the States which it is proposed should participate in such meetings.

---

57   Fitzmaurice and Redgwell (n 29) 39. See also Fitzmaurice (n 7). See further Chapter 18.

1972 Space Liability Convention, 961 UNTS 187

Art IX

A claim for compensation for damage shall be presented to a launching State through diplomatic channels. If a State does not maintain diplomatic relations with the launching State concerned, it may request another State to present its claim to that launching State or otherwise represent its interests under this Convention. It may also present its claim through the Secretary-General of the United Nations, provided the claimant State and the launching State are both Members of the United Nations.

1973 Convention on International Trade in Endangered Species of Wild Fauna and Flora, 993 UNTS 243 ('CITES')

Article XIII

International Measures

1. When the Secretariat in the light of information received is satisfied that any species included in Appendix I or II is being affected adversely by trade in specimens of that species or that the provisions of the present Convention are not being effectively implemented, it shall communicate such information to the authorized Management Authority of the Party or Parties concerned.

2. When any Party receives a communication as indicated in paragraph 1 of this Article, it shall, as soon as possible, inform the Secretariat of any relevant facts insofar as its laws permit and, where appropriate, propose remedial action. Where the Party considers that an inquiry is desirable, such inquiry may be carried out by one or more persons expressly authorized by the Party.

3. The information provided by the Party or resulting from any inquiry as specified in paragraph 2 of this Article shall be reviewed by the next Conference of the Parties which may make whatever recommendations it deems appropriate.

1976 Convention on the prohibition of military or any hostile use of environmental modification techniques, 1108 UNTS 151

ARTICLE V

1. The States Parties to this Convention undertake to consult one another and to co-operate in solving any problems which may arise in relation to the objectives of, or in the application of the provisions of, the Convention. Consultation and co-operation pursuant to this article may also be undertaken through appropriate international procedures within the framework of the United Nations and in accordance with its Charter. These international procedures may include the services of appropriate international organizations, as well as of a Consultative Committee of Experts as provided for in paragraph 2 of this article.

1979 Convention on Long-Range Transboundary Air Pollution, 1302 UNTS 217 ('LRTAP')

Article 5: Consultations shall be held, upon request, at an early stage between, on the one hand, Contracting Parties which are actually affected by or exposed to a significant risk of long-range transboundary air pollution and, on the other hand, Contracting Parties within which and subject to whose jurisdiction a significant contribution to long-range trans-boundary air pollution originates, or could originate, in connection with activities carried on or contemplated therein.

1992 United Nations Framework Convention on Climate Change, 1771 UNTS 107 ('UNFCCC')

Article 10 SUBSIDIARY BODY FOR IMPLEMENTATION 1. A subsidiary body for implementation is hereby established to assist the Conference of the Parties in the assessment and review of the effective implementation of the Convention. This body shall be open to participation by all Parties and comprise government representatives who are experts on matters related to climate change. It shall report regularly to the Conference of the Parties on all aspects of its work. 2. Under the guidance of the Conference of the Parties, this body shall: (a) Consider the information communicated in accordance with Article 12, paragraph 1, to assess the overall aggregated effect of the steps taken by the Parties in the light of the latest scientific assessments concerning climate change; (b) Consider the information communicated in accordance with Article 12, paragraph 2, in order to assist the Conference of the Parties in carrying out the reviews required by Article 4, paragraph 2 (d); and (c) Assist the Conference of the Parties, as appropriate, in the preparation and implementation of its decisions.

19.2.3   The Settlement of Disputes

MARPOL

Settlement of disputes
Article 10
Any dispute between two or more Parties to the Convention concerning the interpretation or application of the present Convention shall, if settlement by negotiation between the Parties involved has not been possible, and if these Parties do not otherwise agree, be submitted upon request of any of them to arbitration as set out in Protocol II to the present Convention.

CITES

Article XVIII
Resolution of Disputes
1.   Any dispute which may arise between two or more Parties with respect to the interpretation or application of the provisions of the present Convention shall be subject to negotiation between the Parties involved in the dispute.
2.   If the dispute can not be resolved in accordance with paragraph 1 of this Article, the Parties may, by mutual consent, submit the dispute to arbitration, in particular that of the Permanent Court of Arbitration at The Hague, and the Parties submitting the dispute shall be bound by the arbitral decision.

LRTAP

Article 13: SETTLEMENT OF DISPUTES If a dispute arises between two or more Contracting Parties to the present Convention as to the interpretation or application of the Convention, they shall seek a solution by negotiation or by any other method of dispute settlement acceptable to the parties to the dispute.

1980 Convention for the Conservation of Antarctic Marine Living Resources, 1327 UNTS 47

Article XXV

1. If any dispute arises between two or more of the Contracting Parties concerning the interpretation or application of this Convention, those Contracting Parties shall consult among themselves with a view to having the dispute resolved by negotiation, inquiry, mediation, conciliation, arbitration, judicial settlement or other peaceful means of their own choice.

2. Any dispute of this character not so resolved shall, with the consent in each case of all Parties to the dispute, be referred for settlement to the International Court of Justice or to arbitration; but failure to reach agreement on reference to the International Court or to arbitration shall not absolve Parties to the dispute from the responsibility of continuing to seek to resolve it by any of the various peaceful means referred to in paragraph 1 above.

3. In cases where the dispute is referred to arbitration, the arbitral tribunal shall be constituted as provided in the Annex to this Convention.

1982 United Nations Convention on the Law of the Sea, 1833 UNTS 3

SECTION 2. COMPULSORY PROCEDURES FOR BINDING DISPUTE SETTLEMENT

Article 286
Application of procedures under this section

Subject to section 3, any dispute concerning the interpretation or application of this Convention shall, where no settlement has been reached by recourse to section 1, be submitted at the request of any party to the dispute to the court or tribunal having jurisdiction under this section.

Article 287
Choice of procedure

1. When signing, ratifying or acceding to this Convention or at any time thereafter, a State shall be free to choose, by means of a written declaration, one or more of the following means for the settlement of disputes concerning the interpretation or application of this Convention:
    (a) the International Tribunal for the Law of the Sea established in accordance with Annex VI;
    (b) the International Court of Justice;
    (c) an arbitral tribunal constituted in accordance with Annex VII;
    (d) a special arbitral tribunal constituted in accordance with Annex VIII for one or more of the categories of disputes specified therein.

2.   A declaration made under paragraph 1 shall not affect or be affected by the obligation of a State Party to accept the jurisdiction of the Seabed Disputes Chamber of the International Tribunal for the Law of the Sea to the extent and in the manner provided for in Part XI, section 5.

3.   A State Party, which is a party to a dispute not covered by a declaration in force, shall be deemed to have accepted arbitration in accordance with Annex VII.

4.   If the parties to a dispute have accepted the same procedure for the settlement of the dispute, it may be submitted only to that procedure, unless the parties otherwise agree.

5.   If the parties to a dispute have not accepted the same procedure for the settlement of the dispute, it may be submitted only to arbitration in accordance with Annex VII, unless the parties otherwise agree.

[...]

Article 288
Jurisdiction

1.   A court or tribunal referred to in article 287 shall have jurisdiction over any dispute concerning the interpretation or application of this Convention which is submitted to it in accordance with this Part.

2.   A court or tribunal referred to in article 287 shall also have jurisdiction over any dispute concerning the interpretation or application of an international agreement related to the purposes of this Convention, which is submitted to it in accordance with the agreement.

3.   The Seabed Disputes Chamber of the International Tribunal for the Law of the Sea established in accordance with Annex VI, and any other chamber or arbitral tribunal referred to in Part XI, section 5, shall have jurisdiction in any matter which is submitted to it in accordance therewith.

4.   In the event of a dispute as to whether a court or tribunal has jurisdiction, the matter shall be settled by decision of that court or tribunal.

[...]

Article 292
Prompt release of vessels and crews

1.   Where the authorities of a State Party have detained a vessel flying the flag of another State Party and it is alleged that the detaining State has not complied with the provisions of this Convention for the prompt release of the vessel or its crew upon the posting of a reasonable bond or other financial security, the question of release from detention may be submitted to any court or tribunal agreed upon by the parties or, failing such agreement within 10 days from the time of detention, to a court or tribunal accepted by the detaining State under article 287 or to the International Tribunal for the Law of the Sea, unless the parties otherwise agree.

2.   The application for release may be made only by or on behalf of the flag State of the vessel.

3.   The court or tribunal shall deal without delay with the application for release and shall deal only with the question of release, without prejudice to the merits of any

case before the appropriate domestic forum against the vessel, its owner or its crew. The authorities of the detaining State remain competent to release the vessel or its crew at any time.

4. Upon the posting of the bond or other financial security determined by the court or tribunal, the authorities of the detaining State shall comply promptly with the decision of the court or tribunal concerning the release of the vessel or its crew.

1985 Vienna Convention for the Protection of the Ozone Layer, 1513 UNTS 293

Article 11: Settlement of disputes

1. In the event of a dispute between Parties concerning the interpretation or application of this Convention, the parties concerned shall seek solution by negotiation.
2. If the parties concerned cannot reach agreement by negotiation, they may jointly seek the good offices of, or request mediation by, a third party.
3. When ratifying, accepting, approving or acceding to this Convention, or at any time thereafter, a State or regional economic integration organization may declare in writing to the Depositary that for a dispute not resolved in accordance with paragraph 1 or paragraph 2 above, it accepts one or both of the following means of dispute settlement as compulsory:
   a. Arbitration in accordance with procedures to be adopted by the Conference of the Parties at its first ordinary meeting;
   b. Submission of the dispute to the International Court of Justice.
4. If the parties have not, in accordance with paragraph 3 above, accepted the same or any procedure, the dispute shall be submitted to conciliation in accordance with paragraph 5 below unless the parties otherwise agree.
5. A conciliation commission shall be created upon the request of one of the parties to the dispute. The commission shall be composed of an equal number of members appointed by each party concerned and a chairman chosen jointly by the members appointed by each party. The commission shall render a final and recommendatory award, which the parties shall consider in good faith.
6. The provisions of this Article shall apply with respect to any protocol except as provided in the protocol concerned.

1989 Basel Convention on the Control of Transboundary Movements of Hazardous Wastes and their Disposal, 1673 UNTS 57

ARTICLE 20 SETTLEMENT OF DISPUTES

1. In case of a dispute between Parties as to the interpretation or application of, or compliance with, this Convention or any protocol thereto, they shall seek a settlement of the dispute through negotiation or any other peaceful means of their own choice.
2. If the Parties concerned cannot settle their dispute through the means mentioned in the preceding paragraph, the dispute, if the Parties to the dispute agree, shall be submitted to the International Court of Justice or to arbitration under the conditions set out in Annex VI on Arbitration. However, failure to reach common agreement on submission of the dispute to the International Court of Justice or to arbitration shall not absolve the Parties from the responsibility of continuing to seek to resolve it by the means referred to in paragraph 1.

3.   When ratifying, accepting, approving, formally confirming or acceding to this Convention, or at any time thereafter, a State or political and/ or economic integration organization may declare that it recognizes as compulsory ipso facto and without special agreement, in relation to any Party accepting the same obligation:
       (a)   submission of the dispute to the International Court of Justice; and/or
       (b)   arbitration in accordance with the procedures set out in Annex VI.

Such declaration shall be notified in writing to the Secretariat which shall communicate it to the Parties.

UNFCCC

Article 14 SETTLEMENT OF DISPUTES
1.   In the event of a dispute between any two or more Parties concerning the interpretation or application of the Convention, the Parties concerned shall seek a settlement of the dispute through negotiation or any other peaceful means of their own choice.
2.   When ratifying, accepting, approving or acceding to the Convention, or at any time thereafter, a Party which is not a regional economic integration organization may declare in a written instrument submitted to the Depositary that, in respect of any dispute concerning the interpretation or application of the Convention, it recognizes as compulsory ipso facto and without special agreement, in relation to any Party accepting the same obligation:
       (a)   Submission of the dispute to the International Court of Justice; and/or
       (b)   Arbitration in accordance with procedures to be adopted by the Conference of the Parties as soon as practicable, in an annex on arbitration.
       A Party which is a regional economic integration organization may make a declaration with like effect in relation to arbitration in accordance with the procedures referred to in subparagraph (b) above.
3.   A declaration made under paragraph 2 above shall remain in force until it expires in accordance with its terms or until three months after written notice of its revocation has been deposited with the Depositary.
4.   A new declaration, a notice of revocation or the expiry of a declaration shall not in any way affect proceedings pending before the International Court of Justice or the arbitral tribunal, unless the parties to the dispute otherwise agree.
5.   Subject to the operation of paragraph 2 above, if after twelve months following notification by one Party to another that a dispute exists between them, the Parties concerned have not been able to settle their dispute through the means mentioned in paragraph 1 above, the dispute shall be submitted, at the request of any of the parties to the dispute, to conciliation.
6.   A conciliation commission shall be created upon the request of one of the parties to the dispute. The commission shall be composed of an equal number of members appointed by each party concerned and a chairman chosen jointly by the members appointed by each party. The commission shall render a recommendatory award, which the parties shall consider in good faith.

1992 Convention on Biological Diversity, 1760 UNTS 79

Article 27. Settlement of Disputes

1. In the event of a dispute between Contracting Parties concerning the interpretation or application of this Convention, the parties concerned shall seek solution by negotiation.
2. If the parties concerned cannot reach agreement by negotiation, they may jointly seek the good offices of, or request mediation by, a third party.
3. When ratifying, accepting, approving or acceding to this Convention, or at any time thereafter, a State or regional economic integration organization may declare in writing to the Depositary that for a dispute not resolved in accordance with paragraph 1 or paragraph 2 above, it accepts one or both of the following means of dispute settlement as compulsory:
    (a) Arbitration in accordance with the procedure laid down in Part 1 of Annex II;
    (b) Submission of the dispute to the International Court of Justice.
4. If the parties to the dispute have not. in accordance with paragraph 3 above, accepted the same or any procedure, the dispute shall be submitted to conciliation in accordance with Part 2 of Annex II unless the parties otherwise agree.
5. The provisions of this Article shall apply with respect to any protocol except as otherwise provided in the protocol concerned.

1998 Rotterdam Convention on the Prior Informed Consent Procedure for Certain Hazardous Chemicals and Pesticides in International Trade, 2244 UNTS 337

ARTICLE 20 Settlement of disputes

1. Parties shall settle any dispute between them concerning the interpretation or application of this Convention through negotiation or other peaceful means of their own choice.
2. When ratifying, accepting, approving or acceding to this Convention, or at any time thereafter, a Party that is not a regional economic integration organization may declare in a written instrument submitted to the Depositary that, with respect to any dispute concerning the interpretation or application of the Convention, it recognizes one or both of the following means of dispute settlement as compulsory in relation to any Party accepting the same obligation:
    (a) Arbitration in accordance with procedures to be adopted by the Conference of the Parties in an annex as soon as practicable; and
    (b) Submission of the dispute to the International Court of Justice.
3. A Party that is a regional economic integration organization may make a declaration with like effect in relation to arbitration in accordance with the procedure referred to in paragraph 2 (a).
4. A declaration made pursuant to paragraph 2 shall remain in force until it expires in accordance with its terms or until three months after written notice of its revocation has been deposited with the Depositary.
5. The expiry of a declaration, a notice of revocation or a new declaration shall not in any way affect proceedings pending before an arbitral tribunal or the International Court of Justice unless the parties to the dispute otherwise agree.

6. If the parties to a dispute have not accepted the same or any procedure pursuant to paragraph 2, and if they have not been able to settle their dispute within twelve months following notification by one party to another that a dispute exists between them, the dispute shall be submitted to a conciliation commission at the request of any party to the dispute. The conciliation commission shall render a report with recommendations. Additional procedures relating to the conciliation commission shall be included in an annex to be adopted by the Conference of the Parties no later than the second meeting of the Conference.

2001 Stockholm Convention on Persistent Organic Pollutants, 2256 UNTS 119

ARTICLE 18 Settlement of disputes

1. Parties shall settle any dispute between them concerning the interpretation or application of this Convention through negotiation or other peaceful means of their own choice.
2. When ratifying, accepting, approving or acceding to the Convention, or at any time thereafter, a Party that is not a regional economic integration organization may declare in a written instrument submitted to the depositary that, with respect to any dispute concerning the interpretation or application of the Convention, it recognizes one or both of the following means of dispute settlement as compulsory in relation to any Party accepting the same obligation:

    (a) Arbitration in accordance with procedures to be adopted by the Conference of the Parties in an annex as soon as practicable;

    (b) Submission of the dispute to the International Court of Justice.
3. A Party that is a regional economic integration organization may make a declaration with like effect in relation to arbitration in accordance with the procedure referred to in paragraph 2 (a).
4. A declaration made pursuant to paragraph 2 or paragraph 3 shall remain in force until it expires in accordance with its terms or until three months after written notice of its revocation has been deposited with the depositary.
5. The expiry of a declaration, a notice of revocation or a new declaration shall not in any way affect proceedings pending before an arbitral tribunal or the International Court of Justice unless the parties to the dispute otherwise agree.
6. If the parties to a dispute have not accepted the same or any procedure pursuant to paragraph 2, and if they have not been able to settle their dispute within twelve months following notification by one party to another that a dispute exists between them, the dispute shall be submitted to a conciliation commission at the request of any party to the dispute. The conciliation commission shall render a report with recommendations. Additional procedures relating to the conciliation commission shall be included in an annex to be adopted by the Conference of the Parties no later than at its second meeting.

19.3 CASE LAW

19.3.1 Negotiation and Consultation

CASE
ICJ, *Fisheries Jurisdiction (United Kingdom v. Iceland)*, Merits, Judgment, ICJ
Reports 3 (1974)

31. A series of negotiations between representatives of the two countries soon followed
and continued throughout May, June and July 1972, in the course of which various
proposals for catch-limitation, fishing effort limitation. area or seasonal restrictions
for United Kingdom vessels were discussed, in the hope of arriving at practical arrangements for an interim régime pending the settlement of the dispute. By 12 July
there was still no agreement on such an interim régime, and the Icelandic delegation
announced that new Regulations would be issued on 14 July 1972 which would
exclude all foreign vessels from fishing within the 50-mile limit after 1 September
1972. The United Kingdom delegation replied that, while ready to continue the
discussions for an interim régime, they reserved the United Kingdom's rights in
areas outside the 12-mile limit and would seek an Order for interim measures of
protection from the Court. The new Regulations, issued on 14 July 1972, extended Iceland's fishery limits to 50 miles as from 1 September 1972 and, by Article 2,
prohibited all fishing activities by foreign vessels inside those limits. Consequently,
on 19 July 1972, the United Kingdom filed its request for the indication of interim
measures of protection.

[...]

33. On 17 August 1972 the Court made an Order for provisional measures in which,
inter alia, it indicated that, pending the Court's final decision in the proceedings,
Iceland should refrain from taking any measures to enforce the Regulations of 14
July 1972 against United Kingdom vessels engaged in fishing outside the 12-mile
fishery zone; and that the United Kingdom should limit the annual catch of its
vessels in the "Sea Area of Iceland" to 170,000 tons. That the United Kingdom has
complied with the terms of the catch-limitation measure indicated in the Court's
Order has not been questioned or disputed. Iceland, on the other hand, notwithstanding the measures indicated by the Court, began to enforce the new Regulations
against United Kingdom vessels soon after they came into effect on 1 September
1972. Moreover, when in August 1972 the United Kingdom made it clear to Iceland
that in its view any settlement between the parties of an interim régime should be
compatible with the Court's Order, Iceland replied on 30 August that it would not
consider the Order to be binding upon it "since the Court has no jurisdiction in the
matter".

> **CASE**
> RIAA, *Lake Lanoux Arbitration (France v. Spain)*, Arbitral Tribunal, 12 RIAA 281;
> 24 ILR 101 (16 November 1957)

128: The reality of the obligations thus undertaken is incontestable and sanctions can be applied in the event, for example, of an unjustified breaking off of the discussion, abnormal delays, disregard of the agreed procedures, systematic refusals to take into consideration adverse proposals or interests, and more generally, in cases violation of the rules of good faith.

19.3.2 Judicial Dispute Settlement

> **CASE**
> ICJ, *Gabčíkovo-Nagymaros Project (Hungary v. Slovakia)*, ICJ Reports 7 (1997)

140. It is clear that the Project's impact upon, and its implications for, the environment are of necessity a key issue. The numerous scientific reports which have been presented to the Court by the Parties – even if their conclusions are often contradictory – provide abundant evidence that this impact and these implications are considerable.

In order to evaluate the environmental risks, current standards must be taken into consideration. This is not only allowed by the wording of Articles 15 and 19, but even prescribed, to the extent that these articles impose a continuing – and thus necessarily evolving – obligation on the parties to maintain the quality of the water of the Danube and to protect nature. The Court is mindful that, in the field of environmental protection, vigilance and prevention are required on account of the often irreversible character of damage to the environment and of the limitations inherent in the very mechanism of reparation of this type of damage.

Throughout the ages, mankind has, for economic and other reasons, constantly interfered with nature. In the past, this was often done without consideration of the effects upon the environment. Owing to new scientific insights and to a growing awareness of the risks for mankind – for present and future generations – of pursuit of such interventions at an unconsidered and unabated pace, new norms and standards have been developed, set forth in a great number of instruments during the last two decades. Such new norms have to be taken into consideration, and such new standards given proper weight, not only when States contemplate new activities but also when continuing with activities begun in the past. This need to reconcile economic development with protection of the environment is aptly expressed in the concept of sustainable development.

For the purposes of the present case, this means that the Parties together should look afresh at the effects on the environment of the operation of the Gabčikovo power plant. In particular they must find a satisfactory solution for the volume of water to be released into the old bed of the Danube and into the side-arms on both sides of the river.

141. It is not for the Court to determine what shall be the final result of these negotiations to be conducted by the Parties. It is for the Parties themselves to find an
agreed solution that takes account of the objectives of the Treaty, which must be
pursued in a joint and integrated way, as well as the norms of international environmental law and the principles of the law of international watercourses. The Court
will recall in this context that, as it said in the North Sea Continental Shelf cases:
"[the Parties] are under an obligation so to conduct themselves that the negotiations
are meaningful, which will not be the case when either of them insists upon its own
position without contemplating any modification of it" (ICJ Reports 1969, p. 47,
para. 85).

19.3.3 Advisory Opinions

ADVISORY OPINION
ICJ, Legality of the Threat or Use of Nuclear Weapons, Advisory Opinion, ICJ
Reports 226 (1996)

27. In both their written and oral statements, some States furthermore argued that any
use of nuclear weapons would be unlawful by reference to existing norms relating
to the safeguarding and protection of the environment, in view of their essential
importance. Specific references were made to various existing international treaties and instruments. These included Additional Protocol 1 of 1977 to the Geneva
Conventions of 1949, Article 35, paragraph 3, of which prohibits the employment
of "methods or means of warfare which are intended, or may be expected, to cause
widespread, long-term and severe damage to the natural environment"; and the
Convention of 18 May 1977 on the Prohibition of Military or Any Other Hostile Use
of Environmental Modification Techniques, which prohibits the use of weapons
which have "widespread, long-lasting or severe effects" on the environment (Art. 1).
Also cited were Principle 21 of the Stockholm Declaration of 1972 and Principle 2
of the Rio Declaration of 1992 which express the common conviction of the States
concerned that they have a duty "to ensure that activities within their jurisdiction or
control do not cause damage to the environment of other States or of areas beyond
the limits of national jurisdiction". These instruments and other provisions relating to the protection and safeguarding of the environment were said to apply at all
times, in war as well as in peace, and it was contended that they would be violated by the use of nuclear weapons whose consequences would be widespread and
would have transboundary effects.

28. Other States questioned the binding legal quality of these precepts of environmental
law; or, in the context of the Convention on the Prohibition of Military or Any Other
Hostile Use of Environmental Modification Techniques, denied that it was concerned
at all with the use of nuclear weapons in hostilities; or, in the case of Additional
Protocol 1, denied that they were generally bound by its terms, or recalled that they
had reserved their position in respect of Article 35, paragraph 3, thereof. It was
also argued by some States that the principal purpose of environmental treaties and

norms was the protection of the environment in time of peace. It was said that those treaties made no mention of nuclear weapons. It was also pointed out that warfare in general, and nuclear warfare in particular, were not mentioned in their texts and that it would be destabilizing to the rule of law and to confidence in international negotiations if those treaties were now interpreted in such a way as to prohibit the use of nuclear weapons.

29. The Court recognizes that the environment is under daily threat and that the use of nuclear weapons could constitute a catastrophe for the environment. The Court also recognizes that the environment is not an abstraction but represents the living space, the quality of life and the very health of human beings, including generations unborn. The existence of the general obligation of States to ensure that activities within their jurisdiction and control respect the environment of other States or of areas beyond national control is now part of the corpus of international law relating to the environment.

30. However, the Court is of the view that the issue is not whether the treaties relating to the protection of the environment are or are not applicable during an armed conflict, but rather whether the obligations stemming from these treaties were intended to be obligations of total restraint during military conflict. The Court does not consider that the treaties in question could have intended to deprive a State of the exercise of its right of self-defence under international law because of its obligations to protect the environment. Nonetheless, States must take environmental considerations into account when assessing what is necessary and proportionate in the pursuit of legitimate military objectives. Respect for the environment is one of the elements that go to assessing whether an action is in conformity with the principles of necessity and proportionality. This approach is supported, indeed, by the terms of Principle 24 of the Rio Declaration, which provides that: "Warfare is inherently destructive of sustainable development. States shall therefore respect international law providing protection for the environment in times of armed conflict and cooperate in its further development, as necessary."

31. The Court notes furthermore that Articles 35, paragraph 3, and 55 of Additional Protocol 1 provide additional protection for the environment. Taken together, these provisions embody a general obligation to protect the natural environment against widespread, long-term and severe environmental damage; the prohibition of methods and means of war- fare which are intended, or may be expected, to cause such damage; and the prohibition of attacks against the natural environment by way of reprisals. These are powerful constraints for all the States having subscribed to these provisions

32. General Assembly resolution 47/37 of 25 November 1992 on the "Protection of the Environment in Times of Armed Conflict" is also of interest in this context. It affirms the general view according to which environmental considerations constitute one of the elements to be taken into account in the implementation of the principles of the law applicable in armed conflict: it states that "destruction of the environment, not justified by military necessity and carried out wantonly, is clearly contrary to existing international law". Addressing the reality that certain instruments are not yet binding on all States, the General Assembly in this resolution "appeals to all States

that have not yet done so to consider becoming parties to the relevant international conventions".

[...]

33. The Court thus finds that while the existing international law relating to the protection and safeguarding of the environment does not specifically prohibit the use of nuclear weapons, it indicates important environmental factors that are properly to be taken into account in the context of the implementation of the principles and rules of the law applicable in armed conflict.

34. In the light of the foregoing the Court concludes that the most directly relevant applicable law governing the question of which it was seised, is that relating to the use of force enshrined in the United Nations Charter and the law applicable in armed conflict which regulates the conduct of hostilities, together with any specific treaties on nuclear weapons that the Court might determine to be relevant

19.3.4 ITLOS

CASE
ITLOS, *MOX Plant (Ireland v. United Kingdom)*, Provisional Measures, Case No. 10, ITLOS Reports 95 (3 December 2001)

84. Considering that, in the view of the Tribunal, prudence and caution require that Ireland and the United Kingdom cooperate in exchanging information concerning risks or effects of the operation of the MOX plant and in devising ways to deal with them, as appropriate.

CASE
ITLOS, *"Volga" (Russian Federation v. Australia)*, Prompt Release Judgment, ITLOS Reports 10 (2002)

68. The Tribunal takes note of the submissions of the Respondent. The Tribunal understands the international concerns about illegal, unregulated and unreported fishing and appreciates the objectives behind the measures taken by States, including the States Parties to CCAMLR, to deal with the problem.

ADVISORY OPINION
ITLOS, Responsibilities and Obligations of States Sponsoring Persons and Entities with Respect to Activities in the Area, Advisory Opinion, Case No. 17, ITLOS Reports 10 (Seabed Dispute Chamber) (1 February 2011)

147. With respect to customary international law, the ICJ, in its Judgment in Pulp Mills on the River Uruguay, speaks of: a practice, which in recent years has gained so

much acceptance among States that it may now be considered a requirement under general international law to undertake an environmental impact assessment where there is a risk that the proposed industrial activity may have a significant adverse impact in a transboundary context, in particular, on a shared resource. Moreover, due diligence, and the duty of vigilance and prevention which it implies, would not be considered to have been exercised, if a party planning works liable to affect the régime of the river or the quality of its waters did not undertake an environmental impact assessment on the potential effects of such works. (Paragraph 204)

148. Although aimed at the specific situation under discussion by the Court, the language used seems broad enough to cover activities in the Area even beyond the scope of the Regulations. The Court's reasoning in a transboundary context may also apply to activities with an impact on the environment in an area beyond the limits of national jurisdiction; and the Court's references to "shared resources" may also apply to resources that are the common heritage of mankind. Thus, in light of the customary rule mentioned by the ICJ, it may be considered that environmental impact assessments should be included in the system of consultations and prior notifications set out in article 142 of the Convention with respect to "resource deposits in the Area which lie across limits of national jurisdiction".

QUESTIONS

1. Should there be an international environment court?
2. Do you think that non-adversarial methods of dispute settlement are better for friendly relations between states for environmental law?
3. Critically assess the roles of the International Court of Justice and the International Tribunal for the Law of the Sea in being a competent forum for settling environmental disputes.

FURTHER READING

BOOKS

M Bowman and A Boyle (eds), *Environmental Damage in International and Comparative Law: Problems of Definition and Evaluation* (Oxford University Press 2002)

J Collier and V Lowe, *The Settlement of Disputes in International Law* (Oxford University Press 1999)

S Forlati, M Moïse Mbengue and B McGarry (eds), *The Gabčíkovo-Nagymaros Judgment and Its Contribution to the Development of International Law* (Brill 2020)

C Romano, *The Peaceful Settlement of International Environmental Disputes: A Pragmatic Approach* (Kluwer 2000)

T Stephens, *International Courts and Environmental Protection* (Cambridge University Press 2009)

CHAPTERS

A Boyle, 'Environmental Dispute Settlement' in *Max Planck Encyclopedia of Public International Law* (2009)

M Fitzmaurice, 'Environmental Law and the International Court of Justice' in V Lowe and M Fitzmaurice (eds), *Fifty Years of the International Court of Justice* (Cambridge University Press 1996)

A Lehman, 'International Environmental Court' in *Max Planck Encylopedia of Public International Law* (2018)

T Meshel, 'Optional Rules for Arbitration of Disputes Relating to Natural Resources and/or the Environment: Permanent Court of Arbitration (PCA)' in *Max Planck Encyclopedia of Public International Law* (2016)

T Stephens, 'The Settlement of Disputes in International Environmental Law' in E Techera, J Lindley, K Scott and A Telesetsky (eds), *Routledge Handbook of International Law* (2nd edn, Routledge 2020)

ARTICLES

A Akhtarkhavari, 'Power, Environmental Principles and the International Court of Justice' (2009) Australian Yearbook of International Law 91

R Bilder, 'The Settlement of Disputes in the Field of International Law of the Environment' (1975) 144 Recueil des Cours 139

A Boyle, 'The Environmental Jurisprudence of the International Tribunal for the Law of the Sea' (2007) 22 International Journal of Marine and Coastal Law 369

A Boyle and J Harrison, 'Judicial Settlement of International Environmental Disputes: Current Problems' (2013) 4 Journal of International Dispute Settlement 245

M Doelle, 'Climate Change and the Use of the Dispute Settlement Regime of the Law of the Sea Convention' (2006) 37 Ocean Development and International Law 319

D French, 'Environmental Dispute Settlement: The First Signs of Spring?' (2007) 19 Hague Yearbook of International Law 3

R Jennings, 'The Role of the International Court of Justice in the Development of International Environmental Law' (1992) 1 Review of European Community and International Environmental Law 240

R Jennings, 'Need for an Environmental Court' (1992) 20 Environmental Policy and Law 312

N Klein, 'Litigation over Marine Resources: Lessons for the Law of the Sea, International Dispute Settlement and International Environmental Law' (2009) Australian Yearbook of International Law 131

M Koskenniemi, 'Peaceful Settlement of Environmental Disputes' (1991) 60 Nordic Journal of International Law 73

C Payne, 'Environmental Impact Assessment as a Duty under International Law: The International Court of Justice Judgment on Pulp Mills on the River Uruguay' (2010) 1 European Journal of Risk Regulation 317

A Postiglione, 'A More Efficient International Law on the Environment and Setting Up an International Court for the Environment within the United Nations' (1990) 20 Environmental Law 321

DP Ratliff, 'The PCA Optional Rules for Arbitration of Disputes Relating to Natural Resources and/or the Environment' (2001) 14 Leiden Journal of International Law 887

P Sands, 'International Courts and the Application of the Concept of "Sustainable Development"' (1999) 3 *Max Planck Yearbook of UN Law*

T Scovazzi, 'State Responsibility for Environmental Harm' (2001) 12 Yearbook of International Environmental Law 43

T Stephens, 'The Limits of International Adjudication in International Environmental Law: Another Perspective on the Southern Bluefin Tuna Case' (2004) 19 International Journal of Marine and Costal Law 177

E Valencia-Ospina, 'The International Court of Justice and International Environmental Law' (1992) 2 Asian YB Int'l L 1

J Viñuales, 'The Contribution of the International Court of Justice to the Development of International Environmental Law: A Contemporary Assessment' (2008) 32 Fordham International Law Journal 232

PART IV
ENVIRONMENTAL LAW AND INTERNATIONAL LAW

20
Trade and the environment

20.1 INTRODUCTION

International trade law has the capacity to overlap with international environmental law, and this gives rise to problems of regime interaction. The main reason for this is twofold: (1) international environmental law does, at times, place restrictions on trade; (2) trade law generally requires trade liberalisation, but it allows for exceptions related to human, animal or plant health, or the conservation of natural resources and thus scope for environmental considerations to operate within the trade regime. At the outset, it is important to recognise that the two regimes may either complement each other, or they may conflict. The problem of conflict may loom larger, but the interactions between the two regimes are not predicated upon a conflict. There is, moreover, a recognition that trade and the environment may also be 'mutually supportive': (1) trade can lead to transfers of more environmentally friendly technologies; (2) poverty and environmental degradation are closely connected, and wealth generated from free trade may alter behaviour in developing countries towards more environmentally friendly practices. Of course, given the great range of concerns covered by international environmental law, it may be that trade may be more supportive of certain sorts of environmental benefits than others – for example, while pollution from certain gases, such as sulphur dioxide, declines with economic development, production of carbon dioxide increases with economic development.[1] Furthermore, in some cases, trade itself may directly or indirectly be a cause of environmental harm.[2]

Interactions between trade and environment take place in two main contexts. First, an environmental treaty may take account of trade matters. Second, an environmental issue may arise under a trade treaty. With regard to the former, few environmental treaties directly take account of their interaction with trade. Some treaties, e.g., the Biosafety Protocol, recognise the mutual supportiveness of trade and the environment, but usually only in their preambles. In terms of substantive interactions, some environmental treaties seek to place restrictions on trade. This may be in the form of a requirement of prior informed consent for trade in a reg-

---

[1] D Bodansky and J Lawrence, 'Trade and the Environment' in Daniel Bethlehem, Isabelle Van Damme, Donald McRae, and Rodney Neufeld (eds), *The Oxford Handbook of International Trade Law* (OUP 2012).

[2] Ibid.

ulated substance. Alternatively, the treaty may ban the trade in particular substances outright. Examples of treaties of both types are provided in the first section of this chapter.

Even if an environmental treaty does not directly regulate trade, measures taken in order to meet targets under or attain the objectives of an environmental treaty may involve restrictions on trade. Where the particular type of trade restriction is *prima facie* prohibited, the question is whether *bona fide* environmental regulation constitutes an exception under the relevant trade treaty. The main institutional settings where such conflicts arise are in the multilateral trading system under the World Trade Organization and its associated treaty instruments. In the first place, this has the consequence that questions of trade and the environment tend to be raised within a trading context. This raises the prospect that a 'trade perspective' may dominate the evaluation of the proper balance. Second, the primary instruments under which the question of breach falls to be assessed are trade treaties. The three most significant of these are (i) the General Agreement on Tariffs and Trade 1994, (ii) the 1979 Agreement on Technical Barriers to Trade, and (iii) the 1994 Agreement on Sanitary and Phytosanitary Measures. The GATT provides restrictions on tariff barriers to trade, but within its exceptions it allows both for measures 'necessary to protect human, animal or plant life or health' and 'relating to the conservation of exhaustible natural resources'. The TBT Agreement, which covers product regulations, provides that measures to protect the environment constitute a legitimate objective of a technical barrier to trade. The SPS Agreement, which covers food safety and animal and plant health, is perhaps the most far-reaching of the trade agreements to engage with environmental matters. This allows for certain technical barriers, in particular where the measure is justified on a scientific basis or is in line with international norms and standards. In addition to its primary instruments, the WTO also set up a forum for the discussion for trade and environment interactions, named the Committee on Trade and Environment.

The third section of the chapter gives examples of the approach taken to trade and the environment in recent free trade agreements. There are chapters in these treaties dedicated to the protection of the environment. These can expressly cover a wide range of environmental topics, from ozone pollution to illegal fishing. Perhaps most significant are the following points: first, the provisions of the treaties seek explicitly to define the balance to be drawn between environmental concerns and the concern that environmental regulation might be used to undermine trade. Second, they seek to regulate the relationship between the trade agreement and other environmental treaties, including by committing parties to the implementation of certain other environmental treaties.[3]

---

[3]   See USMCA, art 24.8(4).

20.2   ENVIRONMENTAL TREATIES DEALING WITH TRADE

1973 Convention on International Trade in Endangered Species of Wild Fauna and Flora, 993 UNTS 243

Article II
Fundamental Principles
1.   Appendix I shall include all species threatened with extinction which are or may be affected by trade. Trade in specimens of these species must be subject to particularly strict regulation in order not to endanger further their survival and must only be authorized in exceptional circumstances.
2.   Appendix II shall include:
    (a)   all species which although not necessarily now threatened with extinction may become so unless trade in specimens of such species is subject to strict regulation in order to avoid utilization incompatible with their survival; and
    (b)   other species which must be subject to regulation in order that trade in specimens of certain species referred to in sub-paragraph (a) of this paragraph may be brought under effective control.
3.   Appendix III shall include all species which any Party identifies as being subject to regulation within its jurisdiction for the purpose of preventing or restricting exploitation, and as needing the co-operation of other Parties in the control of trade.
4.   The Parties shall not allow trade in specimens of species included in Appendices I, II and III except in accordance with the provisions of the present Convention.

[…]

Article X
Trade with States not Party to the Convention
Where export or re-export is to, or import is from, a State not a Party to the present Convention, comparable documentation issued by the competent authorities in that State which substantially conforms with the requirements of the present Convention for permits and certificates may be accepted in lieu thereof by any Party.

1987 Montreal Protocol on Substances that Deplete the Ozone Layer, 1522 UNTS 3

Article 4: Control of trade with non-Parties
1.   As of 1 January 1990, each party shall ban the import of the controlled substances in Annex A from any State not party to this Protocol.
1 *bis.*   Within one year of the date of the entry into force of this paragraph, each Party shall ban the import of the controlled substances in Annex B from any State not party to this Protocol.
1 *ter.*   Within one year of the date of entry into force of this paragraph, each Party shall ban the import of any controlled substances in Group II of Annex C from any State not party to this Protocol.

1 *qua.* Within one year of the date of entry into force of this paragraph, each Party shall ban the import of the controlled substance in Annex E from any State not party to this Protocol.

1 *quin.* As of 1 January 2004, each Party shall ban the import of the controlled substances in Group I of Annex C from any State not party to this Protocol.

1 *sex.* Within one year of the date of entry into force of this paragraph, each Party shall ban the import of the controlled substance in Group III of Annex C from any State not party to this Protocol.

1 *sept.* Upon entry into force of this paragraph, each Party shall ban the import of the controlled substances in Annex F from any State not Party to this Protocol.

2. As of 1 January 1993, each Party shall ban the export of any controlled substances in Annex A to any State not party to this Protocol.

2 *bis.* Commencing one year after the date of entry into force of this paragraph, each Party shall ban the export of any controlled substances in Annex B to any State not party to this Protocol.

2 *ter.* Commencing one year after the date of entry into force of this paragraph, each Party shall ban the export of any controlled substances in Group II of Annex C to any State not party to this Protocol.

2 *qua.* Commencing one year of the date of entry into force of this paragraph, each Party shall ban the export of the controlled substance in Annex E to any State not party to this Protocol.

2 *quin.* As of 1 January 2004, each Party shall ban the export of the controlled substances in Group I of Annex C to any State not party to this Protocol.

2 *sex.* Within one year of the date of entry into force of this paragraph, each Party shall ban the export of the controlled substance in Group III of Annex C to any State not party to this Protocol.

2 *sept.* Upon entry into force of this paragraph, each Party shall ban the export of the controlled substances in Annex F to any State not Party to this Protocol.

3. By 1 January 1992, the Parties shall, following the procedures in Article 10 of the Convention, elaborate in an annex a list of products containing controlled substances in Annex A. Parties that have not objected to the annex in accordance with those procedures shall ban, within one year of the annex having become effective, the import of those products from any State not party to this Protocol.

3 *bis.* Within three years of the date of the entry into force of this paragraph, the Parties shall, following the procedures in Article 10 of the Convention, elaborate in an annex a list of products containing controlled substances in Annex B. Parties that have not objected to the annex in accordance with those procedures shall ban, within one year of the annex having become effective, the import of those products from any State not party to this Protocol.

3 *ter.* Within three years of the date of entry into force of this paragraph, the Parties shall, following the procedures in Article 10 of the Convention, elaborate in an annex a list of products containing controlled substances in Group II of Annex C. Parties that have not objected to the annex in accordance with those procedures shall ban, within one year of the annex having become effective, the import of those products from any State not party to this Protocol.

4. By 1 January 1994, the Parties shall determine the feasibility of banning or restricting, from States not party to this Protocol, the import of products produced with,

but not containing, controlled substances in Annex A. If determined feasible, the Parties shall, following the procedures in Article 10 of the Convention, elaborate in an annex a list of such products. Parties that have not objected to the annex in accordance with those procedures shall ban or restrict, within one year of the annex having become effective, the import of those products from any State not party to this Protocol.

4 *bis.*   Within five years of the date of the entry into force of this paragraph, the Parties shall determine the feasibility of banning or restricting, from States not party to this Protocol, the import of products produced with, but not containing, controlled substances in Annex B. If determined feasible, the Parties shall, following the procedures in Article 10 of the Convention, elaborate in an annex a list of such products. Parties that have not objected to the annex in accordance with those procedures shall ban or restrict, within one year of the annex having become effective, the import of those products from any State not party to this Protocol.

4 *ter.*   Within five years of the date of entry into force of this paragraph, the Parties shall determine the feasibility of banning or restricting, from States not party to this Protocol, the import of products produced with, but not containing, controlled substances in Group II of Annex C. If determined feasible, the Parties shall, following the procedures in Article 10 of the Convention, elaborate in an annex a list of such products. Parties that have not objected to the annex in accordance with those procedures shall ban or restrict, within one year of the annex having become effective, the import of those products from any State not party to this Protocol.

5.   Each Party undertakes to the fullest practicable extent to discourage the export to any State not party to this Protocol of technology for producing and for utilizing controlled substances in Annexes A, B, C, E and F.

6.   Each Party shall refrain from providing new subsidies, aid, credits, guarantees or insurance programmes for the export to States not party to this Protocol of products, equipment, plants or technology that would facilitate the production of controlled substances in Annexes A, B, C, E and F.

7.   Paragraphs 5 and 6 shall not apply to products, equipment, plants or technology that improve the containment, recovery, recycling or destruction of controlled substances, promote the development of alternative substances, or otherwise contribute to the reduction of emissions of controlled substances in Annexes A, B, C, E and F.

8.   Notwithstanding the provisions of this Article, imports and exports referred to in paragraphs 1 to 4 *ter* of this Article may be permitted from, or to, any State not party to this Protocol, if that State is determined, by a meeting of the Parties, to be in full compliance with Article 2, Articles 2A to 2J and this Article, and have submitted data to that effect as specified in Article 7.

9.   For the purposes of this Article, the term "State not party to this Protocol" shall include, with respect to a particular controlled substance, a State or regional economic integration organization that has not agreed to be bound by the control measures in effect for that substance.

10.   By 1 January 1996, the Parties shall consider whether to amend this Protocol in order to extend the measures in this Article to trade in controlled substances in Group I of Annex C and in Annex E with States not party to the Protocol.

Article 4A: Control of trade with Parties
1.   Where, after the phase-out date applicable to it for a controlled substance, a Party is unable, despite having taken all practicable steps to comply with its obligation under the Protocol, to cease production of that substance for domestic consumption, other than for uses agreed by the Parties to be essential, it shall ban the export of used, recycled and reclaimed quantities of that substance, other than for the purpose of destruction.
2.   Paragraph 1 of this Article shall apply without prejudice to the operation of Article 11 of the Convention and the non-compliance procedure developed under Article 8 of the Protocol.

Article 4B: Licensing
1.   Each Party shall, by 1 January 2000 or within three months of the date of entry into force of this Article for it, whichever is the later, establish and implement a system for licensing the import and export of new, used, recycled and reclaimed controlled substances in Annexes A, B, C and E.
2.   Notwithstanding paragraph 1 of this Article, any Party operating under paragraph 1 of Article 5 which decides it is not in a position to establish and implement a system for licensing the import and export of controlled substances in Annexes C and E, may delay taking those actions until 1 January 2005 and 1 January 2002, respectively.
2 *bis*. Each Party shall, by 1 January 2019 or within three months of the date of entry into force of this paragraph for it, whichever is later, establish and implement a system for licensing the import and export of new, used, recycled and reclaimed controlled substances in Annex F. Any Party operating under paragraph 1 of Article 5 that decides it is not in a position to establish and implement such a system by 1 January 2019 may delay taking those actions until 1 January 2021.
3.   Each Party shall, within three months of the date of introducing its licensing system, report to the Secretariat on the establishment and operation of that system.
4.   The Secretariat shall periodically prepare and circulate to all Parties a list of the Parties that have reported to it on their licensing systems and shall forward this information to the Implementation Committee for consideration and appropriate recommendations to the Parties.

1989 Basel Convention on the Control of Transboundary Movements of Hazardous Wastes and their Disposal, 1673 UNTS 57

ARTICLE 4
GENERAL OBLIGATIONS
1.   (a)   Parties exercising their right to prohibit the import of hazardous wastes or other wastes for disposal shall inform the other Parties of their decision pursuant to Article 13.

(b)   Parties shall prohibit or shall not permit the export of hazardous wastes and other wastes to the Parties which have prohibited the import of such wastes, when notified pursuant to subparagraph (a) above.

(c)   Parties shall prohibit or shall not permit the export of hazardous wastes and other wastes if the State of import does not consent in writing to the specific import, in the case where that State of import has not prohibited the import of such wastes.

2.   Each Party shall take the appropriate measures to:

...

(d)   Ensure that the transboundary movement of hazardous wastes and other wastes is reduced to the minimum consistent with the environmentally sound and efficient management of such wastes, and is conducted in a manner which will protect human health and the environment against the adverse effects which may result from such movement;

...

(g)   Prevent the import of hazardous wastes and other wastes if it has reason to believe that the wastes in question will not be managed in an environmentally sound manner;

...

5.   A Party shall not permit hazardous wastes or other wastes to be exported to a non-Party or to be imported from a non-Party.

1998 Rotterdam Convention on the Prior Informed Consent Procedure for Certain Hazardous Chemicals and Pesticides in International Trade, 2244 UNTS 337

The Parties to this Convention,

Aware of the harmful impact on human health and the environment from certain hazardous chemicals and pesticides in international trade,

...

Desiring to ensure that hazardous chemicals that are exported from their territory are packaged and labelled in a manner that is adequately protective of human health and the environment, consistent with the principles of the Amended London Guidelines and the International Code of Conduct,

Recognizing that trade and environmental policies should be mutually supportive with a view to achieving sustainable development,

Emphasizing that nothing in this Convention shall be interpreted as implying in any way a change in the rights and obligations of a Party under any existing international agreement applying to chemicals in international trade or to environmental protection,

Understanding that the above recital is not intended to create a hierarchy between this Convention and other international agreements.

Determined to protect human health, including the health of consumers and workers, and the environment against potentially harmful impacts from certain hazardous chemicals and pesticides in international trade,

Have agreed as follows,

Article 1
Objective

The objective of this Convention is to promote shared responsibility and cooperative efforts among Parties in the international trade of certain hazardous chemicals in order to protect human health and the environment from potential harm and to contribute to their environmentally sound use, by facilitating information exchange about their characteristics, by providing for a national decision-making process on their import and export and by disseminating these decisions to Parties.

...

Article 5
Procedures for banned or severely restricted chemicals

1. Each Party that has adopted a final regulatory action shall notify the Secretariat in writing of such action. Such notification shall be made as soon as possible, and in any event no later than ninety days after the date on which the final regulatory action has taken effect, and shall contain the information required by Annex I, where available.

2. Each Party shall, at the date of entry into force of this Convention for it, notify the Secretariat in writing of its final regulatory actions in effect at that time, except that each Party that has submitted notifications of final regulatory actions under the Amended London Guidelines or the International Code of Conduct need not resubmit those notifications.

3. The Secretariat shall, as soon as possible, and in any event no later than six months after receipt of a notification under paragraphs 1 and 2, verify whether the notification contains the information required by Annex I. If the notification contains the information required, the Secretariat shall forthwith forward to all Parties a summary of the information received. If the notification does not contain the information required, it shall inform the notifying Party accordingly.

4. The Secretariat shall every six months communicate to the Parties a synopsis of the information received pursuant to paragraphs 1 and 2, including information regarding those notifications which do not contain all the information required by Annex I.

5. When the Secretariat has received at least one notification from each of two Prior Informed Consent regions regarding a particular chemical that it has verified meet the requirements of Annex I, it shall forward them to the Chemical Review Committee. The composition of the Prior Informed Consent regions shall be defined in a decision to be adopted by consensus at the first meeting of the Conference of the Parties.

6.   The Chemical Review Committee shall review the information provided in such notifications and, in accordance with the criteria set out in Annex II, recommend to the Conference of the Parties whether the chemical in question should be made subject to the Prior Informed Consent procedure and, accordingly, be listed in Annex III.

...

Article 12
Export notification
1.   Where a chemical that is banned or severely restricted by a Party is exported from its territory, that Party shall provide an export notification to the importing Party. The export notification shall include the information set out in Annex V.

2000 Cartagena Protocol on Biosafety to the Convention on Biological Diversity, 2226 UNTS 208

Recognizing that trade and environment agreements should be mutually supportive with a view to achieving sustainable development,

Article 7
APPLICATION OF THE ADVANCE INFORMED AGREEMENT PROCEDURE
1.   Subject to Articles 5 and 6, the advance informed agreement procedure in Articles 8 to 10 and 12 shall apply prior to the first intentional transboundary movement of living modified organisms for intentional introduction into the environment of the Party of import.

Article 10
DECISION PROCEDURE
...

2.   The Party of import shall, within the period of time referred to in Article 9, inform the notifier, in writing, whether the intentional transboundary movement may proceed:
   (a)   Only after the Party of import has given its written consent; or
   (b)   After no less than ninety days without a subsequent written consent.
3.   Within two hundred and seventy days of the date of receipt of notification, the Party of import shall communicate, in writing, to the notifier and to the Biosafety Clearing-House the decision referred to in paragraph 2 (a) above:
   (a)   Approving the import, with or without conditions, including how the decision will apply to subsequent imports of the same living modified organism;
   (b)   Prohibiting the import;
   (c)   Requesting additional relevant information in accordance with its domestic regulatory framework or Annex I; in calculating the time within which the Party of import is to respond, the number of days it has to wait for additional relevant information shall not be taken into account; or
   (d)   Informing the notifier that the period specified in this paragraph is extended by a defined period of time.

Article 11
PROCEDURE FOR LIVING MODIFIED ORGANISMS INTENDED FOR DIRECT USE AS FOOD OR FEED, OR FOR PROCESSING

1. A Party that makes a final decision regarding domestic use, including placing on the market, of a living modified organism that may be subject to transboundary movement for direct use as food or feed, or for processing shall, within fifteen days of making that decision, inform the Parties through the Biosafety Clearing-House. This information shall contain, at a minimum, the information specified in Annex II. The Party shall provide a copy of the information, in writing, to the national focal point of each Party that informs the Secretariat in advance that it does not have access to the Biosafety Clearing-House. This provision shall not apply to decisions regarding field trials.

2. The Party making a decision under paragraph 1 above, shall ensure that there is a legal requirement for the accuracy of information provided by the applicant.

3. Any Party may request additional information from the authority identified in paragraph (b) of Annex II.

4. A Party may take a decision on the import of living modified organisms intended for direct use as food or feed, or for processing, under its domestic regulatory framework that is consistent with the objective of this Protocol.

5. Each Party shall make available to the Biosafety Clearing-House copies of any national laws, regulations and guidelines applicable to the import of living modified organisms intended for direct use as food or feed, or for processing, if available.

...

8. Lack of scientific certainty due to insufficient relevant scientific information and knowledge regarding the extent of the potential adverse effects of a living modified organism on the conservation and sustainable use of biological diversity in the Party of import, taking also into account risks to human health, shall not prevent that Party from taking a decision, as appropriate, with regard to the import of that living modified organism intended for direct use as food or feed, or for processing, in order to avoid or minimize such potential adverse effects.

9. A Party may indicate its needs for financial and technical assistance and capacity-building with respect to living modified organisms intended for direct use as food or feed, or for processing. Parties shall cooperate to meet these needs in accordance with Articles 22 and 28.

Article 16
RISK MANAGEMENT

1. The Parties shall, taking into account Article 8 (g) of the Convention, establish and maintain appropriate mechanisms, measures and strategies to regulate, manage and control risks identified in the risk assessment provisions of this Protocol associated with the use, handling and transboundary movement of living modified organisms.

2. Measures based on risk assessment shall be imposed to the extent necessary to prevent adverse effects of the living modified organism on the conservation and

sustainable use of biological diversity, taking also into account risks to human health, within the territory of the Party of import.

3.   Each Party shall take appropriate measures to prevent unintentional transboundary movements of living modified organisms, including such measures as requiring a risk assessment to be carried out prior to the first release of a living modified organism.

2001 Stockholm Convention on Persistent Organic Pollutants, 2256 UNTS 119

ARTICLE 3
Measures to reduce or eliminate releases from intentional production and use
1.   Each Party shall:
(a)   Prohibit and/or take the legal and administrative measures necessary to eliminate:

[...]

(ii)   Its import and export of the chemicals listed in Annex A in accordance with the provisions of paragraph 2; and

2.   Each Party shall take measures to ensure:
(a)   That a chemical listed in Annex A or Annex B is imported only:
(i)   For the purpose of environmentally sound disposal as set forth in paragraph 1 (d) of Article 6; or
(ii)   For a use or purpose which is permitted for that Party under Annex A or Annex B;
(b)   That a chemical listed in Annex A for which any production or use specific exemption is in effect or a chemical listed in Annex B for which any production or use specific exemption or acceptable purpose is in effect, taking into account any relevant provisions in existing international prior informed consent instruments, is exported only:
(i)   For the purpose of environmentally sound disposal as set forth in paragraph 1 (d) of Article 6;
(ii)   To a Party which is permitted to use that chemical under Annex A or Annex B; or
(iii)   To a State not Party to this Convention which has provided an annual certification to the exporting Party. Such certification shall specify the intended use of the chemical and include a statement that, with respect to that chemical, the importing State is committed to:
a. Protect human health and the environment by taking the necessary measures to minimize or prevent releases;
b. Comply with the provisions of paragraph 1 of Article 6; and
c. Comply, where appropriate, with the provisions of paragraph 2 of Part II of Annex B.

The certification shall also include any appropriate supporting documentation, such as legislation, regulatory instruments, or administrative or policy guidelines.

The exporting Party shall transmit the certification to the Secretariat within sixty days of receipt.

(c) That a chemical listed in Annex A, for which production and use specific exemptions are no longer in effect for any Party, is not exported from it except for the purpose of environmentally sound disposal as set forth in paragraph 1 (d) of Article 6;

(d) For the purposes of this paragraph, the term "State not Party to this Convention" shall include, with respect to a particular chemical, a State or regional economic integration organization that has not agreed to be bound by the Convention with respect to that chemical.

20.3   WTO LAW

20.3.1   Legal Instruments

1994 General Agreement on Tariffs and Trade, 1867 UNTS 187

Article III: National Treatment on Internal Taxation and Regulation

1. The contracting parties recognize that internal taxes and other internal charges, and laws, regulations and requirements affecting the internal sale, offering for sale, purchase, transportation, distribution or use of products, and internal quantitative regulations requiring the mixture, processing or use of products in specified amounts or proportions, should not be applied to imported or domestic products so as to afford protection to domestic production.

2. The products of the territory of any contracting party imported into the territory of any other contracting party shall not be subject, directly or indirectly, to internal taxes or other internal charges of any kind in excess of those applied, directly or indirectly, to like domestic products. Moreover, no contracting party shall otherwise apply internal taxes or other internal charges to imported or domestic products in a manner contrary to the principles set forth in paragraph 1.

[...]

5. No contracting party shall establish or maintain any internal quantitative regulation relating to the mixture, processing or use of products in specified amounts or proportions which requires, directly or indirectly, that any specified amount or proportion of any product which is the subject of the regulation must be supplied from domestic sources. Moreover, no contracting party shall otherwise apply internal quantitative regulations in a manner contrary to the principles set forth in paragraph 1.

Article XI: General Elimination of Quantitative Restrictions

1. No prohibitions or restrictions other than duties, taxes or other charges, whether made effective through quotas, import or export licences or other measures, shall be instituted or maintained by any contracting party on the importation of any

product of the territory of any other contracting party or on the exportation or sale for export of any product destined for the territory of any other contracting party.

Article XX: General Exceptions

Subject to the requirement that such measures are not applied in a manner which would constitute a means of arbitrary or unjustifiable discrimination between countries where the same conditions prevail, or a disguised restriction on international trade, nothing in this Agreement shall be construed to prevent the adoption or enforcement by any contracting party of measures:

(a)   necessary to protect public morals;

(b)   necessary to protect human, animal or plant life or health;

...

(g)   relating to the conservation of exhaustible natural resources if such measures are made effective in conjunction with restrictions on domestic production or consumption;

1994 WTO Agreement on Technical Barriers to Trade, 1868 UNTS 120

Article 2: Preparation, Adoption and Application of Technical Regulations by Central Government Bodies

With respect to their central government bodies:

2.1   Members shall ensure that in respect of technical regulations, products imported from the territory of any Member shall be accorded treatment no less favourable than that accorded to like products of national origin and to like products originating in any other country.

2.2   Members shall ensure that technical regulations are not prepared, adopted or applied with a view to or with the effect of creating unnecessary obstacles to international trade. For this purpose, technical regulations shall not be more trade-restrictive than necessary to fulfil a legitimate objective, taking account of the risks non-fulfilment would create. Such legitimate objectives are, *inter alia:* national security requirements; the prevention of deceptive practices; protection of human health or safety, animal or plant life or health, or the environment. In assessing such risks, relevant elements of consideration are, *inter alia:* available scientific and technical information, related processing technology or intended end-uses of products.

1994 WTO Agreement on the Application of Sanitary and Phytosanitary Measures, 1867 UNTS 493

Article 2

Basic Rights and Obligations

1.   Members have the right to take sanitary and phytosanitary measures necessary for the protection of human, animal or plant life or health, provided that such measures are not inconsistent with the provisions of this Agreement.

2.   Members shall ensure that any sanitary or phytosanitary measure is applied only to the extent necessary to protect human, animal or plant life or health, is based on

scientific principles and is not maintained without sufficient scientific evidence, except as provided for in paragraph 7 of Article 5.

3. Members shall ensure that their sanitary and phytosanitary measures do not arbitrarily or unjustifiably discriminate between Members where identical or similar conditions prevail, including between their own territory and that of other Members. Sanitary and phytosanitary measures shall not be applied in a manner which would constitute a disguised restriction on international trade.

4. Sanitary or phytosanitary measures which conform to the relevant provisions of this Agreement shall be presumed to be in accordance with the obligations of the Members under the provisions of GATT 1994 which relate to the use of sanitary or phytosanitary measures, in particular the provisions of Article XX(b).

Article 3

Harmonization

1. To harmonize sanitary and phytosanitary measures on as wide a basis as possible, Members shall base their sanitary or phytosanitary measures on international standards, guidelines or recommendations, where they exist, except as otherwise provided for in this Agreement, and in particular in paragraph 3.

2. Sanitary or phytosanitary measures which conform to international standards, guidelines or recommendations shall be deemed to be necessary to protect human, animal or plant life or health, and presumed to be consistent with the relevant provisions of this Agreement and of GATT 1994.

3. Members may introduce or maintain sanitary or phytosanitary measures which result in a higher level of sanitary or phytosanitary protection than would be achieved by measures based on the relevant international standards, guidelines or recommendations, if there is a scientific justification, or as a consequence of the level of sanitary or phytosanitary protection a Member determines to be appropriate in accordance with the relevant provisions of paragraphs 1 through 8 of Article 5.(2) Notwithstanding the above, all measures which result in a level of sanitary or phytosanitary protection different from that which would be achieved by measures based on international standards, guidelines or recommendations shall not be inconsistent with any other provision of this Agreement.

Article 5

Assessment of Risk and Determination of the Appropriate Level of Sanitary or Phytosanitary Protection

1. Members shall ensure that their sanitary or phytosanitary measures are based on an assessment, as appropriate to the circumstances, of the risks to human, animal or plant life or health, taking into account risk assessment techniques developed by the relevant international organizations.

2. In the assessment of risks, Members shall take into account available scientific evidence; relevant processes and production methods; relevant inspection, sampling and testing methods; prevalence of specific diseases or pests; existence of pest — or disease — free areas; relevant ecological and environmental conditions; and quarantine or other treatment.

3. In assessing the risk to animal or plant life or health and determining the measure to be applied for achieving the appropriate level of sanitary or phytosanitary

protection from such risk, Members shall take into account as relevant economic factors: the potential damage in terms of loss of production or sales in the event of the entry, establishment or spread of a pest or disease; the costs of control or eradication in the territory of the importing Member; and the relative cost-effectiveness of alternative approaches to limiting risks.

4.   Members should, when determining the appropriate level of sanitary or phytosanitary protection, take into account the objective of minimizing negative trade effects.

Article 10
Special and Differential Treatment
1.   In the preparation and application of sanitary or phytosanitary measures, Members shall take account of the special needs of developing country Members, and in particular of the least-developed country Members.

20.3.2   Case Law

CASE
ILM, *United States, Reformulated Gasoline*, 35 ILM 603 (1996)

Taken together, the second clause of Article XX(g) appears to us to refer to governmental measures like the baseline establishment rules being promulgated or brought into effect together with restrictions on domestic production or consumption of natural resources. Put in a slightly different manner, we believe that the clause "if such measures are made effective in conjunction with restrictions on domestic product or consumption" is appropriately read as a requirement that the measures concerned impose restrictions, not just in respect of imported gasoline but also with respect to domestic gasoline. The clause is a requirement of even-handedness in the imposition of restrictions, in the name of conservation, upon the production or consumption of exhaustible natural resources.

There is, of course, no textual basis for requiring identical treatment of domestic and imported products. Indeed, where there is identity of treatment – constituting real, not merely formal, equality of treatment – it is difficult to see how inconsistency with Article III:4 would have arisen in the first place. On the other hand, if no restrictions on domestically-produced like products are imposed at all, and all limitations are placed upon imported products alone, the measure cannot be accepted as primarily or even substantially designed for implementing conservationist goals.[42] The measure would simply be naked discrimination for protecting locally-produced goods.

...

The chapeau, it will be seen, prohibits such application of a measure at issue (otherwise falling within the scope of Article XX(g)) as would constitute
(a) "arbitrary discrimination" (between countries where the same conditions prevail);
(b) "unjustifiable discrimination" (with the same qualifier); or
(c) "disguised restriction" on international trade.

...

"Arbitrary discrimination", "unjustifiable discrimination" and "disguised restriction" on international trade may, accordingly, be read side-by-side; they impart meaning to one another. It is clear to us that "disguised restriction" includes disguised discrimination in international trade. It is equally clear that concealed or unannounced restriction or discrimination in international trade does not exhaust the meaning of "disguised restriction." We consider that "disguised restriction", whatever else it covers, may properly be read as embracing restrictions amounting to arbitrary or unjustifiable discrimination in international trade taken under the guise of a measure formally within the terms of an exception listed in Article XX. Put in a somewhat different manner, the kinds of considerations pertinent in deciding whether the application of a particular measure amounts to "arbitrary or unjustifiable discrimination", may also be taken into account in determining the presence of a "disguised restriction" on international trade. The fundamental theme is to be found in the purpose and object of avoiding abuse or illegitimate use of the exceptions to substantive rules available in Article XX.

CASE
ILM, *United States - Import Prohibition of Certain Shrimp and Shrimp Products*, 38 ILM 118 (12 October 1998)

127. We begin with the threshold question of whether Section 609 is a measure concerned with the conservation of "exhaustible natural resources" within the meaning of Article XX(g).

...

128. ... Textually, Article XX(g) is not limited to the conservation of "mineral" or "non-living" natural resources. The complainants' principal argument is rooted in the notion that "living" natural resources are "renewable" and therefore cannot be "exhaustible" natural resources. We do not believe that "exhaustible" natural resources and "renewable" natural resources are mutually exclusive. One lesson that modern biological sciences teach us is that living species, though in principle, capable of reproduction and, in that sense, "renewable", are in certain circumstances indeed susceptible of depletion, exhaustion and extinction, frequently because of human activities. Living resources are just as "finite" as petroleum, iron ore and other non-living resources.

129. The words of Article XX(g), "exhaustible natural resources", were actually crafted more than 50 years ago. They must be read by a treaty interpreter in the light of contemporary concerns of the community of nations about the protection and conservation of the environment. While Article XX was not modified in the Uruguay Round, the preamble attached to the WTO Agreement shows that the signatories to that Agreement were, in 1994, fully aware of the importance and legitimacy of environmental protection as a goal of national and international policy. The preamble of the WTO Agreement – which informs not only the GATT 1994, but also the other covered agreements – explicitly acknowledges "the objective of sustainable development"[107]:

...

130. From the perspective embodied in the preamble of the WTO Agreement, we note that the generic term "natural resources" in Article XX(g) is not "static" in its content or reference but is rather "by definition, evolutionary". It is, therefore, pertinent to note that modern international conventions and declarations make frequent references to natural resources as embracing both living and non-living resources. For instance, the 1982 United Nations Convention on the Law of the Sea ("UNCLOS"), in defining the jurisdictional rights of coastal states in their exclusive economic zones, provides:

ARTICLE 56

Rights, jurisdiction and duties of the coastal State in the exclusive economic zone
1.   In the exclusive economic zone, the coastal State has:
    (a)   sovereign rights for the purpose of exploring and exploiting, conserving and managing the *natural resources, whether living or non-living*, of the waters superjacent to the sea-bed and of the sea-bed and its subsoil, ...(emphasis added)
The UNCLOS also repeatedly refers in Articles 61 and 62 to "living resources" in specifying rights and duties of states in their exclusive economic zones. The Convention on Biological Diversity uses the concept of "biological resources". Agenda 21 speaks most broadly of "natural resources" and goes into detailed statements about "marine living resources". In addition, the Resolution on Assistance to Developing Countries, adopted in conjunction with the Convention on the Conservation of Migratory Species of Wild Animals, recites:

> Conscious that an important element of development lies in the conservation and management of *living natural resources* and that migratory species constitute a significant part of these resources;... (emphasis added)

131. Given the recent acknowledgement by the international community of the importance of concerted bilateral or multilateral action to protect living natural resources, and recalling the explicit recognition by WTO Members of the objective of sustainable development in the preamble of the WTO Agreement, we believe it is too late in the day to suppose that Article XX(g) of the GATT 1994 may be read as referring only to the conservation of exhaustible mineral or other non-living natural resources. Moreover, two adopted GATT 1947 panel reports previously found fish to be an "exhaustible natural resource" within the meaning of Article XX(g). We hold that, in line with the principle of effectiveness in treaty interpretation, measures to conserve exhaustible natural resources, whether living or non-living, may fall within Article XX(g).

132. We turn next to the issue of whether the living natural resources sought to be conserved by the measure are "exhaustible" under Article XX(g). That this element is

present in respect of the five species of sea turtles here involved appears to be con-ceded by all the participants and third participants in this case. The exhaustibility of sea turtles would in fact have been very difficult to controvert since all of the seven recognized species of sea turtles are today listed in Appendix 1 of the Convention on International Trade in Endangered Species of Wild Fauna and Flora ("CITES"). The list in Appendix 1 includes "all species *threatened with extinction* which are or may be affected by trade." (emphasis added)

CASE
EC, *Measures Affecting Asbestos and Asbestos-Containing Products*, WT/DS135/AB/R (12 March 2001)

167. As for Canada's second argument, relating to "quantification" of the risk, we con-sider that, as with the SPS Agreement, there is no requirement under Article XX(b) of the GATT 1994 to quantify, as such, the risk to human life or health.[156] A risk may be evaluated either in quantitative or qualitative terms. In this case, contrary to what is suggested by Canada, the Panel assessed the nature and the character of the risk posed by chrysotile-cement products. The Panel found, on the basis of the scientific evidence, that "no minimum threshold of level of exposure or duration of exposure has been identified with regard to the risk of pathologies associated with chrysotile, except for asbestosis."[157] The pathologies which the Panel identified as being associated with chrysotile are of a very serious nature, namely lung cancer and mesothelioma, which is also a form of cancer.[158] Therefore, we do not agree with Canada that the Panel merely relied on the French authorities' "hypotheses" of the risk.

168. As to Canada's third argument, relating to the level of protection, we note that it is undisputed that WTO Members have the right to determine the level of protection of health that they consider appropriate in a given situation. France has determined, and the Panel accepted[159], that the chosen level of health protection by France is a "halt" to the spread of asbestos-related health risks. By prohibiting all forms of amphibole asbestos, and by severely restricting the use of chrysotile asbestos, the measure at issue is clearly designed and apt to achieve that level of health pro-tection. Our conclusion is not altered by the fact that PCG fibres might pose a risk to health. The scientific evidence before the Panel indicated that the risk posed by the PCG fibres is, in any case, less than the risk posed by chrysotile asbestos fibres[160], although that evidence did not indicate that the risk posed by PCG fibres is non-existent. Accordingly, it seems to us perfectly legitimate for a Member to seek to halt the spread of a highly risky product while allowing the use of a less risky product in its place. In short, we do not agree with Canada's third argument.

...

174. In our view, France could not reasonably be expected to employ any alterna-tive measure if that measure would involve a continuation of the very risk that

the Decree seeks to "halt". Such an alternative measure would, in effect, prevent France from achieving its chosen level of health protection. On the basis of the scientific evidence before it, the Panel found that, in general, the efficacy of "controlled use" remains to be demonstrated.[168] Moreover, even in cases where "controlled use" practices are applied "with greater certainty", the scientific evidence suggests that the level of exposure can, in some circumstances, still be high enough for there to be a "significant residual risk of developing asbestos-related diseases."[169] The Panel found too that the efficacy of "controlled use" is particularly doubtful for the building industry and for DIY enthusiasts, which are the most important users of cement-based products containing chrysotile asbestos.[170] Given these factual findings by the Panel, we believe that "controlled use" would not allow France to achieve its chosen level of health protection by halting the spread of asbestos-related health risks. "Controlled use" would, thus, not be an alternative measure that would achieve the end sought by France.

CASE
EC, *Measures Affecting the Approval and Marketing of Biotech Products*, WT/DS291/R WT/DS292/R WT/DS293/R (29 September 2006)

7.74   We note that like most other WTO Members, Argentina, Canada and the European Communities have ratified the Convention on Biological Diversity and are thus parties to it.[249] The United States has signed it in 1993, but has not ratified it since.[250] Thus, the United States is not a party to the Convention on Biological Diversity, and so for the United States the Convention is not in force. In other words, the Convention on Biological Diversity is not "applicable" in the relations between the United States and all other WTO Members. The mere fact that the United States has signed the Convention on Biological Diversity does not mean that the Convention is applicable to it.[251] Nor does it mean that the United States will ratify it, or that it is under an obligation to do so. We have said that if a rule of international law is not applicable to one of the Parties to this dispute, it is not applicable in the relations between all WTO Members. Therefore, in view of the fact that the United States is not a party to the Convention on Biological Diversity, we do not agree with the European Communities that we are required to take into account the Convention on Biological Diversity in interpreting the multilateral WTO agreements at issue in this dispute.

7.75   Turning to the Biosafety Protocol, we note that it entered into force only on 11 September 2003, i.e., after this Panel was established by the DSB. Among the WTO Members parties to the Biosafety Protocol is the European Communities. Argentina and Canada have signed the Biosafety Protocol, but have not ratified it since.[252] Hence, they are not parties to it. The United States has not signed the Biosafety Protocol. While this does not preclude the United States from ratifying the Protocol, the United States has so far not done so.[253] Accordingly, it, too, is not a party to the Biosafety Protocol. We do not consider that the rules of the Biosafety Protocol can be deemed to be applicable to the United States merely because the United States participates in the Protocol's Clearing-House Mechanism. It follows that the Biosafety Protocol is not in force for Argentina, Canada or the United States.[254] We deduce from this that the Biosafety Protocol is not "applicable" in the relations between these WTO Members and all other WTO Members.

[...]

7.1521   The European Communities observes that, in view of the fact that the underlying science is still in a great state of flux, it has chosen to apply a prudent and precautionary approach to identifying, assessing and managing risks to human health and the environment arising from GMOs and GMO-derived products for which marketing approval has been sought.

7.1522   As an initial matter, we note that, in our view, Annex C(1)(a), first clause, does not preclude the application of a prudent and precautionary approach to identifying, assessing and managing risks to human health and the environment arising from GMOs and GMO-derived products. As we have said, we consider that Annex C(1)(a), first clause, allows a Member to take the time that is reasonably needed to determine with adequate confidence whether its relevant SPS requirements are fulfilled. Consistent with this, we consider that a Member which finds it appropriate to follow a prudent and precautionary approach in assessing and approving applications concerning GMOs and GMO-derived products, might, for instance, be justified in requesting further information or clarification of an applicant in a situation where another Member considers that the information available is sufficient to carry out its assessment and reach a decision on an application.[1300] Whether a particular request is a reflection of genuine caution and prudence or whether it is a pretext to delay the completion of an approval procedure would need to be determined in the light of all relevant facts and circumstances.

7.1523   It is apparent from the foregoing observations that we perceive no inherent tension between the obligation set out in Annex C(1)(a), first clause, to complete approval procedures without undue delay and the application of a prudent and precautionary approach to assessing and approving GMOs or GMO-derived products. Nevertheless, it is clear that application of a prudent and precautionary approach is, and must be, subject to reasonable limits, lest the precautionary approach swallow the discipline imposed by Annex C(1)(a), first clause. Indeed, if a Member could endlessly defer substantive decisions on the grounds of a perceived need for caution and prudence in the assessment of applications, Annex C(1)(a), first clause, would be devoid of any meaning or effect. In applying the provisions of Annex C(1)(a), first clause, it is therefore important always to bear in mind that Annex C(1)(a), first clause, implies as a core obligation the obligation to come to a decision on an application.

[...]

7.90   Up to this point, we have examined whether there are other applicable rules of international law which we are required to take into account, in accordance with Article 31(3)(c) of the Vienna Convention, in interpreting the WTO agreements at issue in this dispute. We now turn to examine whether other rules of international law could be considered by us in the interpretation of the WTO agreements at issue even if these rules are not applicable in the relations between the WTO Members and thus do not fall within the category of rules which is at issue in Article 31(3)(c).

[...]

7.93   In the light of the foregoing, we consider that a panel may consider other relevant rules of international law when interpreting the terms of WTO agreements if it deems such rules to be informative. But a panel need not necessarily rely on other rules of international law, particularly if it considers that the ordinary meaning of the terms of WTO agreements may be ascertained by reference to other elements.

7.94   This approach is consistent with the Appellate Body's approach in US – Shrimp, as we understand it. In that case, the Appellate Body had to interpret the term "exhaustible natural resources" in Article XX(g) of the GATT 1994. The Appellate Body found that this term was by definition evolutionary and therefore found it "pertinent to note that modern international conventions and declarations make frequent references to natural resources as embracing both living and non-living resources".[270] Thus, as we understand it, the Appellate Body drew on other rules of international law because it considered that they were informative and aided it in establishing the meaning and scope of the term "exhaustible natural resources".[271] The European Communities correctly points out that the Appellate Body referred to conventions which were not applicable to all disputing parties. However, the mere fact that one or more disputing parties are not parties to a convention does not necessarily mean that a convention cannot shed light on the meaning and scope of a treaty term to be interpreted.[272]

7.95   In the present case, in response to a question from the Panel[273], the European Communities has identified a number of provisions of the Convention on Biological Diversity and of the Biosafety Protocol which it considers must be taken into account by the Panel.[274] The European Communities has not explained how these provisions are relevant to the interpretation of the WTO agreements at issue in this dispute. We have carefully considered the provisions referred to by the European Communities. Ultimately, however, we did not find it necessary or appropriate to rely on these particular provisions in interpreting the WTO agreements at issue in this dispute.

CASE
EC, *Brazil - Measures Affecting Imports of Retreaded Tyres* WT/DS332/AB//R (3 December 2007)

151. This does not mean that an import ban, or another trade-restrictive measure, the contribution of which is not immediately observable, cannot be justified under Article XX(b). We recognize that certain complex public health or environmental problems may be tackled only with a comprehensive policy comprising a multiplicity of interacting measures. In the short-term, it may prove difficult to isolate the contribution to public health or environmental objectives of one specific measure from those attributable to the other measures that are part of the same comprehensive policy. Moreover, the results obtained from certain actions—for instance, measures adopted in order to attenuate global warming and climate change, or certain preventive actions to reduce the incidence of diseases that may manifest themselves only after a certain period of time—can only be evaluated with the benefit of time.[243] In order to justify an import ban under Article XX(b), a panel must be satisfied that it brings about a material contribution to the achievement of its objective. Such a demonstration can of course be made by resorting to evidence or data, pertaining to the past or the present, that establish that the import ban at issue makes a material contribution to the protection of public health or environmental objectives pursued. This is not, however, the only type of demonstration that could establish such a contribution. Thus, a panel might conclude that an import ban is necessary on the basis of a demonstration that the import ban at issue is apt to produce a material contribution to the achievement of its objective. This demonstration could consist of quantitative projections in the future, or qualitative reasoning based on a set of hypotheses that are tested and supported by sufficient evidence.

CASE
United States, *Measures Concerning the Importation, Marketing and Sale of Tuna and Tuna Products*, WT/DS381/AB/R (16 May 2012)

384. We agree with the United States that an international standardizing body must not privilege any particular interests in the development of international standards. In this respect, we note that the TBT Committee Decision states, under the heading "Impartiality and Consensus", that:

> All relevant bodies of WTO Members should be provided with meaningful opportunities to contribute to the elaboration of an international standard so that the standard development process will not give privilege to, or favour the interests of, a particular supplier/s, country/ies or region/s.

385. With respect to the Panel's finding that the AIDCP remains open to all Members on a non-discriminatory basis since any State or regional economic integration organization can be invited to accede to the Agreement on the basis of a decision by the parties, the United States asserts that a body in which Members may participate by invitation only is not a body that is open. The United States stresses that becoming a party to the

AIDCP is not an option available to at least all Members; it is an option available only to those Members invited. For the United States, it follows therefore that not all Members have the ability to participate in review or revision of the definitions at issue. Mexico responds that being invited to accede to the AIDCP is a "formality".

[...]

386. The question whether a body is "open" if all WTO Members or their relevant bodies can accede pursuant to an invitation has to be decided on a case-by-case basis. It is conceivable that an invitation might indeed be a "formality". In our view, this would be the case if the invitation occurred automatically once a Member or its relevant body has expressed interest in joining a standardizing body. A panel must therefore carefully scrutinize the provisions, procedures, and practices governing accession to a standardizing body before concluding that it is "open to the relevant bodies of at least all Members".

CASE
EC, *Seal Products*, WT/DS400/AB/R WT/DS401/AB/R (22 May 2014)

5.198. However, the notion of risk in the context of Article XX(b) is difficult to reconcile with the subject matter of protection under Article XX(a), namely, public morals. While the focus on the dangers or risks to human, animal, or plant life or health in the context of Article XX(b) may lend itself to scientific or other methods of inquiry, such risk-assessment methods do not appear to be of much assistance or relevance in identifying and assessing public morals. We therefore do not consider that the term "to protect", when used in relation to "public morals" under Article XX(a), required the Panel, as Canada contends, to identify the existence of a risk to EU public moral concerns regarding seal welfare.

5.199. For this reason, we also have difficulty accepting Canada's argument that, for the purposes of an analysis under Article XX(a), a panel is required to identify the exact content of the public morals standard at issue. The Panel accepted the definition of "public morals" developed by the panel in US – Gambling, according to which "the term 'public morals' denotes 'standards of right and wrong conduct maintained by or on behalf of a community or nation'".[1251] The Panel also referred to the reasoning developed by the panel in US – Gambling that the content of public morals can be characterized by a degree of variation, and that, for this reason, Members should be given some scope to define and apply for themselves the concept of public morals according to their own systems and scales of values.[1252] Canada does not challenge these propositions on appeal. In addition, we note that, although Canada indirectly questions the existence of EU public moral concerns regarding seal welfare by contending that the Panel ought to have considered the similarity of animal welfare risks in both terrestrial wildlife hunts and seal hunts, Canada does not directly challenge the Panel's finding that there are public moral concerns in relation to seal welfare in the European Union.

20.4   FREE TRADE AGREEMENTS

2018 United States-Mexico-Canada Agreement

Preamble

[…]

RECOGNIZE their inherent right to regulate and resolve to preserve the flexibility of the Parties to set legislative and regulatory priorities, and protect legitimate public welfare objectives, such as health, safety, environmental protection, conservation of living or non-living exhaustible natural resources, integrity and stability of the financial system, and public morals, in accordance with the rights and obligations provided in this Agreement;

[…]

PROMOTE high levels of environmental protection, including through effective enforcement by each Party of its environmental laws, as well as through enhanced environmental cooperation, and further the aims of sustainable development, including through mutually supportive trade and environmental policies and practices;

CHAPTER 24 ENVIRONMENT

Article 24.1: Definitions

For the purposes of this Chapter:

environmental law means a statute or regulation of a Party, or provision thereof, including any that implements the Party's obligations under a multilateral environmental agreement, the primary purpose of which is the protection of the environment, or the prevention of a danger to human life or health, through:

    (a)   the prevention, abatement, or control of the release, discharge, or emission of pollutants or environmental contaminants;

    (b)   the control of environmentally hazardous or toxic chemicals, substances, materials, or wastes, and the dissemination of information related thereto; or

    (c)   the protection or conservation of wild flora or fauna, including endangered species, their habitat, and specially protected natural areas,

but does not include a statute or regulation, or provision thereof, directly related to worker safety or health, nor any statute or regulation, or provision thereof, the primary purpose of which is managing the subsistence or aboriginal harvesting of natural resources; […]

Article 24.2: Scope and Objectives

1.   The Parties recognize that a healthy environment is an integral element of sustainable development and recognize the contribution that trade makes to sustainable development.

2.   The objectives of this Chapter are to promote mutually supportive trade and environmental policies and practices; promote high levels of environmental protection and effective enforcement of environmental laws; and enhance the capacities of the

Parties to address trade-related environmental issues, including through cooperation, in the furtherance of sustainable development.

3.   Taking account of their respective national priorities and circumstances, the Parties
recognize that enhanced cooperation to protect and conserve the environment and
the sustainable use and management of their natural resources brings benefits
that can contribute to sustainable development, strengthen their environmental
governance, support implementation of international environmental agreements
to which they are a party, and complement the objectives of this Agreement.

4.   The Parties recognize that the environment plays an important role in the
economic, social, and cultural well-being of indigenous peoples and local communities, and acknowledge the importance of engaging with these groups in the
long-term conservation of the environment.

5.   The Parties further recognize that it is inappropriate to establish or use their environmental laws or other measures in a manner which would constitute a disguised
restriction on trade or investment between the Parties.

Article 24.3: Levels of Protection

1.   The Parties recognize the sovereign right of each Party to establish its own levels
of domestic environmental protection and its own environmental priorities, and to
establish, adopt, or modify its environmental laws and policies accordingly.

2.   Each Party shall strive to ensure that its environmental laws and policies provide
for, and encourage, high levels of environmental protection, and shall strive to
continue to improve its respective levels of environmental protection.

Article 24.4: Enforcement of Environmental Laws

1.   No Party shall fail to effectively enforce its environmental laws through a sustained
or recurring course of action or inaction[3] in a manner affecting trade or investment
between the Parties,[4,5] after the date of entry into force of this Agreement.

...

3.   Without prejudice to Article 24.3.1 (Levels of Protection), the Parties recognize that
it is inappropriate to encourage trade or investment by weakening or reducing the
protection afforded in their respective environmental laws. Accordingly, a Party
shall not waive or otherwise derogate from, or offer to waive or otherwise derogate
from, its environmental laws in a manner that weakens or reduces the protection
afforded in those laws in order to encourage trade or investment between the
Parties.

Article 24.8: Multilateral Environmental Agreements

1.   The Parties recognize the important role that multilateral environmental agreements can play in protecting the environment and as a response of the international community to global or regional environmental problems.

2.   Each Party affirms its commitment to implement the multilateral environmental
agreements to which it is a party.

3.   The Parties commit to consult and cooperate as appropriate with respect to environmental issues of mutual interest, in particular trade-related issues, pertaining
to relevant multilateral environmental agreements. This includes exchanging

information on the implementation of multilateral environmental agreements to which a Party is party; ongoing negotiations of new multilateral environmental agreements; and, each Party's respective views on becoming a party to additional multilateral environmental agreements.

4.   Each Party shall adopt, maintain, and implement laws, regulations, and all other measures necessary to fulfill its respective obligations under the following multilateral environmental agreements ("covered agreements"):

(a)   the Convention on International Trade in Endangered Species of Wild Fauna and Flora, done at Washington, March 3, 1973, as amended;

(b)   the Montreal Protocol on Substances that Deplete the Ozone Layer, done at Montreal, September 16, 1987, as adjusted and amended;

(c)   the Protocol of 1978 Relating to the International Convention for the Prevention of Pollution from Ships, 1973, done at London, February 17, 1978, as amended;

(d)   the Convention on Wetlands of International Importance Especially as Waterfowl Habitat, done at Ramsar, February 2, 1971, as amended;

(e)   the Convention on the Conservation of Antarctic Marine Living Resources, done at Canberra, May 20, 1980;

(f)   the International Convention for the Regulation of Whaling, done at Washington, December 2, 1946; and

(g)   the Convention for the Establishment of an Inter-American Tropical Tuna Commission, done at Washington, May 31, 1949.

5.   Pursuant to Article 34.3 (Amendments), the Parties may agree in writing to modify paragraph 4 to include any amendment to an agreement referred to therein, and any other environmental or conservation agreement.

[...]

Article 24.22: Conservation and Trade

1.   The Parties affirm the importance of combatting the illegal take of, and illegal trade in, wild fauna and flora, and acknowledge that this trade undermines efforts to conserve and sustainably manage those natural resources, has social consequences, distorts legal trade in wild fauna and flora, and reduces the economic and environmental value of these natural resources.

2.   The Parties commit to promote conservation and to combat the illegal take of, and illegal trade in, wild fauna and flora. To that end, the Parties shall:

(a)   exchange information and experiences on issues of mutual interest related to combatting the illegal take of, and illegal trade in, wild fauna and flora, including combatting illegal logging and associated illegal trade, and promoting the legal trade in associated products;

(b)   undertake, as appropriate, joint activities on conservation issues of mutual interest, including through relevant regional and international fora; and

(c)   endeavor to implement, as appropriate, CITES resolutions that aim to protect and conserve species whose survival is threatened by international trade.

3.   Each Party further commits to:

(a)   take appropriate measures to protect and conserve wild fauna and flora that it has identified to be at risk within its territory, including measures to conserve the ecological integrity of specially protected natural areas, for example grasslands and wetlands;

(b)   maintain or strengthen government capacity and institutional frameworks to promote the conservation of wild fauna and flora, and endeavor to enhance public participation and transparency in these institutional frameworks; and

(c)   endeavor to develop and strengthen cooperation and consultation with interested non-governmental entities and other stakeholders in order to enhance implementation of measures to combat the illegal take of, and illegal trade in, wild fauna and flora.

4.   In a further effort to address the illegal take of, and illegal trade in, wild fauna and flora, including parts and products thereof, each Party shall take measures to combat, and cooperate to prevent, the trade of wild fauna and flora that, based on credible evidence,[33] were taken or traded in violation of that Party's law or another applicable law,[34] the primary purpose of which is to conserve, protect, or manage wild fauna or flora. These measures shall include sanctions, penalties, or other effective measures, including administrative measures, that can act as a deterrent to such trade. In addition, each Party shall endeavor to take measures to combat the trade of wild fauna and flora transhipped through its territory that, based on credible evidence, were illegally taken or traded.

5.   The Parties recognize that each Party retains the right to exercise administrative, investigatory, and enforcement discretion in its implementation of paragraph 5, including by taking into account in relation to each situation the strength of the available evidence and the seriousness of the suspected violation. In addition, the Parties recognize that in implementing paragraph 5, each Party retains the right to make decisions regarding the allocation of administrative, investigatory, and enforcement resources.

6.   Further, each Party shall:

(a)   take measures to enhance the effectiveness of inspections of shipments containing wild fauna and flora, including parts and products thereof, at ports of entry, such as improving targeting; and

(b)   treat intentional transnational trafficking of wildlife protected under its laws,[35] as a serious crime as defined in the United Nations Convention on Transnational Organized Crime.[36]

7.   In order to promote the widest measure of law enforcement cooperation and information sharing between the Parties to combat the illegal take of, and illegal trade in, wild fauna and flora, the Parties shall endeavor to identify opportunities, consistent with their respective law and in accordance with applicable international agreements, to enhance law enforcement cooperation and information sharing, for example by enhancing participation in law enforcement networks, and, as appropriate, establishing new networks with the objective of developing a strong and effective worldwide network.

[...]

Article 24.25: Environmental Cooperation

1. The Parties recognize the importance of cooperation as a mechanism to implement this Chapter, to enhance its benefits, and to strengthen the Parties' joint and individual capacities to protect the environment, and to promote sustainable development as they strengthen their trade and investment relations.

2. The Parties are committed to expanding their cooperative relationship on environmental matters, recognizing it will help them achieve their shared environmental goals and objectives, including the development and improvement of environmental protection, practices, and technologies.

3. The Parties are committed to undertaking cooperative environmental activities pursuant to the Agreement on Environmental Cooperation among the Governments of Canada, the United Mexican States, and the United States of America (ECA) signed by the Parties, including activities related to implementation of this Chapter. Activities that the Parties undertake pursuant to the Environmental Cooperation Agreement will be coordinated and reviewed by the Commission for Environmental Cooperation as provided for in the ECA.

CHAPTER 32 EXCEPTIONS AND GENERAL PROVISIONS

Article 32.1

1. For the purposes of Chapter 2 (National Treatment and Market Access for Goods), Chapter 3 (Agriculture), Chapter 4 (Rules of Origin), Chapter 5 (Origin Procedures), Chapter 6 (Textile and Apparel Goods), Chapter 7 (Customs Administration and Trade Facilitation), Chapter 9 (Sanitary and Phytosanitary Measures), Chapter 11 (Technical Barriers to Trade), Chapter 12 (Sectoral Annexes), and Chapter 22 (State-Owned Enterprises and Designated Monopolies), Article XX of the GATT 1994 and its interpretative notes are incorporated into and made part of this Agreement, *mutatis mutandis.*

[…]

3. The Parties understand that the measures referred to in Article XX(b) of the GATT 1994 and GATS Article XIV(b) include environmental measures necessary to protect human, animal, or plant life or health, and that Article XX(g) of the GATT 1994 applies to measures relating to the conservation of living and non-living exhaustible natural resources.

QUESTIONS

1. Can trade restrictions under MEAs be reconciled with the trade liberalisation objectives of international trade law?
2. 'Far from showing hostility to environmental concerns, the WTO Appellate Body strikes a good balance between unjustified restrictions on trade and the prevention of environmental harm.' Discuss.
3. In what ways, if any, does the inclusion of environmental regulation in FTAs address concerns about the integration of environmental law and trade law?

FURTHER READING

BOOKS

P Delimatsis and L Reins (eds), *Trade and Environmental Law* (Edward Elgar 2021)

K Gallagher, *Handbook on Trade and the Environment* (Edward Elgar 2008)

A Goyal, *The WTO and International Environmental Law* (Oxford University Press 2006)

L Gruszczynski, *Regulating Health and Environmental Risks under WTO Law* (Oxford University Press 2010)

J Munro, *Emissions Trading Schemes Under International Economic Law* (Oxford University Press 2018)

RH Steinberg (ed.), *The Greening of Trade Law: International Trade Organizations and Environmental Issues* (Rowman and Littlefield 2002)

E Vranes, *Trade and the Environment: Fundamental Issues in International Law, WTO Law and Legal Theory* (Oxford University Press 2009)

CHAPTERS

D Bodansky and J Lawrence, 'Trade and the Environment' in D Bethlehem, I Van Damme, D McRae and R Neufeld (eds), *The Oxford Handbook of International Trade Law* (Oxford University Press 2012)

VM Tzatzaki, 'Restrictive Measures When Trading Water: May GATT Protect Us from Water Scarcity' in *Yearbook of International Environmental Law* (2021)

ARTICLES

Special Issue: Trade and the Environment at WTO+20 (2014) 23(3) Review of European, Comparative and International Environmental Law 285

E Brown Weiss, 'Environment and Trade as Partners in Sustainable Development: A Commentary' (1992) 86 American Journal of International Law 700

E Brown Weiss, 'Integrating Environment and Trade' (2016) 19(2) Journal of International Economic Law 367

S Charnovitz, 'The WTO's Environmental Progress' (2007) 10(3) Journal of International Economic Law 685

B Cooreman, 'Addressing International Environmental Concerns Through Trade: A Case for Extraterritoriality?' (2016) 65 ICLQ 229

PH Sand, 'Enforcing CITES' (2013) 22 Rev Euro Comp & Int Env Law 251

G van Calster, 'Trade and Environment in the EC and the WTO – A Legal Analysis' (2003) 6(2) Journal of International Economic Law 540

JD Werksman, 'Trade Sanctions Under the Montreal Protocol' (1992) 1 Review of European Community & International Environmental Law 69

21
The protection of the environment in armed conflict

21.1   INTRODUCTION

The protection of the environment in armed conflict is a pressing area of international law which merits further consideration. Indeed, the adverse and destructive effects of armed conflict on the natural environment has been a long-standing source of deep concern for the international community. In the International Committee of the Red Cross ('ICRC') Guidelines on the Protection of the Natural Environment in Armed Conflict, the ICRC has observed that:

> Armed conflicts continue to cause environmental degradation and destruction, affecting the well-being, health and survival of people across the globe. The consequences of this damage persist for years or decades after wars end, leaving indelible impacts on the lives of local populations.[1]

The international legal framework that governs the protection of the environment in armed conflict can broadly be categorised in two streams: the legal framework of international law protecting the environment, comprising customary international law, general principles and treaty obligations; and the laws of armed conflict, i.e., international humanitarian law ('IHL'). This is not to say that the former is not applicable during times of armed conflict. On the contrary, the general presumption is that the legal framework pertaining to the environment applies even during armed conflict, unless it is explicitly stated otherwise. The ICRC has stated:

> The outbreak of an international or non-international armed conflict does not in and of itself terminate or suspend the application of rules of international law (whether treaty or customary) protecting the natural environment in peacetime, either between States party to the conflict or between a State party to the conflict and one that is not. Thus, other rules within different branches of international law may, depending on the context, and in whole

---

[1]   Guidelines on the Protection of the Natural Environment in Armed Conflict, International Committee of the Red Cross ('ICRC Guidelines'), p. 11.

or in part, complement or inform the IHL rules protecting the natural environment in times of armed conflict.[2]

Within the multilateral setting, there has been ongoing interest in the protection of the environment during armed conflict, e.g., in 1992, the General Assembly ('GA') adopted GA Resolution 47/37, entitled 'Protection of the environment in times of armed conflict', which *inter alia* urges all states 'to take all measures to ensure compliance with the existing international law applicable to the environment in times of armed conflict'.[3]

In 2013, the International Law Commission ('ILC') decided to include the topic 'Protection of the environment in relation to armed conflicts' in its programme of work and appointed two special rapporteurs in 2013 and 2017, Marie G Jacobsson and Marja Lehto respectively. The first reading adopted at the ILC's seventy-first session in 2019 gave rise to the Draft Principles on the Protection of the Environment in Relation to Armed Conflict.[4] In the commentary to these draft Principles, it is worth noting that the draft principles were 'prepared bearing in mind the intersection between the international law relating to the environment and the law of armed conflict'.[5] Breau points out that 'this intersectionality is an important contribution to this field as these principles apply before, during and after, an armed conflict'.[6]

The International Committee of the Red Cross ('ICRC') released the 2020 ICRC Guidelines on the protection of the natural environment in armed conflict ('2020 ICRC Guidelines'). According to the Commentary, these Guidelines represent the ICRC's reading of the status of customary international law and focus on how the rules of IHL protect the natural environment;[7] and represent the ICRC's efforts to 'raise awareness of the need to protect the natural environment from the effects of armed conflict'.[8]

Generally, it is accepted that the rules of international environment still apply during times of armed conflict. The International Court of Justice ('ICJ') has opined that:

> while the existing international law relating to the protection and safeguarding of the environment does not specifically prohibit the use of nuclear weapons, it indicates important environmental factors that are properly to be taken into account in the context of the implementation of the principles and rules of the law applicable in armed conflict.[9]

---

[2]   Ibid., p. 20.

[3]   GA Resolution 47/37, Protection of the environment in armed conflict.

[4]   ILC Draft Articles on Protection of the environment in relation to armed conflicts (2019) ('ILC Draft Articles') A/CN.4/L.937.

[5]   International Law Commission, 'Report of the Work of the Seventy-first Session' (2019) UN Doc A/74/10 (29 April to 7 June and 8 July to 2019) p. 215.

[6]   Susan Breau, 'Protection of the Environment during Armed Conflict and Post-Conflict' in Erika Techera and others, *Routledge Handbook of International Environmental Law* (2nd edn, Routledge 2020) 440.

[7]   ICRC Guidelines (n 1), p. 13.

[8]   Ibid., p. 14.

[9]   Legality of the Threat or Use of Nuclear Weapons, Advisory Opinion, ICJ Reports 1996, p. 226, para. 33.

The GA convened in 2017 a conference to negotiate a legally binding instrument to prohibit nuclear weapons, leading towards their total elimination, and adopted the Treaty on the Prohibition of Nuclear Weapons, which entered into force on 22 January 2021.[10] There are, of course, other multilateral environmental agreements (MEAs) that continue to apply in situations of armed conflict. The ILC's 2001 Articles on the Effects of Armed Conflicts on Treaties is instructive in this regard. Article 3 stipulates:

> The existence of an armed conflict does not ipso facto terminate or suspend the operation of treaties:
> (a) as between States parties to the conflict;
> (b) as between a State party to the conflict and a State that is not.

Further, according to Article 7, treaties relating to the international protection of the environment continue to operate in whole or in part, during armed conflict. The ICJ has opined that:

> while the existing international law relating to the protection and safeguarding of the environment does not specifically prohibit the use of nuclear weapons, it indicates important environmental factors that are properly to be taken into account in the context of the implementation of the principles and rules of the law applicable in armed conflict.

In the ICRC Commentary to its 2020 Guidelines, it is stated:

> [...]rules of international treaty law that protect the environment may continue to apply alongside IHL during times of armed conflict. This continued application is subject to two exceptions. The first is when it is expressly stated that a specific rule, or part of it, does not apply during armed conflict. The second is when, provided that it is not expressly stated that a rule does apply during armed conflict, its application is incompatible with the characteristics of the armed conflict with an applicable rule of IHL. This potential incompatibility between a rule of international environmental law and IHL must be considered on a rule-by-rule basis, but where a rule of international environmental law is more protective of the natural environment than the parallel rule of IHL, this difference should be interpreted as incompatibility only if there are clear reasons for doing so.[11]

Within the IHL framework, there appear to be two broad categories by which the environment is protected: rules of IHL that express direct protection; and rules of IHL that afford indirect protection. In terms of more specific treaty obligations in relation to the protection of the environment, the Convention on the Prohibition of Military or any other Hostile Use of Environmental Modification Techniques ('ENMOD Convention') adopted in 1976 is perhaps the most notable treaties. Accordingly, states parties have an obligation *inter alia* to not engage in military or any other hostile use of environmental modification techniques having

---

10   C.N.478.2020.TREATIES-XXVI.9 (Depositary Notification).
11   ICRC Guidelines (n 1), p. 22.

widespread, long-lasting or severe effects as the means of destruction, damage or injury to any other state party.[12] The First Additional Protocol to the Geneva Conventions relative to the protection of Victims of International Armed Conflicts ('AP1') provides rules directly aimed at the protection of the environment: 'it is prohibited to employ methods or means of warfare which are intended, or may be expected, to cause widespread, long-term and severe damage to the natural environment';[13] and that:

> care shall be taken in warfare to protect the natural environment against widespread, long-term, and severe damage. This protection includes a prohibition of the use of methods or means of warfare which are intended or may be expected to cause such damage to the natural environment and thereby to prejudice the health or survival of the population.[14]

Further, attacks against the natural environment by way of reprisals are prohibited.[15]

With respect to the latter, it is generally understood the natural environment is civilian in character.[16] Accordingly, the natural environment is considered civilian objects and thus is protected under the rules of IHL that protect the environment, unless some parts or elements become military objectives, 'that is, if, by their nature, location, purpose or use, they make an effective contribution to military action and their total or partial destruction, capture or neutralization, in the circumstances ruling at the time, offers a definite military advantage'.[17] It is the ICRC's view that 'all parts of the natural environment are civilian objects, unless they have become military objectives'.[18] Another indirect way that rules of IHL can protect the environment is by restricting attacks against works or installations containing dangerous forces which could have severe effects on the surrounding natural environment, e.g., nuclear electrical generating plants.[19] Rules of IHL can also protect the natural environment by providing rules on specific weapons.[20] Further, there is also the 'Martens Clause', which provides that until the adoption of more specific rules, inhabitants and belligerents are 'under the protection and the rule of the principles of the law of nations as they result from the usages established among civilised peoples, from the laws of humanity and the dictates of public conscience'.[21] Sand and Peel view that 'there is no reason why these should not encompass environmental

---

[12] Convention on the Prohibition of Military or any other Hostile Use of Environmental Modification Techniques 1976 ('ENMOD Convention') Article 1.

[13] Article 35(3), Protocol Additional to the Geneva Conventions of 12 August 1949, and relating to the Protection of victims of international armed conflicts (Protocol I) of 8 June 1977 ('Protocol I').

[14] Protocol I, Art 55 (1).

[15] Ibid., Art 55 (2).

[16] ICRC Guidelines (n 1), p. 17–18.

[17] Ibid., p. 18.

[18] Ibid., p. 19.

[19] E.g. Article 56(1) and (2); see also ICRC Guidelines, ibid., p. 19.

[20] ICRC Guidelines, Part III.

[21] 1907 Hague Convention IV Respecting the Laws and Customs of War on Land, 3 Martens (3rd) 462, Preamble; ILC Draft Articles on Protection of the environment in relation to armed conflicts (n 4), Draft Principle 12.

protection.'[22] Notably, the applicability of these rules in relation to the natural environment may not always be so straightforward and is an area of scholarly debate.

21.2 LEGAL INSTRUMENTS

21.2.1 Legally Binding Legal Instruments

1976 Convention on the prohibition of military or any hostile use of environmental modification techniques, 1108 UNTS 151

Article I
1. Each State Party to this Convention undertakes not to engage in military or any other hostile use of environmental modification techniques having widespread, long-lasting or severe effects as the means of destruction, damage or injury to any other State Party.
2. Each State Party to this Convention undertakes not to assist, encourage or induce any State, group of States or international organization to engage in activities contrary to the provisions of paragraph 1 of this article.

Article II
As used in article I, the term "environmental modification techniques" refers to any technique for changing – through the deliberate manipulation of natural processes – the dynamics, composition or structure of the earth, including its biota, lithosphere, hydrosphere and atmosphere, or of outer space.

Article III
1. The provisions of this Convention shall not hinder the use of environmental modification techniques for peaceful purposes and shall be without prejudice to the generally recognized principles and applicable rules of international law concerning such use.
2. The States Parties to this Convention undertake to facilitate, and have the right to participate in, the fullest possible exchange of scientific and technological information on the use of environmental modification techniques for peaceful purposes. States Parties in a position to do so shall contribute, alone or together with other States or international organizations, to international economic and scientific co-operation in the preservation, improvement and peaceful utilization of the environment, with due consideration for the needs of the developing areas of the world.

---

[22] Philippe Sands and Jacqueline Peel, *Principles of International Environmental Law* (4th edn, Cambridge University Press 2018) 832.

1977 Protocol additional to the Geneva Conventions of 12 August 1949, and relating to the protection of victims of international armed conflicts (Protocol I), 1125 UNTS 3

Article 35 — Basic rules
1.   In any armed conflict, the right of the Parties to the conflict to choose methods or means of warfare is not unlimited.
2.   It is prohibited to employ weapons, projectiles and material and methods of warfare of a nature to cause superfluous injury or unnecessary suffering.
3.   It is prohibited to employ methods or means of warfare which are intended, or may be expected, to cause widespread, long-term and severe damage to the natural environment.

[...]

Article 55 — Protection of the natural environment
1.   Care shall be taken in warfare to protect the natural environment against widespread, long-term and severe damage. This protection includes a prohibition of the use of methods or means of warfare which are intended or may be expected to cause such damage to the natural environment and thereby to prejudice the health or survival of the population.
2.   Attacks against the natural environment by way of reprisals are prohibited.

Article 56 — Protection of works and installations containing dangerous forces
1.   Works or installations containing dangerous forces, namely dams, dykes and nuclear electrical generating stations, shall not be made the object of attack, even where these objects are military objectives, if such attack may cause the release of dangerous forces and consequent severe losses among the civilian population. Other military objectives located at or in the vicinity of these works or installations shall not be made the object of attack if such attack may cause the release of dangerous forces from the works or installations and consequent severe losses among the civilian population.
2.   The special protection against attack provided by paragraph 1 shall cease:
      a)   for a dam or a dyke only if it is used for other than its normal function and in regular, significant and direct support of military operations and if such attack is the only feasible way to terminate such support;
      b)   for a nuclear electrical generating station only if it provides electric power in regular, significant and direct support of military operations and if such attack is the only feasible way to terminate such support;
      c)   for other military objectives located at or in the vicinity of these works or installations only if they are used in regular, significant and direct support of military operations and if such attack is the only feasible way to terminate such support.
3.   In all cases, the civilian population and individual civilians shall remain entitled to all the protection accorded them by international law, including the protection of the precautionary measures provided for in Article 57. If the protection ceases and any of the works, installations or military objectives mentioned in paragraph 1 is

attacked, all practical precautions shall be taken to avoid the release of the dangerous forces.

4. It is prohibited to make any of the works, installations or military objectives mentioned in paragraph 1 the object of reprisals.

5. The Parties to the conflict shall endeavour to avoid locating any military objectives in the vicinity of the works or installations mentioned in paragraph 1. Nevertheless, installations erected for the sole purpose of defending the protected works or installations from attack are permissible and shall not themselves be made the object of attack, provided that they are not used in hostilities except for defensive actions necessary to respond to attacks against the protected works or installations and that their armament is limited to weapons capable only of repelling hostile action against the protected works or installations.

Table 21.1 Examples of multilateral environmental treaties that directly or indirectly provide for their application in times of armed conflict

1954 International Convention for the Prevention of Pollution of the Sea by Oil (OILPOL)
1972 Convention Concerning the Protection of the World Cultural and Natural Heritage (World Heritage Convention)
1972 Convention on the Prevention of Marine Pollution by Dumping of Wastes and Other Matter (London Convention)
1973 International Convention for the Prevention of Pollution from Ships (MARPOL)
1976 Convention for the Protection of the Marine Environment and the Coastal Region of the Mediterranean (Barcelona Convention) and its Protocols
1979 Convention on Long-Range Transboundary Air Pollution
1982 United Nations Convention on the Law of the Sea (UNCLOS)
1983 Convention for the Protection and Development of the Marine Environment of the Wider Caribbean Region
1987 Convention on Wetlands of International Importance especially as Waterfowl Habitat
1997 Convention on the Law of the Non-Navigational Uses of International Watercourses (Watercourses Convention)
2003 African Convention on the Conservation of Nature and Natural Resources

1997 United Nations Convention on Non-Navigational Uses of Watercourses, 2999 UNTS, A/51/869

Article 29 International watercourses and installations in time of armed conflict
International watercourses and related installations, facilities and other works shall enjoy the protection accorded by the principles and rules of international law applicable in international and non-international armed conflict and shall not be used in violation of those principles and rules.

21.2.2 Non-Binding Legal Instruments

1972 Stockholm Declaration

Principle 26

Man and his environment must be spared the effects of nuclear weapons and all other means of mass destruction. States must strive to reach prompt agreement, in the relevant international organs, on the elimination and complete destruction of such weapons.

1982 World Charter for Nature

5.   Nature shall be secured against degradation caused by warfare or other hostile activities.

20.   Military activities damaging to nature shall be avoided.

1992 Rio Declaration

Principle 24

Warfare is inherently destructive of sustainable development.

States shall therefore respect international law providing protection for the environment in times of armed conflict and cooperate in its further development, as necessary.

International Law Commission Seventy-first session Geneva, 29 April–7 June and 8 July–9 August 2019

First reading
Protection of the environment in relation to armed conflicts
Part One Introduction

Draft principle 1
Scope
The present draft principles apply to the protection of the environment before, during or after an armed conflict.

Draft principle 2
Purpose
The present draft principles are aimed at enhancing the protection of the environment in relation to armed conflict, including through preventive measures for minimizing damage to the environment during armed conflict and through remedial measures.

Part Two [One] Principles of general application

Draft principle 3 [4] Measures to enhance the protection of the environment

1.   States shall, pursuant to their obligations under international law, take effective legislative, administrative, judicial and other measures to enhance the protection of the environment in relation to armed conflict.

2.　　　In addition, States should take further measures, as appropriate, to enhance the protection of the environment in relation to armed conflict.

Draft principle 4 [I-(x), 5]
Designation of protected zones States should designate, by agreement or otherwise, areas of major environmental and cultural importance as protected zones.

Draft principle 5 [6]
Protection of the environment of indigenous peoples
1.　　　States should take appropriate measures, in the event of an armed conflict, to protect the environment of the territories that indigenous peoples inhabit.
2.　　　After an armed conflict that has adversely affected the environment of the territories that indigenous peoples inhabit, States should undertake effective consultations and cooperation with the indigenous peoples concerned, through appropriate procedures and in particular through their own representative institutions, for the purpose of taking remedial measures.

Draft principle 6 [7]
Agreements concerning the presence of military forces in relation to armed conflict
  States and international organizations should, as appropriate, include provisions on environmental protection in agreements concerning the presence of military forces in relation to armed conflict. Such provisions may include preventive measures, impact assessments, restoration and clean-up measures.

Draft principle 7 [8]
Peace operations
  States and international organizations involved in peace operations in relation to armed conflict shall consider the impact of such operations on the environment and take appropriate measures to prevent, mitigate and remediate the negative environmental consequences thereof.

Draft principle 8
Human displacement
  States, international organizations and other relevant actors should take appropriate measures to prevent and mitigate environmental degradation in areas where persons displaced by armed conflict are located, while providing relief and assistance for such persons and local communities.

[...]

Part Three [Two] Principles applicable during armed conflict

Draft principle 12
Martens Clause with respect to the protection of the environment in relation to armed conflict. In cases not covered by international agreements, the environment remains under

the protection and authority of the principles of international law derived from established custom, from the principles of humanity and from the dictates of public conscience.

Draft principle 13 [II-1, 9] General protection of the natural environment during armed conflict

1. The natural environment shall be respected and protected in accordance with applicable international law and, in particular, the law of armed conflict.

2. Care shall be taken to protect the natural environment against widespread, long-term and severe damage.

3. No part of the natural environment may be attacked, unless it has become a military objective.

Draft principle 14 [II-2, 10]
Application of the law of armed conflict to the natural environment
The law of armed conflict, including the principles and rules on distinction, proportionality, military necessity and precautions in attack, shall be applied to the natural environment, with a view to its protection.

Draft principle 15 [II-3, 11]
Environmental considerations
    Environmental considerations shall be taken into account when applying the principle of proportionality and the rules on military necessity.

Draft principle 16 [II-4, 12]
Prohibition of reprisals
    Attacks against the natural environment by way of reprisals are prohibited.

Draft principle 17 [II-5, 13]
Protected zones
    An area of major environmental and cultural importance designated by agreement as a protected zone shall be protected against any attack, as long as it does not contain a military objective.

Draft principle 18
Prohibition of pillage
    Pillage of natural resources is prohibited.

Draft principle 19
Environmental modification techniques
    In accordance with their international obligations, States shall not engage in military or any other hostile use of environmental modification techniques having widespread, longlasting or severe effects as the means of destruction, damage or injury to any other State.

ICRC Guidelines on the Protection of the Natural Environment in Armed Conflict

PART I: SPECIFIC PROTECTION OF THE NATURAL ENVIRONMENT UNDER INTERNATIONAL HUMANITARIAN LAW

Rule 1 – Due regard for the natural environment in military operations.

Methods and means of warfare must be employed with due regard to the protection and preservation of the natural environment.

Rule 2 – Prohibition of widespread, long-term and severe damage to the natural environment.

The use of methods or means of warfare that are intended, or may be expected, to cause widespread, long-term and severe damage to the natural environment is prohibited.

Rule 3 – Prohibition of using the destruction of the natural environment as a weapon.

A.   Destruction of the natural environment may not be used as a weapon.

B.   For States party to the Convention on the Prohibition of Military or Any Other Hostile Use of Environmental Modification Techniques (ENMOD Convention), the military or any other hostile use of environmental modification techniques having widespread, long-lasting or severe effects as the means of destruction, damage or injury to any other State Party is prohibited.

Rule 4 – Prohibition of attacking the natural environment by way of reprisal.

A.   For States party to Protocol I additional to the Geneva Conventions (Additional Protocol I):

    i.   Attacks against the natural environment by way of reprisal are prohibited.

    ii.   Reprisals against objects protected under the Protocol are prohibited, including when such objects are part of the natural environment.

B.   For all States, reprisals against objects protected under the Geneva Conventions or the Hague Convention for the Protection of Cultural Property are prohibited, including when such objects are part of the natural environment.

PART II: GENERAL PROTECTION OF THE NATURAL ENVIRONMENT UNDER INTERNATIONAL HUMANITARIAN LAW

Rule 5 – Principle of distinction between civilian objects and military objectives.

No part of the natural environment may be attacked, unless it is a military objective.

Rule 6 – Prohibition of indiscriminate attacks.

Indiscriminate attacks are prohibited. Indiscriminate attacks are those:

A.   which are not directed at a specific military objective;

B.   which employ a method or means of combat which cannot be directed at a specific military objective; or

C.   which employ a method or means of combat the effects of which cannot be limited as required by international humanitarian law;

and consequently, in each such case, are of a nature to strike military objectives and civilians or civilian objects, including the natural environment, without distinction.

Rule 7 – Proportionality in attack.

Launching an attack against a military objective which may be expected to cause incidental damage to the natural environment which would be excessive in relation to the concrete and direct military advantage anticipated is prohibited.

Rule 8 – Precautions.

In the conduct of military operations, constant care must be taken to spare the civilian population, civilians and civilian objects, including the natural environment. All feasible precautions must be taken to avoid, and in any event to minimize, incidental loss of civilian life, injury to civilians and damage to civilian objects, including the natural environment.

Rule 9 – Passive precautions.

Parties to the conflict must take all feasible precautions to protect civilian objects under their control, including the natural environment, against the effects of attacks.

Rule 10 – Prohibitions regarding objects indispensable to the survival of the civilian population.

Attacking, destroying, removing or rendering useless objects indispensable to the survival of the civilian population is prohibited, including when such objects are part of the natural environment.

Rule 11 – Prohibitions regarding works and installations containing dangerous forces.

A.   Particular care must be taken if works and installations containing dangerous forces, namely dams, dykes and nuclear electrical generating stations, and other installations located at or in their vicinity are attacked, in order to avoid the release of dangerous forces and consequent severe losses among the civilian population.

B.   i.   For States party to Additional Protocol I, works or installations containing dangerous forces, namely dams, dykes and nuclear electrical generating stations, may not be made the object of attack, even where these objects are military objectives, if such attack may cause the release of dangerous forces and consequent severe losses among the civilian population, subject to the exceptions specified in Article 56(2) of the Protocol. Other military objectives located at or in the vicinity of these works or installations may not be made the object of attack if such attack may cause the release of dangerous forces from the works or installations and consequent severe losses among the civilian population.

     ii. For States party to Protocol II additional to the Geneva Conventions (Additional Protocol II) and non-state actors that are party to armed conflicts to which the Protocol applies, works or installations containing dangerous forces, namely dams, dykes and nuclear electrical generating stations, may not be made the object of attack, even where these objects are military objectives, if such attack may cause the release of dangerous forces and consequent severe losses among the civilian population.

Rule 12 – Prohibitions regarding cultural property.
A.   Property of great importance to the cultural heritage of every people, including such property which constitutes part of the natural environment, must not be made the object of attack or used for purposes which are likely to expose it to destruction or damage, unless imperatively required by military necessity. Any form of theft, pillage or misappropriation of, and any acts of vandalism directed against, such property is prohibited.
B.   For States party to Additional Protocols I and II, as well as for non-state actors that are party to noninternational armed conflicts to which Additional Protocol II applies, directing acts of hostility against historic monuments, works of art or places of worship which constitute the cultural or spiritual heritage of peoples, including when these are part of the natural environment, or using them in support of the military effort, is prohibited.

Rule 13 – Prohibition of the destruction of the natural environment not justified by imperative military necessity.
The destruction of any part of the natural environment is prohibited, unless required by imperative military necessity.

Rule 14 – Prohibition of pillage.
  Pillage is prohibited, including pillage of property constituting part of the natural environment.

Rule 15 – Rules concerning private and public property, including the natural environment, in case of occupation.
  In occupied territory:

A.   movable public property, including objects forming part of the natural environment, that can be used for military operations may be confiscated;
B.   immovable public property, including objects forming part of the natural environment, must be administered according to the rule of usufruct; and
C.   private property, including objects forming part of the natural environment, must be respected and may not be confiscated;

except where destruction or seizure of such property is required by imperative military necessity.

Rule 16 – The Martens Clause with respect to the protection of the natural environment.
In cases not covered by international agreements, the natural environment remains under the protection and authority of the principles of international law derived from established custom, the principles of humanity and the dictates of public conscience.

Recommendation 17 – Conclusion of agreements to provide additional protection to the natural environment.

Parties to a conflict should endeavour to conclude agreements providing additional protection to the natural environment in situations of armed conflict.

Recommendation 18 – Application to non-international armed conflicts of international humanitarian law rules protecting the natural environment in international armed conflicts.

If not already under the obligation to do so under existing rules of international human-itarian law, each party to a non-international armed conflict is encouraged to apply to that conflict all or part of the international humanitarian law rules protecting the natural environment in international armed conflicts.

PART III: PROTECTION OF THE NATURAL ENVIRONMENT AFFORDED BY RULES ON SPECIFIC WEAPONS

Rule 19 – Prohibition of using poison or poisoned weapons. The use of poison or poisoned weapons is prohibited.

Rule 20 – Prohibition of using biological weapons. The use of biological weapons is prohibited.

Rule 21 – Prohibition of using chemical weapons. The use of chemical weapons is prohibited.

Rule 22 – Prohibition of using herbicides as a method of warfare. The use of herbicides as a method of warfare is prohibited if they:
A. are of a nature to be prohibited chemical weapons;
B. are of a nature to be prohibited biological weapons;
C. are aimed at vegetation that is not a military objective;
D. would cause incidental loss of civilian life, injury to civilians, damage to civilian objects, or a combination thereof, which may be expected to be excessive in relation to the concrete and direct military advantage anticipated; or
E. would cause widespread, long-term and severe damage to the natural environment.

Rule 23 – Incendiary weapons.
A. If incendiary weapons are used, particular care must be taken to avoid, and in any event to minimize, incidental loss of civilian life, injury to civilians and damage to civilian objects, including the natural environment.
B. For States party to Protocol III to the Convention on Certain Conventional Weapons, it is prohibited to make forests or other kinds of plant cover the object of attack by incendiary weapons, except when these are used to cover, conceal or camouflage combatants or other military objectives, or are themselves military objectives.

Rule 24 – Landmines.

A.   For parties to a conflict, the minimum customary rules specific to landmines are:

    i.   When landmines are used, particular care must be taken to minimize their indiscriminate effects, including those on the natural environment.

    ii.   A party to the conflict using landmines must record their placement, as far as possible.

    iii.   At the end of active hostilities, a party to the conflict which has used landmines must remove or otherwise render them harmless to civilians, or facilitate their removal.

B.   For a State party to the Anti-Personnel Mine Ban Convention:

    i.   The use of anti-personnel mines is prohibited.

    ii.   Each State Party must destroy or ensure destruction of its anti-personnel mine stockpiles.

    iii.   As soon as possible, each State Party must clear areas under its jurisdiction or control that are contaminated with anti-personnel mines.

C.   For a State not party to the Anti-Personnel Mine Ban Convention, but party to Protocol II to the Convention on Certain Conventional Weapons as amended on 3 May 1996 (Amended Protocol II to the CCW), the use of antipersonnel and anti-vehicle mines is restricted by the general and specific rules under the Protocol, including those requiring that:

    i.   All information on the placement of mines, on the laying of minefields and on mined areas must be recorded, retained and made available after the cessation of active hostilities, notably for clearance purposes.

    ii.   Without delay after the cessation of active hostilities, all mined areas and minefields must be cleared, removed, destroyed or maintained in accordance with the requirements of Amended Protocol II to the CCW.

Rule 25 – Minimizing the impact of explosive remnants of war, including unexploded cluster munitions.

A.   Each State party to Protocol V to the Convention on Certain Conventional Weapons and parties to an armed conflict must:

    i.   to the maximum extent possible and as far as practicable, record and retain information on the use or abandonment of explosive ordnance;

    ii.   when it has used or abandoned explosive ordnance which may have become explosive remnants of war, without delay after the cessation of active hostilities and as far as practicable, subject to its legitimate security interests, make available such information in accordance with Article 4(2) of the Protocol;

    iii.   after the cessation of active hostilities and as soon as feasible, mark and clear, remove or destroy explosive remnants of war in affected territories under its control.

B.   Each State party to the Convention on Cluster Munitions undertakes:

    i.   never under any circumstances to use cluster munitions;

ii. to destroy all cluster munitions in its stockpiles and to ensure that destruction methods comply with applicable international standards for protecting public health and the environment;

iii. as soon as possible, to clear and destroy, or ensure the clearance and destruction of, cluster munition remnants located in cluster munition contaminated areas under its jurisdiction or control.

PART IV: RESPECT FOR, IMPLEMENTATION AND DISSEMINATION OF INTERNATIONAL HUMANITARIAN LAW RULES PROTECTING THE NATURAL ENVIRONMENT

Rule 26 – Obligation to respect and ensure respect for international humanitarian law, including the rules protecting the natural environment.

A. Each party to the conflict must respect and ensure respect for international humanitarian law, including the rules protecting the natural environment, by its armed forces and other persons or groups acting in fact on its instructions or under its direction or control.

B. States may not encourage violations of international humanitarian law, including of the rules protecting the natural environment, by parties to an armed conflict. They must exert their influence, to the degree possible, to stop violations of international humanitarian law.

Rule 27 – National implementation of international humanitarian law rules protecting the natural environment.

States must act in accordance with their obligations to adopt domestic legislation and other measures at the national level to ensure that international humanitarian law rules protecting the natural environment in armed conflict are put into practice.

Rule 28 – Repression of war crimes that concern the natural environment.

A. States must investigate war crimes, including those that concern the natural environment, allegedly committed by their nationals or armed forces, or on their territory, and, if appropriate, prosecute the suspects. They must also investigate other war crimes over which they have jurisdiction, including those that concern the natural environment, and, if appropriate, prosecute the suspects.

B. Commanders and other superiors are criminally responsible for war crimes, including those that concern the natural environment, committed by their subordinates if they knew, or had reason to know, that the subordinates were about to commit or were committing such crimes and did not take all necessary and reasonable measures in their power to prevent their commission, or if such crimes had been committed, to punish the persons responsible.

C. Individuals are criminally responsible for war crimes they commit, including those that concern the natural environment.

Rule 29 – Instruction in international humanitarian law within armed forces, including in the rules protecting the natural environment.

States and parties to the conflict must provide instruction in international humanitarian law, including in the rules protecting the natural environment, to their armed forces.

Rule 30 – Dissemination of international humanitarian law, including of the rules protecting the natural environment, to the civilian population.

States must encourage the teaching of international humanitarian law, including of the rules protecting the natural environment, to the civilian population.

Rule 31 – Legal advice to the armed forces on international humanitarian law, including on the rules protecting the natural environment.

Each State must make legal advisers available, when necessary, to advise military commanders at the appropriate level on the application of international humanitarian law, including of the rules protecting the natural environment.

Rule 32 – Evaluation of whether new weapons, means or methods of warfare would be prohibited by international humanitarian law, including by the rules protecting the natural environment.

In the study, development, acquisition or adoption of a new weapon, means or method of warfare, States party to Additional Protocol I are under an obligation to determine whether its employment would, in some or all circumstances, be prohibited by applicable rules of international law, including those protecting the natural environment.

21.3   CASE LAW

ADVISORY OPINION
ICJ, Legality of the Threat or Use of Nuclear Weapons, Advisory Opinion, ICJ Reports 226 (1996)

30. However, the Court is of the view that the issue is not whether the treaties relating to the protection of the environment are or are not applicable during an armed conflict, but rather whether the obligations stemming from these treaties were intended to be obligations of total restraint during military conflict. The Court does not consider that the treaties in question could have intended to deprive a State of the exercise of its right of self-defence under international law because of its obligations to protect the environment. Nonetheless, States must take environmental considerations into account when assessing what is necessary and proportionate in the pursuit of legitimate military objectives. Respect for the environment is one of the elements that go to assessing whether an action is in conformity with the principles of necessity and proportionality. This approach is supported, indeed, by the terms of Principle 24 of the Rio Declaration, which provides that: "Warfare is inherently

destructive of sustainable development. States shall therefore respect international law providing protection for the environment in times of armed conflict and cooperate in its further development, as necessary."

31. The Court notes furthermore that Articles 35, paragraph 3, and 55 of Additional Protocol 1 provide additional protection for the environment. Taken together, these provisions embody a general obligation to protect the natural environment against widespread, long-term and severe environmental damage; the prohibition of methods and means of warfare which are intended, or may be expected, to cause such damage; and the prohibition of attacks against the natural environment by way of reprisals. These are powerful constraints for al1 the States having subscribed to these provisions.

32. General Assembly resolution 47/37 of 25 November 1992 on the "Protection of the Environment in Times of Armed Conflict" is also of interest in this context. It affirms the general view according to which environmental considerations constitute one of the elements to be taken into account in the implementation of the principles of the law applicable in armed conflict: it states that "destruction of the environment, not justified by military necessity and carried out wantonly, is clearly contrary to existing international law". Addressing the reality that certain instruments are not yet binding on all States, the General Assembly in this resolution "[a]ppeals to all States that have not yet done so to consider becoming parties to the relevant international conventions".

   In its recent Order in the *Request for an Examination of the Situation in Accordance with Paragraph 63 of the Court's Judgment of 20 December 1974 in the Nuclear Tests (New Zealand v. France)* case, the Court stated that its conclusion was "without prejudice to the obligations of States to respect and protect the natural environment" (Case, ICJ Reports 306 (1995), para. 64). Although that statement was made in the context of nuclear testing, it naturally also applies to the actual use of nuclear weapons in armed conflict.

33. The Court thus finds that while the existing international law relating to the protection and safeguarding of the environment does not specifically prohibit the use of nuclear weapons, it indicates important environmental factors that are properly to be taken into account in the context of the implementation of the principles and rules of the law applicable in armed conflict.

34. In the light of the foregoing the Court concludes that the most directly relevant applicable law governing the question of which it was seised, is that relating to the use of force enshrined in the United Nations Charter and the law applicable in armed conflict which regulates the conduct of hostilities, together with any specific treaties on nuclear weapons that the Court might determine to be relevant.

1. Critically assess and explain the main principles underlying the ILC draft environment.
2. Should MEAs apply during armed conflict?
3. Do you agree that the current protection of the environment is inadequate and insufficient?

BOOKS

L Boisson de Chazournes and P Sands (eds), *International Law, the International Court of Justice and Nuclear Weapons* (Cambridge University Press 1999)
R Grunawalt, J King and R McCLain (eds), *Protection of the Environment During Armed Conflict* (Naval War College 1996)
K Hulme, *War Torn Environment: Interpreting the Legal Threshold* (Martinus Nijhoff 2004)
DH Joyner, *International Law and the Proliferation of Weapons of Mass Destruction* (Oxford University Press 2009)
E Koppe, *The Use of Nuclear Weapons and the Protection of the Environment During International Armed Conflict* (Hart 2008)
G Plant (ed.), *Environmental Protection and the Law of War* (Belhaven Press 1992)
R Rayfuse (ed.), *War and the Environment: New Approaches to Protecting the Environment in Relation to Armed Conflict* (Martinus Nijhoff 2014)
C Stahn, J Iverson and JS Easterday, *Environmental Protection and Transitions from Conflict to Peace: Clarifying Norms, Principles, and Practices* (Oxford University Press 2017)

CHAPTERS

C Gray, 'Climate Change and the Law on the Use of Force' in R Rayfuse and SV Scott (eds), *International Law in the Era of Climate Change* (Edward Elgar 2011)
J-M Henckaerts and D Constantin, 'Protection of the Natural Environment' in A Clapham and P Gaeta (eds), *The Oxford Handbook of International Law in Armed Conflict* (Oxford University Press 2014)
D Montaz, 'The Use of Nuclear Weapons and the Protection of the Environment: The Contribution of the ICJ', in L Boisson de Chazournes and P Sands (eds), *International Law, the International Court of Justice and Nuclear Weapons* (Cambridge University Press 1999)
S Vöneky, 'Armed Conflict, Effect on Treaties' in *Max Planck Encyclopedia of International Law* (2011)
S Vöneky and R Wolfrum, 'Environment, Protection in Armed Conflict' in *Max Planck Encyclopedia of International Law* (2016)

ARTICLES

M Bothe, C Bruch, J Diamond and D Jensen, 'International Law Protecting the Environment During Armed Conflict: Gaps and Opportunities' (2010) 92 International Review of the Red Cross 569
A Bunker, 'Protection of the Environment During Armed Conflict: One Gulf, Two Wars' (2004) 13 Review of European Community and International Environmental Law 201
J Goldblat, 'The Prohibition of Environmental Warfare' (1975) 4 Ambio 186
LJ Juda, 'Negotiating a Treaty on Environmental Modification Warfare: The Convention on Environmental Warfare and Its Impact on the Arms Control Negotiations' (1978) 32 International Organization 975

I Peterson, 'The Natural Environment in Times of Armed Conflict: A Concern for International War Crimes Law' (2009) 22 Leiden Journal of International Law 325

R Rayfuse, 'Editorial: War and the Environment: International Law and the Protection of the Environment in Relation to Armed Conflict: Introduction to the Special Issue' (2013) 82 Nordic Journal of International Law 1

D Shelton and A Kiss, 'Martens Clause for Environmental Protection' (2000) 30 Environmental Policy and Law 285

R Tarasofsky, 'Legal Protection of the Environment During International Armed Conflict' (1993) 24 Netherlands Yearbook of International Law 17

C Voigt, 'Sustainable Security' (2008) 19 Yearbook of International Environmental Law 163

J Wyatt, 'Law-Making at the Intersection of International Environmental, Humanitarian and Criminal Law: The Issue of Damage to the Environment in International Armed Conflict' (2010) 92 International Review of the Red Cross 593

INDEX